"WE HAD AN OBJECTIVE IN MIND"

THE U. S. FOREST SERVICE IN THE PACIFIC NORTHWEST 1905 to 2005

A CENTENNIAL ANTHOLOGY

Pacific Northwest Forest Service Association

THE PACIFIC NORTHWEST FOREST SERVICE ASSOCIATION
PO Box 5583
Portland, OR 97228
www.oldsmokeys.org

PNWFSA
PO Box 5583
Portland, OR 97228
www.oldsmokeys.org

ISBN-13: 978-0-9768723-0-6
ISBN-10: 0-9768723-0-7

Library of Congress Control Number:
20059904076

Printed in the United States of America by
Maverick Publications · Bend, Oregon

TABLE OF CONTENTS

EDITOR'S INTRODUCTION

This is a book of stories about the Forest Service in the Pacific Northwest - an area that includes the Pacific Northwest Region of the National Forest System, also called Region Six or R-6, and the Pacific Northwest Research Station. Our stories begin with the early Rangers, men who began with not much more than a badge, a horse, meager camp-out gear and orders to manage the newly established National Forests for "the greatest good, to the greatest number, in the long run."

The stories are full of tales about the hardships and difficulties of starting a new venture. The full collection of stories records growth and change as the Forest Service matures, including stories that bring to life fires and floods, the Civilian Conservation Corps, the first smokejumpers, and experiences that chronicle the evolution of multiple-use management from World War II to the present. The reader will experience the beginnings, the growth spurts, and everyday life as told by Forest Service employees and their families. Each of the six chapters covers a unique time period in Forest Service history.

In 1945, the first club of Forest Service retirees began operations in the Pacific Northwest. It was called "The 30 Year Club" and was open to Forest Service employees and retirees. Many of the original 30 Year Club members had worked for the Forest Service since the early 1900s, and they felt it important to record their experiences. In 1947 the club began publishing an annual newsletter, called "TIMBER-LINES."

Along with a mix of current news about retirees and their activities, each issue included reminiscences by club members about their days in the Forest Service. Occasionally there was a story about the old days from the perspective of a family member. The issues of TIMBER-LINES contain a rich lode of stories from the early 1900s into the 1970s. They are the inspiration for this book.

The Pacific Northwest Forest Service Association (PNWFSA), the official name of the Club after gaining non-profit status in 2001, decided these and other stories describing the Forest Service in the Pacific Northwest from 1905 to 2005 should be shared with a wide audience. The purpose of this book is to celebrate the 100th anniversary of the Forest Service and to add to the festivities of the Forest Service National Reunion in Portland in 2005,

Most of the stories in this book are from TIMBER-LINES and the newsletters, while others are the result of direct solicitations for this book. In many cases, we selected pieces from longer stories in TIMBER-LINES. In some cases, parts of stories by the same author but appearing in separate issues of TIMBER-LINES have been combined. Some punctuation has been updated to current standards. Editor comments at the beginning of each chapter introduce the era described by the chapter. Editorial notes within a story are in [brackets].

In some chapters there are a number of selections from the same author, e.g. Grover Blake and M. L. Merritt in Chapter One; H. C. "Chris" Chriswell in Chapter Three; and Bob Bjornsen in Chapter Four. These authors were prolific contributors to TIMBER-LINES and their stories are both relevant and interesting.

Information about the author, provided with each story, came from a variety of sources. Sometimes there was conflicting information, particularly dates. If the information shown is incorrect, I apologize. The error is mine for not researching deeply enough.

The title of this book, <u>WE HAD AN OBJECTIVE IN MIND</u>, was selected from a longer quote by longtime Ranger Grover Blake. This simple quote, appearing at the beginning of Chapter One, captures the spirit and determination of the early day Forest Service that has provided motivation for the agency through the entire century.

Finally, these stories are presented with minimal interpretation. They speak for themselves, describing the ever-changing and continuously evolving growth of the Forest Service in the Pacific Northwest through descriptions of everyday experiences. Enjoy your reading!

-rolf anderson, editor

ACKNOWLEDGEMENTS

It took a lot of people to nurture into reality the idea floated by Wendall Jones in one of the Pacific Northwest Forest Service Association (PNWFSA) newsletters. Acknowledgements have to start with recognition of the hundreds of Forest Service retirees, employees, and family members who, between 1947 and 2005, wrote stories about their experiences. Over 1,000 stories from past issues of Timberlines, a handful of stories from "Sampler of the Early Years" Volumes I and II, and more than 100 stories submitted in response to our request for contemporary stories were collected and reviewed. We are indebted to every author that contributed a story. Our book wouldn't have been possible without this huge collection to select from.

We began this publishing adventure with lots of ideas, but no real knowledge about how to proceed. Advice and counsel about publishing and self-printing was offered readily by Gary Asher, Carol Ann Bassett, Skye Blaine, Susan Butruillle, John Dewitz, Jim Freeman, Larry Gold, and Mike Thoele. Gil Davies and Les Joslin were especially helpful. Kathy Bulchis, Paul Jeske, John Marker, Al Matecko, Bev Pratt and Susan Skalsky contributed advice, ideas, or other assistance along the way.

Another group of people we are indebted to are those who contributed specific information to enhance stories or background information. These are Rita Glazebrook, Ed Graham, Jon Lilligren, Kermit Link, Frank McKinney, Cindy Miner, Elmer Moyer, Marsh Nelson, Ruth Ann Nicklin, Mary Paterson and Jack Smith. Jerry Williams was an information source we tapped continuously. Joani Bosworth, Bob Boyd, Paul Clayssens, Sarah Greene, Terry Holtzapple, Tom Irasci, Chris Kelley, Bob Leonard, Cheryl Mack, Jim Mayo, Rick McClure and Fred Swanson helped in our search for photos. Tom Stewart transcribed the first draft of National Forest Establishment Dates, at the time a much more complicated table than the current form. Vern Clapp, George Grier, Tracii Hickman, Doug Porter and Mike Running helped with our grant applications.

Dallas Emch and Rob Iwamoto were major supporters, providing the use of a Willamette National Forest computer, printer and copier, and copy paper to transform our review drafts from a CD to hard copy.

Neal Forrester, Gregory Koester, Vickie Petsch, Kathy Ragan, Donna Short, and Marlee Stubblefield gave hands-on help to make this happen. Allison Reger was indispensable, always ready to respond to our needs for assistance, including escorting us from the building security station, reserving and providing access to a computer, and walking us through unfamiliar procedures.

John and Bonna Wilson took on the task of handling and shipping the mail orders.

The PNWFSA Board of Directors were supportive from start to finish, providing both encouragement and funding.

We simply wouldn't have a book without the time and energy put in by our Photo Editors Dick Connelly and Dick Buscher, the hours Paul and Marcia Caruso spent scanning copies of mimeographed pages of TIMBER-LINE articles into computer files, and the days spent editing by Pam Wilson, Kathy Barrett, and Mike Kerrick.

Foremost was the ever-present vision, standard-setting, sounding board, encouragement, and overall guiding hands of Phil Hirl, Wendall Jones, and Dave Scott.

All of the above – every bit – was volunteer, contributed time and energy. We are overwhelmed by the willingness of everyone to be a part of this project, and grateful beyond words. Our appreciation and thanks extend to all of you.

CREDITS and RECOGNITION

Designing the front and back covers turned out to be an adventure in itself. We started with ideas and photos by Dick Buscher, Steve Coady, and Dick Connelly. Then Pam Druliner and Dick Connelly did a photo shoot at the High Desert Museum in Bend, with the assistance of Bob Boyd. Pam continued incorporating ideas into design work resulting in the final products. Maverick Press assisted with the finishing work. The front cover utilizes a standard handout map compiled by the Forest Service and the Bureau of Land Management. The back cover photo is by Dick Connelly.

All text photos are from USDA Forest Service National Forest and Ranger District files unless otherwise noted.

Stories are from the following sources:

*Issues of TIMBER-LINES, a Pacific Northwest Forest Service Retirees Association (30 Year Club) publication. PNWFSA maintains a complete set of TIMBER-LINES and its successor newsletters.

*A story by Charlotte Wood from "Sampler of the Early Years" Volume II, Forestry Wives Club of Washington DC, 1986, is used with permission from Forest Service Women.

*Stories were submitted in response to a 2003/2004 request for latter day stories for this book.

Some TIMBER-LINES stories have also been published in personal memoirs.

TIMBER-LINES stories in this book by Forest Service wives Dorothea Burgess, Eva Poole, Mildred Nelson and Lillian Olson, and Forest Service daughter Emma Matz were reprinted in "Sampler of the Early Years", either Volume I, Foresters' Wives Club of Washington DC, 1980, or Volume II, Forestry Wives Club of Washington DC, 1986. The current name of this organization is Forest Service Women.

"WE HAD AN OBJECTIVE IN MIND"

Pacific Northwest
Forest Service
Association

OldSmokeys

"It was a great privilege to be associated with the fine group of young men who were a part of the Forest Service fifty years ago and thereafter. I like to reminisce of those days. We had many hardships to overcome. The work was hard and hardships many, but it was a joy and a pleasure because we had an objective in mind, we felt we were getting somewhere and we were playing a part in conserving our natural resources for 'the greatest good to the greatest number in the long run,' quoting Secretary Wilson. I feel that the Nation owes a great debt to the founder of the Forest Service, Gifford Pinchot, and the conservation-minded President, Theodore Roosevelt, who saved for all the people the remnant of our diminishing timber resources. "

-Grover C. Blake

CHAPTER ONE

1905 to 1918 MILLIONS of ACRES and a FEW GOOD MEN

In the early 1900s Harold Langille was a trouble-shooter for Division R of the General Land Office, Department of the Interior. He traveled Oregon and California inspecting the "field force," arbitrating complaints against the Forest Reserve system and explaining the benefits of conservation to the public. He was good at what he did and was well respected. Langille resigned in November 1905, nine months after the Reserves were transferred to the Bureau of Forestry in the Department of Agriculture. Looking back, in 1941, he wrote, "By now, the Forest Service was a lusty youth. Erased was Division R, gone were the days of assessor, referee and adjudicator in the field. Unavoidably the old order changed, and with the change dissolved those factors which lent zest and stimulation to the blazing of new trails. I resigned."

At the same time, a group of young men was learning about this new government agency. These men thought the ideas of wise use and conservation made great sense. They saw adventure and challenge in managing these Reserves and they liked the objective of placing local managers close to the ground. They became the new order and their stories begin in this chapter.

3

The stories about the early days of the Forest Service, from 1905 until the end of World War I in 1918, are full of tales about the hardships and difficulties of starting a new venture. Everything was new – the concept of conservation and wise use tied to active management of the natural resources rather than leaving them untended and open for exploitation, and the job itself, including methods and procedures for accomplishing the work.

The workforce was small, with only a few hundred people in the Pacific Northwest. This group was an unlikely mix of woods-wise, practical local men who were the early forest guards and Forest Rangers, and college-trained foresters from the newly formed forestry schools, who were called Forest Assistants or Technical Assistants. All of them were dedicated to the principles described in the Use Book, a small volume one could tuck in his field jacket pocket, containing the "Regulations and Instructions for the Use of the National Forest Reserves".

Public response ranged across the spectrum, from outright hostility by those who felt the government presence inhibited their own interests, to suspicion and wait-to-see, to support from those who embraced the concept of conservation of public-owned resources and saw management of Forest Reserves as a welcome change from the sometimes chaos of uncontrolled use.

At first, management was a direct line from the Washington Office to each Reserve/National Forest headquarters. There was no District (Regional) Office until late in 1908. Alaska was part of the North Pacific District until 1921. Forest Supervisors operated much like latter-day District Rangers. Many Ranger Districts had just one employee, the Ranger. A few forest guards were hired for the summer. Sometimes several Rangers on a Forest were brought together for a couple of weeks to work jointly on projects.

The work ethic overshadowed everything else. They did whatever it took to get the job done, often working late into the evening or on weekends. They worked alone, a long way from home, never really knowing when they would return. They were at the mercy of the weather and the unknown backcountry. They stood up to those using the National Forests illegally.

These early employees started with little or nothing. There were few trails, almost no roads, few buildings or other structures such as barns and corrals, and no lookouts.   Budgets were small.   Building infrastructure was a major struggle.

In spite of all their trials and tribulations, the early workforce established a spirit and legacy of dedication to purpose, innovation, and camaraderie that set the tone for the Forest Service for the next 100 years.

This chapter includes stories about The Beginning, Joining Up, Acceptance and Support, All in a Day's Work, Wives' Tales, Horses, Fire, Grazing, Homesteads, Recreation, Timber, Research, Administration and Improvements.

THE BEGINNING: "-a vigorous and active organization-"

<u>Melvil "M. L." Merritt</u>   *Merritt worked for the Forest Service from 1909 to 1941.   His assignments included Forest Assistant on the Washington and Whitman NFs, Forest Supervisor of the Deschutes NF, Operations in the District Six Office, and Assistant Regional Forester in Alaska and Region Six.*

When on February 1, 1905, administration of the national Forest Reserves was shifted from the Department of the Interior to Agriculture, the forestry personnel of Interior came with them. From this start the Forest Service, as the old Bureau of Forestry was thereafter called, soon became a vigorous and active organization. It operated under the principle of *the greatest good to the greatest number in the long run.*   Gifford Pinchot, our first chief, was a dynamic leader and organizer - a great crusader.

Much has been written about the early Forest Service and its problems: how virgin forests were studied, managed, and made to produce; how users of range and timber were brought into line; how trails, bridges, houses, barns and fences, and eventually telephone lines and roads were built; and how this publicity-supported-enterprise became well managed and profitable. Not so much has been said or is known of the men who did the work. Particularly the first group of hardy public-spirited people who adopted the objectives of conservation - then a new term. These people set about their job of caring for the Reserves and winning the western communities to the conservation idea.

5

Altogether we have the names of about 90 men in the Region Six area who came into the Forest Service from the Department of the Interior in 1905. Many of these old Interior men accepted the conservation ideas and became the solid backbone of the organization. Some dropped out immediately for business or personal reasons. A few lacked ability or temperament and were dropped. A very few were victims of drink (we now call them "alcoholics"). Those that stuck, together with new recruits and the few technically trained men that served as leaven for the whole loaf, soon shook the Forest Service down into an active Bureau that adjusted itself to everyday problems.

Those first groups contributed much. A few became leaders - more were doers - qualified woodsmen who worked long and faithfully for small pay and with little regard for days or hours of work. All of them deserve high praise and commendation for a job well done.

<u>Henry "H. E." Haefner</u> *Haefner began his career in 1908 as a Forest Assistant in Washington DC and then in Arizona. He worked on the Siskiyou NF from 1909 to 1925, then worked in timber management on the Cascade/Willamette NF and in the R-6 Regional Office. He retired in 1944.*

It was necessary to pick men for these early Ranger jobs who understood the people, who could live among them and hold their own with them. Men who could carry on the Rangers' work largely on their own initiative because of the long distance from headquarters and the lack of adequate transportation and mail facilities. The roads were very poor and there were few telephone lines. It took about three days of traveling by rail, stage, horseback or afoot to reach the Supervisor's headquarters [of the Siskiyou NF] from these stations under favorable conditions and often twice as long in mid-winter.

<u>J. M. Schmitz</u> *Schmitz started work on the Mt. Rainier Reserve in 1902. He was appointed Ranger in 1905, then transferred that same year to the Wenaha Reserve as Ranger in Charge, and then named Forest Supervisor stationed at Walla Walla. He resigned from the Forest Service in 1912.*

The first inspection, in 1906 by E. T. Allen, was very favorable, stating that the Rangers were of the cowboy-woodsman type. Well, they were necessary. We took over the Forest in the rough and it required that class of man to handle it successfully. A college education wasn't necessary, although education could be a big help.

Each Ranger had more work laid out for him than could possibly be done. He was supposed to inspect each sheep camp every week to see how it was grazed. Sheep camps were moved every week, and if a Ranger had from ten to fifteen bands of sheep in his District, and as it would take a day for each camp, it just couldn't be done because of the other important work. Most Rangers had a guard to help during the fire season and when a fire was discovered it had to be fought with what help there was at hand. There was no telephone and to go out for help would have taken five or six days. By then the fire would have burned itself out or be beyond control.

<u>Grover C. Blake</u> *Blake began work for the Forest Service on the Deschutes NF in 1909 as a forest guard. He advanced to Ranger in 1910 and in 1911 his area became part of the newly established Ochoco NF. In later years he was a Ranger on the Malheur and Umatilla NFs, and worked with the Civilian Conservation Corps program on the Umpqua NF. He retired in 1944. In addition to contributing a number of stories to TimberLines, he wrote and self-published his autobiography, <u>Blazing Oregon Trails</u>.*

The Forest Service was a growing youngster of four years of age when I became one of the so-called custodians of the National Forests. The Blue Mountains of eastern Oregon had been a hotbed of conflicting grazing interests, and the first big job was to regulate the grazing use in the face of almost universal opposition from the sheep and cattle owners. The *kiddish-looking* young men who wore the Forest Service shield were considered a sort of pest to be tolerated and ignored. It took time to sell ourselves and the Forest Service policies to the stockmen and other users. We had no maps of any degree of reliability, so for several years a lot of effort was put into surveying, retracing land office survey lines and building dependable maps. This work was done, for the most part, in connection with claims work and allotment boundary surveys. We were required to spend considerable time examining and reporting on valid and invalid homestead claims which dotted the Forest areas, and had to deal with numerous applications under the Act of June 11, 1906 [this Act is described by Duffy Lewis in the Homesteads section of this chapter].

7

The Ranger force of that early day was, for the most part, raw recruits. They were woodsmen, yes, but foresters, not yet. They were to become foresters through the tough school of experience, study and such conferences as the 1909 meeting at Mt. Vernon. Their chief assets were health, stamina and a capacity for learning. The Ranger went forth equipped with a badge, a <u>Use Book</u>, map, compass, marking hatchet, a few other articles and a good supply of blank forms, cloth notices, and posters, also a month's food supply, and pack and saddle horses. There were no telephone lines so the Supervisor would likely not hear from the Ranger for several weeks. In the meantime, he had worked on a large assortment of jobs. His duties were many and his job was rather hard, but he was deeply interested and he loved his work.

When it first became the policy to give summer jobs on the Forests to students taking forestry in college, the idea did not meet with favor with most Rangers, who preferred to place experienced woodsmen in the short-term positions because of their experience and dependability. The students required considerable supervision. They learned quickly as a rule and soon became good help, but there were some exceptions.

I recall a certain Ranger meeting when the plans for the following summer were being mapped out and the Supervisor put this question to a certain Ranger: "Jess, how many college students can <u>YOU</u> use this summer?"

The Ranger was lost in thought for a moment or two and then replied, "Not very many. I'm going to be awfully busy this summer."

Well, anyway, those boys, for the most part, were quick to learn and wide awake and became very helpful in the work program.

<u>Melvil "M. L." Merritt</u> *Merritt was transferred from the Washington NF to the Whitman NF as a Forest Assistant in 1910.*

It was midwinter when I arrived [in Sumpter, Oregon]. Four feet of packed snow lay on the level. I reported at the Forest Service office near the railway station and introduced myself to Henry Ireland as his new Forest Assistant. He had had one of these college foresters before, and their experience together had not been a happy one. So I got a pretty fishy eye from Mr. Ireland, himself a graduate of the *school of hard knocks*. But there I was and he made the best of it. I took a room in the hotel and set about making myself as useful as I could. After we became acquainted, Henry Ireland was one of my best supporters.

<u>Albert H. Cousins</u>   *Cousins joined the Forest Service in Washington DC. He came to the newly formed District Six Office in 1908 as the first head of accounts. He was in charge of the National Supply Depot in Ogden, Utah from 1917 to 1920, when he returned to District Six as the fiscal agent. He moved to the Washington Office in 1943 and retired in 1944.*

When District Six was established and its personnel organized, the employment of women clerks in the Supervisor's office was not looked upon with favor and the policy was established to employ men only - the idea being that a woman clerk could not handle the *rough* work required in the administration of a Forest, such as assembling and shipping fire tools, rustling fire fighters, etc. Such work properly was for a *two-fisted* Ranger or forest officer. However, it was not long before it became apparent that there was another element in forest officer's work which had not been taken into consideration. That was PAPERWORK - reports, letters to Forest users, etc. Such work proved to be too much for the *two-fisted* Rangers and Supervisors. Their experience with paperwork was practically nil. Under such conditions the idea grew that perhaps women did have a place in the Forest organization and so *lovely woman* got her foot in the door. The result was very satisfactory and you know the rest of the story.

Not only did the Supervisors and other forest officers welcome these women assistants and the clearance of paperwork, but probably the *two-fisted* Rangers welcomed them more than anyone else.

<u>Harry M. White</u> *White started with the Forest Service in 1910 as the forest clerk on the Chelan NF. He was clerk on the Columbia and Rainier NFs and worked in the District Six/Region 6 Operations Office. He retired in 1949.*

I had known nothing about the Forest Service, and had everything to learn. But I soon saw that the Service, being very new, had many big jobs to do which had nothing to do with technical forestry. There were, at the time, 150 National Forests, all in the West. Prior to 1908, they had been supervised from the Washington Office. In that year, six regional headquarters were established, each in charge of a District Forester, with several assistants handling the different activities.

District Six, the Northwest Pacific Region, comprised nearly all of the National Forests in Oregon and Washington, and the two very large Forests in Alaska. Few of the Forest Supervisors and none of the Rangers had degrees in forestry, but they knew how to do the work that had to be done. Such forestry graduates as there were handled the reconnaissance job and the few timber sales. Although I was a clerk and could seldom get out into the Forest, all these activities, most of which I understood, were a challenge to me.

A very important reason for my continuing in the Forest Service was the quality and dedication of the personnel. The dedication was partly due to the environment in which we worked and the objectives impressed upon us by the leaders. It was largely due to the spirit instilled in the organization by the first Chief Forester and great conservationist, Gifford Pinchot. Imagine a Forest Supervisor in charge of and responsible for a domain of perhaps a million and a half acres of mountainous land carrying varying types of vegetation; heavy stands of Douglas-fir or Ponderosa pine timber at the lower elevations and shading into alpine timber and grasslands at the higher elevations, all to be protected and improved and managed for perpetuation and wise use of timber and other resources. This vast domain was divided into five or six Ranger Districts, each in charge of a District Ranger responsible for all activities in his District; and for all of the workers handling their jobs in a way to gain the respect and cooperation of the public, which wasn't easy in the early days but was accomplished as the years went by.

Thornton T. Munger *Munger was a leader in research throughout his Forest Service career from 1903 to 1946. He began as a Forest Assistant working out of the Washington Office. When the District Six Office was established in November 1908, Munger was transferred to Portland as head of the one-man Silvics Section.*

When Gifford Pinchot, or G. P. as he was affectionately called, took over in 1905, the administration of the 63 million acres of Forest Reserves, all in the West, he had an unusual corps of helpers. First, there were the Forest Supervisors and Rangers in the west, held over from the Department of the Interior, mostly men of the frontier, many of them politicians, many middle-aged. Then, second, there was in Washington a group of young technical men, practically all in their twenties, graduates of the new forestry schools at Cornell, Yale, and Michigan, who were already in the Bureau of Forestry of the Department of Agriculture. This young group was full of the crusading spirit, eager to make a success of the national forest enterprise. As tenderfoot easterners they went west, learned to ride and pack, made examinations for new National Forests, worked on timber sales, acted as forest assistants to the non-technical Supervisors, and in many cases replaced them. Meantime, other high-type young westerners were attracted to this live, new Forest Service, in many cases by Gifford Pinchot's own magnetic personality – men like E. T. Allen, the Langille brothers, H. D. and W. H. They became the backbone of the Ranger force and several rose to the top of the ranks. It was a problem to weld this mixed group into a loyal, trustworthy, hard-working unit, but it was done quickly.

One favorite criticism of the Forest Service was that the administration was from bureaucrats in Washington, DC – 3,000 miles away, and that seemed a long way then. So Pinchot did something to better the Service and to spike this criticism that was quite unheard of in government circles in those days. He decentralized the Forest Service. He divided the West into six districts and then divided the Washington Office – men, women, and messenger boys – into seven groups. One group stayed in Washington and the other six, totaling 377 persons, entrained for the west – Denver, Missoula, San Francisco, Albuquerque, Ogden and Portland.

Though the West liked this local administration, they didn't like the Pinchot policies and certain interests were frank in saying so. The famous land-looting cases of the Northwest were still fresh in the public mind, and government foresters were no more popular with land locators than revenue agents are with moonshiners. A then-conservative Portland daily paper, the Oregonian, described the men who had just arrived from Washington as *callow youths rushing around throughout the Northwest carrying shiny briefcases and talking glibly about 'the field' not even knowing what the term meant.* One editorial writer stigmatized the *minions of the Forest Service* as *reeking of musk and insolence.* This group of young foresters was so fair-minded, so open-minded, so intelligent about local problems, and so public-spirited that they soon won the support and understanding of the users of the National Forests. People began to see the wisdom of the National Forest system and liked it better than the old free-for-all grab-bag system. Pinchot's wisdom in decentralizing his bureau had been demonstrated. The Forest Service made good. Foresters came to be hailed as the saviors of natural resources.

On the foundations begun by G. P. and Secretary Wilson on February 1, 1905, and strengthened with the decentralizing move on December 1, 1908, the Forest Service has built an important structure in the life and economy of the whole country. It has contributed a share in the development of the west which it would be hard to overstate. This place it still firmly holds.

JOINING UP: "-there were some openings with the Forest Service-"

<u>Fred Cleator</u> *Cleator started work on the Wenatchee NF in 1908 and was named Deputy Forest Supervisor of the Colville NF in 1910. In 1919 he was assigned to Recreation Planning for District Six. He retired in 1943. This story is from a 1956 article in the Seattle Times, reprinted in TimberLines.*

Cleator first felt an urge to work in the Forests when he was en route to a job as storekeeper and acting as postmaster at a salmon cannery near Petersburg, Alaska, in 1903. On his way through Seattle he saw an article in a newspaper about the new occupation of Forest Ranger, which just was coming into existence. He wrote a letter asking his father to get him some information on the subject.

"He sent me a little book all right," Cleator says, "and said he thought I might make $65 a month at it if I was good. I studied that primer of forestry and then went to the University of Minnesota on my $600 in savings. I lacked half a term's credit when I left school in 1908, so didn't get a degree."

12

"I took a Civil Service examination and without knowing I had passed, went to Powers, Oregon, to work for a logging company. Three days after my arrival, I received a telegram saying I had passed and to report to Washington, DC, on July 1 [1908]. It was already June 28 and I had no money - I got to Powers 'on biscuits,' as we say."

"My boss said there were no trees in Washington, DC, and I'd better telegraph and explain and ask if I could go to the job without reporting at headquarters. In reply I was told to be in Wenatchee, July 1. I borrowed money to get there. From then on I was in the Forest Service."

<u>Charles S. Congleton</u> *Congleton was appointed forest guard on the Blue Mountain (West) Reserve in 1907. He quickly advanced to Assistant Forest Ranger and then to Deputy Forest Ranger. He spent his entire career on the Paulina Ranger District, which was also part of the Deschutes and then the Ochoco NF. He resigned in 1927.*

The period from December 1904 to the spring of 1907 was spent doing general ranch work on the Billy Congleton Ranch in Paulina Valley and the Laughlin (the old Triangle) Ranch.

In April 1907, three or four of the Paulina Valley ranchers signed a petition certifying as to my general reliability and qualifications for Forest Ranger and recommending me for this job in the Paulina area. Accordingly, armed with this petition, I made application to A. S. Ireland, Forest Supervisor of the Blue Mountain West Forest Reserve with headquarters in Prineville, Oregon. On April 15, 1907, I was hired as a forest guard. There were no specific headquarters, but Paulina was my mailing address.

During 1907 the work consisted mostly in searching out section corners, running out and marking Forest boundary, counting sheep and working out allotment boundaries between sheep permittees. At a meeting held the previous winter, there had been allotments made to permittees and the boundaries shown on a map, but no one knew where these were on the ground. Frequently, when the map boundaries were located on the ground they were found impractical and adjustments had to be made. This was further complicated by misunderstanding by the permittees on where the lines were and the fact that there were more sheep permittees than the area could accommodate. Regarding numbers, C. H. Adams of the Washington Office, while inspecting the upper drainages of Mill Creek and Marks Creek in 1907 said, "This is the heaviest stocked piece of National Forest range in the United States." These areas had a band of 1200 sheep on about every four sections. There were no inside fences and cattle and horses permitted at this time often ranged over adjoining sheep range as well as on the area on which they were permitted.

Melvin M. Lewis *Lewis was hired as a Protective Assistant on the Siskiyou NF in 1907. He was appointed District Ranger in 1919 and Deputy Forest Supervisor in 1924. He transferred to the Columbia NF in 1935 and retired in 1945. Lewis' son Frank has stories in Chapter Four (All in a Days' Work) and Chapter Five (Fire).*

I well remember the first job that I worked on - April 1, 1907. M. J. Anderson, then Supervisor of the Siskiyou National Forest, informed me that I had been selected for a job with the Forest Service. I was assigned to boundary survey work with Fred Merrill and George Woolridge and told that we should get together our camp equipment and food supplies and arrange for transportation out to where our work was to begin. We hired a livery team for $3.50 and arranged for an early start the next morning. No expense accounts in those days! The Service did not even own an ax or a shovel; we supplied our own for the little old <u>Use Book</u> stated that those should be a part of our equipment.

On arrival at the end of the road on Slate Creek, we moved into an old prospector's shack near where our work was to begin. It was nip and tuck for a few nights to see whether we stayed or turned over the place to a colony of skunks that were denned up beneath the floor. We soon left this camp to the skunks and moved our camp three or four miles out along the line. Backpacking was the way we moved camp.

In those days from 8:00 am until 5:00 pm on the job constituted a day's work and the work week was six days. Sunday was reserved for shaving, washing clothes and taking a bath in the creek - if you felt tough enough to withstand the shock of the ice cold water. We spent nearly two months on the job and during this time met up with an old miner by the name of Wilson who had a mining location adjacent to

14

the Forest boundary and who seriously objected to our running a line across his claim and threatened to feed us a dose of goose shot unless we cleared out. We informed the old timer that we did not crave the dose of shot and since it was nearly time to quit work for the day, we returned to our camp and formulated plans for dealing with the situation.

It was agreed that next morning Woolridge, who was somewhat of a daredevil, would buckle on his old six gun and go back ahead of Merrill and me and, if possible, separate the old man from his shotguns. When we arrived some minutes later, we saw George and the miner some distance from the cabin looking in some bedrock where he had done some mining. The old miner did not discover us until we had nearly completed running the line along the property. When he saw us he started for the house. It was then that George saved the day by telling the old fellow that if there was to be any gun play that he would be in on it. The old fellow cooled down and finally gave us permission to camp at his place.

We hired his old horse to pack our camp into the place where we stayed for nearly a week. The old man had supper with us every night and seemed real sorry when it came time for us to move on. We loaned him our <u>Use Book</u> to read while we were there and told him that we did not know much more than he did about the Forest Service but thought that it was a step in the right direction. We told him that the timber locators would be shut out, which he allowed was a "dad-burned good thing since those polecats had caused him a lot of trouble by trying to file a claim on his mining property." Before we left the old fellow was very friendly to us and offered his belief that the Service was probably a good thing for the country.

Our methods were sometimes crude, but in those days of pioneering, drastic action was sometimes necessary in order to obtain results.

<u>Gilbert D. Brown</u> *Brown began his Forest Service career in 1906 as Assistant Forest Ranger on the Cascade Range Reserve. He was transferred to a Ranger job on the Fremont NF in 1907, advanced to Deputy Forest Supervisor in 1908, and to Forest Supervisor in 1910. He was Forest Supervisor on the Wenatchee NF from 1931 until his retirement in 1940.*

Learning that the Fremont Forest Reserve in eastern Oregon was to be put under administration, I applied for a transfer and in April 1907, was assigned to the Fremont at Silver Lake as Ranger in charge of that District. It was here that my real forestry work began.

Upon arriving at Silver Lake I found a vast area of Forest without telephone lines, roads, or trails, and transportation was entirely by saddle horse and pack outfit. The work consisted of running and posting Forest boundary lines, reporting on June 11 claims (most of which were fraudulent and had been filed in order to get timber and were later rejected), forest improvements, grazing trespasses, issuing range stock crossing permits, etc.

The fire problem was not great on the Fremont for several years, partially because of the over-grazing.

Ira E. Jones *Jones was forest guard and then Ranger on the Whitman NF from 1908 to 1924. He was Superintendent of Construction for the Whitman, Umatilla, and Wallowa NFs from 1924 to 1934. He worked with the Civilian Conservation Corps and Works Progress Administration Programs on the Siuslaw NF beginning in 1934 (he directed the construction of many of the coastal campgrounds) and retired as Assistant Forest Supervisor in 1942.*

I first worked for the Forest Service in the spring of 1908. I had the title of forest guard and was paid at the rate of $900 per year. I furnished two horses and boarded myself (no travel expenses on the Forest). You could buy a good uniform for $15.00 and a Stetson hat (stiff brim that would fall off at the least touch) for $3.00.

In 1909 I started as forest guard (same salary) on the North Powder Ranger District. For an outfit I had an old blueprint put out by some LaGrande Abstract Company, a Use Book, and a large single bit marking axe weighing about two pounds. This had a *U.S.* stamp on the end

The Ranger told me to start running Forest boundary. I said, "Where shall I start?"

He said, "Go find a place, and start in." So I took my saddle horse and pack outfit and started west. In about two days I found a starting point near Anthony Creek. From there I ran and marked the boundary north and northwest to the Grande Ronde River where I met Ranger W. W. Hawley who had been running boundary from the west. We retraced and reblazed old survey lines and ran new lines where the Forest boundary followed interior land subdivision lines. We posted cloth boundary notices so that they were inter-visible, signed by James Wilson, Secretary of Agriculture,

After completing this stretch, the North Powder Ranger and I checked on grazing. We traveled together with our pack outfit and saw all allotments. After the grazing season I was sent to Beaver Creek country to check on the work of building a dam and the laying of a pipeline by the City of LaGrande (for their city water supply).

<u>Grover C. Blake</u> *Blake describes the circumstances that led him to join the Forest Service and his first days as forest guard on the Deschutes NF.*

I have been thinking about that summer of 1906, when I was camped up on Old Baldy on what is now the Ochoco National Forest, with a band of sheep. Old Baldy has since had her name changed to Spanish Peak, but that change in name did not change her general appearance very much.

These Blue Mountain timberlands had recently become a part of the National Forests. Many stockmen had long summered their flocks and herds upon the rich forage of the Blue Mountain ranges and there was keen competition for the choice grazing areas in those days. Range wars were common and many sheep and a number of men had been killed. Creation of the National Forests, followed by restriction of the grazing privileges, was looked upon by most stockmen as a deliberate attempt on the part of the government to deprive them of their free and unlimited use of the land for grazing. They were bitter and antagonistic and Forest officers had few friends among them.

A few men had been appointed that year as forest guards to carry on field administration of the new National Forests. One of these men was J. D. "Bert" Fine. He came to my camp one day during the summer of 1906 and made the camp his headquarters for some three

17

weeks. He was wearing the first Forest Service badge I ever saw. It was not quite as large as a saucer but several times the size of the largest now in use. I was to wear a like badge later.

Bert and I talked a lot about the new Forest Service and studied the Use Book together. It sounded like *good medicine* to me and I became much interested and in sympathy with the Forestry program. The following year I took the civil Service examination for Forest Ranger and served thirty-three years.

"It will be necessary to keep a daily diary of your activities. Write down everything you do each day and why you do it." Thus spoke Schuyler Ireland, first Supervisor of the Deschutes National Forest as he briefed me on the job ahead when I reported for duty in 1909.

A group of starry-eyed young men, with scant knowledge of what the future held for them, set forth to clear the way for the huge Forest Service which we have today. I had been notified that I was eligible for appointment as a Forest Ranger. The U. S. Civil Service Commission had apparently arrived at that conclusion from a look at results of a recent civil Service examination. In my pocket was a letter from Supervisor Ireland instructing me to report for duty with a saddle horse and a pack horse fully equipped with saddles, camp outfit, etc. He said I should leave my horses at a certain Ranger Station and go to Prineville and take the oath of office.

"OATH OF OFFICE"...There was something thrilling about those three words and they had a tendency to make me feel important. Then there was the "APPOINTMENT," an official looking document stating that I was being given the title of forest guard at a salary of $900 per year. Supervisor Ireland, a kindly man, sat down with me and pointed out some of the things which I would be expected to accomplish during the coming season, including the diary mentioned above. He left with me the impression that this diary should show that my huge salary was being earned. He left the matter of dealing with the complicated grazing problem and other responsibilities of the time for future conferences. He proceeded to fit me out with forms for monthly reports, free use forms, stacks of boundary notices, fire warnings, driveway notices and many other forms and notices. He

Ranger with his children at an Ochoco NF portal – c1915

also furnished me with a marking hatchet, compass, carrying case, badge (about three inches in diameter), a Use Book, stationery and a good supply of other materials. That pack horse had a load!

[He told Doug Ingrahm and I] to hie forth up Mill Creek on what is now the Ochoco National Forest and proceed to mark the said Forest boundary. Well, Doug and I (Doug with his breakfast foods, corn starch, tea and dainties, and me with my bacon and beans) pitched our camp at a little meadow which later became Cabin Ranger Station.

This was before the days of the horse pasture so our leading activity was hunting for straying pack and saddle horses. I could write a book on how those pesky horses schemed to bring gray hairs to our young heads by hiding away in distant nooks and crannies known only to horses equipped with minds of evil. However, Doug and I found time to keep our badges shined and to mark 25 or 30 miles of boundary before somebody found us and put us to counting sheep as they entered the Forest at the old Trout Creek counting corral.

When Doug and I ventured forth that bright spring day, we were young and the world was ours. We were starting to build our future and we had no idea of what was in store for us. This was years before plans for marriage and a home had entered the picture. We were overwhelmed with our new responsibilities.

C. C. McGuire *McGuire began his Forest Service career as a forest guard on the Washington NF in 1909. He received a Ranger appointment in 1910 and was a Ranger until he resigned in 1918. He returned to the Forest Service as a Senior Ranger in 1930. He was Assistant to the Regional Office Training Officer when he retired in 1941.*

On May 1, 1909, I was appointed as a forest guard on the Washington NF. The Forest Supervisor fitted me out with a badge, the Use Book and a marking hatchet. He told me to go to Finney Creek and establish headquarters at the Finney Guard Station. Sixteen miles of trail from Sauk City, the end of rail transportation, to the guard station, had been built the previous year and the winter storms made it impassable except on foot. The one major bridge at Gee Creek was out and in many places the trail was obliterated by slides.

I was told that $300 was set aside to repair the trail and build a bridge across Gee Creek. I was to spend the entire amount and if any surplus was left after maintenance work was done, I was to build a new trail continuing on to Little Deer Creek.

I arrived at old Sauk City at night. The next morning with a pack of beans and bacon on my back, I set out for the Finney Guard Station 16 miles away. I found many logs and slides in the trail and noted that Gee Creek ran through a box canyon about 60 feet wide.

The Finney G.S. was an old log cabin on an abandoned homestead claim. Never before or since have I seen so many mice. They were as thick as flies around a honey pot.

As soon as I had fixed something to eat, I started killing mice with a stick of stove wood, but headway was slow. So I took a five gallon oil tin and cut the top out. Next I got a piece of wire and strung a milk can on the wire and laid it across the opening in the oil can. I put about four inches of water in it and placed a small rock in the water so that just a small portion of the rock extended above the water line. Then I was ready to bait the trap by tying two pieces of bacon on opposite sides of the milk can. Then, with a flat stick leaning from the floor to the top of the oil tin, I was ready for business.

In a few minutes a mouse ran up the stick and not being able to reach the bait, he jumped the few inches necessary to get the bacon. When he lit, the can rolled on the wire axis and Mr. Mouse was in the drink. Soon another went after the bacon and he too went into the drink. The war was on! The rock extending above the water was only big enough to accommodate one mouse and a battle started to see who should have the perch. Their squeals attracted others and soon a procession was moving up the stick, some jumping for the bait and others just diving in to see what the commotion was all about.

Twice that night I emptied the can of dead mice. My first count was 62 and at least as many more on the second count. Business tapered off then for even a mouse will get smart. I spread my bedroll on the old bough bunk and crawled in. In a few minutes mice were in bed with me. That I couldn't take so I moved outside. Mice were even nesting in my boots by morning. The season was pretty well over by the time I got them thinned out enough so I could be comfortable in the cabin. The next morning I hiked out the 16 miles to Sauk, hired a man to help me, purchased about 60 feet of 1 1/4 inch rope and so started to spend the $300.

With the rope and a Spanish windlass we swung two 20" stringers across the box canyon, split puncheon for decking and in three or four days had the bridge in and proceeded with the maintenance. When that job was completed, I still had enough money to build three miles of new trail. My instructions were to spend all the money, so to make it come out even I worked the man two hours and 20 minutes on the last day and the book was balanced. Is it necessary to draw a comparison between then and now?

There were no fires that year and in the absence of further instructions I started posting the Forest boundary, tacking up with wooden pegs the old cloth signs signed by Secretary Wilson and blazing in accordance to instructions in the Use Book.

McGuire took the Ranger Exam in the fall of 1909, after his first summer working for the Forest Service. He received his appointment the following year.

In October 1909, sixteen potential Rangers assembled at the [Washington NF] Supervisor's headquarters in Bellingham for a three-day test of their fitness to become Forest Rangers. The examination was conducted by Supervisor Park and his assistant, A. A. Parker. It is interesting to compare the agenda with latter-day requirements and qualifications.

As memory serves me, the following tests were given:
(1) From the foliage, identify ten species of trees grown on the Mount Baker [NF] – give common and technical names – if you can spell the latter, more power to you.
(2) Fall a tree ten or more inches in diameter with an axe. In giving this test, a stake was driven in the ground about 20 feet from the tree. The victim was allowed to select the point where the stake was driven. All he had to do then was to fall the tree so that it would drive the stake further into the ground. His skill was determined by the nearness of the tree bole to the stake. Only

three candidates out of the sixteen survived that test, one man actually driving the stake. Most trees went wide of the mark with some trees falling in the opposite direction.

(3) Figure magnetic declinations on the four quadrants of the compass. In those days it seems no one thought of the idea of setting off the compass dial.

(4) Run and pace a triangle, prepare the field notes and compute the acreage.

(5) Demonstrate your ability to use a seven-foot cross-cut saw.

(6) Tell the boss man what ingredients and how much of each you would use in preparing a batch of biscuits.

(7) Build and put out a campfire (no accent on getting the last spark).

(8) Pack a horse. This was a toughy – the pack consisted of two loosely tied sacks of oats, an axe, a mattock, a shovel and a cross-cut saw. Also, five days' supply of grub for one man – all unpacked and a conglomeration of cooking equipment. Not only was your skill tested, but you worked against time. Many would-be Rangers fell by the wayside on this test. One bewildered candidate got the packsaddle on backwards with the britchen over the horse's head and used the breast strap for a double cinch. Next he picked up his lash rope and cinch and after he walked around the horse a couple of times, he gave up in despair remarking, "There is no ring on this saddle that will fit the big hook on the end of this rope."

There may have been other tests but they are now forgotten. Anyway, only the following four men survived the three-day test; Ralph Hilligoss, Carl Bell, Grover Burch, and C. C. McGuire.

Harry M. White *White worked 39 years as forest clerk on three Forests and in the District Six/Region Six Office in Operations.*

In the later years of the nineteenth century, there still were fine stands of oak, hickory, maple, and other hardwood species in the hills of southern Indiana, where I grew up. Settlers coming down the Ohio River in pioneer days had carved their farms out of the unbroken forest, felling and burning the trees and planting their crops among the stumps. The forest was an obstruction to agriculture and had to be gotten rid of, with much hard labor.

In my boyhood this clearing process was still going on and we often put in a crop on *new ground*. So far as I remember no one in that part of the country thought of conserving the Forests, and certainly no one visualized a National Forest in the Ohio Valley. Nothing about forest conservation was taught in the public schools.

It was not until 1907 that I saw the western mountains with their magnificent stands of conifer timber and matchless scenery. That year I traveled to California and back, and from then on I was a westerner at heart. Up to that time I knew little or nothing about the Forest Service, although I had heard of the segregation of large areas of the public domain in Forest Reserves.

The summer of 1909, a couple of former Hoosier schoolmasters were batching in the outskirts of Salida, Colorado, and often saw a Forest Ranger riding past their cabin. My buddy remarked that he seemed to have a nice job - nothing to do but ride around. It seems that some of the early employees didn't have a much better idea of what a Forest Ranger was for. E. T. Allen once said that when he received his first appointment and appeared before D. B. Sheller, old-time Supervisor of the Washington Forest, and asked about his duties, D. B. scratched his head awhile and finally said, "You're a Ranger ain't cha? Well, get out and range."

Living in Washington DC during the winter of 1909-10, I was as homesick for the western mountains as any kid ever was for home and mother upon his first adventure into the world. I was determined to return to the West and thought it would be nice to have a job to go to. So when the Forest Service decided that clerks in Forest Supervisor's offices should be men and an examination was announced, I passed it.

And so it was that on a day in June, 1910, I got off the train at Wenatchee, Washington, and took the boat up the Columbia River to Chelan Falls, forty miles and seven hours away. From that point a four-horse stagecoach took me another five miles to the little town of Chelan at the foot of the lake. Little did I suspect that beginning the next day I would be on the Forest Service payroll for nearly thirty-nine years. The reason for staying was that I liked the Forest Service ideals, the personnel, and the work, and I have never ceased to do so.

24

When I went to work Forest boundaries had just been revised and our Forest was comprised of the Chelan and Entiat drainage areas, about 800,000 gross acres. The rest of the orginal Chelan had become the Okanogan with headquarters in the town of the same name. My Supervisor was George Milham. He had been a homesteader in the Upper Methow Valley, then had become a Forest Ranger and been promoted, probably because of native ability above average. His *book larnin* was limited, but he knew the work and had good judgment and considerable executive ability. I liked him and we became good friends. The headquarters force consisted of the Supervisor and clerk, so I was alone when George had to be in the field. As soon as he felt that I could be depended upon, he let me know that I should go ahead with the work in his absence, and not stack up all the mail to await his return. That put me on the spot. I had to study the books and the files and learn as fast as possible. George also had the idea that the Forest clerk could do his job better if he got out into the Forest whenever possible and saw conditions and work on the ground. So he arranged field trips for me whenever he could, even though he had to type some letters by the hunt-and-peck method, and he took me with him to grazing meetings and had me in on conferences with Forest users. I was grateful to him for this, both while on the Chelan and afterward.

The first District officer I met was Charles H. Flory, Chief of Operation, who was at Chelan when I arrived. I had always liked to climb hills and mountains, to see what was on the other side; so the first Sunday I took off up Chelan Butte, which rose about 2,800 feet above the town and afforded a grand view of the Big Bend wheat fields and meadows to the east and a sea of rugged mountains to the west. To my surprise, I found Flory already on top - he liked to climb up and look around too. A couple of years later I met C. J. Buck, Chief of Lands, who was then spending much time on Forest homestead work. I also met Howard K. O'Brien, Chief of Grazing, and his successor, Thomas P. MacKenzie. O'Brien taught me more about filing than anybody else (these pioneer foresters were versatile - they had to be).

In 1913, I was called to Leavenworth, where Albert Cousins, Chief of Accounts, explained a new accounting system to Emmet Springer, Clerk on the Wenatchee, and me. At that time the complete Forest accounting system was kept on a few 8" x 10" cards. How simple compared with what it later became! The next year a handsome young man came along to make entry surveys; that was Kirk Cecil. In July 1913, Oliver Ericson was assigned as Forest Assistant, just after he had graduated from the University of Washington. He was the first graduate of a western forestry school that I met; the others were from eastern and midwestern schools.

So, gradually I got acquainted with several of the District Officers and other foresters, and a little forestry and other knowledge rubbed off on me. In the winters of 1913 and 1914 the Division Chiefs and other District Office men and two or three Supervisors wrote correspondence courses for the Rangers, covering a variety of subjects, most of which I had never studied or on which I had only a smattering of information. I was, therefore, glad to be permitted to work on these courses. To write the lessons and review the papers must have taken a lot of the time of these busy men. It was a fine thing for them to do.

It must be difficult for men of a later generation to visualize conditions as they were in the National Forests during the first two decades of the current century. In our little Forest, conditions were crude indeed during the five years I was there. We had few roads, good trails, telephone lines and buildings. The annual allotment for improvements, including maintenance, was generally less than $700, plus a very small amount from the Ten Per Cent Road Fund. A windfall appropriation in 1908 had permitted the building of a 50-mile telephone line up the lake [Chelan], but otherwise communication was over a few farmers' lines. Until 1914 not a single lookout was established. The few guards rode the trails or cross-country and looked for smokes from vantage points along the way. If a fire was seen at a distance, they could judge its location only by using a small crude compass and by their knowledge of the country. Then it could be reported only by riding a long distance. As I look back over the later years, when large fires burned on both sides of the lake, it is a wonder to me that the whole country didn't burn over in the earlier years.

My introduction to the Forest Service came in an exceptionally bad fire year, yet there were only two fires of any size on the Chelan;

about 500 and 300 acres, as I remember. But that situation really put me up against it, for the Supervisor and the District Ranger, Jack Blankenship, were on the larger fire and far out of communication when the smaller one broke out on a hot Friday afternoon in mid-August. It was on a steep slope to Twenty-five Mile Creek and Jack's wife called the office in great excitement. There I was, a six-weeks-old employee, alone, inexperienced, and with no knowledge of the country, and "Sheridan 30 miles away!" Then occurred one of those instances - and there must have been many such on the various Forests - which gladdened the hearts of the Forest Service pioneers, an instance of hearty cooperation by a man who understood what the Forest Service was trying to do and was all for it. His name was Gaines. He lived on a fruit ranch up the lake and had a telephone on the Forest Service line. He cut in on our conversation and offered to go to the fire with his boys and two other men, five in all. So the initial attack was made early that evening.

Walt L. Dutton   *Dutton was appointed Forest Guard on the Fremont NF in 1911. He finished forestry school in 1913 and was appointed Assistant Forest Ranger. He transferred to the Cascade NF in 1915. He worked on the Wallowa NF, was Forest Supervisor of the Malheur and Whitman NFs, worked in Grazing in the R-6 Office, and was Chief of the Division of Range Management in the Washington Office when he retired in 1953.*

When Scott Leavitt was principal of the Lakeview, Oregon, high school before he became a Forest Ranger, he talked a great deal about the new Roosevelt-Pinchot forestry movement. He even predicted that someday many major colleges and universities would carry courses leading to degrees in forestry. Lynn Cronemiller (later State Forester for Oregon) and I took Scott's advice and entered the School of Forestry at Oregon Agricultural College (now Oregon State University) in the fall of 1909.

I received my first appointment [in 1911] as forest guard at $900 per annum and was assigned to the Paisley District of the Fremont Forest under District Ranger Jason Elder. Cronemiller and I reported for duty to Forest Supervisor Gilbert Brown at his office in Lakeview, Oregon.

Gilbert instructed us to go to a place known as Ingram Guard Station, fifty miles northwest of Lakeview, and repair a pasture fence which

27

we would find had been broken down by the weight of winter snows. He then issued us the equipment then considered standard for forest guards. Each signed for the following items: double-bitted axe with scabbard, Forest Service marking hatchet, claw hammer and tacks, long handled shovel, standard Forest Service compass with Jacob staff, tally register, 7' x 9' tent, Dutch oven, two canvas saddle bags (only the Rangers could have leather saddle bags), a good supply of variously worded James Wilson cloth posters, Forest Service green-backed note book, two pencils (one Faber #3 and one indelible), a large Forest Service brass badge to be worn over the left shirt pocket, and finally, the national flag which was to be flown even in temporary camps.

We furnished our own saddle and pack horses, saddles, and horse feed and boarded ourselves - all on $75.00 per month. There was no uniform allowance in those days but we felt nattily outfitted in khaki-colored shirt and trousers, green tie, stiff-brimmed Stetson hat and laced boots with trousers tucked inside. Our left shirt pockets sagged a bit with the weight of the big brass badge.

The Forest Supervisor came downstairs to help us pack. A small crowd of curious but friendly onlookers had gathered to watch the proceedings. But that didn't bother us at all. We had already been taught how to throw a *squaw hitch* - probably the most ineffective hitch known to packers - and we used it then. We also used this hitch later that fall when we took the Ranger examination in Albany under the direction of Supervisor MacDuff. Doubtless Mac graded us down because we didn't know how to throw a diamond. Later, of course, we became reasonably adept at throwing an assortment of hitches.

The first night out from Lakeview we camped at Jack and Jenny Buttes on the Chewaucan River just south of the Gaylord place. We had read somewhere that Forest Rangers began their day with a cold dip in a mountain stream. So, next morning before breakfast we did just that - plunged right into the Chewaucan River which, at the time, was running high and cold from melting snows off Gearhart Mountain. After that, as I recall, we did without cold morning dips.

Next day, about midafternoon, we figured we had reached Ingram Station. But, except for the remnants of a wire fence, there was nothing on the ground to identify the site. Here was a poser. Other pastures in the vicinity also needed repair and our problem was to find out which was located on the Ingram Station site. Somehow we seemed to feel that a wrong decision here would jeopardize our future careers. Besides, we didn't want to put in a lot of hard work fixing the other fellow's fence! It was then and there that we made our first practical use of some of the technical knowledge gained from our forestry course.

It was as simple as finding a section line in a stand of lodgepole pine, following the blazes until we came upon a section corner, reading the inscriptions on the corner stone and witness trees, and learning that we stood at the SW corner of Section 19, T. 34 S., R. 17 E., WM. Only then were we sure we had located the Ingram Station pasture. That was fifty-eight years ago as of this writing and few, if any, accomplishments since then have produced the same degree of inner satisfaction.

<u>Jack Groom</u> *Groom wrote this story about his father, Fred, who took the Ranger exam at the Whitman NF Forest Supervisor's Office in 1911. Fred was the first Ranger to be stationed at Dale, Oregon and retired as a District Ranger on the Whitman NF. Jack Groom was a long term Forest Service employee and has two stories in Chapter Three (All in a Day's Work and Grazing).*

Fred Groom was a self-educated man having attended school near Ukiah, Oregon, only until the age of 12. At that time it was necessary for him to drop out of school to help make a life for himself and his mother following the death of his father. However, during the remainder of his formative years he read everything he could get his hands on including many of the classics. And so it was at the age of 28 he heard that there were some openings with the Forest Service for a job as a Forest Ranger. He studied hard to master the subjects he would have to know in order to pass the Ranger's examination. In 1911, along with about fifteen others, he took this test at the Forest Service headquarters in Sumpter, Oregon. All who took the examination were local men like himself except for two Forestry graduates from an eastern school.

Besides the technical examination, part of the test had to do with the requirement that each one demonstrate his ability to saddle and pack two horses as if he were going on a trip into the back country. All the materials including blankets, tarps, ropes, eggs, canned goods and other provisions were stacked alongside the saddles and packbags. Two fairly gentle horses were provided. This, of course, was *old hat* for local boys. Fred was the first to volunteer. He quickly completed the loading, got on the horse and galloped down to the end of the lane and back. The two eastern boys waited until the last, carefully observing each of the others. Finally, one of them took his turn. By that time, old Nell, the packhorse, had become considerably disenchanted with the whole setup. She had been forced to gallop down this same lane and back over a dozen times and couldn't really see that she was getting anywhere. So when she started out with this young man's pack, the cinches not being in their usual place and the pack not feeling too solid, she must have decided that this was her opportunity to unload. She started bucking and the pack came apart throwing cans and everything else in the load out into the brush alongside the road. Old-timers reported years later finding unopened cans at a considerable distance from the old road and wondering how in the world they ever got there.

ACCEPTANCE AND SUPPORT: "-to achieve acceptance and support was clearly a challenge-"

Dahl Kirkpatrick *Kirkpatrick, also a long-term Forest Service employee, wrote this story about his dad, John, who reported to the Rainier NF in 1908 to begin his career as Forest Ranger. John spent his entire career on this area of the Rainier, which later became part of the Columbia NF, and retired in 1934. Dahl began his career in 1928 on his fathers Ranger District. He worked on the Columbia, Siuslaw, and Mt. Baker NFs and in the R-6 Regional Office. He was the Assistant Regional Forester for Timber in R-3 when he retired in 1965. John Kirkpatrick's grandson and great-granddaughter also work for the Forest Service. Four generations!*

At the outset [1908] the [Randle] community attitude toward the Forest Service could only be characterized as hostile. The establishment of the [Rainier] Forest had removed land from homestead entry and had otherwise had the effect of inhibiting the liberties of the settlers who had been accustomed to helping themselves to anything they wanted from the public lands. The feeling was widespread that the development of the country would be seriously retarded by the coming of National Forest administration. To achieve acceptance and support for Forest Service program and objectives in the face of this universal ill will was clearly a challenge.

There were no Forest Service-built improvements in the District save the house and barn at the station and the telephone line to Lewis. What few trails existed were largely unimproved ways of travel through the country that had been used by Indians and early day prospectors. There was a very poor wagon trail from the valley settlements across a low divide into the Cispus River drainage immediately to the south of the Cowlitz Valley. This had been built by the few settlers in the Cispus area and augmented by the efforts of people cutting shingle bolts along the Cispus River. The river was used to transport the bolts to shingle mills in the developed country on the lower Cowlitz. There were no forest fire lookouts and for a year or two after dad's arrival on the job, there was no money to hire seasonal personnel. It was strictly a one-man show.

Early work included examination and reporting on the few Forest homestead claims established within the Forest boundaries under the Act of June 11, 1906. It was often necessary, too, to survey lines along the boundary of National Forest-private lands to settle disputes or prevent trespass. Another early activity which consumed a lot of time in the early stages of administration on the District was making and supervising the sale of shingle bolts at various points on the District; especially in Cispus which was six or seven hours by horseback from Randle. Spare time was occupied with improving the pasture at the headquarters station.

The following note of [John Kirkpatrick's retirement] event was reported in the Region Six Administrative Bulletin, the "6-26": "In the spring of 1908 a stranger came to the valley. He was afoot leading a pack horse loaded with bedding and a few personal effects. At the post office he inquired for the Forest Service mail and asked the way to the Ranger Station. He was regarded with suspicion and disdain. In the fall of 1934 in the high school gymnasium a program sponsored jointly by the Grange, Garden Club, Ladies Aid, High School, Odd

Fellows and Rebeccas was attended by some 250 residents of the valley of all ages and all walks of life. They had gathered there to express their appreciation of the efforts of the 'man who led the horse'." The piece went on to identify my dad as the man in question.

<u>Grover C. Blake</u> *Blake remembers the challenge facing early Forest Service employees to gain public acceptance.*

How well I remember the fight made by Gifford Pinchot with the backing of Theodore Roosevelt to save the remaining natural resources for the benefit of all the people and for the *greatest good to the greatest number in the long run.* It was a courageous fight against great odds - the powerful, well-financed and well-entrenched private interests, including the timber barons who wished to exploit the remaining timber lands and others who desired to gain private control over power sites and other natural resources.

<u>John D. Guthrie</u> *Guthrie's work in District/Region 6 included his 1907 experience, then in Information in 1920 and as Assistant District Forester in 1922. He also worked in the Washington Office Civilian Conservation Corps program and in Information and Education. He retired in 1943. Guthrie wrote some 200 articles on forestry and related conservation subjects throughout his career, and also edited and published two books of poetry written by Foresters and Rangers.*

Although not in D-6 when the District was established, I was here in 1907 and did work on the Siuslaw, Mt. Hood, Deschutes and Crater Forests, and know somewhat of the condition of public sentiment in those days. And so I may be pardoned for a word or two on the public's attitude toward forestry and foresters of that day. Those were the days of the *timber barons* and *malefactors of great wealth.* In the eyes of the average lumberman, foresters were mere microbes, hardly worthy of serious attention. The famous timber fraud cases of the Northwest were still fresh in the public mind, and the *government* was none too popular in these parts. When the press did notice us, it was to ridicule, revile, malign and misrepresent. We were the blockers of progress; we were the lockers-up of natural resources; the name of Gifford Pinchot was *anathema maranatha* to many papers and many of the people of the region. One of the leading local papers was an especially bitter enemy of the Service and Mr. Pinchot.

We all know how different is the attitude of the press and the public today. What has brought about that change? Surely it didn't just happen. I believe it is almost entirely due to the high character of Forest Officers throughout the twenty years since 1908. If I am right, then no higher compliment can possibly be paid to the Service as an organization than that its members were honest and loyal and at all times tried to be fair and yet faithful to their trusts as guardians and managers of the public's properties.

<u>Thornton T. Munger</u> *Munger visited Rosland, near present day LaPine, Oregon, for the first time while on assignment from the Washington Office.*

Rosland then consisted of a store, hotel, stage and feed stables, the Ranger's 2-room house and office (the former saloon) and a couple of residences. But it was the biggest town in 10,000 square miles. In a letter written while there in 1908, I said, "It is a hotbed of land squabbles, and the air is full of them. The Forest Service is more talked of than any other subject, and though the people are very polite, some of them are awfully sore at the Service. Many of them have gotten claims fraudulently and got caught by the Service, or are trying to get timberland and claim that it is agricultural. Nearly everyone who passes through town is looking for a place to locate."

<u>Henry "H. E." Haefner</u> *Haefner worked on the Siskiyou NF from 1909 to 1925.*

A short distance below the West Moore Ranger Station [Siskiyou NF in about 1908] an old schoolmate of Ranger Walter J. Jones resided on a ranch, but these men were never on very friendly terms. The rancher's house was close to the road leading from the station to the settlements on the coast. The road ran across his land. The Forest Service had the right to use the road by agreement but the rancher soon began to resent its use by the Forest Service and especially by Walter. The rancher had several boys growing up, the oldest of which soon became a man in size and strength though still very young. When the boy was about 19 years old, a powerful youngster weighing about 190 pounds, he blocked the road one morning as Walter was on the way to the settlement. The boy's family was inside the house looking out of the windows to see what would happen. Walter sensed that a showdown would have to come sooner or later and now was as good a time as any. They went at it with bare fists and Walter knocked that boy or man down four or five times before he had enough. After that there was no more trouble about using the road.

C. P. Cronk *Cronk was a forest guard on the Siuslaw NF in 1910 and 1911, and Assistant Forest Ranger in 1911. In November 1910, he took two Forest Service donkeys from Eugene to Hebo.*

This was approximately 225 miles and 22 days from Eugene. Because the night stops were more or less routine, only one stands out. I discovered that in the Willamette Valley, east over the Coast Range from the Siuslaw National Forest, a Ranger was still an oddity. A bit north of Corvallis I inquired at a house if I might put the burros in a fenced pasture I had noticed. There was hesitancy, but finally it was decided that the burros could be taken care of and I could sleep in the barn and get supper and breakfast. After supper the boys of the family brought out copies of the Youths' Companion to show me a series of articles on the Forest Ranger and to ask questions about the life of a Ranger. A couple of hours later, as I asked the man of the house if he would give me a call as he went out to the barn in the morning, he said, "If you don't mind sleeping with the boys we can put you up in the house." I had talked myself into a bed.

J. M. Schmitz *Schmitz was Forest Supervisor of the Wenaha Reserve at the time of this story.*

The Wenaha Forest [Reserve] was mainly a grazing Forest with not much saw timber, so the timber sales were not very heavy. But it was the wood lot for farmers for miles around the north, south, and west sides, and would now come under free use. The work involved was so great and there was so much more important work, we had to use every possible short cut. We would advertise certain dates when all who wanted free use of timber permits could get them at Cloverland, Peola and La Grande, but the west side permits could be handled from the Supervisor's office in Walla Walla whenever required. Each permit was for a certain designated dead wood area. No record was kept of the amount of wood taken. Some may have taken more than the permit called for, but on the whole I believe they took less. At one time we had the record free-use business of all the Forests.

34

Once in 1905, two parties from Dayton wrote saying they had some wood cut, and what were they to do about it? I made a sale to them at a small stumpage price, which I reported to the Portland office. I was severely criticized for making the sale, the office saying it was a clear case of trespass and it should have been reported as such. But if we had made trespass cases of all the wood taken without permit from the Forest in 1905, there would have been hundreds of them which would have caused a tremendous amount of work. However, what I was anxious to avoid was the creation of hard feelings against the Forest. On a Forest where practically every foot was in use, we needed the cooperation of those users, and if we antagonized them for every little wrong done, they could cause a lot of trouble.

Hugh V. Anderson   *Hugh Anderson, also a Forest Service employee, wrote about his father, Milton J. Anderson, when Milton was Forest Supervisor of the Siskiyou NF. Milton began his forestry career with the General Land Office in The Dalles, Oregon in 1902 at the age of 42.*

One of the few times I recall that my father ever wore his Forest Service uniform other than to Ranger meetings, he ended up shoeing a horse in it.

My father and I came out of the woods at the Southern Pacific Railroad Station between Roseburg and Grants Pass, Oregon, called West Fork [in 1908 or 1909]. It was from here that the mail was being carried by pack train through the mountains to Illahee on Rogue River and from there on down to the town of Gold Beach at the mouth of the river on the Pacific coast. Our purpose was to catch the next train south to Grants Pass which was the Siskiyou headquarters.

Our uniforms had been left at the small hotel as we had gone into the Forest, so we washed up and dressed for the return trip. We had about forty-five minutes to spare before train time so walked over to the railroad station where the natives usually gathered. On our way over we noticed a circle of men struggling with a horse which they had securely tied and wrapped with rope and which they had thrown to the ground. It developed that they were trying to put shoes on one of the animals of the mail pack train.

35

My father was known as a practical joker, so when he remarked that if he only had thirty minutes he would show them how to shoe the horse, there followed some joking in which it was pointed out that he had the time. In the end several bets were made that he could not accomplish the job. Dad removed his stiff Stetson hat and his Forest Service coat and cautiously approached the animal which he had ordered released from the many entangling ropes. At least ten minutes were spent in getting a hand on the horse's neck where he petted him gently. The frightened animal calmed down almost immediately, perhaps due in part to the fact that he had previously practically exhausted himself. In any event, my father proceeded to pick up that horse's hooves, one by one, measure the horseshoes to the foot, cold spring the shoes, and tack them on as only an expert could do. He gleefully collected his bets and in his much-bedraggled condition, with horse hair and dirt clinging to him, we barely caught the train.

The men at West Fork, of course, did not know that my father had served an early apprenticeship as a fancy carriage ironer at the Union Iron Works in San Francisco. Nor did they know he had been a blacksmith in eastern Oregon after returning from the Alaskan gold fields. He had become more proficient in the shoeing of horses than in ironing fancy carriages.

The feat he had performed in shoeing the horse was told far and wide in the community. It demonstrated his ability of a kind, but it gained their respect of him as a man among them. He and the type of Forest Service men who served in the early period served it well.

Harold E. Smith *Smith began his career in 1911 as a Ranger on the Paulina NF. His District became part of the Deschutes NF in 1915. He transferred to Alaska in 1919, where he was a forester, District Ranger, and Deputy Regional Forester. He retired in 1945.*

During the winter of 1917, following our entry into World War One, I was commissioned to sell war bonds for the government, ex-officio and without extra compensation. As a further contribution to the war effort, I was glad to take on this extra work.

My territory laid along the fringe of the high desert southeast of Bend, Oregon. By 1917, the high desert was fairly well populated by newcomers and the old settlers were fretting about the fencing of their former grazing lands. Houses were mere shacks, box-car type construction, where the wife held forth in order to meet the homestead law requirements. The breadwinner of the family usually sought gainful employment elsewhere, often in the lumber industry at Bend.

These were the type of people I had to deal with in trying to sell war bonds. The usual reply was "We would like to help but we do not have the money." Once in a while I could sell a $25.00 bond but seldom anything of a larger denomination. One day I noticed that the Sloan sheep had moved to the east spur of Pine Mountain, some four miles from my station. It occurred to me that I might be able to sell a bond to the herder. I waited till late in the evening and rode over to his camp. The sheep and three border collies as their chaperones had bedded down for the night. I gladly accepted the herder's invitation to step inside the tent for it was a bit cold and windy. Inside, the little Yukon stove maintained a comfortable degree of warmth.

There was nothing elaborate about the camp, strictly a temporary abode devoid of things not essentially necessary. Camps of this type are moved every few days as the sheep drift from one grazing area to another. The herder was about 50 years old, dressed in the typical winter garb of the profession, mackinaw coat and blue jeans. He was no paragon of cleanliness, yet not too grimy, considering that camp water had to be hauled some ten to fifteen miles. I saw no reading matter and assumed that he had no time for literary indulgence. His was a seven-day-a-week job, beginning at daylight, when the sheep began to move, and ending well after dark when he had finished his camp chores. Tomorrow would be a repeat of today.

I sized up the situation and decided there would be no point in bringing up the subject of a bond sale. On the other hand, I had ridden four miles for this interview. To quit now would be admitting defeat before the first gun was fired. After filling him in on the latest developments of the war, I asked if he would be interested in buying a bond. He thought he would and I thought, "This is going to be easier than I figured." My next question was, "How much can you handle, about twenty-five?" Yes, he thought twenty-five would be all right.

When I handed him the application to sign, made out for $25.00, he said, "I didn't mean twenty-five dollars, I meant twenty-five hundred."

My heart skipped a beat and I wondered if I had heard him correctly. "Surely you don't carry that amount of money up here," I said.

"No, I don't carry any money with me. I don't need it up here. Sloan furnishes everything I need so I just let my wages accumulate," he replied.

I proceeded to write an order on Sloan for $2500.00, which the herder signed along with the application for the bonds. I thanked him, mounted and headed the old sorrel out across the sagebrush.

Next morning I cranked up the Model T and drove over to the Sloan Ranch, on the theory that if the fellow was in his right senses I wanted to clinch the deal before he had a chance to change his mind. When I presented the order to Mr. Sloan and explained the reason behind it, he was very cooperative. "Yes, we can take care of that," he said.

And so I drove back with Sloan's check in my pocket. Amount $2500.00 made payable to the Treasurer of the United States of America.

ALL in a DAY'S WORK: "-it was hard work physically, but we were young and enjoyed it-"

Melvil "M. L." Merritt *Merritt's first job with the Forest Service was as a Forest Assistant on the Washington NF in 1909.*

[Fred] Brundage came in that night, a young forester just out of Yale. My spirits were up again. We worked together most of the rest of the summer and fall, first staying with the Allens, then moving up river and operating from our own camps. Each day, working separately, we would climb the hills to timber line at about 3,500 feet. We sketched in the upper limits of tree growth on the map and estimated the stand per acre, recording the main species. In this way we crisscrossed the timber slopes on both sides of the river, moving camp upstream as the work progressed. The river was crossed on *log jams*, of which there were several. It was hard work physically, but we were young and enjoyed it. We covered the Suiattle River drainage up to and including Milk Creek, flowing directly out of Glacier Peak. The water of this stream was milky in color, hence the name. Several other parts of the Forest were also covered.

There were many interesting incidents during this work. It rained a great deal, and, later in the season, snowed. At times, traveling was very disagreeable. We cooked our own food, except the few days at Allen's camp. Rice was the principal starch item. Each of us carried a rifle and usually one or the other would come in at night with a pheasant or grouse. So far as I know, this was before the days of game laws. While our diet was simple, it was ample and appetizing. One of our camps just above Buck Creek was under an Indian shelter, a pole frame with shake roof and no sides. It was waterproof from the top and quite comfortable. However, something was eating our food that was not securely covered, and food had to be carried in on our backs. From the odors, we concluded that the culprit was a civet cat. The thefts were at night. We could hear the rustling among our supplies, but eliminating the animal by shooting seemed a case of where the cure might be worse than the disease. Another solution was required. I had some bi-cloride of mercury tablets for use in case of infection. A few of these were crushed and spread on a slice of buttered bread and left as the only easily accessible food. That night the rustling was heard as usual and in the morning the treated bread was gone. This is the end, we thought, but the following night, much to our surprise, our visitors returned. So again bread was treated, but with a heavier dose. That night our visitors again paid us a visit - but they never returned.

Dahl Kirkpatrick *This is another story by Dahl about his father, John, while John was Ranger on the Rainier NF.*

The suppression of fires during the summer season with very limited authority to hire help, and the absence of adequate communication and poor or non-existent travel routes to the fire vicinity made the job formidable to say the least. Endless hours of excruciatingly hard work with nothing but hand tools was common. One very extreme example illustrates the problem faced by the early-day Ranger. In the summer of 1909, Forest Supervisor Allen was in the Yakima area visiting the east-of-the-Cascades Rangers. A fire was reported to him that was said to be menacing the Yakima Indian Reservation in the Potato Hill area on the Cascade Divide, some ten miles north of Mt. Adams. Mr.

Allen immediately telegraphed his office in Orting with instructions to have Ranger William McCullough go to Randle and join my dad and a hired local man and go handle the fire. McCullough probably came by train to the Morton area and by freight wagon or afoot to Randle. The three men with their camp outfit and tools packed on a horse required five days of hard travel through unmapped forested country with no trails or at best very poor miner and Indian trails to reach the fire. It was too extensive for them to control but they stayed with it until their food nearly ran out. With nothing left but a large pot of beans, they decided there must be an easier way home, so rather than going back down the Cispus as they had come, they struck out across country and finally, after nearly three days, reached the Cowlitz Valley just west of the village of Lewis. To be certain that the beans wouldn't be spilled, Ranger McCullough carried the bean bucket in his hand two days until the contents were consumed.

Grover C. Blake *Blake wrote this story about an event on the Umpqua NF involving two of his fellow Forest Service employees.*

Back in June 1909, Vern Harpham and Volney Oden of the Forest Service ventured forth from Roseburg with saddle and pack horses to build a horse pasture at Diamond Lake. After four days of hard travel over the best trails available at that time, they reached their destination and made camp on the south shore of the lake. Harpham says that there was no trail that could be called a trail up the river at that time but it was possible to take a horse over the route by working around windfalls, along the face of rocky bluffs and by crossing some dangerous fords.

Oden and Harpham pitched camp and settled down to fence a pasture which was badly needed for the saddle and pack stock of Forest officers, but before they could get under way, Oden took sick with the measles and Harpham found it necessary to convert their camp into a hospital with himself as doctor, nurse, cook and bottle washer. He stored up a great supply of fire wood. He knew that within ten days or so there would be another case of measles in the camp and they were entirely dependent upon themselves for survival. They were probably the only human beings within an area of several hundred square miles. Vern tells me George Bonebrake, Bob Watson and two others had gone to Big Camas to build a log cabin some 25 miles from Diamond

Lake, but there was no means of communication so dealing with the measles was their own, private affair. They weathered the ordeal successfully and, as soon as he was able, Vern walked out to get assistance, their horses having strayed away and gone out to Beaver Marsh.

Blake describes a confrontation with a bear.

The only trail in my District [on the Deschutes NF] in 1910, other than game trails and a few Indian and trappers trails, was one constructed in 1908 by the Forest Service along the summit of the Blue Mountains called Summit Trail. Summit Trail passed through several Ranger Districts and maintenance was performed by the Ranger [District work] force. Rangers C. C. Hon and W. A. Donnelly, forest guard Zevely and I got together on August 4, 1910, to do the necessary maintenance work through our respective Districts. The first night we camped under the north rim of Mt. Pisgah where a small meadow provided horse feed. Shortly after making camp I killed a deer and Hon and I dressed it and hung the meat in a tree, taking what we could carry in the darkness to our camp. Early the following morning the four of us met at the spot to carry the rest of the meat in.

Hon and Donnelly were the first to arrive. While waiting for Zevely and me, a very huge bald-faced grizzly bear reared up on a nearby log to sniff the scent coming from the venison. They were afraid to shoot as their guns were light and they had only three cartridges so decided to wait for Zevely and me. They thought the bear had laid down behind the log, but when we arrived the bear had departed. Ranger Hon described the bear as much larger than the common black bear and as having a head and neck of snow white. His huge track was frequently seen after that, but, to the best of my knowledge, he never again revealed himself to human eye.

<u>J. Fred McClain</u> *McClain began with the Forest Service in 1906 on the Imnaha NF. He was a Ranger at Joseph for 30 years, retiring in 1939.*

Two old prospectors I met on the Imnaha River at the Forks, Sam Davidson and J. Roy Harvey by name, put in four years looking for a ledge that had pieces of float but could not locate the ledge. They

41

said this float contained a metal which would be in great demand in the near future. It was in 1907, and they said they were quitting and said if I happened to be on Boner Flat, a high plateau between the middle and south forks of the Imnaha River, to go to their cabin where I would find one quart of old Scotch whiskey with the seal unbroken and a half quart with the seal broken. Later that summer I crossed Boner Flat looking over some sheep range. I went to this old cabin and sure enough, there was the old Scotch.

Another old prospector, a Mexican by the name of Manuel Lopaz, had a mine in the Lake Basin area. He wanted the whole Lake Basin set aside for him to pasture his six horses. This caused quite a lot of trouble as he was always into it with some sheepherder or camptender, and at one time he shot a French sheepherder in the foot. One of my trips up into the Lake Basin was to settle an argument between him and a camptender.

After the trouble between them was settled, he asked me to go with him as he wished to show me the rich mineral deposits in his mine. He led me to the entrance of his tunnel which started from a small cave inside of a sheer wall 100 feet high and reached by a rope ladder leading down to this small depression in the wall. I hesitated going down the ladder in such a dangerous place, but he assured me that it was perfectly safe. So, I followed him down and went into his tunnel to find the same formation in the tunnel as outside - no sign of mineral bearing ore. In going back up the ladder, after he had climbed out, I caught hold of the rope in a way that turned it part over and say, did I try to lose weight! The ropes on both ends of the ladder were cut over half in two! I think this put a grey hair or two in my head as the rope was very old. Upon my arrival at the top I asked him why this was done. He said it was caused by the wind blowing the ladder back and forth against the wall. I told him it certainly made a very smooth cut! I watched him very carefully when in his company after that.

On one of my trips up into the Lake Basin in early summer, I stopped at one of the beautiful lakes which was still covered with snow and ice except for a small opening at the foot of the lake. My curiosity caused me to walk around this opening to see if I could locate any fish. Did I ever get a wet ducking when I stepped on an area of a large snowdrift! It proved to be covered with a coating of ice and I slid into the lake

42

over my head. I scrambled out and went to my horse for matches out of my saddle pockets and a hatchet. Then I built a fire. I took off my clothes to dry by the fire, but not for long. I had to scramble to put my clothes back on again in a hurry as the mosquitoes came by the millions - lit all over my body and began boring their bills into me. Needless to say, I did not wish to be host to their feast. I mounted my horse and rode back down the trail, thankful for a wind which helped dry my clothes by the time I reached the settlement.

<u>William G. Weigle</u> *Weigle began his forestry career in the east in 1904 with the Bureau of Forestry. He worked on assignments throughout the west and in North Carolina from 1905 to 1910. (He was a Forest Supervisor in northern Idaho during the 1910 fire holocaust.) He was Forest Supervisor in Alaska from 1911 to 1919 while this area was part of District Six. He was Forest Supervisor of the Snoqualmie NF when he retired in 1933.*

In 1911, Assistant Forester Lage Wernstedt of the Cordova, Alaska, office outfitted a lone river boat to be used in a timber investigation of Bremner River, an eastern branch of the Copper River. He and another man traveled by train from Cordova to a point where the Bremner entered the Copper River, crossed Copper River and started up the Bremner. The Bremner was swift so the boat in most places had to be pulled along the shore until they reached a canyon where the rocky shores made progress very slow. They had their provisions, bedding, camera, guns and all their equipment for a month's camping in the boat. There were places in the rocky canyon where one would have to hold the boat line while the other climbed around the rocks and relieved the other man by taking the line. In one place, the swift water jerked the line out of Lage's hand and down the river went the boat and all the equipment. The boat landed on a little island in the middle of the stream where it was impossible to reach. They had no means of crossing the Copper River to get back to Cordova. It was approximately 100 miles to Chitina and not a house in that distance. The country was rough the entire distance, with plenty of Kodiak bear, but it was good huckleberry country so the bears were well fed. This left little danger of the bear bothering anyone as long as you kept away from them.

At their first camp out, they had abandoned a small pot of beans which, with the berries, was all the provisions they had for four days.

They finally arrived at the Chitina River, a branch of the Copper. The little railroad town of Chitina was on the north side. An Indian offered to take them across the Chitina River, but he wanted a dollar. Since they had no money, he finally put them across. Just by luck, I happened to be at Chitina that day so the Indian got his dollar! The boys were foot sore, tired and hungry, so I ordered them a good steak dinner. The next day we went to Cordova on the train.

One day, Ranger McDonald of Cordova took his boat, *The Restless,* out to Hinchinbrook Island to scale some timber. He anchored his boat and walked a mile to the timber and just as he reached the timber, he ran into a big Kodiak bear. His monthly report card read, "I went to Hinchinbrook Island to scale some timber. I was fully a mile from the boat and met a big Kodiak bear at 12:01. Reached the boat at 12:02."

Ranger McDonald and I left one day in *The Restless* for Katalla, about 100 miles south. In order to protect ourselves from the ocean winds, we traveled through the muddy waters of the Copper River delta and its thousand or more islands. In making short turns, the nose of the boat would run into the bank and plough out buckets of razorback clams. These clams, at that time, were not used commercially, but by 1925 there were a dozen canneries in the Cordova region depending upon the Copper River clams. We continued south through the islands, but when we left their shelter we got caught in a heavy storm and had to tie up behind a little island for three days. We thought the wind subsided enough to sail through a small inlet into Katalla but just before we got in, a strong gust of wind blew us up on a rocky shore and punched three holes into the hull of our boat. We had a canvas, some thin boards, and tar on the boat to make temporary repairs, but when we were ready we had to pay $50.00 to have the boat pulled into the water.

Duffy Lewis *Lewis took and passed the Ranger exam in 1912, but didn't receive a Ranger appointment until after graduating from forestry school in 1913.*

In the spring of 1912, having passed the Ranger's exam, I was assigned to the Gardiner District [on the Siuslaw NF], as Acting Ranger, Pete Rice having resigned. The District was about 40 miles long and 20 wide, along the Pacific Ocean from Coos Bay north to a

44

point just south of Florence. There was no railroad at that time and the only road was a dirt one from Gardiner to Florence. The land was cut up by many creeks, and wherever the bottomland was wide enough, there were beautiful dairy ranches operated by the most hospitable folks I have ever known. To this day, their homes are second homes to me. The only means of transporting ranch products was by boat on rivers and lakes.

I soon found that my boat, scow and horse were nearly useless. The boat (when I could get the engine to run) would be at the wrong end of the river and the scow and horse on the wrong side. I finally got rid of them and used the mail boats, and hiked the rest of the time. I seldom tell people how far I used to hike because it is pretty hard for me to believe it myself! It was on one of these hikes along the Florence-Gardiner road (at night) that I had quite an experience. It was so dark that when I held up my hand I could barely see the outline. Suddenly there was a "BOO-BOO-BOO" and a violent stamping of feet. I nearly had the *blind staggers*.

I said "what the h---?"

A voice said, "God, I thought you was a bear." We lit a match and looked at each other. We had never seen each other before nor since.

Our Supervisor at that time was very frugal, to say the least. When I had to go to Coos Bay, the fare was around $7.00, but with my $75.00 a month salary as an Acting Ranger, I could hardly stand much of that. Passengers for the Coos Bay stage would ride the stern-wheeler *Eva* from Gardiner to the mouth of the Umpqua. When I got ashore I would start walking down the beach. [Since there was no road, the stage used the beach as the route of travel.] When the stage came up behind me, I glanced back to see which side the curtain was on (it was always on the windy side). Then, as it passed me on the blind side, I would hop on the trunk rack. This gave me a ten-mile lift to a convenient location just before the stage reached Ten Mile Creek. I had to leave it there lest they discovered how I had been able to keep up with them for the last ten miles. From there I still had to walk the ten miles or so to Coos River. What a contrast to the way employees in government cars get over the District now.

45

William F. Burge *Burge worked for the Forest Service for 41 years on the Okanogan and Chelan NFs.*

My first experience with some of our *struggles* was in 1915 when [Okanogan National Forest] Supervisor H. M. Hale sent me as a special grazing guard into the high mountains to supervise some ten bands of sheep. These bands of sheep were made up mostly of dry sheep and were all 1200 to 1400 head bands.

No permittee had an allotment. All 10 bands were sent to the Ashnola country, and it was my job to place these sheep on summer range. I had no idea how large an area it took for a band of sheep, but I soon realized I had a tough problem. First, I had to fight my way through the mountains without any trails except for the driveway which had been opened up in 1913-14. I reached the Ashnola on June 12, and had already contacted seven bands on the driveway. By July 1, I had nine bands on feed, but realized I had to find more feed. My problem was to push them further on, but none wanted to move. I called all the packers together and we agreed on the necessity of going beyond Ashnola. So five packers and myself started cutting a trail across the Pasayten River, about 12 miles cross country through some very heavy timber. We finally managed to cut through. Around July 20, we had four bands moving into what I supposed was all US land but very soon discovered we had two bands in Canada. The herders refused to come back so remained in Canada some 30 to 35 days!

Our next struggle was for trails. There were a few trails made by trappers and miners in this area, but all were in need of marking and relocating so one could follow them. This was especially true in the sheep ranges where trails and driveways were needed to get to them. I can recall an allotment of money for some 35 miles of trails, from Pasayten River Crossing to Kettle Camp on the Mt. Baker. I had found an area that would carry two bands, so I wanted to cut through, and I mean *cut through*. There were areas of steep slopes covered with overhanging brush too thick to walk through for some 3-1/2 miles. I had two old-timers agree that they could, and eventually did with my help, cut this trail through for $250. Think of it! Thirty-five miles for $250 and all of it on steep ground. These three men furnished themselves and two horses each, a saddle horse and a pack horse, all for $80 per month. The work was mostly done with double-bitted axes as these old devils could not work on a saw together. We later called this Kettle Camp Trail as the area up this hill represented a kettle.

If you are camping alone in bear country and some of them are grizzly, better tie up your horses near your bed for the night. I once had a grizzly pass within 12 feet of my bed. Was I scared? Well, sure, but I had agreed long before that I would never shoot a bear - unless he started the fight. Since Mr. Grizzly never started anything, I left him alone. He was later killed by a Mr. Peterson who was paid to find and kill him as he was a sheep killer. Peterson said he weighed 1200 pounds. About the horses, yes, they woke me up but I did not have to be told to lie quiet since Mr. Grizzly was avoiding them as much as possible and kept a safe distance from them.

Black bears are night prowlers and have killed many sheep in the Cascades. Once he becomes a killer, he has to be shot before you can stop his killing. I have seen as many as 80 sheep killed within a few minutes in one night by one black bear. One slap with his big paw is sure death to a sheep. He gets to know dogs and can slip into a band on the other side of camp. By the time the dogs find him, he has made his kill. Therefore, a sheepman had to kill whenever he saw a bear and sometimes, perhaps, has killed the wrong bear.

<u>William G. Weigle</u> *Weigle was a Forest Supervisor in Washington and Alaska in District/Region 6.*

In looking back over the first half century of the activities of the Forest Service, the early field officers met up with many conditions that required the judgement of a seasoned statesman, the know-how of every kind of mechanic, and the physical endurance of a superman. Even so, the periods of greatest difficulties furnish the most pleasing memories.

What old-timer in the Forest Service does not look back with pleasure to the time when he surveyed with pride the completion of a Ranger Station that cost six hundred dollars or less?

Again his stooped shoulders straighten up when he thinks of drilling

47

holes in solid granite, loading them with dynamite and shooting off a pinnacle rock, and listening to it go thundering down the mountain one thousand feet or more. Just to get a space 12 feet square to build a lookout house on a 7000 to 8000-foot-high mountain. Then the stringing of two parallel wires fitted with trolleys from a point 3000 feet or more down the mountain up to the lookout site on account of the absence of a trail. The trolleys being fitted with wire baskets carrying rock going down to furnish power to pull a load of lumber going up.

What a joy it was to know that the bridge was completed and that you had swam old Dobbin across this dangerous stream for the last time.

You were again happy when you got a telephone line into Elk Canyon and, of course, the Forest Service had to be neighborly and accommodating so the settlers were given the privilege to tie on. Next August, during a bad fire bust, you wanted the use of the line badly and Sister X says, "Get off the line!"

You were a new man in the District, 40 miles away from a blacksmith, shop, store, or anything that could give you help in time of trouble, and how well you slept that night when you learned about Old Bill Fixit over in the next canyon who would teach you how to shoe a mule or splice a cable.

In the Forests of the open country, horses were used everywhere from the start, but the Forests of District Six, in the early days, had few roads and continuous trails. Hence means of travel over the Forests was to a great extent on foot, and in going from one watershed to another no one thought 20 to 30 miles a day on foot called for any overtime pay.

Although the early forester had many unfavorable conditions to meet, there was some recompense in addition to the small pay he received. While on a trip, if he was so inclined, he was free to benefit from the wonderful fishing conditions in most of the large streams. Anyone not familiar with trout fishing in streams of Oregon and Washington prior to the time they were opened up by roads and trails would consider the truth a fish story.

Packing lumber for a new house at Price Creek Guard Station,
Wenaha NF – 1916

Price Guard Station at the head of the South Fork of the Walla Walla River,
Wenaha NF – 1916

In looking back over the Forest Service work of years gone by, the old-timer has the pleasure of many pleasing memories and a feeling that he is glad he made forestry his life work.

<u>Grover C. Blake</u> *Blake reflects on the early part of his 35-year Forest Service career.*

The few of us old timers who are left and who used the trails in the horseback days look back across the span of years to the days of our youth and cannot refrain from certain nostalgic feelings. Those were carefree days. We were not crowded. There was room for everyone. As *Old Dobbin* jogged along at about two and a half miles per hour, the rider encountered no speed limit signs. When night came he made camp beside the trail. Maybe caught a mess of trout for supper and bedded down for the night to arise at daybreak and continue unhurriedly toward his destination. Vern Harpham could point out the charms of the country-side to his heart's content as he sped along on horseback without upsetting the nervous systems of fellow passengers.

I am glad it was my privilege to live in the horse-and-buggy days. To me it was the saddle and pack-horse days. It is easy to forget the trials and hardships of those days of inconvenience as we enjoy the comforts and freedom of our present age.

WIVES' TALES: "-what heroines those wives of the old Service were-"

<u>J. M. Schmitz</u> *Schmitz was the Forest Supervisor of the Wenaha NF from 1905 to 1912.*

I can't speak too highly of the wives of the Rangers, living as they did in cabins or small houses in isolated places but with never a complaint. They always met you with a pleasant smile, made you as comfortable as possible even if you did come in rather dirty after two weeks in the hills. I'm sure we all appreciated it.

<u>Scott Leavitt</u> *Leavitt left his job as principal of Lakeview high school to join the Forest Service. He took the Ranger exam in 1907 and was one of the first Rangers on the Fremont NF. In later years he was a Forest Supervisor in Minnesota and*

50

Montana, a US Congressman from Montana, and then the Assistant Regional Forester for Information and Education in the Regional Office of the Lake States Region.

Of course there were no Ranger Station houses on such a new Forest [Fremont NF in 1907-1909]. I was in an old cabin one summer and out with a tent and my pack outfit the next. My first headquarters on the Chewaucan Ranger District had to be a one-room cabin which a cowman had been using to store salt. The salt was moved out and Mrs. Leavitt and I moved in with our two babies. It was many miles from town or a ranch. A dim wagon trail ran by, used by stockmen permittees mostly. There was a little stream of good water. Add a fence and corral built by a departed homesteader. All about was the forest of yellow pine, bright in the sunshine and somber in the storms. Mrs. Leavitt was then, of course, just a girl in her very early twenties. With a baby boy less than a year old and a little girl of three, she no doubt felt the Forest closing in on her when dusk was gathering and I was off somewhere on my horse.

No story of those early days of the Forest Service is complete without a tribute to the wives of the oldtime Rangers. To be sure, there were humorous incidents which my wife now recalls, such as the time the Supervisor came by when I was out on my District and found her with a black eye. He cocked a questioning eye at my later explanation that I had gone away without leaving her enough wood and she, in breaking up a limb with the axe, had caught a flying chip in her eye. At that, I guess, even the truth didn't leave me blameless.

But there was also the time I was out with a sheepman locating an allotment line. We followed a section line by the old blazes, left our horses at a place too steep to ride, and then, far away from our horses, discovered that the survey crew had blazed only one side of the trees. It got dark and a storm blew up, so we built a fire and spent the night in the rain. Early in the morning we rode to his camp and it was afternoon when I got back to the cabin. Then I realized what it had meant to my wife. She had gone out to the corral time and again to see if my horse had come back without me. She had called and listened and gone back to her babies to wait. We men, of course, took that sort of experience as part of the work, but I realize now what heroines those wives of the old Service were. Elsie and I have celebrated our own golden anniversary ahead of that of the Forest Service, but we remember those days.

<u>Zella Zeigler Manwarren</u>   *Manwarren began her Forest Service career on the Umpqua NF and was Chief Forest Clerk on the Columbia NF at the time of this story. She later worked for the National Park Service, Region Six Division of Grazing and the Pacific Northwest Experiment Station. She retired in 1955.*

This was in the days of the old Columbia Forest, about 1917, and a good Supervisor encouraged the Forest Clerk to take vacation trips on the Forest, to learn the *lay of the land* and topography, etc. of the Ranger Districts. Two weeks vacation was being enjoyed at Spirit Lake Ranger Station, where lived the Ranger, his wife and baby daughter, Marie. Also on duty there at the time was Ray Chapler, Forest Assistant. Incidentally, the Supervisor [Fred Brundage] was also present for a few days to see that the work and the vacation were progressing nicely.

This particular evening, the five adults were enjoying a lively game of 500 after a satisfying meal cooked on the little old wood stove, including roast salmon with tomato sauce (the salmon were running to the head of the lake that fall) and fresh huckleberry cobbler. The baby had gone to sleep after having been rocked by Chap in the Station's homemade wooden rocking chair - some of you can imagine that rocking chair; perhaps even see the same. Chapler had a knack for putting little girls to sleep since he had several in his home and he was blessed with a fine baritone singing voice. During the course of the evening, the sleeping infant was awakened several times by the 500 players and particularly by Chapler's hearty laugh.

Marie had a good excuse for she was asleep in the ladies' loft bedroom above the large lower room and there was typical loft flooring and a big opening where the ladder-stair came through. Well do I recollect that stair, for I had ridden 27-1/2 miles on horseback into Spirit Lake and was still painfully climbing that stair-ladder. At about the fifth awakening of the baby, the Ranger's wife told Chap he had been warned and if he laughed so loudly again and woke Marie, he would have to do the rocking and singing act again. Later we all had our suspicions that Mrs. Ranger already had her plans laid, for Chap was an inveterate tease and had made our lives miserable for several days because we couldn't ever get the upper hand.

Well, the baby was soon startled out of sleep again and Mrs. Ranger went up the stairs to bring her down. Soon she came down with a bundle of blankets and a sober determined air, and Chapler got into the rocking chair and held out his arms for Marie. He settled down and began a lullaby and gentle rocking of the bundle when all at once the bundle began to squirm wildly and a very agitated cat dropped into Chapler's lap. This poor stray cat often got into the loft through numerous openings in the cabin roof and had been fed by the women but scarcely tolerated by the men. Yes, Chapler was for once paid back for his teasing and the rest of us could hardly get to sleep that night for laughing.

<u>Kirk P. Cecil</u> *Cecil began with the Forest Service as a forest guard in Montana. During his career he was Regional Surveyor-Draftsman for District Six, District Six Inspector for Roads and Trails, and Forest Supervisor of the Umatilla and Columbia NFs. He retired in 1949.*

During World War I, when men were scarce, the nursery on the Siskiyou needed weeding and watering, otherwise two years of fir seedlings would be lost. So Mrs. X staked her two-year-old toddler with rope at the end of the rows and day after day did the watering and weeding - without pay.

[<u>Frank E. Lewis</u> wrote that according to his mother, Sadie Lewis, the wife of Mel Lewis, Ranger on the Paige Creek District of the Siskiyou NF, she and her sister-in-law were hired during WWI to weed the tree nursery because of the lack of manpower due to the war. An official visited from the Portland office inspecting nursery operations reported that he didn't think use of funds to hire relatives was appropriate.]

Again, on the Okanogan, near the Canadian line, the Ranger's wife, Mrs. Y filled a vacant lookout job, taking her two small children to the tall peak for the summer. This was all well and good but soon her compass readings (no fire finder then) were found erratic and erroneous and that threw the works into a tizzy. The Supervisor fumed and the Ranger returned to repeat his training. His readings to other peaks were correct. The wife made readings and they were

53

incorrect. Ranger took readings with wifey looking over his shoulder. "See", sez he, "do it this way," and the readings were, yes, incorrect. A *steely* silence - and - well, need it be added that the foundation of this story was in the days between the era of whale bones and the two-way stretch!

<u>Lura Esther Cooley Osborne</u> *During the summer of 1909, Esther Osborne, a bride from New England, accompanied her husband, William B. (Bush) Osborne, a young Forest Assistant, while he was making the first extensive reconnaissance of the Oregon National Forest. "Bush" Osborne's inventive talent is described in a story by Harry M. White at the end of this Chapter and also in Chapter Two. Mrs. Osborne wrote long letters home. This is an excerpt from one of them.*

The Ranger, who had been a packer for sheep men and knew the country thoroughly, was to guide the Forest Assistant (William B. "Bush" Osborne - who went on to make many outstanding contributions to fire prevention programs, including inventing the Osborne Firefinder used extensively in lookouts) through a pathless tract to a certain ridge, and I was to stay alone until their return. Mentally I had prepared to enjoy my own society for four or five days, and to fear not man or beast, but I must confess I was pleased, when at the last moment, they decided to take me.

That peaceful Sunday morning, while the people at home were walking along the elm-shaded streets to church, our little cavalcade started. The Ranger rode ahead, leading a pack horse. I followed, and the Forest Assistant walked behind, prodding Gypsy. Skillfully we were guided through the bewilderingly dense Forest and maze of fallen logs and underbrush. I had to recover from considerable surprise when my pony jumped the first log, but I didn't fall off, and soon log jumping became the least of the troubles. We climbed steadily, leaving the heavy timber below us, and scrambling over sharp rolling stones. I dared not look back any although I realized the view must be grander than I had ever seen. My eyes were glued on the jagged rocks over which the horse ahead was being dragged, and my whole energy was concentrated in keeping my pony at his heels. How the loosened stones rattled down and down below us. To hold them under the horses' hooves, I was even glad of patches of grease bush, through which we had to break our way, although it slapped our faces unmercifully and tore my skirt in shreds. Spicy but sickeningly sweet is the smell of the grease bush. When we gained the crest I drew a long breath, and it was well I caught it before I was told that now we had to go down, cross the river in the bottom of the canyon and climb the opposite side.

How I rode down I don't know. I kept telling myself that our guide could find a way if anyone could, that the horse ahead was getting down and mine must. Surefooted as goats, those ponies slid and crawled until we reached the bottom. We forded the river only to find that we must make a detour around the head of a gorge, too deep to cross. Our progress was very slow, because the men had to cut a path through alder thickets. I didn't mind this jungle as much as I did the rolling stones, but it was harder for the others. At times it was only by standing in his stirrups that the Ranger could see over the rhododendron far enough to pick a trail. Gypsy thought this an opportune moment to die, fell down and could not or would not rise until we transferred her load to my riding pony. To lighten the other pack, we threw away an elk horn we had found, a perfect specimen about six feet long.

We struggled on hoping to find horse pasture, and, fortunately, about seven o'clock when darkness and fatigue had nearly the best of us, we happened upon a brook and bit of grass. A drizzling rain began to fall, but I drew my soft hat over my face, rolled my boots in my coat and slept, blissfully unconscious that the rain might change to fog so dense that the men could not find their way forward or back.

In the chill gray morning we started, and were soon drenched with water from the brush. Presently we struck a swamp, and I was astonished to see the horses smell their way through the mire and walk logs like cats. About ten we came unexpectedly upon a luxuriant green meadow, hemmed in by woods, with a clear stream flowing at its edge. We were afraid of a storm, so pitched the tent and built a lean-to under lodgepole pines. This name, of Indian significance, is descriptive, for the slender straight trunk is conspicuously like a pole and little hidden by the small branches of the short crown and by the needles born in stiff brushes near their tips. The back of the lean-to was made by piling three logs on each other against a bank. About seven feet in front two poles were driven in the ground, a third laid across the tops. To this a canvas was fastened by pegs and stretched down to the upper log at the rear, thus forming a slanting roof which caught the heat from the big fire in front and made a warm shelter.

Our general plan was to stay in one place for several nights, using the camp as a basis for trips into the surrounding country. It was necessary to travel through the timber in order to investigate its condition and form an estimate of the amount; also to scan its extent from high peaks which were good lookout points. These side expeditions were usually made on foot through the steepest and roughest regions, where even the mountain horses could not go. Although the Forest Assistant was gone from breakfast time till dark, there was no time to be lonely, for dishes had to be washed in the frying pan, and clothes in icy rivulets, firewood gathered and supper cooked.

We returned to the settlement by another route, moving every day and never stopping to make a camp. We grew dirtier and wearier at every stage, and talked much of baths and of sleeping between sheets when we reached the *hotel*. Can you imagine our disappointment when the abundant supply of hot water we had long desired was handed to us in a two quart pail? Clean clothes and supper refreshed us, but the luxury of bed and sheets was very enticing to our tired muscles. Before we could fall asleep, we were subjected to the attacks of certain voracious red bugs, which caused excessive irritation to the flesh and spirit. In desperation we lighted the lamp and tried to annihilate them, but they crawled from the board wall faster than we could kill them.

At midnight we gave up our frantic effort, dressed and slipped outdoors. From our pack we took blankets and a candle. By its wavering light we fled across a footbridge, which hung over the river, to the woods, and slept there, thankful to escape "the comforts of civilization" and go back to "that terrible wilderness."

Our expeditions continued, but in future we avoided spending the night at the *hotel*. The first of September found us camped beside a little lake sunk in a basin formed by encircling ranges. Lying on a knoll under a lonely Engelmann spruce, I used to look over a grassy stretch, shaded with lavender daisy-like flowers, pinkish fireweed and goldenrod, growing on single spikes, to the sparkling blue lake. The farther edge was fringed by tall dark firs, but the mountain sides, which shut it in, were scarred and desolate. The sun beat down upon naked rocks, red earth, gray tree trunks, lifeless in the sunlight, motionless in the breeze. A year before, fire swept away a virgin forest, full of life and growth, thick shadows, gentle motion (little wind stirred in summer). A veritable cemetery was left, the blackened limb and bark fallen away and the whitened shaft-like trunks glinting in the light.

The lake was full of trout, pretty fellows with rainbow stripes along their gleaming sides. At twilight we went fishing - that is, the Forest Assistant cast his fly and I sat in a cross section of log (the seat of the raft) and watched day change to night. Once it seemed as if a film gathered over my eyes in the veiled moment before the starlight. All color faded from the sky leaving it and the water a soft gray. Grayer rose the distant peaks, each nearer range grew darker and darker, that by the shore was only a degree less black than the trees at the rim. No line of light separated them from the inverted image, which was equally still, and reflected tone for tone the wonderful veil drawn over heaven and earth.

HORSES: "-the whole job depended on good horseflesh-"

<u>Fred P. Cronemiller</u> *Cronemiller worked on the Fremont NF from 1913 to 1917, when he was transferred to District Five. He was the Assistant Regional Forester, Division of Wildlife Management, Region Five when he retired in 1957.*

In the old days one was horse feed conscious. The whole job depended on good horseflesh and camps were not made where there was no feed. Plans for making certain camps often had to be changed when it was found livestock grazing had eliminated all of the horse feed.

<u>William F. Burge</u> *Burge wrangled horses for 41 years on the Okanogan and Chelan NFs, beginning in 1915.*

Did you ever get up in the morning, 50 miles in the *hills*, and find your horses gone? Well, this happened to me once or twice but I soon learned how to keep them with me. Camp where you can pasture your horses in back of you so they have to pass camp to get away. Use a

57

good bell and keep one ear listening. Keep your shoes and pants close by as you might suddenly need them in the dark. In parts where Lodgepole are handy, put up a fence across the trail. This will save you many a sore foot.

<u>Grover C. Blake</u> *Blake was a Forest Guard on the Deschutes NF at the time of this story.*

On May 6, 1909, Forest Guard Douglas C. Ingram and I were sent to Mill Creek, northeast of Prineville, to survey and mark the Forest boundary. We made camp and hobbled our four horses. They all disappeared during the night and strayed away, hobbles and all, and it took us two days to find them. During the next several years, hunting for straying saddle and pack horses required a large percentage of our time. Eventually, we were able to build enclosures here and there for holding horses, but before this was accomplished, keeping our saddle and pack stock with us was a major problem.

<u>Fred Wehmeyer</u> *Wehmeyer started as a forest guard on the Okanogan NF in 1912 and was District Ranger on several Okanogan and Chelan NF Ranger Districts into the 1920s. He was then District Ranger on two Ranger Districts of the Umatilla NF. He retired from the Forest Service in 1945.*

I often wonder if those who now use modern roads and trails ever fully appreciate the cost in pain and misery, besides dollars, of building them in the days long gone by. Every mile of trail was constructed by someone being stung by bees. Nearly every down log, if rotten, contained yellowjacket nests and the air itself was full of insects. Horse flies, deer flies, gnats, no-see-ems, and mosquitos were so thick that one breathed with difficulty. In those days, when exploring for future trail routes, we generally camped on a ridge and packed water. There we could clear a spot and build smudge fires for the horses. The horses would stand head to tail in the smoke and tears rolled down their cheeks. They would venture off to eat only when a breeze brought a temporary lull to the hordes of ravenous flies and mosquitos.

Keeping an eye on the horses was an endless job because, if they thought there was any chance of getting away, they would take off. I remember a story of Ranger Jamison of Loomis, Washington, who was back in the Toats Coulee country, about his horses wandering off during the night. He started trailing them and soon met another person doing likewise. They struck up an immediate and casual acquaintance. Jamison introduced himself as the local Forest Ranger and the other fellow said, "I am a prospector, been prospecting these mountains for the past twenty years." He then added, "That ain't exactly the truth as I've hunted horses fifteen of those years."

Gilbert D. Brown *Brown was on the Cascade Range (South) Reserve in 1906, when he was sent to two fires on the north end of the Reserve. He was then dispatched to a third fire on the Oregon Reserve.*

When the fire was under control, we were sent to another fire above Detroit where I was left in charge. This fire lasted a week or so when I was requested to secure two horses and an outfit. I went to Marquam, Oregon, where I had taught school the winter before and found two ponies which cost me $15.00 each; one of which was unbroken. I packed her and rode the other one - a wild little mustang and tough as steel. I secured an old saddle and pack outfit, some camp equipment and headed south, past Colton, toward the Clackamas River. The second day I apparently did not pull the pack cinch tight and the pony turned the pack but since it was well tied it remained intact until I could catch her and repack. Going down the steep winding grade to the river this pony refused to follow the trail so I decided to lead her. She also refused to be led! I pulled on the lead rope and instead of following around the switchback, she rolled down to the trail below - without dislodging the pack! She got up onto her feet and I then drove instead of leading her.

Near the river where the trail turned sharply to the left, instead of turning, that critter jumped into the river! I managed to get a rope onto her and pulled her with my saddle pony onto a sandbar and unpacked. Everything was wet - flour, sugar, etc. After spreading everything out on the bank to dry, I picketed the horses in a meadow near the river and went to look for the camp of a fire guard who was to show me the trail on the way south. Unable to locate his camp I found a gentle old saddle horse in the meadow and decided to see if he would go to camp. My hunch proved correct. I got onto him bareback, without a bridle, and he took me down the river about a quarter of a mile to the camp where I found the guard asleep.

The next day I started up the mountain over an old Indian trail which was difficult to follow. That night, finding no feed for the horses, I tied them to a tree and waited for daylight. About 10 o'clock in the morning I reached the top of the ridge and saw the heavy smoke rising from the fire I was supposed to take charge of.

Ira E. Jones *Jones was a Ranger on the Whitman NF at the time of this story.*

In 1913, Superintendent Ireland [Forest Supervisor of the Whitman NF], who had been Master of the Sumpter Masonic Lodge, was asked to conduct a funeral at Audry, about 30 miles south. We had a team of young and partly broken mules. We thought this would be a good trip for them so we hired a two-seated hack, hitched them up and started off. The front seat was set high up, and the brake was worked from it. I drove and Henry Ireland worked the brake. R. M. Evans and Harry Wilson, a local jeweler, rode in the back seat.

We made it all right until we reached the top of the Whitney Hill and started down. Henry shoved the brake handle forward, but it jabbed the mule in his rump and away they went. It was about two miles to the bottom of the hill. Every attempt to use the brake only made them go faster. The road was narrow and crooked, but fortunately, it was early morning and we met no one. We made the bottom and after half a mile got them slowed down, but we all lost our hats!

We made the rest of the trip OK. On the way back we gave a ride to a man who had been fishing in Camp Creek. When we stopped to let him off at the Whitney mill, one of the single trees dropped off. The mule gave a jump, the tongue dropped down, and away they went again. After a short distance the tongue ran into the ground and broke. We all jumped out. I got mixed up with the lines and was dragged 30 or 40 feet before I got loose. Aside from ruining a suit and losing some skin, I came out all right. The team broke loose, ran into the slab pile at Whitney and stopped.

Harold E. Smith *Smith was a Ranger on the Paulina and Deschutes NFs from 1911 to 1919.*

Lady and I joined the Forest Service at Bend, Oregon, on July 1, 1911. For the next eight years Lady contributed much to the cause of conservation. She became quite proficient on fire patrol. On boundary work and timber cruising she would do my pacing for me while I sat in the saddle and recorded her steps on the tally register. She would stand perfectly still while I took my compass shot then resume walking when she heard the compass lid click shut. A slight pressure of the knee against her shoulder would bring her back on course when she occasionally veered off line. Thus I found her more valuable, in the area where I worked, than a seventy-five dollar-a-month field assistant.

Trailing a band of cattle up the north slope of the Paulina Mountains, Deschutes National Forest, for the purpose of checking on the number of cattle and ownership of same, I came across a fire burning merrily in a thick carpet of pine needles. It evidently had been started by a cigarette butt dropped by one of the cowpokes. The fire was only about ten feet in diameter but conditions were right for rapid spread. Having no tools, I put *Old Doll* into a long swinging trot around the fire. By the end of 75 to 100 turns the pine needles were pretty well submerged in the volcanic soil. I parked Doll on the sideline and finished the trench by kicking away whatever loose duff still remained in the trail. It didn't take long for the fire to eat its way to the inner edge of the trench and die out for lack of fuel. Upon catching up with the cattlemen they denied having any knowledge of the fire.

To *Old Doll* this was just another example of the many services she and many others of her kind were called upon to perform. In fact very few segments of pioneer history would be complete without paying high tribute to horses and the faithful services they rendered. Just to mention a few, it was Doll who made the 36-mile run from Pine Mountain to Bend in 3 hours and 48 minutes. What was the hurry? No hurry, just jogging along. Again it was Doll who carried me, on a snow-flecked night, from East Butte to Pine Mountain, ten miles over the old   fire road, in just 55 minutes flat. Had we been in a hurry, I think that time could have been shortened considerable.

And also it was Doll who packed the doors, windows, shingles and hardware to the top of Paulina Peak (1915) for the lookout house. Dick and Jack, the two little mules, handled the longer-timbers on narrow gage sleds.

FIRE: "-this policy of keeping down fires-"

<u>C. C. McGuire</u> *McGuire was on the Washington NF at the time of this story.*

During the summer of 1910, Herman Johnson and his assistant named Wolff came to my station one evening after hiking in twenty-five miles from Marblemount [on the Washington NF]. While traveling along the Goat Trail, they sighted a smoke about three miles to the south. We did not know just where the fire was, but the next morning early we all set out to find it. There were no crossings on the Skagit River so we went back down Goat Trail hoping to get a compass shot on the smoke. No smoke was visible so we continued on down to what is now Newhalem to see if we could get across the river at that point. No crossing, so we hiked back to Reflector Bar and continued on up the river to Deer Park where there was a *go-devil* swung across the river. A go-devil is a cable strung across the river with a cage suspended under the wire in which one could sit and pull himself across. We crossed on this contrivance and worked our way down the river by dark that night. We arrived at a point just across the river from my cabin which we had left early that morning. After the hard, all-day hike, we were just 300 yards closer to the fire than when we started.

Early the next morning we were on our way again and arrived at the fire about 5 PM. It covered about three acres. After three day's work, we got it corralled and partially mopped up. We did not get that last spark but evidently our lines held. The next night we were camped again 300 yards from the cabin with the river between us, shelter and grub. We did not like the idea of climbing back up over a spur of mountains to the go-devil, so the next morning I explored about a mile down the river where I found a tin boat about the size of a bath tub, moored and sunk but on my side of the river. Later I found that the boat belonged to Glee Davis who had filed a claim under the Act of June 11, 1906, across the river. I got the tub bailed out and though it leaked badly, it would float. Having considerable experience in handling Siwash canoes, I decided I could pilot this one. While it was a one-man craft, if we were going to all get across, it must carry two. The fact that we are all still here indicates that crossing was made safely. Just another day's work in the life of a Forest Ranger.

<u>Henry "H. E." Haefner</u> *Haefner tells another story about Ranger Walter J. Jones on the Siskiyou NF in the 1910 – 1920 period.*

Walter J. Jones was well known in the Chetco District when he took over his Ranger duties. Some of the younger men in the community had been his schoolmates as a boy and later he had worked and hunted with them. The early fire seasons were very tough with the *light burners* at their old tricks, but they reckoned without Walter. He traveled light with two horses during the fire season and often showed up next morning fifteen or twenty miles from where he had camped the night before and ran most of the light burners to cover the first year. This policy of keeping down fires was resented by many of the local people, especially stockmen, and they were hostile to the Ranger because of the energy and vigor he showed in enforcement. He soon jailed the worst fire-bug for a year and then made it so uncomfortable for that individual when he got out that he left the country for over ten years.

Another of the chronic fire-bugs on the District was an old miner of over 70 years who had cabins on Upper Diamond and Bald Face creeks in the most inaccessible parts of the District. He was a confirmed *light burner* and it required a day and night ride of about 40 miles over very poor trails for the Ranger to get to the fires he started. The old man had the advantage because of lack of manpower to watch him. After a few trips to put out his fires, Walter bluntly told him to lay off or he would catch him and put him in jail, and hard feelings grew up between the two men. Both men went armed and Walter exercised care that the old man did not shoot him from ambush. A year or two later the old man was brought to trial for a fire he set and was sentenced to one year in jail. He was paroled to his brother, an early day mining camp judge, who acted as his attorney. The old man and his brother, who was over 80, were Civil War veterans and this was the only thing that prevented him from going to jail. Many of the rest of these *light burners* became more cautious in their activities along these lines. Walter had the fire situation well in hand after the first year or two.

During those early years he seldom used over 10 to 15 men in a fire fighting crew and most often had less. He believed in quick and early action and took such dynamic action that few of his associates could stand the pace he set. Greatly handicapped by lack of men, equipment, and adequate trails he nevertheless almost single-handedly established a fire record for that area that has never been surpassed.

Grover C. Blake *Blake was a Forest Guard on the Deschutes NF at the time of this story.*

[My first fire occurred] on August 31, 1909. It was on a sheep range and when I reached it, I found two sheep men carrying water from a creek about one-fourth mile away in camp kettles in an effort to extinguish it. They had been doing this for a full day and had accomplished little. So far as these men knew there was no way to fight fire but by use of water. When we trenched around it and mopped it up in a couple of hours by using shovels they were somewhat amazed.

A. H. "Hal" Sylvester *Sylvester began his Forest Service career on the Wenatchee NF in 1908. He was Forest Supervisor of the Wenatchee NF from 1909 until he retired 1931. It is said he named over 3,000 features in the area of the Wenatchee NF.*

In 1909 the Wenatchee received its first baptism of fire under Forest Service administration. Our fire bill was about $6500, more than all of the rest of the District put together, and I was called on the carpet to make fitting explanation. In 1910 came the great fires in Idaho. Compared with them the District Six fires of that year were insignificant, but standing by themselves and in comparison with the previous year they were tremendous. The fire costs on many of the District Six Forests far exceeded my 1909 costs, while the Wenatchee dropped to $4400, and the District first learned something of its fire problem. It was in 1909 that some of our men were fired on by an unseen rifleman as they worked on the Derby Canyon fire. No casualties except a hole in a hat.

J. M. Schmitz *Schmitz was the Forest Supervisor on the Wenaha NF at the time of this story.*

The Grand Ronde fire in 1910 was the only one that amounted to much. That was discovered in time, but the Ranger thought it wouldn't do much damage. I happened to get there just as it was getting a good start. I sent for men and got a good crew on short notice from the Eden country and Elgin. All did their best, especially Eden people as their homes would be in danger if we couldn't control it. Our main work was done from three to eleven o'clock in the morning when the trenching and backfiring was done. The rest of the day about half of the crew had to patrol the fire line. We gained some each day, and finally ran it down the bluff into the Grand Ronde River 2000 feet below. The area burned was about 1000 acres, but the damage was not great as the timber was of little value. I couldn't have asked for a better crew. There were no eight-hour day men and no sit-down strikes. Some of the Eden settlers nearly stampeded on me, wanting to drop back about five miles and start backfiring from there. I couldn't blame them much as their homes were in danger, but I told them my plan and promised that if it failed we would fall back and try again. Fire losses were kept down because most of the Forest was heavily grazed and because of the good work of the Rangers.

Fred Cleator *Cleator was on the Colville NF at the time of this story.*

Once upon a time when I was a Deputy Supervisor on the Colville Forest in 1910, we, similarly with foresters in Idaho, suffered the toughest fire season of many a year. Fires burned unreported. Rangers worked with axes and shovels for a month on the same fire without seeing each other, and maybe not even aware of each other.

Fire-fighters, even as nowadays, had little money for tobacco. Uncle Sam allowed no charge back on payrolls, and commissary for the Forest Service was undreamed of, at least on the Colville. We boys in the Service, averaging around $100 per month, couldn't afford to loan very much for knickknacks like tobacco.

So in desperation I wired our problem to the District (now Regional) Forester. "Firefighters no work without tobacco."

Promptly we received an answer by wire. "Buy beans, Buck". We went ahead and bought a large supply of a variety of *beans* which very much resembled tobacco in flavor - if you get me. Anyway, the firefighters were completely soothed and content.

65

Well, a few years later when things were better, and worse in many ways, I was detailed to Portland. I tried in devious ways to find out which Buck, Shirley or C. J., was so smart as to think up so cheap, poetic and effective a telegram as "Buy beans, Buck". I HAVE NEVER LEARNED WHICH. But, thought I, how handy to be a Buck with no responsibility for signature, while I with the undersigned cognomen must forevermore be acutely conscious and able at all times to defend the signature of Fred Cleator.

<u>Alvin "Ag" or "Andy" Anderson</u> *Anderson began his career in the early 1950s. He worked on the Rogue River and Siskiyou NFs and was a Timber Management Assistant on the Siuslaw NF when he retired in 1977. His wife Marci served as a lookout for several seasons. Anderson sent this news article, "Forest Ranger Lived Like An Eagle" by Marjorie O'Hara of the "Oregonian", dateline Medford, Oregon, 7/21/97, to Rich Reeves, who then sent it to TimberLines in the fall of 1999.*

As Forest Service lookouts return to their summer posts in southern Oregon this year, they like to remember Dan Pederson, a man who felt the only way to keep an eagle eye peeled for forest fire was to live like an eagle.

This is what Pederson did for 11 years on the windy top of Brush Mountain, a U.S. Forest Service lookout station [on the Siskiyou NF] in southern Oregon in the early 1900s. Pederson was 40 the summer of 1915 when he was sent to Brush Mountain where there was only one convenience, (a telephone to the Guard station). He set his compass on a post stuck in a pile of rocks and went to work scanning the timbered mountains for that telltale puff of smoke that could mean fire.

His station didn't suit him. He wanted a higher point, and he spotted one – right on the top of a huge Shasta fir that stood nearby. This could be just like home, he figured, to a man who had worked on sailing ships as a youth. Pederson got an axe, auger and a pair of pliers and went to work. There was no plan. He started at the ground and bored holes a foot deep into the trunk of that mighty fir. He stuck two-inch yew pegs into the holes to make a spiral ladder. Up he went, limbing and peeling, perching on the pegs he had anchored while he pounded in the next ones. He cut yew poles and bent and wired them

66

Early lookout on the Ochoco NF
(prior to the establishment of a District 6 Safety Officer)

to the ends of the pegs as he took his stairway toward the sky. Finally, 104 feet up, he reached the spot he wanted and topped the tree.

Friends helped him build, then hoist to the top, a five-by-five foot platform that weighed 250 pounds. Pederson was proud of his dry-land crow's nest. It gave him a place for his fire-finder, and he put his map board on rollers so it could revolve around his perch. But then something else started to bother him. The telephone was at the bottom of the tree, near where he slept, and it was troublesome and time-consuming to scramble down to make his fire calls.

To remedy this situation, he rigged two buckets on a cable and counterbalanced his weight with rocks. One good yank on the cable would drop him down to the phone. Another would shoot him back up to the perch with little time lost. Few visitors ever used the homemade elevator. The hardy souls who made it to the treetop lookout preferred to clutch the rungs of the sturdy ladder as they climbed to the dizzy height.

Dahl Kirkpatrick *Dahl wrote this story about the 1918 Cispus Fire on the Rainier NF during the time his father, John, was a District Ranger.*

The widely known and extremely damaging Cispus fire started on June 12, 1918, and burned without effective control for most of the summer. It burned some 52,000 acres before it was over in spite of the best efforts that could be mounted to stop it. The greater part of the burned area had been initially burned in 1902, but the boundaries of that earlier fire were extended into substantial areas of virgin old growth timber at several points around the perimeter of the older bum. That fire had killed an old-growth Douglas-fir forest and in the intervening 16 years some of the big snags were down, the ground was covered with bark, fallen limbs, herbaceous growth and some coniferous reproduction. All in all the old burned area was as hazardous a situation imaginable and presented extreme resistance to fire control efforts.

By 1918 auto and truck transportation to the Cowlitz Valley was practical but there was nothing aside from the original settlers-shingle bolt cutters wagon road from the edge of the Cowlitz Valley at Judd Siler's farm across the low divide to the Cispus. The only communication facility was a single-wire grounded circuit telephone line from Randle which terminated at the Tower Rock Guard Station where the base fire camp was established.

Fighting the fire because of its immense size was extremely difficult for several reasons. Manpower was in short supply because it occurred during the final year of World War I. The lack of trails to any part of the fire area except the southwestern quadrant made movement of men and supplies impossible or very tedious. Communication as mentioned, except to the headquarters camp, was non-existent, so control tactics could not be well coordinated. All material used in the suppression effort had to be hauled by wagon from the end of motorized transportation some twelve miles over the primitive road to the base camp. From there, over very inadequate horse trails, many of which were built as a part of the suppression effort, it was a pack horse chance. Ultimately, line camps on the perimeter of the burn were as far as one or twenty miles from the base of supplies at Tower Rock.

To overcome the manpower problem the Army was called upon for help and provided some 300 conscientious objectors with their supplies and equipment to supplement the local forces. Though the military people were not as effective as the locals man for man, the fact that they came in self-sustaining units was a great plus.

While the fight was being mounted against the main Cispus fire, another fire broke out in the upper reaches of the Cispus watershed in the Hamilton Butte area. It started in another old burn and consumed some 30,000 acres. This fire missed joining up with the Cispus fire by only a mile or so near Blue Lake. It was manned largely by military personnel directed by local experienced men. The entire suppression effort dragged out most of the 1918 summer. I recall that dad [John Kirkpatrick], who acted as Fire Chief for the total suppression operation on both projects, was away from home for a solid month at one stretch. On at least two occasions there was real concern for his safety. In one instance, in the early stages of the fire he was scouting afoot ahead of the flames to plan the attack. An afternoon run of the fire cut him off from returning to the Tower Rock base camp. He was

69

able to make it to the flank of the fire by crossing a steep fuel-choked canyon and spent the night with a prospector at his cabin. He returned to the base camp the next day through the burn which by then had cooled down, much to the relief of Supervisor G. F. Allen who was visiting the camp. The latter had been very evasive when my mother had phoned the night before to talk to dad.

Another later time, when going to one of the outlying line camps, dad rode his horse to a point where the trail entered the burned area. He dismounted, tied the bridle on the back of the saddle and started the horse back to camp before proceeding on foot. The horse failed to return by the next day and a search was initiated only to find that Prince had been dilatory about returning to camp and had been cut off by an afternoon run of the fire. He was trapped by snags burning and falling across the trail. The searchers rationally assumed that John had made it to his destination okay. They sent the horse home to Randle for mother to nurse back to health. His mane ends were singed off and he was blistered on his muzzle and on his chest and flanks where the hair was short or non-existent. At first he had no interest in eating and rather than drinking he would put his muzzle in the water trough and keep it in there for extended periods. In due course he fully recovered, with the administration of ointments applied to his blistered skin by my mother.

The writer's contribution to the Cispus fire suppression effort was limited to the following. At the end of June the fire had been in progress for nearly 20 days and was still increasing in size. A delegation of officials from the Portland District Office consisting of Mr. Melvin Merritt and Mr. Charles Flory, both Assistant Regional Foresters concerned with Administration and Fire Control, came to check on efforts being made to control the conflagration. By prior arrangements made by phone, the visitors were to be met at the terminus of the auto road at Judd Siler's with saddle horses for the trip to the base camp. In the absence of any help at the Randle Ranger Station it became my duty to meet the visitors at Siler's and accompany them to Tower Rock. Mother helped me get the horses up from the pasture and saddled. I rode one and led two to Siler's and waited for the auto to arrive.

In due course it came, the dignitaries unloaded and we proceeded to

70

the Cispus Fire. The camp was on the other side of the river which we had to ford, but the water was low at this season and presented no serious problem. My dad and the visitors concluded their review of the suppression action and plans by noon of the next day. Mr. Flory along with Forest Supervisor G. F. Allen and I returned to Siler's by late afternoon July 2, 1918. The dignitaries got into the auto and drove away, leaving me to bring the horses home some five miles. I can't recall whether or not they thanked me, doubtless they did, but as an eleven-year-old, I'd expected something more than thanks! Anyway, I had gotten to see my dad and sleep with him in his bedroll on the ground the night of July 1. His diary for that day says, "Mr. Flory came in today. Dahl came with him over from Randle." I at least got my name in the official record of the fire! (An interesting footnote is that I succeeded Charles Flory as Supervisor of the Mt. Baker National Forest some 24 years later.)

By present day standards the firefighting efforts employed in the great Cispus Fire seem puny indeed. In 1918 the employment of three or four hundred men in the suppression of a single fire was almost unheard of in the region.

GRAZING: "-grazing protection was of the utmost importance-"

J. M. Schmitz *Schmitz recounts grazing management experiences when he began his work on the Wenaha NF, first as a Ranger, then as Forest Supervisor.*

On August 8, 1905, I arrived in Walla Walla to act as Ranger-in-Charge and soon thereafter as Supervisor of the Wenaha National Forest, having been transferred from my position as Ranger on the Rainier National Forest. I found a few supplies, a typewriter and a letter press awaiting me. As there was no office, I did all the work in my room.

Stockmen began to call to see what it was all about. Most of them had the idea that their stock would be excluded from the Forest. I assured them that such would not be the case. I also learned that the Forest was practically surrounded by small stockmen and that a large part was being heavily overgrazed. The main reason for the overgrazing of

71

the interior was that each spring long before the range was fit to graze there would be a race to get the sheep over the divide and located on the best camps. I then realized the hard work it would take to get things organized and on a good working basis.

On my first trip around the heads of the Walla Walla and Wenaha Rivers and Mill Creek I found that the map of the interior was all wrong. I had a good small compass and taking my bearings from Walla Walla, I found that Table Rock was about two miles north of the state line instead of on it as shown on the map. Then from Table Rock I could locate other buttes approximately before returning to Walla Walla to correct the map.

In September I had three guards appointed, only one of which, Mose Kinnier, turned out to be good help. On September 23, H. D. Foster, Forest Assistant, arrived, but I had to use him as a clerk. We took a trip to the Touchet and Tucannon to look over the lay of the land and to get data on settlement claims. As to grazing inquiries I told everybody that a meeting would be called in the fall. Two new guards, T. P. Mackenzie and 0. T. Green were appointed - both good men.

From November 14 to 28, Harold Foster and I took a trip along the eastern part of the Forest to see settlers and to work on the map. We found the map all wrong but did not have time to correct it in the field. The Rangers were called in to help get out the best map possible for use at the stock meeting.

The stock meeting was called for December 18-25 at the Walla Walla Court House. A great number came, although only about 300 of them had stock on the Wenaha Forest. Superintendent D. B. Sheller was there. He was a good organizer and kept the crowd in a fine humor. We finally arranged a committee of three cattlemen and three sheepmen to divide the sheep and cattle ranges. Each group tried to claim about all the range. Finally after an all day confab, an agreement was reached.

Then came the tug-of-war for the individual sheep allotments. All admitted that a reduction of sheep was necessary and as the one-band men couldn't be reduced, it fell on the two- and three-band men. This was accomplished without much trouble. The division into individual allotments took some time.

The Oregon man claimed all the Oregon range for Oregon sheep. Both Mr. Sheller and I told the committee to disregard the state line and allot the range according to prior use. The Washington sheep men were in the majority and so could outvote the Oregonians, leaving out some of the Oregon prior users for personal reasons.

The last day of the meeting was mainly used for making out applications for grazing permits. After they were all stacked up, I asked Superintendent Sheller what to do with them. He said if it were up to him, he would send them to Washington, DC, and let them do as they pleased with them. However, by the regulations I would have to approve or disapprove them anyway, which I did. I do not remember the number of stock applied for or approved nor the permits issued. Approving applications and sending out notices took about two weeks work for Mr. Foster and me.

The committee's rejection of Oregon sheep applications was going to cause trouble, and a move was being made to exclude Washington sheep from Oregon. As I did not want to leave room for a just complaint, I called a meeting at Pendleton, for which I got a good old-fashioned call-down from the Washington Office, saying I had no right to call a second meeting and that if the committee had made a mistake, let them shoulder the responsibility. However, the meeting was a success and all were fairly well satisfied. Apparently all the Oregon legislature could do was to pass an inspection law saying all Washington sheep had to be inspected at the state line, but the actual inspections died out after a few years.

The foregoing will give some idea of the amount of work it took to get an overgrazed Forest organized. The field-work was yet to come. The cattle were given a general allotment in each locality, the permits ranging from one head up to a few over a hundred head. The sheep men were given individual allotments with a description and map. All this was no small task. The clerical work fell on H. D. Foster who was capable and very willing.

As grazing protection was of the utmost importance, (the early fieldmen) had to know stock and range. They had to be woodsmen and able to take care of themselves and their horses under all conditions. They must see that each sheep man got located on his allotment. The fact that there were very few infringements on each other's allotments or of sheep on cattle range shows the good work of the Rangers and the fine cooperation of the stockmen, especially of the sheepmen. But some of the herders were not too careful as to the boundaries of their allotments.

All disputes were quietly and satisfactorily settled in the field by getting the parties interested on the disputed area. Although it cost me several rides to the heads of Walla Walla River and Mill Creek, I did not want to give the impression that the Forest was being run in a highhanded manner, but was willing to overlook little mistakes and to treat the stockmen in a friendly and neighborly way. By doing so we received their cooperation in fire protection which was of great value.

The first season, 1906, went much smoother than I expected. With only rough and loggy trails the Rangers got about surprisingly well, looking after the grazing and keeping down fires. They fought the fires with what help they could get from some of the stockmen or herders. It was lucky for the Rangers and also for myself that I had done a large part of the mapping, helped with all of it, and had seen practically all of the Forest, so that when a sheep man came to the office asking for more range, I didn't have to refer it to the Ranger but could point out where he could use a rough or loggy part of his allotment and have range enough. All left satisfied. A few times I went with them to the allotment to show them range the herders hadn't wanted to use.

Each Ranger had more work laid out for him than could possibly be done. He was supposed to inspect each sheep camp every week to see how it was grazed. Sheep camps were moved every week, and if a Ranger had from ten to fifteen bands of sheep in his District, and as it would take a day for each camp, it just couldn't be done because of the other important work. Most Rangers had a guard to help during the fire season, and when a fire was discovered it had to be fought with what help there was at hand. There was no telephone and to go out for help would have taken five or six days. By then the fire would have burned itself out or be beyond control.

74

<u>Grover C. Blake</u>   *Blake describes the introduction of grazing management activities on the Blue Mountain Reserve/Deschutes National Forest.*

I doubt if any Supervisor in Forest Service history ever shouldered a heavier load than did A. S. Ireland when, on April 1, 1906, the vast Blue Mountain Forest Reserve was dropped in his lap.   He was entirely unfamiliar with the area.   Since 1896 or 1897, he had been a Ranger on the Cascade Forest Reserve but had not seen the Blue Mountains. With his office and headquarters in the residence he had rented for himself and family on the banks of the Ochoco in Prineville, he faced the responsibility of bringing under Forest Service regulation a vast and strange territory which later contained several present day National Forests. His domain was the most intensely grazed area in the west. His job consisted in part, the settlement of grazing disputes, regulating the grazing of vast herds of sheep, cattle and horses and establishing allotments for each separate unit. While dealing with this explosive problem he was expected to change the existing unfriendly public sentiment to a friendly one.   An examination and separate report was demanded on each of the many land claims (many fraudulent) within the Forest Reserve boundaries. The Supervisor was required to appoint and train a staff of field men to enforce regulations and help with general administration of the ranges.

Supervisor Ireland was authorized to open the ranges in 1906 to all stock grazed the previous season, upon payment of the grazing fee. The opening of the grazing season was to be deferred to June 1 for cattle and June 15 for sheep. It was estimated that 30,000 cattle and horses and 340,000 sheep had grazed the ranges in 1905, but the numbers to enter this range under permit in 1906 were 32,170 cattle and horses and 247,000 sheep. The opening up of the ranges to all stock in 1906 gave Mr. Ireland and his field force a little time to become familiar with the ranges and study the grazing problems. Besides himself and one Forest assistant, Mr. Ireland had an authorization of seven field men for his vast territory for the field season of 1906 as follows:

75

```
1 Supervisor at $1,200 - 11 months        $1,100
1 Forest Assistant at $1,456 - 12 mos.     1,456
1 Deputy For. Ranger at $1,000 - 12 mos.   1,000
2 Asst. For.Rangers at $900 - 12 mos.      1,800
4 Forest Guards at $720 - 6 months         1,440
                                          $6,796
```

Expenses

Travel	Equipment	Communications	Shelter	Protection
$150	$50	$50	$75	$0

With the knowledge gained during the 1906 grazing season, Supervisor Ireland began formulating plans to increase the efficiency of the Reserve and to improve administration for 1907 which included the reduction in numbers of permitted stock on the badly overgrazed ranges.

Many stockmen were bitterly opposed to government regulation of grazing and the way in which administration was being conducted. Many complaints were made to the Supervisor as well as to the Washington Office. They seemed to feel that the government was not only depriving them of their established rights but unjustly charging them for something that was already theirs. Meetings were held and problems and complaints weighed and considered. Objectives of the Forest Service were explained and future benefits to both the ranges and the users thereof were pointed out, but the demands upon the Forest Supervisor continued to be very great. He had his hands full and naturally made mistakes. He was between two fires - the Washington office demanding compliance with regulations on one hand and the stockmen opposing this procedure on the other. Forest officials met with the stockmen at The Dalles in November 1907. This meeting was followed by another at Prineville in January 1908, with L. F. Kneipp, Chief of the Office of Control in attendance. Mr. Kneipp later made a lengthy report on his observations and findings from which I will quote the following paragraph:

Supervisor Ireland was a stranger in the country. His Rangers were not familiar with the work or were they particularly good men, and the grazing conditions were so complicated and involved that the stockmen despaired of ever getting them straightened out. In fact they refused to attempt to do so at the first meeting held by the Supervisor. Mr. Ireland, inexperienced and a stranger to local conditions, then had to undertake the work of sifting out the chaotic mass of claims and counter claims. Something like twenty of the stockmen present at the Prineville meeting stated that he had done better than anybody had expected him or any other man to do. Numerous mistakes were made, but not as many nor as serious ones as were expected.

J. Fred McClain *McClain describes the grazing management job and tells two related stories.*

I will try to relate some early experiences which happened on my District on the Imnaha NF. As you know, the early Rangers had large areas or Districts to supervise, and in order to cover the entire District - much of which was isolated and with a lack of roads, trails, or even ways - it was necessary to cover the greater part by saddle horse. I would start out on a saddle horse leading my pack animal carrying full camp outfit consisting of groceries, cooking utensils, and bed and armed with the Use Book and a copy of Teddy Roosevelt's proclamation to bring the public to understand what the intentions were. These intentions were to conserve the timber, forage, wildlife and all commodities on the Forests and to get the cooperation of the people in bringing about these ends, as at this time range wars were just starting. Just across the Snake River from my District one sheepherder had been killed and numerous sheep and cattle shot, the sheep by the cattlemen and the cattle by the sheepmen. This made it imperative to bring about as much harmony as possible among the two factions, cattlemen and sheepmen, and also to make fair divisions of both cattlemen and sheepmen.

The early divisions were made in the Supervisor's Office by the representatives of the stockmen and the forest officers. Maps of the allotments were set up and descriptions of each allotment or unit were written up. Of course, these first tentative maps and descriptions had to be checked in the field. When complaints came in, the Ranger took the people concerned and rode over the range and settled the differences right on the ground. The men were consulted and most always agreed, but when they did not agree the Ranger settled it in their presence and made the change, if any, on the map.

I remember one case where three sheepmen were concerned over the division of some winter range. They consisted of two Frenchmen and one American. It was in February and in zero weather. We rode all day during which time the two Frenchmen dismounted five times to fight but never struck one blow. This trip proved to be very satisfactory, however, as the lines we established prevailed through the years and we never had any more trouble from these men.

Once it became necessary for me to stop overnight with one of the Frenchmen. We arrived at his headquarters at 9:00 pm, cold and hungry. They ushered us through the kitchen where the whole meal was in a large iron kettle, steaming hot. I guess I made some kind of facial expression as I smelled the contents of that kettle which consisted of meat, cabbage, corn, rice, beans and garlic; the garlic in the largest proportion. As I emerged from the washroom a camptender motioned for me to follow him into the cellar. He produced a quart bottle of Old Red Top, contents of which I lowered about four fingers. I was then able to stow away a large quantity of the contents of the kettle without even tasting the obnoxious garlic.

I received a letter late in August (1906) from H. K. O'Brien in which he instructed me to not let the Nez Perce Indians come in on the Day and Clemons Cattle range with their ponies as was their yearly custom in the hunting season. Sure enough, one morning in early September I saw a great dust coming up the trail, and Beith [the rider for Day and Clemons Cattle] said, "Here comes the Indians." I got on my horse and rode down the trail to meet them.

I motioned them to stop as they had about four or five hundred horses and were heading for Cold Springs to camp. They said they did not savvy. In fact, they pretended to not understand any English at all. As more Indians kept coming I saw Joe Albert and Culley, the Indian interpreter, with whom I was very well acquainted, and who I knew talked and understood good English. By this time, Philip McFarland and his daughter Nora came up. After I explained to them they could not camp and graze their horses on this range, they all moved back down Horse Creek below the Forest boundary and camped. They

78

stayed there for about two weeks, and from this camp they wrote numerous letters to A. C. Smith, an old lawyer who lived in Enterprise at that time, and who was a great friend of the Indians. He also wrote them that they could not graze on National Forest lands without permit.

Grover C. Blake *Blake was District Ranger on the Deschutes NF in 1910. In 1911 his Ranger District became part of the newly formed Ochoco NF.*

During the season of 1910 renewed efforts were made to get the cattle owners to make reasonable efforts to keep their stock on the allotted range [on the Deschutes NF]. Salting plans were made and were half-heartedly put into effect by some permittees. In a few instances, line riders were employed, but little success was attained until the cattle owners were organized into associations and drift fences constructed. It was several years before this was accomplished, however.

All permittees were furnished with blueprints and written descriptions of their allotments so their employees could locate their own allotment boundaries and get along until the Ranger could reach them. If they ran into difficulties they could notify the Ranger and get help. Constant cattle trespass called for many written notices to owners promising legal action, and trespass reports to the Supervisor's office. On July I, 1910, I was given a short-term guard to help with the administration of my vast territory.

On July 1, 1911, I was again at the Trout Creek entrance counting sheep into the Forest. I counted in from two to four bands per day for 15 days and then followed up by rushing from allotment to allotment assisting the men in charge getting established and getting their allotment boundaries located. Forest Guard C. M. Irvine was assigned to assist me during the 1911 field season. It was this year that we began organizing the cattle and horse permittees into stock associations. The first one for my District was the White Butte Cattle and Horse Association organized on November 11th. In this way we were able to deal with all the users of one allotment as a unit through their advisory board, thus greatly simplifying administration.

By the end of the 1911 season allotment lines were so definitely established and the men in charge of the stock were so familiar with them that I was able to devote more time to building horse pastures and trails.

Fred Wehmeyer *Wehmeyer was a forest guard on the Okanogan NF at the time of this story.*

Early in September of 1912, I heard the Forest Service [Okanogan NF] needed a few men to cut driveway. I applied in person to Ranger R. W. Flournoy and was sworn in as a forest guard at $75.00 per month - such a sum of money in buying power I never again achieved, though I worked on through the years until February 1945.

The work was done under the supervision of Supervisor H. M. Hale and Assistant Supervisor Vernon Harpham. Two crews were started on separate sections of the trail. The one to which I was assigned was under the leadership of Ranger Flournoy. I had a dozen men including Harry Green, an excellent camp cook, and a packer, Paul Heaton, who continued in Service until his retirement. The work was almost entirely by axe and saw, and we hacked out miles and miles of trail twelve feet wide. The route was almost entirely through dense lodgepole thickets. This lodgepole was beautiful timber; six, eight and ten inches in diameter and standing fifty to seventy feet in height. The stands were so dense that after felling and cutting into lengths and piled along the road-trail, they made fences five or six feet high that ran for miles. Sheepmen later named these places tunnels.

At that time much of the area had never been traveled or explored. Wildlife had little or no fear of man and we kept the cook's mulligan rich with stewed fool hen or ptarmigan, usually caught with a shoe lace or knocked down with a small pole or rock.

At that period of Forest Service development any meager funds received went into tools or material. The Supervisor then assembled his Rangers and they went to work. Hale or Harpham were usually in one or the other camps swinging an axe or helping consume huge quantities of beans and mulligan. As I remember, the work was highly dangerous but the men were deployed in such a manner there was little danger to themselves or others and that they were only allowed one mistake. That was a grand time in life – huge quantities of camp grub, large evening campfires and bull sessions. The tide of life was young with strength and stamina a grizzly bear might admire.

As everything must, the job came to an end near the Canadian line and in a blizzard. The morning we packed to leave it was bitter cold. The snow was about eight inches deep and still falling. Canvas, rope and hobbles were stiff and unmanageable. We started out trying to get to lower altitude in hopes of getting below the storm. Shortly after we started one of the boys saw a deer and could not resist the chance. This called for general readjustment of all the packs as we couldn't leave the meat. We took a shadowy trail down a creek canyon where the brush swept us with nearly every step. Since we were hurrying we went without dinner and as the days were short, it was dark at 4 pm except for the reflected light of the snow. We kept looking for a place to camp but found nothing appearing favorable.

Finally, in deference to the horses we stopped on a slight bench near the creek. This was the only time I ever saw the cook out of humor. With fourteen hungry men, everything a soppy mess, darkness and no dry fuel, we couldn't blame him. We found a large dead lodgepole and after splitting out a section of the heart we soon had a fire going. With everyone flying into the work, we soon had tents and canvas spread, horse equipment hung up to drip and out of reach of porcupines, and, we hoped, safe from wood rats. A full belly and a large campfire soon put the world in proper focus. Damp beds, though not pleasant, can be tolerated as one soon *steams* himself warm.

The next day we walked to Winthrop, Washington, about 30 miles distant where we settled up with the store. The grub bill was a total of $14.00 per man for a field trip of six weeks. I still drool when I think of the meals we ate. Hot dutch oven bread drowned in tea garden drips, kettles of red beans boiled with fat back, mulligans, dried fruit, rice, biscuits baked a golden brown in the reflector, coffee brewed over the fire and with a heavenly aroma, bacon, eggs, butter and an appetite that made everything something superlative. Only one accident marred the trip. A poor chap's axe deflected and sliced into his boot nearly severing the big toe. A clean dish towel and lots of pitch plastered the wound. After a day with his foot held high to staunch the blood flow, he returned to duty. Those days were simple and no compensation forms to worry over.

Ira E. Jones *Jones was a Ranger on the Whitman NF at the time of this story.*

In the spring of 1917, a sheep bridge at the Allison Mine [on the Whitman NF], across the North Fork of the John Day River washed out. The D. O. Jusii sheep allotment was just across the river. Without a bridge it was necessary to trail the sheep five or six days to reach the allotment, so decided to move them across the Desolation cattle range. There was some private land on the range leased by Ben Colvin. He told us not to cross, but we thought we could make it without getting on the private land. So Ranger Judy and I went down to handle it.

Colvin had gotten the road supervisor to refuse permission for the sheep to use the county road. I called the county commissioner and got his permission to put the sheep over the road if we agreed to clean it out afterwards, which we did. Then I called Colvin, told him the sheep were at Desolation Creek bridge and that if he wanted to see them cross to be there early in the morning. Next morning at daylight he was there, and said, "Don't cross them sheep." The herder was told to start them. Colvin got in his car, drove to Pendleton and got a lawyer to write a letter demanding damages, but no damages were ever paid, and the sheep reached their allotment without further difficulty.

Later, listening in on the party line at the Dale Ranger Station, the Ranger's wife heard two women talking about this deal. One said, "It looks like when the Forest Service starts anything, they always go through with it, as the Deputy Supervisor and a Ranger did when they put the sheep across the cattle range."

HOMESTEADS "-the land problems did cause considerable hard feeling-"

Duffy Lewis *Lewis describes the work created by the Act of June 11, 1906.*

After graduation [1912], I returned to Oregon, and was appointed District Ranger of the Gardiner District [Siuslaw NF]. My work was mostly with homestead examinations, including a number of final examinations so the homesteaders could *prove up*. As most of them showed good faith, I had little trouble. But there were also the June

11th [1906] claims which were a horse of a different color. These claims allowed the homesteader of any land that was better for agriculture than for timber to be homesteaded. The Forest had been closed to entry by homesteaders, but when it was thrown open about this time, there were a flood of applications. The applicant had only to take the description of the claim from a map, but the Ranger had to double-run the forties, make a topographic map and cruise the timber. As most of these claims were on rough land, with perhaps a half an acre of flat land, it was a real headache. There were hundreds of applications.

<u>Melvil "M. L." Merritt</u> *Merritt was Forest Supervisor of the Deschutes NF from 1912 to 1916.*

The critical problems on the Deschutes at that time [1912] related to land. There was a tremendous boom in homesteading going on in central Oregon then and for a few years later. Much of the high desert of central Oregon was being located by hopeful settlers. Many hundred, probably thousands, came to Oregon in high hopes, expecting to duplicate the experience of their fathers in the fertile Mississippi Valley, where good land had been waiting for them. Even in Iowa first settlers had plenty of privations, but they could grow crops, get water and stock feed on their own land. That wasn't possible for most settlers here. Nearly all used up their savings. This was a different country – it required capital, larger operations and the learning of new agricultural processes. No doubt the experience was a necessary one, but it was mighty tough for the individuals who tried it and worse on their wives.

These events had their effect upon adjoining National Forests. Although Forest land was withdrawn from entry, land chiefly valuable for agriculture could be listed for homestead entry under the act of June 11, 1906.

When I came to the Deschutes there had been several hundred applications for homestead. A rather liberal policy had been followed and many areas were approved. Though the climate was adverse, timber values were low and folks did have a chance. When I arrived this problem was at or past its peak. Many protested the rejection of their applications; some appealed to the Secretary of Agriculture.

Several formal hearings were held by the Secretary's representative. The best Forest land was better than desert homesteads. At least there was wood and water and hardy garden crops could be raised.

Some troublesome situations developed. For example, a homesteader named House applied for the high mountain meadow (and adjoining lodgepole) land west of Davis Lake. His application was rejected, properly I think, before my time. House had not accepted the rejection. Instead, he moved right onto the land, built a cabin, dug a well and there he was, though he hardly raised a garden. A few others did likewise. He made the usual appeals. As I arrived on the scene, the wheels of law enforcement had turned to the point where the Portland U. S. Marshall had, at the request of the Forest Service and after proper legal consideration, sent a deputy to Davis Lake to arrest House.

The deputy took him to Portland for trial. Here House contacted Senator Lane and explained his predicament. He was trying to develop a bit of land at Davis Lake. He had erected a home on it and was farming the land but the Forest Service had arbitrarily refused his application, had harassed him, and now, finally arrested him. No doubt he told of other examples of settlement being discouraged by the Forest Service. Senator Lane, with senatorial sympathy, listened to his story and, it was reported, told him to go back home and leave things to him. Confronted with this support, the U. S. Attorney dropped the case and House returned to Davis Lake.

A long-used wagon road along the west-side of Davis Lake passed right in front of House's cabin. Each spring sheep were driven to their summer range over this road. Come sheep traveling time, following House's trip to Portland, a Mr. Jones, who had the grazing allotment above Davis Lake, arrived with his sheep as usual. At the House claim he was met by Mr. House, adequately armed with a rifle, and denied passage. Jones repaired to the nearby Forest Ranger Ed Mann. Ed protested to House - pointed out the long use of this route as a public road and sheep driveway, and the impracticability of taking sheep through the lodgepole thickets back of his house. Mr. House was not impressed. There followed much consultation regarding

84

Homesteader cabin on the Deschutes NF – c1915

Forest Service tool box on the South Fork of the Nooksack River,
Washington NF – c1916

proper legal procedure, including a personal trip to Klamath Falls to see the county attorney. Naturally, federal attorneys were now wary of the case. So back to Davis Lake, where Jones' sheep were meanwhile eating non-permitted forage (I don't suppose they cared).

Jones again, at the Ranger's suggestion, brought his sheep up to the House crossing, Ranger Mann with him. There was House and his rifle, this time stoutly reinforced by his wife. Mann again asked permission for the sheep to cross the road. According to the report that came to me, House refused and threatened Mann with bodily harm - eventually attacking him, not with the rifle but with fists - his wife helping. Mann kept away from the wife and gave House the beating of his life. Jones took the sheep through to his summer range and House retired to his cabin. Next morning Mann, whose cabin was close, saw House hitch up his horse to his single wagon, load up his household belongings, put his wife on the seat beside him and drive away. They were never seen in that locality again.

The land problems did cause considerable hard feeling and brought criticism on the Forest Service until finally Chief Forester Graves decided to eliminate the lodgepole pine area around La Pine and south to Crescent, which was done.

C. C. McGuire *McGuire was a Ranger on the Washington NF from 1910 to 1918.*

During the formative years of the Forest Service areas, there was much resentment against barring such areas from homestead claims. The value of timber lands was beginning to be appreciated, with the result that many homestead claims were located on the Forests, not with the idea of founding a home, but to secure title to timberlands. Unscrupulous locators made a business of locating people on National Forest lands. It fell to my lot to examine many of these entries to determine if they were bona fide, that the homestead laws were being complied with and if there were ulterior motives involved.

The Finney Creek country [Washington NF] was particularly plagued with these land grabbers. In the examination of over fifty claims throughout the Forest, only one was found which was at all suitable for agriculture and on which the claimant had made an honest effort to comply with the homestead law. Unfortunately for this claimant, his holdings were on unsurveyed lands where he had only squatter's rights. In 1905 he joined the Klondike gold rush and was away from his cabin for five years with the result that the Forest Service contested his claim for non-occupancy. The claimant told the exact truth and as a result lost his claim. In view of the fact that so many fraudulent claims were passed to patent, I always felt that we might have closed our eyes as a reward to an honest man.

Typical of these claims which passed to patent was the C. E. Montgomery claim on Cumberland Creek. I examined his claim and found it laid on a mountain-side wholly unsuited for agriculture, but it was covered with 5,500,000 board feet of merchantable timber. While the homestead law did not require a definite portion of the land be placed under agriculture, it did require that the land should be the home of the claimant and that agriculture be pursued with due diligence. In this case the claimant resided in Bellingham where she taught school. Her residence was sketchy and amounted to less than two months per year. The cleared area under cultivation measured sixty-two feet by one hundred feet with a three-foot log lying the long way through the area. In addition there were seven stumps six to twelve inches in diameter. Not over two-thirds of this plot could be cultivated.

Miss Montgomery conducted her own case before the Register and Receiver of the General Land Office and proved herself a better lawyer than a homesteader for she won the suit and was granted a patent. Then she had a white elephant on her hands. The area was so isolated that lumbermen were not interested and, of course, no one would think of buying the land for agriculture. After many years had past she finally sold the land back to the Forest Service for $800. This case is typical of many homestead entries. Forest Rangers A. B. Conrad, Ralph Hilligoss and I almost acquired the title of professional witnesses in appearing for the government in contesting claims to areas whose only value was the timber thereon.

<u>Shirley Buck</u>   *Buck began his career in 1906 as a clerk on the Cascade Range Forest Reserve.   He also worked in Idaho and as an Inspector stationed in Portland.   He joined the District Six office when it was established in 1908, where he was Chief of Maintenance, District Budget Officer, and Regional Purchasing Agent.   He retired in 1942.   This story took place sometime between 1911 and 1915.*

About the time heat generated by the Act of June 11, 1906, reached its highest point, I was sent to help Supervisor Cryder of the Paulina Forest check up on his June 11 situation.   Our work was going well and without much incident until one day word was received that a squatter in trespass at Davis Lake would be pleased to kill the Supervisor if he would just take time out to come over.   Supervisor Cryder was not of the timid sort and, besides, here was a case of saving face which meant much to him because he had lived in the Orient.   After a brief consideration Mr. Cryder said he would go at once and did I want to go along?   Unnecessary question!   Of course I did not want to go, but here also was a case of saving face - my own to be specific.   So, speaking in a casual manner which I by no means felt, I said, "Oh, yes, I would like to go.   Seeing a Supervisor killed will be a new experience."

Well, unarmed, we started.   I wondered enroute whether the killer, if it turned out that way, would care to have a surviving witness.   Our light wagon, which made plenty of noise, announced us a long ways ahead. Rounding a short turn in the road near the lake we saw a man standing in front of a cabin, gun barrel resting on forearm.   He was about 40 yards distant.   We drove on up to him and spoke to him.   He made a muttering reply not understood by us.   He made no move to shoot, and I'm sure we made no effort to provoke him.   We then drove on about 60 yards and made camp for the night.   It would not be the truth to say we did not sleep any, but it would be a great untruth to say we slept much.   We saw nothing more of the man and after an early breakfast we were on our way.

It was reported afterward that the man did not shoot, he said, because he did not want to kill someone he did not know and that someone was me.

J. Fred McClain *McClain describes a meeting with a squatter (circa 1909-1912) when he was a Ranger on the Wallowa NF.*

There was a squatter settlement on the Imnaha River known by other settlers as *squatters*, among whom one outstanding man was designated as the king of the squatter settlement. These squatters caused a lot of trouble as they were always complaining about the cattle which were allotted on adjoining range. One day I finished counting the cattle allotted to this adjoining range and started down the river. Suddenly a cowboy overtook me and said a man, whom stockman called the *King of the Squatter Kingdom*, had come down the road and forbid their driving the cattle up the road to their range. I told him to tell the men to start the cattle up the road.

Sure enough there was the man sitting by the side of the road. He bade me "Good Morning," and suggested I dismount and talk, which I did. Presently the cattle were driven by us by their owners. The *King* never said a word, didn't even mention the cattle or men who drove them by. However, he went to great detail in describing how our government should be run and ended up by asking why the Forest Service was taking charge of this country. He said he had never been notified that there was a Forest Reserve. I then took out of my saddlebags a copy of Teddy Roosevelt's proclamation and had him read it. After doing so, he handed it back to me with the comment "Freak Legislation." I mounted my horse and rode back down the river.

RECREATION: "-high recreation potential-"

Melvil "M. L." Merritt *Merritt was Forest Supervisor of the Deschutes NF from 1912 to 1916.*

John Curl strongly advocated development of East Lake, [Deschutes National Forest] as a recreational center. A hot spring there, he said, had great possibilities, a prediction since borne out. He interested a local man, Fred Shintaffer, in the project. Fred helped build the road to East Lake and took out a five-year permit for a resort, the first term permit issued on the Deschutes. Between them, also, they caught and transported a number of fish to East Lake which, at that time, had none. Later Curl arranged for fish planting from the State hatchery. The area has become a good fishing ground.

Stylish angler on the Metolius River, fishing from what was at that time
the site of a proposed hotel, Deschutes NF – 1916
(Photo by C.J. Buck – future Regional Forester.)

<u>Rudo L. Fromme</u> *Fromme began his Forest Service career in 1905 in the east, then worked in Idaho and California before coming to District Six. He was Forest Supervisor of the Kaniksu in District 1, the Klamath in District 5, and the Siskiyou, Olympic, Rainier, Deschutes, and Mt. Baker NFs in District/Region 6. He retired in the 1943.*

It was the fall of 1915, as I remember it, when The Forester [Chief of the Forest Service], Henry S. Graves, voiced a desire to travel across the south end of the Mt. Olympic National Monument. Seattle and Grays Harbor mining men had been petitioning the government to return this area to National Forest status because of the purported presence of valuable minerals and lack of outstanding scenery or other reasons for remaining in a Monument status.

The plan was to cross the South Fork Skokomish-Quinault divide from upper Hood Canal to Quinault Lake, then by road to Hoquiam, where Mr. Graves was scheduled to address a Chamber of Commerce banquet five days hence. Ranger Hilligoss assisted us with horses the first two days to reach the divide. There is where the horse trail ended. It was a wild guess as to whether even a foot trail would be found from there on down to the East Fork Quinault. Besides Mr. Graves, George Cecil and myself, F. H. Stannard, mining promoter of Seattle, had attached himself to complete a foursome in this cross-country gamble; not gambol, as we soon learned. Stannard had asserted, in advance, that he knew this route.

The fog was extremely heavy when we started our foot-work down through soggy, wet mountain meadows to the head of what was then Success Creek. The map indicated the travel distance as probably ten to twelve miles to where we would be meeting Ranger Ernest Paull with saddle horses to carry us the remaining twenty miles to Quinault Lake. As we started dropping down one of the creek branches, we began to encounter canyon country. Bull-headed Stannard claimed that an old man-made trail would be discovered if we kept close to the creek to where it dropped into definite canyons. I, bull-headedly, contended, based on District Ranger Chris Morgenroth's statement, that there was no trail, that the most practical foot route was upper side hill.

With Stannard intermittently spying bits of elk or deer trail as the real thing and me side-hilling it high above, Graves and Cecil were alternately clamboring down or up, following the wrong leader. This got them pretty winded, while Stannard and I got in the same condition from yelling at each other. The only thing that kept going steadily was the rain. A cold lunch of imported summer sausage and erbswurst soon had Cecil's stomach doing handsprings, even though he, personally, as well as the rest of us were practically doing the creeps. Stannard, by this time, was out of the canyon, but dragging his seat even more than the forestry contingent. We eventually waited for him in the sullen downpour. His alibi was that his pack was far heavier than any of ours, due to special maps and other data, which he wished to present at the Hoquiam meeting. I suspected the *other data*, so traded packs for a spell. As soon as he spurted ahead, I looked inside and found a badly rain-soaked suit of street clothes and shoes, together with a *half-ton*, more or less, of rock samples picked up during our progress. (We had all agreed beforehand to send our street clothes by railway express from Seattle). I dumped most of the rock by the wayside.

We did not reach the East Fork Quinault that day. Darkness caught us on a small half-level bench above another canyon, probably the lowest one on the creek, but the going was too gloomy to find out for sure. We huddled together in front of a large, old Douglas-fir, reclining our soggy wet backs against soggy, wet packs, and intermittently chipping off flakes of old bark to maintain a semblance of camp fire throughout the long night. Snoring was also intermittent, but not so the rain. (In his speech preceding that of Mr. Graves at the Hoquiam banquet, Stannard spoke of our stopping for the night as follows: quoted in the press - "Impenetrable darkness stopped further travel that day, so we sat in the gloom of a fitful campfire while a Quinault downpour continually drenched us from head to toe. When we awoke, we found to our alarm that we had been perilously perched on the very brink of a canyon a thousand feet deep.")

Well, the foggy dew of approaching daylight finally inspired our creaking joints to further effort onward to those much yearned-for saddle horses. Nobody had the stomach for a cold breakfast, even though the hard tack was no longer hard and the summer sausage had washed away some of its high protein zip. Ah-hah! Eureka!, etc., we could now see an opening ahead. It meant the East Fork Quinault valley and - ? - ! Let's draw a somber veil over that heavy-hoof-dragging travail. There was no Ranger Paull and no horses. Signs of camp break-up indicated that they had just left, but who in our party had the zip to try to overtake them? There was, of course, no telephone line at that time nearer than Quinault Lake, our destination. There was, however, twenty miles of easily visible horse trail to follow except for four or five fordings of the river in the first ten miles, at anywhere from knee to hip deep. As District Forester George H. Cecil said rather pointedly to yours truly, "It was a damn poorly planned trip."

In fairness to the Ranger, I could add that when we finally hobbled into the old Quinault Lake log hotel, we learned that he had waited three full days for our appearance, then assumed that we had changed our plans. He left principally because he had been out of feed for man or beast for 24 hours. However, he had made the mistake of reading my directions too hurriedly, taking the date for our departure from Hood Canal to be the date for our expected arrival at the mouth of Success Creek. I later changed the name of this creek to *Graves* on a new map we were preparing, to better fix in memory this harsh, but certainly unintended, Olympic initiation of the Chief Forester.

C. C. McGuire *McGuire was a Ranger on the Washington NF at the time of this story.*

In January 1917, a bill to create a Mount Baker National Park was reported on favorably by the Public Lands committee. This aroused a storm of protest particularly by the mining interests. Many public hearings were held and the discussions became super-heated. The tempest died when Congress failed to pass a bill.

Then the Mount Baker recreation area, consisting of 125 sections of scenic country, was set aside. No timber to be cut for commercial purposes and mining to be carefully supervised so the scenic areas would not be destroyed. This ended the agitation for a National Park and all factions became boosters for a highway from the town of Glacier to Austin Pass, or as the area is now called, Heather Meadows.

Forest Service camp shelter with a split hollow larch log roof on
Heliotrope Ridge, Washington NF – c1916

Forest Ranger transporting cutthroat trout in milk cans to stock streams
above falls blocking fish access, Washington NF – c1916

Albert Wiesendanger *Wiesendanger started as a messenger in the District 6 Office in 1909 and was transferred to the Oregon NF in 1916. Other than an assignment in the R-6 Regional Office from 1931 to 1934, he was a Ranger on the Oregon/Mt. Hood NFs until 1948, when he became the Executive Secretary of Keep Oregon Green for another 32 years.*

The Columbia Gorge, with its spectacular forested cliffs, had long been recognized as one of the prime scenic resources of the Pacific Northwest. Long before the turn of the century it had been easily accessible via railway, steamboat and buses. When the Columbia Gorge Scenic Highway was opened, the area became accessible to highway traffic. Certain factions within the Portland Community, concerned with the preservation of scenic values, took up the problem of how to prevent the degradation of the Oregon bank of the Gorge, that might result from unrestricted tourist development. Two Portland organizations in particular took an active interest in the preservation of the Oregon bank; the Portland Chamber of Commerce and the Progressive Business Men's Club of Portland of which Forest Supervisor T. H. Sherrard was very active. Certainly their support played a crucial role in Forester Henry Graves' decision to recommend to the Secretary of Agriculture that an area some 22 miles long and 4 to 6 miles wide (13,873 acres) along the Oregon bank of the Gorge be designated as the Columbia Gorge Park Division of the Oregon National Forest.

Secretary David Houston's order to that effect, dated December 24, 1915, appears to mark the first time the Forest Service dedicated an extended area to purely recreation use. The order prohibited timber sales and the distribution of permits for homesites. Having closed the Columbia River Gorge Park to the development of summer cabins or private resorts, the Forest Service found itself forced to assume greater responsibility for recreational facility development than it had done in other areas of high recreational potential. During the summer of 1916, the Oregon National Forest developed the Eagle Creek Campground within the Park. Because the area was already so readily accessible and popular, the new camping area could not be merely another undeveloped site set aside for the use of campers, as had most earlier *campgrounds* in the National Forests.

At Eagle Creek, for the first time, the Forest Service undertook the construction of a public campground in the modern sense. Facilities included camp tables, toilets and a Ranger Station. The Forest Service plans for recreational use in the Park did not end with the dedication of the campground in July 1916. Even then work was progressing on a 13-1/2 mile long Eagle Creek Trail to Wahtum Lake. Built specifically for recreational use, the trail purposely sought out scenic routes, even tunneling at one point behind a waterfall. The easy accessibility and great beauty of the Columbia Gorge Park assured its rapid acceptance by the public.

TIMBER: "-we were getting curious as to how much timber we had-"

Melvil "M. L." Merritt   *Merritt was a Forest Assistant on the Washington NF at the time of this story.*

After Christmas 1909, Supervisor Park asked me to estimate the timber on a projected railway right-of-way up the Cascade River from Marblemount to the summit. I went to Marblemount by stage, crossed the river on a skiff and walked. There were from six inches to a foot of snow on the ground and it was heavy going. About 15 miles above Marblemount was an old unused log cabin where I camped. It was good shelter from the weather but not rodent proof. The first night wood rats ate the leather strings from my high-topped shoes as well as several good-sized holes in the shoes themselves. Fortunately, I had suspended my food supply from a rafter and it was untouched. I was quite disturbed about the shoes and even considered returning for replacements. However, I converted the heavy cord from around my slab of bacon to shoe strings and wore my leaky shoes. The railroad was never built.

C. C. McGuire   *McGuire was a Ranger on the Washington NF at the time of this story in 1912.*

That summer we were getting curious as to how much timber we had, so I spent several weeks on extensive reconnaissance. Fred Brundage and M. L. Merritt had made a pretty complete inventory of the Suiattle River drainage in 1909. To carry out the work in the Glacier District, I started at the west boundary near Glacier. The method used was to go to the summit noting timber enroute, then offset one mile along the summit, cross the valley to the opposite summit, sampling the timber enroute, then offset another mile and repeat. In this manner, I worked out the Nooksack River, Canyon Creek and Chilliwack Creek drainages. It was interesting work and I might have covered more territory if I had refrained climbing every high peak enroute just to see what was on the other side. However, I did get a speaking acquaintance with most of my District and made mental plans of places where I might someday build a trail.

<u>Grover C. Blake</u> *Blake was a District Ranger on the Deschutes NF at the time of this story.*

On January 1, 1910, my salary was raised from $900 to $1,100 per annum. On February 3, 1910, Ranger W. J. Nichols arrived at my homestead and informed me that he, Rangers W. A. Donnelly, C. S. Congleton and I were to go to the head of Badger Creek, near the summit of the Blue Mountains, on the Mitchell-Big Summit Road, at about 5,000 feet elevation and do insect-control work on an infested area of lodgepole pine. After I engaged a settler to stay at my homestead and care for my horses, Ranger Nichols and I went to Mitchell where we met Congleton and Donnelly. We engaged a livery team and driver to deliver our supplies and camp outfit. On the morning of February 5, the livery rig loaded up and started out, but stalled in the deep snow and was forced to turn back. We then equipped a bobsled with four heavy horses to break through and finally reached our destination. We made camp in an old rough lumber cabin which had been a homesteader's residence.

This cabin did a very good job of keeping out the snow but none of the cold as it was thoroughly ventilated with cracks between the boards. It was by far the coldest cabin I was ever in. The snow was four or five feet deep, but we would beat out a trail from tree to tree, fall the trees, dig them out of the deep snow, buck them up and pile and burn them. It was bitter cold and each night the water would freeze solid in the pail. The ancient range stove smoked constantly and kept the cabin filled with smoke when in use. It was hard to imagine a more uncomfortable situation. But I never heard a word of complaint from anyone throughout the assignment and jokes about our plight were a common diversion. We battled away at the job until February 17th without accomplishing very much, although we put forth every effort to make a showing. One of the boys went out at this time and reported

Ranger Grover Blake cruising beetle killed pine on the Deschutes NF – 1910
(Grover Family Photo)

conditions to Supervisor Ireland, who called the job off until weather conditions and the snow situation improved.

We returned to our respective headquarters and I devoted the next month to assisting stockmen with applications for grazing permits, attending to free use business, and marking boundary at the lower elevations. On March 21st I returned to the insect control job with Ranger Donnelly and on March 25th Rangers Congleton and J. C. Gilchrist arrived. Ranger Nichols was assigned to another job. We continued our work of cutting and burning bug-killed lodgepole pine trees. Winter conditions still prevailed at this high elevation, but we worked until April 7th when Gilchrist returned from a trip to the outside with orders from the Supervisor to discontinue the work, and so ended the insect control project.

Incidentally, we tackled this job without any previous training or any information on the subject of insect control and had only a vague idea of what should be done. Later we were to learn that all the trees we had felled and burned had been killed the previous year, had been abandoned by the beetles and were no longer infected. It will be remembered that we had no expense accounts in those days so the venture for us was a financial problem of a personal nature.

<u>Melvil "M. L." Merritt</u> *Merritt was a Forest Assistant on the Whitman NF at the time of this story.*

The Forest Service [Whitman National Forest in 1910] soon had an application from Frank Gardenier, under the name of the Baker White Pine Lumber Company, to purchase timber on several sections northeast of Austin. This cruising I did alone; running compass, pacing distances, mapping and estimating volume of timber, staying in a little log cabin on Crawford Meadows. Yellow (ponderosa) pine was new to me and I had much to learn. I made my own volume tables. The ten percent cruise later cut out slightly in excess of the estimate. After the cruise there was much arguing and negotiating in preparing the sale contract. Mr. W. T. Andrews, Forest Service Lumberman from Portland, did this negotiating.

It was the first large sale on the Whitman and, I believe, the first large yellow pine sale in District Six. So both sides to the negotiation were operating in a pioneer field. A minimum price and conditions of utilization were agreed on. We actually cut about 80% of the stand - too much by later standards, but a considerable volume was required to warrant railroad spur building. All brush was to be piled for burning. Final cutting report shows the following volume in board feet cut on this sale: Yellow pine 18,363,000; Douglas-fir 3,511,000; Western larch 3,511,000. Receipts were $46,396.78. Not a large sale at present day prices and standards, but it set a pattern.

Assistant Regional Forester Fred Arnes, Supervisor Henry Ireland, Thornton Munger and W. T. Andrews, particularly, took part in the marking discussion with Ames as the final arbiter and Munger as technical adviser. A working policy was adopted which guided yellow pine sales in that area for several years to come. Marking in the heavy winter snow, often more than four feet deep on the level, involved hard labor. Travel was on snowshoes; a long-handled shovel was used to dig down to ground level for the stump mark which was to remain after cutting.

Before the first sale to the Baker White Pine Lumber Company (Mr. Gardenier) was in operation, application was received for all National Forest timber on the headwaters of the John Day River east of Austin, and a crew under Lumberman W. T. Andrews was organized to cruise it. This crew consisted of Andrews and myself cruising, two compassmen and a cook.

We worked hard and fast. One day Kan Smith, compassman for Andrews, came in with a bad axe cut. He had been carrying a double-bitted axe over his shoulder and accidentally dropped it behind him. It cut his leg above the heel. We bandaged the cut (it was before accident reports) and Smith hobbled around camp for several weeks. Our cook became a compassman and Smith a cook.

We started cruising early each day, returning just before six for dinner and compiled our map data in the evening. This was six days a week. Sunday was general clean-up and odd-job day. Final cutting reports for all these areas show a total cut of 190,745,000 board feet, bringing in $552,550.11.

While cruising, Andrews engaged the local sheep packer to move camp. He failed to show up. When he apologetically appeared, admitting too much celebration, Mr. Andrews told him gruffly that he was being fined just one sheep to compensate us for our inconvenience. He paid the fine.

So started the logging of Ponderosa pine (we called it yellow pine then) in Oregon's National Forests. During the negotiations many government foresters participated; all of those handling sales in the Portland District Office and several from Washington DC. From Portland there were Fred Ames, W. T. Andrews and T. T. Munger. The latter deserves much credit for devising the forestry practices which were adopted. Among the Washington men was Rafael Zon, born in Russia, educated at Cornell, and the Service's authority on silviculture. He spent several days on the project, during which time we *batched* at the Blue Mountain Ranger Station cabin. This two room cabin had but one bed. The lots fell against Zon and he had to sleep on the floor with Andrews. One morning Zon protested he hadn't slept a wink! Woodrats (perhaps mice) had kept running over him, to his great distress. No one extended much sympathy, but as I recall, Zon lived through without damage.

Later, after marking timber, L. B. Palter, E. K. McDaniels and I came into the Blue Mountain cabin from the north. It was cold with deep snow. We were on snowshoes. The John Day River was crossed where it runs through the Blue Mountain meadow. It was six or eight feet wide, three or four feet deep with steep banks and not frozen over. Mac, ahead, crossed on a fence rail. I followed. Pag was some distance back. He started across. Halfway over, the rail broke and Pag was in the water, snowshoes and all. It wouldn't have been so bad, but he lost one of his snowshoes in the water and was hunting for it when Mac went back to see why he hadn't shown up. The lost snowshoe was found, he was dried out, and the next day we snowshoed over the mountains, about a dozen miles to Whitney on our way to Sumpter. The weather was splendid, and it was most exhilarating.

Ira E. Jones *Jones describes scaling on the timber sale Merritt cruised and marked.*

The first large timber sale on the Whitman was made in 1910 to a newly organized company called the Baker White Pine Lumber Company for a tract of timber near Tipton.

I scaled the first logs that were cut on this sale during the winter of 1910. My residence was a 12' x 14' wall tent; no floor, a board bunk and straw mattress. The logging was done by team and sled. Along about mid-January (of 1911) it got down to 30° below zero and the small Sibley stove kept the tent warm for only a few minutes at a time. The floor was frozen except around the stove. When not at work I stayed in bed most of the time. I got to thinking about my folks in Texas, asked for some leave, and took off for a warmer climate.

George L. Drake *Drake wrote this story about a summer job on the Cascade National Forest in 1910. He also had summer employment in New Hampshire and worked for the Forest Service in Alaska and Oregon from 1910 to 1930. He then worked for the Simpson Logging Company in Washington until his retirement in 1954.*

The timber survey crew was working across the river on the slope between the Willamette and Row River, Mt. June country. This was one of the first major cruising projects in Region 6 and why they would pick out this rugged country for a timber sale, I never could figure out. In fact it was one of the last units I understand that has been sold in that area. The country rises very sharply from the river to the summit with lots of cliffs and bad country. The crew had been there since early June, originally under E. M. McDaniels and then later under W. G. Hastings. Hastings was kind of a martinet, and the boys were always comparing the good old days when E. H. McDaniels was running the crew. There had been very little cruising done as I mentioned before and apparently each man in charge of a job of this kind more or less made up his own rules on how the work was to be done.

We used a 33-foot chain to do our measuring. These soon wore out, and we finally wound up using clothesline for a chain. In order to keep tally, we had to use wooden pins and wasted time looking for the pins in that rough brushy country. The cruisers later found you could do a pretty accurate job of pacing even in the country of that kind.

One of the silly things that was done that slowed down the work and certainly added to the fire hazard was the practice of starting out on Monday morning with a pack on your back and enough food for two or three days and then when night came, camping at the nearest water. This added a lot to the inconvenience of going through the brush, especially climbing over cliffs where oftentimes we had to pull up our packs with a rope. The practice also created a beautiful fire hazard in that we built a fire morning and night. I guess the good Lord was with us because we had no fires.

William G. Weigle *Weigle was a Forest Supervisor in Alaska at the time of this story.*

During World War I, England was still in the market for spruce lumber to be used in airplane construction. So they called on the United States to furnish it to them. Someone notified the Washington office of a fine stand of spruce near Lituya Bay located within the shadow of the 16,000-foot Mt. Fairweather and a half dozen other similar mountains on the coast, approximately 100 miles west of Juneau. The Forester requested me to investigate and report the situation.

With our splendid 64-foot boat, *The Tahn*, and the efficient Captain Blodget in command, we started for Lituya Bay. When we arrived outside the bay, a powerful stream of white water and immense chunks of ice were coming out of the narrow entrance into the Bay. We waited outside until it was low tide and the water in the channel got quiet. The channel was unsurveyed and the report was that there was a rock in the middle of the channel. As a matter of precaution l stood on deck and threw a lead line continuously, but we did not hit a rock. We found the bay most delightful. Anchoring in a safe place, we collected our equipment for several days camping.

A helper and I walked about ten miles north where we found the reported spruce and an old miner's cabin where we camped. It was, and I presume still is, a fine stand of spruce from two to five feet in diameter, covering several hundred acres. The area was badly cut up with glacier streams and would have been difficult to log or to care for the logs after you got them. Evidently an earthquake had loosened millions of tons of ice from the face of a nearby glacier that fell down reaching the timber. I had my photo taken with my back against a five-foot spruce and my feet against a chunk of ice as large as a barn. The region was full of Kodiak bear and we both carried rifles, but avoided shooting at them, as a wounded Kodiak bear can cause a lot of trouble. After carefully examining the timber we went back to the boat and found just south of the bay several hundred acres of open ground literally covered with delicious wild strawberries and no one living within miles of them! There were many signs indicating the Kodiak bear were taking their share of the crop.

RESEARCH: "-research was not neglected-"

Thornton T. Munger *Munger began his career with the Bureau of Forestry in 1903. He came west as a Forest Assistant, then was Head of the Silvics Section in District Six from 1908 to 1924. These stories relate some of his early experiences.*

In 1908, I was in Washington DC, preparing for a field study of ash in the middle west when a call came from Inspector W.H.B. Kent for someone to study the "encroachment of lodgepole pine on western yellow pine in Central Oregon." I was soon on the train for Portland where Chief Inspector E. T. Allen and two or three others had offices. The only one I saw when I reported was Shirley Buck, then clerk in the Inspectors' Office.

The next day I started for the Deschutes country, via train to Shaniko and that night by four-horse Concord Stage to Prineville, 64 miles in 13½ hours; thence an 18-hour run by two-horse stage to Bend and Rosland. Arriving at Rosland after midnight, the stage driver said he would find a bed for me in the hotel. After looking with a candle in a couple of rooms and finding them occupied, he spied an empty bed. He said, "It is a good, clean bed. Bill Jones slept there last night and he is O.K."

I bought a horse the next day for $65 from Ranger Beach of the Cascade National Forest which then came to the Deschutes River. For the next three months I roamed the country from Rosland (near the present La Pine) to Pelican Bay [in the Klamath Basin], mostly on horseback, trying to puzzle out the ecological relationship of lodgepole pine to western yellow pine.

It has since struck me how audacious or naive it was for the Washington Office to assign a Forest Assistant with no experience, who had not even seen the two species before, to such a study that now would be assigned only to subject specialists with a Ph.D.

Meanwhile, Chief Forester Pinchot had decided to decentralize the Forest Service and set up six District Offices with a miniature Washington office in each. In December 1908, with some 25 or 30 people from Washington and others recruited locally, the District Six [name changed to Region in 1930] was established in 37 rooms in the Beck Building (northwest corner of Oak and 7th, now Broadway). E. T. Allen was District Forester, Fred Ames, Chief of Silviculture (name changed to Forest Management in 1920 and to Timber Management in 1935), and under him Julius Kummel and I had the one-man sections of Planting and Silvics respectively. Most of the crew were in their twenties.

It is an evidence of the vision, progressiveness and scientific spirit of the Forest Service that even under the pressure to take over the administration of a tremendous acreage of almost unknown and undeveloped public forests with a ridiculously small crew of very young men, research was not neglected. Coincident with the pressing problems of manning, developing and protecting the National Forest, studies were carried on of growth and yield, silvical characteristics of the important species and methods of reforestation.

My first work was as a sort of technical roustabout. I organized and catalogued a library as a necessary foundation for any technical work. I looked into the causes of dying timber reported here and there. I answered questions the Supervisors and the public asked on technical matters; wrote instructions for the field on various subjects.

In a swing through eastern and southern Oregon in the spring of 1909 (400 miles in horse stages and riding eight different saddle horses), I put in two pairs of plots on small timber sales to test "no slash disposal vs. piling and burning." I also started a tiny nursery of 1700 wildings of yellow pine at the Rosland Ranger Station thinking that this pumice country would need some planting; also tried some direct seeding there.

Believing that the most important thing to know about the Douglas-fir region was the rate of growth of its Forests, in July 1909, six of us went into the field, measuring even-aged stands of Douglas-fir in Washington and Oregon. We measured trees and stands up to about 125 years old wherever we could get to them by logging trains, horse stages or walking. We moved often and boarded at farmhouses, logging camps and country hotels, sometimes putting up our tent when there was not room inside. A walk of three or four miles to work was thought nothing of. The study was resumed in 1911. The results gave the first convincing evidence that Douglas-fir forests grew at an astonishing rate, but the industry took little cognizance thereof for many years. In the spring of 1910, I established three permanent sample plots on the south side of the Middle Fork Willamette River in a beautiful 54-year old stand. These were, I believe, the first growth plots of this nature to be established in the west.

In 1910, the Section of Silvics turned its attention to the growth of western yellow pine (now ponderosa pine), and two three-man crews were in the field all summer. In 1913, I was in on the establishment of three 15-acre Methods of Cutting plots on the Whitman National Forest, the first of a large series of plots to study the silviculture of western yellow pine. These plots were laid out by T. J. Starker, E. H. MacDaniels and others.

There being no reliable volume tables for even the major species, a feature of the above studies in Douglas-fir and pine was the preparation of regional volume tables. Later, with the help of forest assistants on the National Forests, we made standard tables of other species, hoping to replace the many *local* volume tables made by cruisers for a special job based on just a few trees.

A four-week circuit in the spring of 1910 started with a voyage on the steamer, *Ramona*, from Portland to Coos Bay. Near Marshfield (now Coos Bay), I went over the logging operations of the C. A. Smith Lumber Company with their Forester, John Lafon, who was trying to install some pioneering good forest practices.

On the sand dunes between Coos Bay and Florence I put in some planting experiments with maritime pine, Scotch broom, willows, etc., to test the practicability of revegetating at least the inter-dunal areas.

Transportation between these points was then by horse stage on the beach at the lowest tide, or, as I did a time or two, on foot with shoes off walking on the wet sand at the water's edge.

From the sand dunes I went over some of the backwoods of the Siuslaw National Forest looking at the results of recent direct seeding in the deforested fern patches. The Ranger at Florence then had a boat, for the only way of getting into the interior was by the river.

Three of the other Districts had experiment stations by 1911, so District Six followed suit. It was placed at Wind River on the Columbia (now Gifford Pinchot) National Forest beside the nursery, largely because it was then thought by some that most of the problems that an experiment station might settle were in connection with artificial reforestation. An office-residence was needed. The statutory limit on any building was then $650 and that was reached before the plumbing fixtures were acquired. So Julius Kummel paid for the toilet, and I for the bathtub. A small greenhouse was built at about the same time, mostly by contributed time of a few of us. It was intended mostly for germination tests.

Odds and ends of exotic trees were planted in the stump land adjoining the nursery in 1912. This was the beginning of the Wind River Arboretum which was considered to be a desirable adjunct of a research agency.

C. P. Willis was in charge at Wind River for a while and did notable work on nursery practice problems. In 1912, the heredity study of Douglas-fir was launched, initially to see if conky trees made good parents. Seed of 120 trees was gathered and the progeny planted on four widely separated National Forests.

In 1913, after interviewing J. V. Hofmann at the Priest River Experimental Forest, he was put in charge at Wind River where he remained until the spring of 1924. Appropriations were meager: $5,514 for 1916, for example, but a lot of productive studies were made.

ADMINISTRATION: "-one of the rules-"

<u>Ed Fenby</u> *Fenby started in Montana as a Forest Expert. He began work on the Rainier NF in 1909, where he advanced to Forest Supervisor from 1930-1933. He was Forest Engineer on the Snoqualmie NF beginning in 1933 and retired in 1950.*

Bill Sethe's entrance to the Forest Service was unusual. After the transfer of the Reserves from Interior to Agriculture in 1905, G. F. Allen became Supervisor of the Rainier Forest. He was also Superintendent of Mt. Rainier Park. In order to carry out Park rules, he hired Sethe to serve as guard at the western entrance. One of the rules was that no one would be permitted to operate an automobile within the Park boundaries after 6:00 pm, presumably a fire protection precaution. The penalty for such was arrest with a $5.00 fine and having the car towed out to the Park boundary by horses. Early in the season, a visitor appeared in his automobile but failed to depart before the 6:00 pm deadline. Sethe dutifully applied the penalties. The man was outraged and threatened Bill's job. In a short time, Superintendent Allen received instructions to discharge Mr. Sethe. This he obediently did by writing a letter to Bill dismissing him. In the same envelope, however, was another letter signed by Supervisor Allen, instructing Bill to report for duty the next day as Forest Guard at Sulphur Springs, (now Packwood) Guard Station. Sethe reported as directed and continued in this same station giving satisfactory Service as Guard and Ranger until his retirement on February 28, 1947.

<u>Loran "Coop" Cooper</u> *Cooper started on the Mt. Hood NF after World War I and was a District Ranger on the Siskiyou and Rogue River NFs. He retired in 1945.*

I am submitting this article showing a little of the contrast between now [1955] and back in 1907, taken from Ranger W. B. Milbury's copy of the Forest Service issue of <u>The Green Book</u>. As you know, this is a small 4" x 7" book with 47 pages devoted to instructions and about the same number of blank pages in the back with the heading "Memorandum of Expenses." The instructions cover such subjects as appointments, salaries, leave, traveling expenses, field purchases, cost keeping, property control, lease of office, lost checks, daily record, etc. - practically the whole fiscal set-up in 47 4"x7" pages! The book also has a very interesting little foreword signed by Gifford Pinchot.

To give you a few figures on travel expenses in the good old days I quote the following, taken from the "Memorandum of Expenses."

1907 - Nov. 6	Dinner, supper, and lodging		$ .75
" 7	Breakfast, dinner, supper, and lodging		1.00
" 8	" " " " "		1.00
" 8	Fare to Coqullle on train		.35
" 8	" on boat to Myrtle Point		.25
" 9	Breakfast, dinner, supper, and lodging		1.00
" 10	Breakfast and dinner		.50
			$4.85

<u>Thomas H. Sherrard</u>   *Sherrard started with the Bureau of Forestry in 1899.   He was Forest Supervisor of the Oregon/Mt.Hood NF from 1908 to 1934, when he went to the R-6 Regional Office Division of Lands, working into early 1941.*

In 1908, none of the thousand and one things that a Supervisor may not do had been thought up. The fiscal regulations did not weigh two pounds. The rain of circular letters had not even been forecast. The <u>Use Book</u> was a convenient little pamphlet that could be carried around in the cuff of your overcoat. There was no one between the Supervisor and the Forester in far-away Washington. Here and there an Inspector might be fairly close on a Supervisor's tail, but on the whole a Supervisor was pretty much on his own.

<u>Harry M. White</u>   *White transferred from the Chelan NF to the District Six Office in the Division of Operations in 1916.*

When I arrived in Portland in 1916, the entire Forest Service organization, including the Columbia and Mt. Hood [Oregon NF until 1924] offices, was housed in the Beck Building, at Broadway and Oak, where it had been established at the time of *The Exodus* from Washington in 1908. There were no Divisions of Engineering, Personnel Management, Education and Information, or State and Private Forestry. Timber Management handled research and the library. There was a Division of Products, which later became a part of the Pacific Northwest Forest and Range Experiment Station. A hydraulic engineer reported directly to the District Forester, while *Ten Per Cent Roads* were handled by an engineer detailed from the Bureau of Public Roads, with general supervision by Operation.

109

In addition to general supervision and allotment work, Operation handled fire control, improvements, personnel, what was called *geography*, including drafting, fire cooperation (both direct and under the Weeks Law, later superseded by the Clarke-McNary Act), and protection of the Oregon and California lands, which had just been revested.

Grover C. Blake *Blake was probably an Assistant Forest Ranger on the Deschutes NF at the time of this story.*

Our first real forestry conference was held in 1909 (November 22 through 26) when the personnel of the Deschutes, Malheur, Whitman and Umatilla Forests gathered at Mt. Vernon Hot Springs for a five day discussion of the current problems and general policies. Incidentally these four Forests had boundaries which differed greatly from those Forests of the same names of the present day. We were three and one-half days by horseback from the Prineville area to the conference and another three and one-half days returning, so we were seven days going and coming and five days in conference including two Sundays and Thanksgiving Day. Supervisors present were Cy J. Bingham of the Malheur, Thos. E. Chidsey of the Umatilla, Henry Ireland of the Whitman and A. S. Ireland of the Deschutes. Incidentally Henry and A. S. Ireland were not related, but A. S. Ireland was a brother to Asher Ireland who served many years on westside Forests and in the Regional Office. The conference opened on the morning of November 22 with W. P. Staley of the District Office in the chair. After a day and a half Mr. Staley was followed by Thos. P. McKenzle, C. S. Judd and Chas. H. Flory in that order to fill out the five days.

Albert H. Cousins *Cousins wrote this story about an audit trip he took as Head of Accounts in the District Six Office.*

The Service commenced audits of Supervisors' offices early after the establishment of Region Six in 1908. One of the first audit trips I made was in 1911. It was memorable to me, for, as you will see, it entailed a lengthy journey across Oregon and transportation by stages and a railroad not now in existence.

I left Portland one evening on the O.W.R. & N., arriving at Baker City in the morning and left Baker City by the Sumpter Valley Railroad, a narrow gauge road and mixed train for Sumpter, Oregon. Sumpter, even then, was a town where gold mining activities had practically ceased. The headquarters of the Whitman NF were located at Sumpter. Henry Ireland was the Supervisor and Otto A. Zimmerli the Forest Clerk. (Zimmerli retired as Chief of Fiscal Control, Washington DC.)

After inspection of the Whitman, my next point was the Malheur at John Day. To reach John Day, I left Sumpter in the morning on the Sumpter Valley Railway and went to Austin (the end of the line) where Mrs. Austin had an *Eating House.* At Austin, the passengers all piled out for dinner and as I remember we had a good meal as she was noted in that section as a good cook. After dinner the next move was by stage - a regular (to me) *Buffalo Bill* rig; four horses, two seats inside, facing each other and the body hung on straps.

There were eight passengers, including the driver, mailbags, lots of packages and bundles for the trip. I could not figure where it all could be stowed. However, the driver did not seem to be worried. The packages were stowed on the back seat up to the roof. Three passengers were put on the other seat; two passengers occupied the driver's box with him, and the other passenger and I climbed up on the roof and sat on the mail bags. It certainly seemed far off the ground and a rather precarious seat. To make things more uncertain we started up grade. On my side I could look down into a canyon that seemed about a mile deep. However, after a mile or two I got my sense of balance and *risked* looking around at the scenery and even let go of one hand grip.

We jogged along until we reached Prairie City, where the stage unloaded and we had dinner, and then resumed travel to John Day, arriving there as it was getting dark. Passengers who were going through to Burns got *comfortable* on the stage for the night trip. John Day was a wide place in the road but there was a hotel of sorts. The next morning I went to the Malheur office. Cy Bingham was Supervisor and Leigh Pratt the clerk. Each of them weighed 200 pounds or over so a good-sized office was needed to accommodate them. The office was a one-story stone building with thick walls, a relic of the days when the Indians roamed that country. It had iron shutters, a coping around the roof with dirt on the roof as a protection

111

against flaming arrows shot by the Indians. A well was in the back of the building. Once inside, one was fully protected from Indian raids and could get along if there was food enough.

Finishing the Malheur audit, my next was the Ochoco at Prineville. Bingham made arrangements for me to secure transportation on the stage from Dayville to Mitchell. Leaving John Day by stage at 4:00 AM, before breakfast, we arrived at Dayville at noon. After dinner, I left on the stage, a one seat open rig, for Mitchell. Enroute the driver had some *packages* to deliver and each time the rancher stood at his gate awaiting delivery and each time the rancher insisted we stop while he pulled the cork and showed his Western Hospitality (being with the driver I was included in the Hospitality). When we reached the last four miles of the down-grade into Mitchell, the driver whipped up his team, remarking he "would show me there was still some 'life' left in the team in spite of the distance we had traveled." Downhill we went and the team certainly had life in it. I hung onto the seat and prayed the road was straight and not too narrow. (As we jostled along, the bigness and beauty of the October moon seemed to make my trials and tribulations pale and fade away.)

We made it all right and pulled into Mitchell in the evening. I had a room over the Post Office grocery store. After dinner, I met the boy who was to drive me to Prineville, went to bed, and left a call for 6:00 am.

In the morning, the boy was not around and the storekeeper advised me the boy and friends had been playing poker that evening. The sheriff had run them out of town and they were camped outside the town limits. (We passed them on the way out of town and the boy said he was sorry he could not make the trip with me.) The storekeeper had hired, as a substitute, an old man who was somewhat the worse for wear from the night before, but said he knew the way and could make it. We started out and went over the Blue Mountains but took the wrong road and had to climb the mountains again. That put extra mileage on the team and by the time we were in sight of Prineville one of the horses went down on its knees, about all in. We finally pulled into Prineville about 9:00 pm. The livery keeper gave the old man a bawling out for misusing the team and would not let it return to Mitchell for a couple of days.

Forest Supervisor Homer Ross in the first gas-powered fire engine on the
Ochoco NF – 1912

Spacious quarters of the Forest Supervisors' Office in Prairie City,
Malheur NF – 1915

The Supervisor of the Ochoco was Addison S. Ireland. Prineville was a sleepy- looking town, dirt streets and plenty of vacant lots.

After the Ochoco audit, my last point was Portland, via stage to Shaniko, 65-mile trip. Supervisor Ireland and I left by stage at noon Saturday and reached Shaniko early Sunday morning. Enroute, we and others walked a bit up Cow Creek Canyon to stretch our legs and take out the kinks. At Shaniko, there were about ten thousand sheep awaiting shipment and almost as many sheep dogs, it seemed to me, yapping and barking. We stretched out on the hard station chairs until seven when we boarded the Sunday local of the O.W.R. & N. Co. for Portland.

Thus ended one of my first audit trips which took about fifteen days. Three audits were made and a lot of ground covered, touching two railroads only across Oregon.

C. C. McGuire *McGuire was a Ranger on the Washington NF at the time of this story.*

In [1914] word was passed down to the Forests that we must have training camps for the Forest personnel. So, two days were set aside for that purpose. The Supervisor and his Executive Assistant came to Glacier, gathered the personnel around the dining table in the road camp and got down to business.

The Supervisor would read a chapter from one of the manuals. The Executive Assistant then read another chapter. This consumed about one-half an hour.

A compass was then produced and someone immediately asked, "What is that piece of wire wrapped around the needle for?" The argument was on; no one seemed to know but everyone had opinions. Finally, C. C. McGuire volunteered to answer. He said that the magnetic pole attracted the needle and since the earth was round, the magnetic pole exerted not only directional pull, but also a downward pull due to earth curvature. Whether the answer was right or not, it satisfied the curiosity and was accepted. That ended the compass lesson. Another half hour gone.

It was then decided to put out a fire. Accordingly, a brush pile was touched off. An old Fairbanks-Morse pump was put in operation and the fire doused. One more hour gone. Then we were out of soap. Nothing more on the agenda. Everyone agreed it was a fine meeting. The Supervisor and his Assistant returned to their headquarters and the men went back to work.

IMPROVEMENTS: "-so why not leave things as they were-"

Grover C. Blake   *Blake reflects on his early days in the Forest Service.*

As a feller goes about the old fields of activity and travels the old trails, he is reminded again of the hardships of the early years in Forest Service history and how we really enjoyed them. Do any of you boys remember how we used to take our old saddle pony and drag in logs to a site previously selected for a cabin and how we would fit the logs and lay them up to become a one-room cabin with the usual roof extension in front to shelter the saddles? 'Member? How we worked all the daylight hours to get the job done on schedule? How we cut and rived the shakes for the roof and packed them in on the old pack horse and chinked the cracks with moss? How proud we were of the job when it was finished? How thrilled we were when we could fold up the old tent and move into the new cabin out of the storm, build a fire in the little cook stove and settle down to the comforts of home as the rain pattered on the roof? Do you remember the thrills we experienced when a pasture fence was completed, a telephone line hooked up with the outside or a trail opened up through new territory? I doubt if anyone ever got more enjoyment from looking upon a finished job than the early day Ranger who did everything the hard way because there was no other way,

Dahl Kirkpatrick   *This is another story by Dahl about his father John's Ranger District on the Rainier NF.*

The first mechanical equipment to be supplied to the Randle Ranger

Road construction on the Umpqua NF – c1915

Early version of a *minimum impact road* on the Umpqua NF – 1915

District was a construction-type wheelbarrow. It arrived probably in 1911; knocked down and delivered to the store in town by their regular freight wagon from Norton, the ultimate terminus of the Tacoma Eastern Railroad. I can clearly remember how anxious I was to have it brought to the Ranger Station so we could put it together. Ed Fenby, the Technical Forester from the Supervisor's Office was at the Station at that time and he arranged for a farmer coming our way to bring the wheelbarrow from the store. Mr. Fenby and I had it assembled before dad came home from the field that day.

A lapse of several years intervened before any additional equipment was provided. Next to arrive was a light wagon suitable for use with a couple of mules from the pack string. It was used for general utility work around the station and part of the District where roads were available.

Arthur "A. J." Radigan *Radigan was a Ranger on the Colville NF in 1907.*

Back in the fall of 1907, a telephone line was built on the Colville National Forest from Republic to Anglin. This line was partly through timber and partly over open ground. I worked on it. The wire used was No. 12 galvanized and the insulators were No. 16 glass on brackets.

This line was a grounded pole system the entire length unless a tree of suitable size stood directly in the right of way. A suitable tree was one from 10 to 14 inches in diameter. This tree was then topped about 20 feet from the ground and the limbs removed. Bark was peeled off from the top down about two feet and also at the butt. A bracket was then nailed to this stub and the line was attached in the same manner as on regular poles with a Western Union tie. The poles were unseasoned Douglas-fir and Western larch and were installed without stubs or treatment. A few lasted as long as five years.

Almost constantly from the beginning, this line gave trouble. Trees fell across it and the No. 12 wire snapped like string. Brackets were torn loose and split. After a year or two, always traveling by horseback, with the usual tools and extra wire, the repair work which not only was arduous but short-lived led to the conclusion that

117

something must be done. E. W. Wheeler, now across the *Great Divide*, was one of the Rangers who had a lot of this repair work to do. He had visions of a line which would stay together after a tree hit it, so he strung the wire through small porcelain insulators and hung the tie wire to the side of trees. This was about 1909. Two Forest men from the District Office came to view the line and immediately claimed it was not the thing. They said all the slack would creep to the long spans and a lot of other things now forgotten would happen to it; however, three trees were purposely felled across the line within a quarter of a mile of each other and nothing happened except the wire did not break and communication was still uninterrupted.

From this beginning was born our present tree line with all loose ties and oval brown split insulators. When Ranger Wallace Wheeler, formerly of the Wenatchee (now in Region 2) took care of his tree telephone maintenance or construction, he derived much pleasure from the fact that *This was Dad's idea.*

Ira E. Jones *Jones was a Forest Guard on the Whitman NF at the time of this story.*

I first worked for the Forest Service in the spring of 1908. That summer Hugh Rankin (later Forest Supervisor of the Umatilla, Siuslaw, and Rogue River Forests), Ephriam Barnes (later Supervisor of the Minam), Joe Zipper and I built a telephone line from the Grande Ronde River to Cable Cove (at the head of Cracker Creek north of Sumpter). It was a metallic circuit on brackets, and all on trees except across Starkey Prairie where poles were set in cribs. Hugh Rankin had been a telegraph operator so we strung the wires tight and tied them with solid ties like the railway telegraph lines. I don't believe it was ever used as it would break even in a slight breeze.

We had no climbers - used ladders - made these of small poles, with a single nail at each end of the rounds so it would adjust for uneven ground. We built a mile a day, starting at 6 am and working till we had completed our mile.

That year, also, the Whitman built its first cabins -- at Porcupine Ranger Station - and at Anthony Lake. These were of logs about 12" x 16', shake roof, no floors, two windows (no glass) and door of 1" x

12'' rough lumber. They were both contracted and cost about $25.00 each.

<u>Melvil "M. L." Merritt</u> *Merritt was Forest Supervisor of the Deschutes NF from 1912 – 1916 and worked in the District Six Operations Office from 1916 – 1921.*

(When) Henry Ford put out his Model T, many were sold in Bend. I think it was in 1913 that Ranger Earl Austin at Crescent bought a Ford. He did much chauffeuring for the Supervisor. One day, going south from Crescent on a fair dirt road, his speedometer registered the dangerously alarming and very unusual speed of 17 miles per hour. By the end of 1914, however, all Rangers and the Supervisor had cars, all Fords.

This brought to light the poor condition or lack of roads. Most roads were mere ways through the timber with roots and rocks in the tracks. At Crescent, Perry South, who followed Earl Austin as Ranger, organized the local men into volunteer road crews and attacked the roots and rocks vigorously. Soon roads to Crescent and Odell Lakes and south to the Klamath Indian reservation were passably good. This continued until there were usable ways to most lower elevation objectives in this area. Other Rangers acted similarly. Never were so many miles of road built with so little. None were good, but you could drive a Ford over them and by the time I left in 1916, one could drive to every Ranger Station and to most Guard stations on the Forest. Some of these roads later became important travel routes. Ranger Harriman's *China Hat Road* from Cabin Lake Ranger Station north to the Bend-Burns road, and Ranger John Curl's road from Paulina to East Lake are now main roads. I think I was the first person to drive a car to East Lake. Wasn't sure that I'd get back, but did.

About 1917, Mr. Clay M. Allen was secured from the telephone company as our technical advisor. He prepared standard instructions for building grounded tree lines, for installing instruments, for constructing metallic circuit lines where electrical interference made this necessary and for maintenance. He and his ideas were universally accepted, although there was much bantering about his voluminous instructions. A Mr. Adams in Region One did similar work there. They collaborated in the development of design and instructions.

119

Although instructions have since been rewritten, the ideas and practices of Mr. Allen are still being followed. The present Forest Service telephone system is a monument to his foresight.

<u>Grover C. Blake</u> *Blake was District Ranger on the Ochoco NF at the time of this story.*

At this time [1913], public-spirited people were beginning to stir up enthusiasm for good roads. Among the leaders in the campaign for roads was Supervisor [Homer] Ross. He owned an automobile! However, there was plenty of opposition. Many people were afraid of high taxes if roads were built. Many taxpayers said they had always gotten along without roads and did all right, so why not leave things as they were. However, taxpayers kept buying Model T Fords and car owners soon became good road converts. Mr. Ross was anxious to build a road from the south boundary of the Forest on Ochoco Creek to the north boundary on West Branch. He had some money available from the *Ten Percent Road Fund*, which was a portion of the Forest income set aside for roads and trails. He then endeavored to get Crook and Wheeler counties to each contribute an equal amount and eventually succeeded. I was assigned the task of canvassing the settlers and businessmen who would be directly benefited, for donations of cash, labor and materials. I had very good success considering the widespread opposition to the proposed road program. By putting forth extreme efforts we gradually got some so-called *good roads* but they would not even be called roads, as we think of roads today.

It was on May 4, 1916, that I purchased a second-hand automobile (a 1914 Buick) and promised to pay for it. The Supervisor and two of the Rangers already had cars and I could no longer resist. We had no roads fit for auto use in winter and we could hardly call them auto roads at any time of the year, but many were passable for the high bodied cars of that day during the dry summer months.

For several years during the spring and fall months, I kept my car at a ranch about three miles from Beaver Ranger Station and used the buggy and team over the road between, which was not passable for cars. In this way I could get considerable use of the car that I could not have gotten had I kept the car at the station.

During the summer of 1917, I assisted James T. Schuyler, Civil Engineer for the Bureau of Public Roads, in making a reconnaissance survey for a new road across the Blue Mountains to replace the one we built in 1914 and of which we had been so proud at the time. Before we started the work in 1914, the public was astounded when we talked of a road to cost $5,000.00. Now Mr. Schuyler tells them that the estimated cost of the proposed new road was $250,000. How fantastic such an undertaking seemed to be. Yet that road was later built and then put in the *has been* column when the present State Highway No. 28 was opened to travel.

By 1917, the activities for good roads had grown by leaps and bounds. Supervisor Ross believed that the Forest Service should aid the cause as much as possible. I served on committees representing the community in appearing before the county court and state Highway Commission and in carrying on much correspondence.

Crater Forest Newsletter *The following item from the August 1911 issue of the Crater Forest Newsletter notes the arrival of the Forest's first piece of mechanized equipment.*

The Forest is now equipped with one motorcycle. This motorcycle was transferred from the Olympic Forest for use on the Crater Lake Highway. It is proposed to patrol the road in search of careless campers who leave their camp fires, and to catch vandals who shoot insulators along telephone lines. W. E. White is detailed on this job. It is a very difficult one and the machine is having difficulty in running through the very deep pummy dust along this road. White has already worn out lagging belts and reports that his main drive belt is nearly worn out.

Ira E. Jones *Jones was Superintendent of Construction for the Whitman, Umatilla, and Wallowa NFs from 1924 to 1934.*

Road building had quite an evolution. We first started with a plow, a wooden V and a slip scraper. Then we advanced to a Martin ditcher and a Fresno scraper. Starting around a hillside, we first opened a trail by hand then for one horse to walk in and shoveled out by hand until we could get a team over, then used a ditcher until wide enough for a small grader. All rock work was done by hand drilling and using only caps and fuse for blasting.

Thornton T. Munger *Munger was Head of the Silvics Section in District Six at the time of this story.*

Another *first* that I had a part in was the purchase in 1909 or 1910 of the first adding machine in the District Office, a Dalton, for use mostly by Silviculture's computing clerk, Erma Bell, who checked all the scale books used throughout the District - up to that time by mental addition. [Erma Bell Lakes on the Willamette National Forest were named for Erma Bell, after she was killed in an automobile accident.]

Harry M. White *White was on the Columbia NF and in the District Six Office, Division of Operations at the time of these stories.*

The first portable fire pumper I heard of was a heavy *one-lunger* called by the manufacturer the Wonder pump. (Now we have wonder bread. Advertising bally-hoo such as we hear today is not new, it is only more widespread and sillier). In 1915 G. F. Allen and his boys were fighting an early snag fire in the Cowlitz and Charles Flory called me from Portland, wanting to know if he should send up one of these Wonders. I relayed the message to G. F., but he turned the offer down, much to Flory's disgust. This heavy, low-powered pumper, however, was the forerunner of many different types of portable pumpers to come: light, medium, and heavy; two-cycle and four-cycle; one-cylinder, two-cylinder, and four-cylinder.

In 1916, Bush Osborne went from the Mt. Hood to Operation in the District Six Office to work on fire control activities. Recognizing that lookouts must have a more accurate instrument for locating fires than a single compass, he had invented the fire finder that bears his name, and he continued to develop it into a fine precision instrument. He also designed nested mess outfits which were copied in other parts of the country and finally were covered by standard specifications, as were the fire finder and the adz hoe, an excellent digging tool designed by him as a modification of the hazel hoe. It was also about this time that he put together a light-weight, three-day balanced ration for smokechasers which was the basis for continuing development in that field.

A few years later Osborne got the idea of taking panoramic pictures from lookouts to aid in spotting fires and borrowed a couple of cameras from the Geological Survey to experiment with. When these had to be returned he did an outstanding job of drawing plans and specifications for a precision instrument which he named a photo-recording transit. With this instrument, pictures were taken from all lookouts and used not only for the original purpose but for mapping detection coverage. In 1918, just before leaving for an officers' training camp, Bush turned out the copy for the Fire Fighting and Lookout manuals. I remember that very well, for the proofs came from the printer after Bush had gone and I had to read proof on them; thereby learning much about smoke-chasing problems and firefighting technique.

"After WW I, the Forest Service received increased funds for developing more trails, lookout houses and telephone lines, as well as increased funds for fire protection."

-John R. "Ray" Bruckart

CHAPTER TWO

1919 to 1932 PROSPERITY, DEVELOPMENT and PROTECTION

While working conditions remained harsh and difficult, and many facilities throughout District Six continued to be rudimentary, the end of the teens and beginning of the 1920s did bring some change from the austere programs of the early years. The end of World War I ushered in a new era of prosperity, not only for the nation, but also for District Six. Funding became available to implement many of the improvement projects the early Rangers could only dream of. Stories about this era describe an increase in Forest Service programs and activities across the board. In addition, the Forest Service benefited directly from the availability of army surplus equipment, such as the vehicles and the Sibley stove, and indirectly from the war-driven technical advances in mechanized equipment.

Forests were able to hire large seasonal crews for fire protection and suppression activities, and when not on fires these crews were able to work on a variety of other projects. Throughout the 1920s, existing trails were improved and re-routed. New trails were located and constructed. An extensive telephone line system was put in place to connect Ranger Stations with guard stations and lookouts. New guard stations were constructed and lookout towers and cabins replaced tents pitched adjacent to rocky points and rudimentary platforms perched on the top of cut-off tree trunks.

Employment for seasonal workers was extended, benefiting local communities and *short-term men*, the long-time seasonal employees who returned for work year after year.

The use of automobiles in lieu of horses increased. Initially, District Rangers and Forest Supervisors used their own personal cars, with the Forest Service sometimes providing mileage. Eventually District Six began to purchase vehicles for the Forests. Ranger Districts also acquired surplus army equipment, primarily trucks, and the first tractors were developed and tested in the mid-1920s. As a result,

125

District Six Forests increased the construction of roads and bridges as the beginnings of a National Forest road system.

In 1921, the National Forests in Alaska were split-off from District Six, forming the Alaska District, also known then as District Eight.

Some of the stories describe experiences on bad fires in the years 1924, 1926 and 1929. The large fires in the late 1920s led to the origination of lookout firemen, who were trained not only to man lookouts but to also be the initial attack on fires they spotted. The objective was to place firefighters closer to the point of ignition. Central dispatching for all Ranger Districts on a Forest was tried from the late 1920s into the early 1930s.

In 1930, District Six had a name change, henceforth to be called Region Six. And, beginning in 1931, at least one Forest participated in a work program to provide a limited amount of jobs to the unemployed, a precursor to the massive depression-era work programs to come.

This chapter includes stories about Joining Up/Starting Out, All in a Day's Work, Wives and Families, Horses, Fire, Lookouts and Fire Guards, Grazing, Recreation, Timber, Engineering and Construction, Research, Administration and Improvements.

JOINING UP/STARTING OUT: "Although I did not realize it at the time, this was the beginning of my Forest Service career."

Earl D. "Sandy" Sandvig *Sandvig started as a temporary in 1920 and received a permanent appointment in R-1 in 1923. He worked on the Helena, Custer, and Beaverhead NFs in R-1 and in the R-1 and R-2 Regional Offices. He was the Assistant Regional Forester for Personnel Management in the R-6 Regional Office when he retired in 1959.*

As I grew up on a Montana ranch my whole interest in life was ranching. Family persuasion caused me to enroll in the University of Montana as a business major, but my mind was fixed on the ranching industry as a career. Forestry students on the campus were obtaining summer jobs in many parts of the West. It occurred to me a summer job would give me the opportunity to examine the ranches in the area of my job. Inquiry revealed the way to get a summer forestry job was to write to a Forest Supervisor. I picked Prineville, Oregon, and although I was not a forestry student I was offered a job as a road laborer [on the Ochoco National Forest].

Prineville, in 1920, could easily pass for a cowtown in Montana. Board sidewalks, dusty and unpaved streets, put Prineville in the same class as my hometown of Plentywood, Montana. The difference in the two towns rests in the fact that not far from Prineville a real forest is growing while Plentywood is a prairie town.

I found the Forest Supervisor in a small cubicle-like office above a bank. He was a big, robust, outdoor type of fellow who looked like a woodsman. I liked him. His name was Vern Harpham.

While discussing my job assignment, I got a terrible cramp in my belly. Harpham noticed my pained agony and we speculated over what caused it. I told him I hadn't drunk anything but Prineville water since my arrival, but it seemed to have a taste similar to the alkali water I often had in eastern Montana. I added that since I had been drinking western Montana water for several months, I just guessed that my stomach was rejecting Prineville's strongly flavored liquid. Harpham agreed with that diagnosis. He then said he had the proper cure for a bellyache.

From under his desk be brought forth a gallon jug of buttermilk. He urged me to drink heartily from it, then go to the hotel, lie down and report back the next morning. You better believe it, the next morning I was *fit as a fiddle*, ready to perform any service within my capabilities for Supervisor Harpham. Whether it was the buttermilk that cured my bellyache is a moot question. Anyhow, that summer's work on the Ochoco proved to be so challenging and interesting that ranching as a career lost a candidate and forestry gained one. I wouldn't change the decision if I had to make it again.

Gerald J. "Tuck" Tucker *Tucker worked for the Whitman NF seasonally beginning in 1922. He was appointed District Ranger on the Umatilla NF in 1925 and worked as a Ranger on that Forest and the Wallowa-Whitman NF until his retirement in 1963. Tucker wrote and published The Story of Hells Canyon in 1977.*

My first work for the Forest Service was as a day laborer in the summer of 1922 [on the Whitman NF]. Although I did not realize it at the time, this was the beginning of my Forest Service career. The job didn't amount to much and it was a casual, almost incidental and minor episode. It was of very short duration too, only for three days.

I was a ranch-bred boy and knew my way around cattle, horses, loggers, farmers and cowboys. Like a lot of my peers, I discounted the value of higher education and was working that spring of 1922 as a laborer on a county road crew under the neighborhood road supervisor. I felt no envy whatever of the men my age who were still battling the finer points of geometry and the conjugation of verbs.

Then I heard that the local stock association wanted a replacement for the riding and salting job on the Minam cattle range. I wanted that job. I knew the range. I had the horses or knew where I could get plenty of half-broke horses to use for the summer. I went that very evening and talked to Wm. Roulett, the president, and Leonard Parsons, the secretary of the association. I got the job at a salary of $100.00 a month and was to report at once at the Stockman's cabin on the Minam River. This was on a Saturday evening and I had all day Sunday to get an outfit together and get on the job.

I told the road boss my plans and he turned in my time. I got Mr. Bibler, the storekeeper, to open up his store and I got a supply of bacon, beans, etc. to last a couple or three weeks. I loaded a couple of packhorses and headed for the Minam where I arrived at the cabin a few hours after dark that Sunday evening.

This was in April and the cattle needed salt which I proceeded to scatter far and wide during the next couple of weeks. There were no posted salt grounds, but I knew some of the places where it was customary to salt the cattle and I found others. I distributed some of the cattle that were concentrated too much and put them out on good grass areas. Some of the cows were calving and I earmarked the little calves with the marks of their mothers and castrated the bull calves, as I had been told to do. However, I did no branding.

The ranchers were all busy at home putting in spring crops and none of them showed up during this time. About two weeks passed before any of them came in to help or supervise and when they did come, they were well pleased with what I had done. I sent out for more supplies and salt and had two more horses brought in as those that I had been using were getting leg-weary. I also got permission to run in a few off the range to use when I wanted them.

It was about this time that I became acquainted with the local Forest Ranger. Paul Ellis was from New Mexico where he had been a Ranger on the Santa Fe National Forest. He stayed at my camp for several days at a time and we got along O.K. even though I knew it was not possible to get cattle to graze the high, dry, well-grassed ridge slopes after the weather became warm, water scarce, and flies thick. He put in enough time with me that summer to learn quite a lot about handling cattle on that type of range and I learned a few things too.

We were somewhat inconvenienced that spring and early summer by the fallen trees across the Minam River trail and the rockslides that filled the trail in places. So, Ranger Ellis asked me if I would clear the trail as time permitted as he had not been able to hire a trail crew to do the job. For this extra work, he would pay $4.00 per eight-hour day and I was able to keep track of the time spent on clearing the trail.

I sawed and chopped out the logs and shoveled out the rock slides, threw out the loose rocks, and removed a lot of toe-bumpers all of the way from the Forest boundary to the upper end of the cattle range at Chaparral Creek. I did this over a period of two or three weeks working at odd times and without taking time from my first duty to my employer - the stock association. When I added up my time spent on the trail maintenance, it totaled twenty-four hours, or three eight-hour days.

Ranger Ellis rode down the 15 miles of maintained trail one day that summer and was well pleased. He stayed overnight with me and complimented me on the work I had done. As he prepared to make out a time report, he inquired as to the hours spent on the job and I showed him my tabulation of figures for a total of 24 hours. He was amazed and insisted on doubling the hours and paying for a six-day week. I did not object too strenuously and eventually received a check for $24.00.

So, when the next spring rolled around and I was offered a job on the Cove Ranger District by Ranger Ellis at $110.00 per month, and the Minam Stock Association decided to do without a rider because of hard times in the cattle business that year, I accepted the offer. I thought if I could do enough work in three days (not working too hard) to earn six days' pay, that the Forest Service would be a good outfit to work for.

This should not be taken too seriously, nor be construed to mean that the Forest Service has been in the habit of double pay for work done. However, this incident did have some influence in causing me to begin work for the Forest Service. Perhaps of more importance was literature made available to me by Ranger Ellis describing the objectives of the Forest Service, the high ideals of Gifford Pinchot and the principles of conservation advanced by Theodore Roosevelt. I have never regretted making the Forest Service my life work. I believe as strongly as ever in the principles so well initiated by Pinchot and Roosevelt.

I started work for the Whitman National Forest on June 9, 1923 on the old Cove District and remained on that District under Ranger Paul Ellis until September 30, 1923. I had several classifications that summer. First was foreman at $90.00 per month from June 9 to June 30; chaser-lookout at $1080.00 per annum from July 1 to August 31; and then lookout at $1080.00 per annum from September 1 to September 30. Then I was turned out to graze for the winter.

June and the first week or two in July was spent doing maintenance work on trails and telephone lines over the entire District. Then, for the fire season, as lookout on Meadow Mountain.

About July 10th, Keith H. McCool was assigned by Supervisor William F. Ramsdell of the Whitman to fire-chaser work on the Cove District with the station at the Catherine Creek Meadows Guard Station, a one-room log cabin at the upper end of Catherine Creek Meadows. He was also expected to build a pole fence enclosing about five acres near the summit of Meadow Mountain as a pasture for the lookout's horses. To help him in this work, a young man from the Baker country by the name of Page Jeffords was also assigned to the meadows with a pack string of eight mules to act as packer for the District and to pack the fence material, etc.

The lookout station on the top of Meadow Mountain was three and one-half miles from the cabin at Catherine Creek Meadows. I was dispatched to four or five fires that summer and each time McCool was dispatched to take over the lookout station.

All three of us were kept on fire duty until late in September and didn't get to build the fence on Meadow Mountain. We did cut the posts and poles and dragged most of them out along the fence line before we were laid off. We cut the post timbers into 34-foot lengths (out of lodgepole trees) and dragged them with the mules up the mountain from the basin where we cut them. We tied the logs to the packsaddle, one on each side of a mule with the other end dragging on the ground. The next mule had to walk between those of the mule ahead and we had many a mix-up before the mules were trained to do the job without protest.

Fishing was good on the North Fork of Catherine Creek. One evening I went out to get fish for supper. Our Ranger, Paul Ellis, was expected that evening and with McCool, Jeffords and I, we needed quite a number of fish. McCool called after me as I left the cabin, "Get a good big mess of fish!" I got a branch of white fir and went to the horse corral and swatted the horse flies until I had a tobacco can full of those big gray horse flies. Then I went to the creek and in just one hour I caught exactly 80 fish on a plain snell hook baited with those horse flies. We had quite a fish feed that evening.

Meadow Mountain was at the hub of several sheep allotments and the camp tenders passed the lookout quite often. I always had them stop and eat and we became friends; the result was that I had fresh mutton all summer. Every few days one of the camp tenders would butcher a lamb or a big fat wether, and he would deliver the meat to some of the other sheep camps and never fail to leave me a quarter. I soon overcame my aversion to mutton which was ingrained in all cattlemen at that time and I was no exception to the rule. I had quite a lot of visitors, folks on the way to the Upper Minam from LaGrande, Cove and Union, and many of them stopped for a mid-day lunch with me. The mutton was always welcome fare, and helped out on the grocery

131

bill, but I never fail to be amazed at the fact that for the entire time that I worked that summer my grub bill was only $12.50 per month.

After McCool and Jeffords left in late September, I was kept on for awhile to do some trail cutting on the upper reaches of North Catherine Creek. One evening Ranger Ellis instructed me by telephone to take a sack of TNT down from the loft of the Catherine Creek Cabin and bury it out in the meadow. This sack of about 60 pounds of TNT had been hanging in the cabin for a couple of years and none of us except Ellis knew about it. Evidently due to some safety drive in the Forest Service, it had been suggested to eliminate the keeping of all explosives around cabins and Ranger Stations. Either they were to be kept in a powder house or else disposed of. So, I proceeded next morning to follow out the instructions.

I took the sack down quite carefully. It weighed nearer 100 pounds than 60 pounds. I took the sack outdoors and carried it in the meadow a couple of hundred feet and contemplated the job of digging a hole in which to bury it. Then I had a brilliant thought. Why not just leave it there and go back to the cabin and get my trusty 30-30 and shoot the sack and set the powder off? I wondered how much of a boom it would make and took the precaution to stand by the corner of the cabin and sighting around the corner; after careful aim I pulled the trigger.

Well, the boom was awful! The concussion knocked all the dishes off the shelves in the cabin. The stovepipe was knocked off of the roof and I was set back a foot or two. All of the glass in the two windows of the cabin was blown out, and there was a hole in the ground where the powder had been big enough to bury a horse in. After making the best of the situation, recovering the dishes (mostly tin), sweeping up the broken glass and crockery, putting the stove pipe back on, etc., I still had no way to fix the windows.

So it became quite necessary to report to the Ranger that I needed *X number* of glass panes of such and such measurements and enough putty to place them in the windows; also a few dishes. The report was made, not because I wanted to, but because it had to be done. Ranger Ellis came out a few days later with the necessary items and somehow he failed to give me the reprimand that I expected. He stayed a couple of days, helped fix up the windows, went with me to look over the trail work being done and left with final instructlons. All the time I was uneasy and I thought I detected, at times, a look of amusement on his face.

Lloyd R. Olson   *Lloyd started his Forest Service career on the Snoqualmie NF in 1925 on a trail crew. He worked on the Columbia NF, was a Forest Supervisor on the Wenatchee and Mt. Hood NFs, and was Assistant Director of Fire Control in the Washington Office when he retired in 1963.*

Come 1925, Lonzo Hurt got me a job with the Forest Service on the Darrington District [of the Snoqualmie National Forest]. J.R. Bruckart was District Ranger, and Ed Ritter was Protective Assistant. I was assigned to a 12-man trail crew to build a trail along the White Chuck River from Kennedy Hot Springs to White Pass. The crew was a diverse and extremely interesting collection of individuals working under a competent foreman, Hugh Miller. Miller was a true mountain man, working for the Forest Service in season and trapping during the winter. The rest of the crew were old loggers, some younger men who for one reason or another wanted the work and the isolation, one other young fellow, and me.

The cook, Harry Campbell, was something else! He could hold his own anywhere in the bullfest, and he demonstrated by deeds he could hold his own in any kitchen. He regularly turned out gourmet meals on time, with unfailing good humor, sometimes under seemingly impossible conditions. While the kitchen and dining area floor were either dirt, dust, or mud, the rest of the operation, including Harry, was immaculate, including his pill box cap and clothing. He never talked about himself. Others have told me he served as head chef in some major logging camps and hotels. I often wondered, but never dared ask why, with his talents, he would take a cooking job on a trail crew with all its hardships, not to mention low pay.

Speaking of food, a little German, Henry Johnson, knew his groceries. He was one of the hardest working and by far the quietest man on the crew. When he had something to say, it was limited to one-syllable words when possible. In the spring when he was on a three-man trail-maintenance crew, they ran out of food with only one more day to go.

The final morning they decided to cook some oatmeal found in the lean-to where they were staying.

It was generously sprinkled with rat droppings. These were carefully removed before it was cooked. When it was served, Henry refused his share. The other two started kidding Henry about not eating—after all, the rat droppings had been removed. Henry's reply was "When they defecate they urinate." Those were not his exact words. Four letter words were used with a German accent. Henry made his point and breakfast came abruptly to an end. It was a hungry crew that got back to home base that night.

<u>Don Stoner</u> *Stoner began his Forest Service career in 1925 on the Mt. Baker NF as a Junior Forester. He was a District Ranger on the Willamette (twice), Mt. Baker, Ochoco, and Rogue River NFs. He then worked out of the Regional Office supervising log scaling activities until his retirement about 1956.*

The day was July 8, 1925. The place was the Mt. Baker office, Bellingham, Washington. I was greeted by a Mrs. Davis who designated herself as the clerical force. In a small off- room was Bob Campbell, the administrative force. The Supervisor, Harry Parks, was *in the field*, tallying shingle bolts. Get the picture - two people were the office force. There were four Rangers: Grover Burch at Glacier, Charlie Bagnell on the Baker River, Tommy Thompson on the Skagit, and John West at Sauk. My coming increased the year-long force to eight.

My first assignment was reached by road, trail, and packhorse - to Heather Meadows where the original Mt. Baker lodge (since burned) was under construction. My job was rodman for Fred Cleator as he made a topog map of the area. This ran into the fall of the year when I went on my first fires. A never-to-be forgotten experience happened the day after the summer force left. The Ranger had a few dollars for some crib work on Glacier Creek to protect a short road to the District's only campground. He hired a local rancher-logger, Frank Bottiger. I was assigned to help. Frank's gruff greeting was, "Why did they let all the good help go and keep a green kid like you?" My futile explanation involved an attempt to explain the technically-trained Junior Forester position, to which he commented that he would build the cribbing and I could do the technical work of packing rocks to fill it, adding, "Go up to the shed (our 1925 warehouse) and get a peavey, that is if you know what a peavey looks like." Later that fall I cruised a cedar salvage sale at 119 M board feet. Frank logged it and got 120 M board feet scale at the local mill and from then on I had a pal in Frank.

My first winter was real busy (?). The Ranger and I, and again I did the technical work, built a garage from salvage lumber for our Model T truck, the only government-owned car on the Forest because we had about 20 miles of road. We took a day off a month to do the office work - filling out an 874 time report, diary, and a form 26, all for 30 days, 48-hour weeks. If that didn't take up the day we filled out with studying bulletins. My second winter was spent with the new Glacier Ranger, Archie Estes, making bird cage signs and sash cord pully pull-out register booths, along with some office furniture including a fancy rack for our bulletins.

A word about quarters and equipment. The Rangers had government houses at $5 per month. Glacier was $10 since it was in town, but it still had the li'l ole outhouse. Tommy Thompson's office was his dining room table on which he used the standard Oliver typewriter - Ranger peck system. Only the Bellingham office had an adding machine, a standup Burroughs with a big bank of keys and pull lever. At Sauk, John West had partitioned off a room, wedged in a rickety self-paid-for roll top desk and was real proud of his private office. John, an excellent woodsman, was part Indian. He had trouble writing legibly and with his spelling, so the Supervisor gave orders for him to type his diary. This took too much office time - over the one day per month - so some sort of a deal was made on his diary, whatever it was no one knew. Baker River Station was reached only by packhorse up the shingle bolt road from Concrete. The Ranger house here had been built by Ranger Burch before he moved to town at Glacier. Grover built another house after leaving Glacier, at Easton on the Wenatchee, built in the style of upright poles. Winters on the Baker River were made up by caring for the stock, keeping the trail open, shoveling snow, cutting wood, and reading the Use Book. Those were the intermediate early days - there was probably more romance in the original early days.

We did some traveling those days but not much. My memory on travel allowance is a bit hazy but I do remember it was actual expense for a while - you itemized every meal and had to scare up lodging at the Ranger Station somehow. A meal at the Ranger's house was a must payment of fifty cents. Some wives were reluctant to accept payment, but I recall one place where you just about had to lay the four-bit piece by the plate as you sat down or you didn't get served. Along the line somewhere we got high fangled and went to a per diem - would you believe $1.20 to start with? Per diem was a big help to us bachelors. In connection with traveling, all by personal cars, we attempted some recognition of being in official travel status by use of the old Forest Service shield, about a five-inch enamel tag deal - remember? I found an added good use for the one I wired around the radiator cap on my dashing 1928 Essex coach in helping me get by road blocks set up in the Bellingham area to check for liquor running from Canada during the prohibition days.

In April, 1926, I went on my first timber sale - Goodell Creek on the Skagit. It was a ten million board feet sale, a railroad show spur off the city of Seattle main line to Newhalem. High lead and seed trees. The Supervisor broke me in on scaling - he had been there two weeks scaling and had bachelor quarters built under the old city sawmill framing. He furnished the food for the week he was with me, but he was on a diabetes diet, so I had it too for a week. The sale lasted several years giving me the happy experience of living with all the early city of Seattle developments and people in their isolated community reached only by *Toonerville trolley*. In this type of living you get to know every man, woman, child and dog and their hobbies. It was ultimate that everyone looked with favor upon the blossoming romance between the *nice young Ranger* and the equally *nice young school marm*, yet something happened and another case of *withering on the vine* was recorded.

While at this location, in June 1926, I attended my first guard training camp - and it could have been the first for the Mt. Baker. Most of the instruction was in the form of reading by the Supervisor although we did work some problems with the old Forest Service standard compass and Jake staff (before the azimuth compass) and dug some fire line. As opposed to present day field dress with shoulder patches, nameplates, forestry green, etc., I distinctly remember the popular and almost standard bib-overall garb and I have a picture to prove this point.

The year 1926 was a bad fire year on the Skagit. Soon after July 4, the Upper Skagit Fire started and jumped lines methodically every Saturday afternoon until it reached 40,000 acres. In the meantime, the Bacon Creek fire took off on the Lower Skagit and reached 6000 acres. Many thought they would come together and had this country been more heavily timbered, these fires may have well joined up.

Fire behavior then and now is no different but tools and methods certainly are. West side firefighting was all hand tools. Crews were picked off Seattle and other skid roads, shipped by train to Rockport, by *Toonerville trolley* to the Skagit fires, and on the Upper Skagit we hiked 24 miles into the Big Beaver fire camp. Some never made it. Rates were 25 cents an hour; later 35 cents. The standard smoke chaser pack was the saddle bag type pack sack, iron rations, first aid kit, collapsible Stonebridge candle lantern, or bug, water bag, and maybe an old army blanket. Bedrolls might come later by pack train, four blankets in a canvas cover tied with rope, but if you knew how, you could tuck the roll in the canvas ends. I haven't followed the big strides in fire control in recent years but only know in my earliest days that the shovel (long-handled), axe (double-bitted), and hoe (grub) were the stand-by tools; along with saw, (cross-cut or felling) as needed.

<u>John B. "Jack" Smith</u> *Smith began his Forest Service career on the Umpqua NF in 1939 as a temporary. He passed the Junior Forester exam in 1939 and received a permanent appointment in 1941. He worked as a CCC Foreman and Protective Assistant while on the Umpqua, and worked on the Fremont, Wallowa and Willamette NFs, and in R-6 Regional Office in Fire Control. He was Forest Supervisor of the Wallowa-Whitman NF and worked in Fire Control in Washington DC, was Assistant Regional Forester for Resource Management in Alaska, and was Assistant Regional Forester in Region 2 for Fire Control, Air Operations, and Law Enforcement when he retired in 1970. He is a 60+ year member of Society of American Foresters and was chosen as Columbia County, Oregon Tree Farmer of the Year in 1993, and Yamhill County, Oregon Tree Farmer of the Year in 2003.*

I watched and listened as Forest Service people fought practice fires at fire guard training sessions in the late 1920s. This was near the Tiller Ranger Station on the South Umpqua District, Umpqua National Forest. My presence was welcome because my dad and brother worked for the Forest Service and I was always called on to play a few tunes on my fiddle after supper. Also, the training came in handy when the Forest Service or Douglas County Fire Patrol needed a fire-fighter or fire chaser. My brother, Jake, and I had trapped and hunted over a lot of the area, both inside and outside the Forest boundary. Since we knew the country and how to fight fire, we were pretty effective fire chasers.

I was on many small fires (100 acres or less) prior to 1931, but my first full-time job with the Forest Service started that year. I was employed at day labor as a member of the South Umpqua road crew, and like anyone on a new job, I had a lot to learn. I reported to Carl Fisher, the road foreman, at Coffee Pot Creek Camp some 18 miles above Tiller - just me, my packsack, and my bedroll. Furnished was a cook and mess tent and the foreman's tent; some 20-plus workers were assigned four to a tent. Our crew included a powder man, a Cat driver, a part-of-the time truck driver, and a blacksmith.

Most of the men were from the down-river community and I knew many of them. We had an outdoor privy and the wash-up facilities were across the brand new single-lane dirt road next to the river. We had wash basins, water was dipped out of the river and each had his own soap and towel. The river furnished bath water and all one needed to do to wash off the sweat and dust was to pull off the duds and plunge in the always-cold water.

On my first day on the job the crew loaded onto the stake-side truck and moved upriver. After going some distance, the truck stopped and Carl Fisher, the foreman, called my name to grab a pick and shovel and get off the truck. He pointed out a metal culvert - perhaps one of the first ones installed on the South Umpqua Road - and showed me where to put it in a small wash. His instructions were, "Bed it in well and build a rock headwall, and I'll look at it this evening when we pick you up to return to camp." That evening he said, "It looks okay; let's go to camp."

ALL IN A DAYS' WORK: "- this was accepted as part of the job and no one gave it a second thought."

C. Frank Ritter *Ritter writes about being District Ranger on the Umpqua NF. His career included being Forest Engineer on the Olympic NF and work in Fire Control on the Columbia/Gifford Pinchot NF. He retired in 1956.*

When I landed at Tiller [on the Umpqua NF in 1923] there was a house, barn, woodshed, an outside toilet and a lean-to garage and that was all. There was a bathroom in the house which was used for storage of fruit, supplies, etc. The living room, a large desk, plus an Oliver typewriter and two file cases constituted the Ranger's office. There was a bath tub too, but it was not connected to anything. In order to bathe, one pounded a wooden plug into the tub outlet and carried water from the kitchen stove and the pump on the back porch.

The Ranger's salary was around $1200 per annum and he furnished saddle and pack stock. If there was a car needed, the Ranger furnished it too, and I do not recall getting anything for use of the car on official business, but maybe I did. As I recall, there was a per diem allowance while in the field and I believe it amounted to $1.20 per day. Of course, I admit that ham and eggs with toast, coffee and potatoes could be obtained for 25 cents.

I bought a new *Model T Ford* the fall that I moved to Tiller. This was the first car that I had driven. There were only two roads out from the Ranger Station and both were bad. During the winter months there were mud holes, slides and streams without bridges. In 1925 or 1926, after having Guy Cordon [Douglas District Attorney at the time and a U.S. Senator from Oregon from 1944-1955] on a horse trip for a considerable period of time, I drove him to Roseburg. Enroute he stated, "Ritter, you don't drive a car, you ride it."

The South Umpqua District was the first in Region Six to have a *Loveridge work plan.* This was developed after a week or ten days in the field with saddle and pack stock. Earl [last name not identified] carried a stop-watch and recorded the time on all activities. He insisted on trotting the loaded mules in order to speed things up. One morning, just as the sun came over the horizon, Earl looked at his

An early Ranger Station, Bear Valley RS, Malheur NF – c1920
(Grant County Museum Photo)

Forest Service family at the Dale Ranger Station, Whitman NF – 1924
(Photo by Walt Dutton, who has a story in Chapter One, Joining Up)

watch, announced that we should be in the saddle and made a run for his horse. However, in this instance, his impatient desire to stay on schedule did not bear fruit. He failed to untie the tie rope and, of course, the horse was cold.

I suppose that the most gratifying moment in my official career was when the Supervisor called to advise that my Ranger appointment had been approved. I had burned all bridges behind me and all of the blue chips were on the table. I really appreciated that message.

I have enjoyed my career tremendously and I am happy and proud to have been a part of the Forest Service. In addition, I shall always have a warm feeling for what I believe is the finest group of men and women in the world.

<u>C. Otto Lindh</u> *Lindh worked on the Columbia, Olympic, Rainier, Snoqualmie, Umatilla and Willamette NFs and was the Assistant Regional Forester for Fire Control in R-6. He was the Regional Forester in R-3 and R-8 and retired in 1958.*

For the winter of 1923-24, District Ranger Jim Huffman offered free lodging at Spirit Lake Ranger Station [on the Columbia National Forest] to Fred Bradley and two young men provided they kept the building roofs free of snow. In a couple of months they came down with a bad case of cabin fever. They discussed many options to break the monotony. It was decided to play a joke on two miners living in a cabin a few miles north of Spirit Lake.

The *jokers* cut big feet from boards about two feet long, with a big toe and eight inches or so in width. Straps were put on so as to fit a boot like a snowshoe.

When a clear weather period developed with no snow to remove, they tied the big feet and a bite of grub to their packboards, put on their snowshoes and took off on the ice across Spirit Lake for the north. Near the miners' cabin they waited until after dark and the light had been extinguished.

The three put on the big feet and went around the cabin. They screamed, yelled and grunted and threw rocks at the cabin. The cabin light came on and the door was opened a crack for a few seconds. The light was quickly put out again. After about 20 minutes, the three "jokers" traveled to a deserted cabin about one-half mile away to spend the night.

As later told by the miners, they stayed put in the cabin and couldn't sleep a wink. At daybreak, they found all those bigfoot tracks and at once decided they would rather be someplace else. They put on their snowshoes and traveled on trails to the west and south. About noon the next day, they came to the Toutle River and civilization. They were still scared but told their story to any skeptic who would listen. Of course, the story grew as it was retold. I know that in later years, other *jokers* made big-foot tracks in the snow in the Wind River area and in Northern California.

So *Bigfoot* became a legend that is still with us after 60 years. But there is no *Bigfoot*.

<u>Harry M. White</u> *White also describes a "Sasquatch" incident, but places it the summer after Lindh's story occurred.*

In the summer of 1924 I was Acting Supervisor of the Columbia National Forest (now Gifford Pinchot) because the Supervisor had been transferred May 1 and his successor was on an assignment in eastern Oregon that could not be completed until fall. In August, I was at a 2,000-acre fire in the Twin Buttes area west of Mt. Adams when Jim Huffman, District Ranger of the Spirit Lake District, called me on the fire camp telephone. He had a problem.

There was a miner's cabin on the east slope of Mt. St. Helens which had been occupied by an elderly prospector. It was said that he had appeared in Kelso one day in great excitement and told how, during the night, huge beasts had bombarded the cabin with large rocks while uttering ape-like screams. Some of the rocks had gone through the roof and landed on the cabin floor. When daylight came large tracks had been found near the cabin.

The story had gotten into the papers from Portland to Seattle and many people, including numerous reporters from the cities and several Portland policemen, had flocked to Spirit Lake and the area around Mt. St. Helens. Jim was worried, not about the alleged beasts but

142

about the people. He said the woods were full of people, armed with rifles, shotguns, and pistols, and shooting at anything that moved. He was afraid somebody would be shot.

With the fire still not controlled, I couldn't go to Spirit Lake to help Jim out. There was little Forest officers could do anyway. Later, when I returned to Portland, I read a story written by sports editor L. H. Gregory and given a prominent place on the front page of the *Oregonian*. Gregory had gone to Kelso, thence to the Mt. St. Helens area with the Cowlitz County Sheriff and the sheriff's son. He said the purpose of the trip was to try to capture one of the apes, train him as a baseball pitcher, and sell him to Bill Klepper, manager of the Portland Beavers for a million dollars. He confirmed what Jim had told me about the ape hunters and their activities. Jim had showed him a piece of wood that had been whittled roughly to the shape of a large foot and evidently used to make the tracks, except the toes which were made by clenching the hand and pressing the knuckles into soft dirt. Strangely enough the tracks were all of a right foot so the apes must have gone hopping over the terrain on one leg.

Gregory wrote such a fantastic and humorous tale that its publication, in two installments, seemed to put a damper on the whole thing, and I heard no more about it. I guessed the other newsmen realized they couldn't top Gregory's story, so they just gave up.

`John G. Clousten`   *Clousten started with the Forest Service on the Umatilla NF in 1924. He received a permanent appointment in 1934 and was then transferred to the Fremont NF. He was Grazing Staff Officer on the Umatilla NF and worked in the R-6 Regional Office in Personnel Management and Range and Wildlife Management. He retired in 1957.*

The men making up the staff of the Umatilla then [1924], with the exception of [Forest Supervisor] Kuhns, were not technically trained. They were recruits from the fields of ranching, logging, cow punching and sheep herding. They were practical in that they could do many things with their hands and had skills in maintaining themselves in the woods that many of our present-day people will never have to learn. They shod their own horses, ground valves in their own cars, repaired telephones and even rewired them. They fought their own fires, cut their own wood and washed their own clothes. Time was not a factor in their work. If it was necessary to count a band of sheep at 4:00 am they did it and then went about their day's work. They *made a hand* at all the maintenance work on the District whether it was hanging telephone wire, brushing a trail or replacing the foundation blocks under a cabin. They had a know-how at this sort of work which was essential to the times. That was the kind of work that had to be done. Resource management was only a figure of speech and few of them could define it.

They were, though, in spite of their lack of technical knowledge and their short-term view of the Forest Service destiny, as loyal and dedicated a crew as any today.

<u>Howard T. Phelps</u>   *Phelps started work on the Chelan NF in 1923. He worked on the Fremont and Deschutes NFs and in the Division of Operations in the R-6 Regional Office. He retired in 1952.*

My pack trips into the back country of the old Chelan [National Forest] usually coincided with the open season on blue grouse. They were made in late September or early October, after the fire season, and it required little ingenuity to fit them together. A twenty-two rifle completed the strategy. A noble bird for the pot!

One fall we made rendezvous at Eight Mile Ranger Station - Frank Burge, the District Ranger, Glenn Mitchell, Assistant Supervisor and myself - and headed our pack string up Boulder Creek. Here we were joined by Fred Wehmeyer, District Ranger of the Conconully District upon whose District our trip would encroach and whose dry wit and salty humour made him doubly welcome. We traveled north from there, up past the Windy Peak country to Horseshoe Basin. Enroute we holed up at North Twenty-Mile Lookout to sit out a severe fall snowstorm. Glenn was a fabulous camp cook, and he rummaged around among our supplies and some odds and ends left by the lookout, intending to bake a pan of biscuits, but some way he contrived a cross between biscuits and cake. Like the cross between a mare and a jack, the result was wonderful to behold - a sort of chocolate cupcake that melted in the mouth. Glenn was a sure asset on a pack trip.

We laid over a day at Horseshoe Basin for range inspection in a pleasant camp beside a clear cold stream. Someone, probably a herder or camp tender, had felled a fair-sized fir adjacent to the camp and its needles were tinder dry. We suggested to Frank that it was an unsightly fire hazard and should be burned, and since we were now in his District, he was the only man among us with the authority to set it afire. Frank listened skeptically, making an occasional pointed and ribald remark disparaging our ancestry. Finally, goaded by our insistence, he scanned the clear evening sky, tested the wind and reluctantly and I think against his better judgment, set a match to the tree. It went up with a whoosh. Unfortunately, a freak gust of wind caught it as it was going good and carried the flames toward camp, crowning out a small fir near camp and showering sparks and embers over the camp area. One of the packhorses came jack-knifing through camp, scattering dirt and equipment. Frank, beating at his clothes to dislodge sparks while side- stepping the pack-horse and trying to rescue his bed-roll, swore at us, the packhorse, the fire and the wind with picturesque fluency and vigor, while we, almost helpless with laughter amid the general pandemonium, tried to salvage our own gear. Ah! Me! I haven't had such a muscle-tightening belly-laugh since. The remainder of the trip was enlivened by caustic invective against know-nothings who desecrated a man's District and darn near burned up the camp.

Here, Fred left us to return home, having assured himself that we committed no vandalism while on the fringes of his District. Then we headed west along Bauerman Ridge, the trail generally at timberline, to Cathedral Lake set so beautifully in its natural amphitheatre; over Windy Pass where we passed an uncomfortable night in a snow storm; and so to Spanish Meadows. Here, Frank and Glenn spent a day riding the adjacent range, while I made a sashay west across the Ashnola to Sheep Mountain to look at its possibilities as a fireman-lookout point. I found a light tender for the Geodetic Survey staying in a cabin-dugout at the base of the mountain, sporting a summer-long growth of beard, starved for companionship, and fearful that he would be snowed in before being relieved.

The next morning we broke camp and headed down the Andrews Creek trail, and then up the steep way-trail to Coleman Ridge. At the north end of the ridge we parted for the day, Glenn and Frank to ride the Coleman Ridge range while I climbed Remmel Peak to see if it would provide detection for the country north and west. We agreed to camp that night in the meadows at the south end of Coleman Ridge, where it breaks down to the Chewack.

It was about 11 am when I climbed Remmel, where I made a visibility map with some difficulty in the face of a raw wind and returned to my horse somewhere about the middle of the afternoon. I headed south and soon picked up the tracks of my companion's horses and the pack stock. The weather had been threatening all day, and soon it began to snow, large wet flakes slanting on a cold wind. The tracks were soon covered with snow and the country was strange to me so I buttoned up the collar of my mackinaw against the snow and wind and headed for the south end of the ridge and, I hoped, camp.

Dusk was falling when I reached the breaks to the Chewack, the ground was covered with three inches of wet snow, and it looked like a blustery night ahead. I scanned the openings below me, separated by clumps and fingers of timber, for the glow of a campfire or the sound of horse bells. Nothing but snow and wind and rapidly approaching darkness. I rode the upper fringes of the openings for half an hour, stopping frequently to listen for horse bells, with no luck. I had about decided to pick me a down dry log in the shelter of a clump of timber and build a fire before the light was all gone to sit out the night, when the wind brought me the faintest tinkle of a horse bell. I listened, motionless, my horse restless and uneasy, and had about concluded my imagination was playing me tricks, when ever so faintly on the wind came another tinkle. Angling down toward the sound, I soon caught the glow of a campfire, and in a few minutes reached the snug camp Frank and Glenn had made, screened from the wind in a clump of timber.

I was cold and stiff, my stomach empty and growling for food, and that cheery camp and the faces of my camp-mates, who were becoming a bit concerned, looked right good to me. Glenn, always a man to look to the comfort of his horses before his own, helped me with my horse while Frank stirred a savory pot of mulligan bubbling over the fire. Soon I was hunkered down with a heaping plate of mulligan stew and hot black coffee.

That, gentlemen, was without doubt one of the best and most satisfactory meals I ever ate. What was it? Blue Grouse Mulligan, of course.

<u>Grover C. Blake</u> *Blake describes his new Ranger District, on the Umatilla NF.*

On June 1, 1927, after three years on the Malheur, I was transferred to the Asotin District of the Umatilla National Forest with headquarters at Pomeroy, Washington. Here I found the grazing business quite up-to-date and a number of trails and telephone lines had been constructed, but there was a marked scarcity of cabins. The Ranger Station, of greatest importance, had only a very antique, one-room log cabin in a tumble-down condition. The best house in the District was a frame cabin of three rooms on the Wenaha River that could be reached only by trail, and was used only occasionally by maintenance crews. The District was very rugged and accessibility difficult.

In time we succeeded in getting two primary lookouts and two secondary lookouts established and a 90-foot lookout tower on Big Butte.

There was a large volume of small timber sale business in the Asotin District. By using the lumber from a couple of old Special Use permittees' cabins and some cull lumber from an abandoned Special Use sawmill, all of which had reverted to the government by default, and aided by cooperators who hauled the lumber free, $250.00 in Forest Service money, $50.00 donated by the Game Commission and my labor, I managed to get a small house at Clearwater Ranger Station where I made my field headquarters. We also added some mileage to our system of trails and telephone lines in the four years I served on the District.

<u>Ken Wilson</u> *Wilson worked seasonally for most of the 1930s while attending forestry school. He received a permanent appointment on the Willamette NF in 1939 and that same year was transferred to New England. He also worked in R-2 and R-3, the Washington Office, and was the Assistant Regional Forester for the Division of Fire Control in the R-6 Regional Office. He retired in 1973.*

One of the things that has stayed with me down through the years was the casual approach to safety in the woods in those days and how it has changed. Thank goodness! Roy Elliot was District Ranger at Detroit, [on the Santiam NF in 1930] when I reported for work. I remember he hauled me up to the Coffin Mountain Trail and as I started up the trail to Scar Mountain, 17 miles distant, Roy said, "Now be sure and keep a diary of your day's activities and be sure and call in to the office as soon as you get the telephone line up and working." Lookout and firemen's first jobs were to clear out the trails and repair the phone lines. Each morning I would leave the lookout, burdened with an axe, bucking saw, sledge, wedge, roll of #9 telephone wire, supply of split insulators, pliers, connectors, about an 8- or 10-foot split cedar ladder, or tree climbers, and, of course, lunch.

As I recall, it was about ten days before I was able to free the line enough to call in. No one seemed to be at all alarmed. (Note: Even though the District had a couple of trail maintenance crews, it was necessary for most of the summer lookouts and firemen to supplement the work of the maintenance crews to assure that trails and phone lines were clear by the time fire season rolled around.) From a safety standpoint, such a practice of leaving an employee to fare for himself for a week or two without communication, and performing dangerous work in the back country, would have been unheard of only a few years later. However, at the time this was accepted as part of the job and no one gave it a second thought.

To continue along this line, the same philosophy applied if you went to fight a fire in your area of responsibility. You stayed with the fire until it was completely out, or got too large to handle. In the latter case the lookouts who were watching the smoke would report to the dispatcher that the fire appeared to be out of control and additional help would be sent. Strict adherence to the cardinal rule of *stay with 'em 'till they're out* was drilled into us new employees from the very start. I'm sure we would have fewer fires *get away* today if we adhered more strictly to this rule.

Corwin E. "Slim" Hein *Hein worked his entire career on the Deschutes NF, starting in 1928. He was the Forest Engineer when he retired in 1969.*

In spite of the depression years and the bountiful supply of deer on the Fort Rock District, I believe that the smokechasers of those times religiously obeyed the game laws. But what is one to do when a *neighbor* drops a haunch of venison off at your station at 11 o'clock at night? This happened to me [in the early 1930s on the Deschutes NF]. I peeled and buried the hide and ate the delicious viands for breakfast, dinner and supper for several days. Shortly afterward Whit [Ranger Fenton G. Whitney] visited me on a routine inspection and hair-cutting trip. While I was sitting on a stump with Whit cutting my hair, his mongrel dog dug up the deer hide. Whit said nothing and threw the hide in a brushpile. The dog again returned with the hide and received a more discouraging reception from Whit. Neither Whit nor I offered to discuss the matter which was becoming extremely embarrassing to me.

Everett Lynch   *Lynch started work on the Fremont NF about 1927. He also worked on the Mt. Hood NF, and retired in 1954 while District Ranger on the Okanogan NF.*

For some time I've hoped that someone would write a tribute to the old-time short-term man of the Forest Service. But the years pass so now I will try.

Few people today realize the effort the short-term men have given in helping to establish the Forest Reserves on a firm foundation in the many activities in which they worked. Usually each Ranger District had one or two outstanding men who, because of their knowledge of the country, acquaintance with the people of the community and familiarity with the work to be done, were simply indispensable. Most of these men had worked many years for the Service. They were of high moral standards, imbued with loyalty, integrity and industry. The libelous remarks that I have heard on occasion of Forest Service sweat being worth a thousand dollars an ounce were entirely false. Many times I have seen these men work to the point of exhaustion on fires. In other duties they often sacrificed their personal time to complete an urgent improvement job.

As I think back, many golden memories are recalled of the delightful comradeship shared with those many fellow workers. On every District on which I worked, there was always at least one dependable short-term man who helped me get acquainted with local people and with the area of the District. Most always, these men worked the usual five months during the fire season for the Forest Service, and the balance of the year on a ranch, trapped the back country for furs, hunted predators, or cut timber for one of the local saw mills. While working for the Forest Service their pay was largely in their pride of doing a job well. Since they were a part of the organization before the days of social security or other government benefits, they worked for 20 to 25 years and then were shunted aside as being *too old* [because they had reached the age of 62, they could no longer be hired]. That is a sad story.

John R. Montgomery *John Montgomery was a short-term employee on the Diamond Lake Ranger District of the Umpqua NF in the late 1920s and early 1930s. He was a foreman with the CCC program and was named District Ranger at Tiller on the Umpqua NF in the mid-1940s.*

Within the Umpqua National Forest on the Diamond Lake Ranger District lies an old burn known for years as the Fish Creek Desert. Early in the spring of 1925 a Spanish war vet, Emroy Davis, called upon Forest Supervisor Carl B. Neal to inform Neal of his intention to settle on the Fish Creek Desert burn under the homestead laws.

A road camp was established the same year at Cedar Springs, the only spring on the burn. Not far away Emroy Davis set up his headquarters and began his colonization. The Forest Supervisor was a blunt, determined individual who was not above rocking the boat, if necessary, to gain his point. Davis was just as determined he would settle the burn. While on a visit to the road camp Neal went to see Davis at his nearby camp. Neal is said to have asked Davis if he was going to raise bananas, pineapples, oranges or what? Davis' reply was that he was going to pick up all the stray dogs and raise Forest Supervisors.

Davis had some experience as a surveyor and proceeded to lay out the area in homesteads. During the winter he recruited others to join in the venture. In 1926, E. H. Best, another war vet, squatted on the Desert with his family. Best was said to be an ex-Forest Service Ranger with a degree from Montana University and an excellent war record. He was a disabled veteran. Sympathy was definitely on the side of the homesteaders throughout the county, making a conviction for trespassing rather difficult. By the winter of 1926-27, there were four families, 15 people and 9 cabins on the Desert.

The March 18, 1928, issue of the *Roseburg News Review* headed an article, "Davis & Best Lose Fight For Homes - Fish Creek Lands Kept Non-Agricultural - Long Fight Is Ended." The two squatters had served terms in the federal jail and were allowed to leave only after promising not to return to the homesteads.

Despite the terms of his release [from jail], Emroy Davis returned. One incident witnessed by Assistant Forest Supervisor Thomas *Bud* Burgess, Julius Kummel, Timber Staff from the RO, and the whole planting crew happened not far from Cedar Springs in the spring of 1931. While planting we were approached by Emroy Davis. Davis was alone and carried a luger with the holstered grip solidly in his right hand. He ordered us off his land-NOW. Bud asked Davis, "Where is your land, Mr. Davis?"

Davis replied, "Just leave, you talkative SOB." We left and wrote our version of the episode for benefit of testimony for a trial was sure to follow.

It was not long before Loren Cochran and Joe Vogelsand, Deputy U.S. Marshals, appeared with warrants for the arrest of Best and Davis. A strategy meeting was called, with a total of fourteen people involved. Best had settled on an open meadow along the Mountain Meadows Trail called Bridge Prairie. He had good taste as this was probably the only location worth working. It was a nice, level, rich piece of land. The marshals thought it best to keep the two wanted men apart to prevent a joint resistance effort on their part. The marshals and the rest of the crew would apprehend Davis at his cabin. Harold Barker and I were assigned to go to the North Umpqua Bridge on the Mountain Meadows Trail between the camps to keep the *outlaws* apart. The thought was that Davis would make a run for Best's Bridge Prairie homestead. These were exciting times!

Early the next morning Harold and I were dispatched to the bridge. I was to stay in the open at the north end of the bridge and Harold was to conceal himself above the south end of the bridge. We were only there a short time when Best came down the trail headed for the burn. This was something for which we were not prepared. There was a gate on the north end of the bridge to keep cattle on the Mountain Meadows side of the river. The gate was closed and I was on the outside next to it.

I told Best he couldn't leave as there was a warrant out for his arrest. He asked how many were on the Desert. I told him I thought twelve. He said it would take that many to get Davis and that he would go back to his camp, get more ammunition and another gun and would be ready for whoever came for him. I insisted he could not leave and he insisted I could not stop him. We wrestled to the ground. Once loose I pulled out a long bladed pocket knife to cut the strap holding his rifle. I can hear him scream yet . I'm sure he thought I would cut his throat.

About this time Brahan [a friend of Best] and Best's niece appeared on the run headed for the bridge. Harold Barker dashed from his hiding place, pulled his revolver and yelled at Brahan to "STOP!" Brahan kept coming and again Harold shouted, "You Stop!" He stopped and I breathed a sigh of relief. I knew Harold well enough to know if he said stop he meant just that.

We told Brahan and the girl they were free to go and we waited for the marshal's return from Davis' cabin. Time passed and Best wanted us to feed him since he was our prisoner. I offered him my lunch as I had little appetite but he refused, saying I would probably poison him.

After he left us, Brahan had gone to Davis' camp to arm himself before returning to the bridge to dispatch us. As he left the tent with the rifle he encountered the marshal. Brahan growled that he had seen a couple of coyotes on the trail. Cochran, squatting in the tent doorway, suggested Brahan put the gun down and reached out to push the barrel to one side. Brahan threw the rifle on the bed and took off down the North Umpqua in the direction of Roseburg.

It was a long afternoon for us at the bridge, but Cochran finally came and Best greeted him like an old friend. Best and Cochran left for Best's camp to spend the night and prepare for his departure. Harold and I headed for Big Camas. It was a day we would never forget and would not like to go through again.

WIVES AND FAMILIES: "Oh, she can do it!"

Albert Wiesendanger *Wiesendanger was a Ranger on the Oregon NF at the time of this story.*

During the summer of 1919 nearly 150,000 people enjoyed the Eagle Creek Camp Ground [on the Mt. Hood National Forest]. It was at this important location that Mrs. *Micky* Wiesendanger became the first wife of a Forest Ranger to reign over such an important area.

Many, many very fine people came to the door of her Ranger Station to inquire if they could park near the Station their automobiles, mostly Ford cars, as they wanted to hike on up the Eagle Creek Trail overnight. She always obliged them. The Multnomah County police patrolled those days on motorcycles. The Eagle Creek Ranger Station had the last telephone in Multnomah County on which they could report in to their headquarters, or to report a grass and brush fire along the railroad right-of-way caused by a coal burning freight engine. They, too, were given the welcome mat by Cleo Weisendanger. She was Mrs. Public Relations.

Edith Y. Kuhns *Kuhns was a Forest Service clerk before she married. After her husband, John C. Kuhns, retired, Edith went back to school and received a degree from Portland State College in 1966, when she was 73 years old.*

I returned from a brief weekend vacation to find the [Wenaha National] Forest office empty of Supervisor and Ranger, but conspicuous on my desk were three lists: supplies for 25 men, supplies for 50 men, and supplies for 100 men. A brief explanatory note stated: *Bad fire at Mottet Meadows. When we phone you to hire men, buy grub according to these lists. Get tools wherever you can; we'll need plenty. Don't leave the phone.* Those were my complete instructions for what followed during the next six weeks - and I had been Forest Clerk a brief three months.

It was the depletion of the country's manpower during World War I that had given me the opportunity to take the Forest Clerk examination

153

in the first place. With an American Expeditionary Force in France the Civil Service Commission had let down the bars and permitted mere females to compete for the job heretofore restricted to men.

I had been employed several years in a Forest Service District Office where the humdrum compilations of cattle and sheep grazed, timber cut and sold, fires, their acreage and causes and the wildlife census hadn't been especially exciting. I was young and wanting thrills. It was out on the Forests, I analyzed, that things happened. There one had direct contact with stock raising, with firefighting, and with timber cruising, and with the men engaged in these interesting out-of-door activities. I dreamed of open ranges, of timbered slopes and mountain lakes, and possibly there did flit through my mind thoughts of hard-riding cowboys, of stalwart, green-clad Forest Rangers, and of men battling victoriously against odds during that dreaded period of the year—the fire season.

So when women at last were considered eligible for Forest office jobs, I didn't hesitate. As the result of a passing grade, I found myself one day behind a desk in a small upstairs office in the Federal Building in Walla Walla, Washington. Piled high before me were vouchers, property and improvement records and what-not that had nearly overwhelmed the Supervisor in the interim since the previous forest clerk's departure. The Supervisor's expressed delight upon my arrival which I had thought was due in part at least to my own personal appearance was, I concluded later, due only to his great relief at being given an office assistant.

I was amazed at the variety of jobs a Forest Clerk was supposed to handle, the knowledge one was expected to possess. The Civil Service exam hadn't even hinted that cowboy vocabulary might be essential in checking property. A deficit of two alforjas, a surplus of two latigos - it seemed quite reasonable to me that they might be one and the same. But there was something about the Supervisor's reaction to my question, amusement that he suppressed with great difficulty, that revealed how deep was my ignorance. And the improvement records and expense accounts! I studied the thick volume of regulations, determined to master it somehow, though I wondered why training in legal phraseology hadn't been specified as a requisite. "This is a man's job, after all," I thought to myself.

I began eagerly to anticipate my annual vacation when, for a little time, I could put out of my mind all these perplexing problems. I was blissfully unaware, but not for long, that summer vacations were not for forest clerks; that the hotter the weather the closer I would be expected to stay on the job. I could wangle only a brief weekend respite. Here I was, on my own, expected to handle the office end of a Class C fire that in six weeks covered some 10,000 acres along the summit of the Blue Mountains in the southwest corner of Wallowa County, Oregon.

The men were out on the fighting line, the enemy FIRE. All right, I'd fight it too, here in the office. At the thought that I was at last in the thick of things a wave of exultation swept over me. Upon my ability to carry on might depend the outcome of the battle, for men and supplies meant holding the line.

The temperature that had played around in the 90s skipped to new highs. The thermometer recorded 100 degrees, 105, then 110. I had never before lived where, in the heat of summer, doors and windows were closed tight during daylight hours to conserve the cool night air and to keep out the furnace-like blasts from reflecting pavements and brick walls. When it registered 115 degrees I felt I understood the term *All Hell's a-popping* that I had heard used by the men in discussing past fire experiences. And out on the fire line I knew it must be an inferno. The thought of what was happening up at Mottet Meadows, the agony of heat the firefighters were enduring, made me bear my own oven-like existence, though I found myself growing grim with the passing days.

The injunction *Do not leave the phone* I took literally. Phone messages were relayed to me wherever I might be, even for brief periods of time. I turned down opportunities to go riding, though the thought of moon-drenched roadsides and evening breezes was like a vision of heaven to a dweller in eternal fire. Phone calls came at all hours of the day or night, and sometimes, it seemed to me, at the most inopportune times. As surely as I planned to enjoy the luxury of a tepid bath there would be the familiar ring. After one experience, when for several hours I fluttered from phone to tub, from tub to phone, without being able either to bathe or dress, I confined my ablutions to hurried showers, my clothes right at hand and in such order I could fling them on in no time flat.

I handled in routine manner the instructions from the fire line, contacting the employment agency for fallers and buckers, pick and shovel men, timekeepers. I phoned the shops for food supplies, rounded up tools as I could, saw that they were delivered at specified hours at designated places, to be picked up by the trucks. Then calls came through for personal purchases as well, and I shopped for such masculine articles as I could never have dreamed I would buy. Nothing in my past experience had fitted me to shop for loggers' boots, men's work shirts and pants, even undergarments, Copenhagen "snus" [snoose] chewing tobacco. Every item thus purchased had to be charged to the right employee in order that proper deduction be made from paychecks. I was to learn later that such articles, when they reached the front, were sometimes diverted to the men most in need of replacements, to those who had lost their soles -- shoe variety -- in hot ashes, or whose shirts had been almost burned off their backs by sparks.

A phone call one evening requested that I arrange for a District Office man to be on hand the following day to pay off some men being sent out. The Supervisor had realized there was something wrong along the fire line. Instead of his usual route he had reversed his inspection tour. A well-organized alarm system that had made it possible for those *in the know* to sleep when they were supposed to be fighting failed to work in reverse. Five sheepish-looking individuals, who had been rather boastful about *putting it over* on the boss, presented themselves for their paychecks. I was grateful a man was present to give them what they deserved - talk of a special variety. I wondered if, given time, I might not even master that for emergencies; after all they were scriptural expressions.

The District Office representative informed me that because this was an exceptionally bad fire year and an emergency existed, the usual bonded fiscal agent could not be sent to handle the paying-off of men; that, under ordinary circumstances, I would have been bonded to disburse federal funds. In this emergency, however, and because I was well known to the District Office, they would wire me, whenever I requested, $1,000 at a time, to be deposited in my name and to be paid out in personal checks to the firefighters. My own personal checking account had been of such meager proportions that just the thought of that $1,000 at a time in my keeping was overwhelming. It seemed to me that just being able to sign checks for the amount gave me an atmosphere of affluence, and I was quite certain I detected an attitude of deference toward me on the part of the bank tellers that wasn't due to my years.

I felt myself becoming a movie character, in my own mind at least, when word came one afternoon to be ready to contact the Sheriff's office. Trouble with the I.W.W.s [International Woodworkers Union] had developed and they might need outside help to handle the situation. I contacted that officer of the law and he stated he would be ready with men and guns at any time the need arose. Fortunately the expected race to the aid of the endangered didn't have to be run.

Medical care for a 19-year-old firefighter had to be arranged for. His greatest activity had always been in response to the dinner bell, and it was while hurrying to the mess tent, not to work, that he had slipped off a log and fallen, plunging his arms down into hot ashes. Nevertheless, the youngster's predicament somehow appealed to my maternal instincts though I was but a few years older. Questioning elicited the fact that the boy was without funds. I was on the verge of staking him for fare home to alleged parents when the Supervisor intervened, "Don't be soft with him; he'd lose it as he has his own, playing craps."

I knew it was good news when no further calls for firefighters came through. Then men began dribbling back from the hills. What a strange assortment they were. They had been picked up not only on the streets of the town (I recognized this variety—bronzed men just through working in the harvest fields) but from Seattle's notorious Skid Road and Front Street in Portland. When the fire finally was brought under control and only a few needed, the others swarmed like bees. In the office, in the hall, down into the Post Office corridors below, awaiting their turn to receive in cold cash recompense for the hot hours endured at the fire.

An SOS had been sent to the District Office to have a man on hand to check returned bedrolls and to maintain order while I handled timeslips, made deductions, etc. These hundreds of men must be paid as speedily as possible; they deserved quick returns on their investment of sweat and brawn.

But I wasn't too busy to listen in to the conversations around me. When someone in awed tones said, "Here comes the Chief," I glanced up to see the aquiline features of a native American whose dignity and stoicism marked him as a descendant of some great redskin brave. "Gee! You shoulda seen him at the fire," the man I was paying said with little-boy hero-worship evident. "There wasn't any place too hot or smoky for him. Gosh! He'd go right in where things was the worst, where none of the rest of us wanted to go. He sure could take it." Not even the news item in the next day's paper, reporting the Chief's incarceration in the city jail for drunkenness could erase my mental picture of him in the midst of flames and crashing trees.

A big, bulky policeman-like individual sidled up to my desk. Somehow I wasn't surprised when in low, confidential tones, he said, "Better check the bedroll of the Snake Charmer. He's trying to get away with some government blankets. I been on the police force and I sort of suspicioned him and kept my eyes open." But the dunnage bag of the Snake Charmer, a sallow youth, thin almost to emaciation whose only qualification as assistant cook was probably his desire to be as close as possible to food, contained only his own threadbare, ragged bedding and personal belongings. Not so the bedroll of the self-appointed detective, who probably hoped to divert attention from his own by causing suspicion to fall on someone else.

I was having a terrible time getting the deductions right. Who got the size 11 loggers' boots and who the size 42 underwear and the $3.00 wool shirt, blue and green? "I got some unnerwear, lady. Wanta see it?" *Happy* Green, fumbling with his shirt buttons as he came, staggered up to the desk; his *happy* grin in a way offsetting the awesome bashed-in nose that set him apart from his fellows. Questioned as to that physical deformity he would reply, "Ne-er knew how it happened. When I woke up after a fight that's how I looked."

Happy became a familiar figure around the office thereafter. He seemed to feel in some vague way that, having once acquired here the wherewithal to keep him in drinks, he might still have money coming to him. A graduate of the University of Edinburgh, he had slipped far. When the local paper reported his sudden demise - the railroad tracks having proven an unwise bed for a night's repose - I found myself breathing a wordless prayer that *Happy* might have another chance in a new existence to attain what he might have been during his earthly career.

The deductions for tobacco and snuff were the most perplexing. Dire necessity had driven the men to taking even quarter plugs when the quantity brought in on the truck wouldn't go around. I felt my education had been much enhanced when I could estimate the number of chaws to the plug. When the final accounts were drawn up and I realized I would have to pay for some of the discrepancies, I was amused at the thought that, *the treat was on me* and *who'd have thought I'd ever be buying snus for loggers.*

The final report sort of staggered me. In six weeks, $11,000 in cash for labor had passed through my hands. I had purchased groceries enough to stock a good-sized store, and, through purchase of personal garments and boots, added appreciably to the profits of the local merchants. I knew the local doctor and his office force better than my own good health would have permitted and my prestige at the bank was almost good enough for a loan without collateral. Most surprising of all, whatever timidity I might have had at the beginning had completely vanished. I was now a fire-seasoned, full-fledged forest clerk.

Oh, yes, I married the Forest Supervisor, John C. Kuhns, and the next forest clerk on the Wenaha Forest was a man.

Eva Poole *Poole was the District Clerk on two Ranger Districts on the Umpqua NF. Here she tells of her experiences when she accompanied her husband to a remote station.*

On July 5, 1921, (my 19th birthday) Ira and I left Roseburg for Steamboat [on the Umpqua National Forest]; Ira as a guard and I as telephone operator. We went by car as far as Rock Creek, as far as the road was completed. We crossed the North Umpqua River above Glide on the Lone Rock Ferry. We were met at Rock Creek by Abe Wilson, the packer. We were expected to hike in the rest of the way.

159

Telephone operator at Oakridge RS, Cascade NF – c1915—
wives often handled the phones at remote stations

Ira knew that I wasn't up to hiking that distance, so he scouted around and hired a horse for me to ride.

The first night was spent at Boundary about halfway from Rock Creek to Steamboat. Next evening we arrived at Steamboat. I was sort of let down! Steamboat consisted of a lean-to and an open rock pit to cook on. The switchboard was on a tree.

Ira got busy and put up a tent to sleep in and there was a huge pile of split shakes nearby. It wasn't too long until he had built a small but neat one room cabin. I don't remember where we got the small cook stove, but I remember I was soon baking bread, pies and other goodies. We moved the switchboard inside the cabin as soon as he got the roof on. My job was to answer the telephone. One line came over the mountain from Bohemia and the other from Big Camas and Illahee, and other lookouts on the North Umpqua and Diamond Lake Districts.

As I remember, the packer, Abe Wilson, made the trip by about once a week, coming from Big Camas, I suppose, and going to Rock Creek to meet a truck that would have supplies and mail for guard stations and lookouts along his route. We were always so happy to see him coming.

A young man by the name of Harry Hill was a guard and lived in a tent a few miles up Canton Creek. There was no bridge across the North Umpqua, just a swinging *Mule Bridge* across Canton Creek. Then there was a trail crew at Illahee and a few lookouts. It was a big wide world and very scary when Ira had to go to a fire.

I believe a Mr. Rankin was Supervisor of the Umpqua National Forest and Urcess McLaughlin the District Ranger at Glide.

We were told there were no rattlesnakes around there, but we encountered one, one evening after putting out the light in the cabin and going to the tent to bed. It was between the cabin and the tent. It rattled and we must have jumped high and wide - anyway, we cleared it. Ira turned the flashlight on the snake just as it went under the tent floor. We didn't hear or see it again, but every time I looked in my suitcase, I expected to see or hear it rattle.

<u>Dorothy Burgess</u>   *Burgess describes the early years of her married life to Ranger R.C. "Bud" Burgess.*

I am sure it is true that the one who is enjoying himself the most is the one who is relating his own experiences and though they be good or bad, they are more interesting than someone else's. And so with me, though I hope I do not find my only interest is reliving the past, it gives me pleasure to go back over 50 years.

I had come out from Minnesota to teach school in Bend in 1925 when I met Bud, who was a USFS Ranger on the Deschutes Forest stationed at LaPine. Before long we knew there was something special between us. As we discussed marriage, he said he had a house that was completely furnished and all I needed to do was to pack my clothes and move in.

I always accused him of marrying me for my money. I had recently lost my parents and so had a bit of inheritance. He said he was in debt, but could get *leave* (a new meaning for me) if I would finance a trip to Portland. He must have known that women's lib was in the offing, but I was brought up to believe that the man paid for the honeymoon, and so we settled for the Ochoco Inn in Prineville because Bud had a friend who rented a room there by the month and was not using it that particular weekend.

So after our weekend honeymoon in a rent-free room, we returned to *the completely furnished* FS cabin that my groom had provided for me. My heart really sank as I looked at that forlorn Rosland Ranger Station sitting all by itself several miles from civilization. It was two rooms, one a combined living, kitchen and bedroom, measuring about 15 feet by 18 feet, the other was Bud's office with a breezeway in between.

Our living quarters were furnished with a combined heating and cooking stove, a built-in cupboard, a small unpainted drop-leaf table and four straight back chairs with rawhide bottoms and an army cot. The walls were decorated with coyote hides. The only convenience was a pump in the breezeway.

Bud said he was a good cook and would get our evening meal. And so as I kept the tears back and unpacked, hanging my clothes that had been bought in some of St. Paul's better stores, in the corner of the kitchen, Bud prepared our dinner. He had tomato soup with hunks of tomato floating around and cocoa. I thought it was a strange menu but my only comment was as I pushed the hunks of tomato to one side, "It is very good." The next morning when he suggested the same menu for breakfast, I took over.

The dishes were granite and the pots and pans a miscellaneous collection mostly of a size that would accommodate cooking for an army. Now that so many years have elapsed and I know I cannot be thrown in jail, I will admit that I became attached to some of those FS cooking utensils, as I am still using an old, beat up granite roaster, a big granite cup and an antique food grinder.

But I knew I could not go on using granite dishes. Our first morning we went back to Bend. We bought a set of dishes and a few other things, including a day bed that looked quite elegant during the day and was more comfortable at night than a single army cot.

We had boarders from almost the first day of our marriage; a never-ending succession of foresters from the Bend office. They occupied the bunk beds in the breezeway.

While the men were out cruising or doing whatever they had to do, I kept busy cooking and making that one room more livable. I painted the furniture gray and blue - never my favorite colors but the floor was gray, the house was painted gray and of course gray was the standard FS color at that time, so I guess I was just trying to stay in tune. Bud had built a closet in one corner of the room so with our clothes out of sight, the colorful day bed, and some new scatter rugs and the newly painted furniture, it was quite cheery.

At least I thought so until my family came out one by one from Minnesota to see what I had gotten into. I had no parents but I had older brothers and sisters. One sister was so depressed over the way I was living that she only stayed a couple of days. Then too I guess she did not like sleeping in a sleeping bag at the end of the day bed. When my oldest brother came to visit, I can still see him looking around and

163

saying, "Jabes, (a nickname) to think you would ever come to living like this! I think the only good thing about this deal is the fellow you married." They all liked Bud so that made me feel good.

I was afraid of everything! First it was the switchboard. Bud had failed to instruct me how to use it and I thought all I had to do when the phone rang was to say *hello*. Finally after pulling plug after plug I got a voice - Keefer from Crane Prairie. He instructed me how to operate the switchboard. That was a big mistake! From then on I was operator without pay and during the busy fire season I was often there by myself manning the switchboard.

The wild animals frightened me. Bud said to ignore the coyotes as they were more afraid of me than I was of them. I did not believe that and would make a hasty retreat for the house whenever I saw one. One day I heard this eerie noise when I was out walking and looked up to see a great big owl blinking at me. He really scared me as I thought owls were only found in captivity.

I was afraid to stay alone and made myself sick so Bud couldn't leave me for the first couple of times. He solved that by making arrangements for me to stay with the Clarks who operated the store in LaPine. But I didn't care for that and finally decided to be brave and stay alone. As a result Bud's bulldog, Jack, became my good friend. Prior to that I was afraid of him as he seemed to resent me, but from then on he sensed he had to take care of me.

And the car - Bud said I had to drive as it would help him a lot. Shortly after we were married, he wanted to pick up a horse at Crescent, a distance of 20 miles. The highway was glare ice. I was driving and looked at Bud to see that he had his hat pulled over his eyes. When I asked him why he was doing that, he said if he were going to be killed he didn't want to know about it and that when I was going downhill I should take my foot off the accelerator. I said, "What's that?" With those instructions I learned to drive. When we got to Crescent Ranger Station, Mrs. Floe couldn't believe that I had driven for the first time. She really gave Bud a bad time and said that she had been driving for years but Sanford wouldn't think of letting her drive on that icy highway. Bud said, "Oh, she can do it!" And I did! Bud rode the horse home.

One day I heard a knock on the door. I looked out to see a grizzly-haired old man. I quickly latched the screen door, but before I could slam the door in his face he said, "Why, you're Bud's new bride and old Jake wouldn't harm a hair on your head. I just stopped by to see if Bud had any coyote hides to sell." I couldn't believe that I could get rid of those unsightly things and get money for them. When Bud got home that evening he was really pleased. He said Jake had given me twice what the hides were worth.

Then came that first baby and I was afraid something would happen to him. I spent three weeks in the hospital in Bend and when we came home a distance of 30 miles, I had a regular drug store with me. I thought if this is what it takes to raise a baby, he'll never live. Fortunately, he was a good baby and I did not have to use any of those drugs but he was brought up according to all of the government bulletins that I had amassed. I worried if I was five minutes late feeding, bathing or napping him. I wouldn't let anyone near him for fear they would contaminate him. Bob's first Thanksgiving we spent with Bud's brother where there were five children. They had looked forward to playing with their new cousin. I am sure I did not endear myself to them as I kept Bob in the car all of the time we were there. I still marvel at the casual way young mothers care for their babies today.

I was a bit more relaxed with our second son who arrived a year and a half later. With no neighbors, close friends or modern conveniences, it was hard. With Bud's help we did the babies' laundry, but the rest of it went weekly on the mail stage to Bend.

The only time we had fresh meat or vegetables would be the first few days after we had been to Bend and in those days, 30 miles was a long trip. For a few months in the winter we could keep the meat by freezing. Bud did try one summer to have an ice-house but that didn't work and we lost some good meat. Mostly we missed fresh vegetables and to this day, I cannot stand any kind of canned vegetables. We all built up an aversion in later years to ham.

The year before Bob entered school, we spent the winter in Bend on detail and rented an apartment. The boys were entranced by seeing

165

lights go on with the push of a button and a stove that cooked without wood. What really fascinated them was the bathroom. One night we left them with a sitter and when we came home she greeted us laughing. She said the boys had given her a conducted tour of the apartment, explaining all of the remarkable things and when they came to the bathroom, John went over to the toilet, lifted the seat cover and proudly announced, "This is where we wee."

Then came the depression. We sent money to two of my improvident brothers and one came to live with us. We helped Bud's brother who had the five children and Bud's mother and father, who had lost their small savings, came out from Illinois and we rented a small house for them in LaPine and paid for all of their groceries. We did all of this on $144.75 per month. A few years later, Bud got his first raise of $25.00 a month and we thought we were millionaires.

After seven years in LaPine we were transferred to Crescent. Then we had a big house with a bathroom, but our own light plant so we still could not have refrigeration. We were now 50 miles from Bend. The teacher and her daughter came once a week for a bath and I was reminded of our days in LaPine when we would go to the schoolhouse to take showers.

The boys started school in Crescent with the entire class numbering four to six. The children should have had excellent individual training but good teachers did not want to come to those isolated areas and therefore we always got the dregs. That became a worry most of the years the boys were in grade school.

Ida Matz *Matz describes her summer experiences at a Regional cruising camp. Cruising camps are also the subject of stories by M.M. "Red" Nelson in this chapter and by H.C. "Chris" Chriswell in Chapter Three.*

To begin this narration, I feel that you should know who I am. I'm Ida Matz, daughter of Fred A. Matz, who retired in 1946 after 37 years in Region 6. Dad was in Timber Management - Surveying and Cruising - Regional Office. Home was in Portland. The field was National Forests in Region 6.

Dad had gone to the field weeks before school was out. Camp was north of Enterprise near the Washington state line. Dad had written home telling about going from the end of the road by pack outfit to get into the work area, setting up camp beside a creek and getting the crew oriented and work started.

Finally the day came that my brother and I were out of school. Within a day or two, we threw our shoes into the garbage can, climbed into the 1924 Hupmobile touring car with Mom at the wheel and headed east. Summer had started.

The only incidents of the ride that I remember was that the wind blew the canvas top of the car over the wall at Crown Point. Mom stopped, lowered the wooden frame-work and decided there would be no rain all summer so we wouldn't need the top. So we went on. No more problems until the next morning, after overnight at Pendleton. Going up Cabbage Hill *Hup* boiled only because Homer, my eight-year-old brother, had forgotten to release the hand brake. We crept to the top of the hill to the shade of a telephone pole and waited for the motor to cool enough to add water from the water bag. The motor started so we went on.

At Enterprise, Mom went to the Forest Service warehouse to get directions to camp and pick up camp supplies - fresh meat, fruit, vegetables, staples, mail, etc.

By sundown we had arrived at the end of the road where the packer should be. He was gone. The buildings were locked. The note on the door said he would return in four days. Mom cranked the FS phone nailed to a tree until camp answered. She explained the problem to Dad. He told her to park the car so that the morning sun would not shine on the cargo and to camp there; he would be out in the morning.

The next morning Homer and I sat on a split rail fence looking across a dry meadow. We saw sun reflections on metal and ran to meet Dad. On one shoulder was a double-bit axe and on the other was a crosscut saw. Dad had left camp four hours earlier (it was only eight miles from camp to the end of the road) and had opened a road so that *Hup* could go to camp.

167

After Dad had rested, lunched and repacked the car we again went on. Mom drove and Dad led the way on foot or rode the running board - no room on the seat. *Hup* suffered the loss of a fender when a bank gave way while fording a creek. I remember seeing the tents in the woods and how happy I felt. I'm sure Mom must have been even happier. We had arrived.

Camp life was the same as summers past and to come. Good memories include bonfires at dusk, sing-alongs to the wind-up phonograph, star gazing, story telling, good food, sleeping on the ground in a tent, bathing in a creek, damming the creek, taming chipmunks, building towns of *Log Cabin Syrup* cans and going fishing on Friday mornings. Not-so-good memories include pit toilets, electric storms and fear when the phone rang at night and Dad called, "Crew out! Going to a fire!"

Homer and I had chores to do at camp including keeping the wood box full for the cook, water buckets full at the cook tent and wash rack and coloring the maps with colored pencil.

One dumb adventure Homer and I had involved going fishing on a Friday. Mr. Tripp packed our lunch and we headed out to the beaver dam to catch fish for the crews' dinner. We were to be back by 9 o'clock. For some reason we didn't catch fish and since we didn't want to face razzing about being poor fishermen, we didn't go back to camp until we thought everyone would have gone to bed. Nobody had gone to bed! Dad and the crew were looking for us. Mom and Mr. Tripp were waiting in camp. Mom honked the horn on *Hup* and everyone came back to camp. The long day ended and everyone except Dad, Homer and I went to bed. We three had a long, long conversation about our adventure.

Three days later when Homer and I got off our 50-foot hemp tethers and could talk in private, we agreed we had done a dumb thing, and had earned the punishment we received. We never did anything like that again. In later years, Homer and I thanked God that Dad was not a violent man.

Another adventure I had that summer happened on the way back to the tent after a bedtime *pit stop*. I was very excited about the black puppy

I had been playing with. Mom and Dad were not all that excited, and I was told not to go to the pit alone anymore. After we had moved from that camp, Dad explained to me all about baby bears and Mama bears. I really was scared then and realized I had not played with a puppy.

The time came for camp to be moved to another area and Dad insisted that a truck could come to move the gear. After all, if the family car could make the trip a truck should be able to do the same.

A couple of weeks before school would start again, *Hup* went to the garage at Joseph, and the family went to Wallowa Lake. I do not remember how we got there, we may have walked. I do remember the joy of playing with the FS kids that lived at the lake and also remember how awful it was to sleep in a building and in a bed.

In due time, *Hup* was again fit to travel on the highway with a new top and new fender. We kissed Dad goodbye and headed west. Our summer had ended. Dad got home about two months later and we survived the winter knowing another summer would come.

As an adult I know now that the family had the best of two worlds; summer in the field and winter in the city, thanks to the Forest Service.

HORSES: "Those double-darned horses."

H. C. "Chris" Chriswell *Chriswell began his career in 1933. He was on seasonal timber survey and cruising crews on the Olympic, Malheur, Chelan, and Whitman NFs from 1933 to 1937. He was a District Ranger on the Umatilla, Olympic, Columbia, Rogue River, and Mt. Hood NFs. He was the Forest Supervisor on the Mt. Baker NF from 1957 until his retirement in 1971. Chriswell wrote and self-published a detailed book about his experiences titled* Memoirs - Harold C. (Chris) Chriswell – 1933 to 1971. *The stories he submitted to TIMBER-LINES are in his book, along with many others. Chriswell was an Assistant District Ranger on the Umatilla NF at the time of this story. He quotes his District Ranger, Fred Wehmeyer, about the "good ol' days." Wehmeyer has another story about horses in Chapter One.*

One day Fred was cussing forms (one of his pet peeves). He was mad at what he called those *nasty meemos*. He kept referring to the *good ol' days*. Suddenly he swung around in his chair and glared at me.

"What in H—— am I talking about! The good ol' days! I'll tell you what the good ol' days were like. You start up the trail dragging the pack stock behind you. About 3:30 am you start looking for a place to camp with good horse feed. You locate a place and unpack the stock. Then you peel off the saddles and put bells and hobbles on the horses, turning them out to feed. Then you start making camp and getting firewood. You drop everything and bring the horses back to camp. While cooking dinner you notice the bells stop ringing and you go after the horses again. Getting them back you restart the fire and finish dinner. Just before dark you bring the horses close to camp."

"Finally, bone-tired you crawl into your bedroll. Just as you drift off to sleep the bells become silent. Nothing will waken you quicker. You pull on your boots and chase horses half the night. When dawn cracks you're up and chasing horses again, sometimes walking three to seven miles. Hobbles didn't slow them nags. You feed them a handful of grain and then get breakfast. After currying and brushing, you saddle up. By the time you break camp, make up the packs and throw a few squaw hitches the sun is pretty high in the sky. Then you start all over again. That's what the good ol' days were like. Thank God they're long gone."

<u>Grover C. Blake</u> *Blake describes an incident that occurred while he was District Ranger on the Ochoco NF and one when he was District Ranger on the Umatilla NF.*

On July 3, 1920, I witnessed what I believe to be the most unusual of all the unusual spectacles of my career. I saw it with my own eyes and still I don't believe it, so I will not expect the readers of this tale to believe it either. I found a full grown horse fast in the forks of a tree.

Virgil Allison, foreman for Elliott, Scoggins and Wolfe, road contractors, and his wife were riding with me along the Vowell Trail near the summit of the mountain when we saw this horse in the tree not far from the trail. He was an unbroken range horse about three or four years old and probably weighed about 1100 lbs. The tree forked

170

about two feet from the ground and the spread at six feet was not more than 15 inches. The hind feet of the horse were on the ground on one side while his head, neck and shoulders were on the opposite side of the tree with the front feet about four feet from the ground. His body was wedged between the forks until he was pinched as tight as it was possible for him to get. His struggles had worn all the hair and most of the skin off his sides where they contacted the tree.

He tried to fight us when we came near. I took the axe off our pack horse and we started to chop off the smaller fork, about 16 inches in diameter. While we were so engaged, another man, Mr. Bill Peterson, came along and assisted. When the horse was finally released, he was in a bad way and very wobbly. He was able to keep on his feet, however, and soon wobbled away without saying *thank you*. No doubt he had been fast in the tree for at least two or three days.

The question that bothered us was *how did he get there*? The tree stood alone in an opening of considerable size and the only theory I could advance was that a bunch of range horses were standing in the shade of the tree, fighting flies as they would likely be doing at this time of year, and started fighting each other. This horse was cornered somehow and jumped at the only opening he could see. It took a tremendous leap to get his body high enough to get between the forks of this tree. However, it may have happened some other way, I do not know. I have always regretted that we did not have a camera on that day of all days as I realize I need proof.

[*Another horse story by Grover C. Blake*] On the afternoon of April 19, 1928, I was near Cloverland, in eastern Washington, and had just purchased a new saddle horse. I started to go through the mountains to Iron Springs Ranger Station [on the Umatilla NF] riding the newly purchased horse and leading my other saddle animal. Before reaching the edge of the timber on the Iron Springs side, I found myself in a blinding snowstorm and darkness was coming on. Soon the snowstorm, darkness, and the high wind which had sprung up created conditions like a Colorado blizzard. I was soon hopelessly lost. After a time, I knew I was in the settlements but could see nothing and could find no shelter. I passed by the Iron Springs Ranger Station gate without knowing it and kept going.

After a while I realized I was becoming exhausted and that the horses were tiring. I was soaking wet and badly chilled. I felt that I should keep moving to keep up circulation. The snowdrifts were quite deep by this time and it was quite a struggle for the horses at times to get through them. Just as I concluded that neither the horses nor I could keep going until daylight and I would have to figure out some solution quickly, I discovered we (the horses and I) were within a few feet of a building. It was painted red. If it had been white I could not have seen it. I found a door and entered a large barn with stock inside and plenty of hay.

Oh, how pleasant was the feeling to be inside out of that wind and blinding snow. I had some dry matches and got the horses located and fed. It was near midnight. I went outside to look for a house but in the storm, I had no luck. I returned to the barn and found some empty grain sacks and wrapped them around me and my wet clothing and became warmed up eventually. When daylight came, the wind had ceased and I soon got
myself oriented. I then made my way to Iron Springs to warmth, food and dry clothing.

It eventually occurred to me how stupid I had been. If I had changed mounts after the storm struck, the other horse would have taken me directly to Iron Springs Ranger Station. She had been owned by the Forest Ranger who preceded me on the District and had long known Iron Springs as home. I was once saved in a Colorado blizzard by a horse which took me to camp in the face of a blinding blizzard such as once were so deadly to travelers on the plains, and I knew how dependable a horse could be in such a situation. I had *goofed* again and paid dearly for not using my head.

Howard T. Phelps *Phelps describes an all-too-often occurrence while on an overnight pack trip. He was on the Chelan NF, in the late 1920s, at the time of this story.*

Early October in the High Cascades. Clear, sunny days; cold, sparkling night. [District Ranger] Frank Burge and I were camped well up Rock Creek above the Pasayten [on the Chelan National Forest], perhaps five hundred yards from the creek, in the lee of a small clump of alpine firs, near a cold bubbling spring. We were

172

snugly rolled up in our sleeping bags, sleeping the sleep of the just after a hard day's ride. A full moon cast pointed shadows from the firs which patched the valley and bathed the austere peaks which surrounded it with its cold, lovely light. The sky sparkled with a million stars.

Some slight movement roused me from sleep, and peering from under the flap of my sleeping bag I saw Frank propped up on one elbow with an ear cocked toward the lower creek.

"What's the matter, Frank?" I grumbled sleepily.

"Those double-darned horses. They're working down the creek. Liable to take off for home, hobbles and all. Gads! I s'pose I'll have to go get 'em, or we'll maybe be afoot." Frank continued to grumble in his beard, and to listen to the faint tinkle of horse bells on the cold air.

"I'll go get 'em, Frank." My voice didn't sound very convincing, even to myself.

"No. I'll go. But J----! It's cold."

"Sure is, I'll go." My voice was a little stronger but still not very convincing. It was so nice and warm in the sleeping bag.

"They're working down all right. May be to h--- and gone by morning. I'd better be going." Frank's voice sounded just about as convincing as mine.

Myself, thinking - Well, now, can't let Frank take all the responsibility. After all, it's his District, and he's the District Ranger, and we'll both be afoot without horses. But it's hellish cold - summoning all my willpower I threw back the covers and emerged into the cold night air. I pulled on boots and jacket, thinking - I won't bother with pants. I'll run myself into a sweat. I headed the horses about a mile below camp and herded them back up the meadows a little above camp and then started for camp and that nice warm sleeping bag.

I took a quick look to spot the clump of firs at camp. I saw a dozen clumps, and every one looked just like every other. The fire was out.

We had pitched no tent. Nothing to identify camp except a clump of fire. A cold wind was sucking around my bare shanks and my teeth were beginning to chatter. Thinking - now here's the devil to pay and no pitch hot. Can't call to Frank. He'll think I'm one sweet Ranger if I can't find my way to camp after a little excursion like this. But I sure can't afford to wander around looking for that sleeping bag very long.

Taking a bearing on a likely looking clump I headed toward it, and by good fortune and the grace of God I spotted the sleeping bags near another group not too far away. As I crawled gratefully into that nice warm sleeping bag and settled down to sleep, with Frank snoring a lullaby, I thought to myself - lost in the wilds within 500 yards of camp. What a fine Ranger you turned out to be!

FIRE: "The fire got away a time or two-"

Harry M. White *White describes his experiences as a District Six Office Fire Dispatcher in the 1920s.*

There was no District Office Fire Plan in those days, no fire dispatcher on the telephone day and night, and no fire cache. The District Chiefs were listed in priority order to receive night telegrams and phone calls. Long distance telephone service was poor. There were no buses, and this continued into the thirties, so that firefighters, hired through private employment agencies in Portland, had to be transported by train.

In the war years [WW I], and for sometime after the war ended, it was almost impossible to hire good men. I remember signing up 50 men for the Santiam in 1919, of which Supervisor Hall was able to use only 17. Later, when calls kept coming for men on the Portland Creek Fire on the Cascade, we hired 50 more of the hoboes and sent them to Eugene by train in charge of Julius Kummel. Julius wasn't able to get any of them to the fire; the long hike that had to be made was too much. It was on that fire that Chief of Operation A. 0. Waha and several other men had to immerse themselves in the creek to keep from being burned. The labor shortage was still so bad in 1920 that [Rainier NF] Supervisor Fred Brundage had only about 60 men on a 7,000 acre fire on upper Lewis River because additional men worth sending to that isolated area were not available.

Forest and Regional fire plans began to be worked out and improved, though we still had no organized units in the Regional Office for several years and, in fire emergencies, had to call on other Divisions promiscuously to help hire men and do other things we did not have time to do. Usually at such times I was the only man in the Fire Control Office, as the others were in the field. In 1929, when very large fires burned in Washington and later in Oregon, the many firefighters hired in Portland and other cities had to be transported by train. Bus transportation, which was much better, came later. In 1929 and other bad years large quantities of fire equipment had to be purchased after the fires started. This, of course, was handled by the supply officer in Operation.

Henry "H. E." Haefner *Haefner worked on the Siskiyou NF at the time of this story.*

The fire season during the summer of 1924 started early [on the Siskiyou NF]. We had lightning fires north of Rogue River in June and early July; something unusual up to that time. These fires were all under control by July 15 and we went along to the end of August without much trouble, with conditions about normal for that part of the fire season.

On the night of September 1, a dry lightning storm gave us 60 fires, spread over the length of the Forest, with every Ranger District having some. By hard work all of these fires but six were limited to small areas under ten acres. Six reached "C" size - more than ten acres.

On the morning of September 2, I left Grants Pass for Powers, since several fires were reported in that area and in those days no Ranger was stationed there. I arrived at Powers in the evening and contacted Tom Hayes, our fireman, who, with a small crew, had already controlled several fires and was working on the last fire reported in that area.

I left the next morning for Agness after further talks with Hayes and walked to the Thomas ranch on the South Fork of the Coquille, a short distance below the mouth of Rock Creek, a distance of 17 miles. Next day I walked to the Agness Ranger Station on Shasta Costa Creek, a distance of 27 miles. Next morning I helped get out men and supplies to fires in that District. At about 10 am the Supervisor asked me by phone to go to a fire in the *Craggies* west of the Illinois River and south of Collier Creek in a rough, poorly mapped region devoid of trails and with the actual location of the fire unknown because of smoke.

I got two young men at Agness, three saddle horses and a pack horse, some grub and a few tools and left Agness about 1 pm. We rode about twenty-five miles over a very poor trail via Lawson Creek and Horse Sign Butte and arrived at Collier Bar on the Illinois River about 8 pm, long after dark. During our ride across the ridge west of Horse Sign Butte we were able to locate the fire roughly as being about 2,000 feet in elevation above and two miles west of the Illinois River at Collier Bar and two miles south of Collier Creek. At Collier Bar I found a crew of six men under Jack Finch had been sent in from Kerby to meet me.

We got up very early the next morning and were ready to go to the fire before daylight. The deep holes in the river and the big boulders and bluffs in and along the river made traveling in the dark dangerous, so we had to wait for daylight. We went up the river a mile or more, wading it where necessary, and then started up the mountain to the fire, reaching it about 12:30 pm, about four and one-half days after it started.

Jack and I sized up the situation, then sent two men back to camp to get more food and to hunt out a way, as they went back, over which the horses could bring up the camp the next day. The fire had died down and was out in many places and our small crew made good progress mopping up the fire that afternoon and evening. That night we lay down to rest, without any blankets, at the head of a small creek in a little rocky canyon under the edge of the fire. There seemed to be little level ground around there among the rocks to bed down on. We ate some cooked beans with bacon and some frying pan bread - *dough gods*. We slept little.

At dawn we were on the fire again. The fire was dead in some places but burning briskly in others. At noon the two men arrived from our Collier Bar camp with food on their backs but they did not have the horses or the camp. They said the country was too rough and brushy

176

for horses to get the camp up to us. I sent them back for more food and told them to hunt out a route farther to the west away from the *breaks* to the river over which it might be possible to bring up the horses with the camp.

We fought the fire that day with good results but we were getting tired. The brush was very heavy, line building was slow and our tools were getting dull - too many rocks. That night when we quit we estimated that we had about one-fourth mile of line to build to encircle the fire. The fire here was backing downhill slowly and we expected to complete the line early the next morning. That night we lay down to rest, again without blankets, in a small alder swale, inside the fire line, that had been burned over during the afternoon. There was a little spring there so water was handy.

About midnight a strong dry wind came out of the northeast and whipped up fire all around us. It came back up the hill as a crown fire in the brush and went roaring over our lines to the southwest. We were safe in the alders but scared and were glad that nobody got hurt in the crown fire. At the break of day, Jack and I climbed to the top of the ridge and saw the fire still racing off to the southwest with the front a mile or more away. The wind had blown most of the smoke away, and we could see that we had lost the fire. The perimeter of the fire was now three or four times that of the night before and increasing rapidly.

Across the Tincup Creek drainage to the southeast we could see the Pearsoll Peak lookout house through the haze eight or nine miles away. If we could bring in men and supplies from Kerby around Pearsoll Peak and across the Tincup Creek drainage to the ridge we and the fire were on, it would be about fifteen miles shorter than to come in by way of Collier Bar.

We needed help and lots of it if we were going to control the fire. I told Jack that I would take a man and look out a possible horse route to Pearsoll Peak lookout and ask the Supervisor for help if we were going to control the fire. I asked Jack to take his men back to Collier Bar and try to bring up the camp and horses to this point or closer to the fire if he could and to work on this side of the fire while I was gone. I would return as soon as possible and help him.

I took the job of going to Pearsoll Peak myself because somebody had to go and I did not want to send men I did not know for fear they would get lost or get hurt and never get there. The fire was so large by now that our small crew could not make much headway to control it.

Jack divided the food and my man and I got about one-half of a *dough god* and a two-inch square piece of cheese for the two of us. We thought that we could get to the lookout and telephone by midafternoon. We started immediately. It was about 5:45 am. We traveled continuously through the heavy brush along the Tincup Creek divide until about 3 pm but became so thirsty that we gradually left the ridge and headed for the creek for water. We went up this creek past the high Tincup Creek falls until dark and layed out near the creek beside a small fire. We were on the move again at daybreak and finally reached the lookout house about noon, about 30 hours after we left the fire. We were tired, hungry, sweaty and dirty.

I talked with the Supervisor by phone from the lookout and told him about the rapid spread of the fire, its probable size in acres burned over, the number of men, in my opinion, needed to control it and the way to get to it. We then went down to the Anderson Ranch on the Illinois River to get something to eat for the lookout man was not too well supplied with food to feed two hungry men. I knew the people at the Anderson ranch but as my companion and I walked into their yard late in the afternoon they failed to recognize me. My whiskers were long and red and I was gaunt. Both of us looked like tramps.

I returned to Collier Bar where I found Jack Finch camped and still unable to get the camp up the mountain. Most of the fire was now miles away to the southwest. Jack was tired out. He was a good trail foreman for a small crew, a good mountain man and a good firefighter, but he was nearly 60 years old at that time and the rough trip, long hours, lack of rest and inadequate food wore him out. His men were nearly barefoot and their clothes badly torn. Food was running low and it took four days to get more from Kerby. Agness could not be depended on for food supplies. The Supervisor was sending in a new and larger crew by way of Pearsoll. Jack's crew patrolled the fire along the Illinois River and Collier Creek side until the food ran out and then returned to Kerby.

178

I found out later that the new crew missed the route to the fire from Pearsoll that I picked out for them and had such great difficulty cutting a trail through the brush that they never reached the fire. Jack's small crew, my two boys from Agness and myself were the only ones to ever reach the fire. It burned most of the time without anybody fighting it.

I took the two boys I brought from Agness, a saddle horse apiece and one pack horse and tried to go to the front of the fire or find out where it was, by way of Game Lake, Snow Camp and over the rough trail into *Craggies Camp* where I met the Ranger from the Chetco District and two men. This Ranger was a new man on the District that year and did not know the country very well. The fire was estimated to be about four miles northeast of the *Craggies Camp* through a sea of manzanita brush. There was no way to get there from this side unless a trail was cut through the brush which was impossible with the manpower and tools at hand. I returned by way of the Chetco River, Cedar Camp, Johnson Creek and the Anderson ranch. The rains came a few days later. The area burned over was estimated at 5500 acres. The loss of timber and young growth of fir and pine was nil. This was a brush country - manzanita and tan oak.

If we had had one more day of favorable weather or a few more men on the fire line it is possible that we could have completed our fire line, mopped up and held our lines. We got there too late with too little and did not get an extra break in the weather, so lost the fire. I lost about ten percent of my normal weight on that trip and had very little sleep or rest or enough to eat during the time I was on the fire or near it. My clothes were worn out and my shoes were ruined. However, I suffered no permanent ill effects from it.

<u>Lloyd E. Brown</u> *Brown began seasonal work on the Columbia NF in 1920. He received a permanent appointment in Fire Management in 1929. He worked in the Civilian Conservation Corps program on the Columbia NF and in the Regional Office, and supervised the Forest Service Aircraft Warning Service activities for the state of Washington during World War II. He was then Administrative Assistant for the Wenatchee and Mt. Hood NFs, and was the Regional Budget Officer when he retired in 1964.*

In 1924, the District had a project fire in the old Smoky Creek burn [on the Columbia NF]. As the road crew was camped at Little Goose Lake, we were the first crew on the fire. I was assigned to my first job as campfire boss; to order supplies, equipment, men and camp cooks. The fire got away a time or two so we finally had quite a crew on it. One of our problems on the fire was to obtain enough cooks. Finally the Ranger's office sent us two women cooks and four or five women flunkies. To prevent trouble between our men cooks and women cooks we set up another cooking unit and tables across the road from the other unit. This worked out fairly well except all the crews wanted to eat at the women's camp.

<u>Wilmar "W. D." Bryan</u> *Beginning in 1920, Bryan worked most of his career on the Olympic NF. He also had short assignments on the Mt. Hood and Snoqualmie NFs. He was Timber staff Officer on the Olympic NF when he retired in 1960.*

Most of my memories of the 1924-1930 period tie in with fires. I arrived at Quilcene [on the Olympic NF] about August 1924 [as District Ranger] in time to see a fire, starting at Dry Creek on the upper end of the Penny Creek road, sweep to the top of Green Mountain. Neither [District Assistant Bill] Vallad or I had had any previous fire experience. The fire reached a size of about 1700 acres. Most of the crew of about 150 men came from the Seattle *skid road*, a common practice continuing up to the time of the CCC programs. Many of the crew were slick-shod misfits, but there were a few experienced firefighters, and their advice in fire technique was a great help. In view of the present policy it is hard to believe that Vallad and myself were the only overhead. It rained hard on August 25 and resulted in the first real sleep either of us had had for the three weeks.

In July 1925, Snow Creek Logging Company celebrated the approaching end of their sale with a fire. It smoldered for several days before taking off through the Mt. Zion gap to the head of Deadfall Creek. Tom Talbott, R-6 Law Enforcement Officer, was at Quilcene. Since the fire was beyond the sale boundary he suggested District action. Gathering a crew of about fifteen *homeguards* we went up the Little Quilcene trail. The next day Doc Billingsley and about 30 men arrived. The fire was checked on the south side of the Zion gap. A few days later, with the crew in camp for lunch, we were disturbed by a sudden down-valley wind of considerable force and an unfamiliar

Forest Service Buick with fire tools on the Ochoco NF – 1920

One of the earliest Forest Service patrol planes
and crew on the Ochoco NF – c1920s

noise from the slope below us. Because of dense smoke covering the valley for several days visibility was limited to a few hundred feet. Charlie McClanahan went down to investigate and was back shortly with word that a crown fire was coming up the slope.

Throwing the tools in the creek, we headed for the Zion gap burn which had cooled to a point of reasonable safety as long as one didn't stand too long in the same spot. What happened was that the fire in Snow Creek had spread by way of Lord's Lake eastward along Green Mountain and west up the Little Quilcene in the matter of a few hours. I believe this was the first fire for the newly formed *Regional Flying Squadron*, a group of five or six experienced firemen who acted as overhead throughout the region. At any rate, there was help from other Forests. This was also my first introduction to gravity hose lines.

The first time that a fire crew was supplied by aerial drop was in 1929 when lightning fires hit at the head of Tunnel Creek. A crew of about 40 men were working out of a central camp on two fires in rugged country without trails. Included in the crew were Walter Lund and his party of cruisers which also included Allen R. Cochran. J. R. Bruckart, Assistant Supervisor, arranged for two [airdrops] on successive days. Both canned and fresh supplies were packed in burlap sacks together with blankets to offer some protection. The sacks were stacked in a cabin plane with Robert McClay of the Supervisor's staff acting as dropper, or perhaps bombardier is a better word.

The fire camp was located in a small meadow near the edge of a shallow pond. On the first trip the plane circled the camp to get a bearing. On the next circle the plane door flew open and McClay started kicking out the sacks with his feet while holding on to the inside of the plane with his hands. The first two sacks out were filled with bread and both landed in the pond. Bruckart and I had stationed ourselves on a ridge a short distance from and about 200 feet above the camp to spot the fall of the sacks. One sack landed near us and canned corn flew like shrapnel. These were free drops from an altitude of about 300 feet above camp to 50 feet where the plane crossed the Tunnel Creek-Dosewallips divide. Supplies came through in surprisingly good shape. In all, about 60 sacks were dropped in two days and all but one was recovered. The second drop included a copy of *the Seattle Times* with a vivid description of men surrounded by fire being supplied from the air. In the meantime, Frank Ritter, Forest Engineer, with a large crew were building a trail from near Corrigenda Guard Station to the ridge above the fire camp. This trail was built in about three days and from then on the camp was supplied by pack horses.

Les Colvill   *Colvill spent most of his career in Fire Management positions.   He worked on the Deschutes, Fremont, Okanogan, Olympic, and Siskiyou NFs.   He retired in 1958 while in the R-6 Regional Office in Fire Control.*

Centralized forest fire dispatching was the system of fire control practiced in Region 6 during the late 1920s.   The principle characteristic of this system was the reporting of fires to and the directing of initial fire action from one location on the Forest. Reporting was done mostly by telephone over Forest Service single #9 wire telephone lines.   Most of the reporting was by primary lookouts direct to a dispatcher located at the central location.   I was the fire dispatcher for the Deschutes National Forest during the period 1926 to 1931 and located in the Supervisor's Office at Bend.

The principle equipment used consisted of the telephone, plotting board (a steel plate on which was mounted a ½" mile scale Forest map with a 3/16" hole bored at the exact location of each fire finder), a 12" brass protractor, wall maps and filing baskets.   A wander type telephone was hooked up to a four-line plug-and-jack switchboard. The Crescent line terminated at LaPine.   The others came in direct to the switchboard.   Ringing was done manually and four rings was the fire call.

It will not be the purpose of this article to praise or condemn the central dispatching system, but instead to cite a few unusual incidents associated with my dispatching duties.   I mentioned the wander phone because it threatened to end my dispatching career in the early stages. Assistant Supervisor Bill Harriman shared the dispatching room with me and had installed a spring-operated foot pedal to the wander phone so as to cut out the transmitter when listening.   Obviously the pedal had to be released when transmitting.

I constantly got the procedure reversed and to satisfy my own ego doubted the value of such a hook-up. I could not convince Bill so one day when he was absent I disconnected the wire leading to the phone but left the pedal unchanged. The next day Bill had occasion to use the phone and I watched him carefully place his foot on the pedal and the pressing and releasing action required by the conversation. When he had finished, and not satisfied to let good enough alone, I asked if he was convinced the transmitter hookup improved his conversation. He said it did. I told him the hookup was disconnected and braced myself for the blow-up. True to Bill's eccentric manner he just sat quietly looking down and after a moment said softly, "You shouldn't have done that."

On another occasion I was talking to Walker Mountain Lookout approximately 60 miles distant and due to interference was having difficulty getting my message across. I must have been shouting pretty loud because Supervisor Carl Neal, whose office was two doors down the hall, came busting in thoroughly mad and asked who I was talking to. I replied, "To Walker Mountain."

He said, "Why don't you use the telephone?" and stalked out slamming the door.

My loud voice was not all bad. On occasions during a fire bust and with windows open, people would gather on the sidewalk and get fire information first-hand. Even now my wife reminds me to lower my voice when talking over the telephone, but I counter it was this voice coming through the open window of the dispatcher's office at Bend that caught her attention and proved irresistible.

<u>John G. Clousten</u> *Clousten was a Fire Dispatcher prior to his permanent appointment on the Umatilla NF in 1934.*

In 1927 I was put on the job of central dispatcher for the [Umatilla NF] where I stayed until the fall of 1934. This job was a man-killer. On the telephone from 6 am until 9 pm seven days a week from late June until fall rains without relief wore one thin and made one *edgy*. Hard physical labor is much easier. This came to be realized eventually as did also the facts that District Rangers were too

184

frequently not accepting their responsibilities in fire control. Also it happened that dispatchers were usurping the Ranger's direction of his short-term force and control was becoming confused. The system was generally abandoned in the Region about 1934 and 1935.

Don Snyder *Snyder was a trail construction foreman on the South Umpqua RD on the Umpqua NF in the late 1920s, working for Frank Ritter during Ritter's last year as District Ranger. He then went to work with the Southern Pacific Railroad for some 40 years.*

Willard Cook was at Fitzgerald Fire Station [on the Umpqua NF in 1928]. According to what I was told by Slick Barrow at Dummont Fire Station, Willard had been snoozing on his cot in the shelter there when he woke up about 10 pm. He heard a cracking noise as if a tree might be breaking up, so he called Barrows at Dummont and told him about what was going on. They agreed that he (Willard) should leave the receiver off the hook so if anything happened Barrows could hear the noise. Willard went out to try to locate the problem. A large tree nearby with diseased roots finally fell right across the shelter and across the bed and smacked the telephone. Barrows heard the noise of the tree hitting, then silence, so he got permission to go see. He found a badly scared Willard Cook, who promptly quit and never came back.

That is why I was asked to take over the station by Glen Voorhies. A while later Glen moved me and my belongings to a flat about where the old shelter had been. I found a nice large tent, a cook stove, built a fence around it and, of course, had a telephone on a tree. I got started improving things a little, such as building a hitch pole for horses. We (Barrows and I) cut a few dead snags - one with yellow-jackets under the bark.

One evening at almost dark, with the moon just coming up, I got a report from Tiller Ranger Station to get ready to go to a fire nearby, reported by Walter Lervill from Grasshopper Lookout. After waiting some 15 to 20 minutes, [the Ranger's wife] Gladys Ritter called to tell me that they finally decided that it was the moon coming up on the horizon through the snags on the crest of the mountain. Mrs. Ritter joked that it was the moon all right, and probably had a lot of *shine* with it. These were prohibition times; moonshine was considered an essential commodity by some of the local people on the South Umpqua.

Lyle Anderson *Anderson worked on the Mt. Baker and Siskiyou NFs and in the R-6 Regional Office. He was on the timber staff on the Rogue River NF when he retired in 1969.*

The summer of 1929 was a bad fire season on the Glacier District of the Mt. Baker. I was still in college and working as Headquarters Fireman. Ranger Ralph Cooke was spending the week with the Canyon Creek Trail crew. Supervisor L. B. Pagter was at Glacier at the time.

Soon after a lightning bust we started getting reports from our lookouts and several from the Canadian side of a sizeable fire on Fiddle Creek. Forty men were recruited and 30 head of packstock hired from Charley Bourne. A daylight start to the US Cabin on the Chillawak, 25 miles by trail, was scheduled. From there they would have to build seven miles of trail to reach the fire. We figured two and a half to three days at the best to get men on the fire.

Realizing that we had a bad one on our hands, Mr. Pagter wired Portland for instructions. That night the following five-word reply came from Fred Brundage, Chief of Fire Control: KEEP IT OUT OF CANADA. We did.

ECHOES OF 1929 *The following excerpts are from the District Six Newsletter, "Six Twenty Six" Volume XIV, Number 1, of January 1930.*

"In many ways 1929 served us poorly. It withheld our accustomed rain and snow and thereby harmed our ranges, retarded our tree growth and made our drouth-weakened trees more liable to insect damage. There was revived the charge by some irrigation regions that the lowered waterflow is due to sheep-grazing. Nineteen twenty-nine gave us a fire season of ferocious severity in many places, of huge losses and costs, and of unheard-of length. A seven-thousand-acre fire in the last days of November! The fire campaign put many of our men under a gruelling strain. And, of most vital concern, it took from us Doug Ingram, contributed heavily to the development of the disease which took Jim Huffman, and cost the lives of five of our fire fighters.

186

Nineteen twenty-nine will never be forgotten by District Six."
C. M. GRANGER, Regional Forester

Other news and comments in this issue include the following;

Colville Forest: Willis Ward reports reaching a forest fire on November 22, 1929, after walking across Empire Lake on ice. The fire was *a mile long and a quarter of a mile wide.* He returned to Republic and notified Ranger Buckley that the fire was on his District and he was welcome to it. Antifreeze was procured for the government truck to go to the fire. The weather had been zero for a week.

Rainier Forest: Otto Lindh reports the humidity at Currant Flat was 2% on October 31, east winds were blowing and about 1600 elk hunters were on the eastern side of the Forest.

Whitman Forest: Keith McCool reports finding an old bear and her two cubs that were killed by lightning while up a fir tree during a storm on August 1, 1929. The fire went out.

Colville Forest: While on the Dollar Mountain fire, Ira Jones left some duds in a laundry at Kettle Falls. A week later he returned figuring on a change of clothes only to find the laundry had moved to a different town, taking his clothes with them.

<u>C. Frank Ritter</u> *After his term as District Ranger on the Umpqua NF, Ritter worked on the Olympic and Columbia/Gifford Pinchot NFs. In 1956, looking back on his later years, he wrote, "Presumably, my most worthwhile accomplishment over the last twenty years has been the imparting of fire suppression techniques to the incoming younger men at schools for fire overhead and on the ground. It is estimated that I have personally trained not less than 1000 men, including cooperators, at these schools."*

In 1929 on August 5, while on a fire on the Olympic, the District Office called me to go to the Dollar Mountain Fire on the Colville. I was on fires every day from August 1 to December 1. Thanksgiving Day dinner was taken on the fire line. These fires were the Dollar Mountain, approximately 100,000 acres; the Chelan (incidentally the fire on which Doug Ingram was burned), acreage not known; and the Interrorem fire, 9,000 acres, on the Olympic. Fred Brundage was the Regional Fire Control man at that time.

John B. "Jack" Smith *Smith tells about fighting his first large forest fire.*

The Forks of the River (Acker Divide) fire [on the Umpqua National Forest] probably occurred in late September [1931]. I never got back to my road camp where I had worked. Most of my crew, including the foreman Carl Fisher, went to the fire. This was my first big fire.

The area had been a beautiful old growth stand of Douglas-fir when hit by a crown fire in the extremely bad fire year of 1910. I talked to a rancher who, with some neighbors, had tried to fight that fire but could do nothing but in his words, "to throw away his shovel and run like hell." Following the 1910 burn, the deer population mushroomed and the area was very popular for deer hunting until it brushed up. In 1931, 21 years after the crown fire, the area was mostly a sea of snags with a 20-year-old pole stand below. In the dry fall of 1931, the fire started near or, perhaps, on the Acker ranch; burned hot, spread over a large area and set spot fires in the snags a mile or more ahead of the main fire.

The road crew was the main firefighting force and made camp in the green timber a mile or so outside the old burn where the fire was raging. It burned on both sides of the Acker Divide trail for several miles and, of course, burned up the telephone line. Our camp was some ten miles from a road, and there was little or no food or bedding for a couple of days. Carl Fisher killed a deer with his Luger, and we ate boiled venison. For a couple of nights we envied Gene Rogers, the Ranger, who had his saddle for a pillow and a saddle blanket for bedding.

We had falling saws and several sets of fallers but there were too many snags, and it was apparent the fire movement was faster than the fallers. There was a decision to blast down a line of snags prior to building the fire line. Springboard holes were chopped in the snags, loaded with fast dynamite (I think 60% - maybe 40%). It was quite effective in getting the snags down, faster than with the two-man falling saws. But it was a fiasco. The snags were splintered, fell every direction, and when the fire got to them, it really burned hot and crossed the line.

H. C. "Chris" Chriswell *Chriswell tells a story that occurred when Fred Wehmeyer was District Ranger on the Chelan NF. After passing the Ranger exam, Wehmeyer received an appointment on the Okanogan NF and, over time, was Ranger on nearly every District of that Forest, and the Okanogan NF, which merged with the Chelan NF in 1920.*

When Fred was at Chelan, he was plagued with grass fires that burned up onto the Forest. He became expert at handling them. One dry summer day a fire broke out on the east side of Lake Chelan. Fred called the Supervisor at Okanogan and asked P. T. [Harris, Forest Supervisor] for 200 men. Remember, a Ranger was supposed to *calculate the probabilities*. The next morning P. T. sent 30 men to Chelan as the fire crowned up the mountain. By evening it became evident to Fred that P. T. considered 30 men more than enough to man the fire. He went back to town, marched into the theater, shut down the show and drafted every able-bodied man to fight the fire. It wasn't long before he was transferred to the small Touchet District on the Umatilla. One of the drafted men was a small town politician.

LOOKOUTS AND FIRE GUARDS: "The most exciting events I experienced were on the lookout."

Wilmar "W. D." Bryan *Bryan was a seasonal on the Olympic NF at the time of this story.*

My first job with the Forest Service and the Olympic [National Forest] started June 1, 1920, assisting A. A. Griffin, Forest Examiner, in relocating the Lake Quinault summer home lots. I recall discussions as to the size of the lot to be set aside for Forest Service use. The lot on which the present District Ranger's office stands was considered adequate to hold all future improvements.

Midsummer found me at Salonie Guard Station, Quinault District, hiking the gravel highway between the Forest boundary and Quinault watching for fire. My father, visiting for a few days, asked what I would use to put out a fire if I found one. I hadn't thought of that. He suggested I carry a shovel, which I did for the rest of the summer.

After a winter at school I returned to work in late May 1921. A windstorm the previous February had caused heavy blowdown extending from Quinault along the coast to near Lake Crescent. A special appropriation of about $300,000 had been provided for extra protection on this area of high fire hazard. Snider Ranger Station, designated as headquarters for the increased protection force and equipment, was a beehive of building activity where only a shake cabin had stood before. I arrived there in late May. Oliver Erickson, Assistant Supervisor, was in charge. The District headquarters were in Port Angeles where Chris Morgenroth was District Ranger.

A few days later I moved to Forks and the Peterson ranch as fire dispatcher. The Army Air Corps of Fort Lewis contracted to fly a daily patrol. Planes were equipped with radio to be used in reporting fires as soon as spotted. A receiving set was installed and manned by the Army Signal Corps at the Peterson ranch. The Peterson ranch was selected because it had the only cow pasture suitable for a landing field. The dispatcher, with Forest Service phone lines to the Hoh, Bogachiel and Snider, received reports of fires from the army operator and sent them on to the appropriate guard or crew. The set-up didn't work, mainly because radio equipment was quite crude in those days, especially transmission from the plane.

Grover C. Blake *Blake faced some fire detection challenges when he was transferred to the Malheur National Forest, and then again when he moved to the Umatilla National Forest.*

After serving as Ranger in one District for 15 years [1909 to 1924] during which time the boundaries were changed several times and the name changed twice [Blue Mountains to Deschutes to Ochoco], I was transferred to the Burns District on the NF with headquarters at Burns, Oregon. This was an automobile District and I had little use for the two good horses I had brought from the Ochoco. I could drive the car within walking distance of nearly any point in the District.

When I arrived at Crow Flat Ranger Station to take over the Burns District, there was no one to show me around or to introduce me to the

Fire lookout near Sisters on the Deschutes NF – 1921 – any volunteers?

new territory so I found my way around alone. There was a short-term man located at Calamity Guard Station near Drewsey and a lookout fireman at West Myrtle Butte on the opposite end of the District. When I reached Myrtle Butte on my preliminary rounds, I found it to be a butte covered with a heavy stand of mature timber with a commanding view when an opening could be found between trees. An Osborne fire finder was set up on a wobbly table about four feet high, constructed of small, round sticks wired together with emergency telephone wire. When a smoke was sighted, the lookout fireman would proceed to carry the table and fire finder to a spot from which the smoke would be visible between trees. He would set the table down and orient the finder as best he could, as the table wobbled and shook, then take a reading and report.

I sized up the situation and said to the guard, "Don't you think we can rig up a better setup than this?" He thought it might be worth a try. So we felled two fir poles about 75 feet in height and I prevailed on a road maintenance crew not far away to send a team and driver over and drag the poles over to one of the tallest trees. I found some lumber and nails and we made a 50-foot ladder and got it raised to the side of the tree. At the top of the ladder we built a platform. Then we made a 30-foot ladder and pulled it up the side of the tree until it rested on the platform. Now we were up 80 feet and another platform was made. About three feet above the upper platform we cut the tree top off and set up the fire finder on the stub. We now had a platform which did not wobble and in a permanent location. Three years later when I left the Malheur for the Umatilla we were still using the tree lookout. I have been informed that a steel tower later replaced our tree lookout on West Myrtle Butte.

[*Another story by Grover C. Blake*]

Figuring out a way to overcome handicaps became a way of life in the activities of early Forest Service personnel. I remember one instance where we were able to develop a lookout on a point having a commanding view of a large area of our protection unit after many frustrations. After serving as Ranger for 15 years on the Ochoco and several years on the Malheur where Walt Dutton was Supervisor, I was transferred to the Umatilla NF and to a District which lacked an adequate detection system. There were several guard stations manned by firemen who did patrol duty on horseback and visited points of observation to look for fires along their patrol routes, but there were no established lookout stations.

The point that seemed to me to be ideal for lookout purposes was known as Big Butte. The Supervisor felt this butte was not for us since it was on private land and outside the National Forest. I never liked to give up without a try so I went to the county seat and learned that the land belonged to Frank Farrish of Farrish Lumber Company. I then went to see Mr. Farrish and placed our problem before him. He was more than willing to cooperate and said they would gladly donate the land needed.

In due time I surveyed out the land and got a legal description of five acres and the land was deeded to the United States. Our troubles were not ended though. We learned that the taxes were several years in arrears and would have to be paid before *Uncle Sam* would have a clear title. I went again to the county seat and explained our troubles to the assessor and county clerk. They agreed to *forgive* the taxes on the five acres and clear the title. Then we learned that Uncle Sam could not accept a gift but could buy the land. A check was sent to Farrish Lumber Company good for one dollar in cash and the deal was closed and the top of Big Butte belonged to the United States.

There was much to be done before Big Butte would develop into the kind of a lookout we wanted it to be. It was a timbered mountain and it seemed that the best way to clear the view was to put the lookout and firefinder above the tree tops. This would require a 100-foot tower. When the workload provided the time, Assistant Supervisor Lester Moncrief came over from Pendleton and he and I headed for Big Butte.

After several weeks of work, setbacks, and frustrations, we completed a tower, surmounted by a snug eight foot cabin which housed an Osborne fire finder. I marvelled at the nerve of Lester as he placed the last shingle on top of the pyramid roof topping the little cabin 100 feet up, and sliding down to land on a staging he could not see!

Anyway, another world had been conquered.

<u>Ralph F. Cooke</u>   *Cooke worked for the Forest Service in South Dakota in the early 1920s and was hired on the Mt. Baker NF in 1924 as a Guard.   He was appointed Ranger on the Mt. Baker NF in 1926.   He worked on the Gifford Pinchot NF and was Timber Staff Officer on the Mt. Hood NF when he retired in 1959.*

In the spring of 1924, I applied to Supervisor Park of the Mt. Baker NF and was sent to the Sauk Ranger Station headquarters for the old Suiattle-Finney Creek District. The pay was $125.00 per month.

District Ranger John West was a hard-working ex-logger and natural woodsman. My station was to be the Finney Creek Guard Station, so after a few days the Ranger and I made back packs of about 60 pounds each and hiked 16 miles to the Station. The trail was impassable to horses until the guard got it cleaned out, which was not until late summer. My main job was a three-way patrol to watch for fisherman fires and go up on a lookout point in case of a lightning storm. One day I would patrol 14 miles up Little Deer Creek and back. The next day was an easy one - only five miles into Big Deer Creek and back. The third day I hiked out ten miles to the end of the telephone line and reported in.

On one of these latter trips West told me there had been a shooting in a town near the Forest and the sheriff was looking for a man that was supposedly headed into my area. I asked the Ranger what I should do, as I didn't have a gun. He said to, "Borrow one from the wanted man, as the sheriff said he was carrying two." The next few days I kept hoping I wouldn't meet this fellow and wondering what to do if I did meet him. He was caught before he got to the Forest.

<u>Thomas "Tommy" Thompson</u>   *Thompson started with the Forest Service in 1905.   He was a District Ranger on the Washington NF from 1909 until 1924, when it was renamed the Mt. Baker NF.   He continued as Ranger until he retired in 1943.*

The first big fire that I had on the Skagit District [on the Washington NF] was in Skagit Canyon in the year 1922 just above what is now Diablo. It was undoubtedly started by someone working on the tunnel which was to take water down through the mountain to the Newhalem powerhouse. The fire covered several thousand acres according to my memory.

The next big fire was eight miles up Big Beaver Creek on July 1, 1926. No one saw it until July 4th. It eventually covered about 50 thousand acres, as I recall. There were nearly 400 men on it in, two or three fire camps at one time. That was a lot of firefighters in those days. C. C. McGuire was fire boss. The fire burned until the rain came about August 20. However, there were men working on it until around the 1st of October. When we first obtained control of the fire it was not anywhere as large as it finally turned out to be. About the middle of July, I went all around the fire; there was a fire line completely around it and only two small smokes were visible, but during the night a hot northeast wind started the fire up and set it roaring over our heads. It's a wonder that someone wasn't killed. We had to go back into the burn in order to be safe. That wasn't the only blow-up. Three or four days later there was another hot wind and the fire went three or four miles. That first blowup occurred in the nighttime. There were several such runs at intervals. I think that it was the big fires in 1926 that started everyone thinking about discovering the fires more quickly and agitating for the establishment of lookouts. In 1926, the only lookout on my District was on Sourdough Mountain, so we had gone from the period 1917 to 1926 with only one lookout.

Harry M. White   *White describes the evolution from Fireman to Lookout-Fireman.*

Many of the firemen [in the late 1920s] were stationed in the valleys where their view was limited. Gradually they were moved up on secondary lookout points, where they could provide detection when not chasing fires. Thus the position of lookout-fireman was created and soon that title applied to a majority of the short-term positions. The employment of married men was also encouraged so that the wife could act as lookout when her man was sent to a fire.

Carroll E. Brown   *Brown began seasonal work with the Forest Service in 1928, with his twin brother Carlos (Tom), on the Columbia NF. He received a permanent appointment as a CCC Foreman in Wisconsin in 1934. He worked on the Wenatchee, Mt. Hood, Olympic, Gifford Pinchot, Siuslaw, and Fremont NFs, and the R-6 Regional Office. He was the Forest Supervisor on the Rogue River NF when he retired in 1967.*

I was then (1929) assigned to the Pine Creek Guard Station [on the Columbia NF], twelve miles east of Cougar by trail. Ranger Wang visited all of the outlying stations, including Pine Creek. I decided to treat him with an apple pie. I called Mrs. Campbell at the Lewis River Guard Station near Cougar for instructions. I made the pie, we tried to eat it, but gave up. It was awful. After the Ranger left, I called Mrs. Campbell and told her my sad story. Finally, she said, "Carroll, did you soak those dried apples before you baked them?"

I meekly said "No." That was my first and last apple pie that I have made.

Following the [trail and telephone line maintenance] work in the Mt. Margaret country [in 1930], I was assigned to Vanson Peak to help a carpenter build a lookout house. It was an Aladdin, 14 x 14 feet. The lumber was pre-cut, packaged in bundles for pack horses, and marked for its location on the building plans. It was packed from Spirit Lake to Vanson over the 37 switchbacks on Goat Mountain. After completing the house I stayed on as lookout for the remainder of the year. As lookout I received $4.00 per day with board.

Carl "Slim" Albrecht *Albrecht worked his entire career on the Mt. Hood NF, retiring in 1965.*

The most exciting events I experienced were on the lookout. The first year was 1930. The packer packed me into Beaver Butte on the Mt. Hood National Forest. No roads were in there then. When we got there it was just a knob sticking out on a ridge. The first thing I saw was a three-sided pole shack with shakes on the sides. I looked in - it was empty, no stove, no bed. That didn't bother me as I had been working trails and telephone lines before and slept out part of the time wherever we were at the end of the day. There was a telephone line coming into the cabin. The packer dug out a small phone and we set that up. Next he came up with a fire-finder. We set this up on a rock slide about 100 feet from the cabin where we could see north and east. We oriented it and unpacked my belongings. Besides my bedroll, I had a skillet and a kettle, also a canteen. My place to cook was out on the rock slide by the fire-finder. The place to get water was about a mile down the trail at a spring that cattle used every day.

196

Getting back to the lookout cabin, I slept on the ground. Next day I found some telephone wire so I cut some poles and hung them from the rafters, (yes, I had an axe and saw) and cut smaller poles and laid them across the other poles, cut some boughs for a mattress and that was my bed for the summer. I ate like a horse and kept the packer busy bringing groceries up every week or two. He was the only one I saw all summer.

I spotted several fires that summer but never got to go to one. Most were lightning caused. One strike hit close to the cabin while I was out at the fire-finder and melted the plates together on the end of the magnet [on the phone]. I had to cut them apart with my pocket knife so I could ring in to headquarters at Clackamas Lake. Another struck the fire-finder and turned it upside down on the ground. Luckily I wasn't standing there at the time. It got pretty cold up there, but cooking outside, I always had hot rocks to put in my bed to keep warm.

The second year up there was a lot more eventful. I got a five-gallon can to pack my water in and bought a sheepherder stove, and talked the Ranger into letting the packer pack me up a steel cot. That was quite a luxury. I also had a 22 revolver and when I was lucky I would get a grouse to supplement my bacon.

There was this cougar that would follow me when I went after water. The trail being dusty where the cattle walked, I would see the cougar's tracks in my track when I came from the spring. I tried all summer to get to see him. I would hide in the brush, or I would wait on a high point overlooking the trail, but never got to see him.

Bears would visit the spring also. I would get to see them once in awhile. I had a camera that year and tried to get a picture of them but could never get close enough. One day when going after water, I saw what I thought was a big black cow coming through the pole patch. I kept going and looked up. It was not a cow but a huge bear! It did not see me, or hear me, and we met on the trail. I hollered at him and he gave a big woof and took off down through the trees on a dead run, then turned around and came back to the trail. He reared up on his hind feet and came toward me. I let him get within about 15 feet from me, and I figured I must do something so I fired my 22 over the top of his head. He let out a woof and took off down through the pole patch, but turned around and came back again three more times. Each time I would fire over his head. The last time he followed alongside about 30 feet away frothing at the mouth and snapping his teeth. He followed until I came out in the opening at the lookout, then sat there swinging his head back and forth. A few days later, an Indian rider came by and I told him about the bear. He said, "Oh, you seen that old grizzly!" It scared me then, but I never saw him again.

The tracks of his front feet were as large as a dinner plate and the toes of his hind foot tracks were longer than my shoe tracks and I wear a size 12 shoe! When he reared up on his hind feet, it looked like I could lay my two hands spread out between his ears.

Corwin E. "Slim" Hein *Hein relates several stories about smoke-chasing and lookouts.*

Experienced smokechasers used many ingenious ways of finding and putting out fires. The most unique example in my memory was when Frank Stratton was sent alone to control a small lightning fire. When he arrived at the fire it was confined to a small spot about 30 feet from the ground in a large ponderosa pine. Frank, being inclined to use his head to save his hands, sized up the situation. With his gallon canteen on his back he climbed a nearby jackpine and by swaying the jackpine came near enough to the spot fire to dunk it with a small amount of water on each swing. Several sways and several dunks later the fire was out, and no doubt that big ponderosa pine still stands. I suppose this could have been called a one-gallon fire.

Smokechasers must have been a hardy race in those days. Hardhats, walkie-talkies, pumpers and borate planes were unknown. One or two men were dispatched to small fires and were expected to find and extinguish them without further help, and in most cases they performed up to the Ranger's expectations. I recall very few accidents or serious injuries among the smokechasers.

With today's [1971] swing toward aerial fire detection and the wholesale removal of lookout stations as being of no further use, it will be surprising to the under-30 group to know that in 1930 the pendulum was at the opposite end of its swing and nearly all firemen were being *kicked upstairs*. Construction of lookout facilities was being rushed in every quarter, and hardly a township of the Forest was without its lookout-fireman atop a likely butte or pinnacle. Even lowly Pilot Butte on the fringe of the desert was manned, although no permanent structure was ever built there.

The strategy was to have 100 percent detection coverage and a fireman within 30 minutes of any possible fire. Sitting on a lookout irked some of the old guards who had for many years been located at a comfortable ground station.

A keen spirit of competition for first discovery and rapid travel time to fires soon developed and the lookout-fireman system proved to be extremely efficient and effective. The lookout's day was made if he got a first discovery on a fire in another lookout's territory. There was no overtime or fire differential pay in those days. Pay was $90 to $100 per month for 31 long days, and you were lucky to get a trip outside for supplies after daylight hours at intervals of 15 to 20 days.

GRAZING: "Demand for range was heavy at this time."

John G. Clousten *Clousten worked on the Umatilla and Fremont NFs and in Personnel Management and Range and Wildlife Management and in the R-6 Regional Office.*

Having been graduated in Animal Husbandry with emphasis on beef production, I was, naturally, interested in grazing although my technical training in that aspect of the business was meager. In fact, few men in Region Six at that time had the qualifications and training we now consider necessary to do a good range management job. In the mid-twenties, Button, Horton, Peterson and Ingraham were working on range appraisal and trying their best to give to Rangers and others what knowledge they had of the fundamentals of forage management. It was a rough task. Dealing with people who had no concept of plant-soil-animal relationships and who believed in but didn't know the Aristotelian theory that plants fed from the roots, they had two strikes on them before they began.

Indeed, not only this region but the whole Forest Service was permeated with misconceptions of the degree of use under which forage plants could survive. A stock saying of the time was, *The opens and flats are grazed pretty short but the stock haven't used the timber feed yet.* The key area, key-species concept and the selective grazing nature of animals was not yet recognized.

Another factor working against good management was the annual authorization letter sent to each Supervisor. This letter authorized the grazing of a definite number of cattle units and sheep units on each Forest and that number could not vary more than ten percent either way from the previous authorization. Most Supervisors took this as a requirement that the full number be grazed and many livestock associations and individuals knowing about it insisted that the authorization be filled. Consequently there was no opportunity to take advantage of dropouts to reduce the use because the vacancy was filled by issuance of temporary permits which accrued to preference in three years.

Demand for range was heavy at this time too because this was an era of large sheep numbers. It seemed that every new Irish immigrant could, within two or three years, acquire a band of sheep. It mattered little whether he had feed for them. He could always trail them from one small leased plot to another, more often than not on National Forest driveways. Many bands spent nearly the entire summer on the driveways of the Umatilla, Malheur, Whitman and Wallowa Forests going and coming from small leased headquarters. Private range land was at a premium and twenty-five cents an acre rental was a common fee. Naturally the sheep took the last mouthful.

No one can now be blamed for such conditions. There was ignorance throughout the Service and the livestock industry of what was happening.

NOTES from "THE OCHOCOIAN", (Newsletter published by Ochoco NF), February 1928. *The following two excerpts are reprinted from TIMBER-LINES.*

February 15 was the final date for accepting grazing applications. In totaling up those on hand, we find that we have applications for 101,884 sheep, 11,053 cattle and 263 horses. This shows a decided swing to sheep. Cattlemen have apparently sold down so low that there are insufficient numbers to take up all of the range; hence it looks like another case of granting temporary sheep permits on at least some portions of the cattle ranges for the season 1928. We prophecy that by 1929 there will be at least nearly enough cattle to fill out the estimated carrying capacity. It will be a fine thing to hold the numbers to the minimum again for the coming season so that we will be getting prepared for an intensive division of range and intensive management which will surely follow within another year or so if stock prices continue good. - V. V. Harpham, Forest Supervisor

Since W. J. Hodgson, "Curly" Hodgson, and the Williams Land and Livestock Company have proved that it is practical to run sheep on the dry range in the Dry Mountain section by hauling water for them, we have applications for twice as many sheep as there is room for. This spring the Williams Company propose to open up the remainder of the unused range on the south side of Big Ridge by building four additional miles of road to be used in hauling water for sheep. This new strip can be used early in the season, perhaps June 1 to June 30. Water will be hauled a distance of 2-1/2 miles. A small fee will be charged for use of this unit during the coming season. - E. W. Donnelly, Forest Ranger, Snow Mountain District

Gilbert D. Brown *Brown was Forest Supervisor on the Fremont NF for 21 years, from 1910 to 1931.*

The wild-horse problem on and adjoining the Fremont NF was solved by a big roundup and sale. After advertising in the newspapers that all unpermitted horses found on the Forest would be rounded up and sold unless claimed by their owners, I proceeded to secure three men who were skilled in such work and started the roundup. Some of the horse owners thought that it could not be done so were not in too much of a hurry to get their unpermitted stock off of the range. However, we gathered approximately 300 head of horses proving that it could be done. I was accused of hiring horse thieves for doing this work and in one instance this may have been true! Some of the horses were claimed by the owners who paid $5.00 per head to cover the cost of gathering. The rest, mostly unbranded and of little value, were sold and removed from the area.

George M. "Mike" Palmer *Palmer began his Forest Service career as a lookout on the Whitman NF. He was appointed Forest Ranger in 1926. In addition to the Whitman NF, he held District*

Ranger positions on the Malheur and Fremont NFs. He retired from the Fremont NF in 1959 or 1960.

In 1928 I went to Unity as the District Ranger of Burnt River District. I had a good farmer background and the Forest Service grazing regulations, technique and policies were really my dish. I spent a lot of time, both official and personal, studying and applying these techniques, policies and regulations. Several of the permittees were sure I was wrong and one fellow remarked, I remember his words real well, that the trouble with the Government regulations was that some young fellows didn't know any better than to believe them. John Kuhns ran the Whitman in those days and John believed in decentralized administration. So I fought it out mostly on my own knowing that I had good backing if my judgment and decisions were up to par.

RECREATION: "Which would you rather have, sheep or recreationists?"

Fred Cleator *The Seattle Times printed an article about Cleator on January 8, 1956, on the occasion of his retirement. The following excerpts are from that article.*

Cleator was among the first government foresters in [the state of] Washington. He was instrumental in defining some of the boundaries of this state's National Forests. He did much of the original reconnaissance of the Pacific Crest Trail and named approximately 500 obscure lakes and other places in the forested areas of the state. He made a similar record in Oregon.

In 1919, he was assigned to recreation planning for the Forest Service. In this capacity he laid out summer home sites in Rainier (now Snoqualmie) National Forest and on the White and Naches Rivers.

"That was the start of summer-home work. We backed the home-sites away from the highway, out of the dust. Instead of using engineering lines, I made plats to fit river and shoreline, providing isolation, but not too much of it. I found that persons who thought they wanted to get away from it all, soon got too much of being alone. I made it so they could see a light in the distance."

Driving for pleasure through big pines on the Deschutes NF – 1925

"I also prepared a formula reserving at least a third of each area for public use; the summer-home people and the concessionaires talked loudly, but the picnickers hadn't a voice. I wanted them taken care of. Our plan has paid off big."

The Columbia Highway just had been developed and the demand was for another road between Crater Lake and Mount Hood through the National Forests. Cleator was selected to ride through the area and see if such a route was feasible. He had nine horses, a packer and cook. Sometimes a Forest Ranger joined him for a time. The party followed disconnected trails made by miners and Indians and Cleator put out signs the entire length of the Skyline Trail, later part of the Cascade Crest system. He also stocked lakes with trout taken to road ends in hatchery trucks. His means of communication was carrier pigeons.

"My report did not say it was impossible to build the road," Cleator says, "but I warned that some years one could not get over it. The idea gradually petered out." In 1927, Cleator did similar exploration in Washington, walking from Darrington to Lake Chelan.

George Jackson *Jackson began with the Forest Service as a part-time office boy for the District Office in Portland in 1917. In 1920 he became a member of seasonal timber cruising parties where he worked on at least nine different Forests. He received a permanent appointment on the Deschutes NF in 1937. In 1950 he became the Regional Check Scaler for Region Six, and from 1957 to his retirement in 1966 he coordinated scaling activities in the six western Regions and the Alaska Region.*

Around 1920 a popular week-end trip and hike was to climb Larch Mountain [on the Mt. Hood National Forest] to watch the sun come up over Mt. Hood. Transportation from Portland was by the *Oregon, Washington Railroad and Navigation Company*, now the Union Pacific Railroad. Trains would leave the *City of Roses* in late evening and arrive at Multnomah Falls about midnight. The hike over the Larch Mountain Trail was timed to arrive at a viewpoint on Larch Mountain right at sunrise. There were no roads into this area in those days.

The original lookout tower on Larch Mountain, in 1920, consisted of a small cabin built on top of two large, tall Douglas-fir trees that had

Transferring a camp outfit from a hayrack to boats on Odell Lake for transport to the head of the lake, Deschutes NF – 1920
(Photo by Fred Cleator who has stories in Chapter One, Joining Up and Fire, and Chapter Two, Recreation)

Throwing a diamond hitch, Umpqua NF – 1930

been topped. To reach the cabin, a stairway zigzagging from one tree to the other from the ground to the top was built. On a windy day the tower would sway giving the occupants quite a thrill. Some years later a modern tower replaced this old one.

Ralph F. Cooke *Cooke was a headquarters fireman on the Mt. Baker NF in 1925.*

One day while working in the office on fire reports I heard [Mt. Baker NF] Supervisor Park and Ranger [John] West in a discussion of opening a range in the head of the Suiattle River to sheep. I heard the Supervisor say, "John, which would you rather have, sheep or recreationists?"

The Ranger shifted his Copenhagen a time or two, then answered, "Sheep, by gosh; they furnish a herder with them."

TIMBER: "I was appointed as timber sale officer."

Harry M. White *White transferred from the District Office in Operations to the Columbia NF as head clerk in 1920.*

My first impressions of westside logging [on the Columbia NF in 1920] were anything but good. Operations were in progress in the Wind River Valley and at the west side of the Forest outside, and on small sales inside. Early loggers had come from the *Lake States*, where they had driven the rivers. Rather than construct an expensive railroad from the Columbia River some 20miles to their main camp, the Wind River Lumber Company had elected to drive the river, even though this meant taking the logging locomotives and donkey engines apart and hauling them, with all other equipment, by teams and wagons over a very poor road. It was not a profitable operation. Much of the cedar was smashed and numerous fir logs were damaged. I understood that in nearly a quarter century of operation, before it finally quit, the company never declared a dividend.

In those days, of course, logs were yarded and loaded with wood-burning donkey engines. The locomotives also burned wood. It seemed impossible to get spark arresters that would completely prevent the escape of sparks. Most of the timber stands were defective and, under prevailing market conditions, close utilization could hardly be practiced. Many trees were left standing as not worth cutting, and any logs not deemed one third good were left in the woods. Logging methods knocked down most of the under-sized trees. The result of all this was an unholy mess.

I was amazed at the chances the loggers took with fire. They were there to get out logs as fast as possible - to *highball*. Fooling around with fire prevention equipment and using enough time and men to do a good job at slash burning were not popular. Sometimes engines had to be shut down because the fire prevention and suppression equipment required by timber sale contracts and state law was not in place. It was very difficult to get slash burned at what was judged to be the proper time, and if an accidental fire started, it was almost impossible to keep action going on it until it was out. Loggers would fight like demons to stop a fire, and even risk their lives to save equipment, but mopping up was something else. As a result there were instances, too numerous to detail here, where large areas were burned, with heavy losses to the loggers and the government, by fires that either should never have occurred or should have been confined to small areas.

During those years little attention was given to seedlings and saplings by loggers and the public generally. These baby trees were often spoken of as brush and, especially in the ponderosa pine region, there were advocates of light burning to get rid of the *brush*. It was common for newspaper reporters, writing about fires that did not spread to mature stands of green timber, to say there was no damage. Many people seemed not to understand that we couldn't have adults if we killed the children.

Sanford Floe   *Floe began seasonal work on the Rainier NF in 1919. He was appointed District Ranger on the Deschutes NF in 1922 and transferred to the Olympic NF in 1927 where he was a District Ranger until his retirement in 1959.*

Early March 1920 I was part of a crew sent to the Cispus [on the Rainier National Forest] to set up a planting camp. [The Cispus area experienced major fires at least twice in the early 1900s - once in 1902 and again in 1918. The 1918 fire covered over 50,000 acres. See Ranger John Kirkpatrick's experience on this fire in Chapter One.] Everything was brought in by pack string. The camp was at the *Claybank* a mile or so above Camp Creek on the bank of the river.

When camp was set up I returned to Randle repairing the telephone line on the way. There I met [District Ranger] Ed Fenby and Julius Kummel for the first time. [Kummel was the Chief of the Section of Planting in the Office of Silviculture responsible for reforesting large burns.] One morning the crew assembled at McKay's Store and I overheard Ed Fenby reporting to Supervisor G. F. Allen in Tacoma by telephone. In answer to some question by the Supervisor about the crew Ed remarked, "Part of them are setting around the stove telling stories of the Civil War and the others are playing marbles in the street."

We followed the pack string into camp. The mules were loaded with trees and grub. The crew carried their bedrolls and personal effects. There were about 24 planters. The camp was considered luxurious as we had tents with Sibley stoves and kerosene lanterns. I was informed the old-timers got along with a brush wickiup and an open fire in front. We were divided into two crews and trained in planting by Fenby and Kummel.

Wilmar "W. D." Bryan *Bryan worked for the Forest Service for about 40 years, mostly on the Olympic NF.*

In the fall of 1922, I had taken the Ranger's examination and was appointed the following spring, 1923, as Timber Sale Officer on the Quinault Shingle Company sale [on the Olympic NF]. Their mill was at Neilton. This sale was for dead cedar from an area then known as the Quinault Burn, extending from about the Salonie Guard Station to Neilton and westward in places almost to the Indian Reservation boundary. Most of the burn was well stocked with small saplings. The cedar was removed either in bolt form with horses or in logs by ground-lead donkey and thence by narrow gauge railroad to the mill. Considering the heavy volume of cedar removed the reproduction came through in good shape.

[District Ranger] Hartsuck resigned the fall of 1923, and as the only other employee on the District, I was designated Acting District Ranger until Joe Fulton arrived from Quilcene in July 1924. The principal sale during the winter was the Furness sale on Canoe Creek. This was a selective cut sale of sorts, since only the most decadent cedar was marked for cutting, yarded by horses and towed to the

Bailey mill located at the lower end of Lake Quinault near the site of the present Indian Service headquarters. Travel to the sale area was by Forest Service boat. The boat, formerly a captain's gig with service in the Canadian Navy proved unwieldy for a single oarsman. To offset this, the District had purchased an outboard motor, possibly the first motor built by Evinrude. A typical lake crossing started with 30 minutes or more in attempting to start the motor, finally resigned to rowing with pauses for further goes at the motor with success usually attained a few hundred feet short of the opposite shore. The homeward voyage was frequently a repeat performance.

<u>Walter J. Buckhorn</u> *Buckhorn was in government service nearly 40 years. He was an Entomologist with the R-6 Regional Office when he retired in 1962. In 1961, he received the first Annual Forest Protection Award from the Western Forestry and Conservation Association. This story was published in TIMBER-LINES in 1962.*

In the 1920s when Walt was first employed on a Forest insect survey and control project, he conceived and advocated aerial surveys as being better and less costly than the ground methods then in use. He emphasized that early suppression is the key to control of insect outbreaks. In those early days he purchased an airplane and became a pilot and airplane mechanic in an effort to demonstrate the practicability of his idea. Loss of the airplane in a crash in which Mr. Buckhorn was not involved postponed the day of aerial surveys for 20 years.

<u>Corwin E. "Slim" Hein</u> *Hein tells some stories about "bug hunting."*

Insect enemies of the forest were created for a purpose, no doubt at the same time trees were created. Early in this century, forest managers becoming concerned with the bugs' depredations, researched, studied and began control measures. The old-timers were mostly concerned with the infestations of western pine bark beetles in the ponderosa stands of eastern Oregon. Because the technical name *Dendroctonus brevicomis* was too unwieldy for the woodsman of that time, the term *brevi* or just plain *bugs* was used. Early Rangers were instructed to be on the lookout for beetle infestations and report their findings. The story among the old *bug hunters*, as the beetle control men were dubbed, was of the early-day Ranger who glued a *brevi* to a paper and submitted it to his Supervisor with the following bit of doggerel beneath:

> This is the beetle dendroctonus,
> The killer of the pine.
> He lives on pitch,
> The son of a -----;
> And to kill him will take a long time.

His observations were more true than he realized. In spite of all the control measures taken, the *brevi* is still very much alive.

Autumn of 1929 brought the first bug control projects on the Deschutes in the Fox Butte burn of 1926. The fire-weakened timber was heavily infested with *brevis*. Control procedure was to make a 100 percent cruise of the project area with a team of one compassman and two spotters who marked the trees and located them on an eight inch-to-one mile map sheet. Treating crews of from two to four men followed later, falling marked trees and peeling the bark on the top two-thirds of the log, and with the aid of pitchy wood or dry needles placed under the log, burning the bark sufficiently to kill the over-wintering brood of bugs.

Living accommodations in the camp were meager, with six to eight men in a squad tent with a Sibley stove in the center and bedrolls on the ground. Can't remember that I ever slept more soundly, though. Water was hauled in from Cabin Lake Ranger Station in barrels, and our bathing facilities consisted of tin basins and *Lava* soap on a wash-bench of poles. There were no R&R trips to town, and after several weeks in camp the B.O. index was pretty high! Who could tell, though, when everyone smelled the same? These long tours in the woods did a lot in the way of family planning, however. There was no population explosion in those days.

In 1930, the Deschutes had a bug project near Long Butte, again treating timber in the 1926 Fox Butte burn area. Two feet of snow fell one night, collapsing the World War I squad tents we were living in and making us snowbound for the ensuing two weeks. Hiking was a bit difficult, but work never stopped. Finally Mart Baty, an old Fort

Rock homesteader, and Mr. Buckholz, a Bend trucker, left Bend with a load of groceries but were forced by deep snow to stop that night 15 miles short of our camp. They had lots of grub but no cooking utensils, so Mart, an ingenious cuss, started flaking off a square-point stable shovel Buck had on the truck. Buck asks, "Whatcha gonna do with that?"

"Fry some bacon and eggs." Mart keeps on chipping.

"I won't eat 'em," declares Buck. Mart, when telling of it later, said, "When he smelled the bacon frying, his belly got the best of him."

They reached camp the second evening with the groceries, most essential of which was salt. We had run out of salt a week before and Avon Derrick, being raised on a cattle ranch, 'lowed we'd sure lose our calves if we didn't get some salt pretty soon.

Every bug hunter aspired to become a member of the spotting crew, as this was considered less arduous and more interesting than felling trees and chipping bark. It was an unwritten law that to become a spotter one had to eat some brevicomis larvae. Now, this isn't as bad as it sounds. The larvae is pure white, about the size of a grain of rice, and all its life has dined on nothing but good clean pine bark. The flavor is very much like that of pinon pine seeds. It's really little different from eating shrimp.

M. M. "Red" Nelson *Nelson began working for the FS in 1930. For the next few years he worked summers with cruising crews on the Olympic NF, in eastern Oregon and in Alaska. He was a prolific contributor to TIMBER-LINES. He received his permanent appointment on the Mt. Baker NF in 1935 and was a District Ranger on the Siskiyou NF and Timber Staff Officer on the Umpqua NF. He went on to hold Fire Control positions in the Washington Office and in R-5, was Regional Forester in R-9, and was a Deputy Chief in the Washington Office when he retired.*

In the 1920s and '30s the Regional Offices of the Forest Service had summer timber cruising parties to cruise large areas on different National Forests. Cruising parties made a rather accurate contour map by running strips on the ground - usually two per 40 acres - and measuring or estimating the diameter and height of trees on the strip

211

and recording it by species. This, of course, was before use of aerial photos. The summer parties were made up of college students in forestry.

The parties were headed and camps run by the head Regional Timber Cruiser. In District/Region 6 it was Fred Matz. He gave special training to the students. A student job on the cruising party was considered most desirable - his first chance to work at *real forestry* as opposed to fire control jobs. Many of the later FS leaders served in such cruising parties and were sometimes referred to as *the boys* of Fred Matz because Fred had made some of the early appraisals of the student's ability to advance in the Service.

I worked in such cruising crews in the Northwest and Alaska. The camps were most often way back in the country (often beyond end of roads). They were made up of 10 to 15 summer forestry students, the boss and a cook. There were few visitors. Mail did not come often - perhaps every two or three weeks. There was no radio to listen to and it was before days of TV. Crews went to camp for the summer - there was no *going to town*. Thus the need for making their own entertainment. Half the fun must have been doing it without the knowledge of their stern boss.

My first job in such a timber cruising camp was in 1930, the end of my sophomore year. It was on the Hoh River (now in the Olympic National Park) on the Olympic National Forest under the leadership of Lester McPherson, a recent graduate. It was real *back country* in those days. I got to camp by taking a ship (over-night) from Seattle to Port Angeles. The FS met us in a truck and we drove down the west side of the Olympics a short distance below Forks to the end of the road. We then took our backpacks and headed up the trail. Being an area of very high rainfall, much of the trail was such muddy country that the trail was covered with *puncheon*; split poles laid across the trail like railroad ties except next to each other, upon which we walked. We did not get to our camp that night, but stayed at the *stump ranch* of a German couple who had homesteaded on a meadow. They fed us both dinner and breakfast, and we slept in their hayloft.

The next day we hiked up the Hoh River to our first camp. It was strictly a tent camp with sleeping tents plus a larger one for a combination of cooking, dining and storage. The table was of cut poles upon which was rolled a top made of canvas with staves made of lath. That was so it might be rolled up for moving to next camp. It was covered with the usual oilcloth. The camp was moved a number of times in summer to keep us closer to our work. A few days before each move some of us would go to the new camp site to cut wood to dry for the cook and cut poles for the tables, tents, etc. The cooks were always very good (including baking) but most often were alcoholics trying to stay away from the booze for the summer.

Each sleeping tent had a Sibley stove for keeping warm on cold nights. That type of stove was like an ice cream cone set upside down with stove pipe going straight up. There was no bottom - it sat upon the bare ground. It had a small door for putting in wood and a small hole for draft which was controlled by how much dirt you put in front of it or over it. It made a good hot fire quickly. Many nights, even though not cold, we would build a fire in the Sibley so we could sit about it and spit on the hot side to listen to it sizzle. Again, homemade entertainment! That went with storytelling. We called it *Lying and Bragging*.

We had not camped on the Hoh too long before the FS packer came in on a Saturday (we worked six days per week) with mail and supplies. He had a couple of cougar-hunting hound dogs. He went on up river to Jackson Guard Station where there was grass for his mules. Before noon on Sunday, District Ranger Sanford Floe came into camp with his horses. He unpacked and prepared to stay for Sunday dinner, a big affair in the camp served in the early afternoon.

The phone rang and it was the packer to tell the Ranger that he had killed a cougar that morning. We had never heard of anyone eating cougar meat, but apparently it was common in the Olympics. The Ranger said, "Put it in the pan." He saddled up and left before the big dinner was served. We decided it must surely be worth eating and delicious besides. Later the packer gave our camp a hindquarter of the cougar. The day we were to serve it we had an inspector from the Regional Office, one George Drake. I recall we considered him an *old man* and wondered if he could keep up with us as he went to accompany my group for a day in the field. (He just died and I now learn that he must have been only 37 at that time!) In trying to make some fun for ourselves we decided to keep it a secret from him that he would be eating cougar that night. It backfired because he was wise to the ways of those woods and recognized it as cougar on the first bite. Actually it was very tasty meat, between beef and pork.

ENGINEERING and CONSTRUCTION: "I remember the excellent abilities and expertise of the two men who built the bridge."

John R. Montgomery *Montgomery describes an early-day bridge building project.*

For many, many years Big Camas Ranger Station, located on the Umpqua National Forest of southwest Oregon, was accessible only by horse trail. In the second decade of this century Forest Supervisor Carl B. Neal recognized the need for improved access and a road from Diamond Lake to Big Camas was initiated. Beginning at Diamond Lake, heading west through pumice flats covered with lodgepole pine, it crosses gentle terrain and many small streams over its 25-mile length.

Prior to 1925 the road had been completed to within eight miles of Big Camas. A camp was established about half-way through the unfinished section at Cedar Springs on the Fish Creek burn in the spring of that year. Several smaller streams had been crossed with low log bridges, but the biggest remaining obstacle remained. Fish Creek, a major tributary of the North Umpqua, required a concerted effort in men and material to complete the span.

Deputy Forest Supervisor George Bonebrake was the project manager. C.C. Hon was the camp superintendent and Nora Wilson the camp cook. There were approximately 25 total crew members. Elmer Brooks and Fred Krowcher did the bridge building. Others felled and bucked the Douglas-fir timber and made planking for the 84-foot Howell design span. My job was to skid the timbers from the woods to the bridge site, about half a mile using a team of horses.

The only timbers I couldn't handle were the two main stringers that were 12 inches by 24 inches by 84 feet long which were skidded one at a time with an old WW-160 Holt tractor. These were pulled over a

214

false bridge (temporary structure) by a winch constructed on site and powered by the bridge crew. Round, peeled logs were hand-hewn by broad axe. In fact, other than rods, bolts, spikes and plates, all material was native.

Some of my fondest memories of that summer include the kitchen fare. As the youngest member of the crew, I had become Nora's favorite. She always made sure my plate was full and I was encouraged to return for seconds. I'll never forget the pineapple pie she made!

A two-lane concrete structure has replaced the single-lane log span we built that summer of 1925. Parts of the old skid trail are still visible. I cannot think of it but remember the excellent abilities and expertise of the two men who built the bridge. Using almost exclusively their brains, brawn and natural materials, the link between Diamond Lake and Big Camas was forged.

R. O. Walker *Walker started to work for the Forest Service on the Columbia NF in 1928. In the spring of 1929 he transferred to the Regional Office where he worked at the warehouse and in Procurement. He retired in 1959.*

The first job I had was on the Weyerhaeuser old railroad line to Camp 11. There were two of us clearing out ties and cutting short cuts. Dee Teal was the cat skinner. We stayed at the old Yacolt Motel. Our transportation was an old Reo 3/4-ton truck. We had to pull out the vine maple clumps with an old army two-ton Holt tractor. Dee Teal backed into a clump. I said, "Dee, if we hook onto the clump this way, I think it would come out easier."

Dee said, "Young man, if I want any advice, I will ask for it."

I hooked onto it as he advised. Dee started out with the Holt wide-open. At the end of the chain there was a hole. The tractor hit the hole. Dee got bucked off and scrambled on all fours into the tall ferns. When he got up, he asked, "Did you know that hole was there?"

"Yes," I said.

He asked, "Why didn't you tell me?"

I replied, "You told me that when you wanted any advice, you would ask for it." After that we got along fine.

RESEARCH: "Congress made possible a Regional Experiment Station."

Thornton T. Munger *Munger recounts some research activities in the 1920s.*

In 1924, Congress made possible a Regional Forest Experiment Station in the Pacific Northwest to replace the local Wind River Experiment Station. Much to my surprise, District Forester Cecil asked me if I would like to be its director. I was happy in silviculture (now timber management) under Fred Ames, but I accepted this pioneering opportunity at a salary of $3900. So the Pacific Northwest Forest Experiment Station was born on July 1, 1924.

Assistant Forester Clapp, believing in having the Experiment Stations, like the Madison laboratory, affiliated with a university, invited cooperation from local institutions, but much to my satisfaction none was proffered. On Clapp's principle that the Experiment Stations should be physically as well as administratively separate from the District Offices, we rented four little rooms in the Lewis Building, a half-mile from the District Forester's offices.

We had an allotment for the year of $26,000. Our crew consisted of Miss June Wertz (whom we stole from the District Office); A. G. Simson, resident officer at Wind River; Leo A. Isaac, recently forest assistant at Wind River; R. E. McArdle, fresh from the University of Michigan; a stenographer and myself.

Initially, the pine country of central Idaho was assigned to our Station since it so closely resembled the Blue Mountains of Oregon. Isaac made an exploratory trip through there in the fall of 1924 with Assistant Forester Chet Morse of D-4, but that District decided they wanted to have their own Experiment Station and not be appended to the Pacific Northwest Station. The matter was dropped and our territory limited to Oregon, Washington and Alaska.

A Thornton Munger experiment in snag-falling—Wind River Experimental
Forest Station compound and nursery fields in the background,
Columbia NF – late 1920s

Our first project was a resumption of the 1909 to 1911 study of the yield of Douglas-fir. I quote from a reminiscent letter of McArdle's about the start of this project. "Thornton Munger, as I was later to learn more fully, was not a man to waste time. On July 3, he took me to Yacolt, Washington, to select a place to begin work on the yield study, and on July 4, (which heretofore I had thought was a holiday, but that was before I began working for the Forest Service) he moved me and my crew in his personal car to Yacolt. We spent that afternoon measuring sample plots."

The first Natural Area in this region (if not in the whole west) was one of 160 acres at Wind River, Washington, set aside after considerable remonstrance, in 1926. It was later enlarged to 1180 acres. At first these were called *virgin timber reservations.*

Leo A. Isaac *Isaac began with the Forest Service on the Okanogan NF in 1920. He transferred to the Columbia NF in 1924 to work at the Wind River Experimental Forest, beginning a long career in research with the PNW Experiment Station. He was the lead scientist in the silviculture of Douglas-fir and known widely as "Mr. Douglas-Fir" for his innovative and pioneering research with this species. He retired in 1956.*

In May 1924, I was transferred to the Wind River Experimental Forest (Carson, Washington), the cradle of forest research in the Pacific Northwest. There for the second time in my life I started work in forest research.

Bits of information gradually piled up. For the first time in the history of forestry the flight of tree seed was accurately measured, the life of seed in the soil determined and many causes of seedling mortality revealed. Col. Bill Greeley said, "Go ahead Leo and pile up these bits of information. Every one of them is a building stone, and when you get enough together, we will help you build a foundation with them." He meant a foundation of silviculture for Northwest tree species.

And everyone did help. If I named the important people that I worked for and with down through those years there would not be room for the rest of my story. In addition to work in reforestation there were studies of growth and yield, of species composition and plantation density, of thinning, pruning, selective logging and so on down the line. There were battles with bugs, and disease and with fires and politicians; I never decided which one was the worst, but it was fun while it lasted.

<u>Richard E. McArdle</u> *Some years ago Dave Bernstein wrote an article about Bob Marshall, focusing on his activities in the Northwest. He noticed that Marshall and Richard McArdle had been assigned to the PNW Station in 1924. On speculation, he wrote to McArdle (who was then Chief of the Forest Service) to see if there had been any contact. In return, he received a long detailed letter, part of which was published in Timber-Lines. Bernstein thought it was a very interesting look at a couple of our country's leading foresters early in their careers. Among other things, it illustrates the future Chief McArdle's legendary total recall and gives an insight on Marshall, who later became the Forest Service's first Chief of the Division of Recreation and Lands in the Washington Office as well as a leading proponent for a Wilderness system.*

When Bob Marshall was first detailed to the Douglas-fir yield study, our first job was to locate and remeasure some permanent plots near Wind River. These plots were on Panther Creek. My diary says that we left Hemlock Ranger Station (now Wind River Ranger Station) at 8 am on September 16, [1924] and went up Panther Creek by the Warrens Gap trail and were packed in by Elvin Blaisdell. I don't think Bob had had much camping experience. We did a full day of work before starting to set up camp. I disliked setting up camp so I said I'd do that job. John McGinn (the other member of the crew) and I set up the tent and fixed up some sort of table while Marshall collected firewood. I thought he'd find a dead cherry or some other dry standing tree.

As usual at that time of year it was raining. As usual also it got dark early in dense timber. We couldn't figure what had happened to Bob. When he finally showed up he was dragging some very small green hemlocks. McGinn located a small standing dead tree and after some delay we got a fire going. But when I looked at the ends of the hemlocks Bob had cut, I could understand why Leo Isaac had told me that Bob had broken every thermometer the Station had because he used a thermometer like an axe - and an axe like a thermometer. It was my mistake. I should have made sure that Bob knew how to make

219

a fire in a rainy forest. All of us were wet to the waist because we had had to wade through high salal underbrush so two members of the crew were pretty upset. But Bob was not and never lost his good nature the whole time he was with me - except one time when he was measuring trees and stepped in a yellow jacket nest.

Marshall never had proper field clothes, at least in 1924. He said he had so many half-worn-out dress suits that he wanted to wear them out. When he stepped on the yellow jackets they swarmed inside his pants legs and stung him rather severely on certain tender parts of his anatomy. I can still hear Bob shrieking "Oh dear, Oh dear ..." as he ran around trying to get rid of the yellow jackets.

McGinn was a gent with a hair-trigger temper and when he heard Bob's *cussing*, he shouted at Bob, "If you have to cuss, for God's sake cuss like a man." I tried to catch Bob when he passed us on one of his frantic circuits so that I could rip his pants off, but I couldn't catch him. I was really sorry about Bob because he was stung extremely badly. This incident was the late afternoon of the one and only day Bob worked in Oregon. I tried to persuade him to let me get him to a doctor, but he absolutely refused. I was sorry I let him talk me out of that. But he said he was leaving early for Portland next day anyway and would see a doctor there. I never knew if he did or not.

But to get back to the camp on Panther Creek. By mutual agreement McGinn and I decided that perhaps we should not ask Bob to cook any of the evening meals. One crew member would leave early and have supper ready when the other two came in. Bob insisted - a dozen times a day - that he should take his turn in fixing the evening meal. He was that way - always willing to do his full share and more of the work. Finally, Bob beat on me so much that I told him, OK, it will be your turn Friday evening (we planned to pack out after work on Saturday, assuming we could finish).

McGinn had to have fish on Friday and had grandly offered to catch all the fish we needed, but I thought I'd better be sure and took along two cans of salmon. Bob asked what he should cook for the Friday dinner. I told him that we hadn't much left so to cook whatever he could find but save enough for breakfast [Saturday].

As near as I could reconstruct that Friday evening meal, Bob used every piece of a six-man mess kit, using a larger kettle when he had no space in the pan he was using. First, he told me that he had sliced our one remaining loaf of bread (this was before the days of bakery sliced bread) and toasted each slice laboriously over a big fire. Then he combined the toast with (as near as I could figure) two or three cans of evaporated milk, one or two cans of peas, the two cans of salmon, and I don't know what other ingredients.

When McGinn and I got in, Bob had what looked like gallons of what he told us was a salmon souffle. Oh yes, he had found half a dozen big lemons and because he thought salmon needed a touch of lemon juice he added the juice of all the lemons. He was crouching over a raging fire with the biggest kettle sitting in a bit of water in the biggest frying pan. He said it was a rather make-shift double boiler. Bob thought the *souffle* tasted fine, but to McGinn and to me it tasted like lemonade with salmon and peas.

McGinn told me privately that he was going to get up early and beat Bob to the breakfast-fixing job. About three in the morning I was awakened by light on the tent flaps. First I thought we hadn't extinguished our fire but then I knew that wouldn't be true because it was raining. I looked out and there was Bob making breakfast. He had used the rest of the flour and had made hotcakes which he was stacking on a nearby log. Had a stack about a foot high. I was tempted to awaken McGinn and decided perhaps I shouldn't. I went back to bed.

Three hours later when McGinn and I got up, Bob was making what he called *broiled eggs*. He had hard-boiled all the rest of our eggs, shelled them (or maybe he didn't) and was frying the whole eggs in copious grease. Told me that he had this inspiration during the night and his ambition was to make this new dish, *broiled eggs*, the national dish of the US. The eggs were like golf balls. I couldn't cut one and when I tried to do it, the egg bounced off into the brush. It was typical of Bob that he took our dissatisfaction with his breakfast in good part, perfectly good-natured.

Maybe I shouldn't have put that in my recollections of Bob Marshall. I am sure that he learned everything that he needed to know before many years. He wasn't stupid by a long shot. Far from it. His mistake was to try to do more than his share of the work. He wasn't a shirker at any time I knew him.

If you write up anything about Bob Marshall I hope you will stress his many good qualities. He was generous to a fault; he would give the shirt off his back and throw in the coat for good measure. In fact, he would insist on it. He was smart, genuinely brainy. I never heard him say an unkind word about anyone. He never sought credit for what he did but went out of his way to give the credit to other people. If anything that I have written in this letter makes you think that McArdle didn't appreciate Bob Marshall's many good points please scratch it out. Many times in the years between 1924 and 1939 when he died (I think of a heart attack), I laughed at Bob, but he always laughed with me. In my book he was OK!

Thornton T. Munger *Munger continued research activites in Alaska, even after Alaska was made a separate District.*

Alaska was a part of District Six until 1921, but our responsibility for research continued. When, in 1927, it seemed probable that there would soon be some big pulp timber sales on the Tongass National Forest, I was told to explore the silvical problems of southeastern Alaska and suggest methods of cutting that should be employed. I had about six weeks there that summer, mostly in company of Ray Taylor, Charles Flory and other Forest Officers. I saw the principal logging areas from Ketchikan to Juneau and Sitka, especially Prince of Wales Island. I enjoyed that summer living on Forest Service boats, but not the land work in devil's club, salmonberry and other prickly wet brush, laced with moss-covered decaying logs.

I wrote a lengthy report on the boat coming back to Seattle recommending various research projects that should be undertaken, and venturing some suggestions as to methods of silviculture to be employed in these spruce-hemlock forests. It was some years before the big timber sales materialized and meanwhile Alaska (Region 10) took up its own research.

ADMINISTRATION: -"The Supervisor had noted the lack of detail in my diary-"

Rudo L. Fromme *Fromme was Forest Supervisor on the Olympic NF at the time of this story.*

Reading in a recent issue of the *NW Forest Service News* concerning the [spring Forest] Supervisors' Meeting takes my mind back to a meeting of this nature at a time when the social hour preceding the final banquet was not so easily handled. This was in the spring of 1920, if my memory isn't fooling me, just a few months after the passage of the national prohibition law. Spiritous beverages had taken to the bushes, giving way to *Bevo Beer* and other even less sizz-sudsing slush. Our banquet that spring was held at the Multnomah Hotel, and it shortly took on the appearance of an open defiance of the above legal restrictions. I'll title this particular affair SMITH'S SENSATIONAL SECESSION FROM OUR SYLVAN SERVICE.

His name was Smith C. Bartrum, long-time popular and voluble Supervisor of the Umpqua. It had come to us by the grapevine during our sessions that this was to be Smith's last appearance at a Forest Service gathering. We were, therefore, not too surprised when we had taken seats at the several group tables to see him rise to his feet and step to the end of the head table as if to unceremoniously sound off his sob-song before the meeting became involved in its orderly program.

"Fellows," said he, glancing toward the middle of the head table, "with due respect to the presence of Chief Forester Henry S. Graves and District Forester George Cecil, this is a sad occasion for me." Now, turning toward us lesser lights, he continued, as near as I can remember at this long lapse of time as follows: "Circumstances, which I shall not attempt to explain, have engendered my resignation from a Service for which I have given the best years of my life and, I might add, gladly so. Such an unusual occasion, I think you'll agree, justifies an unusual ceremony. I desire to leave the Service in the best of spirits so have ordered the best of spirits for our mutual celebration of the many past years of cordial fellowship."

During this last more bouyant remark, he was waving the come-on signal toward the service door where a flock of waiters were nervously waiting, with trays held high, to speedily supply our several group tables with high-ball glasses, *White Rock*, cracked ice and dark bottles bearing conspicuous whiskey labels. Meanwhile, Bartrum finished with, "Mix your own, boys, to suit your varied tastes. The treat is all on me."

But, what about the head table? There, matters appeared to be getting a bit out of hand, to say the least. Even at the very start of Bartrum's remarks, Mr. Graves seemed to be looking at him with some apprehension. As Smith continued, he appeared to grow increasingly nervous, and, when the speaker started his play on spirits, he turned toward Cecil and seemed to be urging him to start a back-fire. He was apparently trying to get him to comprehend that we were rapidly approaching a hazard. Well, when the waiters started distributing the delectables among the *boys*, he could contain himself no longer. He rose to his feet with jaw set and dark eyes flashing.

This went unnoticed by most of the *boys*, as they were thirstily watching the waiters. Charles Flory (Chief of Operation) and I were, however, watching the Chief Forester quite closely. We were in on the gag with Smith; we three constituting the program committee. Just as Mr. Graves was about to take the protest action into his own hands, Cecil was seen to be pulling him back to his chair by the coattails and whispering into his near ear. George had to give away the stage secret, that the whiskey was nothing more than apple cider, and quite tame cider at that, as the *boys* soon learned to their apparent sorrow. However, they responded with good-natured laughter, and both Graves and Cecil beamed with peaceful delight.

Cecil told us afterward that Mr. Graves had been quite definitely unnerved and had urged him to, "Stop this crazy deal at once!" That, "It was strictly against the law and would be bound to get into the morning papers!" I was glad that we had finally seen fit to tip Cecil off to this hoax just before the banquet. Bartrum was opposed to this, but Flory and I both knew something about Mr. Graves' serious and conscientious nature from having studied (?) under him at Yale. It could have easily backfired and jumped the fire trail.

<u>Ira E. Jones</u> *Jones reflects on jobs and job titles.*

When I first started work on the Whitman there were seven Ranger Districts. Each Ranger had only one guard, on duty only during the summer months. In the early 1920s you could not get a raise without a change in title (due to the old statutory roll). One of the peculiar results of this was at one time on the Whitman there were four men with the title of Forest Supervisor - R. M. Evans, Johnnie Irwin, Otto Zimmerli and myself. I have had a great many official titles during my FS career, among them laborer, forest guard, Deputy Ranger, Ranger, Deputy Supervisor, Supervisor, National Forest examiner, superintendent of construction, project engineer, and Assistant Supervisor. There may have been others.

<u>Grover C. Blake</u> *Blake was a District Ranger on the Ochoco NF at the time of this story.*

The Supervisor had noted the lack of detail in my diary and had written me about it. As often happened in those days, Forest officers would exchange notes that were not intended for the record. So when I received his letter, I picked up a piece of scratch paper and a lead pencil and made a reply which was intended for the waste basket file. Imagine my surprise several weeks later when I received my February 14, 1921, issue of the SERVICE BULLETIN, published by the US Forest Service, Washington DC, and saw my memorandum to the Supervisor on the front page. The Service Bulletin article is quoted verbatim as follows:

EIGHT HOURS - UNCLASSIFIED:

"Efficiency is a wonderful thing; we all probably try to attain it. Working plans and Schedules of Work have their uses. Diaries come in the Forest Service Scheme. Most field officers in small communities, who try to be neighborly and helpful and at the same time follow their Schedules of Work and keep their diaries up oftentimes have troubles that inspectors don't dream of. Here's an Oregon Ranger who had his. The Supervisor wanted to know why his diary wasn't in more detail; the Ranger told him:

You have no doubt noticed that I have been charging a large portion of my time as Miscellaneous Headquarters Work. I have been bunching the work this way for convenience as that seemed to cover many jobs. To list separately every job of 15 minutes or half-hour during a day would make the diary bulky and require considerable time. During the past season I have never had to worry about finding something to do tomorrow or next week. Instead, I have at numerous times taxed my wits to pick out the important jobs that could be left undone to provide time for doing more important ones. Yet since you mention it, I can see that a person reading my diary and having no other source of information would most likely get the impression that I was simply killing time, with nothing to do.

As you know, the larger part of the headquarters work during the past several months at Beaver Ranger Station was made necessary by the building of the new highway. The road builders tore away fences and other improvements and left trash, broken posts, parts of stumps, fence wire and litter of all kinds in their trail to be cleaned up by me. In this way a great deal of my time was taken up without making a showing.

It very frequently happens that a day is entirely lost from the plan of work that each of us has. Perhaps I would start in the morning on a job that had been planned in advance for the day and the following is typical of the way it turns out:

As I begin work Engineer Smith comes along and requests that I walk up the road with him and inform him whether his plan for rebuilding the irrigation ditch which the road builders had destroyed would be satisfactory. We spend a half-hour looking the ground over and talking over details. Mr. Smith uses up 15 additional minutes telling about some experiences on the battlefront in France during the World War.

I receive a call to the telephone and spend 15 minutes getting connected up with my party and five minutes in conversation (it is not at all unusual for me to spend an hour during a single day at the telephone on official business). I start out to work, impatient at the delay, hang my coat on a post just as a man arrives very much exhausted. His Ford is stuck in the mud on the Fish Creek Hill. He explains that it never acted that way before but his engine is *not working right*. Will I help him? Sure. I help him out and if we are lucky and do not have to tinker with the car too much I get back to work and upon looking at my watch am surprised to find it is 11:45 am.

I have just noticed that a bunch of Bar B cattle have broken into the pasture and proceed to saddle a horse and chase them out, and get to dinner a half hour late. My wife wants to know why I did not split some wood before I went chasing those cattle. I try to explain but get balled up and make a mess of it; then go back to work with family relations more or less strained.

Just as I get my coat hung on the post and my gloves on, Ryan, foreman for the contractors on the highway, arrives and would like to borrow my steel tape to measure some culverts. He only wants it for an hour or so. Ed Black rides in on horseback at this time and he feels very badly about the manner in which the Forest Service manages the grazing business. He offers some suggestions as to how we could make things better in his particular case, spends 37 minutes telling me what a bum Ranger I am and how the Forest Service is conspiring to put him out of business, gets the load out of his system and goes his way feeling better.

I am called to the telephone to explain to Mrs. White how to corn beef, and to Mr. Green what to do for a sick horse. Mrs. White takes up fourteen minutes of my time and Mr. Green exactly eight. While I am thus engaged, Jones' dogs chase a bunch of cattle through the fence, tearing down eight panels, and I work until dark cobbling it up again.

I sit down to write up my diary for the day. I begin to enumerate the many things done and decide that if I write all this stuff that pretty soon I will need help to carry my diary and I am tired and don't feel like writing anyway, so I enter it as follows: "Did miscellaneous headquarters work – unclassified, 8 hrs."

H. J. Stratford *Stratford worked for the Forest Service as Principal Clerk in Nevada and Idaho prior to and after WW I. In May 1923 he transferred to the Whitman NF as principal clerk at $1600.00 per annum. He was Administrative Assistant on the Whitman NF, and in Fiscal Control and a Fiscal Inspector in the R-6 Regional Office. He retired in 1956.*

During Mr. Kuhn's regime as Forest Supervisor, the Whitman [National Forest] was selected as a *guinea pig* of Region 6 to participate in Keplinger's Correspondence Course on Cost Accounting and to place in operation this very complex cost accounting system. The Whitman carried the old and new systems for four years until the new system, which provided for depreciation of Forest Service improvements, was adopted universally by the Forest Service. Periodically, group meetings were held throughout the region by myself and representatives from fiscal control, where the provisions of the new cost system were analyzed and discussed. The system, after a few years of operation, broke down of its own weight; it was too time-consuming and impractical for all general purposes.

Lloyd E. Brown *The training school Brown describes was held in the late 1920s or possibly early 1930s.*

Region Six held its first Ranger Training School at the Hemlock Ranger Station, Wind River District [Columbia NF] from October 5 to November 3 [in the early 1930s]. The instructors and trainees were housed in a semi-circle of small tents between the Ranger's Office and the cookhouse. Allen H. Hodgson, R-6 Chief of Personnel, was in charge of the school. The instructors were: Glenn Mitchell, Arthur D. Moir from Region One, K. C. Langfield, R. Thomas Carter, Ray Buckart and Ross Shepeard. The trainees were: Ervin Peters, L. D. "Bob" Bailey, Ray Hampton, Avery Berry, Lewis Neff, Vondis Miller, George Fisher, John Hough, R. J. Wilbur, Henry Tonseth, LeRoy Olander, Charles Rector, Herman Horning, Charles Overbay, E. D, Wilmouth, Harold E. D. Brown, Fred Ramsay, Fenton Whitney, Lloyd Fullington, Ralph Brown, Henry Harryman, C. H. Young, Frank Lightfoot, Wade Hall, A. E. Kenworthy, William Hallin, R. Nevan McCullough, Edward P. Cliff, Waldemar Anderson, Axel Lindh, Paul Taylor and Peter Wyss.

I was working at the Station during the school term. When the instructors and trainees went on field trips, I took half of them in the two-ton District fire truck, and Carlos "Tom" Brown hauled the rest of them in the fire truck from the Herman Creek Ranger Station on the Mt. Hood.

John R. "Ray" Bruckart *Bruckart began his career on the Snoqualmie NF in 1909. He went on to be Forest Supervisor of*

228

the Columbia, Olympic and Willamette NFs. He retired in 1954 as the "last of the older group of Supervisors".

My time on the Columbia Forest, 1930 through 1935, was a period of severe unemployment. During 1931 to 1932, the Forest Service was allocated funds to provide a limited amount of employment. A snag-felling project was started in the Yacolt Burn and during the winter we provided work for a limited number of men with families from Vancouver and vicinity.

Because of the nature of the work, men assigned to this snag-felling project were required to be experienced woodsmen. In order to spread the work as much as possible, the crews numbering 12 to 24 men were changed every month. Clark County cooperated in selecting men to be employed on the work relief snag-felling project. This was before the Roosevelt Administration and the Works Progress Administration, the Civilian Conservation Corps or other relief programs.

IMPROVEMENTS: "Automotive equipment began to come into use."

Gilbert D. Brown *Brown was Forest Supervisor of the Fremont NF from 1910 to 1931. He tells about working through the bureaucracy to buy the Forest's first truck.*

In looking over some of my old records I find letters covering the difficulty in securing motor transportation for the Forest Service 45 years ago. After building many miles of roads on the Fremont, necessity for motor transportation was very acute. Most livery stables had been turned into garages but did not have trucks or cars for rent. In 1919, I tried to get permission to rent or purchase a $900.00 Ford truck. After considerable correspondence and delay I was authorized to rent such a truck at $100.00 per month, and in case of purchase, the amount of rent paid was to be deducted from the purchase price. I was finally permitted to rent the truck, if available, under these conditions. After one year's delay, the Secretary of Agriculture authorized the purchase which because of the amount of rental already paid, caused the purchase price to be materially reduced.

(Following are portions of Mr. Brown's letter of June 5, 1919, to the District Forester, Portland)

"I wish at this time to call your attention to the necessity of a light truck for use on this Forest. This truck is needed especially during the fire season which has just started and which from present indications promises to be an extremely bad one. We now have one fire on and adjacent to the Forest which covered several hundred acres before we were able to put it under control. I have not been able to get men to do the improvement work which was contemplated for the month of June in order to have available some force to be used in case of fire. Our regular protective force, as you know, is inadequate for ordinary protection during this month."

"I have found it impossible to hire a truck or suitable car to haul a few men and supplies. A few years ago teams and wagons were available for hire. The motor truck and tractor have at the present time supplanted the horse team and it is now almost impossible to hire a team. The livery stables have been replaced by garages, but they do not have sufficient trucks to assure us of one in case of need. I can hire a Ford truck and hold it in reserve for $100.00 per month and we pay all operating expenses and keep it in repair. This, however, is not good business when one can be purchased with low gear transmission and body complete for less than $1000.00. The truck chassis as sold by the Ford Company is $661.00 delivered in Lakeview. The low speed transmission would cost $135.00 installed, and a suitable body could be made locally for approximately $100.00, making a total cost of $900.00. The Ford truck, so equipped, would answer every purpose on this Forest and I am convinced would be the most practicable and economical machine for our use."

"To summarize, fires are bound to occur. Labor is very scarce. A few men can be rapidly transported to the average fire by auto and thus save the necessity of a large crew. Teams are slow at best and at present are not available. Automobiles or trucks cannot always be secured when needed. In order to handle the situation efficiently, provision must be made to have at least one truck or auto available at once. In order to do this it is necessary to hire one by the month or own one."

"I wish, therefore, to urgently recommend that a truck be purchased at once for this Forest, preferably a Ford. If this is not possible, I wish authority to hire one at the stated price of $100.00 per month. The Ford people here are willing to rent us a truck under the conditions stated and deduct any payment made from the purchase price in case we are able to purchase later. This consideration would allow us the use of the machine pending any delay in securing authority to purchase, and since there is no other dealer within a reasonable distance, they would undoubtedly furnish the truck if purchased."

This was the District Forester's reply on June 13, 1919: "Your need for a light truck is fully appreciated in this office and it is hoped that funds will permit furnishing one to you. We are not able to say at this time whether this can be done, but it is suggested that you do not hire one by the month until July 1. On that date, if it is not possible to purchase one for you and it is absolutely necessary in order to provide for the adequate protection of your Forest, the rental of a machine to be held in reserve will be approved."

On July 10, 1919, Mr. Brown replied: "Since July 1 has passed and I have not received notice that a truck would be purchased for this Forest I fear that perhaps you have not found it possible to buy one and since the use of a machine is absolutely necessary for the adequate protection of this Forest I secured on July 1 a new Ford truck equipped with the Moore low speed transmission, constructed a light body suitable for our use and now have the machine on fire work.

The fire hazard is now greater than it has been at any time for several years. There has been no rain whatever since April 20 when there was only .02 of an inch. A truck was badly needed last season as several times when fires occurred I was compelled to use my Dodge to haul men, tools and supplies because it was not possible to hire a car.... A touring car is not suitable for such work and for that reason I consider that during the past two years I have paid out of my own pocket for the Government, above the mileage secured, at least $800.00 in using my own car for fire protection and other Forest Service work. This would be done again this season if necessary but it seems unnecessary since other branches of the Government are supplied with cars or trucks. The Forest Service has purchased for the Supervisor of the Modoc Forest [across the state line, in California, in District Five] a Ford roadster for his official use. The State Highway Department has four cars here for use on the road surveys. The Water Board has a Ford.

Practically all ranchers and stockmen now find it necessary to use cars or trucks in handling their business. The Forest Service here is as much or more in need of such transportation that most other persons so provided."

On July 15, 1919, the District Forester replied: "Your letter of July 10 leaves little if any doubt as to the urgent need of a truck for use in connection with fire protection. You may know that we had arranged to purchase four trucks in June, one of which was to be assigned to the Fremont, but in view of the serious fire situation in District One, the Forester found it necessary to cancel all proposed purchases of equipment."

"We are now starting out in the fiscal year with little if any G. E. contingent, and it does not appear that we shall be able to accomplish much in the way of the purchase of trucks and other equipment during this fiscal year...Accordingly, your action in renting a truck by the month is approved, in view of your definite statement that in case of emergency you could not rent a truck. You should not, however, plan to retain this truck for a longer period than is absolutely necessary."

On June 17, 1920, the Forester requested authority from the Secretary of Agriculture to purchase the following truck:

One Ford Worm-Driven truck, equipped with windshield, Moore Four-Speed Transmission, 30" x 3" pneumatic tires in front, and 32" x 3" solid rubber tires in rear.

The request was approved.

Harry M. White *White describes the acquisition of mechanical equipment after World War I.*

It was while I was on the Columbia that automotive equipment began to come into use. In 1920, we obtained a Moreland truck and a two-ton Holt crawler tractor, surplus Army equipment, which were a big help in road construction and maintenance. In 1922, we acquired a couple of Army five-ton Holt tractors from which the armor plate had been removed and new graders to go with them. In 1921, we bought a three-quarter ton Reo pickup on which I learned to drive. Then we

Sign board in the Ochoco NF where Summit Road leaves
Mitchell-Summit Prairie – late 1920s

purchased a Model T Ford with Ruckstell axle, which was handy on the nine-foot, or narrower, roads that wound among the trees and with which I burned up the Columbia River Highway at 30 miles per hour. From then on improvement in transportation and road-building equipment was rapid.

Shirley Buck *As a long-time Regional Purchasing Agent, Buck was called the father of R-6 procurement and contracting.*

The first trucks were purchased during 1921 when there was a serious blowdown on the Olympic NF. The District Forester was authorized to buy three trucks. Reo was the low bidder; they supplied their renowned *Speed Wagon.*

One truck was assigned at the Portland Warehouse. Horace Whitney and I drew the coveted job of delivering two trucks to the Olympic NF. There were no paved roads; neither were there any bridges across the Columbia, so we drove them to Goble, Oregon, and crossed on the ferry. We reached Centralia, Washington, late the first night, Piedmont on the second night and our destination, Crescent, on the third.

Thornton T. Munger *Munger was Head of the Silvics Section for District Six, performing research on the Columbia NF, at the time of this story.*

In the early 1920s a Model T Ford was purchased to facilitate transporting a reconnaissance crew. This was the first passenger car to be purchased by the Forest [Columbia] in this District. There being no way to license it, I designed and had made at a sign shop two identification plates. Soon thereafter the government bought many official cars.

Richard E. McArdle *McArdle began his Forest Service career with the Pacific Northwest Forest and Range Experiment Station in 1924. He was Dean of the University of Idaho School of Forestry and Director of Forest Experiment Stations in Colorado and North Carolina. He worked in the Washington Office and was the 8th Chief of the Forest Service from 1952 to 1962.*

234

We had a bicycle tire valve soldered to the gas tank under the seat so we could force-feed the gas when we had to go up steep hills – the only other way was to drive backwards up the hill.

<u>Dahl Kirkpatrick</u> *Kirkpatrick continues his reminiscences about the Rainier/Columbia NF when his dad was a District Ranger.*

The first motorized vehicle [at Randle Ranger Station on the Rainier NF] was a Pierce Arrow two- or three-ton truck with solid tires and very rigid springs. It had the steering wheel on the right side and a seat wide enough to accommodate five people - one on the outboard side of the driver. No windshield, no top and with a most temperamental carburation and electrical system. It was a military surplus item from WW I and must have arrived in 1919 - a real white elephant.

Soon thereafter a White one-ton truck was transferred from the Army which we were told had been built to carry an ambulance body. It had a utility box instead and was equipped with pneumatic tires, a four-speed gear-box and had roller bearings in the engine. This was an excellent machine but had to be shared with other Districts on the Forest when work programs required it. It came in 1920 or 1921, I believe.

In about 1919, my dad bought a Dodge touring car, and one of the seasonal employees, Frank Kehoe, had a Ford chassis on which he had built a pick-up type box. Both of these vehicles were used in a limited way on a mileage basis for official work.

Finally by the middle of the 1920s, a Dodge screen-sided panel-type rig was assigned to the District - the first automobile suitable for the transportation of District personnel. It must have come along in 1924 or so. By the early 1930s, pick-ups were becoming common as were modern type trucks used for fire and general utility purposes.

With the beginning of road construction work came the first motorized road construction equipment. It was in 1925 that the first tractor was assigned to the District - a two-ton Cletrac. It was soon equipped with a homemade bulldozer of sorts which was designed by and built under the direction of T. P. (Ted) Flynn, an engineer from the regional office. Ted's strange machine is believed to be the prototype of the modern day bulldozer, though it was very elemental and primitive by today's standards. Ted has been credited with being the *father of the bulldozer* and his first one was built at Randle. It was enough of a novelty that it was photographed by a Pathe News team and was shown widely in the movie houses in the area - about a one minute news clip.

<u>Harry M. White</u>   *White describes more improvements in equipment.*

While working with the rubber companies, [Osborne] Bush developed the light-weight, single-cotton-jacketed, rubber-lined hose that would stand better than 600 pounds hydrostatic pressure per square inch and still was very much lighter than the standard mill hose in common use around logging camps. In the later years, the engineering laboratory under Ted Flynn played an important part in equipment development. The laboratory men undoubtedly accelerated the development and improvement of chain saws, not so much, perhaps, by their own ingenuity as by the influence their ideas and work had on the chain saw manufacturers.

<u>Larry K. Mays</u> *Mays started as a seasonal in 1928, and received a permanent appointment in 1931. He worked on the Columbia, Fremont, Umatilla, and Deschutes NFs and in the R-6 and R-8 Regional Offices. He worked in the Washington Office and headed the Office of Internal Audit when he retired in 1966. He was working as a seasonal on the Columbia NF at the time of this story.*

In the spring of 1930, the Forest Service Region Six used D. L. Beatty from Region One to help test the use of semi-portable radio transmitter-receivers. Beatty worked out of Tacoma, Washington, and took the first eight sets to Wind River near Carson for training operators.

I was selected as an operator and trained for about one week at Wind River in July 1930. My set was #7 and weighed 72 pounds, complete with semi-portable batteries, aerial, counterpoise, ropes, insulators, etc. We transmitted in International Morse Code but received in

236

voice. The central station was at Wind River, manned by Squibb, an ex-Navy communication man.

Following our training, I took my set back to the Spirit Lake Ranger District, Columbia (now Gifford Pinchot) Forest. I was foreman of a Way Trail crew in the Mt. Margaret country and the radio was our only means of communication, other than foot messenger, throughout the summer of 1930. Carroll Brown was also a Way Trail foreman that summer in the Mt. Margaret country and helped with the radio when we combined our camps. He was also at Arab Shelter when I left to take the training at Wind River.

The radio worked very satisfactorily except for two incidents, as I recall. Once the water power went out at the dam and the central station at Wind River was off the air for several days. The other time we were without communication was due to a mishap in moving our camp. The radio gear was on a mule who got into a yellow jacket's nest. He ran off bucking, kicking and bumping into trees. We finally ran him down, but when the radio was set up in the new camp, it didn't work. I finally found a broken filament in one of the tubes. The packer took the broken tube to Spirit Lake and in about two weeks brought out a replacement tube. From then on, we were able to maintain our twice a day contact with the central station.

R. C. "Bud" Burgess *Burgess was a District Ranger on the Deschutes NF at the time of this story. He worked on the Willamette and Whitman NFs and was with the Bureau of Land Management in Lakeview, Oregon when he retired in 1962.*

Chain saws in 1931 were written off as too dangerous and temperamental to be practical! We tried one or two on some clearing work on the Deschutes that fall at Crane Prairie Reservoir. A. G. Angell was in charge of a Ranger crew and a few key forest guards. Chuck Overbay and Fenton G. Whitney were young Rangers with hair on both head and chest at the time. I believe these saws were Evinrudes and we were cutting through jackstrawed lodgepole pine. The power saws would bind and kill the engine, and we would try to get them started again. We were out several starting cords and may have sawed a few more logs than the boys with short tie hack saws, but not too many more! Our final report was that they were plenty dangerous and a man-killer to pack around.

"Meantime the 3C program landed on us. This brought a profound change and an expansion not only of work, but of ideas among field personnel. It also brought wider recognition of the meaning of conservation among the people. The 'old days' were gone. The new Forest Service was born."

-John G. Clousten

CHAPTER THREE

1933 to 1945 The CCCs, a DEPRESSION and WAR

This era was bracketed by two major events, each with long-term impacts and consequences to the Forest Service. The *Great Depression* spawned the Civilian Conservation Corps (CCC) program and related public works activities. World War II generated accelerated timber sales to provide wood for aircraft construction and a new use for lookouts, as 24-hour airplane tracking stations under the Aircraft Warning Service.

The major part of the regular budget during this period went to seasonal fire control forces and fire protection. Other important activities focused on developing the transportation system (trails and roads) and improving and adding to facilities.

Most of the new construction work was performed by the CCCs, who built roads and bridges, trails, buildings and campgrounds. They also fought fire and planted old burns. Another benefit of the CCC program was the conversion of a number of long-time seasonal employees to full-time employment to supervise CCC work projects.

Several Experimental Forests were established and new Wild Areas were proposed. Timberline Lodge was constructed and opened for business and part of the Olympic National Forest went to the creation of the Olympic National Park.

Several stories describe activities on large fires in southwest Oregon in 1936 and 1938. The war brought fire and tragedy to the Pacific Northwest, described in stories about a bomb dropped by an airplane and one attached to a grounded balloon.

Firsts and improvements included the trial use of radios and chain saws, aerial fire drops and the beginning of the smokejumper program.

This chapter includes stories about the Civilian Conservation Corps, All in a Day's Work, Wives' Tales, Horses and Mules, Fire and Lookouts, Grazing, Recreation, Timber, Research, Administration and World War II.

CIVILIAN CONSERVATION CORPS: "Try to imagine a crew of 275 inexperienced men, or I should say, boys, assembled in a very short time, to be organized and started on a program that was tangled in government red tape."

M. M. "Red" Nelson   *Nelson provides a good overview of the establishment of the Civilian Conservation Corps program.*

In the early 1930s the entire country was in a deep depression. Many people were without work, jobs were almost impossible to find, money was very scarce, people were going hungry. In 1932 Roosevelt was elected President and almost immediately started a number of relief programs. The CCC [Civilian Conservation Corps] was established to aid young boys. Many 200-man camps were established in the forested areas of the entire country. Although there was an overall CCC organization in Washington DC, to coordinate the entire program much of the work in running it fell to the Forest Service. They planned the work projects, supervised the work, and trained the boys to work and in other skills (i.e. reading, math). Most of the CCC camps were run by the Forest Service either directly or through its cooperative programs with the State Forester, but there were also some camps run by the National Park Service, Soil Conservation Service and others.

George Morey   *Morey began work for the CCCs in 1933. He then worked for the Siskiyou and Rogue River NFs, retiring in 1963.*

The Civilian Conservation Corps program started in southern Oregon in May 1933. It was through this program that many of the first roads and trails were built in eastern Curry County.

CCC's building a mess hall at Camp Rock Creek,
Rager Ranger District, Ochoco NF – 1933.

CCC crews at noon mess, Camp Rock Creek, Rager Ranger District,
Ochoco NF – 1933

My remarks are made around Company #1650 [on the Siskiyou NF] which convened at a tent camp on the old Mt. Reuben Road and remained there for a few months. It was then moved to a more permanent location at Rand near Galice.

I was an enrollee from the start of the program and want to say that it was about the best thing that had happened to many of us since the crash of 1929. Our pay was $30.00 a month; $5.00 was given to me on payday and Edna was sent a check for $25.00. I only worked for this amount for one month and then was promoted to leader which paid $45.00 a month.

Try to imagine a crew of 275 inexperienced men, or I should say, boys, assembled in a very short time, to be organized and started on a program that was tangled in government red tape. In addition, this project was supervised by two different departments. However, after a few weeks the kinks were mostly ironed out and the result was one of the finest operations with the most lasting good results of any undertaking since the depression started.

The Army was in charge of the camp, that is, subsisting, clothing, and the general welfare of the men. During the initial program, the camp was staffed with regular army officers, consisting of a commanding officer, a mess officer, a first sergeant, a contract doctor and a civilian educational advisor. The project work was supervised by the Forest Service.

Getting back to the organization of the camp: our main contact while at the base camp was with an old regular Army sergeant. I believe that 45 years later, 90% of the enrollees of the 1933 period will recall the old sergeant and his method of operation. His manner never changed around the clock; the snarl was permanent. He gave one the impression that if you were properly greased and had your ears pinned back that he could swallow you. During the time that he was in camp I never heard him say a pleasant word to or about anyone.

Being an old Amy regular he carried the same mannerisms and methods of supervision to the CCC camp as prevailed in the army. It was a common thing, especially in the morning, to hear him tell someone to *shut up*. He also liked to get away from the camp and *live*

A common mode of transportation for CCC crews – c1933

Camp Rager CCC crew constructing a range fence on the Ochoco NF – 1933

it up. One night in Grants Pass, he became involved in a brawl with some of the local citizens and came out the loser, arriving back at camp about dawn and reported to the company doctor that he had fallen down the steps leading to the officers' latrine. It looked, to the men, as though each step had bitten a chunk out of him as he passed by. That is about all I recall about the old sergeant. It is not to our credit that we never tried to be friendly to him. There may have been a real human being hidden behind that mask.

The assistant to the sergeant was an enrollee from Illinois, Lee Miller, who had been a railroad employee and had spent much of his spare time in a gym, boxing. He was a good fighter in the ring, and his nose was decidedly flat from the punches he had taken with the gloves. The administration was not altogether popular with the men, and Lee acted as a stabilizer for the company. He had a good personality, and the athletic program he conducted at the camp made him a favorite with the personnel.

As the men arrived in camp they were issued clothing consisting of World War I uniforms, beds which consisted of blankets and a bag filled with straw for a mattress, and a mess kit. Then came time to assign duties and jobs. It is not known just what methods were used to get the men on the job and the program rolling, but I believe that a list of the jobs to be done was written on a large chart and a roster of the men placed alongside. The men's names were listed alphabetically from A to Z and starting with A, assignments were made.

It went like this. A name was called, the man stepped forward and received the news that he would be head cook. The next one would be second cook and so on until all the jobs were filled. I'm sure this was the method employed because when they got down to the Ms and called my name, I was informed I was to be a *powderman unlimited* and would head up a crew blasting trees from the right-of-way. Up to this time, I had never any more than seen powder, let alone used any of it.

Many of the enrollees had the same trouble I did with results that were less than acceptable. On the second day of my job as powderman, after studying the blasters' manual thoroughly, I attempted to remove a 50-inch Douglas-fir tree from the edge of the road. It was the

CCC crew mopping up a fire on the Ochoco NF – 1934

CCC crew falling snags in an old burn on the Ochoco NF – 1934

practice in those days to blast the trees from the right-of-way. In doing so, the tree and the stump were both removed at the same time and went down the mountain and out of the way. The manual indicated where to dig the holes and how much powder it would take to blast out a tree of a given size. Each inch required a certain amount of powder.

After getting the holes filled with powder and all tamped in, I started to get second thoughts and doubted very much if that amount of powder would do the job. At this early stage of my career, I did want to be a success. So to be safe, two large holes were dug under the tree and two more boxes of stumping powder were tamped in. The result was that the tree went down the mountain all right and with it about 100 feet of the road. It took several days to repair the road enough to let the trucks over it. In the meantime, the crews walked the three miles to work in the morning and back to camp in the evening.

Along about this time, someone discovered a couple of hundred pounds of bacon on the garbage dump resting on the tin cans and other debris. Upon investigation it came out that the cooks had discovered a small amount of mold on some of the meat and had made the decision that all of it was spoiled. The kitchen operation was given the long look and the result was employment of a professional cook to supervise food preparation. The quality of the chow improved as did the morale in the camp.

I was detailed to the Peavine country and another tent camp for the purpose of cutting winter wood for the main camp. The quarters consisted of several tents for the men and one large tent that served as a cook house and mess hall. We had been there only a few days when we were visited by a large bear. The animal would eat the garbage and anything else available. One night the cook heard a noise in the mess tent and upon investigating found himself face to face with the tallest, meanest and ugliest animal that he had ever seen. The bear was just finishing a large pan of stewed prunes on top of the dining table when surprised by the cook and the difficulty was that the cook blocked the only door to the tent so the bear went out the back of it where there was no opening and in so doing, took the tent with it. In just a few seconds the tent was a shambles. The cook finally found his way up and out of the debris, and we all crawled out of bed to work the rest of the night restoring the cook tent and salvaging the rations.

The pilfering bear came back each night and seemed to get bolder as time went on. With each visit we found our supplies damaged and, by this time, the men were becoming nervous, and no one was able to get a night's rest without interruption. We plotted to fool the bear and encourage her to go elsewhere to hunt for food. We secured an old oaken barrel, the old 52-gallon type. Holes were bored near the open end, and several 90-penny spikes were inserted with the sharp ends slanted toward the inside and bottom of the barrel.

The idea was that the bear would be able to squeeze its head past the nail points to get at the food, but would not be able to draw back out, as the nails would bite into the neck just back of the ears. In theory, it seemed like a good idea, but here is how it worked; the barrel was baited with some choice bits of food and placed in front of the tents where the men could watch all the happenings that moonlit night.

It wasn't long before mamma bear arrived and stuck her head into the barrel, eating the last scrap of food. When she started to back out it was evident that her head was firmly held by the spikes near the bottom. What happened next lasted about fifteen seconds. The animal panicked and holding her head and the barrel high in the air, started to run. She had just gained top speed when she hit a large fir tree squarely in the middle. The impact sounded like a car hitting a stone wall and the barrel literally exploded, throwing staves and binders several feet in all directions. That freed the animal and allowed her to retreat to other parts, no doubt to nurse a headache.

In the spring of 1934, I was sent to Gold Springs as assistant to Homer Jones. We had a crew of 100 men. The road toward Marial was completed to the Marble Ledge and the road headed for the Coquille was finished to the Boliver Saddle. A new lookout tower was erected on Ninemile Mountain.

A short time before we broke camp for the winter one of the trucks with 30 men aboard failed to negotiate a curve and rolled down the mountain through thick brush. Three men were hurt quite seriously;

one was in critical condition. All others received cuts, scratches and abrasions on their arms, legs and backs.

Dr. Faucett of Glendale was called and he gave medical aid to the seriously injured. Walter Barklow and I gave first aid to the rest. Here's what we did. We filled a two-quart pan about half full of Army iodine and with a two-inch paint-brush we lined the men up and had them strip. We then went down the line painting everything that looked red. A good generous supply of the Army remedy was splashed on the wounds. It may be that the iodine hurt some of them more than others and it may be that some could just naturally yell louder. At any rate, I'm sure that anyone who had been passing by and not having known of the situation would have been convinced that a mass execution was in progress.

Ralph A. "Sparky" Reeves *Reeves started with the FS in 1941. He worked on the Umpqua, Rogue, and Siskiyou NFs. He was Fleet Manager on the Siskiyou NF when he retired in 1973. Sparky's son, Rich, also worked for the Forest Service and has a story in Chapter Four.*

There was the time in 1937 when we were stationed at Big Camas Ranger Station in charge of a 50-man CCC side camp out of Diamond Lake on the Umpqua NF. Margaret and I lived in a tent house one-quarter mile from the Ranger Station along with our new son, Rich. The Ranger was Harold Bowerman, with Assistant Kelly Churchill and office helper Winnie Churchill.

The 50-man crew and one powder foreman, Van Cleveland, in charge of stump blasting, were building road from Big Camas Ranger Station toward the Steamboat Ranger Station on the Umpqua River. The brushing crews had cut out the brush on the right-of-way, the fallers cut the trees, and the buckers cut the logs to length so that they could be logged by a Forest Service team of matched black horses driven by teamster Guy Fender.

One day the CCC crew had finished their day and returned to camp. Guy had a few more logs to move so that the dozer could push out some shot stumps so another section of truck trail or pioneer road could be built. While pulling a log, one horse slipped and fell onto a one-inch stob that one of the brush cutters had cut off about six inches above the ground at an angle of about 60 degrees. The stob punctured the horse's stomach, and when the horse regained its feet, about 18 inches of intestine was protruding from the wound.

Guy ripped off his undershirt, wet it from a canteen hanging on the hame of one horse, removed a line from the harness, pushed the intestine back in, wrapped the line around the horse and pad, truss fashion, and radioed the Ranger Station from the stock truck.

The phone lines were a-buzz with the news, and the Supervisor's office in Roseburg, with Vern Harpham as Forest Supervisor, was advised by a local vet to destroy the horse. The doctor at the CCC camp at Diamond Lake got word of the situation and said, "Let me try!" The Doc received permission from the Supervisor's office. J. R. Montgomery drove him from Diamond Lake to Big Camas where he picked up water, ropes, about ten CCC boys and myself and drove the two miles out to the job.

The doctor brought along a bottle of tranquilizers from the camp infirmary and asked Guy if he could get a handful into the horse's mouth, which he did. In about five minutes we pushed the horse over into a bed of fir boughs, wound-side up, removed the undershirt that was used for the pad, removed the lines, and Doc cut away the hair as best he could.

After tying the horse's rear feet to a stump, and with the CCC boys holding the horse's head and front feet, the doctor washed the wound and stitched it up. We made a girdle of canvas and copper blasting wire. We got the horse up and into the stock truck and to the Ranger Station just as dark set in. Prognosis: No feed for 12 hours; if after that the horse got around for two days, he would be OK.

The horse and his mate were subsequently transferred to the Tiller Ranger Station for the winter.

M.M. "Red" Nelson   *Nelson describes a unique plumbing feature in CCC camps.*

One feature in all CCC camps that I thought was kind of unique was the system for the flush toilet. I have never again seen one in use. It was made up of a long concrete trough with toilet seats on top. The trough had a slight downgrade. At the head of the trough was an open tank affair with water running into it at all times. The open tank was hinged on a counter balance so that when it became full it automatically dumped into the trough, flushing it into the septic tank system. It was simple, cheap to build, required little maintenance, and with ever running water, it never became a freeze-up problem.

<u>Ira E. Jones</u>   *Jones supervised the Works Progress Administration program for the Siuslaw NF when he got involved in the politics of hiring and firing. He later helped deactivate the program.*

During the depression I was loaned to the Resettlement Administration and had charge of Works Project Administration workers on the Siuslaw Forest. We had three main camps in former CCC camp buildings. They were located at Mapleton, Cape Creek and Hebo. At one time we had 44 side camps with as high as 1100 men. All foremen positions had to be approved by the Democratic Chairman. I remember one man sent out who was absolutely no good as a foreman. I fired him and got a call from the Portland Resettlement to come to Portland and get squared up with the state Democratic Chairman. I went in. The Chairman was at the Congress Hotel. I had known him many years at Pendleton, so I told him the man he had sent out was no good as a foreman. He said, "I know, but he is my father-in-law and I have to take care of him." However, he was not sent back to me.

When we first set up camp we used porcelain dishes. These were condemned so we bought heavy restaurant chinaware. When this work project was abandoned, all camp equipment was surplus and was distributed to Forests in R-6. At the final closing we had a surplus of 900 pounds of dry beans. The Forests that got the dishes had to take a supply of beans.

ALL IN A DAY'S WORK: "-we worked up quite a lather and had several miles to go at sunset."

<u>Sanford Floe</u> *Floe was a District Ranger on the Olympic NF from 1927 to 1959.*

In October 1933, the Hoh Valley [in the Olympic National Forest] was opened to elk hunting after some 20 years of closure. There was an estimated 2000 people in the area. This was four or five times the number expected and created a *Coxey's Army* situation. Biologist Jack Schwartz, two experienced guards and myself were the local Forest officers in the area. The state Game Department had five or six protectors there also. In addition to these the following observers from other agencies were on hand: Leo K. Couch representing the U.S. Biological Survey; Mr. M. P. Skinner, a former National Park naturalist now representing the Boon and Crockett Clubs; Mr. David Madsen, Supervisor of Wild Life Resources for the National Park Service; and Foster Steele representing the Regional Forester.

The first night a former Forest Service employee visiting among the camps accidentally shot a hole in the gasoline lantern pressure tank in a tent. He and two others had to be hospitalized for burns. In rapid succession, a hunter was shot and killed at the head of Owl Creek, miles from a road, and it took the combined efforts of all Forest and Game Department people to get the body out. A party of hunters tried to ford the Hoh River in a truck drowning one of them. A hunter shot himself in the leg about six miles out in the timber, and his partners were so exhausted they could not guide us back to him. We did find him, however. Someone shot a white horse being used to pack out elk meat. Then we had four or five inches of rain in 24 hours, marooning hundreds of people on the wrong side of the river from their camps. Flood stage continued several days. All kinds of craft were pressed into service for ferrying people, but the best were Indians with dugout canoes. There were hundreds of other small incidents; the usual percentage of lost people, car wrecks on the congested road, disputes over who killed the game, camps placed too close to the river bank washed away when the river rose while the owners were out hunting, and so on. One night we were awakened by a pounding on the station door. A somewhat drunk hunter said his partner had not returned to camp. Questioning him got little helpful information. Finally *grasping at straws* I asked how his partner was dressed. In reply the man said he had on a red hat. Since everybody in the area was wearing a red hat, I took considerable ribbing from my partners for not being able to identify the man immediately from his useful (?) information.

251

<u>Ken Wilson</u> *Wilson was a fire guard at the Marion Lake Guard Station on the Willamette NF in 1934. The Willamette was formed by combining the Santiam and Cascade National Forests in 1933.*

WARNING: DON'T READ THIS EPISODE JUST BEFORE EATING

The log cabin at Marion Lake [on the Willamette NF in 1934] was a two-room structure with a living room-bedroom all in one and a separate kitchen. As was the case with many of the early cabins, the ceiling was simply lodgepole-pine poles approximately two inches in diameter laid side by side.

One morning I was frying bacon on my wood stove when I noticed a pop! pop! popping in the frying pan and on top of the stove. Seemed to be coming from the pole ceiling, so I scrambled up on a stool and took a look by lighting a match. Guess what! Right over the stove was a dead pack rat, well-populated with maggots, some of which had obviously been falling into my frying pan. So much for breakfast. I told you not to read this before eating.

<u>Corwin E. "Slim" Hein</u> *Hein told a story in Chapter Two about deer poaching in the early years of the depression. Here is another one, a few years later.*

Ranger Henry Tonseth and I made several winter deer counts in the mid-thirties along the desert edge of the Fort Rock District [on the Deschutes NF] near Cabin Lake Ranger Station. It was fun and fairly easy going on webs and skis as the terrain was quite level. The timber to the west and north had been in the Paulina Game Refuge since 1924 and the deer population was at a high level. Herds of 50 to 150 were common. Following one rather strenuous day we went northeast from Cabin Lake and after about ten miles decided we had enough and dropped in at the old Harrison ranch where Reub Long and two other bachelors were wintering. Reub insisted that we stay overnight and as it was snowing, we accepted and bedded down in the tack room with horseblankets for covers.

The next morning it was still snowing so we kegged up 'til noon. I went out to see what the dogs were barking about and saw Jack Parker,

252

a local trapper, approaching with a backpack and a rather suspicious *limb* sticking out the top. Jack and his partner were wintering at the Foster Well, trapping coyotes and bobcats in the Devil's Garden. Jack announced that they were out of spuds and coffee. Reub threw Jack's pack on the grain bags on the porch and had Jack partake of some lunch. When Jack was ready to leave the spuds and coffee were in his pack and the *limb* was not.

What was it that Jack had brought in his pack? Well, when one is the guest of a neighbor it is not proper protocol to snoop in other guests' baggage.

Soon after Jack left, Henry and I headed for the Derrick ranch via Foster Well and stopped at the trapper cabin for a drink of water. Near the cabin was a mound of coyote and bobcat carcasses bigger than their woodpile. We allowed that Jack and his partner's trapping had saved the lives of far more deer than we suspected they had harvested for table fare. Let sleeping dogs lie!

Hein tells about his experience traveling to two lookouts in the middle of a cold and snowy winter.

In the winter of 1934, Les Hunter and I were given the job of taking panoramic pictures from several of the Deschutes lookouts. Due to the absence of haze it was deemed best to take them in winter.

One of the points was Broken Top Lookout which was located on Tam McArthur Rim above Three Creek Lake. We loaded our gear including a small Cletrac on a truck and set out. Running into snow about five miles west of Bend, we transferred our gear to the cat and took off over the snow. That worked OK for about another five miles when we had to abandon the cat, leaving our bedrolls and other gear, and proceed on skis. We had not the best ski equipment and knew little of the art of skiing uphill. That darned camera and tripod weighed a good 40pounds, so we worked up quite a lather and had several miles to go at sunset. Luckily it was a moonlit night and we zeroed in on the lookout about 8 o'clock.

The door on both lookout and garage were facing the east. The prevailing wind had whipped the ground clean on the west side and deposited the snow high and hard against the doors. Luckily the garage doors had swung partly open and Les, being the smaller of the two, was able to step over the top of the door and onto the snow inside. A barely visible shovel hanging on the wall saved the day, or as it was, the night. After shoveling four cubic yards of snow from the lookout door, we found the door well secured by ice on the threshold. We finally made it and found a good supply of food, a kerosene lamp, a one-man bed and no blankets. We cooked our supper and hit the sack. This was about the first of February but due to some freakish weather it got very little below freezing that night. The next day was warm and cloudless - perfect for taking the pics. Each film spanned 120 degrees. The arc from azimuth 120 degrees to 240 degrees and from 240 degrees to 360 degrees were taken in the morning and from 0 degrees to 120 degrees in mid-afternoon. Therefore it was a bit late when we packed up and headed for home.

I don't know how many times I took spills on the way down with that camera on the Trapper Nelson coming down on the back of my head. We got to Bend with the cat and truck at 10 pm, plumb tuckered out.

Our next trip was to Black Butte Lookout. The trail up the south side was clear of snow so we had a packer take our gear up, however, he did not stay to pack us down. The air was so calm the next morning that the stove would not draw. The kindling would smoke a little, then choke out. Les finally crawled out the cupola window with a kerosene soaked rag, touched it off and dropped it down the stovepipe. Success! I still have a snapshot of Les while he was on the roof in his longjohns.

Jack Groom   *Groom worked on the Whitman, Umatilla, and Fremont NFs, and in Lands and Recreation in the R-6 Regional Office. He retired in 1977. He has a story in Chapter One (Joining Up) about his father, Fred Groom.*

When I was Ranger [at Unity on the Whitman NF] I was the only year-round employee. Because the workload was so light in the winter, I was assigned to other jobs in the Supervisor's Office to help with reports or to other Districts to help with timber sale preparation. I thought of the first few days I spent there as the new Ranger in April 1936. Saturday, upon my arrival, I found a hand-written note on the desk from Gene Wilmouth whose place I was taking. The note said that he had to leave early to go to his new District at Cove so I would have to take a trip he had scheduled for the following Monday.

I was to go to a certain ranch at 4 o'clock in the morning to meet the fence maintenance man for the cattle association. So, I was there at the ranch on time. Two horses were already saddled and we took off. I discovered my companion was totally deaf, but it was amazing that he could understand everything I suggested if he agreed, but if he didn't, he couldn't understand a word. Anyway, at 10 o'clock that night and after 40 miles on that horse, we got back. At about 8 the next morning several local people came to see if I was still alive and to see how many cushions I had in my chair. I could find only one!

Later it was revealed that I was the talk of the whole valley. Evidently this was a sort of initiation. I suppose they might have concluded that although this new Ranger was pretty green, he had survived the first test! Little did they know the real test - I hadn't been on a horse for seven years. Perhaps this initiation was a little rough, but in looking back, I believe that this day had much to do with my friendly acceptance by this community of ranchers.

<u>Lyle N. Anderson</u>   *Anderson worked on the Mt. Baker and Siskiyou NFs.*

In the fall of 1936, I rented two houses at the Riverbanks Farm from old Doc Helens to house my 12-man sugar pine reconnaissance crew [working on the Siskiyou NF]. I tried to locate section corners and run as many of the section lines as I could to familiarize myself with the country before the crew started running their mapping strips.

One morning I spent a couple hours trying to locate a section corner alongside the Redwood Highway just west of the community of Wonder. I finally got into my pickup and spread my topog map over the steering wheel to study it. Across the highway was a rundown shack. I was soon approached by a bearded young man, quite typical of the modern day hippies, who stepped up to the car window reeling off a string of scriptures from the Bible. He then opened the car door and wanted me to get out, kneel down and pray with him. In my flustered state, I finally blurted out, "Say, do you know where that damned section corner is across the road from here?"

255

He straightened up, folded his arms and calmly replied, "Only God knows where that section corner is." He probably was right, for to my knowledge, no one has ever found it.

<u>Gail C. Baker</u>   *Baker started as a temporary in 1933. He received a permanent appointment in 1934. He worked on the Shasta and Plumas NFs in R-5 and the Siskiyou, Malheur, Mt. Hood, and Deschutes NFs in R-6. During WWII he was assigned to the "Synthetic Rubber Project" in Texas. He was the Regional Dispatcher in the R-6 Fire Control office when he retired in 1970.*

While on the Malheur NF in 1937, I was hunting deer on the Long Creek District with Ranger Willis Ward, Supervisor Ed Birkmire, Assistant Supervisor Chet Bennett, game biologist Oliver Edwards and Portland sportsman Ed Averill. We spread out and were hunting on Rudio Mountain. Willis Ward was directing the hunt since it was on his District. He told us all to meet in a saddle on Rudio Ridge. If Willis got there first, he was to signal. When he got there he turned his gun barrel skyward and fired a shot.

Now Willis did not realize his telephone line from the Rudio fireman station to the Rudio Mountain lookout ran up the mountain and through that very saddle. He was quickly aware of it when his signal shot cut his No. 9 telephone line in two. He stood in astonishment as his telephone line went singing through each insulator as it ran a mile and half down the mountainside.

When the rest of the party arrived at the saddle, Willis was chagrined and beside himself in telling us what had happened. Needless to say his hunting trip was over for that day as he had to go to the fireman station and get come-alongs, pliers and tree spurs to restring the telephone line. He had to do it as soon as possible since in those days the No. 9 telephone line was the only means of communication between the lookouts and headquarters.

Another story by Gail C. Baker. The Gasquet Ranger District was part of the Siskiyou NF for many years. The District was transferred to the Six Rivers NF in Region Five in the 1940s.

It happened when we were being transferred from John Day to the Gasquet Ranger District in 1939. Gasquet District was still part of the Siskiyou in R-6 at that time. It has since been transferred to the Six Rivers NF in R-5.

In those days most transfers of personnel were made in the spring before fire season. The Forest Service did the moving by using one of the big red fire trucks that was used in the summer to move Regional fire cache equipment to fires throughout the Region. The Regional fire cache was then on Yeon Street in Portland, and Roy Walker was in charge of the caches. When my move came up, Roy brought over one of the big red fire trucks to move us from John Day to Gasquet.

We were living in a small rental house on the outskirts of John Day. There was an old barn on the place and the owner who lived there before us had chickens. When they moved they left one old hen on the place. Soon she wanted to set, so we sent to Montgomery Ward and got a dozen day-old Rhode Island chicks and gave them to her.

At that time we only had a handful of belongings and wanting to make out somewhat of a decent load for Roy and the big red truck, I crated the dozen chickens and added them to the load. Even that did not make much of a load. So we arranged through Ranger Mike Palmer, who knew the Langs who owned the Rose City Upholstery on Sandy Boulevard in Portland, to pick up a sofa and matching chair on our way through. We also arranged to pick up a set of springs and mattress and other things a short distance from the Rose City establishment.

I had Roy drive the truck via Portland and stop first at the Rose City Upholstery, where I would meet him and help load the living room set. Everything worked out fine, but, since it was only a short distance from the Rose City Upholstery to the next stop, we did not bother to tie the load on securely. As Roy drove the truck down Sandy, the chicken crate fell off and broke wide open. The dozen chickens were loose in the middle of busy Sandy Boulevard. I honked the horn and got Roy's attention. He and I caught every one of those chickens without losing a one! That was in 1939. What do you think would happen if you tried to do that today?

The chickens and the rest of our things arrived safely at Gasquet, and we served fresh eggs and fried chicken to dignitaries from the Regional Office and to Forest Supervisor Ed Cliff on their inspection trips to the District. Probably helped me get a *Satisfactory* rating.

<u>Don Peters</u> *Peters began his Forest Service career as a seasonal lookout on the Mt. Hood NF in 1935. He continued to work seasonally on the Mt. Hood, Umatilla, and Malheur NFs, and in California until he received a full-time professional appointment on the Fremont NF in 1943. He was a District Ranger on the Fremont from 1945 to 1955, and Fire, Recreation, and Lands Staff Officer on the Deschutes NF from 1956 until his retirement in 1974.*

In the early spring of 1939, I and my wife, Ollie, reported to Ditch Creek Guard Station, my first duty station of several to be occupied that summer on the Heppner District of the Umatilla Forest. My official title was Administrative Guard - a glorified assistant to Ranger Fred Wehmeyer as pertained to grazing allotment administration and otherwise a right-hand man in fire matters to Chris Chriswell, then Assistant Ranger. Days were long and weary from riding many miles in company with sheep allotment camp tenders and cattle association riders or cowhands.

Upon being hired for the season by Supervisor Carl Ewing, we were informed that we would be occupying the Ditch Creek Guard Station, but somewhere along the line Ranger Wehymeyer hadn't been in on the planning or otherwise informed. Upon arrival at our duty station we were informed that the station was occupied. The only possible structure having a roof was a small woodshed without floor, stove, sink, bed or cupboards. An extra small wood stove was found around the compound and by use of some sheets of asbestos the roof and walls were protected against fire. A few rough boards were nailed against two sides of the shed and supporting parts to support a bed frame and mattress. Some discarded apple boxes were nailed to the walls for cupboards and other storage.

That took care of cooking and sleeping facilities but you might ask— what about the dirt floors? This problem was resolved by several buckets of water carried daily, applied to the earth floor and then vigorously swept with a broom. Within a few days the dirt hardened

Forest Boundary Patrol at Windigo Pass, Umpqua-Deschutes NFs – 1938

Mill Creek Ranger Station Compound, Ochoco NF – c1940s

and presented no great dust problem. For myself, having been used to eating in logging, sheep and cow camps, this was not a new experience. However for a city girl of 19 without similar experience, I surely admired and still do, the intestinal fortitude it took to accept such a rugged change in lifestyle to make a marriage work. We lived in that set-up approximately six weeks before being transferred to Ellis Guard Station which was to be the center of our activity for another part of the summer.

Fritz Moisio *Moisio started as a temporary in the early 1930s and received a permanent appointment on the Mark Twain NF in R-9 in 1932. He worked on the Mt. Hood, Mt. Baker, Siuslaw and Okanogan NFs in R-6 and was in Watershed management in the R-6 Regional Office when he retired in 1969.*

Seattle City Light anchored their boomsticks on Ross Lake [on the Mt. Baker NF] by means of cables fastened to stumps on the lake floor. The stump ties were made when the lake was drawn down. Floating debris that settled to the bottom along with uncut brush hindered this work. One April day [in the late 1930s or early 1940s] when the humidity was low and the fuel sticks way down, a crew making stump ties burned the debris around a stump. The fire escaped control and threatened to spread from a point opposite Devils Creek to the US-Canadian border. City Light assumed responsibility and secured Forest Service assistance.

The FS provided technical and overhead supervision. The fuels in the immediate green timber were, for the most part, moist. The main concern was the felled, bucked and cold-decked timber within the boundaries of the reservoir. In addition to their own and the contractors' crews, City Light secured firefighters from Seattle's *skid road*. Some were hired without being screened and a few who had been on grape juice all winter reached the fire line in poor physical condition. One such skid-roader on his way to camp at the end of his shift took a shortcut by wading the ice-cold Skagit below Jack Point. He made it to shore but that's all - his heart stopped and first aid failed to revive him.

Since I had first-hand knowledge and other details concerning the death, Mr. Currier, headworks superintendent, and Dr. Rueb, deputy coroner, wanted me to dispatch and accompany the body to

Newhalem. Because of the draw-down, it was necessary to tote the body to a point below Cat Creek where the Forest Service boat was beached. Fred Berry and I had quite a time with the stretcher bearers we had recruited. They were so superstitious that during each rest stop we lost a bearer. By the time we were within a half mile of the boat, Fred and I were the bearers. We made it to the boat and by evening reached City Light Floating Camp.

Here we contacted [District Ranger] Tommy Thompson. Tommy informed us Mr. Currier had called that arrangements had been made for the high-line to lift us and the body over the dam to a City Light boat in the morning and other City Light transportation would be available to take us from Diablo to Newhalem. It was warm and we asked Tommy where we could best keep the body. Tommy said he'd find a place after supper, so we left the body in the FS boat while we washed and had dinner. After dinner we were assigned bunks and Tommy came along with a flashlight, saying he had a good place for the body. So once again Fred and I were bearing the body and followed Tommy into the cook's walk-in ice box. We deposited the body within the available floor space. As we closed the door, I asked Tommy, "How about the cook?"

Tommy answered, "He's got what he needs for breakfast. It's best to keep this quiet or nobody will get any sleep."

Next morning early as Fred and I were walking towards the mess hall. Tommy approached and said, "I think you fellers had better get your breakfast in Newhalem. Early this morning Stan Aldo saw the cook going over the hill white as a sheet." When the high-line was lifting us over the dam, I had the feeling Tommy had really set us up. Whenever I travel over the North Cascade Highway, I stop at an overlook near Ross Dam and give Tommy and the Skid Road gentleman a salute of respect, and each time I hear Tommy saying, "We put it over on them fellers," and the Skid Roader chuckles, "Yeh, yeh, we sure did, Tommy."

WIVES' TALES: "-locating on a Ranger District meant a lot of new experiences for me."

<u>Mildred G. Nelson</u> *Mildred and her husband, M. M. "Red" Nelson, went to high school together in California, at San Fernando High. Mildred had a short career as a registered nurse before she married "Red". From then on she was a stay at home mom, raising two sons. One son, Marsh, was an engineering technician, working almost forty years on the Shasta-Trinity NF in R-5. Another son, Gordon, was a forester in private industry. "Red" Nelson, who had a long career in management with the Forest Service, has several stories in Chapters Two and Three of this book.*

My life with the Forest Service started in 1936 when I married M. M. "Red" Nelson who only months before had received his permanent appointment as a junior forester. He was assigned as Assistant Ranger on the Naches District of the Snoqualmie NF. Some say, in those days, when you married a Forest Service man you also married the Forest Service. There is some truth in that, but I have no complaints - both have been good to me. I was no young kid when we were married, being a registered nurse and working at my profession. I wasn't, however, wise to the mountains or backwoods because I was raised in the Los Angeles area and was a *city girl*. So coming north and locating out on a Ranger District meant a lot of new experiences for me. As I think back there were experiences that would be impossible to have in this day and age.

One example: All of my belongings were packed up for moving and came north with me on the train. As the train crossed some of the desert lands south of Yakima it suddenly stopped out where there was nothing in sight but sagebrush. It stopped to pick up some Indians that had flagged it. It made me feel like I was riding a stagecoach waylaid by Indians. I was glad my mother was with me.

We were married in Seattle in mid-August on a weekend. In those days it was unheard of for a Forest Service employee to have any leave during the fire season. Red felt lucky at even getting the Saturday morning off. That means a pretty short honeymoon before being back to work at the Ranger Station on Monday morning. In fact one might say our honeymoon was at the Naches Ranger Station.

You should understand what the Ranger Station was like. It is located on the eastern side of the Cascade Mountains in pine country about 40 miles upriver from the apple growing community of Naches and about 60 miles from Yakima. It was on a large flat with the American River on one side and mountains on the other side with the Naches Highway running through it. The Ranger's office and three year-long residential homes were on the mountain side. On the river side were the warehouses, workshops, corrals, barn and some small summer dwellings and a building for work crews labeled *the Bunk House*. At one end of the flat was a CCC [Civilian Conservation Corps] camp with 200 boys and their foremen and Army camp personnel.

It is natural that a bachelor Assistant Ranger did not occupy one of the dwellings even though it was labeled *Assistant Ranger*. He lived in a room above the office and ate at the CCC camp. It was also natural that if he married in mid-fire season he still didn't rate one of the year-long dwellings until fall. What he did rate was the only unoccupied building, which was the *Bunk House*.

So the *Bunk House* became our honeymoon cottage. It was designed for a crew of eight. It had a good size kitchen with a very large Lang wood range, a table to seat eight, running water (in summer), sink, and cupboards. The main room was surrounded with built-in lockers so each man could have one. When we moved in that room was filled with cots and mattresses. The third room was the bath. It had an open shower, wash basins, a urinal and a toilet like I had never seen. It was designed for cold weather winter use when water would freeze. So, it had no usual water trap in the bowl and no normal water holder. There was a metal tank up above that filled with water only as you sat. The seat stayed up at an angle until sat upon which then opened a spigot to fill the tank above. When you got up from the seat the strong spring caused the seat to fly up. That shut off the water to the tank and also opened a valve to flush the toilet. It worked fine, but first you had to learn to hold down the seat with one hand while you slid off. Red kept telling me how much better it was than just having a *biffy* out back. A year later another newlywed couple lived in this *Bunk House* and his mother-in-law came to visit. She swore the young forester had fixed the contraption just to irritate her.

The wood range was another thing that took some learning for a city girl. There was no electricity at the Ranger Station. I had to learn to light a Coleman lantern, clean chimneys, make best use of candles, and learn NOT to USE an electric toaster, oven, refrigerator, washer, vacuum, iron, stove, etc. The wood range took a lot of practice. I let the fire go out three times while I was baking my first cake. I also burned many a slice of bread making toast on top of the stove. Red did not complain, because he said he was in high school before he learned there was a way to make toast without first burning it on top of the stove then scraping it over the sink. Later he did learn from the fire camp cook that if you sprinkled salt on top of the range then toasted the bread, you could do a fine job. It worked, too.

Ranger Ray Hampton and wife Ramona gave us a gasoline iron as a wedding gift. It scared me, but Ramona had me over to her house to train me how to use it. She got it all pumped up and put some gas in the container used to heat the combustion unit. Then she lit it. There were flames three feet high! Nonchalantly she opened the back door and threw it out in the back yard. My NEW IRON! But she saved burning down the house!

Country shopping was a new way for me. There was no refrigeration, not even an old ice box, so I had to learn to make out with canned goods or things that did not easily spoil. There was some help through community use of a root cellar built like a cave back into the hill. It kept things a bit cooler in summer and from hard freezing in winter. The nearest store was at Naches, 40 miles away, but most real shopping was done in Yakima, even further. Usually once a week one of the four or five families at the Ranger Station would furnish a car and drive to Yakima with some of us wives going or sending our order list with those that did go. It took some time for me to get over going to such stores as Penny's and seeing old Indian women sitting on the floor in the isles with their back next to the warm glass showcases.

As Thanksgiving approached I sent my grocery order to town with some of the other wives and asked them to bring me a chicken. Imagine the surprise on my *city girl* face when I took it out of the bag. It was a whole chicken (as ordered). When they said *whole* they meant *whole*! All I can say is that it was dead and the only thing missing was some blood from having its throat cut. We worked for hours getting it ready to cook. It took a reference book, time and patience before it was defeathered, dressed and stuffed. I learned chicken anatomy firsthand.

Social events at an outlaying Station were not many - perhaps a dance at some distant Grange Hall every month or so. The District personnel had to make their own entertainment. Having a newly-married couple on the flat made one such opportunity. It was called a *shivaree*. That is where the people all wait until you are well settled in bed then all come calling on you en masse with much noise, pan beating, bell ringing and horn blowing. I had never heard of such a thing, but Red was wise to it. Guessing when it might occur, we turned the gas light off early (but stayed up in the dark). Sure enough they came - a jolly lot! We were prepared with beer and refreshments. Our first party was a success!

We had not been established at the Ranger Station too long when one day the *crank-your-own-number* phone rang with my number - two longs and one short. It was Red calling to say, "The Indians are coming! Come over to the office quick!" I did not know what to expect but followed the orders. It was a large group of Yakima Indians, mostly on horseback but with a few horse and buggies. They had been up on the Ranger District in the high country picking their annual supply of blueberries. A colorful parade was going back to their reservation. I shall never forget one old, old Indian woman on a swayback horse who looked as if she had spent her life on that horse and they had grown old together.

Nelson was left alone when her husband was sent to a fire in southwest Oregon.

We had been married six weeks when one Friday evening the Ranger sent us into Seattle to deliver something to the Supervisor's office on Saturday morning (a work day until noon at that time). We did the job then seriously considered staying to attend a university football game. But, Red said it was still fire season so we better get back. We returned and had not been back more than an hour when the Ranger got a call telling of a most serious fire situation on the Siskiyou Forest and all of southwest Oregon. They were sending CCC crews from most all camps in the region, and Red was to go also but not with the

CCCs. He was to take our car, drive back to Seattle, pick up Ranger Paul Piper and head for Oregon. He soon left his bride to go firefighting. The next morning, I think it was September 26th, the battery-powered radio carried reports that the Oregon coastal town of Bandon had burned to the ground the night before. It was a bad period of dry east winds that came after many loggers and ranchers had started their usual fall burning. There were many large fires; it looked like a long siege and it was!

I was stuck in a strange backwoods area without even a car (no matter about that because at that time I did not know how to drive). The other people at the Ranger Station were especially good to me and made me feel at home. Fire season ended on the Snoqualmie and one of the dwellings next to the office became vacant so I got lots of help moving from the *Bunk House* into a real house - even had some furniture. Red kept me informed as he went from one fire to another getting a world of experience in running crews, scouting fires and running fire camps.

I knew he would not ask to be relieved as long as he could be getting more experience that he thought valuable. So when I had some friends visit me from California, I joined with them and they drove me down the Oregon coast to the town of Coquille. It was then the GHQ for all of the fire area and Red was there, by that time running the service and supply end of the firefighting. I remember the devastated look of what had been the town of Bandon. I guess every home had a fireplace. All that was left was a sea of standing chimneys - all else was burned to the ground all the way to the edge of the sea. Lives had been saved by taking boats out into the ocean.

I also learned about gorse! It looks something like scotch broom with its yellow blossoms. It grows bigger and in very low humidity becomes very volatile. It was growing rampant in and near Bandon and was the culprit that made it impossible to save the town once it caught fire in the high winds. I stayed at Coquille with Red the last week or more as he finished up shipping out men and supplies and writing purchase orders for the last of supplies, phone service, warehouse and office rent. He was the very last of the imported Forest Service overhead to leave the area.

We had a leisurely drive back to Naches and arrived six weeks after he had left. We had been married six weeks, then he had gone firefighting for six weeks. In another six weeks we would be leaving to return to the Siskiyou. Red was to be the District Ranger on the Page Creek District at Cave Junction (now called the Illinois Valley District). Before Red left Coquille, Supervisor Glen Mitchell had come to him and offered him the Ranger job.

Nelson describes her experiences as the Ranger's wife at the Redwood Ranger Station on the Siskiyou NF.

My next experience was different and really enjoyable. The Redwood Ranger Station was all new, having been moved to town from out at Page Creek. It was called *Redwood* because the buildings were all finished in beautiful redwood siding. We had a fine new home with three bedrooms, 1-1/2 baths, full basement, furnace, fireplace, dining room and electric power, but we still cooked on a wood range. It was only a short walk to *downtown* Cave Junction with its post office, store, motel, two eating places, garage, and service station, but I did learn to drive so that I might go into Grants Pass (30 miles) for most major shopping. We arrived a week before Christmas in 1936. The Forest Service moved our household belongings in a stakeside truck (about one-third loaded). They consisted of one easy chair, two barrels of dishes, pots and pans, one trunk, two Navajo rugs and one saddle. The big house was quite bare at first, but the day before our first Christmas a new settee (which had been ordered) came, so for Christmas we could both sit before the fireplace without having to sit on each other.

Part-time telephone operator was one of my volunteer jobs at the Ranger Station. This was because there was little commercial telephone service in the Illinois Valley. The Forest Service had a main line running into Grants Pass and numerous lines out of the Ranger Station to lookouts, guard stations, etc. These lines also served a National Park Service CCC camp near Oregon Caves, the Gasquet Ranger Station and the CCC camp located over the mountain to the southwest. All calls to those locations had to be switched in the Ranger's office or at his home after working hours. Thus when Red was in the field I had much telephone operating to do. There was an interesting feature to the switchboard. Each line had a *howler* hooked into it. That was so that someone in the field could hook onto the line with a small hand phone without a ringer and still be heard by a buzz in the howler. Also it meant that one could hear all that was said on the line without the receiver being plugged in. Thus I kept up pretty well on all that was going on in the District.

I recall some evening phone use where Irene Cribb, wife of one of Red's guards, was giving cooking lessons for the various young fellows on lookouts. She gave a lesson in baking a cake. Later Jimmy Miller on Pearsoll lookout reported that his was burned black on both top and bottom but when he cut that off the center was pretty good.

Irene was an excellent cook and she and Art used her cooking as a fire prevention tool on the Illinois River area. Being in the depression era, there were a lot of would-be-miners scattered along the river panning for gold trying to eke out a living. Some of them were not adverse to setting a fire with the thought of gaining some wages from the Forest Service for fighting fire. One of the forest guard's duties was fire prevention. Art and Irene would invite the local people to the guard station for cribbage tournaments and some of Irene's cooking. They kept on the good side of their would-be-fire-setters. Irene even baked cupcakes that Art would leave at their diggings. One miner told Irene how good they were, but that they had a tough crust. They learned he had eaten the paper cup they had been baked in.

We were close to the Oregon Caves and liked to take guests there for dinner on a warm summer night and stay for the campfire program put on by the musically inclined student workers at the lodge. The best party at the Caves was the night Irene and Art Cribb were married at a campfire wedding. Red and I were best man and bridesmaid. It was a formal wedding and gave Red a chance to wear his tux left from college days - the first time I had seen him in a tux, and the last time until after we retired and started doing some travel by ship.

I was very concerned the first time Forest Supervisor Glen Mitchell came out to the District. I knew he was an excellent cook so inquired about what to feed him. I was told to feed him anything but be sure to have a good dessert. My experience with dessert was something like that of lookout Jimmy Miller, so I went across the highway to my friend who baked me two pies. We passed with flying colors. It was

268

easy to cook for Ed Cliff [when he became Forest Supervisor]. The main thing was to have lots of hot sauce, salt and pepper. He used quantities of all even before tasting the food.

Living at Cave Junction was surely being in town compared to Naches, but still it was a town without a doctor, dentist, bank or many such things considered for town living. Our dentist was located over in Crescent City on the California coast. Our trips over there had some advantages; we could stop to visit with the Gasquet Ranger's family (in our time the Merle Lowdens and the Gail Bakers); we could always have a seafood dinner; and we always went to the waterfront to buy three large crabs to take home. They cost three for $1.00 - quite a difference from what I paid the other day (1979) which was one crab for $3.50.

While we were at Cave Junction some progress was made: a movie house opened, two older brothers moved in and started a weekly newspaper, and an old retired doctor moved into the valley. We had to use him twice. First, when I was splitting kindling to start a fire in the furnace I miscalculated and chopped my finger. He sewed it up but it has been crooked ever since. The second time was when our son Marshall was about two years old (he was born in summer of 1937). Red had fenced a small area as a playpen for him in our yard. First time he used it was with a guard's youngster, Sunny Handsen, and they had some small garden tools. Next thing I knew, Sunny had used the hoe on Marshall's head. The blood was all over his face, and the new *old* doctor had another sewing job. Needless to say we never again got Marshall into that playpen.

When I went to Grants Pass I usually bought groceries by the case. I discovered a store that sold catsup by the gallon (#10 cans) and checked out with two such cans. The clerk asked if I ran a restaurant. My answer was simple, "No, but my husband loves catsup." It was well known that every lookout and guard better have catsup available when the Ranger came to stay overnight on an inspection. He claimed it was the only thing that made some of their cooking eatable. He may have thought the same about my cooking, but he never said so. I claim his love of catsup came in the years of his bachelorhood developed for his own cooking.

Nelson recalls the occurrence of a number of large fires on the Siskiyou NF in 1938.

In the days of our assignment on the Siskiyou it was well known as the *Fire Forest* of the Region. They had lots of lightning fires plus lots started as incendiary by the local people who really believed in burning (especially along the coast). Consequently, it was a rare year that there were not large fires where the Siskiyou played host to overhead from all the Forests of the Region. In fact, they decided, following the 1936 season, to fill all of the six Districts with vigorous young Rangers. Then they sent Les Colvill to be Assistant Supervisor with instructions to *teach those kids how to prevent and fight fires.* The Rangers included Merle Lowden, Ed Marshall, Kermit Lindstedt, Whitey Norgard, Loren Cooper and Red. Within a year or so, Boyd Rasmussen and Gail Baker were also Rangers. Also Ed Cliff came to be the Forest Supervisor replacing Glen Mitchell.

Being the wife of a Ranger on a District with a heavy fire load meant being disturbed many times during the night when he would be called for a fire or a lightning storm in progress. In those days the Forest Service was the only firefighting agency for all of the private land in the entire Illinois Valley so there were house fires to be fought as well as forest fires. I recall one night when he went out three times. About 9 pm a lookout reported a fire up on the Caves Highway. It was small and he was back in an hour, but said it had been set by an arsonist. About 11:30 pm there was another; he was gone again - same cause. Then about 1 am the same thing. This time, however, the lookout, who was a local chap, had been watching the lights of a car in a logged area where the fire started. [The lookout was Fritz Morrison, a native of Grants Pass and attending Oregon State College Forestry school. Morrison joined the Forest Service upon graduation and was second in command at the Boise Interagency Fire Center when he retired.] He could tell Red just which house in the town of Kerby the car stopped. When that fire was out, Red called a friend in the State Police. Early in the morning they made an arrest and the arsonist spent a good many months in jail. That put an end to the incendiary problem on that District for the rest of our time there.

When we had a lot of lightning fires going at the same time, or a big fire, there was always lots of activity at the Station. I recall getting up one morning in 1938 and looking out to see 200 men sleeping on our front lawn. They had been bused in from Portland as firefighters. Then, Red also ran a Regional Remount Station so we had lots of activity with pack horses being sent out to pack supplies. There were about 60 horses besides Red's District string of mules. In non-fire times it was interesting watching the three packers breaking horses, or branding or shoeing them.

The 1938 fire siege was the big one on the Siskiyou. It started when Cooper on the Galice District had a project fire set, followed by Lowden with lightning project fires. Then we had bad dry lightning storms for two nights in a row. Red had 54 fires reported to take action on. The last one reported was way back on Nome Creek and took a tired crew 16 hours to get to it. It became big. In the meantime, Ed Marshall's *friends* on the Chetco started one for him in a bad place and in bad weather which made it the biggest. With all that fire and smoke covering the whole area, the lookouts couldn't see a new fire if it did start. The Indians on Lindstedt's Agness District knew this, so they went out and set one for him that became project-size even before discovery. That means of the six Siskiyou Districts, five of them had big project fires at the same time.

When Red's crews caught the Nome fire, he moved a camp onto the backside of the bigger Chetco fire (by then on his District too). I recall that he sent me a radio message on the occasion of our second wedding anniversary. It was from a fire camp so far back that it took pack trains two days to make a round trip. But I learned that anniversary messages from isolated places came to be expected when one marries into the Forest Service on August 8th.

This vigorous group of young Rangers made for some good times when they were called into Grants Pass to attend Ranger Meetings. In those days the meetings were used to prepare the yearly work plans so they lasted for a week or more. The Rangers' wives and babies also came to town and all stayed at the Pine Tree Motel. We wives had great times together even if much of it was washing diapers. (Those Rangers were vigorous in more ways than one!)

The Gold Beach Ranger's home was probably the finest in the Region. A reason for this was that in the days of the CCC and other depression

271

funding, the Supervisor had much to say about what type of work was done. Glen Mitchell believed in improved housing and Station buildings. This differed from where we had been on the Snoqualmie where the Supervisor wanted roads and recreation improvements. Up there, the residence buildings, (even in their cold climate) didn't have basements, furnaces, fireplaces, storm doors or even screens for the windows. The Siskiyou had a full time architect and even a shop making myrtlewood furniture. Red's office was paneled in Port Orford cedar which has a rich color.

We were glad we had the chance to spend three years on the Ranger District before Red became a staff officer on the Umpqua. We moved to Roseburg in 1940 and stayed there ten years - through and after the war. The *city girl* had made it to town! Yes, town, with churches, doctors, dentists, high school, lodges, service clubs and even milk delivery.

<u>Charlotte Wood</u> *Charlotte Wood's husband, Jack Wood, spent a long career with the Forest Service in Region Six and Washington DC. This story is taken from a longer version first appearing in "Sampler of the Early Years, Volume II", published by the Forestry Wives Club of Washington DC in 1986. The club is now titled Forest Service Women.*

In the spring of 1937, Jack was appointed as junior forester on the Colville NF. At that time Republic, Washington, was the headquarters. Its population was 510. He left me in Seattle in March, and after six months of looking for a rental house, he was successful and returned to move me and our 18-month-old daughter to our new house. [The Colville NF has a history in both Region 6 and Region 1. Administration of the Forest was transferred from R-6 to R-1 in 1943, although a portion remained in R-6 as part of the Chelan NF. Then, in 1974, administration was transferred from Region 1 back to R-6.]

The little cottage was our first house. After living there about six weeks, we learned that the house had been sold. Our landlord offered us another rental which would be available in June when the school year was over and the teacher-tenants left. The rent for this two-bedroom house was $20 per month. It had a living room with a wood heater, kitchen complete with wood stove and icebox, and in what had been the closet of the master bedroom, a bathtub. There were neither hand basin nor toilet. The outdoor toilet was in the garage/woodshed building.

After thinking about winter temperatures of 20 degrees below, I went to talk to our landlord. I didn't exactly make him an offer he couldn't refuse, but I did suggest that we could pay $25 a month if he would install a toilet and hand basin. He thought the hand basin entirely unnecessary. "After all," he reasoned, "Jack could shave in the kitchen sink." But he succumbed when I said I just couldn't have people brushing their teeth in the sink and I couldn't stand whiskers in my breakfast. Before cold weather, we had a complete bathroom.

This house had another point of interest. It occupied a hillside with the front of the house at street level and the back porch on stilts with a steep stairway from the backyard. The view over the housetops was toward a large building containing the local bordello, known as *Buttercup Hill* by the natives. Each group of girl residents of Buttercup Hill stayed only a few weeks on a sort of rotation basis being then replaced by others. They were required to have health examinations every week, and although they could come into town to shop, they were not allowed to speak to anyone on the street.

Life in Republic was very different from life in Seattle where Jack and I were raised. I soon learned to enjoy the friendliness of small-town living.

H. C. "Chris" Chriswell   *Chriswell was an Assistant District Ranger on the Umatilla NF at the time of this story (1937-1938).*

Some of the older Rangers had their wives travel with them. They were as much a part of the Forest Service as their husbands. On horse trips they would camp-tend, cook and take care of the stock. Iris went with me whenever she could. After guard school most of my work [on the Umatilla NF] was follow-up training of guards and lookouts, followed by range inspection *and other duties as assigned*. When spending a day with a guard, Iris would visit with his family. The guards became our best friends; they were wonderful.

We often got home late Friday night from a week's trip. Iris would shop Saturday morning while I worked in the office. We would load everything in the car Sunday evening and head out again to the District to make camp. It was a busy and eventful life.

There was a shelter and fenced pasture at Long Prairie. We camped there and turned my rented horse out in the pasture. He was a good horse but defied all my efforts to catch him in the morning. One day Iris went out, walked up to him and put the halter over his neck. We learned later that the horse had been ridden to school all winter by a girl. From Long Prairie, I could spend the week inspecting several sheep allotments and training a few guards. We visited the young couple on Wheeler Point lookout. One day, after inspecting a sheep allotment, I returned to camp about 5:00 pm to find Iris and the car gone. I assumed she was visiting her friend at Wheeler Point, so I prepared dinner. I called the lookout but no answer. Just as I was ready to call Heppner, the lookout drove up in his car.

"Our wives left the lookout in your car after lunch for a short ride. About two hours ago, they walked back to the lookout. Your car is stuck in the mud down on Wineland Meadow. I got permission to leave to go down and get it out but got my car stuck too. After I got my car out I came here."

When we arrived at the meadow there was my car out on the lush green grass, down on all axles. Iris excitedly explained, "We saw a lake on the map and decided to go swimming. We came to this pretty meadow where the road ended. I could see the road leaving on the other side so all I had to do was drive across." I patiently explained that no one would ever dream of crossing that wet meadow in the summer. It didn't dry out until September.

We pried on the axle ends with poles, stuffed bark, rotten wood and other material under the wheels until the car was out of the mud. Then we *paved* the short distance back to solid ground with more bark. Then we rigged a *Spanish windlass*. I tied my long one inch rope to the car and the other end to a nearby pine tree. About 50 feet behind the car I dug a hole and jabbed a sturdy post into it. We used a long pole, putting one end against the post and wrapped or looped the rope around the end. Pushing the pole around and around the post gave us the power of a lever and wrapped the rope around the post like a capstan. We got the car out without difficulty. We hadn't heard of the handyman jack yet and used the *Spanish windlass* several times. Late that fall we walked into Wineland Lake, the only lake on the Heppner District. It was small and covered with lily pads, definitely not suitable for swimming.

HORSES AND MULES: "It became common knowledge that Agate would unload his boss, the Supervisor, now and then on a cold morning."

<u>H. C. "Chris" Chriswell</u> *Chriswell has a story about Ranger Fred Wehmeyer and horses in Chapter Two. Here, Chriswell tells two stories about his own adventures with burros and horses.*

We had two burros at Baker Creek while we were performing the R-6 cruise and map work [on the Olympic NF] in 1934. The cook fed them any left over hotcakes from breakfast. While we were eating, the burros would be getting closer and closer to the open end of the cook tent. They would stretch their necks out and then walk their bodies up to their heads. They did this over and over very slowly. We could look up and they would be a foot or two closer, but we never noticed them move. I don't know where they learned to do this, but before long their heads would be inside the tent.

Chriswells' second story occurred when he was the Assistant District Ranger on the Umatilla NF in 1937.

Oh yes, there was one other bit of training [from Fred Wehmeyer, District Ranger at Heppner on the Umatilla NF]. "This ol' horse's name is *Nuts*. He's been in the Forest Service family so long he probably knows more than we do. Watch him. He'll fool you goin' out but he'll go H—— bent when you turn him towards the barn. Give him his head and he'll take you any place on the District you want to go." Nuts had been ridden by forest officers for several years. I could hang on the saddle all manner of maintenance tools that dangled and jangled. I would stand up in the saddle to replace a low-hung split insulator, dropping cut-off No. 9 wire about his ears. He wouldn't move a muscle. Upon meeting a bear, Nuts would calmly stand there watching the bear until it finally ambled away. With a grazing map in one hand I would point Nuts towards where a sheep camp was indicated. Before long there would be the camp.

275

M. M. "Red" Nelson   *Nelson tells about some of his early experiences with horses.*

In 1935 I started my regular FS career on the [Mt. Baker National] Forest, being assigned as a junior forester at the Ranger Station at Marblemount. One morning Ranger Tommy Thompson asked if I knew how to pack a mule. He had determined it was time to build a privy at one of the established lookouts and needed to take some lumber up to do the job as well as some rolls of #9 phone wire to replace the upper part of the line which was then buried under much snow. I told him I knew something about packing and how to throw a diamond hitch, but had never packed lumber. Tommie says, "You're my man." He had another fellow working but I recall Tommie saying, "He doesn't know the breast strap from the crupper."

He also said he would go up and show me how to load lumber on a mule. He did. Some of the lumber was eight feet long so it was packed with the forward end up over the neck of the mule and the other end sticking out rather wide on each side of the mules (the lumber thus in a kind of a *V* shape). I was soon off on my own leading the saddle horse loaded with the phone wire and the two mules loaded with lumber. The Ranger was an excellent packer (had to be with a million acre District and about 12 or 15 miles of road). But I still had to stop and repack the loads a number of times.

As I got near the lookout, the snow became quite deep and the trail had only been broken by the lookout walking in. The lumber would rub in the snowdrifts. Then I started to cross a small stream that ran down under the snow on the trail. One mule dropped into that. The lumber caught, and he was flipped upside down and over the bank. The lumber sticking out on each side served like ski poles and kept the mule on his back as he slid down a steep snow bank with all four feet pawing the air. I thought that would be the last I would see of him, but in a few hundred feet he hit a tree and stopped. I cut off the pack and retrieved the mule (unhurt except for his dignity). From that point on to the top, the lumber packing job had to be handled by the lookout - board by board.

In 1936, at Naches Ranger District (then on the Snoqualmie NF), I was a full time Assistant Ranger so obligated to buy my first saddle horse

($50) and saddle ($5) - total cost a bit over a third of my monthly pay. Much of the inspection work in summer was in the back country requiring horses and mules for transportation. In December of that year, I was made Ranger on the Siskiyou NF at Cave Junction, Oregon. A look at a map made it clear that much of my work would require a horse (only one of six lookouts had a road to it) so I suggested to Supervisor Glen Mitchell that the FS pay for transporting my saddle horse to the Siskiyou. I was disappointed when he turned me down. But, he said they had plenty of pack and saddle stock and the government would furnish the horses for the Ranger. Besides, he said, if you like your own horse you would not like to use it on the Siskiyou because natural feed (meadows) were very few and far between and you always had to pack grain to subsist and it was a hard country on the pack and saddle stock. He was right.

Nelson shares some background about the Regional Remount Station on his Ranger District on the Siskiyou NF.

When I took over the Ranger District I also assumed considerable responsibility for horses and mules! I had my District string of seven or eight mules plus saddle horses and also five or six burros used with trail maintenance crews. I also had full responsibility for the Regional Remount Station. It had about 65 head of horses maintained at my Ranger Station for use in packing on fires any place in the Northwest (also used some in Northern California). In addition, each fall, all of the string of mules and the saddle horses from the other five Ranger Districts were assembled at my Ranger Station.

I was responsible for getting winter pasture for the whole herd, about 110 head. We usually got the pasture in the Medford area and drove the whole herd to the pasture and return in the spring. It was a two day drive each way. I recall one year when spring was late in coming and the rented winter pasture played out. We rented another pasture for a month but it was located nearly 40 miles away. One of my packers, a summer fire guard and I went over early one morning, caught us some riding animals and started the drive to the new pasture. The first ten miles were at a full gallop! The route required crossing a ridge of mountains. As we neared the top of a logging road the road divided into many branches and we had different horses taking each different branch. It was a big round-up job before getting them headed down the other side on a narrow trail. It was well after dark and raining hard before we got them into the new pasture. Needless to say part of me was too sore to comfortably sit down the next day. After returning the whole herd to my Station in the spring, the other Districts would come for their pack strings.

In the mid-1930s the Forest Service, in much of the west, found that supplying fire camps on large back country fires was becoming a problem because the number of pack strings that might be rented for use on fires were becoming fewer and fewer. The answer was for the Forest Service to maintain some remount stations to be sure to have pack animals to go on large fires. Region One out of Missoula, Montana, established a remount station with brood mares and jacks and raised mules for their supply of remount pack animals. Later, in the 1940s, their mule production was great enough so they were even supplying mules for some Ranger Stations in Oregon. We used mules from such a shipment on the Umpqua NF.

Region Six decided to establish a remount station on the Siskiyou NF for use in the Northwest. In 1935 or spring of 1936, Ken Blair, the Redwood Ranger and Frank Folsom of the Regional Office made a horse buying trip to eastern Oregon for animals to establish the remount. I know it was in operation in 1936 because as an Assistant Ranger I was assigned as service chief on the large Sandy Fire (one of many being handled by the FS during the late fall conflagration situation). We determined that we needed to establish a fire camp a good distance back from any road. Otto Lindh was Division Boss in charge of that camp. My responsibility was to keep the camp supplied. I heard about the new remount station and ordered packers and pack animals to pack to Otto's camp.

A couple of months later I was made Ranger with responsibility for the remount station. It was then that I began to really learn about the remount. The animals bought for it were, in general, range horses and had not been broken to carry a pack. The remount packers had a big job just breaking horses. Some were impossible to break so the packers and I were allowed to *horse trade* - always trying to upgrade the pack strings. That was in the days before the Siskiyou rated an administrative officer on the staff. Later Ernie Shank was assigned in such a job and discovered in the manual that *horse trading* was not allowed without getting out bids and other paper work that made it not worthwhile. By that time, however, we had a pretty good string of working horses.

There were many interesting experiences in operation of a remount. When at the station the stock had to be fed twice a day. They ate a lot of hay in a season. I had to buy hay and some of that was done in the packer's *off season*, meaning that I was the only one available for the unloading and stacking of the hay bales in the barn - a back breaking job! After each horse was broke to pack, they had to be shod before used on the rocky trails. We hired a special horseshoer to help the packers with that job in the spring. Then it was up to the packers to replace shoes as needed. Horseshoeing went on for several weeks in the spring. Some horses did not like it, so a special sling rig was used to hold up the horse and a special method used in tying up their flailing hind legs until the metal shoe could be heated in the forge, pounded out to fit the shape of the hoof and then nailed in place. Spring always had something interesting at the horseshoeing shed. If the animal had not yet been branded with a US that was also done at shoeing time while we had a fire going in the forge to heat the branding iron white-hot. The bad odor of burning hair was common.

One year we had a young jack burro and decided to try to raise a couple of mules using mares in our pack string. We built a special corral for the jack to keep him away from the jennie burros. We put mares in with him but he would have nothing to do with them. My packers claimed it was because he had previously been with jennies and liked them better.

Nelson relates one more horse story, this one is about a horse and Ed Cliff before Cliff became Chief of the Forest Service.

In 1962 Ed Cliff became Chief of the Forest Service. It was only a few weeks after John Glenn had made his famous trip into space. A family meeting was held in the USDA auditorium which Information and Education promoted as a *Launching of the New Chief.* They even had a dummy rocketship on the stage. Some of us were called upon to say a few words. I thought it might be a good time to say that this was not the first time Ed Cliff had been launched and tell the story of the first launching.

279

In the late 1930s one of our horses at the Redwood Remount Station [on the Siskiyou NF] was a beautiful pinto. His name was Agate. He was not a stallion and really not a gelding either. That was because he had been *cut proud*. We called him an *original*. As such, he was a kind of a nuisance. If in a corral with geldings he was always fighting with them. If in a corral with mares his stallion instinct became pronounced. But he was a good strong horse so my packers and I decided he would be more useful as a saddle horse rather than being used in a pack string. They broke him to ride.

When Ed Cliff came to the Siskiyou as Forest Supervisor he needed a saddle horse to get around in that unroaded Forest. He chose the beautiful Agate even though he had not been fully broken and tended to buck now and then. It became common knowledge that Agate would unload his boss, the Supervisor, now and then on a cold morning or early in the spring.

On a back-country inspection trip Ed was making with Ranger Boyd Rasmussen they had been gone a week and Agate had behaved fine. On their last day as they headed toward the Powers Ranger Station, Boyd commented to Ed something like, "I am not going to be satisfied until I see Agate buck you off." Well, they had not gone far and were riding a steep trail around a mountainside with a cover of thornbush, when sure enough Agate launched Supervisor Ed Cliff high into the air and down the hill into the thornbush. As you can expect there was one mad Supervisor climbing out of the brush patch and accusing his Ranger of having jogged Agate with a stick to cause the bucking. Boyd steadfastly denied it for many years. Good thing he did for he was, perhaps, closest he had ever come to being demoted or fired.

When Chief Cliff took the podium he told the story in greater detail. Also, how he enjoyed that horse, Agate, and had him transferred to the Fremont Forest when he moved to Lakeview to be Forest Supervisor. Agate still had his game at bucking but Ed did not mind because Agate was still a fine beautiful strong horse and also made a good show in local parades. (Probably the local Lakeview people were like Boyd and looked forward to seeing a contest between Ed and Agate?) The Regional Safety Officer, however, considered Agate a safety hazard and recommended disposal. Ed refused, but it is said that when Ed left for Region 4, the new Supervisor Larry Mays could not stand the pressure from the Safety Officer. That was the end of Agate's Forest Service career.

It is also understood, in later years, Boyd did admit that all he had done was toss a small pebble that happened to land under Agate's tail. And that ends this tale!

<u>Fritz Moisio</u> *Moisio was a District Ranger on the Mt. Baker NF at the time of this story, in the late 1930s or early 1940s.*

It was the beginning of a new year [on the Mt. Baker NF]. Last year's files had not been closed and folders had not been prepared for the current year. Paper was piling up and we were getting behinder and behinder! But that's how things got every other year or so on a fire District like the Skagit. Art Hall, Forest Administrative Officer, provided us a pay period for temporary clerical assistance. Clarence McGuire hired Dolly. She had previously worked for the Skagit and Baker River Districts on similar assignments.

One day when passing through the office, I noted something was bugging Dolly, so asked if the office rigamarole was getting her down. She replied, "It's nothing like that, but I was wondering why the Forest Service filed their pack stock under 0 - SUPPLY PROPERTY? It seems so cruel and inhumane. Take that *Monkey* mule for instance; he has more personality than many people. I think they should be filed under K - PERSONNEL."

My answer, "That's a great idea. Dolly. They would fare better under PERSONNEL, and at retirement age they'd be retired on a pension of eastside grown alfalfa and oats."

After this bantering I forgot all about office details until one day Blackie Burns said, "I can't find the pack stock files. We lost *Maude* when she slid into the canyon in packing to Hidden Lake lookout. I need to 858 her, add *Blaze* to our records, and update the others."

Bells began to ring in my head, so I suggested looking under K - PERSONNEL and that is where Blackie found the lost mules. Upon his inquiry how they got there, I said, "Sometime when we're on annual leave and having a tall cold one at De Silvia's I'll tell you, but for now just think about the fantastic possibilities."

Blackie asked, "What possibilities?"

I said, "Well, for instance, if one of those critters kicked you, you could prepare a personnel case against him."

To this he responded, "Yeah! It's about time I brought charges against that ornery *Lightning* mule and recommend the Forest Supervisor transfer him to the Darrington District."

FIRE and LOOKOUTS: "I don't know, John, it's your fire."

John G. Clousten *Clousten was on the Fremont NF in the mid-1930s, the likely time of this occurence.*

Jess Mann, in one horrible moment, taught me what it meant to accept one's own responsibility when he said upon my asking what I should do with the largest fire I had seen up to then, "I don't know, John, it's your fire."

David D. Walker *Walker was a lookout and a forest guard on the Mt. Hood NF from 1933 to 1942.*

Fire is always a tough and relentless enemy. Some of the men I worked with on fires will always be very close to me, as real friends who were there with what it takes when needed.

Roger Sherman was with me on the North Wilson Fire [on the Mt. Hood NF]. It was a small tough fire on the edge of an old blowdown. We would have plenty to work on if we failed to control it. We worked all night but there was still a tall hemlock with a snag top inside our line. Although we could see no sign of a lightning strike on the tree and no smoke was visible at its top, we decided to make a bed and fall the hemlock into it well away from the blowdown. We finished our first cut and had started on the back cut when wisps of smoke started rising from its snag top. We didn't have long to wait - thirty feet of the tree's top broke apart - limbs and all, to come hurtling down at us. As a rule the safest place is close to the tree, but this time it didn't seem to be the answer. A sky-full of debris came plunging at us. We ran from the tree to escape. Roger tripped and landed face down. I yelled, "Roll, Roger! Quick!" He did. A second later a huge limb stood like a dagger in the spot he had vacated. Burning bark, rotten wood and limbs were piled around the base of the tree, and we had to cool them with dirt before we could finish falling it. It took us most of the day to mop up. As we started back the rain poured down and soaked us good on the way to our cars on East Gate Road.

<u>M. M. "Red" Nelson</u>   *Mildred Nelson talked about the 1936 Siskiyou NF fires in her story. Here, Red Nelson describes an incident when he was on those fires.*

While assistant Ranger in the fall of 1936 the great conflagration of southwest Oregon [and the Siskiyou NF] occurred - the one that burned the town of Bandon. Most CCC camps in the northwest sent crews to fight those fires. The crew from Naches was sent by train. I was not sent with our CCC crew but went separately as part of the fire overhead. I was in the town of Gold Beach one morning talking to the Regional Fire Chief when ten busloads of CCC firefighters rolled in to be organized and assigned to some of the numerous fires.

The Fire Chief Jack Campbell had been the District Ranger on that District during World War I. I recall him seeing the ten buses of CCCs and stating, "How things have changed. In 1918, when the entire Smith River drainage was one big fire, there was only me and two other fellows fighting it - and one of those was sick!" Yes, the CCC program did represent great improvement for all forestry agencies in protection of their land from fire.

<u>H. J. Stratford</u>   *When he was in fiscal control in the Regional Office, Stratford was the paymaster on practically all R-6 Project Fires.*

The experiences most outstanding over the past 20 years since my assignment to the Regional Office have been my fire details on project fires as Assistant Disbursing Officer and member of the service and supply unit in charge of timekeeping and related activities.

Some amusing and different experiences in connection with fires occurred. One in particular that is outstanding was in connection with the Siskiyou fires of 1936. Men recruited were mostly transients from

Burnside and 2nd in Portland. Fires were wide spread over a considerable area. Men, upon release, were paid at the fire camp by payroll from the Supervisor's office in Grants Pass and some men were transported to Portland by bus and paid in the office of the Regional fiscal agent. The Fiscal Office at this time was located in the Mayer Building.

For some unknown reason not determined at the time, some men were sent to Portland for checks without time reports. This created an immediate problem. The fire camp at Carpenterville on the Coast Highway south of Coquille was contacted by telephone and radio time and again, but still time reports did not show up. This was serious and extremely embarrassing to say the least. Men sat around the corridors and lobby of the Mayer Building in their filthy clothes, and unwashed, awaiting their checks. Outbursts were common every hour or so. This persisted for three days. To tide them over, [Albert] Cousins [Regional Fiscal Agent] advanced each man $1.00 per day on three different occasions. In a final effort to get the men's time I was sent to the Carpenterville Camp. After considerable searching and research, the time was located and Fiscal Control was advised of time due each man. Men were eventually paid and order again restored to the Mayer Building.

<u>Wilmar "W. D." Bryan</u> *Bryan was a timber sale officer on the Olympic NF in 1937.*

Schafer Brothers proved a good outfit to work with [on the West Fork Satsop Timber Sale in 1937, on Olympic National Forest], but sometimes were rather extreme in carrying out their responsibilities. For example, lightning set a fire high up on the northeast side of Anderson Butte in moss-covered rock outcrops. After several attempts at dry mop-up, Elmer Due, camp foreman, closed the logging, called in the crew of 150 men, including fallers and buckers, set up a seven-pump relay with over a mile of hose extending from the Satsop River to the fire. The fire covered about 800 square feet before it was sluiced down the mountain side.

<u>Al "Tyke" Sorseth</u> *Sorseth was a local boy from the Sweet Home community when he signed up for lookout duty on the Cascadia Ranger District in 1938. He received a permanent appointment in 1948 and worked on the Malheur and Willamette NFs. He*

was Recreation Staff Officer on the Willamette NF when he retired in 1977.

The fire detection lookout stations and the people who worked on them three-fourths of a century ago are fast becoming historic. With few exceptions, the original buildings do not exist and those who manned them are fewer every year. I spent four seasons as a lookout fireman starting in 1938. A lookout fireman was also a smokechaser if he was the closest one to a lightning fire. My boss was Cascadia District Ranger R.C. Burgess who was one of six Rangers on the Willamette NF.

From my lookout on Twin Buttes there was no visible development except the construction in progress of the South Santiam Highway, connecting the Willamette Valley to eastern Oregon. This (1938) was seven years before the first commercial advertised timber sale would be made on the Cascadia Ranger District.

Some folks ask what one does on a 14' x 14' lookout all day. Well! There was always ordinary housekeeping, cooking, cutting firewood, cleaning, required washing of all windows every two weeks, answering roll call at 7:00 am, reporting to the Ranger Station every hour, carrying water from a spring 1-1/2 miles away (and a 1200 feet vertical fall), maintaining the last mile of trail to the lookout, plus other odd jobs such as painting, sharpening tools and digging garbage pits. *Bon Ami* for washing windows was standard Forest Service issue. All tasks done beyond the sound of the telephone had to be done <u>before</u> roll call at 7 am.

All food and supplies were hauled by pack mules, and lookouts were required to have food on hand for at least six weeks without new supplies. Since the closest neighbor was eight to ten miles away, we *opened* grouse season once in a while. We quickly learned how to ration the canned and dried provisions.

All communication was by telephone. Since several lookouts were connected by party line, we could visit in the evenings and it was amazing how often the conversations turned to what we cooked or baked on our little wood stoves. Cooking was a new experience for most of us! We often *played checkers* by telephone. We drew a

285

Pack train of supplies headed for a lookout on the Umpqua NF – 1940

checkerboard on our table top and each partner would make the moves for both sides, using dried prunes and apricots for checkers, or two different colored beans. Lima beans were always great!

As a note of interest, some lookouts were manned by forestry graduates, which indicated limited job opportunities. (Dick Skiles, who was a forester on Chimney Peak lookout, spent his working career with J. K. Gill Company in downtown Portland. J. K. Gill was one of the first graduates of the Oregon State School of Forestry.)

In the late 1930s the District Ranger and the Forest Fire Staff Officer inspected each lookout station once or twice a year. I always had to roll out my fire backpack for inspection and prove that I was familiar with all of it. The pack included three days of rations in cloth bags with Roman numerals printed on them, a *mill bastard* file (I didn't know it had such a fancy name!), three seven inch tallow candles for the foldable Stonebridge lantern, matches, and of course a Pulaski and a small *lady shovel*. After all contents of the pack were inspected, I had to roll it all up in a small canvas tarp in a standard way and put it on a Klack packboard, ready to go.

My pay on the lookout was $73.00 per month with $5.00 deducted for my quarters. Duty time was seven days per week and overtime wasn't a consideration. I really felt fortunate to have a job and I look back on my summers on lookouts as an invaluable experience. I shall never forget them. I heard one radio commentator describe a lookout as one who sits on top of the mountain and opens the window each morning and shouts "Lookout!!!"

My ensuing Forest Service career was filled with many experiences that I value. The Forest Service was good to me and my family.

Bob "Rob" Mercer *Mercer began work for the Forest Service in 1934. He worked on the Umpqua, Columbia, and Rogue River NFs and was in the R-6 Regional Office in Engineering when he retired in 1962..*

The great Chetco fires [on the Siskiyou NF] burned many thousands of acres in southwestern Oregon in 1938. My first notice was a phone call from the Regional Fire Dispatcher telling me to get to a Forest

287

Service airstrip on Smith River in northern California to assist in aerial supply of a major firefighting operation.

I was there by dawn and found several planes and their pilots on the strip as parachuted packages of food, supplies and tools were being loaded into the ships. Among the pilots was my friend, Larry Sohler, who as soon as he saw me came over and told me that it was at his request that I had been detailed.

A low, dense ceiling of smoke hung a few hundred feet overhead and Larry explained that only the tips of the highest mountains projected above the smoke plateau. As the fire camps destined to receive the supplies were buried somewhere in the blanket of smoke, delivery to and location of these points was truly a hazardous procedure. Larry almost paid me a compliment, which would have been a shock to us both, by telling me that he would not fly with a greenhorn and that we two worked well together.

Larry's *Travelair*, stripped to provide maximum cargo space, was finally loaded to my satisfaction, as I was the one who would get the stuff airborne through the door-less opening and proper stowing of chutes and freight was a must.

We bumped down the pasture strip at first light and began the long climb upward through thousands of feet of dense smoke. The experienced forest firefighter prays for and banks on abatement of vicious winds during the night and early morning hours. The aerial supply crews are just as interested in the quiet, cooler dawn hours as we're more likely to find the smoke stabilized and easier penetrated. Our cargo was destined for a remote fire camp in an otherwise inaccessible canyon somewhere east of Mount Emily, (the Siskiyou Mt. Emily, not the one overlooking La Grande in eastern Oregon). We sagged down into the smoke until we could locate the hazy mound of Mount Emily, but try as we would the lower ridges and canyons were not to be seen, even faintly.

Such flying is extremely dangerous and bears no promise of success, so we climbed back on top and soon saw other planes circling above the smoke, unable to even find the Smith River canyon and the strip we had flown out of. What a happy feeling!

To the south, Mt. Shasta shone white in the first rays of the rising sun, and to the east and north the white peaks of the Cascades were visible, but no opening was visible over the airstrips of Klamath, Medford, Roseburg or Eugene. Larry shook his head at the prospects and we turned our attention westward. The heavy quilt of smoke blanketed the entire shoreline north and south, but the ocean was plainly visible along the well-demarked border of the smoke.

We figured that our best bet was to get out over the ocean, drop down to near sea level and see if we could sneak back under the ceiling. We could, and we did. We found the long curving beach below Crescent City and could see by the narrow margin of wet sand that the tide was beginning to ebb. This was no place to tarry. Larry shrugged his shoulders. I braced myself in the doorway so that I could prevent cargo from being thrown out the door with parachutes attached if we hit rough going. We knew from experience that parachutes and freight draped around the horizontal stabilizer were not conducive of ease of mind.

Once committed, there was no chance to change our minds. Larry did his usual superlative job of flying by setting down that heavily loaded plane on a narrow curved strip of wet sand with surf reaching for one wheel and dry sand the other. By the time we jumped down on the sand, a second plane slipped under the smoke ceiling and followed our tracks to safety. Fortunately for the three that followed, the surf swept ashore to smooth the wet sand and obliterate wet tracks before each one came in.

We had a rush of awe-stricken locals who had probably never seen so many planes in so narrow a track. About midmorning a sea breeze swept back the smoke and we all took off for base and refueling. The air cleared enough to permit some nearby flights from the strip adjacent to the Gasquet Ranger Station. Our objective, I believe it was called Green Camp, did not clear so we prepared for another dawn attempt. Radio messages from the fire camp indicated a serious lack of food. We were ready to give it our best, come dawn.

The clear upper air above the smoke was being laced with the first horizontal rays of the rising sun as we made our elevation and headed northwest toward our hoped-for destination. Again we eased down into the smoke until Mount Emily could be seen. From here we knew the bearing to the camp and knew the elevations of local high points. We were soon circling over a valley between two smoke-obscured ridges, striving to detect anything at all below us that might indicate a camp, a stream, anything.

I was lying flat on the floor with my head out the door when I was sure I detected a rectangular dot below us. It had to be the camp, perhaps a tent or some other target someone had sense enough to prepare. I yelled to Larry to put the plane in tight bank right and hold it there. As the ship banked almost vertical, I began to get the packages and chutes out as fast as possible. The object of this was to set up a trail of at least three chutes at different levels as guides.

Soon everything was out except a big quarter of beef, which I had to wrestle from the front of the plane to the back door. Try doing that some day against all the G's of centrifugal forces. I yelled at Larry to come and help me. I could see his shoulders shaking as he laughed, but his attention to the flying never wavered. At last I got the beef partly out the door, attached one chute to hopefully slow the descent, but the chute failed to open. However it seemed headed straight for the target and at the last second the chute opened and collapsed to hide the target, which couldn't have been very big as the chute was only about eight feet square.

Larry wasted no time in getting that *Travelair* up and out of the canyons and I slid into the co-pilot's seat for the trip home. We were congratulating ourselves first for finding the camp, and second for actually hitting the target. We were barely on the ground when the radio operator rushed up and told me that an infuriated cook was threatening me with a painful death if he ever caught me. It seemed that he had worked long hours in the construction of a split table for cutting up the quarter of beef they were expecting. The monster portion of precious beef had struck the table dead center and left only a low mound of mixed beef and splinters. Let's hope he was exaggerating, at least a little. We never met.

We flew for several days before a southwest wind brought a welcome rain in from the ocean and the firefighters had their first chance to corral the spread of their fires. Larry and I had one other little thrill while on the Chetco fires. We were up and flying over a great redwood forest when the motor developed a hiccup. Redwoods are huge and tall and 12 to 14 foot diameter stumps are no pushover for a light plane. A large clearing appeared in the otherwise unbroken forest and Larry spiraled us down into the cavity. The landing was rough but successful and the trouble proved to be of sparkplug origin and easily replaced.

A sort of aisle between the tallest trees offered the best opportunity for escape and we made it with redwood branches not many feet from our wing tips.

<u>Larry K. Mays</u> *Mays tells several stories about developing improvements for fire control activities - radios (he also has a story about radios in Chapter Two), water drops, smokejumpers, and power saws. Mays experience with power saws was not too different than that of R. C. "Bud" Burgess almost ten years earlier, as described in Burgess' story in Chapter Two (Improvements).*

In the summer of 1938, there was a fire on the Agness District of the Siskiyou Forest. Jack Campbell was Chief of Fire Control then. Kermit Lindstedt was District Ranger and Glenn Mitchell was Forest Supervisor.

I recall Bernie Payne was packer boss on that fire, Phil Paine and Jaenkes Mason were also around on the Rogue River side. Henry Haeffner was a scout and of course there were others. We went into Dry Diggins and spent the night on the north side of the fire. The next day, Kerm Lindstedt and I went around the west side of the fire with a saddle horse and an *S set* radio. Kerm wouldn't ride the horse so I rode it with the *S set* on the saddle. It used a 14-foot antenna and I had a 30 minute schedule with Lake 0' the Woods lookout, about three or four miles away, reporting the fire edge location by coordinates. I had to get off the horse, put the antenna up in a tree and call the lookout. The radio worked perfectly.

After several contacts, I removed the insulator from the end of the antenna and drug the wire behind the horse, (which luckily was gentle). With the *S set* on the saddle horn, and, in motion, I called the lookout and had a very satisfactory conversation with him. To my knowledge, this was the first mobile use of radio.

Later that fall, we put the *S set* on a packboard and by using a half wave-length whip antenna, (seven feet), we had a very useful mobile radio. The next year the handi-talkie was developed by Harold Lawson and the radio crew at the Portland Radio Lab on 122 Street (Mt. Hood Office site). Afterward the U. S. Army developed the walkie-talkie and commercial outfits have since developed many mobile two-way radio sets.

After many suggestions by the public and inventors on how to put out forest fires, the Forest Service decided something must be done. A Stinson Reliance airplane was purchased in 1939 in the Lake States, and Harold King was assigned as pilot. After experimenting with scooping up water from lakes in Region Nine, the plane was sent to the California Region, to be used on bombing brush fires. The Madison Lab was to develop a wetting agent more efficient than water. This project was managed by Mr. Truax of the laboratory.

The California people cut a hole in the floor of the aircraft. A delay fuse inside a five gallon can was activated when the can was released through the hole in the floor. After some unsuccessful experimentations in Region Five, the plane and pilot were sent to the Northwest. Al Davies was assigned to the project in fire control and under Otto Lindh got quite a lot of experience that summer.

We flew out of the Troutdale Airport and we blew up a lot of cans. If over rough terrain, the can either exploded high in the air with no wet spot on the ground, or the can hit the ground without exploding. In either case it was not effective. The project ended when a can blew up in the rear of the airplane. The pilot, Harold King, took a pretty dim view of that.

Dave Godwin, assistant to the national fire control chief, Roy Headley, was in the Northwest, actively related to the airplane project. I well remember Mel Merritt, Chief of Operation, saying, "There is nothing as effective as a man on a fire. Why don't you drop a man?" There had never been a premeditated parachute jump over rough ground at that time. We told Mr. Merritt that you would tear a man to pieces if

Smokejumpers at North Cascades Smokejumper Base,
Okanogan NF – c1939

Fire Lookout – can you identify it?

he landed in the brush and rocks or other rough country. Mel said, "Wrap him up like a cocoon. You fellows drop eggs, radios, and other perishables, so drop a man." The smokejumpers were initiated. There had been a number of parachute jumps made over good ground previously. For instance, Tom Fearson had made some jumps off the Post Office roof in Ogden, Utah. The officials stopped him as being too dangerous.

Dave Godwin developed the smokejumper suit and other paraphernalia. We signed a contract with the Eagle Parachute Company, of Los Angeles, California, and went to the Chelan Forest to test out the items and ideas. Lage Wernstedt and Al Davies represented the region under Otto Lindh. They had a panel truck at Parachute Meadows on the Methow near Twisp, Wash.

The procedure at that time was to somersault out of the airplane and when the jumper saw the horizon on coming around, he pulled the ripcord. The first employee of the parachute company pulled the ripcord all right, but the big mitten that Dave Godwin had put on him caught the airstream and knocked off his face mask and helmet. The side of his face was split open from the chin to the ear. He was hauled in the panel truck to the Wenatchee hospital.

The next day, the number two man tried it and when he pulled the ripcord he didn't pull hard enough to free all the pins on the back pack, and had to pull again. He was upside down on this second tug and his leg got fouled in the lines, dislocating his hip. He also was taken to the Wenatchee hospital in the panel truck.

The following day the number three man tried it. He made a good opening and was coming down in good shape when he floated by the top of a high Larch snag. Being the first solid thing he had seen, he reached out and grabbed the top of the snag. When the air collapsed his chute, the top of the snag broke off and he came down too fast. The chute caught the air again but he landed too hard, so he also was taken to the Wenatchee hospital.

That night there was a lot of conversation around the stove and no one was about to try another jump. Finally, one fellow volunteered and thus saved the project. The next day he made a perfect opening, descent and landing. Before the weather closed in, there had been 59 jumps made by parachute in the fall of 1939 in Region Six. Lage Wernstedt suffered a stroke and there were other casualties, but the project was launched and was a success. Frank Demy developed the slotted chute which was steerable. Francis Lufkin, a guard on the Chelan, became interested and [subsequently] had a very interesting career in smoke jumping. Walt Anderson, fire assistant on the Chelan, was knocked out when his head hit the ground after a jump.

The Ogden Fire Conference took place in the spring of 1940. Axel Lindh was Fire Control Chief in Region One; Otto Lindh, his brother, was Fire Control Chief in Region Six. Otto sold the smoke jumper idea to Axel for the Continental Unit in Montana at that conference in Ogden. The first jump to an actual fire was made in Region One in 1940. There were 14,000 or more jumps made to actual fires before an injury was sustained that one could not walk away from.

Early in 1940, Mill and Mine Company of Seattle demonstrated a power saw to a group of foresters at Wind River, Washington. Power saws were then permitted only on forest fires and other emergencies. Many people thought the use of such saws would put many men out of work. Otto Lindh arranged to use two or three power saws on the first suitable fire. The Tumble Creek Fire on the Detroit District of the Willamette Forest was one such fire and the saws were ordered. At that time, an automotive mechanic had to be present to keep the engine running. While they knew little about handling timber, they were good engine mechanics.

I met the two Mill and Mine men with their three power saws at the mouth of the Brietenbush River near the Tumble Creek Fire. I told them they could fall any or all of the trees on the hillside along the fire's edge. They replied, "Oh no, we can't operate these saws on anything but level ground."

I then told them, "Yes, but the fires don't know that and most all our snags and burning trees are on steep ground."

The men stood firm so I told them to go down along the river and start falling on nearly level ground. These fellows used a Pulaski tool to remove the undercut which was made by two saw cuts into the tree.

On about the third tree cut, they didn't hold enough wood on one side. The tree spun around, jumped off the stump and landed on one of the saws, flattening it so badly the fellows loaded up their equipment and headed back for Seattle.

Later I wrote Otto Lindh a memo saying that power saws were a long way off, if they could ever be developed to a practical state. Well, the War came along in 1942. Use of power saws were permitted in the woods. McCullough developed a light-weight engine and Ted Flynn, Forest Service Equipment Lab, developed a good chain and the unit was off to the races. I wished many times I could retract that memo on the impracticability of power saws.

GRAZING: "That week I learned what 'feed lot counts' really meant."

<u>Laurence D. "Bob" Bailey</u> *Bailey worked on the Oregon NF as a temporary in the early 1920s. He received a permanent appointment on the Fremont NF. He worked on the Malheur NF and was the District Ranger on the Chesnimus Ranger District on the Wallowa NF when he retired in 1953.*

The back side of the [Dog Lake] District, [Fremont NF] was open sheep range [in the 1930s]. The adjoining area was public domain, open to every sheep outfit to range free from *snow off to snow on*. The only boundary markers were now and then a tin sign saying *National Forest Boundary*. The sheepherders were all Irishmen, ranging far and wide. I'd find them miles inside the Forest where there was some feed. The usual answer, "I'm lost."

I had learned they use a can of condensed milk a day. I'd casually glance over their can pile and say, "You have been here five days." No argument. I'd just move them back to the public domain.

<u>H.C. "Chris" Chriswell</u> *Chriswell was an Assistant District Ranger on the Umatilla NF at the time of this story.*

Fred [Wehmeyer, District Ranger on the Heppner District of the Umatilla NF] had Assistant Rangers in constant succession but there were periods when the position was vacant. Henry Fries was an administrative guard at Opal Guard Station who filled the gap. He performed much more than a new Assistant Ranger could do for a season, and it was, perhaps, a bitter pill to have a green person like me come in and take over. Upon meeting Henry [in 1937] I told him I was there temporarily for one purpose only and that was to learn the work on a Ranger District. I asked him for his help. From then on Henry went out of his way to help me in every way he could.

The work plan for April read, "Three days - make feed lot counts of cattle in the Spray area. Fries to assist." That looked good on paper but how in the world did you do it? Well, bright and early one morning I was riding in a pickup with Henry headed for Spray. The work plan was wrong. I assisted Henry. He was aware that I barely knew which side of a horse to climb up on. I had already learned that darn near everything was done on horseback in the cow country. The gates had vertical levers to open and close them from the saddle. The horses knew how to help in this. I have even seen an association rider mending fence from the saddle. If he couldn't reach a break, it didn't get mended. I was approaching Spray with considerable trepidation. Henry noticed my nervousness. "When they hand you a horse just climb on like you know what you are doing. Not because the cattlemen are watching you but because the horse is. If he thinks you are scared of him he'll pile you for sure. The men would only laugh at you, but the horse might kill you."

That week I learned what *feed lot counts* really meant. You were expected to lend a hand in any activity going on. I pitched manure, slopped pigs, chased cows, fed stock, helped brand calves and other interesting chores. Actually a small part of the time was used to count the permitted cattle that would be turned out on the Forest allotment when the range was ready. It would have been insignificant had we not found some strange brands on the cattle of one of the larger permittees. The man was trying to run cattle on the Forest without owning them. This eventually led to cancellation of a long-time permit and the rancher eventually went broke.

George M. "Mike" Palmer *Palmer was a District Ranger on the Malheur NF at the time of this story.*

I went to the Bear Valley District of the Malheur in 1936. On the Malheur, I was with my old boss, Claude Waterbury, and my

Supervisor was Carl Ewing. With these fellows I was a lot happier than I anticipated. Besides Bear Valley Station is about the best place in the world, I think, to summer a bunch of youngsters. My wife and I had accumulated four head by this time.

While at Bear Valley, my old Supervisor, Walt Dutton and a Mr. Woodhead visited the District on a fall range inspection tour. Mr. Loveridge had visited the District during the summer before they came. Mr. Loveridge and Mr. Woodhead were both very much impressed by the things which were not being done in a range management way. As I recall Mr. Woodhead said that parts of the Flagtail allotment were the most overgrazed of any that he knew of in the United States. They made it quite plain that it was the Ranger's responsibility to make plans and execute range management which would improve things.

I figured out a rotation deferred grazing scheme for the Flagtail. Ed Birkmaier and Chet Bennett, who were on the Forest then, helped me finance a fencing program, sell the cattlemen on the deal and put this plan into use. So far as I know, we were the pioneers for extensive rotation, deferred grazing with fenced units on eastern Oregon National Forests.

Jack Groom *Groom was a District Ranger on the Umatilla NF at the time of this story.*

During the fall of 1937, 36 young Rangers, or prospective Rangers, attended a Ranger's training school at the Wind River Training Center which lasted six weeks. It was made pretty clear that our performance at this session, as well as our final interview with Chief of Personnel Mr. Hodgson, would probably have much to do with our future with the Forest Service. Rumor was that if you goofed up someplace you would be shipped to the Fremont. Bill Harriman was the Supervisor there and he was supposed to be able to make or break a man in short order! So far as I knew I got along all right and never gave the Fremont another thought until later.

In 1941, I was the Touchet Ranger [on the Umatilla NF] with headquarters at Dayton, Washington. This was a small District that was combined with the Walla Walla and Pomeroy Districts a few years later. In late summer we were scheduled for a Regional Office inspection by Chief of Personnel Arnold Standing. I was to meet this inspection party at the District boundary between my District and the Pomeroy District. Since this was several miles from any road, we would all be on horseback. A recent notice had been sent out that we must wear the entire uniform whenever we were on duty.

As I was dressing that morning getting ready for my meeting with the inspection party, I kept trying to decide whether I should or should not wear a tie. I knew I was required to wear all of the rest of my uniform. This District was in a stock-raising country and I knew the local stockmen would laugh so hard it would endanger their health if they ran across me dressed in full uniform including a tie while riding horseback in the back country. I was not in the habit of wearing a tie at such times.

I was the first one to arrive at the District boundary, so I sat down on a log waiting for them. I was in a position so that I could see perhaps a mile along the trail where I knew I could see the inspection party as they came up the trail. The first thing I noticed when I saw them even at that distance was the green ties waving in the wind! That evening Supervisor Ewing and Standing really worked me over because I was not in full uniform. I tried to explain my reasons for not wearing a tie, but Standing said this had all been considered when they issued the regulation and that in future I would be expected to be in full uniform while on duty.

Later that evening I told my wife she had better get things ready for a move to the Fremont. Sure enough, six months later I was transferred to the Paisley District on the Fremont. However, to us the Paisley District was a promotion because it was a much better District in many ways. Bill Harriman was very nice to me and spent much time talking about what it was like when he and my Dad were both Rangers in the early days of the Forest Service. And, you know, I never did see a forest officer wearing a tie while in the backcountry on horseback again.

RECREATION, A NATIONAL PARK, AND WILD AREAS: "In October 1937 the President scheduled a trip to the Olympic Peninsula."

David D. Walker *Walker was a lookout and Forest Guard on the Mt. Hood NF.*

The first year [1934] I was on Peavine Mountain [lookout on the Mt. Hood NF] I had 60 visitors. In three years it jumped to 350 for the season. We [David and his wife, Marcelle] liked company and were always glad to see them. Everett Lynch said, "Any couple who can have that many visitors deserve to be down where they will have more contact with the public."

In 1937, we were stationed at Bear Springs. Everett Lynch was still District Ranger, but Paul Dennis was his Assistant. I believe my rating was fire guard. I was in a position at this station to take a more active part in the work of the Forest Service - fighting fire, counting livestock, some cruising, scaling and meeting the public. The guards who came in contact with the Forest visitors had to wear dress boots, breeches and a half Norfolk coat when around their Station. After trying to explain to them the difference between a Ranger and a guard, I found it less confusing to answer their question, "Are you the Ranger?" by stating, "The District Ranger is at Clackamas Lake, but I am in charge here. May I help you?"

A few of our Forest visitors seemed to be under the impression that our station was a combination restaurant and grocery store where they could buy what they needed. In most cases, if it was some small item we were able to help them. One lady wanted to buy the food we had just cooked for our dinner and became quite upset when we refused to sell. Another demanded the use of our toilet because she refused to use the one by the registration booth even if it did look clean. She stated flatly, "I will have nothing to do with a restroom which is used by the general public!" But 98 percent of the so-called general public were just fine and certainly made up for the others.

Packstring crossing a suspension trail bridge, Umpqua NF – c1940s

Boy Scouts getting directions from a Fire Guard at Big Lake,
Willamette NF – 1940.

<u>John R. "Ray" Bruckart</u> *Bruckart was Forest Supervisor of the Olympic NF during the final deliberations about establishing an Olympic National Park from portions of the Forest.*

In November 1935 I was assigned as Supervisor of the Olympic Forest to fill the position of H. L. Plumb, who was being transferred to the Regional Office as Assistant Regional Forester in charge of State and Private Forestry.

I was happy with my assignment to the Olympic, having previously spent about three years on the Forest as Assistant Forest Supervisor. However, I had not anticipated the controversy that was developing between the Forest Service and the National Park Service and their supporters over a proposal to create a national park as set forth in a House of Representative bill introduced by Congressman Walgren. There was a 300,000 acre national monument in the central part of the Forest that included Mt. Olympia. The monument was created about 1906 primarily for the preservation of the large number of Roosevelt elk that made their home in the Olympics.

The Forest Service had always administered the land within the monument until 1933, when all monuments on most public lands were transferred to the National Park Service for administration. The Park Service immediately established a monument headquarters in Port Angeles. Preston Macy, a very personable Park Ranger from Mt. Rainier National Park, was placed in charge. Without doubt his principal duties were to promote the support for the establishment of the proposed National Park.

Congressman Walgren had proposed to create a National Park in the Olympics to include the monument and a few thousand acres around it. The policy of the Forest Service (opposition to the National Park) was backed by Secretary of Agriculture Henry Wallace. However, he was no match for Harold Ickes, the Secretary of the Interior in the Roosevelt administration.

The Park Service sought and largely obtained public support from many preservation- minded organizations and worked diligently to persuade the local people around the peninsula of the economic advantages that would be gained by having a National Park on the

302

Olympic Peninsula. Also there was nationwide support sought and to a degree obtained from many so-called conservation groups. While there was local support for the establishment of an Olympic National Park, particularly around Port Angeles and Forks, there was strong opposition in the Grays Harbor area.

The controversy continued through 1935, 1936 and 1937, which culminated in President Roosevelt's intervention. In October 1937, the President scheduled a trip to the Olympic Peninsula. I was advised by the Regional Forester to report to the Regional Office in Portland to make plans for the President's trip which was to take place in about ten days.

A party was organized headed by Regional Forester C. J. Buck, his secretary Mildred Sinnott, Allan Hodgson, H. L. Plumb and myself. The party drove around the peninsula deciding various things to be accomplished before the Presidential party arrived. This among other things consisted of assembling materials with photographs explaining Forest Service management policies to be made available to news people traveling with the President.

The balance of the party returned to Portland while I stayed in Olympia to implement plans on-the-ground that had been decided upon by the Regional Forester and his staff. Later, Herb Plumb and I were directed to meet Colonel Starling, Chief of the White House Secret Service detail, in Port Angeles and accompany him over the route the President would travel. This included a brief inspection of the accommodations at Lake Crescent Inn on Lake Crescent, and short stops at the Snider Ranger Station where the Ranger with the assistance of CCC enrollees were scheduled to put on a brief demonstration of forest fire prevention. Assistant Regional Forester Ed Kavanaugh was to read a script prepared by Rudo Fromme explaining the action taking place.

A stop was made at the Bloedell Logging Company camp where plans were made for a high climber to demonstrate topping a tall Douglas-fir tree. A rest stop was planned at Kalaloch. Inspection was made of the Quinault Lodge where the party would have lunch. From Quinault, the route to be covered went through Hoquiam, Aberdeen, Montesano and

303

on to Olympia. Colonel Starling was pleased with the Forest Service plan for the trip. The trip with Starling ended in Olympia at 2 am.

Plans for the President's trip were completed October 1, 1937, and on the afternoon of October 2, the Presidential party arrived at Port Angeles on a U.S. destroyer from Victoria, BC, at about 4 pm. A fleet of Forest Service sedans with drivers was assembled for members of the party with the addition of two large sedans for the President and the Secret Service detail. Lloyd Olson reports he drove a car Number 13 with off-duty Secret Service personnel.

The City of Port Angeles had erected a grandstand along the route of travel for the benefit of the local school children. The proponents of the proposed National Park had erected a large sign at the grandstand which read, "Please give us a National Park, Mr. President." The sky was overcast and gloomy as the party moved through Port Angeles and by the time it reached the eastern boundary of the Forest at Lake Crescent, it was dark and arrangements had to be made to illuminate the large sign the Forest had erected at this point that read "Welcome to the Olympic National Forest."

The Presidential party stayed for the night at the Lake Crescent Inn where dinner was served and lodging was provided. The President, his Secret Service bodyguard and his valet occupied a small guest cottage adjacent to the main resort building. After dinner, Senator Schwellenbach, several Congressmen and other interested officials, including Regional Forester Buck and Superintendent Thomelson of the Mount Rainier National Park, were invited to meet with the President and discuss the legislation as proposed by the Walgren bill.

This legislation, if and when enacted, would change the status of possibly a half million acres of National Forest land and place it in a National Park. This proposal was vigorously opposed by the Forest Service and vigorously supported by the National Park Service. The proposal had the support of many outdoor groups, the local press in Port Angeles and elsewhere around the state. The Forest Service position was supported for the most part by the press at Grays Harbor and by some organized groups in that area. Much time had been spent by the Regional Office and the Olympic Forest personnel presenting the Forest Service position in the controversy.

The meeting with the President was the final effort by the Forest Service and the Park Service to present their views. As the meeting progressed, Regional Forester Buck asked me to come to the meeting and explain to the President the different forest types, cutting practices, and in general the forest land use management of the Olympic Forest and to answer any questions the President might ask. The meeting was attended by the President's son James, Congressman Smith from Aberdeen, Walgren from Everett, Senator Schwellenbach and other politicians.

After reviewing the maps which the President had spread out before him, he stated among other things that the proposal as outlined in the Walgren Bill did not include nearly enough area. He stated that in the Yellowstone Park, the vegetation was being damaged by the large number of visitors and for that reason, it was necessary to greatly enlarge the area to be included in the proposed park. Also, a substantial strip to the west along the coast should be included in the proposed park boundaries. He stated that the name of the park should be changed from the *Mt. Olympus National Park* to *Olympia National Park*.

All of the President's suggestions were carried out in a revised park bill which was enacted into law during the summer of 1938. Of course this was a major disappointment, but considering the strength of the proponents including the President of the United States and the Secretary of the Interior Harold Ickes, it was fortunate for the people of the northwest that the entire Olympic Forest was not included in the Park.

<u>Sanford Floe</u> *Floe was the District Ranger at the Snider Ranger Station when President Roosevelt visited the Olympic Peninsula.*

The President and party stopped at Snider Ranger Station where a display of road building and fire suppression equipment was to be shown and operated. The CCC crew was lined up for inspection and Ed Kavanagh made a speech. I was mounted on my saddle horse with a packed mule in tow. Though the portable fire pump had been started every day for several days and about five minutes before the show, it would not start when scheduled in the show. The excitement of everyone was transmitted to my horse and mule and I had to leave the area or take over the show as a rodeo. Everyone was relieved when this deal was over.

Ward W. Gano *Gano began his career with the Forest Service in 1934, as an engineer in the R-6 Regional Office. He was the resident engineer for design and construction of Timberline Lodge in the 1930s. He worked in R-1 and the Washington Office and returned to R-6 in 1961 as the Regional Engineer. He retired in 1973.*

The modern day skier can agonize over the ski lift rates [Timberline Lodge, Inc.] established for the first year of operation [on the Mt. Hood NF circa 1937]: 35 cents - single ride; 50 cents - round trip; 3 rides (one way) for $1.00; all day for $2.00.

The lift construction costs were reported as follows:

Forest Service (materials, equipment, handling, but no labor)
Ski lift proper $30,265
Power plant $16,990
Silcox hut $ 4,155

Total $51,410

Works Progress Administration (no breakdown available)
Labor $30,000 approx.

Edward P. "Ed" Cliff *Cliff began his Forest Service career on the Wenatchee NF in 1931. He worked in the R-6 Regional Office and was Forest Supervisor of the Siskiyou and Fremont NFs. He worked in the Washington Office and in R-4 and was Regional Forester in R-2. He was head of the National Forest System in the Washington Office, and the 9th Chief of the Forest Service from 1962-1972.*

We were sincerely interested in preserving wilderness in those days [on the Siskiyou NF]. The Kalmiopsis plant had been recently discovered up here on the *Craggies* by Dr. and Mrs. Leach of Portland, Oregon. It was a new species, new to science, a beautiful plant as you know. After they discovered it, people started going in and grubbing it out and hauling it out in wholesale lots to sell in their nurseries for horticultural purposes. They would take it up to Portland where the commercial nurserymen would sell it for high prices. There were people going in there with backpacks to pack the stuff out in rather large quantities.

At first, the only place they were aware that it grew very abundantly was around the *Craggies.* That's where the scavengers started taking it out, so the Forest Service set up the *Craggies Botanical Area* in an effort to protect this rare plant. They drew up some rules against taking out live material. Well, we soon found out that Kalmiopsis extended way beyond the *Craggies* area. We started having the trail crews, packers and the fire people mark on a map all the places they found Kalmiopsis in the back country.

The maps showed quite a wide distribution so one of the ideas of setting up the *Kalmiopsis Wild Area* was to give added protection to Kalmiopsis. It was my decision to recommend establishment of a Wild Area and to name it the Kalmiopsis Wild Area. When I was transferred to the Fremont Forest, I did the same thing. I set up the *Gearheart Mountain Wild Area.* I studied that area personally, wrote the report and sent it in and it was approved. In those days, we didn't have many public hearings over wilderness areas, we didn't have any protests, we didn't have any real back-biters, we just decided to do these things and we did it.

The main opposition I ran into on the *Kalmiopsis Wild Area* was in the Forest Service. I submitted the report in 1941, and World War II started about a month later. The proposal was approved by the Portland Office and sent on to Washington. Washington sat on it because there was some chrome mining in the area. Washington decided that as long as the war was going on and there was a need for strategic minerals, they should not set the area up. Well, I was transferred back to Washington in 1944 and I asked what happened to my report. They said, "Well, we're sitting on it."

So I said, "Well, let's take it out from under your seat." It was another year or two before the Chief approved it in 1946.

TIMBER: "We all wore corked boots, tin pants, hickory shirts, cruising vest and a red felt hat."

H. C. "Chris" Chriswell *Chriswell describes several experiences while a member of the Regional cruising crew on the Olympic and Whitman NFs.*

While cruising on the Olympic in 1934, our compass line brought us to a small cliff that dropped vertically without any hand- or footholds. We explored to left and right but could find no way down. Then we noticed a small Douglas-fir tree growing about three feet from the cliff. Hank Harrison suggested we jump out, grab the tree, and slide about 30 feet down to the ground. I said I would if he went first. [He did, then I did.] We added a half pace to our pacing.

I was bragging about the good fudge I could make when we were camped up Baker Creek on the Satsop River. Hank talked me into trying it. Well, something went wrong. The fudge wouldn't harden. We left it on the table in the mess tent hoping it would harden during the night. In the morning, there was a drowned mouse in it. He must have died happy.

While at the old flea-infested Snow Creek Guard Station we worked in Jimmy-Come-Lately Creek. We wondered how this creek had gotten its name. Fred [Matz, Chief of Timber Surveys in the Division of Timber Management in the Regional Office] described many features he had named through the years. He had followed strict Board of Geographic Names rules and so spent a lot of time talking to people that lived in the vicinity of a feature. The early pioneers and settlers called things as they saw them and many of the names were unprintable on our maps. Fred told of one such name. "This large creek needed a name on our maps. After asking several locals I found out its only name was *Mouse-turd Creek*. Well, I fussed around with that name for a couple of months. Finally I solved the problem and on the new map placed the name *Ratchet Creek*.

We all wore corked boots, tin pants, hickory shirts, cruising vest and a red felt hat. In the back of the vest we carried an Alligator slicker, folded up to about four by six inches. Just before noon we would locate some pitch (we mostly worked in DF types as hemlock wasn't

308

considered merchantable!) and build a fir bark fire. By crossing the slabs of bark in the form of a square we would build up a small hut-like structure. We would drop lighted slivers of pitch down the hole at the top and soon have a fine lunch fire. This would dry out our tin pants and we could toast a sandwich. The folks up the Hoh River stated that the Olympic Peninsula would never have been settled without pitch and fir bark.

In 1937 I was an Assistant Ranger at Heppner and [Bernie Payne] was an Assistant Ranger at Leavenworth. Meeting Bernie in Pendleton, I accompanied him to Baker where Fred Matz was organizing a cruiser party with us and Whitman personnel. We drove all the way around and set up camp out of Long Creek. The November-December weather was miserable. Everything was muddy except when a freeze came along. Bernie and I teamed up as one of the two-man parties. I ran compass and mapped while Bernie tallied the trees. We had each done so much of this over the years that we could move fast in that gentle pine country. No matter how fast I paced (sometimes running), Bernie kept right with me in cruising.

We had developed a hatred for snags from fire suppression work and decided to burn down all we could find. It was easy to start a fire in a check of a pine snag. On the return strip we would often go over ten chains and chunk up some fire that wasn't smoking up much. We burned a lot of snags that fall.

We ran the required daily cruise strip and got back in camp by about 3:30 pm. We also got into trouble. Much later, as daylight was fading, the other crews would come dragging in, tired and muddy. There would be Bernie and me warm and dry, enjoying a before-dinner drink. What was worse, Bernie was winning all the Whitman boys' spare change in the nightly poker sessions.

Fred Matz questioned our accuracy. He made a check cruise on our work. Finally, he agreed that my pacing and mapping were OK. When he worked up the tally sheets, Bernie was off only 1/2 of 1 % in volume. Fred should have known this would be the result. We called Bernie *Old 1/2 of 1%* for years.

Fred solved the problem by making us complete an extra mile of cruise strip. We were all thankful when the job finished a couple of days before Christmas.

<u>M. M. "Red" Nelson</u>   *Nelson was Timber Staff Officer on the Umpqua NF at the time of this story.*

I had only been assigned to the Umpqua a few months [in 1940] when Ranger Avery Berry came into Roseburg with a young man named Elton Jackson. Jackson owned two tractors and had done well with them in growing a potato crop in the Klamath Falls area so he also had $10,000. He and a chap named Green, who was a sawmill man and also had $10,000, wanted to become partners, buy a National Forest sale of sugar pine and build a mill at Tiller.

I was called into the Supervisor's office to be in on the discussion. Before the meeting was over the Supervisor and Ranger had agreed to make the sale, and the discussion went to how much per thousand we would charge for the sugar pine. They talked in the range of $2.00 per thousand. After the meeting I returned to my desk and told Ray Hampton about the meeting and that they seemed to be setting the price by negotiations. I said that I always thought the proper way was to make an appraisal. I'll never forget his comment to me which was, "That is why you are the Timber Staff man, you at least know there should be an appraisal, even if you don't know how to make one."

He was right, I did have a lot to learn. I got a sugar pine appraisal that had been made on the Siskiyou, and I went to the Rogue River Forest and got a lot of help from Hershel Obye who was then Assistant Supervisor. I collected some basic cost information and selling values of pine lumber and got some help from a fellow in the Regional Office with a title of lumberman. We did make an appraisal and the price was set at $8.00 per thousand board feet, which was more than the Rogue had been getting and about twice the Region 5 rate for sugar pine. But we were marking some excellent pine timber to be cut.

The sale was made and the J & G Company built the mill at Tiller. The Umpqua had again gotten into the timber sale business. We then began to hire some professional foresters (junior foresters). One of the first was Jack Saubert whom we housed in a tent up near the sale. He was followed by Lou Gabel.   Elton Jackson is remembered in Roseburg, not as a logger, but as a rich man and president of one of leading banks of Douglas County.

In 1940, there were only three major sawmills in Douglas County: (1) Roseburg Lumber Company with a mill right in town and probably made a profit mostly by selling sawdust for home heating in town (2) a mill at Glendale which was able to operate because it had a more favorable railroad rate to California than the rest of the county and (3) a mill in Reedsport.   The beginning of World War II with heavy demands for lumber and plywood soon came to completely change the whole economy of the county.   In 1940 we worked with the Chamber of Commerce and supplied information on the timber resource available in Douglas County.   That was printed and used in interviews with lumber people in the State of Washington where supply of logs was going down.   That paid off for when the war demand came, loggers and mill men moved to Douglas County with its relatively untapped timber supply.

We became swamped with requests for sales at the same time that we were short of personnel.   Klamath Falls was a place with excess mill capacity but short on a log supply.   As part of the war effort we determined that we could help the Klamath situation by opening up the Diamond Lake District to timber sales with the logs being hauled over the ridge to the railroad to the east.   So sales were planned and made years before anyone had any idea that we would be harvesting timber in that area.   Those were interesting times and we had a lot of young foresters that were in on it (especially as war ended).   I have always been very proud of that group of men who all had many advancements in the Forest Service but have now all retired.   Included were such men as Rex Wakefield, Joe Elliot, Rex Wilson, Don Allen, Al Davies, Tift Kampman, George Churchill, Milt Andrews and Jack Todd (all of whom were or later became Rangers on the Umpqua); plus LeRoy Bond (later an Umpqua Supervisor) and Johnnie Trotter.   Bert Holtby, Frank Casanova, Lou Gabel, Jack Saubert, Wright Mallery and Jack Smith were among the others.

Virgil R. "Bus" Carrell   *Carrell worked on the Mt. Hood NF from 1942 to 1952, first as a Timber Management Assistant, then as a District Ranger.   In later years he was in the R-6 Division of*

311

Information and Education, a Forest Supervisor in R-2, and was in Programs and Legislative Affairs in the Washington Office when he retired in 1970.

In 1942, I was transferred from Wenatchee NF to the Mt. Hood NF with headquarters at Estacada, Oregon, where the Mt. Hood Forest Supervisor had concentrated efforts to get timber for the War Production Board out of the Clackamas River drainage. The reason for the accelerated cut was that World War II was under way and the War Production Board asked the Forest Service to produce more timber for England, who was making mosquito bombers out of spruce.

The US military wanted plywood and lumber fast. Congress appropriated additional funds to the Forest Service including funds to build roads and to get the timber harvested. There was little or no spruce of aircraft grade, but we had noble fir on the Clackamas River District that was a satisfactory substitute. While other National Forests in the Region had road access, that portion of the Mt. Hood NF with some nine billion board feet of standing quality timber had none or almost none, yet the mill capacity was available. So the Forest Service engineers and later the Bureau of Public Roads (then) built a main access up the Clackamas River, about 23 miles. Loggers built most of the rest to tap Fish Creek drainage, Hillockburn where the noble fir was located along with other species, the Collowash River, the Warm Springs fork of the Collowash River and the main Clackamas River to its beginning. And so the accelerated harvest was underway.

Dwyer Lumber Company had just been awarded a contract to harvest 30 million board feet from an area called Hillockburn, southeast of Estacada. I was told they had taken out three million board feet the previous year and logging was going pretty strong when I arrived. The Regional Office had prepared the sales contract and I was the Timber Management Assistant in charge of the sale for Ranger Weeman.

I also worked on a sale on Fish Creek, so we could produce from there as soon as roads got built that far up the Clackamas River. I believe we made the first sale in Fish Creek in 1943 and it was bid by Dwyer, also. That sale was for about 30 million board feet. Later in the sale period, Bob Dwyer, logging superintendent, asked if we could make a sale on a bench above Fish Creek so that he could make a landing strip for his plane. An employee had had an accident, and by the time he was transferred to Portland, he was nearly dead. It was approved and there is evidence of the strip there yet. It was used to permit aircraft to spot fires by plane and observe slash burning operations. There were a number of examples that it served his injured employees well.

We made another sale in Hillockburn to extract noble fir, which was determined to be a substitute for spruce which England needed for its mosquito bombers. Noble fir had been an undesirable species so far as logging was concerned and we had no good volume tables for it, especially for the large sizes at Hillockburn. We had noble fir that would measure up to 54 inches at diameter breast high. These made what was called aircraft grade logs, 30 inches or more at the top of a 32 foot log and 90% surface clear. A specialist from the Washington Office timber management was dispatched, and we made the necessary volume tables. He was a cruiser, in the tradition of the old cruisers who could estimate the size and height of trees by eye to the inch, but we measured all with tape. I had never climbed so many trees with spurs as I had to, to get to the 32 foot height! Much of the noble fir was in the Oregon City watershed. They approved our plans and we cautiously harvested trees for England. Noble fir ended up at $40 per thousand on the stump before I left. That was high stumpage then for any fir except Douglas-fir.

C. Glen Jorgensen *Jorgensen worked on the Fremont NF in the early 1940s. He went on to work on the Umatilla NF and in Timber Management in the R-6 Regional Office. He was Forest Supervisor of the Gifford Pinchot NF, in the Inspector General's Office, and was the Region Six Assistant Regional Forester for Lands and then for Timber.*

Timber sales were given high priority during the war. Under the War Powers Act, the Forest Service was permitted to sell timber without competition, although intent to sell a noncompetitive sale had to be published in advance. This story concerns the trials, tribulations and confessions of a Fremont NF sale to Weyerhaeuser in the Horseglades area (Section 21, T.34 S., R.14 E.). It is not remembered under what authority the Horseglades sale was made, but when Weyerhaeuser thought they might run short of logs during the winter, the Forest took emergency action to mark the timber for cutting (tree selection).

Ed Cliff was Forest Supervisor and Jim Thompson was Timber Staff Officer. All timber sale work was projected out of the SO in Lakeview. On a Tuesday morning early in January 1943, Verus Dahlin, Jay Hughes and I were sent to the Bly District to mark the section of timber which lay adjacent to the company railroad into Camp 6. We did not go on Monday because we had to wait for Jay to get back from Diamond Lake railroad siding where he had moved Forrest and Annette Jones in ⁻ 30° weather.

We encountered a heavy snowstorm going over Quartz Mountain. As was customary for project crews, we stopped at the Bly Ranger Station to tell Ranger Ross Sheapard where we were going. Ross told us that because of the heavy snowfall we could not drive to Weyerhaeuser's camp. In that event, Verus (our leader) said we would go to Beatty and catch the company speeder into camp. Ross said the railroad was also snowbound. With this news we planned on going back to Lakeview and wait for better weather.

Before we got around to departing, the state patrol stopped in and said the highway over Quartz Mountain was now blocked. We were stuck in Bly. Nothing to do but relax and wait, so the three of us moved our gear into the warehouse (nowhere else in Bly to stay, then, or now). *Swede* (forgot his real name) had a double barrel stove hot and he was doing tool maintenance work. In those days on the Fremont you couldn't leave foresters idle very long before they were playing poker. So it was with us. We found the green front store, got a few snacks, drafted Swede, and we were in business. Other than stoking the stove and occasionally replenishing supplies, we played poker all day and most of the night. By the next day we were fit to be tied, but still could not travel in any direction. We agreed it was better to snowshoe into Camp 6 than sit around, so we drove as far beyond the Obenchain Ranch as we could buck the snow, put on our packs and took off.

We had some 11 miles to go, all up hill. Nothing for timber beasts! It was not long until we put on the snowshoes. In an even shorter time we were into the routine grind of going single file and alternating the

Log scaler using woods calipers to scale felled timber. Ochoco NF – c1940s

lead job of breaking trail. The snow was fluffy and we would sink in over a foot with the bear-paw snowshoes. The day wore on. We stopped often to rest. Our rest stops became longer. The nightlife was taking its toll. With still a few miles to go and darkness approaching, we were showing signs of being dog-tired, but kept encouraging each other onward. We were getting somewhat irrational. (None of us had heard about hypothermia or ever experienced sheer exhaustion.) However, camping in a snowstorm without food or proper gear was not appealing. We struggled under our packs as the grade flattened. Our endurance barely lasted as we dragged into Camp 6 after dark. I cannot remember anything about that first night in camp.

Section 21 was mostly surrounded by Weyerhaeuser land so the section lines were well blazed. The railroad paralleled the west section line. For some reason we started marking strips parallel to the railroad. It was bench-type land and the topography was flat. The timber was a beautiful park-like ponderosa pine type with occasional patches of lodgepole. It was enjoyable getting around in snowshoes. We marked with marking axes, blazing the tree and stamping the blaze with *US*. No chance for stump marks in the deep snow.

It was customary for pine markers to torch a dead snag for lunch fires. One day, Verus said it is about time to eat and whoever finds a snag to yell and we will build a lunch fire. Verus found a good snag and I went over to help him fire it. In a few minutes we had a nice fire going and were getting ready to sit down to eat, when we realized that Jay had not arrived. We were puzzled. There was no logical answer for him not being at the snag. Then we heard a faint *h-e-l-p*. We investigated and found Jay down in a deep hole along side of a broken-off tree that stuck above the snow about four feet. With the intentions of building a lunch fire, Jay had tramped solidly around the stub with his snowshoes, then he took them off and tried to tramp some more along side the stub when he slipped down and was unable to get out without help. We then realized the snow was really deep. While in the hole, we handed Jay his marking axe, which he shoved down handle first and determined that the snow was six feet deep at that spot. This figure was later confirmed by the Highway Department as they reported eight feet of snow at Sun Pass on old Highway 97 north of Chiloquin.

It was snowing hard on another day. I was on the outside marking strip some half mile or more east of the railroad as the end of the day approached. We always marked up to the section line before stopping. Before getting to the line I ran into a patch of lodgepole with scattered over-mature pine that had to be marked. In the process of going from tree to tree, I must have gotten a little disoriented. Darkness overtook me without finding the line which I would have followed back to the railroad. I quit for the day and headed west. Camp was near the southwest corner of the section. Weyerhaeuser had a diesel light plant that ran continuously. I soon observed that the sound of the diesel engine was getting faint. I took a sounding and headed towards the sound. Again the engine sound became faint. I took a new sounding and followed my ear. After an hour or so of trying sound orientation, I came to the conclusion that my ear was not going to lead me out of the woods. It was light enough to see the snowshoe tracks of previous days' marking. The tracks seemed to go every which way. I knew the tracks should have a north-south orientation, except the weaving from tree to tree. Finally by establishing the general directional pattern of the tracks, I made it out to the railroad some distance from camp and avoided the utter embarrassment of lying out in the woods all night when I could hear the light plant in camp.

We finished marking the sale by mid-afternoon on Saturday, packed our gear and walked back to our rig. The snow had been plowed with a bulldozer, leaving hard chunks of snow and ice that made walking very difficult. Upon arrival at the car we found it buried. We had to use our snowshoes to shovel away the snow so we could get the back door open. Then with shovels it took us a couple hours to dig out and get the car turned around. We arrived back in Lakeview around 2 am Sunday morning. Probably the most exhausting week in our entire career.

As most emergencies go, Weyerhaeuser did not cut the timber that winter. In the meantime, I was transferred to the Bly District as Assistant Ranger with timber work 99% of my duties. The following summer Oliver Erickson, ARF for Timber Management; Mr. Campbell, Weyerhaeuser boss in Klamath Falls; Ed Cliff, and Jim Thompson made a tour through the District looking at timber activities. For some reason they checked the winter marking job on

Horseglades Sale, and they did not like it. In due course, I received instructions to blue-out (unmark) trees of specified Keene tree classes.

On a hot August day, Bob Appleby and I went to the sale to change the marking. I had mistakenly told Bob that it would be an easy job in the open park-like stand on flat ground. When we arrived at the sale area, it was unrecognizable. The understory was dog-hair reproduction. We had to almost crawl through the reproduction to find marked trees, and then you had to look up, way up, some 14 feet to see the mark. When we finally found a tree that met the instructions for bluing-out, we realized that we were not properly equipped. One of us said we would have to get a ladder, the other said either that or climbing spurs. We had little enthusiasm for the task to do considering the unpleasant conditions. On the way back to Bly, we stopped at Camp 6 and learned that Weyerhaeuser planned to start logging in the next few days.

Bob and I discussed what we should do about the problem. We rationalized that we had plenty other work to do, the War effort called for production not frills, and once a tree is cut there is no second guessing the decision. Accordingly, we gave the job low priority.

Evidence of my insubordination was soon missing, as Weyerhaeuser cut the sale out during the month of August. Forrest Jones administered the sale and did all the scaling with woods calipers. During that month, 20 million board feet were cut and scaled on the District. Sales activities involved two Weyerhaeuser sales, a sale to Ivory Pine Mills and Ewauna Box Exchange cutting. All the sale administration and caliper scaling was done by Jones and the writer.

The Horseglades Sale was closed with no further incidents. Bob Appleby went into private consulting work, Forrest Jones went to other timber work on the Fremont, and I was transferred in November to Heppner on the Umatilla as Assistant Ranger. Everything was done except one thing. I had not told Ed Cliff or Jim Thompson of my insubordination in not carrying out their (illogical) orders. Not being one to mar my integrity and wanting to clear my conscience, I finally confessed to Ed Cliff. It was done under prudent conditions. Ed was about to retire, I had 30 years service, and the discussion was held during happy hour in a Portland hotel room. The story closed in good humor.

RESEARCH: "-there is plenty of opportunity for pioneering, for originality, for enterprise."

<u>Thornton T. Munger</u> *Munger describes research activities in the 1930s and 1940s, and philophizes about the Forest Service when he retired in 1943.*

Regional Forester C. M. Granger was made national director of the Forest Survey in 1931, and for a while he made his headquarters with us before moving to Washington. During the 1930s the Forest Survey was the dominant project of the Station and took a major part of my time in conferences, administrative details and sometimes in the field. [H.J.] Andrews, with Cowlin as assistant in the office, did a fine job of training and directing a frequently changing crew assembled mostly under the emergency programs.

The Regional Office's section of forest products was transferred to the Station in 1931, and with the growing appreciation that progress in forestry depended upon an understanding of the economic problems and obstacles, as well as the silvicultural problems, a division of economics was set up.

Believing that the setting aside of Experimental Forests primarily for research to be under the jurisdiction of the Experiment Station was a *must*, I rapidly built up a series of five of about 10,000 acres each. The Wind River *research reserve* of 160 acres, so designated in the 1910s, was enlarged in 1932 to two big units. Pringle Falls was established in 1931. Then followed in the next three years Cascade Head, Port Orford Cedar and Blue Mountain. Mostly with CCC and CWA [Civil Works Administration] labor substantial residences, offices and garages were built at most of these experimental Forests.

Meanwhile we had outgrown all the space we could rent in the Lewis Building. In 1933, we moved to the brand new federal courthouse where we had 27 rooms, some specially designed for us - laboratories, assembly room, etc. Before this [Richard E.] McArdle had centered his fire studies in an old garage we rented and fixed up as a laboratory.

The depression years of the 1930s were hectic times at the Station, particularly for Miss Wertz, who had most complicated, ever-changing and expanding payrolling and bookkeeping to do. Our regular appropriations were cut, but were supposedly compensated for by the allotments of emergency funds. No promotions for regular personnel were allowed. In July 1932 annual leave was cancelled and employees forced to take two days off a month without pay. Leave was restored in April 1933, but a flat 15% cut in salary was made which was gradually restored two years later.

First of the New Deal projects came the CCCs. This gave us at the start money to hire some capable foresters who were used to make detailed cruises and maps of two Experimental Forests and to work on the Forest Survey. Under the *National Industrial Recovery Act*, there were various other funds made available to us under constantly changing rules and amounts. There was Works Progress Administration, Emergency Conservation Work and several other programs, all with separate quotas and restrictions. We were fortunate in getting many very capable people for computers, draftsmen, and field assistants. This expedited and enlarged many of our projects far beyond what could have been done with our regular allotment, especially the Forest Survey. But it took a lot of planning, organizing and supervision.

In 1935 the logging economic studies moved to the pine region, as well as mill scale studies conducted by the Division of Products. A new approach to selective cutting in the pine type was developed which we dubbed the *maturity selection system*. A vast amount of data was collected to demonstrate which trees should be cut first for greatest profits, best growth and survival. As a result of these convincing findings, methods of cutting on the National Forests of the pine region, and to some extent on private lands as well, were revolutionized.

[Burt P.] Kirkland and [Alex J. F.] Brandstrom came out with a thesis on selective timber management which strongly implied tree selection cutting in the Douglas-fir region apropos of the practicability of using tractors in this region. I, and others who were silviculturally minded, could not agree with their recommendations, in spite of the short-term

Lineup of log trucks carrying old growth to the Memaloos Scale Station,
Mt. Hood NF – 1943

Research scientist using an increment borer to check growth rings in
Pringle Falls Experimental Forest, Deschutes NF – 1937

advantages of selective cutting. But Regional Forester C. J. Buck took it up and ordered that hereafter every timber sale on the National Forests of the Douglas-fir region was to be on a tree selection basis unless the Supervisor could show some reason why it should not be. Quite a controversy arose. The Kirkland-Brandstrom manuscript was greatly toned down before publication [in 1936]. The Regional Forester opposed publication of a paper I had delivered, but on appeal it was OK'd by the Washington Office [and published in 1939].

Exhaustive studies of the selectively cut areas by [Leo A.] Isaac and others at the Station carried on for several years exposed the undesirability from a silvicultural and fire protection viewpoint of tree selection cutting in most mature Douglas-fir stands. In a couple of years, after sporadic trials, it was practically abandoned on the National Forests. Fortunately throughout the controversy, Brandstrom and I remained the best of friends.

A section of grazing studies was set up in 1937 with G. D. Pickford in charge, later assisted by Elbert Reid.

As the effects of the depression years of the 1930s faded out, the work of the Station was again upset by World War II. Many of the younger men went into one of the military services. The War Production Board and other agencies requested the Forest Service to make all sorts of surveys and studies to expedite the war economy.

The projects were most varied and required from a few man-hours to several man-months each. Some of the subjects we worked on were: requirements for truck tires, planning for an emergency supply of hemlock tanbark and of cork from Douglas-fir bark, current census of production of pulpwood, aero lumber, pontoon lumber, plywood; industry's need for power saws, trucks, loggers' boots, wire, lumber carriers; monthly census of log inventories and of lumber production with analysis of factors affecting production; methods of increasing meat production on western ranges; techniques of planting for camouflage.

The Port Orford Cedar and Blue Mountain Experimental Forests were closed in 1942 *for the duration*, and Pringle Falls in 1944 except for a few weeks in the summers when Morris and I did the routine examinations. I had only a small part in the war emergency projects and directed my efforts mostly to the routine examinations of sample plots and their resulting office work. I tried hard to not let lapse the periodic measurements of our long-time studies, but in some cases the interval was extended from five to six or seven years. Our regular travel allotments were very short in forest management research; in one year Isaac and I each had only $100 for travel, but we stretched it. Soon after the conscientious objectors' camps were started, we obtained the detail to the Station of several selected men who, for two or three years did, for practically no pay, effective work. They acted as caretakers and routine technical assistants at Wind River and Cascade Head and on office compilations.

In 1943, at the age of 63, I put in my resignation in accordance with the then-retirement policy. I must say that I did so reluctantly because I always enjoyed my days in field and office and did not know what I would do from 8 am to 4:30 pm each day. My salary at retirement was $8,059.80 gross.

When my associates suggested a retirement luncheon I assented, provided that I was the only speaker - wishing to escape the encomiums of the orators and the jibes of the jokesters. In that swan song, *The Forest Service Then and Now*, I said, "I don't want to be thought of as one who harps back to the *good old days* as though things were now going to the dogs. Far from it; things are different now; they reflect the times. Then we traveled by horse, now by auto. Each fitted the times; each had advantages. Then we were in an era of small governmental expenditures, and we were thrifty, got lots out of our official allotments and lived frugally. Now we are in an age of extravagant public spending and lavish living, and the Forest Service shares in it."

"However, there is a danger in any government bureau gaining size and strength to the degree that it exerts its power in excess of what the public will stand for. Much of the respect that the Forest Service gained from the public in the early days was due to its being thrifty, delivering the goods, and to the fact that its people were modestly paid and there could be no charge of nest-feathering and extravagance. We may laugh now at the slowness and simplicity, or call it crudity, of the *good old days*, but they had something the modern, mechanized, highly-organized, regimented and manualized Forest Service has lost and might well recapture."

Further on I reminisced, "I would not have enjoyed so much my years in research had it not been for the hope of seeing the results put into practice. I do not care for research for research's sake. But I always had faith that research could greatly promote the practice of better forestry. For years it seemed terribly slow in coming. Even on the National Forests the apathy was most discouraging. Latterly the progress has been very fast; progress among the forward-looking private companies has been particularly gratifying."

I continued my swan song with this hopeful thought, "I have heard some of the old-timers, in speaking of the halcyon days of the past, imply that the interesting days of the Service were gone and now it was merely humdrum. I hope none of the younger men subscribe to that idea. Of course youth has advantages over middle age, but I would not grant that the Forest Service is much past adolescence. It is fun to do firsts; I enjoyed pioneering in putting in permanent sample plots, buying the first official automobile and adding machine for District Six, proposing the first natural area, making the first yield tables, drawing up the first real research program, getting the first of the Regional forest surveys started. But there are lots of firsts yet to be done. There may not be new tree species to discover, but there is plenty of opportunity for pioneering, for originality, for enterprise. There is yet a long way to go before forest management, forest protection, forest utilization, forest land economics are utopian."

ADMINISTRATION: "Cause I don't want anyone in the Supervisor's Office to know about it."

Gail C. Baker *Baker tells about "lost inventory" schemes.*

An unusual incident happened on the Malheur NF while I was stationed there during the period 1937 to 1939. Two bank robbers figured out a scheme to rob the Grant County Bank in John Day. They set fire to the Forest Service warehouse in downtown John Day, and, while all the townspeople rushed to the fire, the two robbers tied up the bank president, Ed Way, and got his assistant to open the bank vault. They took a large amount of money but in their haste to get out

324

of town they turned their car over in a sharp turn between John Day and Mt. Vernon. All the money spilled out on the roadway. The two were captured there and the money retrieved.

Another good part of the episode was the Forest got a new warehouse and an excellent opportunity which they took full advantage of to use the fire to account for lost inventory. Any time property was missing all they had to do was report it burned up in the warehouse fire.

The Siskiyou NF used that same gimmick while I was stationed there from 1934 to 1936. At that time and for some years later the only way to get freight and supplies to the Agness Ranger Station was by boat from Gold Beach. Every once in awhile in making the trip up the Rogue River a loaded boat would sink in the rapids. The Siskiyou NF would then use that for some time to account for lost inventory. Finally after an unusually large loss, Albert Cousins, the Regional fiscal agent at the time, wrote the Forest that with so much equipment on the boat it was no wonder it sank.

H. C. "Chris" Chriswell   *Chriswell was an Assistant District Ranger on the Umatilla NF at the time of this story.*

My training as an assistant Ranger [on the Umatilla NF in 1937 and 1938] was: "With 720,000 acres of protective area this thing is too big for one man. You take the east end and I'll take the west. Later we'll trade." District Ranger Fred Wehmeyer was of the school that you learned by going out and doing things. He felt this weeded the men from the boys. It was successful with me; I've never worked so hard before or since, or had so much fun doing it. "You get all the fun of being a District Ranger without the responsibility," Fred used to mutter.

Fred was an atrocious driver. Like some people of those times, a team of horses would have been simple but driving a car safely just wasn't understood. He received a brand new Plymouth panel as an official car. We soon noticed him driving his personal car. About a week later he drove the panel to the office. He was proud as punch as he pointed to the fenders and entire side of the vehicle. We were appalled! The new car couldn't have looked worse. Fred had run off the Heppner grade coming in from Tupper one evening. He had gotten a rancher to pull him back on the road with a truck. He had spent a week of evenings and two Sundays in his backyard pounding out the dents with a peen hammer. When we timidly asked him why he hadn't taken it to a garage, he glowered at us and said, "Cause I don't want any one in the S.O. to know about it."

In the early spring Fred couldn't wait to see what effect the winter snows had on the District. He would drive up the road as far as he could. Sometimes the snow stopped him but usually it was the mud. Except for about three main roads, including the Heppner-Spray Highway, there wasn't a graveled road on the District. When a snow bank melted it took a couple of days for the frost to leave the ground. For a very short period of time the soil would not support a vehicle. Every year, without fail, Fred would drive onto one of these innocent-appearing places and sink up to all four axles.

Fred told me, "Now you know those Chevy pickups. A bunch of engineers worked for years to design 'em so the bed was almost on the ground when you got stuck. The only thing to do is to lay down in that mud in your clean uniform and slowly worm your way under that low box. You work and struggle to get your shovel in beside the wheel. You rassel and you huff and puff. Finally you carefully work the shovel back out and there is a little bitty piece of mud on it. You take a stick and scrape off the shovel, then take a stick and scrape off the stick." Fortunately for our piece of mind the ground wasn't long in this muddy condition. All summer it was deep dust. Fred always said, "The difference between mud and dust in the Heppner country is about five minutes."

Fred's diaries were something. He had boxes of them under a steel cot in the alcove. Every day was faithfully recorded. The entries were almost all the same: 8:00 started work - 5:00 quit - 8 hours. These entries did not endear him to his Supervisor or the Administrative Assistant. Neither did his stock answer. "H——, if I put down everything I did in my diary I wouldn't have time to do it." Fred worked from dawn to dusk and most of his Sundays. His memos to his Supervisor were eagerly awaited by the office force. The girls usually read them before routing them to the boss, and they enjoyed his humor. The Supervisor often threw them into the basket.

<u>David D. Walker</u> *Walker, a 'short-term man' himself, laments about their role in the Forest Service. A 'short-term man' was a less-than-full-time employee. Everett Lynch wrote about 'short-term men' in Chapter Two (All in a Days' Work).*

I understand the *short-term men* with experience had a much better chance of advancement after 1942. Most of us knew that the Forest Service policy and treatment of their short-term personnel had been handed down from beyond the scope of Region Six or our immediate superiors. It would be hard to estimate what this wasteful practice of losing old hands and training new ones cost the Service each year; or the value of a man with at least three years experience on fire and forest procedure against that of a new hand.

WORLD WAR II: "We were to divide the time between us watching for and reporting planes-"

<u>M. M. "Red" Nelson</u> *The Aircraft Warning Service was set up by the War Department and the Forest Service during World War II. A network of observation points (mostly lookouts) was established to be manned 24 hours per day to watch for and report all air traffic to a regional Filter Center operated by the U.S. Army. This program was funded by the War Department.*

Preparing to man lookout stations to serve year-long in the WW-II Aircraft Warning Service meant: (1) winterization with added insulation; (2) hiring two persons who would be compatible for the winter months of isolation - one to be on duty at all times; (3) building a separate room, usually below the tower, so that the off-duty person could sleep; and (4) equipping the stations with added bed, heating stoves, etc. On the Umpqua we were especially pleased when Wright and Betty Mallery, recently married, agreed to serve on Red Butte.

Although the Army would pay for outfitting of the lookout with new equipment needed, the Umpqua had a firm policy established in its *poor days* to use only second-hand equipment such as beds and stoves. Forest Supervisor Vern Harpham had, for many years, taken on the job of buying such used equipment. He personally liked doing that and he knew every secondhand dealer in Roseburg. He reasoned that for those stations to be occupied by married couples he should buy a double bed. He did that for Red Butte. Not long after Wright and

Ranger Albert Wiesendanger with his streamlined REO fire truck,
Mt. Hood NF – 1941

Aircraft Warning Service lookouts, Mt. Hood NF – c1940s

Betty were in place I recall that Wright registered a complaint. He said, "Since our contract requires one of us to be in the tower at all times why in the world did you equip our small sleeping room with a double bed taking up space needed for storing our winter supplies?" Just shows that our young foresters were thinking better than our old-timers.

Ambrose B. "A. B." Everts *Everts began his Forest Service career in 1927 in Region Five. He worked on the Willamette and Snoqualmie NFs, in Fire Control in the R-6 Regional Office, and at the Pacific Southwest Experimental Station. He retired in 1960.*

Howard Gardner, lookout-fireman on Mt. Emily, heard the plane at 6:24 am. It wasn't the time of day that bestirred the watchful Gardner so much as it was the particular time in history. The date was September 9, 1942, and Mt. Emily was, in addition to being a regular forest fire lookout station on the Siskiyou NF, a link in the far-flung Aircraft Warning Service (AWS). An important link, it might be added, only six and one-half miles northeast of the coast town of Brookings in southwestern Oregon.

During the night, a pea-soup-thick fog had rolled in from the Pacific. It lay, quiescent now, in the still of the morning, shrouding the lower valleys in a mantle of white. Only the higher mountains and ridge-tops thrust into the blue like islands emerging out of the foaming sea.

The plane was of a type unknown to Gardner. It was a small, slow, single-motored biplane with a float hull and with small floats on the wing tips. Gardner rang the relay operator at Gold Beach, 30 miles north of Brookings. "Gold 56," he said, giving his code number, "One plane, type unknown, seen, flying low, two miles east." He took another look. "Circling," he added. The message was forwarded to the Roseburg Filter Center.

That was all for the present. In time the sun climbed high, burned through the fog, breaking it into individual cloud-like portions, drifting now in the rising breeze. As the fog dispersed Gardner searched the unshrouded areas before him. Preceding the night fog a brief but hard-hitting thunderstorm had rumbled across the District. There was the chance of *sleepers* - a delayed, lightning-caused fire - which needs the warmth of the sun and a breath of breeze to fan it into life.

The white plume of smoke was spotted at 12:20 pm. Gardner swung the sighting ring of his Osborne firefinder around and lined it up on the smoke. Then he reached for a lookout report form and filled it out carefully: Station reporting, location by landmarks, azimuth, vertical angle, distance.... Again he rang Gold Beach, only this time it was the Ranger Station, headquarters of the Chetco District. Ranger Ed Marshall answered. "Ed," Gardner said, "I have a fire for you."

Marshall copied Gardner's report and platted the location on the District platting board: Township 40 South, Range 12 West, Section 22. There followed then that brief period of mental exercise that the reporting of a fire always triggers: how many men to send, who they would be, travel time, fuel type, weather conditions.... This section of southwestern Oregon has experienced a number of large and difficult to control fires, including the one that burned the coast town of Bandon in 1936. That one claimed a number of lives.

Marshall was a veteran of many of these fires. He knew that September was the month of changing conditions - damp today, drying east winds tomorrow. Gardner was the closest man to the fire. He was also a skilled woodsman, rangy and rugged, and he knew the country like he did his own back yard. Marshall reached for the telephone. Three minutes later Gardner was on his way to the fire, his smokechasers pack slung across his shoulders. Two additional smokechasers were dispatched from Gold Beach. Snow Camp lookout, sixteen miles north of Mt. Emily, was instructed to dispatch Bear Wallow guard Keith Johnson as soon as he could be contacted by radio. Johnson had a portable radio, an *S* set. This would put radio communication on the fire.

"That," Marshall thought, "should do it." All afternoon he waited for the report. He checked the distance Johnson would have to travel, eight and one-half miles, most of it by trail. He alerted other lookouts, giving them platted location of the fire, instructing them to watch for the tell-tale mushroom of smoke that he hoped they wouldn't see--the proof that he had miscalculated. Too little and too late. "You never know about these sleepers," he said.

330

The first radio report came through at 4:30 pm. The fire was controlled *and it had been started by a bomb!* Marshall mulled that over. Could one of our own patrol planes accidentally have dropped a bomb? The second message from Johnson, at 5:40 pm reported that pieces of steel bomb fragments and parts of a tail fin had been found. That cinched it. Marshall reported the find to the Roseburg Filter Center.

The next morning Marshall and Les Colvill, Assistant Supervisor, who had fire-bossed a number of the large fires on the Siskiyou Forest, hiked into the site of the bombing. The fire was out. They dug up and packed out about sixty pounds of bomb fragments and turned them over to Army and FBI officials. One of the larger pieces had Japanese markings on it.

<u>David D. Walker</u> *Walker's Forest Service career ended with an unfortunate incident.*

My separation from the Service came in October 1942. Mrs. Walker and I had gone to Larch Mountain [on the Mt. Hood NF] for 24 hour duty during the war years. We were to live in the lookout house on top of its 110 foot tower. We were to divide the time between us watching for and reporting planes to the Filter Center.

The tower's welcome to us was far from heart-warming. The wind and rain came in around the lookout windows. Water lay on the floor up even with the threshold. The sway of the tower would almost empty a pan of water left on the stove or table. All our wood had to be packed up 176 steps because it was too windy to pull up and over the guard-rail. I caulked around the windows with dish towels using a hammer and screw driver. This kept the wind and rain out, but we were fogged in most of the time. We could hear planes, but we couldn't even guess their distance or direction of flight.

A flock of geese, headed south, almost crashed into the lookout windows, but were able to stop in mid-air, three feet from the glass - tails pointed straight down, wings braking them to a stop where they hung in balance - honking about the obstruction - then back in formation they continued on their way.

On the third morning of this adventure, I stepped out on the catwalk. It was a sheet of ice! My feet went out from under me and I sailed across the catwalk on the seat of my pants. When I stopped most of my body was hanging out from the catwalk, but I was still clinging desperately to the bottom guard rail with both hands and the point of my chin. Marcelle was sound asleep inside the lookout. With my chin holding part of my weight, I couldn't have yelled anyway. When it's 110 feet to the ground, you can put in a lot of effort to stay on top. When I could feel the catwalk under the seat of my pants again, I pulled myself up to a sitting position and sat there looking out between the guard rails. This time I lacked my usual enthusiasm as I looked down at the Columbia Gorge. I thought, "There is surely something better in life for Marcelle and me!" My promises to her about life in the great outdoors had turned to ashes. Ten years on the Mount Hood plus 176 icy steps up the ladder, a little more money and then this!

I worked my way back inside the house and sat there thinking it over. I woke Marcelle to tell her, "I am quitting the Service!" I said, "The catwalk and steps are covered with ice. Stay inside until it thaws!" She answered, "I know you like the Forest Service, please don't quit because of me." I said, "I can get another job, but not another wife like you; I would never forgive myself if you were hurt!"

I called Ranger Baker to tell him we were leaving, but we would stay until our replacement arrived. I knew I had to act quickly while the steps were icy or I might change my mind. They put a woven wire safety fence around the catwalk on the Larch Mountain tower, but in spite of this, the wife of the man who replaced me fell and broke her arm.

<u>Gail C. Baker</u> *Baker told Wendall Jones this story while they were standing in line for lunch at one of the retiree association's monthly meetings. At the time, Gail was 96 years old with a crystal clear memory.*

Gail Baker was Ranger on the Columbia Gorge Ranger District [on the Mt. Hood NF], headquartered at Herman Creek during WWII. There was a CCC camp there until all the boys went to war. In 1942, they moved in a crew of conscientious objectors as a work force in place of the CCC boys.

Of course Gail had lost a lot of his workforce to the war, also. So Gail went to the CCC camp, now Conscientious Objectors camp, and asked for someone who could be his District clerk. They offered a young man by the name of Charles Davis, who was a certified public accountant. Charlie, later in life, became the well-known Public Utilities Commissioner for the State of Oregon.

Then Gail needed a gardener - someone to take care of the lawns, trees and shrubbery around the Ranger Station compound. The CO camp came up with a landscape architect named Carl Upman. Carl's sister Ulsa was the Garden Editor for *Sunset Magazine* for a number of years. Ulsa gave Adeline Baker an autographed copy of one of her books on gardening because of Adeline's interest in gardening.

The CO camp gave another man to Gail to help with phone line maintenance. This man was Lew Ayers who later became a very prominent Hollywood actor. Gail and the Forest Service worked closely with the high school there in the Gorge, and Gail found a man at the CO camp who was a singer. His name was Lee Goodall. Lee had auditioned before the Metropolitan Opera in New York. Gail said that he sang his own rendition of *Old Man River* for the students and townspeople. Gail still remembers how impressed he was with this man's voice. What could have been more relevant along the banks of the Columbia River than *Old Man River*?

You could say that Gail Baker trained his men very well.

Don Peters *Peters was a District Ranger on the Fremont NF at the time of this story.*

On April 10, [1945] the Bald Mountain lookout [on the Fremont National Forest] called on his grounded line (single line) telephone and stated the word *paper*, the code word for a sighted or downed Japanese balloon. He then gave me his azimuth reading and estimated distance from his lookout and said *tree*, which meant that the balloon had landed in a tree. I confirmed his data without further conversation and then reported the incident to Larry Mays, my Forest Supervisor.

The following day a group of Air Force personnel arrived in vehicles to deactivate either antipersonnel or incendiary bombs and to gather and haul back to military headquarters any remaining parts of the balloon that were not destroyed upon landing. The group consisted of a captain, a lieutenant, a sergeant and several non-coms. I led them to the downed balloon area via vehicle and foot travel over snow. By using back sight and foresight readings on my compass, we found the balloon hanging in a small pine tree with its life-endangering envelope dropping device on the ground.

The captain and the lieutenant examined it from a safe distance with binoculars and determined that it had one unexploded incendiary anti-personnel, but did not have an anti-personnel bomb that may have been released while in flight. There was still danger for reason that if the incendiary bomb exploded it would create intense heat sufficient to kill anyone near it. The Lieutenant told me that his training and experience would enable him to dismantle it without danger and asked me to hold pieces of the mechanism as he worked. I agreed to assist him. After the bomb was disabled the non-coms removed the 30-foot diameter balloon from the tree in which it was entangled and then loaded it and other parts of the balloon into one of the small trucks.

When we returned to the Ranger Station, the lieutenant told Ollie of my experience. She became angry with me for taking chances that, if gone sour, would have left our sons without a father and her without a husband. I admitted that I had taken the word of the lieutenant without thought of danger. What a fool I was!!

Ollie had supper almost prepared and announced *supper is ready*. The non-coms left the dining room and went into the kitchen. She followed them and again told them to come to the table. A whispered reply from one of them informed her that they were not permitted to eat with officers. She then stepped into the dining room and addressed the captain saying, "I don't care what rules you have. In my house I am boss and I want all of you to eat together." The captain immediately nodded his head to the non-coms and expressed approval. After having breakfast with us the following morning the group departed with best wishes from the captain.

John B. "Jack" Smith *Smith was an Assistant Ranger on the Fremont NF at the time of this story.*

I was working in Timber Management on the Umpqua with headquarters at Roseburg, Oregon, during the early World War II years. In November 1943, I was transferred to the Bly Ranger District on the Fremont NF as Assistant Ranger where I was also employed primarily in timber management work. Ivory Pine Company and Crane Mills were at Bly, and Weyerhaeuser also had a large railroad logging operation at Camp Six cutting primarily Weyerhaeuser timber but also cutting National Forest timber sales. Most of the National Forest timber harvested was going into the war effort.

Spike Armstrong was the District Ranger on the Bly Ranger District and both of us were working primarily in timber. Spike administered the District as well. Everything went well on the District; Spike was a joy to work with. We got many things done. The timber work was similar to what I had done on the Umpqua. The timber types were, of course, much different.

On Saturday, May 5th, 1945, six people were killed by a Japanese bomb on the Bly Ranger District. Spike and I happened to be at the Ranger Station that morning when Jumbo Barnhouse, the Forest Road Grader Operator, drove hurriedly into the Ranger Station and bailed out of his pickup. He said, "There's been an explosion on Gearhart Mountain and several people are hurt."

Spike and I gathered up sheets, blankets, and first aid kits, and notified the Supervisor's Office that we were headed to the site. The accident scene was on the shoulder of Gearhart Mountain, perhaps five miles or so from Bly. As we approached, Reverend Archie Mitchell pointed the way for us to hike to the site that was a short distance off the road. The balloon canopy was mostly deflated and partially covered by a snowdrift. It was white. Near the canopy were six bloody bodies on the ground, somewhat like spokes of a wheel. There was little brush, but a fair stand of mature ponderosa pine timber. Everything was quiet; the bodies were close together.

Spike said to me, "Can you check their pulse? I don't think I can handle it." So I checked for pulse and breathing. Mrs. Mitchell and the five young people were all dead. No one was breathing and I could feel no pulse. The bomb that killed them was attached to a Japanese hydrogen balloon that had come over the Pacific Ocean on the jet stream. Forest Service employees were aware that these balloons were coming and we had been instructed how to report them by code to the military if we saw one in the air.

One of the victims was Jay Gifford, about a 12-year-old boy, whose father owned the Standard Oil bulk plant in Bly. A couple of weeks earlier, Jay had found a weather balloon and had been praised by the Weather Bureau for returning it to the Weather Station in Klamath Falls. Apparently one of the group must have touched something that caused the personnel bomb explosion. Nothing could be done and so Spike and I waited. I didn't see Reverend Mitchell after we left the road and Jumbo never went to the site. Spike may have told them that there were no survivors. Apparently Reverend Mitchell had ran to the sound of the explosion and knew that he could do nothing for the victims. He heard the Forest Service road grader and intercepted Jumbo to tell him of the accident. Reverend Mitchell indicated that the group had planned to picnic and do a little fishing in a branch of the Sprague River. He had gone back to the car to get picnic supplies when the group found the balloon and the explosion occurred.

Spike and I were there alone for a short while until the sheriff arrived. Then Forest Supervisor Larry Mays arrived and then the coroner showed up. So there were four or five of us there for perhaps an hour. Nothing could be done. Larry Mays informed us that we had to wait for the Navy people to come from Whidby Island in Washington state. This was enemy action. The Navy people needed to inspect and make sure there were no radiological, biological, or chemical contaminants before anything could be handled or moved.

The Sheriff had duty elsewhere. Larry, the Supervisor, had duty elsewhere. The coroner had duty elsewhere. Spike had duty elsewhere. So I spent several hours alone, safeguarding the corpses. While waiting, I dug a jagged piece of shrapnel from a pine tree and I still have it as a memento of this tragedy.

To explain more about the situation: The balloon canopy, which I thought was made out of rice paper, was laminated together in several layers and was tough. It was filled with hydrogen gas, was launched in Japan, and came over the Pacific Ocean on the jet stream. We knew that these balloons were arriving in Klamath and Lake counties. When they worked as intended, they exploded in the air. We found pieces of this type of paper from other balloons scattered over some of the forest and range land areas in both Klamath and Lake county. The bits of paper from these other balloons were mostly hand size and smaller. Since they arrived with winter winds and storms they did not set fires. The intent of the Japanese was to set the forests on fire, but they arrived at the wrong time of year when the outdoors was wet and sometimes covered with snow. Perhaps a month earlier, on a clear April day, I reported one of the balloons by code to the military. Within minutes, the word came back that I (and others) had reported the planet Venus.

This particular balloon had not functioned as intended. The canopy had partially deflated and there was a snowdrift partially covering it. It was a pleasant day with daytime temperatures probably in the 50s or 60s° F and the nights below freezing. Apparently, the group, except for Reverend Mitchell, was gathered around the cogwheel that suspended under the gas-bag. That is where the explosive was located. They were in a tight circle around it. The powerful explosion and the shrapnel from it killed every member of the group. We had received the first report from Jumbo around 9 am. It was late in the afternoon, almost dark, when the Navy people arrived. They took only a few minutes, but examined the site quite thoroughly with instruments. They said there were no hazards so the bodies could be removed. My memory is that a part of the cogwheel assembly contained an aneroid barometer, several pounds of high explosive in metal containers, and an array of small cotton bags filled with sand, each containing two or three pounds of beach sand. If the balloon descended to a certain level, the cog-wheel would turn, a bag of sand would be dropped and the canopy would ascend. The final act, if the balloon was working as intended, was that the explosion would set off some primacord which would go into the hydrogen gas-filled balloon and explode it. That was the reason we saw lots of small pieces of paper at other places where balloons had worked as intended.

Mrs. Mitchell was a few months pregnant and the youngsters were 12 to 15 years old and they were local neighbor kids so this was hard to take. It was a great shock to the Bly Community. We had held community meetings in Bly to inform the citizens. This was war time, so it was hush, hush to keep the news from getting back to Japan that the bombs were getting to America.

More than 400,000 Americans, mostly military, died in World War II. These six fatalities were the only civilian deaths directly attributable to enemy action in the 48 contiguous United States. The people who died were Richard Patzke, Joan Patzke, Jay Gifford, Edward Engen and Sherman Shoemaker, as well as Mrs. Elsie Mitchell.

Ranger Armstrong and I were commended by the Forest Supervisor for our timely and effective action with regard to this tragedy. I heard no criticism from the public, and we did receive personal thanks from members of the community.

"Then the Forest suddenly became very valuable so the whole attitude, the whole economic picture changed with the advent of the war."

-Ed Cliff

CHAPTER FOUR

1946 to 1969 OPPORTUNITY, EXPANSION and GOOD TIMES

The end of WWII generated a housing boom as veterans returned home and started families. At the same time an increasingly more mobile society sought access to National Forests for recreation activities. This led to a significant transition for Forests in the Region, from activities focused mostly on custodial management to intensive development of the timber resource and the establishment of major road systems. New recreation facilities were constructed, existing facilities were improved, and the first inventory of recreation opportunities on National Forests was accomplished.

Returning war veterans, attending forestry schools on the G.I. Bill, began to find employment with the Forest Service during summer breaks and upon graduation. Some had been enrolled in the CCCs prior to the war and thus were familiar with National Forest activities. A career with the Forest Service appeared to be a good way for these veterans to restructure their lives and care for their families after their war experiences. A decade after the war ended, hiring began to pick up and Forest Service rolls increased greatly in the 1960s.

Interest in Forest Service activities began to draw more attention from a variety of groups, including Congress and other government agencies, the private business sector and an interested public. The Multiple Use-Sustained Yield Act in 1960 codified the long-practiced management principles. The Wilderness Act in 1964, along with other environmental legislation in this decade, signaled major changes for future years. Timber values increased greatly and work became more complex. The increased workload led to a larger workforce, focusing on forestry and engineering skills, but also increasing other disciplines, such as biologists, soil scientists, and landscape architects. Some very large Ranger Districts were split into two or more smaller Districts, and Ranger District compound housing was increased.

Stories describe the 1964 flood, massive spruce budworm control projects, the start of a ski area, and the crash of an airplane carrying the Oregon governor. Outdoor work still required coping with unpredictable weather and difficult terrain, and the workforce still relied somewhat on horses and mules for transporting people and materials, albeit not to the extent of the early years.

This chapter includes stories about All in a Day's Work, Wives and Families, Horses and Mules, Fire and Lookouts, Recreation, Timber, Engineering and Administration.

ALL IN A DAY'S WORK: "So we ended up with cold fingers and sometimes cold, wet feet, and put those wet, re-oiled caulked boots on again the next day."

John B. "Jack" Smith *Smith tells of the fatal airplane crash on the Fremont NF, which killed then Governor Earl Snell in October of 1947.*

This crash occurred on October 28, 1947, some 25 miles southwest of Lakeview, Oregon, on the Drew's Valley District, [on the Fremont NF]. I was District Ranger on the Drew's Valley District and headed up a search party. Merle S. Lowden was Forest Supervisor.

Governor Earl Snell, Secretary of State Robert S. Farrell Jr., President of the Senate Marshall E. Cornett and their pilot Cliff Hogue left Klamath Falls late in the evening of Tuesday, October 27, 1947. They were headed for Warner Valley and the Kittredge Ranch where they planned to land on a dry lake bed. The Kittredges were hosting a goose hunt for these Oregon officials.

The airplane left Klamath Falls about 10 pm (or later) and did not arrive at the Kittredge Ranch. The Kittredge family thought the plane had not left Klamath Falls so the plane was not reported missing until Wednesday morning. There had been a small weather front over Lakeview during the night. The airplane was a Beechcraft Bonanza. The pilot probably planned to follow the highway from Klamath Falls to Lakeview, a distance of about 100 miles, and then fly over the Warner Mountain range another 30 or 40 miles to the Kittredge Ranch which was located in south Warner. The airstrip at Kittredge ranch would be lighted by automobile headlights so the pilot could see enough to land. Lakeview, Oregon, is a mile high in elevation and the route is all mountainous country.

Although the weather was bad, a small search plane flown by Bob Adams got a fleeting glimpse of the crashed airplane Wednesday afternoon. The Forest Service, however, was not informed that the Governor's plane was missing until 2 pm on Wednesday. When I got word that the crashed plane had been sighted on the Drew's Valley Ranger District, southwest of Dog Lake, I ordered a 50-man fire cache, except for tools, and proceeded to set up a base camp some three-quarters of a mile southwest of Dog Lake on the Yokum Valley road. This was the nearest road to the area where the crash had been sighted. A hard surface road extended to Dog Lake, some 20 miles southwest of Lakeview. The three-quarter mile stretch on the Yokum Valley road had light gravel surface. After a few trips with four-wheel drive vehicles, the road became almost impassable even for four-wheel drive vehicles.

We did have telephone and radio communication at the base camp. We had a cook so food and hot coffee was readily available. We provided for sanitation and could handle the 50 or 60 men who showed up to help with the search. Mostly they were Forest Service employees and local citizens. However, there were a couple of state police officers, many members of the press and others.

Although some searching was done late Wednesday, searchers were hampered by cold rain, pitch-black darkness and the rugged terrain. These searches were somewhat disorganized and ineffective. The plane crash was at about the 6000-foot level which was heavily timbered with mature ponderosa pine timber. It is moderately rough country with peaks, rock escarpments and deep ravines.

At daylight Thursday morning, we were well-organized and ready to go. There were about 50 or 60 searchers in the group. I briefed the group on what we would do. We lined up about 50 feet apart in a generally north-south direction. We followed a compass course westerly and told people to stay close enough together to have contact with the person on each side of them. The two state police officers were at the each end of the search line. We did not want people to get lost and wander around in the wet, cold weather. As a signal, one of the state police officers was to fire his pistol three times when the plane was found.

After traveling a half to three-quarters of a mile cross-country, we walked into the crashed airplane. The plane had hit several tall ponderosa pine trees, crashed in a small opening and slid under the pine trees. One of the passengers was thrown out a door that came open; the other three were in the fuselage which was badly damaged. There were no survivors; they were killed on impact. The plane had not burned upon crashing.

The operation went well and the search successful. There was excellent cooperation among lots of people. Many news people were there. But the real work started as we had to carry the bodies back to base camp where they could be loaded on four-wheel drive vehicles and moved to Lakeview. We had carried litters and sheets with us, so we got started moving the bodies immediately.

As is often the case, the carrying was done by a limited number of people. It was a real struggle moving the bodies across the rugged terrain to camp, but we got the job done. We cleaned up the area and closed up the campsite. We also said thanks to many people both Forest Service employees and others who helped.

Governor Snell, Marshall Cornett and Bob Farrell were very popular politicians. Earl Snell has been eulogized as one of Oregon's top Governors with great facility to attract good people around him and to delegate and supervise them in excellent fashion. Marshall Cornett and Bob Farrell were also very popular politicians in leadership positions in Oregon. Each of them was potential Oregon governor in the future if they had lived.

<u>Lee Boecksteigel</u>   *Boecksteigel received a permanent appointment in 1955. He worked on the Wenatchee, Olympic, and Willamette NFs, and was the Forest Silviculturist on the Mt. Baker-Snoqualmie NF when he retired in 1990.*

The time period beginning in the early 1950s was a transition period in the Forest Service from one of lookouts, telephone systems, trails and fighting fires coming to a close and changing to one of managing resources, visuals, mining, recreation and harvesting timber. The timber cut on the Shelton Ranger District on the Olympic NF was high which meant many folks were needed to do the field work associated with preparing timber sales and other resource work.

Crews working the Wynoochee River side of the District stayed at the Satsop Guard Station all week, leaving Monday morning from the main station in Shelton, Washington, and returning Friday afternoon. The guard station wasn't much to write home about. The group of workers staying there got along great, but a lot of spare time was available to all so we invented things to do to help pass the time away. We played cards, pitched horseshoes and fished. I paint this picture because it is this spare time which offered the following story.

At this point in time it had been many years since trails and telephone lines were needed, as well as some of the outlying guard stations on this Forest and others so the *removal/destroy* word went out within the Region. This included the Anderson Creek Guard Station which was built by hand from local trees (hand-split western red cedar) in 1921. The cabin was still in reasonably good condition at the time of disposal (except for the local population of wood rats). It had been expertly made. Except for a splitting axe mark here and there, it was difficult to tell the material had not been commercially produced.

The person who built the station also built a tapered hexagonal flag pole which was, as best as I can remember, about 47 feet 6 inches in length. It was about eight inches at the base and about three inches at the top. It was beautiful. None of the crew who were dispatched to destroy the cabin wanted to destroy the flagpole, so we decided to save it. It took us several evenings (on our own time) to remove and relocate it to the Satsop Guard Station. We had to hand-carry the pole a quarter mile, then pull it up to the top of a railroad trestle via rope (200 feet), lift it on to the bridge deck, then place it on a 3/4 ton pickup which carried it to the Satsop Guard Station (about 4-1/2 miles). While it was hard work, everyone enjoyed doing it and felt like a piece of history was saved.

The Shelton Ranger District and the old Satsop Guard Station don't exist anymore, but a new Satsop Guard Station was constructed and the flagpole is the highlight of the station and exists today.

343

Frank Johnson *Johnson started as a temporary in 1951 on the Cabinet NF in R-1 and received a permanent appointment in 1956 on the Olympic NF. He worked on the Klamath and Six Rivers NFs in R-5, in the R-5 Regional Office, and on the Gifford Pinchot NF in R-6. He was the Group Leader in Timber Management Plans and Silviculture in the R-6 Regional Office when he retired in 1986.*

May 6, 1956, I put my *blues* in my B 4 bag, left the ship in New York and headed west. I had an offer of a job with the U.S. Forest Service in Quinault, Washington. On May 26, I arrived in Olympia to fill out some papers and get hired on. There I found that I would be hired as a temporary, as I had not yet taken *the Test*. The Forest administrative officer also informed me that I had been transferred to some place called Snider, which was near Forks and a place called Sappho. That was a fast transfer. Not only was I not on the job but I wasn't hired yet. With direction from the A.O., I found Snider Ranger Station. It was not difficult as there was and is only one road - US 101. I did not unload my car that night as I was afraid I might be transferred again.

The Olympic NF was having an early spring fire season and no one could go to the woods as there were no fire crews on board. Everyone was complaining about the heat. Having spent the winter on a ship in the tropics I did not think 60 to 65 degrees was hot. I wore my coat. They assigned me to mowing the grass around the Ranger Station. That is not a good thing to do with a Navy lieutenant junior grade. My car was still loaded and I came within an inch and 3/8 of leaving for Seattle and the Navy. However, I stayed for 34 years just to see if it would work out.

Sandy Floe (senior) was the Ranger and had been there for about 30 years. He was a GS-9. The foresters, except me, were all GS-7s. I was a 5, of course. Stan Undi, the timber management assistant, was just more 7 than the others. We had an engineer but he was a forester, too.

Bob Bjornsen *Bjornsen began with the Forest Service on the Fremont NF in 1950. He worked on the Wallowa-Whitman and Gifford Pinchot NFs in R-6, and in Fire Management in R-1 and* *the Washington Office. He was the Director of the Boise Interagency Fire Center when he retired in 1980.*

Those who have worked with Lee Corbin know him as an intensely practical man, one who can do everything from shoe a horse to fix a balky engine. He was the consummate District Ranger who possessed the lost art of being able to perform the hands-on chores on his District, while providing the technical know-how of managing the multiple resources.

I was Lee's Assistant back in the days when we were the only year-long employees on the 500,000-acre Silver Lake District, Fremont Forest [in the early 1950s]. If you've been to Silver Lake, you know it's a long way from nowhere; 80 miles SE of Bend and 100 miles northwest of Lakeview. Really out in the boonies! Of necessity we had to be carpenters, mechanics, plumbers and electricians. There was no way of getting such help within a reasonable time, within a limited District budget, without commercial telephone service. But that was no problem because Lee could do all those jobs with one hand tied behind him.

I was his willing apprentice, go-fer, and general laborer, a learning experience that was to serve me in good stead later on in my career. I marveled at his skill by comparison with my bumbling efforts. He was probably the best jury rigger the FS has seen; taking scraps of iron, rusty bolts and assorted odds and ends to fashion something that worked well. I never saw him make a mistake, that is - until we were erecting a power distribution line for the Ranger Station electrical service from our newly installed Witte, a one lung diesel light plant. Once again Bob was the laborer, climbing the poles with spurs to place insulators and thread the line.

One windy day, as the project neared completion, a splice was required in the heavy line lying on the ground between two poles. The job called for a lot of soldering and insulation wrapping. Lee decided to get out of the wind and instructed me to feed one end of the line into the cab of his pickup, where he could roll the window up and cut out wind flow. He then instructed me to feed the other end through the opposite door. Whereupon he proceeded to do a beautiful job of splicing the line - got the picture?

I knew what was going to happen, but mine wasn't to reason why, only to do or die. The result was a securely spliced line running from one pole through the pickup to the next pole. I thought I had a pretty good ex-Marine vocabulary, but I learned some new ones that day.

Bjornsen was a District Ranger on the Wallowa-Whitman NF in the 1950s.

Remember the old wood-burning furnaces? These were in vogue before heating oil models became available, particularly in rural areas. Such was the case in the old Bear Sleds RD office at Wallowa, Wallowa-Whitman Forest [in the late 1950s or early 1960s].

The furnace was located in the office basement adjacent to a two-cord wood storage area. Living next door in the Ranger's house, I would come over about an hour before opening time to load the temperamental wood-eating monster in an effort to cut the chill when we went to work. This was often an exercise in futility because either a smoldering low-heat fire resulted or a roaring inferno that drove upstairs occupants to open windows in a self-defeating exercise.

Compounding the problem was a lone register near the second-story stairs that was supposed to heat the entire building. It intermittently belched smoke that failed to go up the main flue. If the heat didn't drive one out, the smoke would. Having long since given up trying to repair the infernal apparatus, and having no success in persuading the S.O. to give us funds for a new oil burner, we decided to give the Forest Supervisor a full smoke treatment on his next winter visit.

On the appointed day Supervisor Hal Coons was seated by the open door to my office in proximity to the register. By prearranged signal, District FMO Bill Maxwell stoked the furnace with wet rags and green alder wood to ensure a smoky fire. You guessed it! The old furnace never broke stride as it burned that fuel with a degree of efficient combustion never before achieved and nary a smidgen of smoke to sally forth from the register.

Meanwhile, Bill was frantically stuffing more wet fuel into the firebox ignoring the fact the heat was driving us to work in our shirtsleeves with the windows open. Hal's comment about a "damn good furnace you have there," shot down our last hopes for its replacement.

Frank E. Lewis *Lewis started as a temporary in 1942 and received a permanent appointment in 1950. He worked on the Columbia/Gifford Pinchot, Ochoco, Fremont, Siuslaw, Mt. Baker and Mt. Hood NFs in R-6, in Regional Offices in R-1 and R-6, and at the Beltsville Electronics Center for the Washington Office. He retired in 1980 as Assistant Director of Fire Control (Suppression) in the R-6 Regional Office. Lewis' father, Melvin M. Lewis, has two stories in Chapter One (Joining Up and Wives' Tales).*

The construction of Ross Dam by Seattle City Light in the 1940s, on the upper Skagit River, flooded about 15,000 acres on the Mt. Baker NF. A timber settlement was negotiated and the timber in the basin where the reservoir was to be created was cut below the 1605 foot elevation. Ultimately, a 45-mile double lane private access road was constructed from Hope, British Columbia, to the international boundary near Hozameen Peak at the head of Ross Lake to market the settlement timber - over 15 million board feet.

The city of Seattle sold the logs to Decco-Walton Lumber Company. Their fleet of Kenworth log trucks with 14 foot bunks was used to take the logs, tree length, to the Frazier River at Hope, BC where they were dumped and rafted for towing to the company mill in Everett, Washington.

This operation went on during the 1950s. A company logging camp, housing several hundred men at Hozameen, operated from early spring to draw down in early winter for a number of years. The logging slash was confined south of the Canadian border and burned each spring - about 2,500 acres a year.

The only reasonably safe period to travel the road between Hope and Hozameen was a two-hour window between 5 pm when the last truck arrived at Hope and 7 pm when the Canadian customs office at Hozameen closed for the night. Otherwise, upon meeting one of the trucks, usually loaded with about 25 thousand board feet of logs, a driver had to quickly find a convenient turnout on the side of the road appropriate for clearing the tree length loads of logs and depending upon whether if on a curve, it was to the right or left!

<u>Stan Bennett</u> *Bennett started work in 1939 as a temporary on the Siskiyou NF, and received a permanent appointment on that Forest in 1943 as a District Clerk. He worked on the Siskiyou, Chelan, and Okanogan NFs, and was Lands Staff Officer on the Siuslaw NF when he retired in 1975.*

It was not until after WWII that the western National Forests developed an urgent need for road access. By the 1950s, the right-of-way program on most National Forests required adequately trained specialists to carry out that work. Usually the first contact with a landowner was by the District Ranger or assistant. Land owners usually had some demands and even objections to having a road cross their property. In *the good ole' days*, the Ranger had his easement in hand and landowners welcomed the chance to have an improved road to and across their property. Such was not the case after the 1950s. Rather, it became a very lengthy process and even involved the use of condemnation.

The details of some of these knotty right-of-way cases were not necessarily recorded. For instance, on the Tonasket RD of the Okanogan NF, a road was planned for better access to the Lost Lake Recreation Area. A right-of-way was required over a tract of land owned by a Native American woman. After all preliminary contacts had been made, she still resisted. Everett Lynch was District Ranger and he turned the negotiations over to Bert Wells, an engineer on the project. After a number of trips to this lady without results, Bert noticed that she always had a wad of snuff in her upper lip. The next time Bert arrived, the discussion turned to snuff, and Bert produced a brand new can and offered it to the lady. Easement granted!

Bennett describes another right-of-way case, this one not so easily resolved.

Another right-of-way case with a different twist was across property owned by Chet Sisson on the Little Nestucca River within the Hebo Ranger District of the Siuslaw NF. At the time Rolfe Anderson was District Ranger. Rex Wakefield was Forest Supervisor when the case started, but Tenny Moore inherited the job before the right-of-way was

348

obtained. About 1947 a timber sale was sold that required the construction of a log stringer bridge and some improvements across Mr. Sisson's property. The Forest Service obtained some sort of administrative agreement to conduct timber sale operations over this road while negotiating the easement. That did not include public access.

Ranger Rolfe *Andy* Anderson and Chet Sisson did not see eye-to-eye on the need for public access across the property. Both were equally stubborn, no gray areas in their view. Andy truly believed that anyone would gladly grant the good old FS free access. Sisson thought the right-of-way was worth $1,000,000 or so, and that he would control it forever, even after granting. So there was not much progress. They agreed to mutual dislike and distrust.

Time went on and timber sale activities used the right-of-way agreement across Sisson's property. During a lull in timber sale activity, a survey crew was sent in to survey for a description of the proposed easement. That is when the stuff hit the fan. The survey crew was run off his land by Sisson. A county deputy was brought in to ensure the safety of the survey crew while they completed their task. Then Sisson turned his attention to members of the public who tried to cross his land. He would swear, accuse, entrap, threaten harm, and give then the option of buying their way through. He would tell them it was the Ranger's fault and the public, upset and shaken, would go to the Ranger Station. Andy would try to deal with this and it was tough.

Eventually an adequate easement was secured before Andy left the district in 1966.

<u>Robbie Robertson</u> *Robertson started as a temporary in 1950 and received a permanent appointment in 1952. He worked on the Willamette and Mt. Hood NFs and in the R-6 Regional Office in Timber Management and Operations. He retired in 1989 as Information Resources Manager for the U.S. Fish and Wildlife Service in Portland.*

Remember when almost all Forest roads were one-lane roads with turnouts? And on a full bench road there was an unwritten rule that loaded log trucks took the inside and other vehicles pulled into turnouts? This meant that many miles of Forest Service roads were a random combination of *left hand drive* and *right hand drive*. On the Cascadia Ranger District, [Willamette NF] with checkerboard ownership, the heavy haul roads were actually posted *keep to the right* or *keep to the left* depending on which side of the slope you were on. The signing was done by Willamette National Lumber Company, not the USFS. Most west-side Ranger Districts shared this problem.

Of course, this was before roads were actually designed and built to standards, and log truck drivers had little faith that turnouts on a steep sidehill would hold up under a load of logs.

In the mid-fifties, due to concerns about ever-increasing public traffic, an edict was issued that all roads would be *right hand drive* only. Purchasers and loggers were notified, but in many cases truckers cheerfully continued to drive on the inside anyway.

The result was more demands for enforcement of the right hand drive edict. As I recall, on the Detroit RD of the Willamette, the Straight Creek road had been built in the early 1950s. Starting at the bridge across the Santiam River it had turnouts on the left for about four miles of full bench road with steep dropoffs on the outside. Ercil Wilson was the logger, Wendall Jones was the timber sale administrator, and I was laying out sales. Instead of trying to tell the log truck drivers what they must do, Ercil's crew posted this poem on the Straight Creek bridge where the road began:

> To drive on the left, or to drive on the right,
> Is a subject about which some people would fight.
> But if you want to keep living, and not join the saints,
> Better drive on the side where the other guy ain't.

Somehow this calmed everyone down. Although it didn't stop all left hand driving, at least everyone was looking out for the other guy, and not assuming that the loaded trucks always had the right of way. Eventually, everyone did move to driving on the right.

Wendall Jones *Jones started as a temporary in 1950 and received a permanent appointment in 1954. He worked on the Willamette, Deschutes, Siuslaw, and Mt. Hood NFs, headed the*

350

Timber Sales Program in the Washington Office, and was Director of Timber Management in the R-6 Regional Office when he retired in 1990.

Working on timber sale layout often relied on speed and lots of commitment. In the late 1950s [on the Detroit Ranger District, Willlamette NF] our work time was 8 am to 5 pm, and work time began when you had your caulked boots on, and your cruisers vest loaded where you parked the rig [at the job site]. The work day ended when you returned to the rig. And the work day assumed a one hour lunch. So this translated into leaving the Ranger Station by about 7am and returning at 6 pm or later. And Carl Juhl and I never took an hour lunch - more like 20 minutes unless we needed to build a warming fire. Smoke breaks or coffee breaks had not been invented.

We worked in the snow on areas close to the highway or plowed roads, and stuck to the better ground working on snowshoes. We did not have high-tech clothing or shoes to protect our hands and feet from the cold. Our bodies were fine covered with 100% wool longjohns. We rarely wore rain pants - they were just too constraining on keeping up the pace. So we ended up with cold fingers and sometimes cold, wet feet and put those wet, re-oiled caulked boots on again the next day. The worst conditions were a thawing day with a little wind after an overnight snow. Big blobs of snow came out of the trees right on top of you about the time you were trying to write on a cruise card or field notebook.

Now you think that speed probably interfered with our accuracy? We had a lot of pride and the Willamette NF kept track of sale cruises vs. cutout, including names of cruisers, and made those available to all Districts. Gross overcuts were especially bad for your reputation.

<u>Emil Sabol</u> *Sabol started as a temporary in 1950 and received a permanent appointment in 1952. He worked on the Ottawa NF in R-9, the White River and Routt NFs in R-2, and the Deschutes, Willamette, Rogue River and Olympic NFs in R-6. He then worked in timber management in the R-1 Regional Office and the Washington Office, and was Assistant Director of Timber Management in the R-6 Regional Office when he retired in 1986.*

In 1964, when I was District Ranger at Union Creek on the Rogue River National Forest, the station compound was being visited nocturnally by a hungry black bear. He rummaged through the residential garbage cans and left a mess, as you can imagine. This happened on several nights; it appeared that the problem was not going to be resolved without some sort of action by the residents.

Thinking that it was an errant bruin from the garbage dumps at Crater Lake National Park, we decided to seek the aid of our Park Service friends. Buck Evans, who was then Chief Ranger, agreed to lend us their trailer-mounted live trap. This consisted of a section of six foot culvert mounted on wheels, with a trap door spring loaded to a bait can which hung at the rear of the culvert. The culvert was closed on that end. We loaded the bait can with bacon chunks and drippings, and other goodies which were considered sumptuous bear fare.

We parked that rig in various locations on the station for several nights, but the bear wouldn't bite. Meanwhile, he continued to sample the garbage cans of the station personnel. We despaired of ever catching that guy alive, and were considering turning loose some of the mighty hunters among the station's workforce.

Well, this bear solved the problem for us in the wee hours of the next day. He decided to do a little marauding around the cabins behind Beckie's Cafe, a special use which was situated (and still is) adjacent to Union Creek Ranger Station. It so happened that Mrs. Gene Arias, the wife of our Blister Rust Control foreman, worked part-time at Beckie's and was staying in one of the cabins along with another waitress. The bear strolled across the porch of the cabin and began to sniff and snort near the door. It was about 3:00 am.

What the bear didn't know was that Mrs. Arias was an accomplished hunter and kept a .300 Savage handy in the cabin. Her girlfriend had a .32 Winchester, and together they dispatched the bear right there on the cabin porch. In the morning when I came to Beckie's Cafe for coffee, the ladies showed me their trophy which had already been "skun out" and dressed.

While we were a little embarrassed by our failure with the trap, we were pleased that the problem had been solved by one of our own. I don't remember that anyone had written an environmental analysis for the project.

Wendall Jones *Jones was a District Ranger on the Willamette NF at the time of this story.*

In 1963, I went back to Detroit [on the Willamette NF] as District Ranger. The 1964 Flood so dominated this hitch at Detroit that much of what took place before and after that has faded from my memory. In mid-December, we got an early wet snowfall. There was 16 to 18 inches on the ground at the Ranger Station, and that depth increased geometrically at higher elevations. I don't recall that we had any concern about the snow, but then the temperatures rose sharply and we had significant rainfall amounts. The snow was going fast, but most of the big increase in stream levels occurred after dark that first day of warm wet air. We were awakened very early in the morning (I think it might have been around 4 am) by the State Highway maintenance foreman, to tell us that the highway was out above Idanha, and it looked like a big fill down toward the dam was failing, so the highway was closed.

So we knew we were on our own to take care of the people in the canyon through this mess. We had crews out early to look at FS roads. Most of them were already washed out or closed by a slide. The timing turned out to be a blessing because we had no one blocked behind washouts on the FS roads. We had no communications with Marion Forks people, but the highway folks had talked to their counterparts by radio at Santiam Junction. They could not get to Marion Forks either. So one of our early decisions was to send two or three people on foot to check on the Marion Forks bunch. Gus Kuehne led this mission. He reported 17 major highway outages between Idanha and Marion Forks. A second action was to call a meeting of storeowners and other key people in the area to share problems and solutions. Key decisions were to ration groceries and other key supplies such as gasoline, since it could be weeks before access was restored. We didn't intend to enforce any hard rules - just rely on the cooperation and good will of the canyon folks. There were no law enforcement officers in the area. Everyone was concerned about the childrens' Christmas.

We had one exciting incident at the Ranger Station. It was not yet very daylight, maybe about 7 am, when my wife Jessie called the office on the radio-intercom and excitedly told us the creek was coming through the compound and was going to flood our house. Every available person dropped what they were doing and headed up to our house. Debris, silt and water was all around the house, completely covering the yard. Debris was in the breezeway between the house and garage. The water level was very close to the sills on the house, so we had to act fast. Big Gus Kuehne started to scour a ditch along the foundation with his rubber boot covered feet. This was more effective than a bunch of shovels because he was able to quickly put the water to use to create a drainage to the slope in front of the house. As the water ebbed, up to a foot of silt covered the lawn around the house, and it became very solid before we got around to uncovering the lawn. The damage was done, the house was OK, so we went on to more important crises.

Several houses in Idanha were completely swept away. Fortunately they were all evacuated a few hours earlier. The log decks at both Green Veneer and Simpson's veneer plant were all swept into the reservoir along with all the upstream Forest Service logs and trees. Reservoir cleanup became a huge project in 1965. Both bridges to New Idanha were washed away. One of my people came to me with that news and the fact that they needed some bridge stringers. I told them to help these folks find their bridge stringers on NF land close by and *don't fuss with the paper-work*. I doubt that the trees were ever paid for and I don't regret that. I looked at one flooded home in Idanha. Water was still a couple of feet over floor level. When I saw a light bulb still burning in the house, I decided that was not a good place to be.

One story will illustrate the dangers of being out on the roads on that first day. I went up to the Blowout Road with some of my staff to look at the bridge across the Santiam River. There was a big log-jam above and against the bridge confining the current. The bridge was vibrating erratically. There was concern about getting a piece of equipment in there to lift some of the logs out of that jam. It was decided that it was not worth the risk, so we went out Blowout, to near the Hoover Campground entrance, to make sure we had all the folks off the Blowout road and back across the bridge. We had just gotten

354

Johnny Devereaux and Bruce Kirkland beginning a daunting task on the
Rock Creek Bridge, Wenatchee NF – early 1950s

Road washed out by the 1964 flood, Umpqua NF

back near the bridge when someone called on the radio to tell us that a major slide had blocked the Blowout Road with 20 to 30 foot deep rocks and debris right where we had been standing and talking a few minutes earlier. The Santiam bridge did survive the flood.

We had a different Christmas in 1964. Actually we had planned to go to my parents for Christmas that year.

R. D. "Bob" Strombom *Strombom transferred from the U.S. Corps of Engineers (Civil) to the Mount Hood NF in 1960. He was the R-6 Regional Road and Trail Maintenance and Operations Engineer when he retired in 1985. Strombom's wife has a story in this Chapter also (Freda Vincent Evans, Fire and Lookouts).*

In December 1964, Forest Service, state and county officials in western Washington and Oregon were recoiling from major flooding, the magnitude of which was later classified as exceeding a 500-year flood.

Twenty-five miles upriver from Estacada, Oregon, is Ripplebrook Ranger Station on the Mt. Hood NF. Winter access to Ripplebrook was by way of the Clackamas River Road which was then operated and maintained by the Forest Service above Estacada (now State Highway 224). It did not take long for the residents of Ripplebrook to learn that the Clackamas River had washed out this road and bridges in numerous places. Access from the east was snowed in, so people at Ripplebrook were isolated until access could be restored.

District Rangers Tom Carr and Bob Sorber coordinated with the Supervisor's Office to set up a supply line by helicopter when weather permitted. Some family members were evacuated due to medical needs including a pregnancy or two. The remainder of the staff and families simply went to work making emergency repairs.

Lowell *Gil* Gilbert and his forest-wide construction and maintenance (C&M) crew had the task of getting road access to Ripplebrook. Gil had some great help in assistants Lou Keller and Jack Anderson. Access would have to be by way of Forest Service roads running east toward Timothy Lake and US Highway 26 east of Government Camp. Wet snow, falling daily after the flood, settled upon older packed snow and froze, so their work was cut out for them.

Road access was restored to Ripplebrook in about two weeks using every available daylight hour to complete the snow removal and restore flood damage on the involved roads. Deep drifts were removed by a combination of tracked bulldozers and front-end loaders, down to the final couple of feet of snow. Then front-end loaders removed all but the last few inches. Final plowing was normally done with road graders. A substantial amount of snow had to be trucked away to protect meadows and prevent blockage of streamcourses. Throughout the plowing, the crew operated out of converted buses in a winter camp at the old Skyline Meadows Guard Station.

The restoring of basic access to Ripplebrook is but one story of many throughout the northwest that illustrate how the men and women of the FS worked together to keep flood damage to a minimum and restore access to the National Forests after the 1964 flood.

Robert Schramek *Schramek started as a temporary in 1952 and received a permanent appointment in 1954. He worked in Idaho, and on the Olympic, Malheur, Wenatchee, and Willamette NFs in R-6, and the Jefferson NF in R-8. He then worked in the Office of Inspector General, Department of Agriculture and was the Fire, Recreation, and Lands Staff Officer on the Modoc NF in R-5 when he retired in 1985.*

After a transfer to the Malheur Forest in the dry pine country of central Oregon, I was assigned responsibility to head up the Forest Inventory project for the Malheur Forest. This involved training and supervising crews in setting up permanent plots all across the Forest, and taking measurements of timber volume and growth to determine the sustained yield for the Forest management plan.

The plots were located on a grid set up with aerial photos and were located by using the aerial photos to establish the center point for the first of three plots. This involved driving to a known point and traveling cross-country to locate the plots. I had been putting off going into this one plot, but the season was coming to a close, and I decided to take one of the newer, less-experienced crews for additional training and walk into the location.

357

When we got to the starting point, we found that going in from this direction would involve a walk of about three miles, and a climb over a high rough ridge. I knew about an old logging road that crossed private ranch property and came into the Forest very close to the plot location. I had not wanted to use this route, because it was not a public road, and the owner was a doctor who was out of the country for the summer.

After taking a good look at the ridge we'd have to climb if we stayed on Forest land, I decided to risk trespassing on the doctor's land and apologize to him after the fact. After a short drive we found the old road and drove up to a locked gate where we parked to walk in the remaining half mile to the site.

We had walked about a quarter mile up this dry canyon when we came to another gate. We squeezed under the barbed wire fence and began walking up the road, which made a sharp turn around a big rock cliff. There was a fence bordering the road, dividing the valley into two pasture units, one on either side of the small dry creek bed.

As we came around the curve of the cliff, we were met by the largest bull buffalo that I had ever seen. He must have stood close to six feet tall at the top of his massive humped back, and he looked distinctly unfriendly. I saw that he was protecting a small herd of cows and calves, and he was eyeing us and switching his tail in a very menacing fashion. Fortunately, he was on the back side of the barbed wire fence.

As I watched, the bull walked up to the fence, where he was within about ten feet of us, and began snorting and pawing the dust. I looked around to see if there were any trees, or places to get away from this animal if he should decide to come at us through the fence. I had no doubt that if he wanted to, he could walk through that flimsy fence without slowing up!

There were no trees, large rocks, or any other protection close by. However, I could see that there was another cross fence and cattle guard up the road about 200 yards, where the road entered National Forest land. I quietly told the crew to walk slowly up the road with me and try to ignore the bull. If he remained calm we just might get across the next fence without any trouble. I couldn't think of any reasonable alternative, so we just began slowly walking up the road, watching the bull out of the corner of my eye.

The bull walked up the road along with us, keeping pace with us all the way to the cattle guard. As we walked across the cattle guard and into the Forest, the bull stood at the corner of the fence, watching us until we were out of sight. I breathed a big sigh of relief when we got into the trees, and was thankful for reading an article about the importance of staying calm around wild animals to avoid provoking them into a charge. On our way out to the vehicle, the herd had moved and was nowhere in sight, so the walk out was uneventful.

I told the other District personnel about the buffalo herd, and warned them about the lousy disposition of the herd bull, but didn't know if the herd would be around all summer. This was the first I knew about the doctor having acquired a herd of buffalo. We later learned that this same bull had chased some loggers out of the woods after he had walked across that fence and strayed into the Forest. Later that summer, he chased a lookout back into his tower and scared off a survey crew.

The big surprise came later that summer, when a survey crew with some young high school students in the crew came across the bull on a Forest road, just a mile or less inside the Forest boundary. The kids knew where the buffalo belonged. They talked to him, walked up to him, and two of them, each holding onto one of his horns, gently walked him back down the road and put him through the gate, into his pasture!

It just shows that the attitude you project to an animal makes all the difference in the world.

Hillard M. "Lil" Lilligren *Lilligren began his Forest Service career on the Plumas NF in R-5. He worked on the Siuslaw, Umpqua and Rogue River NFs and was Forest Service Liasion to the Corps of Engineers on the Rogue River NF when he retired in 1973. Lilligren's wife Bunty has a story in this Chapter (Wives and Families). Their son, Jon, was a career Forest Service employee, also.*

Then there was the case of the illegal use of a firearm in the South Umpqua Falls Camp area by a person unknown. I transferred [from the Umpqua NF] to the Rogue River NF in the spring of 1966, where I became the liaison officer representing the Forest in mutual planning with the Corps of Engineers on the three proposed dams involving the Rogue Basin Project.

Several months after my transfer, my friend Homer Oft, the venerable fire control staff man in Roseburg [on the Umpqua NF] called me. He wanted to know if I had ever stored dynamite at the South Umpqua Falls Camp. I said there might be one or two cases in a sheet-metal shed back against the base of the hill. Our nearest explosives storage building was in Roseburg. It wasn't very practical to drive in for a few sticks of powder when needed, and then return the unused explosives to Roseburg every night - a total of 260 miles a day. All my previous requests for a powder magazine on the District had been denied.

On a Monday morning, a Tiller employee driving past the South Umpqua Falls camp noticed a change. The metal storage building was gone. Further examination showed the surrounding trees had bits of metal imbedded in their bark. There were also many small pieces of hide and flesh spread over the area, and a dead deer badly mangled in the vicinity.

It appeared that someone had come down the road on Sunday night, spotted deer over by the metal shed and fired at one of them. The poacher may have hit a deer, but he also hit the dynamite. From the evidence, it appeared that one deer was completely fragmented and the second one only partially so.

No one ever admitted the shooting - but it must have been a big shock to the poacher to see his targets disappear in a bright flash and loud explosion. I think someone was trying to give him a message!

Stan Bennett *Bennett tells one more right-of-way story.*

It was a wet cold day in the 1960s on the Oregon coast as three Forest Service officers drove up the driveway of a middle-aged woman who had recently lost her husband, and whose death had not been fully explained. The three men: John Brillhart, Timber Staff; Carl Juhl,

360

District Ranger of Smith River District; and myself, Lands Staff, all on the Siuslaw NF, were out to satisfy a Congressional Right-of-Way complaint. We wondered if the lady, we'll call her Mrs. Knap, would be serving coffee and doughnuts.

Mrs. Knap lived on land adjacent to NF land on the Smith River District. When Carl met her she was quite opposed to granting any kind of deed to allow the FS to gain access to the NF. After meeting with Mrs. Knap, Carl was told that there was something mysterious about the death of Mrs. Knap's husband. It was rumored that she may have poisoned him.

Well, Carl went a second time, and he had a sample easement, which he went over with Mrs. Knap. She still refused, and, in fact, wrote a letter to her Congressman complaining that the Ranger came to her with an easement in his hip pocket which he whipped out and expected her to sign. Well, you know the story on how those complaints go from the Congressman to Chief to Regional Forester to Supervisor and thence to Ranger, asking to answer the complaint.

So there we were. As we drove up the road, you can imagine our thoughts, wondering if Mrs. Knap was going to serve us coffee and what might possibly be in it. Well she did, and we screwed up our courage to drink it. The meeting was good. Mrs. Knap had her day, came to agreement, and we walked away alive and well.

Dave Jay (with assistance from R. Robert Burns, Merle DeBolt and Myrna DeBolt) *Jay started as a temporary at age 16 in 1953 and received a permanent appointment in 1959. He worked on the Shawnee and Superior NFs in R-9, the Flathead NF in R-1, the Mt. Baker, Mt. Hood, Umpqua, and Gifford Pinchot NFs in R-6, the Targhee NF in R-4, and the Lassen NF in R-5. He worked in Fire and Aviation in the Washington Office and in Regional Offices in R-8 and R-6, and was a Deputy Regional Forester in R-5 when he retired in 1991.*

It was the end of the Thanksgiving weekend in 1968 and our family was returning to the Wind River Ranger Station from my folks' ranch in Oregon. As we entered the Columbia Gorge, it began to snow. We crossed the Columbia River and as we drove through Carson, Washington and up the Wind River, the snow was falling heavily with wet, huge flakes. Suddenly the station wagon just stopped on the unplowed road. The night was darker than the inside of a cow. With difficulty and cold hands (no gloves, of course) I was able to chain up and finally make our way into the Ranger Station. Little did we know what was ahead.

Earlier that year we moved to Wind River District as I followed the late Clay Beal as District Ranger. The station, at about 1000 feet elevation, was known for its heavy rainfall but little was said about snow.

This year it started and didn't stop. For the next four months it snowed often and heavy. At one stretch we had measurable snow for 20 consecutive days. At times, it fell at four inches per hour! By the end of the second week we knew we were in for it. The extensive compound included buildings for the nursery, Ranger District, experimental forest and training center, maybe 25 in all. Most were built 30 or more years earlier with cedar shake roofs.

We met with the nurseryman, Frosty Deffenbacher, and his staff to agree on priorities. First, we had to keep one road open to the Wind River Highway in case of an emergency or a building fire, but we had only hand shovels and a backhoe/front end loader! Next was to shovel roofs. We organized into teams and started - warehouses, offices, bunkhouse, and residences. Meanwhile Skamania County loaned us a snow plow that we mounted on one of our large trucks. Al Blaisdell, with the nursery, gerry-rigged together a rotary plow. Where the parts came from, I don't know.

We began to make headway. The main compound road was open, some driveways were plowed, all the fire hydrants were kept open, everyone was keeping at least one walk open to their house and the snow was coming off the roofs. At first the roofs were dangerous work but as the snow accumulated under the eaves, if or when you slid off, you landed in a huge snow pile. And those piles grew and grew and grew. Pretty soon the endless stuff was threatening to shove the windows in on the houses and offices. We finally covered them with plywood and all the outside light disappeared.

After two months a typical day started with shoveling your walk so the kids could get out to the school bus. An early shift of drivers for the plows would have started about 0330 and the late shift ending after midnight (donated time of course). This was usually Dick Blaisdell, Dick Misner, Gordon Reinhart, Merle DeBolt and Bob Burns among others. While the plow could move the new snow, soon there was no place for it to go and the rotary would cut it back to the rising banks. Soon we were driving through a tunnel. Next was roof shoveling for four or five hours and finally back home to your own roof and walks.

February brought more surprises. The roof-shoveled snow was now piled up to the eaves on most buildings. Any new snow had to be shoveled up and over those piles. Deer were using our plowed roads and walks making plowing difficult. Employees were tired and irritable. Dealing with the snow was like trying to stop the incoming tide. The *London flu* was beginning to thin our ranks. Families in the residences could only see out their upstairs gable windows. Communication with the Forest Supervisor and staff became more tenuous as little of our planned work was getting done. A few *SO types* ventured out and left quickly, shaking their heads.

One morning the manager of the Wind River Fish Hatchery called. "Dave, I've got a problem. The elk have moved into Tyee Springs. It supplies our water for the fishponds. The snow is six feet deep and the elk are making a hell of a mess. Grass and debris is floating downstream and plugging up our intake! Any ideas?" After calls to the Washington Fish and Wildlife, US Fish and Wildlife and Skamania County, we had a plan. The state provided the hay, the county plowed a wide spot in the highway, the hatchery and Forest Service folks (families too) volunteered to feed the elk twice a day. Cedar trees were cut to provide additional browse. It worked and all because of the commitment of some great people.

Warm winds and rain came the end of March. By then nearly 240 inches (20 feet) had fallen. It all settled to about eight feet on the level. Gradually our days returned to normal, but piles of snow persisted into May.

Recently several friends who were there commented on what they remembered. "It was really fun. We didn't have TV or phones. We played games and shared meals with our neighbors. Everyone helped each other out every day. It was like a tight, wonderful family."

WIVES AND FAMILIES: "The ground was completely saturated, with water standing all over, and then the women got to work."

Lillian Olson   *Olson describes finding a way to escape the loneliness when her husband was on campouts for work. Vincent Olson worked on the Columbia, Fremont, Gifford Pinchot and Siskiyou NFs in R-6 and was Forest Supervisor on the North Tongass NF in R-10 from 1964 to 1975.*

My husband [Vincent N. Olson] returned from the army in 1945, and in the fall of that year, I was introduced to my first assignment with the Forest Service at Randle, Washington [on the Columbia NF]. During the next summer and fall, Vince, along with other *timber beasts*, as they used to refer to themselves, was usually in camp somewhere all week cruising timber. Travel to and from camp was always on personal time. They usually came back late Friday evenings and left for camp Sunday afternoon so they could be on the job early Monday morning. This added isolation made me determined to find a more useful way of life, so I volunteered to accompany my husband to camp and serve as camp cook, in spite of my husband's protests. Up to this time, the men had done their own cooking. After a month of volunteer service, the Forest Service put me on the payroll as camp cook.

The cruising camps were usually located five to seven miles from the nearest road and only accessible by trails. All food supplies were packed in by mules. Perishables and fresh meat were usually back-packed in by the men, on weekends. As roads were limited to valley bottoms, the pack was always up-hill. The camp consisted of sleeping tents, a kitchen supply tent and an improvised kitchen under a fly. The table and benches were made from split cedar shakes. It also served as an office for paperwork after supper. A portable Kimmel stove was used for cooking. For those of you who may not be acquainted with a Kimmel stove, it was an ingenious device, best described as a tin box with a stovepipe placed upside down over a gravel pad. It was either hot or cold, depending on the fire which was built under it. I soon learned the value of pitch and old growth Douglas-fir bark when it

364

came to keeping the home fires burning. It also came equipped with another double-walled tin box which could be attached to the flue, to serve as an oven. It was an excellent device for burning pies and biscuits until I learned the fine art of manipulating a proper fire. My cooking skills were derived by trial and error. It was frustrating, to say the least. The most rewarding part of the job for me was the appreciation expressed by the men in the camp. They were always helpful in keeping me stocked with wood and kindling for the morning fires. They never complained and always encouraged me with compliments.

A typical day consisted of getting the men up in the morning, feeding them breakfast, and setting out the makings for lunches. As they were gone until evening, I would make good use of the rest of the day by getting everything ready and cooked for the evening meal. When I wasn't busy cooking, I would tidy up the camp, or if it was raining, I would fire up the Sibley stoves in the sleeping tents so the men could change from rain-soaked clothes in comfort when they returned. One misty morning, after washing the breakfast dishes, I noticed what I thought was a person crossing the stream near camp. I figured someone was returning to camp for some forgotten equipment, but the figure was not familiar so I called out. When the figure went down on all four legs, I realized it was a large bear. I quickly grabbed a large piece of wood, determined to go down swinging. Fortunately, the bear sensed danger connected with his anticipated meal and left.

<u>Bonna Wilson</u> *Wilson wrote a descriptive letter to her parents about her first summer as a Forest Service wife. She was a Forest Service employee only on the Willamette NF, but was a part of the Forest Service as her husband John's wife on the Willamette, Umpqua and Mt. Hood NFs. She taught school in each of the towns they lived in and retired from the Parkrose School District in 1979.*

In early June 1948, my husband of six months, John Wilson, brought me out to Oregon from Iowa to spend our long-delayed honeymoon together on a lookout on the West Boundary District on the Willamette NF. But when we got to Oregon, Ranger Fred Briem offered John a better-paying job doing pre-sale mapping, camping out with Arvid Ellson. (I still think of Arvid as *the man with whom my husband spent our honeymoon.*) That left me alone at the Ranger Station all week, so when an elderly man who had recently gone up to Clark Butte Lookout had a heart attack and had to be brought down, I decided I'd like to go up and make a little additional money.

I spent most of that Sunday afternoon in Ranger Briem's office trying to convince him I could do it, while he tried to talk me out of it. He knew I was a nineteen-year-old girl who had never seen a mountain or a forest before, and he talked about all the strange noises that might scare me - the animals, the wind in the trees, etc. But he finally gave in and hired me - the first woman lookout he had ever hired - and since John had decided to continue working that fall and return to Iowa State for the winter quarter, I ended up staying on the lookout until mid-October.

About two weeks after going up there I wrote the following letter to our parents.

Clark Butte Look Out
Tuesday, July 27, 1948

Dear Folks,

I guess this is as good a time as any to start my story. I'm on about the same level as the clouds today, and besides being fogged in, it's raining and there is a cold wind, so they gave me the day off. Of course, there is no place to go and no way to get there, and since I can't see any farther than my clearing goes, I guess I'll just have to entertain myself. It certainly is a funny feeling to be clouded in. If you look down or across or up all you see is thick, streaky fog - makes you feel like you are in a world all your own. If it weren't for King and the radio it would be pretty lonesome on days like this. King is feeling frisky right now and I'm having a little trouble trying to get rid of him. He puts his big old paws on my shoulders and won't let go until I play with him. That's the disadvantage of a big dog - you do what he wants you to because he's too big to argue with. He learned how to bark the other day and it surprised him so much he hasn't gotten over it yet. I always thought dogs barked like babies cried, but not this kind. I guess I've sort of gotten off the subject, haven't I? I'm supposed to be telling you about life on a lookout. I think I'll make several copies of this - one for Wilsons, one for Van't Hulls, and one to keep so I can show our grandchildren how crazy we were when we were young.

To begin with, I came up here on July 15. We got to the bottom of the trail at about 10:10 am so I left the packers to pack my supplies on the mules, and King and I started up the trail alone. I put King on a leash so he could pull me when the going got tough, but his new surroundings and his first ride in a car subdued him so much he stuck right at my heels, so I just had to see that I got myself up. I had to stop and rest quite often and King got pretty impatient with the whole thing, but we finally got here at 11:20. I thought the pack string would pass me about half-way up since I didn't have John to pull me, but I did better than I expected, and I beat them by about 25 minutes. We ate lunch as soon as we were rested enough, and then I spent the afternoon up in the tower with the Assistant Ranger, trying to learn everything in a few hours that the other lookouts learned in three days of Guard School and almost a month of touring the country on trail work.

This is only a temporary lookout, so it isn't nearly as well equipped as the other ones are. The others are all much higher than this one and they can see much farther. This one is just here to keep an eye on the logging operations going on across the valley on about this same level. There are about ten logging areas right across from me, and since they go up in smoke much easier than green timber does, they have to be watched almost constantly during fire weather. As soon as those areas are grown over enough to be safe they'll discontinue this lookout.

Maybe you'd be interested in some of the things I have to know in order to report a fire. There is really much more to it than I thought there would be. Quite a bit of math is involved and that part of it is a little above my head, but I think I caught on to enough of it to get along. In the first place, we have to know how to read a fire finder. Mine isn't a very good one and it's very inconveniently located up in the tower, so I don't work with it as much as I should. My "tower" is just a little platform built up high in four trees and there is an awful old straight-up-and-down rough ladder leading up to it, so I don't go up there any oftener than I have to. The fire finder is a tube with cross hairs in it, mounted on a round map of the territory. You spin the tube around until you can see the smoke through it, and then you take a reading on it. There is a scale around the map marked off into 360 degrees and then another little jigger called a venier to help read minutes accurately. After you have the smoke spotted in the fire finder you read the degrees and minutes that it is set on, and this is called the azimuth reading. Then there is another little scale going up and down that gives you the verticle angle, or how much above or below you the smoke is.

This is all written down on a lookout report form, together with a description of landmarks that will help the Smokechaser find it easily, the estimated size, distance from the look-out, township, range, section, and subdivision it is in, estimated time it originated and cause, description of smoke, time it was spotted, and any other information you can give. This form is supposed to be completely filled out in not more than 5 minutes and phoned in to the Ranger station. To do it in that short time demands that you know the country backwards and forwards, and that takes a lot of practice. You have to know where all the roads are, the names of all the creeks and where they are located, the names of mountains, and I have to know the names and locations of all these logging areas beside what the other boys learn, but my area isn't as big, so I don't have as many creeks, ridges, etc. as they have.

Another thing we have to know is the difference between false, legitimate, and illegitimate smokes, and they can be very confusing at times. A legitimate smoke is one from a gang mill, a camp fire, a ranch house, etc. and they don't have to be reported, but you have to know where they all are and why. A false smoke might be anything from a light-colored rock slide to dust along a road that could be mistaken for a smoke. That's why we have to know where all the rock slides and roads are - so when it's hazy we won't spot something like that and turn in a false alarm. The illegitimate smokes are the ones we have to watch for. They're the ones caused by cigarettes, lightning strikes, and a hundred other things. We have to record every lightning strike and watch it for five days to see whether or not it develops into a "sleeper" fire.

Other things to know are how to orient a fire finder, how to take readings with a protractor or compass and a map, how to orient maps, how to take back-sight readings (which involves too much math for me), and the fellows have to know how to fight a fire in case there is one close enough for them to go to. This job also includes maintaining trails, keeping the clearing cleaned up, packing water, and sawing and splitting wood, and that's where John earns half my check every weekend.

I guess that's enough about my work. Now I'll describe this place a little. Our cabin is about 10' x 14', fairly new, and you'd be surprised how homey we've made it. There's a cupboard for supplies, but no place for clothes, so John put up an old broom-stick in a corner and I brought up one of the big drapes we had in the trailer to hang around it, and we now have a closet. But that didn't take care of clothes that wouldn't hang, so we packed all our canned goods in orange crates, and then when I had them unpacked I covered them with wrapping paper and hung my old red and white striped skirt around them, and that's our dresser. There's also a little table, two chairs, an old single iron cot, a little wood-burning stove (much better than the one we had at the Ranger Station), and a canvas army cot that John sets up weekends (we store it under my bed during the day). There are a lot of big tools up here - axes, shovel, pulaski, etc. - that were all standing behind the door, so John pounded a bunch of nails in the wall behind the door and hung all the tools up on them to get them out of the way. What would I do up here if I had married a helpless man? We left most of our things down at the Ranger Station, so we've got a lot more room here than we had in our trailer.

I've decided I'm getting paid for being without modern conveniences - not for the work I do. You should see our bathroom(?). It's a little square box with a hole in it down the hill in the woods - very unpleasant on rainy days like this without even a roof over your head. Our garbage pit is down there, too, and the trail going down that way is enough to send you roiling head over heels. Our icebox is also outside. It's a box with two shelves in it and a screen on one side set up on a brace John made for it in the trees where it's cool and shady, and the other part is a hole in the ground with a cover over it to keep milk and meat fresh, which is really quite effective. It's always cool in the shade up here, but very warm in the sun - there isn't any in-between.

Our "running water" is a spring down the hill over 1/4 mile on a steep trail. John does the running, and carries it up on his back in a water pack 5 gallons at a time. He carries up 25 or 30 gallons every week-

369

end, and that's more than enough for drinking, cooking, washing dishes, baths. What's left we use for the laundry every Saturday. You'd get a bang out of seeing me do my laundry. We've got one big wash tub, but for the rinsing water I use a dishpan for the first tub and a pail for the second. It isn't exactly fun doing those big old overalls with a little dribble of water and a wash board, but the hardest part is trying to wring them out by hand. I usually just give up and hang them up wet. The wind gets them dry eventually. The wind is my iron and ironing board, too. We've got the clothes line strung up where the wind hits them just right, so while they dry the wrinkles - part of them anyway - get whipped out. Wearing unironed clothes bothered me at first, but now I just think about what a relief it is to have a vacation from the ironing board.

I'm afraid weekends aren't much of a vacation for John. When he isn't hauling water or chopping wood he manages to find plenty of other things to do. Last weekend he decided the trail up from the water hole was too long and he found a place where he could make a shortcut and save 160 steps, so he got out the "to-be-used-only-in-case-of-fire" pulaski and did some trail building. It's really quite an improvement, and when it gets packed down a little it will be fully as good as the regular trail. If he isn't careful they'll take away his SP-6 and put him on the trail crew.

Now I'll tell you about the scary things there are to see and hear up here. Whenever my imagination starts working over-time I just say, "Easy, Kid. You're getting paid for this," and thinking about those checks calms me down. First on the list is our bear. He enjoys crashing around in the woods just west of the cabin, and the first time I heard him I was plenty glad I was up in the tower. The woods are quite thick there so I've never been able to see him, but he makes enough noise to wake the dead. And then there are the "black ghosts". Clark Butte was burned over in 1919, and there are lots of black jagged snags all over that are pretty eerie looking in the moonlight. There aren't any big trees left here - just tall, thin pole trees that bend double in the wind and make lots of noise. There are some other little noises that made me shudder at first, like strange bird calls that sound like baby wild cats, but now that I'm used to them I don't notice them anymore. We also have several deer that go around snapping twigs in the middle of the night.

I forgot to tell you about our roll call gab fests. Every day at 7:00, 12:00, and 5:00 they put in a general ring from the Ranger station for all the lookouts to make sure that we haven't skipped the country. That's when everyone tells about the deer they saw and the bear they heard. They give us the weather report then and tell us what's going on back in civilization, and on Sunday mornings they even break down and read the funny papers sometimes, but that's when I hang up and go back to bed. Most of the boys have their phones rigged up with strings so they can stay in bed and listen, but the cord on my phone is too short for that, and I'd rather just not listen than stand up for half an hour in a cold cabin. In the evening sometimes everyone gets on the line again and two of the boys play mouth organs and sing for everyone's benefit. I listen for a while now and then, but I just can't see standing beside the phone when all the rest of them are in bed.

I can't think of anything else to talk about except what a lot of noise the logging trucks make going up the mountainside, so I might as well call this the end. I'm not expecting to get any questionnaires after this, but in case you think of anything I skipped let me know. I'll try to send you some pictures later on so you can get a better idea of what I've been talking about. I wish I could get John to write something like this about his work and his camp, but he shudders at the thought. Too much like writing an English theme, I guess.

Love, /s/ Bonna

<u>Pam Devereaux Wilson</u> *Wilson is the eldest daughter of Johnny and Pennie Devereaux. Johnny was a long-time fire control officer on the Wenatchee, Willamette and Siuslaw NFs. Wilson began as a summer clerk on the Willamette NF after two summers as a state lookout, and had temporary jobs with both the Intermountain and Pacific Northwest Forest and Range Experiment Stations. Her first permanent job with the Forest Service was on the Siuslaw NF. She worked in Alaska (R-10) and ran her own business; joining a four-woman team planning new National Wildlife Refuges for the US Fish and Wildlife Service. She was teaching 5th grade when she retired in 2003.*

I grew up on a place frequented by folks with different jobs and different approaches to life. We called it a compound and we called the compound home. Most of my childhood was spent on a Forest Service compound. I am convinced growing up on a compound has had a lasting and positive effect on my life.

I don't remember my first compound home -- Liberty Guard Station. There is a picture of me in a yellow dress on the steps of that house. Nor do I remember much of the Forest Service warehouse in Wenatchee where we lived when my sister Renee was born. We lived on the Cle Elum compound. I remember learning to ride a bike there. But not before I crashed into lilac hedges, garbage cans and darn near every tree growing there. I finished kindergarten and started first grade before we moved to the Lake Wenatchee Ranger Station.

My first real memories come from Lake Wenatchee: home and refuge, playground and retreat, family and forest. I climbed my first mountain, Dirty Face, even though dad was adamantly opposed. I swam in the lake chasing the ice out until it melted. I became comfortable in a quiet forest. I learned to read nestled under a tree or along the lakeshore. On Lake Wenatchee's shore was an immense log lying with its root wad in the lake. Almost 50 years later I close my eyes and see this log, feel its smoothness.

The woods were our playmates. We snuck up to the corrals to watch the mules and horses, entering a spankable offense; made a playhouse in the rocky crags behind the house. In the backyard was a holey rowboat we sailed with our imaginations and a tire swing strung from a huge Douglas-fir. One December, in ten feet of snow, we moved into a house on the Leavenworth compound.

We moved to Entiat after I started 4th grade and lived at Steliko, 13 miles upriver. Crews would play "Mother May I" and "Red Light, Green Light" if we would wash their dishes or sweep the bunkhouse. We cleaned and they played with us for hours after work. Visiting the lookout behind the compound many with times with dad, I told him I wanted to be a lookout when I grew up.

Renee and I got into a wire cage in the warehouse where fire rations were kept. I'm not sure how many cans of pound cake and pilot bread we ate, but enough to make daddy mad. Usually our behavior caused him to be disappointed, but mad... That same warehouse became a dancehall. Floors were slickened with powdered soap and the adults danced for hours amidst the posts. Kids played until we fell asleep atop rolls of firehoses. At Steliko, I learned to ski, skis fastened with bands cut from inner tubes. I camped for the first time with my Camp Fire group at Silver Falls. Mom ice-fished with other women and I learned how to dam a creek to create a swimming hole. We walked everywhere, ate apples off Cooper's trees and climbed up the fire escape on the old school which housed the library. In 1956, the Entiat Valley was on fire. Mom worked in fire camp. Dad was gone all summer and fall.

On the school bus, high school boys use a word I didn't know. It wasn't in the dictionary at school, or in the one at home. Mrs. Peters, the ranger's wife, had been a teacher, so I knocked on her door and asked to use her dictionary. That four-letter word wasn't there either, so I thanked her and told her I had looked in three dictionaries but couldn't find the word. She asked if she could help, so I told her the word. I'm not sure what she answered, but in the minutes it took to cross the compound, she called mom who met me at the door. The word was explained and I was mortified. I think the adults had a good laugh!

At Steliko, I began watching compound work. Mom and I cleaned the office in the evenings. I listened in on dad's tailgate safety sessions early in the mornings. I read lying in a hammock and watched crews leaving and coming back. There was a safety bulletin board painted red and black. On the bottom large white letters read, "Always Alert – Nobody Hurt." At summer's end that board displayed 93 rattlesnake tails, complete with date and place.

We transferred in June of 1959 as I entered 7th grade. We moved to the Rigdon/Salt Creek compound in Oakridge. New forest, new state and new compound families. The District Ranger, Mac McCurdy, told dad that if we wanted a vacation, now was the time. My twelfth summer was our first and only family vacation; we went to Disneyland before fire season began. I finished high school and began college while my family lived here. The compound was far enough out of Oakridge to provide the retreat and nature I had come to need after Lake Wenatchee and Steliko. I often walked to or from school for the quiet. Tom and Mirdza Condron lent me books from their library.

When I brought them back, we drank tea and talked about the book. The time they gave me, I have never forgotten. Mary Lysne, the new Ranger's daughter, became a good friend. Shirley Lysne helped mom sew a purple pleated skirt for Pep Club. I learned to parallel park on that compound. I used the cones but dad refused to let me practice using the trucks! Once I could drive, I spent a lot of time on the forest. I thought I was alone but later found that crews told dad where I was by what trailhead my car was parked at. When I was the Lowell Butte lookout, a steady stream of Forest Service people helped me learn the topography back towards Oakridge.

I think my compound childhood affected every major decision I made – my choice of a husband, the places I chose to live, my choice of college study, my politics and how every job I've had has been outdoors or about the environment, even if I had to make it that way. My reading and definitely my writing can be traced to the places I lived as a child. On every compound, the adults seemed to have a sense of belonging and an understood mission. As a child, it came across as interest in me, in how I was doing and what I was thinking. I thought all adults were this way. Imagine my reaction when the dean of OSU's College of Forestry responded to my declaration that I wanted to be a forester with "over my dead body." Not so long ago, Hilary Clinton reminded us of an old African proverb – *it takes a village to raise a child.* It took a compound to raise me!

Theodora "Bunty" Lilligren *Bunty and her husband Hillard "Lil" Lilligren came to Oregon from Minnesota in 1946. They were stationed at Hebo, Mapleton and Corvallis on the Siuslaw NF, at Tiller on the Umpqua NF and finally at Medford on the Rogue NF. Their longest stay was at Tiller, where Bunty worked for many years at the Tiller and Days Creek schools. Through the years Bunty has pursued life-long interests in history, pre-history, geography, and the natural world.*

This story includes excerpts from a letter Lilligren wrote to her parents describing the devastating 1964 flood. At the time Hillard was a District Ranger. Hillard has several stories in this Chapter (All in a Day's Work, Wives and Families, Timber) and one in Chapter Five (Timber).

374

Thursday, Dec. 24, 1964
Tiller Ranger Station, [Umpqua NF]

Dear Folks -
And a Merry Christmas to you too! Actually, we feel much more like Thanksgiving, as we have much to be thankful for. We are well, together, warm, high and dry, and have food, which is more than lots of other folk around here have, during the "Great '64 Flood"! We are pretty well cut off now tho there is a possibility that "the mail will get thru". We get some news from TV, mostly bad, but apparently the FS radio cannot get in or out. No newspapers here since last Saturday.

Things are calming down a little, and I find events are hazy as to time and place, so for my own peace of mind, I'd like to go back and reconstruct things as they happened, so here goes.

Saturday and Sunday were routine, except for heavy rain. First indication of things to come was when a lawn of one of the new houses gave way, taking out the water line, and water poured into the basement. Sunday night the rain continued, and the river rose slowly.

Monday the river was over 14 ft.! Flood stage at Tiller is 18 ft. Still raining heavily. One of our Bridge group had planned a Christmas luncheon at her home upriver. After lunch, the phone started ringing. The river was at 18.5 ft. and rising over a foot an hour; we were advised to get the heck home fast before slides cut us off. We had a short reprieve, as the rain stopped, and the river crested at 19.5 ft. People living down river had great difficulty getting home, some of them leaving cars and wading, then hitching a ride home. Heavy rain again at night.

[Tuesday morning] the heavy rain and the river rise continued. The 1st Class Mail got thru by ferrying, but no bread or milk deliveries. At noon we were watching huge trees go downriver, roots and all; rain and rise continued. I guess we all began to have ominous feelings after noon, and we began to wander around just looking - no one felt like doing anything. We'd stay outside til soaked, go in for a change of clothes, and back outside again to look around. Dad was upriver, as were most of the men of both Districts, checking damage and looking for trouble spots.

About 3 pm, Dad came in, said water was over the road about 6 miles up river, but it was safe to drive to that point, and he would take me and Sandy [our daughter] up there. [We] stopped at the Pickett Butte Bridge, where water was just barely going under the bridge. A tree, about 100 feet long or more, roots first, hit the bridge, swung around sideways, and in minutes a log jam started, with the old bridge shaking and creaking. Water swirled around the end of the bridge, and we got out of there fast.

It was dusk when we got home, so we went below the house for a last look before dark - the river was at the fence. Sandy and I started to walk down the road to Wilsons - Bonna was just leaving in VW bus to help evacuate a family up river. I heard a peculiar sound - like someone throwing oil drums around - and looked up the hill in time to see a mud slide come down in front of the barn. Sandy ran home to call the office as the new houses were in the path. Some men were on hand, and got there in time to divert the water around behind the barn. People in the houses couldn't hear it, so it was lucky we had been there at that time.

In the office, things were hectic as men were radioing in - slides and water over the road, etc. Finally all men were located, and told to spend the night at South Umpqua Falls Camp. Water came up so fast [on some of the Tiller District men] they stalled the big one-ton Crew Carrier, and a pickup was washed off the road. Ranger John Wilson took the jeep up to pull them out, but in the meantime a slide came down Salt Creek, about a half-mile upriver, and the road was blocked. They waded up to their hips thru water, with logs, etc. still coming down. At 7 pm all men except one were accounted for - he was assumed to be caught upriver between slides, with no radio.

Meantime, rain heavier than ever, river still rising. The ground was completely saturated, with water standing all over, and then the women got to work. Clausons driveway had 4-6 inches of water standing, and it poured over the window-well into the basement; the "crew" got to work with hoes and shovels to try to divert the water - don't think trying to dig a ditch across 8 -10 inches of gravel is easy! It occurred to me I'd best check Lilligren's basement about then. The window well by the front door wasn't overflowing, but was about ready to go over. In the basement a slight crack in the concrete about a foot from the floor had started to leak - ground was saturated down that far apparently - so Sandy and I got the tools out to ditch the water into the front yard. That sod was just as tough as the gravel at Clausons.

The next few hours are the haziest, as rain continued, river rose, and rumors flew. Someone had a spotlight on one of the pickups turned on the river. Porters had another one turned on, and I would estimate half the population of Tiller stood in the rain, watching the river pour over the steel girders on the bridge, and logs piling up on the piers - each one would hit with a terrific whump which shook the ground. The next day we found out the river had crested at 26.7 feet about 9:30 pm. Our sleep was very fitful, with the river roaring outside, and periods of heavy rain we could hear over the roar. The smell outside was very weird, also - damp wood and tons of soil going down the river.

Daylight [Wednesday] showed us a slightly new Tiller. We have visibility all around where there were trees before. Two houses across the river have water lines about 2 ft. up the side. The yards, gardens, and river bank are swept clean, except for a few very vigorous trees.

The rest of the day we spent getting reports from the local area; houses were washed away, others knocked off foundations, and all the big change in scenery. The devastation is incredible to us. The ominous reports of more rain have not been fulfilled, except for a few spotty times and places, so the tension has eased at last, and we can start to pick up the threads and get back to living again. We have actually not suffered at all, but the anxiety and tension of waiting and wondering is terrible.

Maybe by tonight [Thursday] we will be ready for our Traditional Feast of Lobster Tails. The power went off last night at 9 pm, but came on again this morning. We hope it will stay! The phones will probably be out for a long time, tho, as lines and cables are down and tangled up with barb wire, etc. near Days Creek.

Hopefully, my next letter will be more cheerful!!

Merry Christmas, and love to all - - - - Bunty

<u>Hillard M. "Lil" Lilligren</u> *Lilligren was a District Ranger on the Umpqua NF at the time of this story.*

If it is any consolation to the present residents of the Tiller RS, as of the time I transferred in 1966, there was no record of anyone living on the Ranger Station or employed by the Forest Service at Tiller ever having been bitten by a rattler. The station was established at Tiller in 1919.

One Saturday early in the spring when the South Umpqua River was low enough to wade knee deep, my teenage daughter Sandra and I decided to check out a possible aboriginal campsite on the left bank of the river below Dumont Creek Campground. (Sandra's interest in archeology eventually led to a degree in Anthropology from the University of Oregon.)

We waded the river and started climbing over some pole-sized flood-felled timber along the banks. I stepped up on one pole, then down and proceeded onward. My daughter was about 30 feet behind me. Then I heard a soft voice say, "Daddy, there is a rattlesnake here!"

I looked back and saw her standing on the pole I had just left. I said, "Where is it?"

She pointed towards her feet and said, "It's under this log!"

I said, "How do you know it's a rattlesnake?"

She said, "It rattled and I can see the rattles!"

I told her to slowly walk up the fallen pole, and when she was six feet away from the snake, she carefully checked the ground and then stepped down. I then looked for a weapon. All the tree limbs and other chunks of wood debris were too heavy to lift, and all the rocks were large and deeply imbedded in the river sand. There wasn't anything to use on the snake.

I was about to admit defeat, when suddenly I remembered I was carrying a US Army Colt .45 semi-automatic pistol in a shoulder holster. In the rush of searching for a crude weapon, I had completely forgotten it. I shot the snake, severed its head, and put the remainder in a cloth sack we had with us.

With that brief interruption, I moved another 100 feet with my daughter trailing a half dozen steps behind. Then I stopped. I could hear the wildest, loudest, and most persistent rattling I had ever encountered somewhere out ahead of me. There was no brush and only a sparse stand of stunted Douglas-fir ahead of me, so I moved forward.

Following the sound, I saw a medium-sized rattler coiled near the base of a tree about 60 feet ahead of me. I stopped and looked the area over carefully because I didn't believe the snake could detect my presence at that great distance. It should have been rattling at something much closer. I saw nothing, so I moved up about six feet, squatted, and aimed my .45 automatic with a two-hand grip.

The snake coiled, rattled and swung it's head from side to side, always facing me. It seemed like an eternity, but I finally got off a shot, and put the snake into the bag with the other one.

My daughter said, "Daddy, why did it take you so long to shoot the snake?"

I said, "Sandra, when the snake's head went zig, my gun barrel went zag, and it was quite awhile before I was going zig and zag at the same rate the snake was going zig and zag!"

We decided someone was trying to tell us something, so we took our two snakes directly home and popped them in the freezer to serve later to guests who wanted to taste genuine rattlesnake meat.

We never did get back to the suspected campsite, though it was always known by us as *Rattlesnake Flat* after that.

HORSES AND MULES: "We had gone a little over a mile when my horse gave a big groan and fell to the ground pinning my right leg under him."

<u>Pete Foiles</u> *Foiles was a CCC enrollee. He started as a temporary with the Forest Service in 1937, and worked for the National Park Service before coming back to the Forest Service. He worked on the Rogue River, Wallowa, Okanogan, and Siuslaw NFs and was on the Recreation Staff in the R-6 Regional Office when he retired in 1976.*

It was 1948 and I had just been transferred to the Joseph Ranger District on the Wallowa NF. My family and I had moved into the Lick Creek Ranger Station until we could find a house in Joseph. The facilities there included a fenced pasture and a real nice barn. The problem was that the pack rats also thought that it was a real nice barn and had moved in (lots of them). They had made a real mess with bits of chewed leather and packing equipment, rat droppings and odor.

There was also a guard stationed there. His name was Ted. He was an honest, trustworthy fellow with several years experience. One of the jobs assigned to him was to get rid of the rats. He had a 22 rifle and tried shooting them. We got animal traps and tried trapping them using various techniques that we had heard of (including the use of stove pipe). He did get some rats, but it soon became clear that we would never solve the problem in those ways.

The year before I got there, the District had had a rodent control project on which they used poison grain (treated with strychnine). There was one sack left that was kept under lock and key. Ted had worked on that project and knew of the left-over poison grain. He wanted to use it to get rid of the pack rats. I said, "NO, it was too dangerous to use that close to people and domestic animals." But Ted was positive he could use it safely. I finally agreed if all safety steps were taken. The barn had a tack room which could be locked so that no one could enter without a key. Ted placed three cereal bowls with the poison grain in the tack room and locked all entrances to the tack room with Forest Service locks.

I had scheduled a range inspection ride with several permittees for this time. The Forest Supervisor and range staff officer planned to join us

380

and trucked their two saddle horses from Enterprise and put them in the Lick Creek pasture the day before the ride. They then stayed in the guard cabin with Ted. The next morning I got up bright and early and caught the three horses we were to ride and tied them in three stalls in the barn. I poured a can of grain in the feed box for each horse and went to the house for breakfast. After we ate we loaded the horses on the truck to drive 20 miles or so to the Marr Flat Cow Camp where we were to meet to start the ride.

As we were loading the horses, I noticed that the one I was to ride was noticeably clumsy and unbalanced. I commented on that fact, but we all agreed that once he got to moving everything would be okay. But as we were unloading them at the cow camp the horse stumbled and nearly fell for no reason. We saddled up and started out. My horse was still wobbly and not at all sure-footed, and I was getting concerned. We had gone a little over a mile when my horse gave a big groan and fell to the ground pinning my right leg under him. He was dead. Luckily I wasn't hurt and had lots of help getting up. One rider commented that he had had a horse that got poisoned and acted just like this one. It happened that this same permittee was leading an extra horse that he was breaking to ride. He agreed to ride that horse and let me ride his. So we finished the ride, returned to the cow camp and loaded the two horses and drove back to the Ranger Station.

When we arrived at the station, I went directly to the stalls where I had tied the horses. I checked the feed boxes and two of them were clean as one would expect. But the third one, where my horse had been tied, still had a little grain left in it. I examined it and there was no doubt that much of it was the poison grain.

A significant feature of the barn was an overhead loft. Access to the loft was a ladder from the feed box where the poison grain was. The rats used this ladder going up or down from the loft. It was a much used runway for them. I got ahold of Ted and really chewed him out. But he swore by all that was holy that he had not put any poison grain anywhere except in the tack room which was locked. But he was sure that he knew how the poison grain got to that particular spot. He had observed how the rats would fill their cheeks with the grain and then go somewhere to store it for future use. He reasoned that the feed box was an ideal place for that since it was located exactly on their well used route of travel and, of course, the locked doors to the tack room were no barrier to them. They had apparently cached the poison grain in the feed box in a manner unnoticed by me.

The loss of a saddle horse required a report and explanation to the Regional Office, which I did. The people handling the case there did some investigating of the matter and agreed that the explanation was consistent with what was known about the way pack rats act. The report was accepted and the case closed. And that is how the pack rats killed the saddle horse.

<u>Bob Bjornsen</u> *Bjornsen was a District Ranger on the Wallowa-Whitman NF in the late 1950s and early 1960s.*

It was one of those bad yellow jacket summers on the Wallowa-Whitman. The critters were everywhere in the woods - neither man nor beast were safe from their stings. Tom Griffith, Baker Assistant Ranger, and I were working our way horseback up Indian Creek below Anthony Lakes on the Wallowa-Whitman when his horse stepped on a jacket's nest, and all hell broke loose!

We were on the side of a hill when they started their rampage. Tom frantically tried to stay in the saddle as the *Speed* horse turned every way but loose to avoid the stings. Have you ever tried to stay with a bucking horse, head pointed downhill while swatting yellow jackets?

"Turn his head uphill!", I cried, sitting calmly astride my *Smokey* horse as if such a feat were possible. About that time the yellow jackets hit me, and I was grabbing leather too. Miraculously, we both stayed aboard our horses, but not because of our skill at bronco-busting. We got out of there fast and found a safe spot where we rubbed our horses down, all the while dabbing ourselves and the horses with spirits of ammonia, a great remedy for neutralizing bee stings.

Our travails weren't over yet. As we reached a meadow near the ridge, it started to rain hard. The meadow soon became a sheet of water, and we found ourselves in the middle feeling our way towards solid ground. Next *Smokey* went down in a bog to his hocks, pitching me into the mud and slime. I hollered to Tom to stop on solid ground until we could find our way out. Next thing we knew, *Smokey* was on his back, legs in the air, gasping for breath and not responding to our trying to right him. This called for quick action because a horse doesn't last long with his innards pressing against his lungs. Somewhere (perhaps from Blen Holman or Wade Hall) I'd heard that a stick thrust in a horse's anus would cause a violent response - I guess it would with humans too!

I quickly found a smooth stick, and with Tom holding his tail aside, did the job. That horse did a 180° flip, and in a split second landed on solid ground with all four feet planted! The rest of the tale was anti-climatic as we made our way safely to solid ground.

Bob Bjornsen *Bjornsen was the Range and Wildlife Staff Officer on the Gifford Pinchot NF in the early 1960s.*

Most R-6ers know Archie Mills for his sharp humor and as a practical joker par excellence, but how many know of his consumate ability as a horse trader? Indirectly, Roy Bond does and that's how the mysterious McClellan saddle entered the picture.

It all started when Archie heard the Gifford Pinchot NF was in the market for a good saddle horse. Having heard that I was in charge of horse and mule trading on the GP, in addition to being range and wildlife staff officer, he called me to offer a fine sorrel gelding to our stable *no strings attached*. His story was that *Rocky* was just too much horse for the Wenatchee buckeroos, but undoubtedly would give yeoman service to the GP equestrians.

Well now, when you get a *no strings attached* offer from Archie Mills, immediately a glimmer of suspicion arises. So we called various Wenatchee friends to find out the real lowdown on Rocky. Surprise! For once Archie was above reproach - he wasn't trying to pull something on us. Rocky wasn't spavined, cinch bound or lame. His only drawback, as we later learned, was at 17 hands, it took a tall stump to get in the saddle.

The *no strings* was shattered when a few weeks after we took delivery, Archie called and wanted to know when we were sending over the saddle as payment for Rocky. "Now just a G- d - minute" we told him, "you said no strings attached!" With the usual Mill's aplomb he said he'd never have traded such a fine horse without some recompense and furthermore he would see to it that the GP's sterling reputation would be sullied unless we came forth with the saddle, immediately if not sooner! Bang! He hung up. What to do? We couldn't let Archie get the best of us in a horse-trading caper, yet we couldn't ignore his threat to sully our reputation either. Voila! He didn't specify the type of saddle, why not send him a McClellan?

Now anyone who has ridden this famous Army cavalry saddle knows it to be the hardest, most miserable piece of leather equipage ever invented to support a man on a horse. Of course, the FS acquired many of these saddles as surplus property in the early days and a few could be found moldering in remote barns on western Forests. Such was the case on the GP. We located a fully-rigged McClellan, complete with tapaderos, at the old Sunset RS, (now) St. Helen's District.

We built a heavy wood crate and sent it COD to Archie on a Government Bill of Lading (GBL), informing him by letter that his saddle was enroute and the GP's reputation continued to be unblemished. Forest Administrative Officer Stan Norton had assured us that sending a collect GBL would generate no end of paperwork for Archie for some reason known only to business managers.

Archie never acknowledged receipt of the McClellan which gave us great satisfaction in knowing we had one-upped him at horse trading. But the saga didn't end there. Archie conjured up a way to save face by sending the saddle to Roy Bond, collect GBL, of course, upon Roy's transfer to Supervisor of the Malheur. Somehow the McClellan kept following Roy around the country. Where it is today is a story for Archie or Roy to tell.

Epilogue: Rocky, the big sorrel horse, went to Mt. Adams District and turned out to be a real jewel. He was a joy to ride and was given a further name of *Rock Around the Clock*. His only bad habit was biting the unwary in the ribs when he was being saddled.

Later, those McClellan saddles *disappeared* from FS barns. They had become a sought after antique like the old wooden box telephones we hauled to the dump and burned. Why we sent Archie a rare fully rigged McClellan, when several others in much worse condition were available at the time. Maybe Archie won after all?

FIRE AND LOOKOUTS: "Flames, not more than one-quarter mile away, must have been hundreds of feet high."

<u>Wendall Jones</u>   *Jones began his Forest Service career on a seasonal fire crew in 1950.*

My first job with the US Forest Service was on the Fish Lake suppression crew working out of the Willamette NF [in 1950]. We were 12 tough young college punks and a few local Sweet Home boys, and a really tough foreman, Jerry Gabriel. It wasn't much of a fire year, but one interesting fire was the Halls Ridge fire at Detroit, Oregon. They were still disposing of clearing slash in the area of the new Detroit reservoir. They were also clearing for and building new power lines. One of these power line-clearing operations started a fire well up on the ridge above the reservoir clearing.

When we got to the fire, the big threat had been pretty well controlled by local crews. But it needed to be mopped up completely because of the high hazard nearby in the reservoir clearing. So we spent a few days in Detroit, then not unlike a frontier town. Reservoir and dam construction had created a boom in the little village, especially at all the bars. There may have been one man on our crew that was 21, but we all sat up to the bar and drank beer - no questions asked. We stayed at the barracks for the dam workers called Camp Mongold.

The most significant happening on the Halls Ridge fire was a trial in shuttling firefighters to a fire by helicopter. I believe this was the first trial at transporting crews by helicopter in Region 6. I once thought it was the first in the Forest Service, but heard in later years that R5 had done it before. This was a very small ship with just room for one passenger and the pilot and not much gear. We loaded at a clearing in the bottom of what is now Detroit Lake, probably about 1200 feet elevation. The ship had to gain about 2000 feet of elevation to reach the fire, which it did by slowly corkscrewing upward. My recollection is that it took 10 to 15 minutes to get to the little heli-spot on the fire at about 3500 feet elevation. It took all morning to move about 12 of us.

We were all invincible, so thought nothing of this probably high-risk trial. We all made it safely to the fire, but probably could have all walked to the fire in much less total time. Tenny Moore was Ranger at the time, Howard Dean was fire control officer at Detroit, Roy Elliott was fire staff, and John Bruckart was Forest Supervisor on the Willamette NF. The reservoir clearing was a sea of red slash, and fire was the enemy as well as the tool to get rid of that slash.

Jones was in his second summer on the fire crew at the time of this story in 1951.

In mid-August [1951], the Fish Lake suppression crew received orders to go to Detroit to the Sardine Creek Fire. We arrived at Detroit late in the day and were immediately sent up to the end of the French Creek road, which at that time was just below the ridge top between French Creek and Tumble Lake. This was to be our fire camp for the present. We were immediately sent out a trail toward Sardine Mountain that roughly paralleled the present road to Halls Ridge. We could glimpse the smoke and hear the roar as we got out of the heavy timber near the ridge top. The view as we topped the ridge was one I have not experienced in my later fire history. Flames, not more than one-quarter mile away, must have been hundreds of feet high. The roar was that of multiple jet engines and locomotives. The smoke was black, but stayed high over us because of the extreme convection column created. Chunks of smoldering bark and other debris, some a foot square, were falling out of that column. It had blown up running through lots of fell and bucked timber and logging slash.

Fortunately, once the fire cleared the ridge top, there was nothing but huckleberry and beargrass which limited the amount of spotting. As we went further toward Sardine Mountain, we saw several men carrying someone on a stretcher just a short distance ahead of the fire. We dropped our gear and ran to assist them. They were now safe, but just a few minutes slower and they would have been consumed at the ridge top. They had made a stretcher out of hemlock poles and their shirts. That stretcher alone must have weighed 150 pounds, and the man on it was easily a 250 pounder.

One of our crew members was a medical student from Iowa. He peeled the man's eyelids back, checked a couple of other vitals, and his diagnosis was, "He's dead." The man was Frank McDonald, then 56, of Idanha, Oregon. According to *Oregonian* files this was August 21, 1951. We were in no danger because the fire behavior was so violent that the convection was actually pulling very cold air in behind us. When the fire reached the top of Sardine Canyon, it ran out of heavy fuel. There was nothing we could do in the way of effective firefighting, so we helped get these men all back to fire camp. It was approaching nightfall by that time.

<u>Dick Worthington</u> *Worthington worked on the Umpqua, Rogue River, Mt. Hood and Olympic NFs in R-6, and the Klamath NF in R-5. He worked in the R-5 Regional Office and was the National Director of Timber Management in the Washington Office. He was the R-6 Regional Forester when he retired in 1982.*

Around Labor Day of 1955, northern California and southern Oregon experienced a series of the most severe lightning storms ever recorded in that area. Many major fires were started, including the Haystack Fire on the Oak Knoll Ranger District of the Klamath NF which was eventually to exceed 150,000 acres. With the normal air-flow in the area the Rogue River Valley quickly filled with smoke. Not only were the airports closed, most of the State and Forest Service lookouts could not see.

On the Rogue River NF we had a lot of fires but because of the smoke no one really knew how many, how big or where they all were. All of us were pretty busy for more than a week on a *minimum sleep and maximum effort* basis. I remember getting home for the first time in a week after it all started. It was for the first full night's sleep I'd had for the period, only to be rousted out about 4 am to take a logging crew into Crater Lake Park to take over one of their fires.

The fire, about a mile from the highway, was smoldering in very heavy duff. No water was anywhere near so it was a dry mop-up show - just the kind of operation a logging crew absolutely hates! I remember about 10 or 10:30 am as we were eating lunch a yearling bear showed up. We threw him some sandwiches, and he thought we were great. Then we noticed that his paws were burnt and he was obviously in pain because he'd lick them frequently.

One of the crew hiked out to their crew wagon and picked up an old end hook rope. Then, much to my consternation, they lassoed the bear and tied him between a couple of small hemlocks. After using all the burn ointment in our first-aid kits the next problem was to let him loose. Well, we got the rope off of him but I'm quite sure the bear had fewer cuts, scratches and bruises than most of us. The last we saw of him he was just getting into high gear. His hind legs were reaching up about his ears and his front paws were just visible under his rump.

I was always real partial to young bears after that for this one kept a logging crew working on a fire they didn't like by providing an hour or so diversion.

Another fire story by Dick Worthington.

In 1958 the Mt. Baker NF had a bunch of lightning fires east of Concrete. One in Found Creek got big so a bunch of us from around the Region met for *a summer outing on the Skagit.* My part of the fire was from the ridge top down to Found Creek, a distance that got greater every time I walked it. And which, without a doubt, was as far vertically as it was horizontally.

One morning I took a crew of fallers up to a snag patch adjacent to our fireline. The crew was made up of local loggers who had worked together several years. Their bull-buck, whom they held in high regard, was a man close to seventy, but was in top physical shape as was everyone else. We carried saws, gas, oil, steel sledges and wedges, axes, and the bull-buck carried everyone's lunch in a pack sack.

We went up the fireline which was straight up the hill. We'd go as far as we could, turn around and sit with our back to the fire trail to rest. I was in the lead, the bull-buck was in the rear. I noticed on our second stop that the man just ahead of the bull-buck gently opened the packsack and dropped in a fist-sized rock. Everyone saw but no one said anything. On we went, stopping every now and then until we got to the snags. There we had a couple hours of concentrated hard work.

When everything was in order it was lunch-time and the crew eagerly waited for the bull-buck to open his pack sack. You can imagine everyone's reaction as he opened up the pack, looked inside, and exclaimed, "Good Lord, what a bunch of dummies I work with! Here I'm the only one who brought a lunch - everyone else brought rocks." Then he pulled his lunch out, tipped the bag upside down and dumped out about ten rocks. Every time his crew put a rock in his pack he stashed a lunch along the trail.

After watching him nonchalantly start to eat with apparent gusto, one of the more guilty parties sighed, stood up, picked up the pack and headed down the fireline muttering something about smart-ass bull-bucks.

Dave Yates *Yates started as a temporary in 1957, and received a permanent appointment in 1960. He worked on the Wallowa-Whitman, Umatilla, Willamette, and Okanogan NFs. He was the Planning Staff Officer on the Olympic NF when he retired in 1998.*

The summer of 1958 was winding down. My high school and college pal Don Clemens and I were hiking down the Minam River trail with full packs and gear. We were members of the Bear Sleds District trail crew maintaining the high-country trails in the Eagle Cap Wilderness on the Wallowa-Whitman NF. District Fire Control Officer Bill Maxwell was planning to meet us at the Forest boundary trailhead to take us in to town.

When we began this last assignment Bill noticed my boots were just about *shot* and he wasted no words (most of which can't be printed) telling me I needed some new ones. However, in my infinite wisdom of 19 years, I thought I could save some money for forestry school expenses so I told him I'd take the chance I could get by this last hitch.

As fate would have it, with still nine or ten miles to go, a late afternoon lightning storm sent a hard strike into an old pine snag within our view. We called the fire into Bill on our radio and headed for the smoke, just as we had been doing most of the summer when not maintaining trails. By the time we reached the fire it was making a run through dry grass and brush up a steep slope, a few young pine were crowning out, and the snag was throwing sparks all over!

After about ten minutes building line I suddenly realized I had one hell of a *hotfoot*! The worst had happened as the sole of my left boot had come loose and was flapping around completely free of any stitching! I didn't get any sympathy from my *pal* Don, and I knew that if Bill found out I was going to be sore somewhere else! With some luck and hard work Don and I managed to pinch off the head of the fire and stopped its run. To this day it's still a mystery to me why I didn't burn my left foot as we worked that fire. Don later said he'd never seen a one-legged fire fighter swear and dance at the same time while building line and throwing dirt!

Well, if Don thought he'd heard some swearing, the best was yet to come. I finally got up enough courage to tell Bill over the radio that we had controlled the fire but one boot was a total loss and the other one was so badly split it wouldn't last the rest of the hike down the Minam. Those who knew and remember Bill understand that his reaction and response cannot be printed under any circumstances! To make matters worse, my *butt-chewing* was heard by many on the forest over the radio! I was not looking forward to being overnight on the fire, the hike out the next day, and of course, seeing Bill again.

Right at daybreak, here came Bill in the small spotter plane to check our fire status and see how we were doing. As Don and I watched the plane circle low over the fire, out from the window came this very small parachute with a box of new boots hanging from it. Good 'ole Bill had a soft spot after all. The parachute made a perfect landing next to our make-shift camp. I thanked Bill profusely but wondered why all we heard on the radio was a hearty laugh and, "I'll meet you boys at the trailhead."

Have you ever walked ten miles after fighting fire in your socks, with a full pack and gear, with new boots that are too small and don't fit?

Bill Maxwell was from the *old school*. Born and raised in the Imnaha and Snake River country, he was dedicated to the Forest Service, its people and its mission. Highly skilled and experienced in virtually all phases of our work, his specialty was fire - and he was one of the best. He was one of the first FCO's to break the GS-11 barrier. He was a mentor to me and to other *wannabe* young foresters. Bill was special to me then, and he always will be.

<u>Gene Holloter</u> *Holloter started as a temporary in 1954, and received a permanent appointment the same year. He worked on the Kootenai NF in R-1 and the Mt. Hood, Malheur, and Wallowa-Whitman NFs in R-6. He was the Assistant Timber Management Staff Officer on the Colville NF in R-6 when he retired in 1987.*

The lightning-caused Anthony Lake fire occurred on Baker and La Grande Ranger Districts of the Wallowa-Whitman NF in August of 1960. I was stationed on the Hood River RD of the Mt. Hood NF at the time. I'd been there and in the FS for about four years and this was the largest fire I'd been on to that date (about 25,000 acres).

This was one of the earliest *Zone* fires in R6. There were three and I was assigned to Zone 3. The zone camp was on the north end in Porcupine Meadows. I was put on the night shift as crew boss with a pick-up crew out of the Burnside area of Portland, a common source of manpower in those days. It was my first crew boss assignment, other than on clearcut slash burns on my District. My confidence level wasn't the best then and I was thinking the worst of my crew. I was prepared for tool cuts, etc. I found I had a *non-wino* crew member with some logging experience, so I kind of made him my first assistant and gave him a pulaski. Everybody else got shovels. Our section of the line had been constructed and we were widening and improving on it and knocking down hot spots next to the line.

After a while, my *assistant* came up to me and told me *so and so* was not with the rest of the crew. I just knew I'd gotten somebody burned up! I got everybody looking for him and before long someone yelled, "Here he is!" He was sacked out under some brush *outside* the fireline. He had smuggled a jug of wine onto the fire and was sucking on that back under the brush. I was so relieved! I just told him to stay in sight but back out of the way. He was off the crew when we got back into camp that morning, of course.

Porcupine Camp was at about 6500 feet elevation. As I was coming back to my bivouac area after breakfast that morning, an Air National Guard helicopter come down into the meadow. It was the older type *banana* helicopters - a rotor on each end but with only a single engine for power. It was not the twin engine and rotor *Chinook*, that we later used for logging. There was a stock fence across the meadow a ways into it and, a little further down, a single wire radio antennae strung across it about 20 feet high. The helicopter was picking up about six firefighters and their tools to air-lift them into a slop-over up near a bald knob above camp a few miles. It was right at timberline (7500 feet or so). On take-off, the pilot found that he was a little under-powered at even the camp elevation, but he went anyway. He started down the meadow to get up some take-off speed and could not even clear the four foot fence across the meadow. So he backed way up to the head end of the meadow and gunned it down the slot again. That time he cleared the fence, but barely the antennae and the surrounding stand of lodgepole pine. Later that morning, we saw some of the crewmen being shuttled back to camp in vehicles and with some minor injuries. We learned that the helicopter stalled out trying to make it to the drop-off point on top of the knob. When the pilot realized that a crash was inevitable, he smartly laid it over on its side, thereby minimizing injuries to all aboard.

After the fire, a couple of weeks later, I was down to Hood River with my family for groceries. That part of town sits a little above the Columbia River Highway and maybe a quarter mile away. I just happened to glance out towards the highway at the time to see the Air National Guard trucking that same helicopter back to Portland in two pieces. They and the FS had gone up to crash point, chopped the aluminum fuselage in two pieces, and skidded it out to a loading point with cats.

(About seven years later, I was transferred to the Baker RD as timber management assistant and we were still dealing with the aftermath of that fire.)

<u>Bob Bjornsen</u> *Bjornsen describes several incidents that happened during the 1960 Anthony Lakes Fire.*

We were in the back of a bus, remnants of the overhead who fought one of the Wallowa-Whitman's worst fires in this century. As we approached a vista of the Anthony Lakes Burn on this summer day 1986, the talk turned to vignettes of firefighting at its worst.

The Anthony Lakes Fire, as it became known, had its tragedies in the loss of three lives; loss of an air tanker and two helicopters; loss of

Radio operator in a fire camp

Helitac crew landing at a fire, Wenatchee NF – 1968

over 19,000 acres of prime timber. Yet it is the humorous episodes we remember more vividly, mostly because time tends to soften the sadness over the years.

At GHQ we had run out of fire time-slips to sign up the bus loads of Burnside winos who were rolling in to augment the 3000 men on the line. We'd also run out of vehicles to fetch a new supply. So ever resourceful Herb Hadley (honcho line boss) commandeered a Greyhound bus to get more slips. I can see him now tooling down a one-lane Forest road, a lone passenger on a vital mission.

Russ McRory loves to tell the story (with increasing embellishments) about the two young female GHQ secretaries who asked if they could sleep in our trailer because they were afraid, with all those winos in camp, to stay alone in their trailer. He usually fails to mention that they slept in one end of our trailer while we slept on couches at the other end.

Unbeknownst to us, some enterprising prostitutes moved their trailer into the Anthony Lakes Campground (not in GHQ camp at Tucker Flat!) and proceeded to accommodate the firefighters in the Anthony zone. Needless to say they were chased out as soon as they were discovered several days later. A month after the fire, Herb Hunt, W-W administrative officer, called me that he had some claims from firefighters who said they had contracted gonorrhea from said prostitutes and wanted treatment at FS expense.

When that bus of retirees reached the vista point, I was asked what was our control strategy in the early stages of that fire 26 years ago. My answer, "Pray for rain," which it did some 12 days later.

Robert Schramek *Schramek was on the Anthony Lakes Fire also, as a sector boss.*

One of the larger fires that I worked on was the Anthony Lakes fire out of Baker, Oregon. This was about 1960. I was assigned as a sector boss, meaning that I had responsibility for three crews; each crew having about 20 men, with a crew boss in charge of each crew. When I arrived, I was given the assignment and a portable radio and told to keep in touch with my immediate superior, a division boss, who was coordinating the control on about half of the fire line along some six miles of ridge on the west side of the fire.

My sector covered about three miles of fire line and was accessible only on foot along the top of a high ridge. The hottest part of the fire was below us, but the fuels were not very heavy along this section of the fire line, so the division boss and the line boss were not very concerned about extreme fire behavior causing us safety problems.

The line had been built by hand and then widened with bulldozers the day before, so our assignment was to hold the line and prevent any spot fires from burning across the line that would allow the fire to escape. Since the crews were spread out along almost three miles of line, I found that it took me at least two hours to make the trip and get back to the beginning where I planned to eat lunch. We were having problems with supplies arriving from town. Because the fire had grown so quickly, the service organization was not able to keep up with the expanding workforce arriving on the fire from all over the west coast.

We had barely enough hand tools to go around, and the guys on the crews were grumbling that lunches were skimpy and not very good. Fire crews were notorious about eating large lunches. That's understandable when you realize that we often worked 12 to 15 hour days, and the work was hard, hot grueling work, swinging an axe, Pulaski or fire hoe all day in the hot sun!

When I got around to the middle crew on the line, I found that this was a pick-up crew from Portland, mostly Burnside Street unemployed vagrants. The Forest Service rarely used this source of labor, but 1960 was a very bad fire year, and the Pacific Northwest was just about out of fire crews. I didn't expect much out of this crew, after seeing their age and physical condition. After spending some time with them, I was surprised to find that they knew how to pace themselves, and they were able to put in a good honest day's work.

We found there were a lot of smoldering small spots of fire creeping around in deep, dry duff and in old rotten stumps and logs. As the day wore on the wind picked up, and it grew very hot. I was concerned that unless we got these hot spots cooled down we would lose the fire across one or more of these hot spots because our crews were spread so thin.

I got on the radio and asked to meet the division boss to discuss the problem. It took over an hour to get through and another hour to set up a meeting. While he recognized the problem, he said they didn't have any more men to spare, and there was no way to get a water tanker up on this end of the line. I suggested that we could do a lot of good with some back-pack water pumps to work over the hot stumps, but there weren't any available.

When I got back to my pick-up crew I explained to the crew boss what I was told and asked if he had any suggestions. He was an older man, an out of work ex-hobo who had worked part-time on fires for over 25 years. He told me that if I would give him two hours, and watch his crew for him, he would come up with some tools, no questions asked. Well, I had given up on the bureaucracy being able to supply us, so I told him to take off and see what he could do, but I warned him if he wasn't back in three hours, I would see that he lost the day's time.

He was back in a little over the two hours with three brand new back-pack pumps, two canteens of water and a new axe! We distributed the tools, found a spring to fill the pack pumps, and when I got ready to leave to go to the third crew, the crew boss told me to drop by their crew for a late lunch break down at the spring we had found.

I agreed to stop to check on their progress in about two hours. When I arrived at the spring, I found that their lunch menu had been supplemented with a gallon of fresh milk, a gallon of ice cream and two fresh apple pies! To this day I have no idea where he stole that food from, or how he got it up on the fire line without being discovered, but I never had a crew boss with the imagination and ingenuity that this man possessed!

Jack Rae *Rae started in 1959 in fire control on the Olympic NF. He worked on the Mt. Hood NF with the Job Corps program and in fire control. He was with the Bureau of Land Management in Alaska when he retired in 1984.*

This is a story that happened [on the Olympic NF, Hoodsport RD] when the Forest Service was still manning lookouts back in the 1960s.

We hired a married couple to man one of the District's lookouts. They were both teachers working somewhere in California. They had been married over 12 years and were childless. Actually we were more interested in hiring mature adults, if we had the opportunity. Married employees were a plus for lookouts and guard stations. The reason being that we would usually get two people for the price of one.

Lucky for us, this couple was dedicated to the point that when the situation required that the lookout had to be manned because of weather conditions even on the days off, one or the other was always on duty while the other went to town and did the shopping and picked up supplies. This couple really enjoyed their assignment and location. Their lookout was a ground station at the end of a dead-end road. The wife told me I couldn't imagine the stress of teaching high school kids. "We couldn't have found a better summer job. It's like being on a second honeymoon for three months."

To make a long story short, at the end of the season the wife was pregnant. They left to return to school teaching a very happy couple.

Douglas D. Porter *Porter started as a temporary in 1961 and received a permanent appointment in 1963. He worked on the Winema, Siuslaw, Deschutes, and Mt. Hood NFs and was a National Incident Commander from 1994 to 1998. He was acting Forest Engineer on the Mt. Hood NF when he retired in 1998.*

I was hired in the summer of 1961 at the Chemult Ranger District, the year the Winema NF became a National Forest. I received my fire training that summer but was never called to a fire. In the summer of 1962, I think it was July, we were getting pounded pretty good by lightning which had started early in the afternoon. Most of us were put on standby (unpaid) in case we were needed during the lightning bust. My normal job was Engineering but all of us became available for fires during fire season.

Finally I got the call. There was a strike in the panhandle area just outside the Crater Lake National Park boundary. Another person and I took the old International one-ton pumper, our gear and headed out. Our gear consisted of a few tools, ax, shovel, pulaski, radio and some water. We were getting a lot of fire starts out of this storm and folks were very aggressive at getting to them and trying to put them out. I know I was pretty excited as this was my first fire. We arrived at the fire area in about 30 minutes and had to hike about half a mile above the road to where the fire was reported.

There was no problem finding the fire as it was burning pretty good. It was less than an acre and after sizing up the situation, we called for additional help. We started flanking the fire hoping to pinch it off, but it was running pretty fast. I don't know who called for borate but I'm pretty sure it was the fire folks at the District office. We were on the fire about 15 minutes when we received a radio message that a borate plane was on the way and it would contact us when they arrived in the area. It seemed like only a few more minutes when we were contacted again and were told the plane had arrived and would approach from the south and to take the normal position when borate was being dropped. Lay on the ground face down, your head pointing in the direction the plane was coming from and clasp your hands behind your neck.

They said not to look up when the drop came but I guess I just had to look. I could hear the plane coming and soon it was very loud and sounded like it was right on top of us. When I looked up it was all airplane, the biggest damn thing I had ever seen; a B-17 that looked like it was just above the Ponderosa tree-tops. Just moments later, even though we thought we were out of the way, I was completely covered with borate coming down like a heavy rain.

When the B-17 finished its run and left the area we got up to take a look and evaluate the drop. It was a direct hit and the fire was really knocked down. We jumped right on the fire and were able to get a line around it before it became any larger. I was pretty excited on my first fire and especially with the borate drop. The one thing I wanted to note was when we looked over the rest of the fire area we found about 30 feet of a ponderosa pine tree top, 18 inches or so in diameter, lying outside the fire area. In checking out where it came from and how it got there, we found it had to have gone right over us during the drop.

We counted our blessings and were dispatched to another fire. As I recall we had about 235 strikes that day and night and by morning had

Retardent drop by a PBY, Wenatchee NF – 1968

manned 110 of them, of which I was on eight. To this day, I can still see that B-17 and hear the roar of those engines just as plain as the day it happened.

<u>Dave Anderson</u>   *Anderson started as a temporary in 1960 and received a permanent appointment within a month. He worked on the Snoqualmie and Wenatchee NFs and was a Type 1 Incident Commander. He was the Fire and Timber Manager on the Leavenworth Ranger District, Wenatchee NF when he retired in 1992.*

It was the summer of 1965. I was sent to the Union Creek Fire on the Naches Ranger District, Snoqualmie NF, from the Skykomish RD along with other overhead. We arrived at the Natches Ranger Station and met with the Fire Control Officer Harry Aultman. He explained the fire was about 2000 acres and was in the mop-up stage. We would take over the bottom of the fire. Harry explained that one of us would need to be in charge as division boss. I was only qualified as crew boss so I assumed Ole Olsen, who had more experience than I had, would speak up and accept the job. He spoke up all right and said Dave would be the division boss. Harry said "Great!" He explained that to get to the camp would require about a two-mile hike on a trail and that about every couple days a pack string would bring in provisions. Harry also informed us that there was a cook at the camp.

So off we went, about 50 of us, up the trail. After about a mile we met a fellow hiking out. I stopped him and asked who he was, and he said, "I am the camp cook and I quit." I decided to keep that information to myself until we got to camp but was thinking, "Great, now I have 50 people to feed and no cook." So when we reached the camp I gathered everyone together and explained that I needed a couple volunteers to cook for us. In the back of the pack I saw two hands raised. It was Jerry Riseland and Glen Katzendberger who quickly decided that camp duty was preferable to fire line duty. Neither had any experience feeding this many people.

I got busy getting the crews working on the fire and the camp cooks began preparing the evening meal. Things went well for a couple days, the two cooks were doing a great job and the camp was running well. About the third or fourth day Jerry had noticed that a large camp garbage pit, located a couple hundred feet from camp, was supporting a healthy population of flies so he decided to take action. He carried a five-gallon can of gas out to the dump and proceeded to pour the contents on and around the pit. The only problem was he forgot the matches so back to camp he tromped. When he returned with the matches, he lit one and threw it into the pit. Well, of course, a lot of the gas had vaporized causing a substantial explosion and fire, causing burning garbage to be thrown into nearby trees and the surrounding area. Jerry beat a stealthy retreat.

Meantime, up on the fire I got a radio call that there was a substantial smoke coming from below the fire. I turned around and looked down the hill and saw the smoke well outside our fireline. So I did what all good division bosses would do, I ordered a load of retardant from Wenatchee. Then I beat feet down the hill toward the smoke that was quickly diminishing. By the time I got there Jerry and the camp crew had the fire under control. I tried to cancel the retardant but too late, it was on its way. We *utilized* the retardant and never let on what had happened.

Anderson describes another fire-related incident.

The summer of 1967 was very dry. I was stationed at the Skykomish Ranger District on the Snoqualmie NF, working for long-time District Fire Control Officer Norm McCausland. There was a 4000-acre fire, Evergreen Mountain, burning on the District and a complete Forest closure was in effect. About two weeks into the fire, after coming off the line, I was told to report to the Ranger Station. When I arrived, there was a group gathered in the front office and Norm explained that the fire detection plane had crashed. He was looking for volunteers to hike in and locate the pilot.

Apparently what had happened was the observer plane spotted a float plane sitting on Lake Dorothy, a rather large high lake located at the head of the Miller River drainage. The observer plane circled down low to get the wing number off the float plane so that it could be reported as a violation of the Forest closure. The Forest Service observer, Andy Lavigere, wrote the number down and when he looked up he saw that the observer plane pilot, I believe his name was Gus Grames, was flying the plane up the inlet of the lake instead of down the outlet, i.e. up-valley instead of down-valley. The plane, a single engine Cessna, was unable to turn in the tight canyon and did not have enough power to climb out. The plane soon pancaked into the trees.

Although both the pilot and Andy were injured, they began to hike out. It was soon apparent that the pilot was too injured to continue hiking. Andy made the pilot as comfortable as possible and continued hiking out with a broken arm and other injuries. The first portion of the hike was about a mile down a steep gorge following the creek to Lake Dorothy. After reaching the lake, Andy hiked along the trail that bordered the lake and eventually reached the Miller River Road; total distance about five miles. Because of the Forest closure, Andy had little hope of finding anyone on the road as he began hiking down it. Well as luck would have it, on that particular day a seasonal Forest Service employee was riding his motorbike up the Miller River Road and found Andy hiking down. He picked Andy up and brought him to the Ranger Station.

So there was Norm McCausland asking for volunteers to hike in to find the pilot. By this time it was late evening. Myself and Gert Gruenwoldt volunteered. Andy told us that once you get to the inlet to Lake Dorothy you hike up the creek and begin counting the waterfalls as you gain elevation. The pilot will be above the fifth waterfall near the creek.

So off we went. By this time it was pitch dark. After driving to the end of the Miller River Road, we began hiking up to Lake Dorothy, then around the lake. As we started up the inlet we left flagging for the larger crew who were to follow us later with a doctor. We began counting waterfalls. After the fifth waterfall we came to a fork in the creek. We were not sure which fork to follow but decided to try the left fork first. We would travel a short ways, holler and wait for reply. After about eight cycles of *hike, stop, holler and wait*, we heard a faint reply. Soon we located the pilot. He was sitting between two trees. His head was badly swollen, and he was in shock. By the size of his head, I thought he was a large man, but after getting a better look I saw he was of small stature. So we picked him up and set him on a sleeping bag we had brought with us. He was quite cold so we rubbed him and wrapped him up as well as we could. By this time it was after midnight.

We radioed in that we had found the pilot and that he was alive. We were informed that another crew, with a doctor, was on its way. The crew arrived just before daylight and after stabilizing the pilot we carried him to a meadow where a helicopter arrived and evacuated him and the doctor. The rest of us hiked out.

A lot of the credit for the survival of the pilot goes to Andy Lavigere who would not leave the Ranger Station for treatment until he personally talked to whoever was going in to find the pilot. His directions to the injured pilot certainly sped up the rescue and eventual medivac.

Freda Vincent Evans *Evans joined the Forest Service as a resources clerk typist on the Fremont NF in 1963. She transferred to the Mount Hood NF in 1966 where she met and married R. D. "Bob" Strombom, who also has a story in Chapter Four (All in a Day's Work). In 1975 she was promoted to the R-6 Regional Office in Lands and Minerals, retiring in 1983. She kept her fire qualification Red Card current throughout her career, serving in Maps and Plans on numerous fires.*

One morning in mid-August 1966, Freda Vincent Evans finished her breakfast Cashier/Hostess job at Van's Restaurant and walked to work in the Budget and Finance section at the Supervisor's Office of the Fremont NF. As she sat down to her desk she had no way of knowing what an unusual day it would be for her.

Shortly after arriving at her desk, she was told she was immediately going to the Winter Rim Fire Camp and to take her manual typewriter and supplies with her. It was Freda's first time going to a fire camp. There was no opportunity to change clothes or pack a bag. All she had was her typewriter and office clothes, including high-heeled shoes. On arriving at the camp south of Silver Lake, Oregon, she was assigned to the maps and plans group and settled into the job of keeping the paperwork up-to-date.

The camp was located on Winter Rim and included Job Corps enrollees as well as regular fire overhead and crews. During the day, it was decided the wind was right to backfire between the camp and fire in order to remove fuels and increase protection for the camp. Things went well until the wind shifted and sent the backfire roaring directly back towards the camp.

One young man on summer employ with a fire crew tried to outrun the flames and totally collapsed on arrival within the camp. Freda began CPR on him and knew he was coming around when the sleeping bag under his head began getting soaked as he again began perspiring. He later told her that when he came to and saw her, he thought at first he had died and she was an angel. For several years after that he would send her a thank you card and note on the anniversary of the day she revived him - one even from overseas where he was stationed in the Army.

When evacuation of Job Corps personnel was ordered, the school bus driver (who happened to be her brother) asked if he could give the remaining seat to Freda and take her with him. He was told that she was staff and had to remain to help pack up the maps and plans. When the time came to leave, she was one of three remaining people and the camp was surrounded by fire. They loaded into the last remaining pickup and headed down the single lane road towards the highway south of Silver Lake. Sherm Anderson drove, Freda was in the middle and a Regional Fire Control Officer whose name she does not recall sat on her right.

They held their metal hard hats to shield their faces from the heat of the fire. The hardhats got so hot they finally had to drop them on the floor of the pickup to keep from burning their fingers. The memory of driving through the fire remains with her and she still marvels that no trees fell across the road and blocked their retreat. At times there were burning branches on the road but they were able to successfully drive over them without setting the undercarriage or tires afire.

When they reached the highway, the paint was burned from the pickup's sides and the tires damaged by the heat but the three occupants were safe. They were told to leave the pickup and get into another vehicle to take them to the Ranger Station for a rest and debriefing. As she began to dismount from the pickup, Freda needed assistance to get out, stand and walk.

After debriefing at the Paisley Ranger District compound, she was told to get some rest in a crew trailer whose crew was on the firelines. She fancies herself as having been quite a sight with her office dress and high-heels coated with ash and perspiration, but sleep sounded awfully good. She settled in and soon dropped off. Some time later a crash and the sound of something moving across the floor brought her wide-awake. As she jumped up to confront whatever was making the noise, she was struck on the head driving her back onto the bed.

Still conscious, she realized there were no further sounds within the trailer. Soon her mind cleared enough to figure out the first sound had been a curtain rod being blown from the window and the following sounds were the metal end balls from the rod rolling across the floor. With growing awareness, she realized she had been sleeping in a lower bunk and she had hit her head on the top bunk instead of someone hitting her.

While Winter Rim was not a particularly relaxing introduction to fire camps, Freda continued to go on fires whenever called. Her first fire has always remained her strongest memory of fire camps, but she never again went to a fire wearing high-heels.

RECREATION: "-there was a heavy increase in recreation use."

Virgil R. "Bus" Carrell *Carrell was a District Ranger on the Mt. Hood NF at the time of this story.*

In 1946, I was transferred back to the Clackamas River District, [on the Mt. Hood NF] to make the management plans work as the District Ranger. Bill Parke, while Ranger on the Clackamas River District, prepared a recreation use and campground construction plan, which I incorporated into a multiple-use plan. I contacted Fish and Game people to obtain their needs and opportunities on the District. They were included in the plan. The Clackamas elk herd was not increasing. We made a study, which pretty much answered our questions when we found that they were wintering over in the Warm Springs Indian Reservation. So recreation use and demands for summer homes, which I refused to accept, were increasing as roads were built. Fishing was a great attraction. Much of the area was closed to recreation during the early 1940s because of the Three Lynx Power plant located 23 miles up the river from Estacada, Oregon, a security decision. When it was opened again there was a heavy increase in recreation use.

<u>Kenneth "K." Wolfe</u> *This notice from the R6 Recreation Staff was printed in Volume 3 of TIMBER-LINES, in the summer of 1949. Wolfe began work with the Forest Service in 1912 in R-1. His career included working as a liaison with the CCC Program in R-5. He was in Lands and Minerals in the R-6 Regional Office when he retired in 1955. During his retirement he served as Secretary of the Columbia River Gorge Commission.*

Doubtless you have all heard that the Forest Service is departing from its long established custom of making the National Forests available for camping and picnicking without charge. For several years past, Congressional appropriations committees have raised the question of why the Forest Service doesn't get some revenue from its Forest camps. It has been a matter of all out and nothing in, and Congress, at least some parts of Congress, don't seem to like this.

So, for this season, throughout the entire country, there will be Forest overnight camps and picnic grounds here and there where you will have to pay for the privilege of stopping. The charge for parties of six adults or less will be only 50 cents a night for camping and 25 cents a day for picnicking. The scheme is purely experimental and is being tried out on only a very limited basis. In this Region, charges will be made at the following camps:

> Camp Creek and Tollgate - Mt. Hood
> Dead Indian Soda Springs - Rogue River
> Eel Creek and Siltcoos - Siuslaw
> Wolf Creek - Umpqua
> Clear Lake and Paradise - Willamette
> Government Mineral Springs - Gifford Pinchot
> American River and Naches –Snoqualmie

<u>**Lee Boecksteigel**</u> *Boecksteigel tells another story from the early years of his career.*

It was late in the summer of 1957 on the Wenatchee NF. College students had been working all summer putting in permanent inventory plots. Their work schedule was ten days on and four days off.

Supervisor J. K. (Ken) Blair asked those who could, to continue their employment on a similar work schedule into the fall in order to get the resource inventory completed for use in determining the future course of direction for the North Cascades area (now the North Cascades National Park complex).

Enough students to form a crew stayed on. We were transported up to the head of Lake Chelan via the Chelan Ranger District work tug or its *PT* boat. If neither of these were available, we used private transportation, *The Lady of the Lake*. We would debark at Stehekin Guard Station and ride 11 miles via pickup to High Bridge Guard Station where we loaded up our gear on our backs and took off for points via foot. We had been working in the dry east side Ponderosa pine forest where it was warm and dry. We were now going up Agnes Creek where the Ponderosa pine transitioned into west side conditions - cold and wet. This time of year there was heavy emphasis on wet, wet, wet and cold. As mentioned all gear was carried on our backs; work equipment, food and rain gear. No tents to sleep in and no horses to carry the burden. The weather kept getting wetter and cooler.

We tried to stay dry, but it rained all the time and there was no place to stop and dry out. We were continually cold and wet. Because of the extended work period (two weeks without a break), we ran out of coffee. We could put up with many things, but to do without coffee in weather conditions as this was almost unbearable.

We continued to work our way up the Agnes. We were getting tired and thought we would never dry out when we came upon an old trapper's cabin. This cabin hadn't been used in a long time. The windows were gone and the door was partially off its hinges. The cabin itself was about ten feet square and had bunk beds built out of logs. The beds were in a degenerative condition, well filled with wood rat stuff, but we were able to clean them out to the point we could lay out our sleeping bags. We scouted the area around the cabin closely for the making and completion of a makeshift stove. We were successful in this endeavor and constructed a fire. We used our rain gear to close the windows and door. The roof, for whatever reason, did not leak. We found some pieces of candle so we now had heat and light.

Further looking found a small enclosure containing an unopened can of Folgers coffee. There were no *used by* dates on the can back then and we didn't care. What more could we ask for? We were able to dry out, get warm, and enjoy a cup of *Joe* for the first time in days. We felt like we were in the Waldorf Astoria. It was like finding a gold mine. Our spirits were lifted and we thought we went to heaven.

All's well that ends well. We dried out and left. When we left we made sure the somewhat depleted can of coffee and candle stubs were in a safe place for the next people who might be in as dire need as we had been.

<u>Don Peters</u> *Peters was instrumental in establishing a ski area on Bachelor Butte when he was Fire, Recreation, and Lands Staff Officer on the Deschutes NF.*

Ollie [Mrs. Peters] and I were powder snow fanatics. As Recreation Staff, [on the Deschutes NF in the late 1950s and early 1960s] I worked hard and long with District Ranger Ed Parker and Forest Supervisor Jim Egan to obtain the Regional Forester's and Chief's approval for a hoped-for large winter sports ski area development at Bachelor Butte. That name has since been changed to Mt. Bachelor following approval by the Oregon Geographical Names Committee.

The potential applicant consisted of five professional businessmen led by Bill Healy, an ex-10th Mountain Division ski trooper having served in Europe during World War II. Bill was an excellent skier, knowledgeable of all snow types and skiing conditions. Soon thereafter the group incorporated for $50,000. Five board members were elected and Bill Healy became president of the corporation.

A major obstacle remained to be solved before obtaining the Chief's approval. Regulations required that for a new area, publicity must be given by contacting all ski area operators operating on NF land to determine if any were interested. No interest was indicated following our contacts. Had there been any, it would have been necessary to select the highest qualified bidder based on the percentage of annual fee he would be willing to pay. Luckily for the Mt. Bachelor group, no positive replies were received.

Prior to recommending approval to the Chief, Frank Folsom, head of the R6 Division of Recreation and Lands, requested that I return to the RO for further discussion. His reason was that I had been a National Ski Patrolman for ten years, held an American Red Cross First Aid Instructor Card during the same period and had close contact with members and officers of the Pacific Northwest Ski Association. He wanted me to give him more information, including my answers to *what if* situations before presenting his final recommendations to the Chief in Washington D.C.

Mr. Folsom was an old time cross-country skier who had done only a small amount of downhill skiing on steep slopes. He at first discussed my R6 assignment during the winter of 1956-57 when I inspected all ski areas but one on NF lands in R6. The result of my recommendations tightened the rules of administration and required all rope tow operators to discontinue use of solid barriers on their operations. He then seriously told me that the proposed development would be unsuccessful for reasons that the Portland area skiers had three ski areas available at Government Camp near the summit of the Cascades at an elevation of 4817 feet. There were additional facilities at Timberline at an elevation of 6330 feet located a short distance above the actual tree timberline on the lower open slopes of Mt. Hood just above Timberline Lodge.

He then stated that Portland area skiers would not drive 160 miles eastward to Bend then reverse their course and drive another 22 miles to Bachelor Butte and then after skiing a day or two drive back 182 miles to the Portland area. He said skiers in the Salem vicinity would not drive beyond Hoodoo Bowl at Santiam Pass on US Highway 20 with an elevation of 4170 feet and Eugene area skiers would not drive past Willamette Pass on US Highway 58 with an elevation of 5128 feet. Mr. Folsom did not quote the pass and other elevations. I put them in for your information.

In my part of the discussion, I explained that the 9060 foot summit of Bachelor Butte, having potential for the lower ends of downhill ski runs available at 6300 feet, together with its location seven miles east of the Cascade Mountain summit, had much drier snow known to skiers as *powder* and many sunny days. I also told him that skiers coming to Bachelor would spend goodly amounts of money for skiing, clothing, shopping, motel rental, eating and gasoline. I then closed my presentation by telling him that two large sawmills located in Bend had logged their lands and slowed their operations from a three-shift operation to one and as a result created a large unemployment situation. Near the end of our conversation, Mr. Folsom told me that my presentation had merit. A few days later, Supervisor Egan was informed that the Chief had approved issuing a special-use permit. That news when conveyed to the applicant was accepted with appreciation.

After the permit was issued, prior to the start of operation in the fall of 1958, the permittee installed three rope tows and a Swiss-made T-bar. In the summer of 1959, the T-Bar was removed and a Poma-Lift was installed. This was necessary because of not having the capacity to fill the growing demand. To remedy that situation the first chairlift was installed, I believe, in 1960. At the present time [2002] there are ten chairlifts ready to go as crowds demand. One takes skiers to the top of Mt. Bachelor. All rope tows except one for beginners have long been removed. There are four lodges and seventy downhill runs; the longest run is one and one-half miles in length. Fifty miles of Nordic runs are available to cross country skiers during the winter season. Mt. Bachelor Ski Area is now rated as one of the high ranking ski resorts in the nation.

TIMBER: "The annual cut was increasing-"

<u>Hillard M. "Lil" Lilligren</u> *Lilligren returned to the Forest Service from World War II in 1946 as a log scaler on the Siuslaw NF.*

What was the Forest Service safety program in 1946? I really wasn't sure for several years, but these were my earlier experiences! As a 28-year-old forester just returned from military service with the Army Air Corps in Italy in 1945, I finally got a job offer as a scaler on the Hebo Ranger District of the Siuslaw National Forest. All junior foresters those days were scalers as far as I could determine! My previous experience consisted of scaling several cords of pulpwood in my college days at the University of Minnesota eight years previously. I never told the Ranger that.

I had seen Douglas-fir, ponderosa pine and the redwoods as a 12-year-old during an automobile trip to the west coast in 1931, so I wasn't entirely ignorant of western timber types. I drove from Minneapolis to Hebo via Portland with most of my worldly belongings in a 1939 Studebaker, leaving behind my expecting wife who would fly out later.

The man who was assigned to teach me scaling on the District was Homer Hildenbrand, the Ranger's Assistant, who became my lifelong friend. Homer took me down to a local sawmill at Beaver, and showed me how to scale a few Douglas-fir poles suitable for sawing into 2 x 4 studs. Then he took me up to Tillamook and we water-scaled a raft of logs on Tillamook Bay while the tide was running out. After a total of four hours training, I became the District scaler. I couldn't complain - I'd been through the *great depression* and nearly five years of World War II so I was very lean and very hungry.

My net paycheck for my first full pay period [two weeks] was about 70 dollars. That just about paid for my wife's ten-day hospital stay when my son was born about a month later. Sound incredible?

Generally I left my quarters at the *side camp* at Hebo at daylight on Monday morning and spent the next four days scaling in the Willamette Valley on cold decks, hot decks, on the ground, on ponds and on river rafts. I came back Thursday night to scale what was necessary on the District and prepare my cutting reports. Saturday and Sunday I stayed home and split wood so my wife could heat the house and cook while I was gone. I believe I scaled about 12 million board feet the first year; which really wasn't much, but I had to drive and walk many miles to do it.

My water scaling became hazardous at times. On some occasions, a log dump operator would take me up the river in a power boat and let me off to scale a raft of logs a mile or more away from the main dump. I was dressed in a cruiser vest, rain clothes, one of those common head-pieces in those days, a red felt hat, stagged-off Levis, and a heavy pair of caulked boots. I carried a scale stick with sharp spud, a bamboo length-measuring contraption, scale tables, scaling books, pencils, a USFS branding axe and often a thermos and a soggy sandwich in the back of my cruiser vest. I had to soak some of my scale books in kerosene to waterproof them so they wouldn't turn into pulp before I could get them back to the Ranger Station.

No one asked me if I could swim! Not that it would have helped. No one ever suggested that I wear a life jacket, and it was a long time before I got a helper. And then he kept falling off the logs into the water, and I had to get rid of him. No one except the log-dump operators or Columbia River Bureau scalers ever knew where I was four days a week.

I guess someone from the Supervisor's Office asked the Ranger one day where I was, and he couldn't tell them. After that, I had to leave a schedule of my field travel, so if I didn't show up on the weekend at least they would know where to start looking.

One of the trickier scaling jobs I had was on the Willamette River one afternoon when the river was in flood stage. I had a raft of western hemlock tops to be taken to a pulp mill. Peter Murphy, Sr. decided to utilize as much hemlock as he could, rare among purchasers in those days. He sawed the larger logs into flooring, and hauled the tops to the valley to be sold as pulp. Those who have water-scaled hemlock know it has a high specific gravity and often sinks when the scaler steps on it. I just couldn't risk this at flood stage. I stood on the bank, estimated the number of logs, and the average length and diameter. I multiplied the average volume times the number of logs, and that was it. I never got my boots wet!

The safety program is a much better one today, I'm sure!

<u>Virgil R. "Bus" Carrell</u> *Carrell was a District Ranger on the Mt. Hood NF at the time of this story.*

The annual cut [in 1946] was increasing with the Hillockburn sale having been increased, more Fish Creek sales, and by this time, we were opening the area near the Collowash River which we called the Sandstone sale area. Most were in the 30 million to 40 million board feet size category of about three years duration; stumpage prices were increasing rapidly. The pressure was for peeler logs and the Sandstone had patches of high-quality peeler grade logs. One large patch was some 85 acres between the bluffs and the road. We decided to take all,

Timber faller at work, Umpqua NF – 1967

burn and plant immediately. Today (2003) it is a beautiful stand which has been thinned. I am told it is 100 feet or more tall with large boles of 24 inches or more in the taller portion of the stand.

Early in the winter of 1946-1947, a crew of professional foresters, LeRoy Bond and Norm Gould, laid out a sale on eight feet of snow, marking boundaries at knee height on the snow, staying in tents and using Sibley stoves for warmth and cooking. They stayed out ten days and came back in for four. The War Production Board was demanding timber products. Road engineering followed and the sale was advertised with the best information we could develop. It wasn't easy sometimes.

Elk Creek Logging Company and Wilson Brothers were purchasing sales in the upper Clackamas and Sandstone Creek area before I left in 1952. By about 1948, the road from Estacada to Three Lynx Power Plant was completed to a one and a half lane standard with turnouts. Log trucks were coming down the Clackamas about every three minutes. Dwyer Lumber Company was logging heavily in Fish Creek. Our total cut for the District was 64 million in 1947 and by 1951, we were logging 110 million board feet per year. A mill was allowed at a site near Ripplebrook to harvest small and poorer quality timber which was marginally or less profitable. A mill closer to the supply made it profitable. The mill and operation was run by Acme Timber Company of Portland, Oregon. The mill is long gone (2003). The site is occupied by the Job Corps Camp. There were steel bridges at Fish Creek, a suspension bridge at the crossing of the Clackamas and a steel bridge across the Oak Grove fork. The suspension bridge was damaged when a log truck driver failed to tie his load properly. It tore down the suspension with bridge, truck and driver falling into the river. He was rescued. The bridge was replaced by a stringer bridge and later a low rail steel and concrete bridge.

These paragraphs illustrate some of the complexities of this Ranger District which led to its classification to GS-11.

<u>Robert Schramek</u> *Schramek worked on the Olympic NF at the time of this story in the early 1950s.*

I never had the dubious privilege of working with old John, but I talked with several young foresters back in the early 1950s who had.

They assured me that the tales they told were accurate descriptions of the way John trained new foresters.

In those days, timber sale layout was a straightforward job of locating timber stands, surveying and marking the boundaries of clear cut units and cruising the timber for volume and grade, by measuring and/or estimating the individual trees within sample plots within each unit. The field work was strenuous, and the measurements needed to be exact and accurate. The surveys and data were the basis for appraisals that set the minimum price required to bid on the timber, and hundreds of thousands of dollars were at stake. We carried measuring tapes, Abney levels, staff compasses, clipboards, altimeters and cruise cards to record data. We wore cruiser vests to carry most of the gear, but we were usually burdened with axes and Jacob staffs in our hands. All the gear slowed up travel, and limited the effective distance that we could walk in for a day's work.

Since this work was done before the roads were built, or even surveyed, the job usually required staying out in the woods for extended campouts to complete the work. Most sale layout crews tried to do the close work from home. When camping out was called for, it was usually for ten days at a time, with four days off, to make logistics easier and give the forester some time with his family. Usually, we carried in a good tent, camp stove, sleeping bags and some amenities, like lanterns, plates, cups, silverware, a mirror and folding stools to make camp life a little more comfortable.

Not so for John, who prided himself on being self-reliant, and felt that luxuries in camp were an unnecessary burden. In fact, the campsite itself was unnecessary. This was on the remote northwest part of the Olympic NF, where roads were just being built into the back country, and most of the drainages were still roadless and rugged territory.

John was an older forester, who was a skilled and accomplished timber cruiser. New foresters were assigned as a training assignment and to complete the field cruise work. According to the stories, a new forester would arrive at the District office, and John would be ready to leave. With no introductions, they would pile into John's pickup and drive to the end of the road, where they would pack up a few supplies in small day-packs and begin walking.

After several miles of strenuous hiking, they would arrive at a marked unit and John would hand the young forester a set of tally cards in a clipboard and start calling off dimensions. This would go on for four or five hours without any break, then stop for a short lunch break. After maybe 15 minutes, John would get up and announce it was time to go back to work. They would set off again at a brisk pace and continue for another five hours, paying no attention to the time or weather. They would break again for a brief supper, consisting of a couple of sliced potatoes, and some diced ham or bacon, fried up in a filthy old frying pan produced out of the bottom of his old pack, over an open fire.

After maybe 20 minutes, the fire would be put out, and cruising would resume until darkness came making writing impossible. John would look around, find a convenient log or tree root, pull out an old army blanket, lay down and go to sleep. At first daylight, they would be up, and after a short fire and a breakfast of more potatoes, they would resume timber cruising. The routine was rigorous and unvaried. It continued until the cruise was complete, or the junior forester simply revolted or collapsed.

They told me that anyone who completed a two-week training assignment under John was considered by the brass in the Supervisor's office to have proven himself and was ready to be taken off probationary status!

Mike Kerrick *Kerrick started as a temporary in 1952 and received a permanent appointment in 1954. He worked on the Willamette, Mt. Baker, and Mt. Hood NFs in R-6, the Six Rivers NF in R-5, and the Coconino NF in R-3. He was the Forest Supervisor of the Willamette NF in R-6 when he retired in 1991.*

It was the summer of 1953 on the McKenzie District of the Willamette NF. It was my second summer as part of a two-man mapping crew. Corson Williams was the TMA. He decided to finish the last unit of the original Tidbits sale in one day by putting a crew together, making the long hike in and then laying out, traversing and cruising the unit all in one day. A day none of us will ever forget.

416

The Bureau of Public Roads had built a timber access road to the mouth of Tidbits Creek. From there it was a long haul by trail up Tidbits Creek to the last foot bridge and cross-country from there to the last unit of the sale. The plan was Corson would lay the unit out using a string line and then begin cruising. My partner and I would traverse the unit following the string line and a fellow from the Supervisor's Office named Al Wiener would also cruise. At the end of the day we would all meet at the last footbridge and head on back to the rig at the end of the road.

We all agreed to the plan and took off to complete our part of it. Corson got us all to the road tag line and then took off at a fast clip saying he would mark up the entrance to the unit real well so we couldn't miss it. My partner and I, along with Al, followed at a slower pace not being in as good a shape as Corson. We found the entrance to the unit and began traversing the unit; Al paced into the unit and began his first cruise line.

Sometime shortly after lunch the plan went awry. Al slipped and fell and in the process twisted his ankle; no one but Al knew his problem. Being a gritty guy he continued on, but at a much slower pace to finish his cruising assignment. Meanwhile Corson finished the layout and his part of the cruising job. We finished the traverse without incident. The three of us all met at the foot log around five or so and waited for Al to show up. We waited and waited and yelled and yelled all with no luck. Corson went back a ways and yelled some more. Still no Al. At dusk we decided it would be prudent to cross the log and wait for Al. It got dark and still no Al. It was obvious he had a problem. Corson decided, knowing Al was woods-wise and could take care of himself, that the rest of us should hike out the trail to the end of the road, go back to McKenzie Bridge, get help and come back for Al in the morning.

By now it was pitch black and under the old growth forest you couldn't see the hand in front of your face. Corson's caulked boots hurt him; so today he was wearing sneakers, he thought he could feel the trail. He took the lead and cautiously *felt* his way along the trail, the two of us right behind. Every time Corson would stop to get his bearings we would all collide. There were many collisions as we

417

made our way out. We finally made it to the rig around midnight and headed back to town.

We alerted folks about Al and got a short night's rest. We were up early the next morning and with a search party headed back to Tidbits Creek. We found Al about three miles up the trail limping along. He had fashioned a crutch from a cedar limb to support his twisted ankle. We were all relieved. Al was madder than a wet hen that we had left him, but calmed down a bit when we told him our story. Al had finished his part of the cruise and had started cross-country to join us at the foot log. Darkness fell, he twisted his sore ankle again and decided to *hole up* for the night. He started out as light broke in the morning managing to cross the foot log by sliding along on his rear and had made it down the trail a mile or so by the time we found him.

Corson Williams later went on to be timber staff on the Six Rivers NF, a job I would follow him in, in 1970. Al Wiener went on to be the chief timber appraisal person in the Chief's office. Whenever our paths would cross, which they did several times over the years, we would talk about the time we left Al for a night in the woods!

<u>Joe Gjertson</u> *Gjertson started on the Flathead and Salmon Ranger Districts in R-1. He worked on the Chelan, Umatilla and Malheur NFs in R-6, and was the Range and Wildlife Staff Officer on the Wenatchee NF when he retired in 1979.*

Between 1953 and 1958, three major budworm control projects were completed in Eastern Oregon. All three used the very effective hydrocarbon, DDT with oil, at the rate of one gallon per acre.

The first aerial spray project attempted by the Forest Service was accomplished out of Meacham on the Umatilla NF. I was selected to be the first unit supervisor by Carl Ewing, probably because I was handy being Ranger on the Pendleton District. Weeks before spray date, a makeshift runway was carved out of a scab ridge near the whistle stop of Meacham. Lindberg had not included Safety Hints for this type of project. They would come much later.

Fortunately we drew a good contractor, (Bob) Johnson Flying Service out of Missoula, Montana. Bob had probably the last three Ford tri-motors still operational. They were capable of hauling heavy payloads

418

at slow speeds. He used his Cessna for our daily observation flights. While following a Ford enroute to a spray block, he nonchalantly barrel-looped around it which was not in *Lindberg's* book, but quite impressive to me. I noticed the Ford pilot reach out and manually activate his windshield swipe after a spray run. Great planes!

Around mid-project Johnson called in a C-47 to cover the long-run blocks. His army pilot had received experience in WW II hedgehopping over Europe. I decided to try a spray run in this ship. I crawled up in what was left of the navigator's cage and braced my feet. We taxied as far back as we could to get enough airstrip, brakes were set and the engines revved to a howl. We were off like a scalded cat and barely cleared the timber. Our spray block was a box canyon known as Devil's Gulch. Our pilot lowered his flaps and called for *landing gear down*. The added drag would put us on treetop level to get maximum coverage (a move to impress me, undoubtedly). We were fast approaching the rock-slabbed dead-end when he lifted the flaps and barked, "Up landing gear!" Nothing happened, a malfunction. Somehow we made a spectacular one hundred-eighty without clipping off a swath of timber and made it back to base.

In 1954, I was transferred to the Long Creek District on the Malheur. Incidentally, another budworm infestation appeared, engrossing much of my District. Just a coincidence that I was *experienced*, so the Forest appointed me unit supervisor of the Fox project. We found a level stretch on private land out of Fox and before long had a pretty good strip, even with dust palliative spread full length. This camp was to become better known as *Rag City*. We scrounged tents from region-wide sources and some were doozies. But we gleaned a good mess tent with two good male cooks and a flunkie. We fed around 50 people.

Twenty-five Stearmans were lined up on the apron plus a couple C-47s. The contractor, Art Butler, had installed makeshift motorcycle seats against the dashboards of the Stearmans for pilot safety. A week went by with little incident other than a few midnight disturbances by Long Creek permittees concerned with real or imaginary range problems.

Charlie Munger had been having marital problems. On his early takeoff, his Stearman was observed tooling along too low to clear the ridge enroute to his block. He pulled up too late and crashed into a mountain just below a state lookout. A returning pilot reported, "Charlie bought the ranch!" A pickup was available. With demerol kit in hand, I was off for the crash site.

At the scene of wreckage I surprisingly found Glen Jorgensen, with Munger laid out next to his totaled plane. The big engine had led interference for him. Glen had been visiting his son David, a lookout for the state. Munger was in deep shock and bleeding from the mouth. I administered a shot of demerol and made him lie still. Doctor Jerry of Canyon City had been radio-notified and arrived shortly after, driving his make-do panel *ambulance*. After a cursory inspection, he administered another shot of demerol. I held the plasma jug high during the bumpy ride down the mountain to Jerry and Martha's hospital.

Munger was lifted on to the x-ray table, alive. Every bone in his head was broken except the skull proper which had been protected by his small helmet. Flesh had been shorn from both knees down the shins. Dr. Profit of John Day did an expert job of wiring up Charlie's jaws and teeth. Munger didn't fly again but emerged a solid person, capable of gainful employment. Our contractor was heard exclaiming, "See? I knew those motorcycle seats would do the job!"

A few years later I was transferred to the Blue Mountain District of the Malheur. In 1958, the RO decided we needed a million acres sprayed for a massive budworm infestation on the lower Malheur and Whitman Forests. "No!", I said to Supervisor Mal Loring, "I don't think a Ranger should be saddled with a budworm project during his heavy field season." We made a trip to Portland to discuss the proposed project. The job would be divided between headquarters at John Day and Baker.

Returning home, we stopped for coffee. Mal purchased a cigar and said, "Congratulations, unit supervisor, have a cigar."

With help of a practical engineer like Joe Wells, we smoothed off a good airstrip on the flat above John Day. When a plane left that strip,

High-lead logging landing, Siuslaw NF – 1968

Spruce budworm spray project, Wenatchee NF – 1976

it was committed. We constructed headquarters at the airstrip. Benton Howard was project director and John Whiteside technical advisor, both capable men. Ace Flying Service was our contractor. They somehow uncovered some WW II PBYs from the Navy and remodeled them to carry copious loads of goop. Fresh out of cosmoline, these big babies appeared to be the ticket for spraying mountain terrain. The boss also convinced some capable Navy pilots (on leave) to fly the planes. A few Stearmans were added to cover small, tight blocks like around Strawberry Mountain.

One morning we heard a loud "MAY DAY! MAY DAY!" on the dispatcher's radio. The PBYs were radio equipped.

The return message was, "Dump the load!" We could see the ship approaching town with the engine belching smoke. The pilot jettisoned his load squarely on a farm house and a new sedan car. DDT dribbled out of the open bays on the low circle approach to the cleared runway. He landed safely on one engine. That triggered a stream of cars, headlights on, up from the valley. Complaints were loud about poisoned truck gardens, cars splattered, livestock spooked, fish kills and more. My comments about saving a pilot's life had little effect. Besides, we killed every mosquito and fly in the valley. We killed some fish in the local streams but anadromous runs returned fairly close on schedule.

Control of the insect was upward of 98%. I cannot begin naming all the good people who made these three projects go. Guys like Alex Jaenicke, Paul Dennis, McPherson, Ron Primozic, Art McKee, Bob Hribernick and scores of others come to mind. Our purpose was *to control the spruce budworm with no lost-time accidents, no forest fires, no loss of wildlife, and no damage to equipment.* Considering the newness of the work and the long, sustained hours of bone-weariness experienced by all, I personally submit we did our damndest.

<u>Bob Bjornsen</u> *Bjornsen was a District Ranger on the Wallowa-Whitman NF at the time of this story in the late 1950s or early 1960s.*

It all started one fall at Thorn Creek Guard Station near the Imnaha River, Wallowa-Whitman Forest. Chesnimnus Ranger Blen Holman and I had been checking some winter C&H [cattle and horse] allotments and had decided to mix a little chukar hunting with the work at hand which was really to hunt elk up in the Red Hill country. Of course you realize this was before purity codes were invented to spoil mixing work with pleasure.

For some unremembered reason we decided to saddle up the horses and head for Thompson Meadow Guard Station about dusk. We hadn't gone far up the trail when it turned darker than the inside of a cow and began to rain and sleet in buckets full. Our trusty horses had to pick their way up the trail without our guidance while we sat miserably in the saddle wondering whose idea this was in the first place. As lead rider my main worry was whether Blen's trail crew had limbed trees high enough to keep from sluicing me out of the saddle.

Eventually we arrived at Thompson Meadow with numb feet and hands so cold we could hardly unclaw them to take the rigging off the horses. Blen had been mumbling all the way about having killed the last of our bottle of spirits the night before at Thorn Creek. I let him grumble until the fire was lit in the old sheep-herder's stove before I brought out a reserve flask hidden in my bedroll. And so we whiled away a few hours listening to the wind whistle through the cracks in the old cabin.

During the night the wind picked up and really began to howl. We could hear branches breaking off the trees and an occasional tree going down. Our main concern was that one didn't topple onto the cabin.

Next morning the storm had passed and we decided to inspect the damage along the Thompson-Billy Meadows road driving a pickup truck that had been conveniently left at the guard station. We hadn't gone far before it became apparent there was enough blowdown of merchantable timber to warrant a salvage sale. A quick cruise was in order so with Blen tallying and driving and me shooting the diameter and heights out the window we sampled a swath along the ridge all the while marveling how the numerous hunter camps escaped being crushed by some of the falling giants.

Then it was off to Enterprise to call Owen Aydelott, W-W timber staff officer, that an estimated ten million board feet of high quality pine had blown down and help was needed to put it up for sale by spring. Naturally Owen wanted to know the particulars, especially how we arrived at the volume estimate. We danced around the latter when I said, "I'd seen some blowdown in my day, but this was the worst I'd ever seen and time was of the essence."

Owen rose to the occasion and sent an SO crew out to help the understaffed District people get the sale ready. A year later Blen and I heaved a sigh of relief to learn the sale cut out within one percent of the cruise volume. After all our reputation as pickup seat timber cruisers was at stake.

ENGINEERING: "We were able to do the ten miles of location, design, and construction staking and keep ahead of the construction crew."

D. O. "Jack" Frost *Frost started as a temporary in 1945, and received a permanent appointment in 1949. He worked on the Mt. Hood, Wenatchee, and Wallowa-Whitman NFs, at the Pacific Northwest Experiment Station, in the Washington Office and in the R-4 Regional Office. He was the Regional Engineer in R-3 when he retired in 1986.*

On one five-month vacation from college (I ran out of money), I worked with Norm Gould and three others [on the Mt. Hood NF] to lay out and prepare over 70 million board feet of timber sales as well as locate and design the needed access roads. We began in the spring on skis and snowshoes in three to six feet of snow, and ended in time for me to re-enter college for the fall term. These timber sales were established under much simpler contracts, laws and regulations than now exist. The multi- and inter-disciplinary input and review was minimal except for the Ranger and timber staff. Even so, the work was technically sound and environmentally adequate. Today the same job would be much better done but at many times the cost.

Road maintenance, Umpqua NF – 1968

Road construction, Umpqua NF – 1969

On one of my first jobs as a junior engineer after graduation, I was assigned to locate, design and stake a new major access road on an emergency timber sale. This route was accessible to construction at only one point, the end of the existing road that dead-ended in the lower part of a canyon. The only work that had been accomplished for the road was a penciled location on a topographic map. The route was a rugged and steep canyon along a large stream.

Upon first arriving at the job site on a Monday morning, my helper and I were met by the road contract construction crew unloading three bulldozers. After some delay, we were able to establish 1000 feet of clearing lines. The clearing work and pioneer road on this section kept the crew busy for the first two days. We found that a 60-foot bridge would have to be constructed about 200 feet beyond the end of the marked clearing. We were able to use the standard R6 log stringer bridge plan and thus eliminate extensive design time delay.

The next day we made further reconnaissance and found that two more log stringer bridges were required in the first two miles due to terrain and topography. We were able to do the ten miles of location, design and construction staking and keep ahead of the construction crew, primarily because of the need to construct the three bridges in the narrow canyon with only one point of access. The construction superintendent was convinced that I made them build the bridges to avoid the embarrassment of construction delay!

With few engineers and foresters and an expanding timber sale program in those days, we were faced with many emergencies, not unlike encountered in fighting a forest fire.

Don Garvik *Garvik's Forest Service career included work on the Deschutes, Okanogan, and Wenatchee NFs.*

In the early months of 1946 most of the veterans returning to the Deschutes NF in Oregon were gathered at the Allingham Guard Station on the Sisters Ranger District. Ken Clark, Dick Harlan, Ray Koski, Lynn McCall and Mike Rastovitch are names that come to mind. Most were working on the extension of the Lower Metolius road. Ken Clark and I, along with an older fellow named Paul

Streibel, were working with Bill Ogletree building a bridge over Jack Creek.

One day a fellow named Barnes, whose first name escapes me, wandered into the Supervisor's Office in Bend claiming to be an equipment operator. Dick Bottcher hired him (at a higher pay grade than any of the rest of us) and sent him to Allingham. He arrived with his army good-conduct ribbon on the bib of his overalls, and immediately began boasting of his prowess with equipment. Needless to say, he was not the most popular man in camp. Ken Bartram, the camp superintendent, who had quite a sense of humor, nicknamed him *Barney Oldfield.*

Barney was assigned to the road project to operate a new D-7 Cat dozer which he promptly got stuck in a boulder patch with the blade sticking straight in the air. Dick Harlan and Lynn McCall managed to rescue him.

When we were ready to pour concrete for the Jack Creek Bridge abutments, Bill asked Ken Bartram for an additional man. Ken said, "Barney, can you operate a manual dragline?" Barney said he never had, but allowed as how he could operate anything the Forest Service had to operate, so Ken told him to go with us to the bridge job in the morning.

When we got to the bridge site, Bill handed Barney a scoop shovel to supply gravel to the concrete mixer. Barney was so irate that he would have quit right then and there but for the fact he didn't know the way back to camp, and besides it would have been quite a hike. He did put in the shift but quit when we returned to camp and we never heard of him again. As I recall these many years later, I don't believe anyone was greatly disappointed.

<u>Bob Bjornsen</u> *Bjornsen worked on the Fremont NF in the early 1950s.*

Believe it or not, there was a time when foresters actually located, designed and staked timber-haul roads. On just such an occasion, Bill Augustine and I found ourselves locating a P-line across Antelope Flat, Silver Lake District, Fremont Forest.

It was one of those early spring days when we were glad to be out in the woods after a long winter in the office. There was a *bite* in the air, but we looked for easy going across the Flat and into the open, old growth pine timber. I was compassman and rear chainman and Bill was rod and head chainman.

Off we went sighting and driving stakes with *gusto*. *Gusto* that is until we hit a shallow lake that would dry up by summer. Do we offset around it, or keep going on a straight tangent? We opted to go straight - which was our first mistake.

As head chainman Bill had to go in first, chaining and driving submarine stakes as he went - ever try to drive a stake under water; our second mistake. Before wading out, Bill removed his pants, placed them in his stake bag and headed into the water in his skivvies. The water was ice cold and crotch deep - need I say more?

Bill became madder and colder by the minute as I fussed with the compass, trying to line him up. The pond was about five chains wide and with a two-chain tape there was no way I could avoid a set-up mid-pond. So off comes my britches and into the water goes Bob - shivering so hard I could hardly run the compass. There we were, two knobby-kneed foresters turning blue in the middle of a lake, when the laughter came. If only a smart engineer had been there to take our photo.

A couple of summers later I would've gladly changed places with an engineer. It was one of those yellow jacket years when the pesky bees were everywhere. I had a P-line crew of two civil engineering students locating a haul road in the Strawberry-Barnes Valley country on the Drews Valley District. We were stung by jackets as a daily routine; seemed like we were always stirring up a nest of them.

But on this particular day no jackets bothered us, that is until late in the afternoon. I came to a new station, jammed the Jacob staff into the ground beside the last stake, settled the compass in place on the staff, and peered through the sight. In those few seconds a swarm of yellow jackets had gone up my pants legs from the jake staff jammed in the middle of their nest. And there goes Bob off through the woods with the swarm following him, all the while trying to get his pants off and get rid of those stinging bees.

Meanwhile, my assistants who had escaped unscathed weren't helping the situation with their laughter. Next, how to retrieve the staff and compass around which the jackets were swarming like banshees? One of the fleet-footed chainmen volunteered to make a dash, grabbing the staff as he zoomed by. It worked fine until he tripped, spread-eagled on a root about ten feet past the nest and became the next victim of their wrath. However, he did manage to scramble to his feet and although severely stung, eventually outran the bees with equipment in hand.

Epilogue: I taught the young engineers how to throw a 2-1/2 chain trailer tape. No big deal, except they learned how to do it left-handed, me being a southpaw and they being right-handers. I even showed them how to throw it right-handed, but they had become accustomed to the southpaw method and stayed with it.

Now for a long-kept secret which has won me numerous bets since I learned it 40 years ago. A right-hander cannot throw a chain a left-hander has taken up and vice versa. I've confounded some of the best chain throwers in the FS with this one, even the ones who could double throw a chain which is probably a lost art today. OK you right-handers, find a southpaw friend and try it out. If you haven't thrown a chain in years, it's like riding a bicycle, you never forget how.

Richard A. Reeves *Reeves received a permanent appointment in 1957. He worked on the Siskiyou, Umatilla, and Siuslaw NFs. He was a Policy Analyst for Planning in the R-6 Regional Office when he retired in 1994. Reeves' father, Ralph A. "Sparky", has a story in Chapter Three (Civilian Conservation Corps).*

In 1960, I was transferred to the Powers Ranger District on the Siskiyou NF. I was to be the District engineer. There to meet me on the first day of work was none other than Ag Anderson. He was the ADR or Assistant District Ranger. Ted Burgess was the Ranger. My official title was supposed to be Assistant District Engineer, with I guess the Ranger being *THE* District Engineer.

Ag told me in his usual gentle manner that the District did not need any engineers fouling up their sale program. Why, the idea of having to survey roads and come back and design them and set construction stakes from the design would do nothing but slow a timber sale down. Quite possibly the District's sale program may not be met for the year and then all heck would break out!

Times were changing though. The old way of Class III surveys were just about gone. That's where a forester went out just ahead of the Cat setting flags at grade. I saw some mighty nice roads built using that method, but the days of side-cast construction were numbered. I worked with Ag for three years and grew to respect him for his down-to-earth knowledge of the land and trees and people.

Phil Hirl   *Hirl received a permanent appointment in the R6 Regional Office in Engineering in 1962, and worked on field assignments to the Mt. Baker and Snoqualmie NFs. He worked on the Malheur and Willamette NFs in Region 6, and the Shasta-Trinity NF in Region 5. He was Assistant Director of Engineering in the R6 Regional Office when he retired in 1993.*

In the summer of 1962, Rob Mercer arranged a detail for me from the RO Bridge Section to the Mt. Baker NF to inspect the construction of four bridges in the Suiattle River drainage. I was to work for Bob Nixon, the contracting officers' representative and Bill Shiley, the Forest Engineer. Chris Chriswell was the Forest Supervisor, Dale Heigh was the Darrington Ranger and Bob Perkse was the Suiattle Ranger.

Joy decided to bring our one-year-old son and come with me. Per diem in those days was $12/day or so, even in Darrington a bit hard to live on. But there was a vacant house on the compound in Darrington which they offered to us. We took it. No furniture but a roof. We brought a playpen, high chair, Coleman stove and sleeping bags/air mattresses. Our son slept in a playpen and Joy and I on sleeping bags. Co-workers brought over a couple of folding chairs and we used an empty spool of high wire cable for a table. Joy got pretty good with meals on the Coleman stove, though she convinced me it was my turn a few times.

Compound living was interesting. I had not yet worked for the Forest

430

Service a year. Though I grew up in mill towns next to National Forests, I did not know a lot about the Forest Service and its culture. I learned a few things that summer. Engineers had an increased pay scale over foresters, starting about in the middle of the pay scale. This was based on the scarcity of potential employees, and some people did not like that. Some of the wives were rather cool to Joy at first, but our next door neighbors didn't care. They were friends and she helped Joy get acquainted with some of the wives.

One day at the bridge site on a creek near the Suiattle River, things slowed a bit, so I decided to take a walk in the woods down to the main river. The river was only a quarter mile from the bridge, so I figured it would be easy to do, but after ten minutes I was lost. All I could see were tall trees that all looked the same. Soon I passed by my footsteps in the dirt, thinking I have been here before. Next time I came upon them I knew I had been there before. Great lesson! After learning I had to fix my bearings, I never got lost again in the woods and later I spent many hours on the Malheur NF by myself locating roads.

Labor Day came and construction slowed so we took a three-day weekend trip. When we got back I found my FS pick up door was unlocked and the truck had been used. I went to Ranger Heigh to complain. In gentle terms he explained, "We had a fire bust when you were gone. We needed your rig. Don't ever leave town again with keys to a FS rig in your pocket." I never did. Anytime I saw Dale again I thought of that learning experience.

In the summer of 1963 I was detailed to the Snoqualmie NF from the RO Bridge Section as COR on three new bridges. They were in different locations, so Joy did not join me for the summer since I had to move from bridge to bridge.

One of the bridges was in Denney Creek Campground east of North Bend. When it was the busiest project and I had to be there most of the time, Joy decided to join me. We set up camp in the campground next to the bridge. Our son was two years old then, and he enjoyed being out in the woods. We did that for two or three weeks. There was a strike in the North Bend area so a lot of people were not getting a paycheck. One weekend day we went into town for groceries. When we returned to camp, it was stripped. All the food and a few other things were gone. They left all the camping gear.

Joy came out again later when I had some bridge maintenance inspections to do on the Naches and Tieton Ranger District. So we set up camp again near Tieton Reservoir. This time we were more careful with our food and put more valuable stuff in the car when we left.

Phil tells a story about an embarrassing moment at a Forest Ranger and Staff Meeting.

Two summers in the field convinced me I wanted to leave the Regional Office for a Forest assignment, and did. I was sent from RO Engineering to the Malheur NF as Assistant Forest Engineer in early 1965.

We had a transportation plan concept for the Malheur NF with identification of major roads and secondary roads. Forest Engineer Phil Heyn got some time at a Ranger and Staff Meeting to present the concept and asked me to do it. I was discussing the major network and how one road led to Drewsey, adding, "--if anyone ever wanted to go there."

Supervisor Al Oard stood up and said, "I am from Drewsey." I wish I had known that. There was a silence in the room.

ADMINISTRATION: "I was asked to program the division of the Clackamas River District into three Ranger Districts."

<u>Virgil R. "Bus" Carrell</u> *Carrell was a District Ranger on the Mt. Hood NF at the time of this story.*

In 1949, I was presented with a Superior Service Award from the US Department of Agriculture for *Outstanding performance in the management of an exceptionally complex Ranger District.* Soon after that I received a P-4 or GS-11 personnel classification which was the first such classification for a Ranger District in Region Six. I was told that it was, also, the first in the Forest Service. The District was called a Division. No other Ranger ever expressed anything but congratulations for my having received the classification or award. I never lost sight of the fact that my employees and co-workers were most instrumental in accomplishing what was asked of us. They were as proud as I.

In 1952, I was asked to program the division of the Clackamas River District into three Ranger Districts, with two to be located at Ripple Brook near the confluence of Oak Grove Fork of the Clackamas with the Clackamas [River]. I worked with the new Rangers to divide property and equipment and prepared the needs for whatever additional was required. I objected to the division because of the topography, one huge drainage. I was overruled with the concern that the District had become a Division, not a Ranger District and was more like a small Forest. I had a crew of 30 to 50 employees by now, making and supervising sales, appraisals, engineering logging roads, maintaining roads and trails, fire control and recreation guards (plus a 20 man hot shot crew in summer). After I left in late 1952, logging continued at a record pace for the Clackamas River Districts, (now three) for a number of years achieving a cut of 125 million board feet or more to meet housing demands and post-war needs.

On September 6, 2003, I had the privilege of attending a 19th reunion of Clackamas River District employees, many of whom were with me in the 1940s and early 1950s. One, Marion "Bud" Unruh, graciously took me up the Clackamas River to see the fruits of our early labors (some 60 years ago) in terms of regrowth from plantings and seeding. It was an emotional trip for me to see tall trees where we once cut. All are now back in fully stocked stands; all drainages are with roads to the end, with campers, fishermen, and outdoors persons everywhere.

Lowell Gilbert *Gilbert's dad (Clarence Gilbert) worked on the Mt. Hood NF in the 1930s. While in high school, Gilbert worked seasonally as a tree planter and emergency fire fighter and continued seasonal work while attending college. He received a permanent appointment in 1948. He spent his entire career on the Mt. Hood NF and was the Forest Transportation Systems Manger when he retired in 1977.*

When the Clackamas Division on the Mt Hood NF was divided into three Ranger Districts in 1952, Roy Bond was assigned as the District Ranger on the Collawash District. This was his first Ranger District. Norm Gould was his Timber Sales Officer and I was his District Assistant.

433

We were given a great Ranger District but no District headquarters. There was no office or even a place to hang your hat. We had a sales program to get out, crews to train, fire season was coming on and we didn't even have a phone to communicate with the work force or the Supervisors Office. With Roy heading up the operation we rolled up our sleeves and started to work.

We took over an old storage building that had been abandoned years earlier by the CCCs at their Station Creek camp. This building was single wall construction with worn out tar paper on the walls and roof. The building did have concrete blocks for a foundation but you could throw any one of the resident rats through the large cracks and holes in the walls. The flooring consisted of half-inch lumber that was warped from the rain that came through the roof. There were no windows, one door, no electricity, no heat, no water, no furniture, no partitions, no office equipment and no telephone lines.

We had no special funding in the current fiscal year for the reconstruction work we were about to undertake. We did have dedicated and determined personnel who thought a seven day work week was standard and fifteen hours was a short day. We borrowed two men from the Lakes District that could pass for carpenters. They hung the windows and doors and put a partition in the building. Portland General Electric brought electricity to the building. All the other work was performed by District personnel.

In one month's time we had a two-room office that did not leak, walls that kept out the wind and rain, a smooth floor to walk on, an oil-fired furnace, a switch-board that provided communications to the outside world and to all of the field stations, and office furniture that was obtained by legal means (and some not so legal). Improvise was the main theme in that first year. We used orange crates for file cabinets which worked surprisingly well when stacked lengthwise up to four deep. We were offered old beat up file cabinets but Roy was wise enough to know that if we accepted them we would never get the new ones that were promised on the next fiscal year budget.

Our adopted building was about 200 yards from the Station Creek bunk house and mess hall. We used these buildings for water and toilet facilities. The Oak Grove Ranger Station, which now housed the newly formed Lakes District, was about a mile down the road. We set poles and ran the phone lines from Oak Grove to our new Collowash headquarters and set up a switchboard and desk phones. Much of the materials used came from the old warehouse at Oak Grove and the warehouse at Clackamas Lake. The central fire warehouse in downtown Portland was a good source for scrounging materials and furniture. The best place for finding needed furniture and materials of all kinds was the Zigzag RS and the old CCCs buildings across the highway. This required much diversion and skill because Ranger Jim Langdon kept a sharp eye out every time we came around with a flatbed or pickup. The lookouts and guards (prior to going to their stations) were put to work splitting shakes that we used on the roof and walls of the building. They also helped with the landscape work and walkways around the office.

By early summer Roy and all his staff had a Ranger Station that looked darn good to us and one that we were all proud of. In June of 1952 we hung a sign in front of our building, ran the flag up the new flag pole and opened the door for business. I'm convinced this work could not have been completed to the standard and time frame that the situation demanded without Roy Bond. All of the men willingly worked weekends and evenings without being asked. Roy always recognized the work progress from the day before and never failed to complement the individuals responsible. Many people did not know what that new Ranger was up against on his first District. Roy Bond took the lack of an office and other handicaps that went with a new District and new personnel in stride. He completed the District work program that first year and set an example that inspired all who worked for him.

Bob Bjornsen *Bjornsen was an Assistant District Ranger on the Fremont NF at the time of this story in 1953.*

In its day, the Wind River Training Center was a premier place for aspiring young Region 6-ers to learn the mysterious ways of managing National Forest business. Just look at the oldtime photos which adorn (or used to) the hallowed halls in the RO. There you would see the likes of a former Chief and Deputy Chief, not to mention countless other stars of yesteryear.

435

My memory of Wind River training was the District Assistant's two-week course in spring of 1953. Ray Lindberg, Regional Training Officer, was our leader and a more dedicated and strict disciplinarian never graced the Center before or since. As a matter of fact it was nearly like my memories of Marine Corps boot camp during the *Big War*. Inside classes were held in the classic timber-and-stone building next to our CCC-built bunkhouse. The forest setting of the center was a splendid place to learn our trade. There we could gaze upon past Ranger School photos, some dating to the ancient 1920s!

Ray had established a curfew of lights out at 2200 and no liberty into neighboring Carson to whet our whistles after a hard day in class. And he enforced it too by random checks to see that we were diligently doing our homework and not *jumping ship*. We couldn't slip out because he could hear a car start from his VIP room in the main building.

You guessed it, his nighttime surveillance was a challenge to a few of us. One night, well into the course, we decided a brew at the local saloon in Carson (some ten miles distant) was in order. Waiting 30 minutes after lights out, we tippy-toed out to the lone civilian car, whose owner was also thirsty, and with care pushed it some one-quarter mile before starting the engine.

Needless to say, we had a rousing good time until the saloon closed in the wee hours, leavened by the fact we had pulled one over on taskmaster Ray Lindberg. Our just desserts came when we cut the engine at the earlier starting place and found we had to push the car up a slight grade all the way to the parking lot. It's a wonder Ray didn't hear our grunting and cursing, although I'm sure he could smell our beery breaths the next day, but he never said a word. Maybe he figured our hangovers were penance enough.

<u>Wendall Jones</u> *Jones was a Timber Management Assistant on the Willamette NF at the time of this story.*

I experienced a different and exciting year in 1958. We became aware that the District was to be split into a Mill City RD and Detroit RD [on the Willamette NF]. Everything north of the reservoir, the

Breitenbush drainage, and of course the Little North Fork area would become the Mill City RD with headquarters in Mill City. There was much anxiety about this. In those days there was no employee or public involvement in the decision-making process. Some employees had a choice of which District they wished to be assigned to. I was definitely going to stay with Detroit. We thought it would be unusual that the Detroit Ranger Station would be on the Mill City RD. There were discussions and humor about splitting up tools, vehicles, supplies, horses, etc. In one morning discussion at the warehouse, the subject came up that there was only one *Ranger saddle*. How was that to be shared? Before thinking about who might be offended, I suggested there was no problem - all we had to do was get a couple of half-assed Rangers.

Frank TerBush   *TerBush worked for the Bureau of Land Managment and the Western Forest Industry Association before coming to work for the Umpua NF in 1960. He was a Regeneration Specialist and Silviculturalist. He was in Research in the Washington Office when he retired in 1980.*

Vondis Miller was Supervisor of the Umpqua NF (1954-1965) in Roseburg, Oregon. He personified everything admirable in the Forest Service (personable, thoughtful and intelligent).

My desk was just outside his door, which was seldom closed. He began each day by checking the incoming mail (possible then, improbable now). Vondis disposed of much of it by tossing it into the wastebasket. He was skilled at turning a colorful phrase. I recall once hearing a particularly heavy thump and looked up. Vondis looked over, grinned, and said, "Frank, much of this stuff should never have come across the plains." Thus did he relieve the burden of WO paperwork on himself and his subordinates. I wonder if his successors are able to follow his good example!

"The environmental movement of the seventies began to loom large on the Forest Service agenda and my job took a sharp turn."

-Ron Walters

CHAPTER FIVE

1970 to 1992 THE ENVIRONMENT, PLANNING and PUBLIC INVOLVEMENT

Environmental analysis and public involvement became major activities as a vocal public expressed strong opinions as to how the Forests should be managed and the Region responded to the National Environmental Policy Act and other environmentally based legislation enacted in the late 1960s. A variety of specialists in the natural resource sciences were hired to accommodate the need for a more regimented environmental analysis for project work. Emphasis was placed on hiring full-time employees, reducing the agency's reliance on a strong core of seasonal employees, and the number of women and minorities increased.

The uniqueness of special areas in Region Six landscapes was formally recognized by the creation of National Recreation Areas, National Scenic Areas, and National Volcanic Monuments. The National Forest Management Act mandated Forest-wide planning, involving a large segment of the workforce, and changing how the Forest Service does business.

Workloads and accompanying budgets remained strong in the first half of this period, but began to decline in the latter half. Recreation improvements were focused on the special areas and timber sales began to look different, with standing green and dead trees left in cutover areas. Social programs, such as the Jobs Corp and the Young Adult Conservation Corps became integral parts of Forest and Ranger District operations, and computers and other electronic systems began to change the way the Region did business.

In the midst of all the change, Mount St. Helens erupted, the Region experienced another major insect infestation, and wildfire continued to take its toll. Stories in this chapter describe these events and activities, and also share the camaraderie of a hunting adventure and a horse trip deep into country without roads.

This chapter includes stories about All in a Day's Work, Wives and Families, Horses and Mules, Fire, Grazing, Recreation, Timber, Research, Land and Resource Management Planning, and Administration.

ALL IN A DAY'S WORK: "In the early 1970s, the Ranger District had totally outgrown its office. We had people working out of one residence and one floor of the warehouse."

<u>Gordon Jesse Walker</u> *Walker worked 31 years on the Rogue River NF, mostly as a packer. He retired in 1983. He wrote and published several books about packing mules and horses and about his Forest Service experiences, including <u>Load 'Em Up, Tie 'Em Down</u>, and <u>Six Years with a Government Mule</u>.*

One year, about Christmas, [Harv Seeley, Forest Supervisor of the Rogue River NF], and I got together in his office and picked a date to inspect the Pacific Crest Trail. The days would be the 22nd, 23rd, and 24th of August 1973. I felt mighty important that day as we sat there making plans for a trip so far in advance. One thing for sure, every activity between then and later would fit around these three days, not in them. On Wednesday, August 22, we headed east from Red Blanket trailhead toward the Sky Lakes country. Harv rode Spook; I rode Patches, and of course, Big Red tagged along behind with his big ears flopping, carrying about 200 pounds of things we needed.

We covered the first two miles rather quickly. The stock clattered across two or three narrow bridges and their shoes caused clanging sounds as we passed over rocky areas. Pumice dust rose from our horses' feet and caused us to squint our eyes and breathe with our mouths closed. The trail was built along the mountainside and around, in, and out of sharp little ravines, some of which had a stream of water cascading down across the trail. The timber was indeed tall. To our left, we could pick out a green-on-white park boundary sign nailed on a tree.

Now and then, the trail passed through a rocky cliff, a perfect place for yellow jackets to build their nests and I told Harv to watch out. About three miles up trail, we started across one of these sites. Spook stopped by a ledge of rock for just a moment. He had bumped against a loose slab of rock and riled up a nest of the yellow beasts. I saw them boil up and shouted at Harv to take off and move out. The nest was right under Spook's belly. I couldn't get past Harv and Spook and it was nearly impossible to turn around and take off down the trail. The nest literally exploded. The last I saw was a yellow mass about two feet across and Spook started moving out with Harv riding like a veteran.

I pushed Big Red out of my way. Patches was beginning to get the message. The big horse plunged off the trail down the mountainside with long, high jumps. Yellow jackets were beginning to make their point. Big Red caught about 20 or 30 somewhere around his britchen and lower belly. Patches was being stung some place because his mouth was open and his eyes were as big as saucers. He carried me down the steep hill for about 70 feet and then jumped a downed tree about four feet high. He was kicking and bucking by now and, to say the least, it was nip-and-tuck to stay in the saddle.

I had been bucked off before, real hard too, but no government horse had enough to him to get the job done. The only time I ever left the saddle was when one turned over with me. Anyhow, when Patches jumped the log, two yellow jackets stung me in the back on my neck. Now, I am allergic to bee stings. The last time I got stung, my body swelled up about one-half inch deep all over. Immediately, I took a pill to counteract the poison.

I told Harv about what might happen. He really got concerned and kept close watch on me. He was perfectly willing to stop the trip, call in a helicopter and take me out, but I assured him everything was OK. The worst thing that happened was that I fell asleep in the saddle somewhere on the Oregon desert and never came to for several miles. Harv's voice finally woke me.

That night, we made camp at the west edge of Cliff Lake in Seven Lakes Basin, about two hours before dark. I unpacked Big Red while Harv unsaddled Spook. We were the only ones at the lake that night. It took me about a half hour to pile the saddles and rigging at the spot where my bed would be and take the horses and Big Red up the mountainside to a nice little hidden meadow.

441

The smell of the campfire smoke reached my nostrils. The aroma of fresh boiled coffee filled the air. Soon, I was at Harv's side watching as he moved from one side of the fire to the other, preparing our meal. Harv is the best camp cook I've ever camped with.

After supper, we talked and enjoyed a sip from the little jug he pulled from his saddlebags. The evening was beautiful. The moonless sky shone with stars, their brightness reflected in the waters of the lake, with the shimmering light from our campfire being dominant.

Next thing I knew, Harv was starting a morning fire. My bed felt so good, and I was in no mood to get up. However, here was the Forest Supervisor already up and ready to go. I was supposed to be tough, but here was the proving ground. So, nothing else to do but roll out, put on my hat, haul on my pants and meet the day with a big fake grin on my face.

Harv greeted me with a hearty "Good Morning" and we set about pulling loose ends together. I went up to look over our horses and mule. It was sort of dark and I had to watch my step in a place or two. Patches nickered and Big Red snorted when I walked up. They stood still as I put on their halters and coiled up the stake ropes.

Harv was working busily around the flames preparing breakfast. The smell of boiling coffee and frying bacon dominated all other odors. I sorted out the different smells coming to me from Harv's breakfast fire and one began to stand out above all the others. It was potatoes, eggs and a little onion mixed in for flavor. Harv had put plates out and had poured me a cup of coffee. He was stirring a frying pan filled with the most wonderful breakfast I have ever seen! The potatoes and eggs were approaching a golden brown. Boy, did they smell good! Harv kept asking if he should call them done, and didn't seem to pay any attention each time I told him yes.

Harv moved the pan toward the edge of our rock ring fire and gripped the handle a little tighter. Suddenly, the most awful thing happened right before my eyes. The collapsable handle released. The pan tipped forward and spilled its contents into the fire. We both stared in unbelief and it took a moment for the sad truth to register. Harv was the first to break the silence with, "Oh God, I think I'll cry." Quickly, he handed me the nearly empty pan and said, "You take what stuck to the bottom." He grabbed a fork and started stabbing some of the chunks that hadn't been consumed by the fire. After the impact of the initial shock wore off, we had a good laugh, ate what few other things we had prepared and broke camp.

That night, it started raining about an hour before dark and we had to hit the sack to stay dry. The next day, we rode from Island Lake to Highway 140 where a truck was waiting for me, and Harv's wife was there to pick him up.

Stephen Kelley *Kelley received his permanent appointment in 1965. He worked on the Wallowa-Whitman, Umatilla, Mt. Hood and Colville NFs in R-6. He was in Land Management Planning in the Washington Office, and was Forest Supervisor of the Huron-Manistee NFs in R-9 when he retired in 1997.*

During the summer of 1973, I was dispatched as Maps and Records Officer to the Rocky Fire on the Barlow District of the Mt. Hood NF. At that time I did not know of the many challenges and opportunities that this Ranger District would hold for me. Halloween, October 28, 1973, I became District Ranger for the Barlow District.

As expected, I knew the District would have a tremendous amount of fire rehabilitation to accomplish during that fall and the next spring. However, upon my arrival I found that the District also had another major undertaking before June 1974 - the establishment of a 50-person, coeducational, residential, contract Youth Conservation Corps (YCC) camp. This was to be the first camp of its type in the Region.

One of several reasons that Barlow District was selected for this camp was that a previously used logging camp (Camp Cody) was located on the District. The existing buildings were to be used to *quickly* and *efficiently* establish a YCC camp and begin operation of the program. Unfortunately, two events had occurred that the District would have to overcome in order to have the YCC camp up and running by its scheduled opening in June.

The first of these events occurred during the Rocky Fire - all the existing buildings at Camp Cody burned to the ground leaving only traces of their previous existence. The planned-on facilities were no longer available for use. The weather also decided to play a role in the process. On Halloween day Dufur experienced an unusual snowstorm and approximately 12 to 14 inches of snow fell and stayed throughout the winter. We were not able to visit the YCC campsite or do any construction until early spring.

Needless to say, there was a lot of hand-wringing (most of it mine) as to how we were to have the camp and program ready for 50 enthusiastic students in less than six months. There was a multitude of tasks to be completed. Sleeping, bathing and mess facilities had to be provided for the students and contract staff. Recreation facilities and conservation programs had to be developed to meet YCC objectives. Property, such as cooking equipment, lockers, linens, cots/bunks, canoes and other recreational equipment also had to be acquired.

Luck smiled on me when I became the Barlow Ranger. There was an abundance of very talented and dedicated District employees who decided the YCC program would be successful. They quickly decided that many *normal* approval processes would have to be forgone in order to successfully open in June. As an example, the process of design, review, redesign, and approval would not expedite construction of the facilities needed at the camp and that process needed to be modified.

Construction of the mess hall was one example. I remember Merle Marshall and Jack Archer proposing that Jack construct the mess hall using the assistance of other district employees. Jack's an excellent carpenter and he led construction of the mess hall with its design coming after construction of the building. This was only one of several buildings that Jack constructed in this manner for the YCC program that year. This building was dedicated at camp opening and became known as the *House that Jack Built*. This approach also occurred with respect to county approval of the septic system. Suffice it to say that you should never look for the drain fields based on the approved Wasco County plans.

Another significant task was the acquisition of all equipment and supplies needed to operate a large camp and its associated programs. Following a lengthy security clearance process, Lou Waikart received military approval to enter any military base and acquire surplus equipment needed for the camp. In addition to fully equipping Camp Cody, Lou also secured much needed equipment for many District workshops on the Mt. Hood.

Cody YCC Camp was successfully opened in June 1974. The facility and program developed by the District folks in that short period of time successfully served the YCC program for many years.

<u>Wendall Jones</u> *Jones was a District Ranger on the Siuslaw NF at the time of this story.*

In the early 1970s, the Hebo Ranger District had totally outgrown its office. We had people working out of one residence and one floor of the warehouse. The building program appeared to be years away. In discussions with Millard Mitchell, Angell Job Corps Director, he was very interested in having his folks take on this job. So he and I started getting support behind plans, designs, and funding. Mitch did not accept *nos* to his requests. Supervisor Tenny Moore was a strong supporter of the Job Corps program.

So we put together an effort to have the Angell carpentry program re-set, to have crews come to Hebo to work on the office, staying in the old Ranger residence and eating at local restaurants. There was foot-dragging by union carpenters, but they had difficulty saying no to Mitch. There was some grumbling from Engineers and Architects, but we had good cooperation from Regional Architect Joe Mastrandrea. The job developed so rapidly that the Job Corps was pouring foundations before the office design was 100% complete and approved. The lead carpenter from Angell was very good to work with. He didn't put up with the grumbling of other union carpenter staff. I think what helped most on the completion of this project was that Millard Mitchell was a 300-pound plus ex-football lineman. He was difficult for anyone to say *no* to.

The end product was a beautiful office and a significantly modified Ranger Station. We dedicated the office in 1974 with Senator Mark Hatfield as the guest speaker. Also participating were Regional Forester Ted Schlapfer, the Job Corps Director, Forest Supervisor and State and County Representatives. The formal dedication was followed by a big feed and a keg at our house with all of the District

Angell Job Corps crew constructing a Ranger Station building,
Siuslaw NF – 1976

Interpreter Joe Meade with visitors at the Lava Lands Visitor Center,
Deschutes NF – 1978

folks, Job Corps folks, and the Regional Forester and new Forest Supervisor Dale Robertson joining in.

Avon Denham *Denham began work on the Montezuma NF in R-2 beginning in the late 1920s. He worked in the R-5 Regional Office, and in Washington DC and was the Assistant Regional Forester for Range and Wildlife Management in the R-6 RO when he retired in 1966.*

Some 15 years ago (mid-1970s), while we were hunting elk in the Wanaha area, we were returning to camp at almost dark. Wright Mallery and Jimmy Wilkins signaled to Al Oard and me, who had just climbed out of a very deep canyon, of some elk grazing on a hill just ahead of us. I had the only scope on my gun so I tried to look through my scope to see if they were bulls. It took some time to get breath enough to hold a gun fairly steady. I finally saw that they were both bulls, one a spike and the bigger bull at least a five-pointer.

The shooting then started, and after several shots, the big bull went down and the other acted like it was wounded. We gathered ourselves and took off to where the elk were last seen. When we arrived some 15 to 20 minutes later, the big bull was dead as a mackerel and was on his back under a windfall. All you could see was feet and horns.

Mallery rushed in and shot the dead elk between the eyes, practically blowing the horns off his head. I asked Mallery why he shot the dead elk and ruined my trophy, to which he said, "I gave him the Coup de Grace." From then on, that area was known, and I hope that it still is, the Coup de Grace Ridge.

Rolf Anderson *Anderson started as a temporary in 1954 and received a permanent appointment in 1958. He worked on the Lewis and Clark NF in R-1, and the Olympic, Umpqua, Willamette, Malheur, and Siuslaw NFs in R-6. He was District Ranger on the Sweet Home Ranger District, Willamette NF when he retired in 1998.*

I was the Area Ranger on the Oregon Dunes National Recreation Area (ODNRA), Siuslaw NF, in the mid-1970s. The ODNRA runs from Florence to Coos Bay between the Pacific Ocean and Highway 101. It is only about 30,000 acres in size, but the small area is packed with home- and landowners, off-road vehicle users, and people looking for a pristine, natural coastal dunes experience.

The ODNRA had only been in existence for a few years when I was there, and one of our major programs was to sort out the land holdings. The legislation that established the ODNRA drew a line running roughly north and south, splitting the area about half-way between the ocean and the highway. The ODNRA was directed to acquire all of the private lands on the ocean side of the line, either by negotiation with willing sellers or by condemnation. The property east of the line and towards the highway could only be acquired if the owner wanted to sell. Condemnation was not an option, thus the owner could continue to own property and live within the boundaries of the ODNRA.

In addition, the entire area within the ODNRA came under standards for construction and maintenance of structures and for landscaping, to ensure the continuation of an overall natural outdoors environment - the reason the ODNRA was established. Needless to say, this created a lot of unrest and uncertainty among landowners.

Two individuals who owned homes and large parcels of land within the ODNRA near the Hauser area were quite uncomfortable. They were within the non-condemnation area, but didn't like the presence of the government and didn't like being held to building and landscaping standards. One of them wanted to build a golf course on his property. Even though a golf course is in an outdoor setting, we didn't think the proposed large expanses of groomed fairways and greens fit the natural environment criteria. The other landowner wanted the right to build a new structure to whatever standard he felt appropriate, notwithstanding the ODNRA standards.

We went round and round with these two landowners. They attended and participated in some of our advisory council meetings addressing the golf course proposal and other property standard issues. They phoned and dropped by the office to state and restate their opinions. The previous Area Ranger, Jerry Hutchins, had set the standard to always document conversations and meetings with all landowners. We would write up who said what, and send the notes to the landowners for verification. Because of the ever-present threat of a lawsuit we wanted as clear a record as possible. These two landowners didn't like that, either. Once they came into my office unannounced and made a great show of setting up and turning on a tape recorder. I'm not sure why, but they were probably attempting to intimidate me. They never did send me a transcript.

One day in the winter of 1976, the Coos County Planning Department held a public meeting to air a number of proposed zoning changes throughout the county. One agenda item was requested by one of the above mentioned property owners. I don't recall the specifics, but I don't think we thought it was a request we should be too concerned about. Nevertheless, since it was within the ODNRA boundary, I decided to attend the meeting to see if there was any reaction from the county or the general public.

I arrived right before the meeting started. There were a number of agenda items, so the room was full. I spied one vacant seat, right in the center of a row in the middle of the room. I edged my way past those who were already seated and sat down. As is usual with those kind of meetings, the chairs were set up too close together so I was rubbing shoulders with the folks on each side of me.

I started to look around, to see if I recognized anyone in the room. Boy, did I! As I looked to my right, the person to my right looked at me. It was the wife of one of the ODNRA property owners! And he was sitting next to her. Her eyebrows shot up! I'm sure mine did, too! But she took the next step. She gasped, "It's you!" Then, in one motion, she raised her purse off her lap and swung it at me. It thumped into my shoulder and upper chest. She then jumped up, pushed past me and left the room. Her husband showed no reaction at all. Maybe it happened too fast for it to register on him. My first thought was, *Assault of a Federal Officer!* Then I turned my attention to the meeting, as by then it was underway.

Nothing more happened that night. Eventually one of the property owners did sue us, taking it to the point of collecting depositions. By the time I gave my deposition, I was on another Forest and lost track of what was going on. To my knowledge the Coos Bay planning meeting incident was never mentioned again.

John Marker   *Marker started as a temporary in 1955, and received a permanent appointment in 1959. He worked on the Allegheny NF in R- 7, the Shasta-Trinity, Sierra, and Sequoia NFs in R-5, and the Rogue River NF in R-6. He worked in Regional Offices in R-4 and R-5, and in the Washington Office. He was the Director of Public Affairs for R-6 when he retired in 1992.*

In 1977 National Forest Roadless Areas were a hot topic of public cussing and discussion. What had started out in the early 1970s as a simple inventory of areas in the National Forests without developed road systems that might be eligible for Wilderness consideration had developed into a full-scale political *dust up* between those for and against more wilderness. By 1977, the Forest Service was engaged in what was called *RARE II*, a second look at the first look at unroaded areas. And the second time around was creating a much louder and more intense public debate than the first exercise.

I was the Public Affairs Officer on the Rogue River NF in 1977 working for Forest Supervisor Don Smith, and had the task of managing the Forest's public involvement role in the RARE II exercise. It was an assignment that thrilled me about as much as a yellow jacket sting. However, with the stellar counsel of Supervisor Smith encouraging me, I, like a good forest officer, did what needed to be done with great skill and good humor. I was also aided in my task by the equally stellar wisdom of the Regional Office.

To add excitement to the project, there was a growing controversy over a piece of roadless land called the Red Buttes, astride the Siskiyou Mountains, the boundary between the Rogue and Klamath NFs and California and Oregon. As the debate over the Red Buttes intensified, the opposing sides recruited high visibility supporters from more distant areas. We were getting a lot of media coverage from Seattle to Los Angeles about the roadless issue in general and Red Buttes, specifically.

As the drumbeats over the buttes and the roadless inventory process increased public attention, folks in the Washington Office decided that one of the major public involvement sessions attended by high-level forest officers would be held in the Rogue Valley. As the planning for this event got under way, I was very happy to have the stellar

450

leadership of both Forest Supervisor Smith and the RO to help with this event which had the potential to become a three-ring circus. And I was even more thankful to have Art DuFault, Assistant Director of the Regional Public Affairs Office become my RO buddy.

Art and I had Rangered together on the Sequoia National Forest in R-5 and had shared many experiences while helping hordes of southern Californians enjoy their national forest without tearing either the forest or themselves apart in the process. But even more important to me was Art's training and experience in dealing with high visibility events. And our *big deal* event was beginning to show indications of such high visibility.

We learned that Max Peterson, Deputy Chief of the Forest Service, would be taking part in the public involvement event, which meant that we definitely had a *big deal* developing. We increased our estimate of people who would want to take part in the public involvement gathering and arranged for meeting space at Southern Oregon State College (now Southern Oregon State University) and brought their event management staff into the meeting preparations.

During one of our planning meetings the subject of security came up. While we expected people with strong opinions to be involved in the presentations, I hadn't given much serious thought to the possibility of any negative behavior beyond loud voices and people ignoring comment time limits. But security people encouraged me to think of other scenarios, some not very nice.

They reminded us we had a major national FS leader taking part in the event, and for some people this would be a grand opportunity to make a major statement, especially if the media coverage was heavy. I had left California only a short time ago and thought I had left all of the nastiness behind. This was Oregon, the mellow state, the state where you were supposed to visit, leave your money and go home - unless you were one of the chosen.

So we cranked up our planning and included discussions with the Jackson County Sheriff and City of Ashland Police. Our public involvement event was becoming something more than just a few people coming in to discuss the use of some National Forest land.

451

But as we talked, it became very clear that our objective should be to eliminate the chances of mischief making and stress the civility of the gathering. However, *just because you're paranoid doesn't mean someone isn't following you* became part of our check-list. The people in the security business reminded us that Oregon did have some individuals capable of stirring up mischief similar to what had taken place on the Berkeley campus and other locations during the Vietnam conflict. Some people were starting to use some of these tactics to draw attention to environmental issues.

As we worked toward the meeting, one issue we paid special attention to was Max's well being. No one thought that there was a major threat to his personal safety, but there was a risk someone could try to do something like throw a pie or some other similar item at him as an attention grabber. So we agreed that several of us would stay very close to him during the event, and college security would take special interest in his well-being while he was in the auditorium.

Finally, the big event took place on a fine August evening, and the public did turn out in sizable numbers. The meeting went well, only a few people tried to create any kind of a scene, and the few incidents were handled with great skill by the meeting moderator and security. At the conclusion, people who had been working the event, including Art and I, thought it might be *Miller time*. After saying thanks to people who had given us so much good help, it was time to leave. Art and I had one more task, to make sure Max got to his motel without difficulty. We headed toward the parking lot with Max not far behind visiting with several Forest Service people.

Suddenly Art looked around and said to me, "Where's Max?" I looked around and he sure wasn't where he was supposed to be, and had been a couple of seconds ago. No, that's silly! Nobody is going to steal a Deputy Chief, but where is he? Well, all of the FS people with us immediately started to search the parking lot and backtrack to the auditorium. Art and I looked at each other and shook our heads. There hadn't been any sign of the *nasty* people at the meeting, and security intelligence reports gave no indication of any serious mischief, but at the moment we had a missing Deputy Chief.

Wilderness Planners Dick Buscher, Archie Mills, and Ralph Kimmerly in the
proposed Alpine Lakes Wilderness, Wenatchee NF – 1972

Hotshot fire crew hiking a fireline, Ochoco NF – 1976

To add to our uneasiness, someone said he had seen Max get into a car with several men. The level of paranoia spiked. People came back from the auditorium and reported no sign of him. We were ready to sound the alarm that we had lost Max. Where in the world had he gone? I didn't want to let my paranoia get the best of me, but it was.

We were about to call law enforcement people with a missing person report, and alert the FS hierarchy of the missing deputy when an old friend of Max walked up and asked if Max had left. When told he was missing, we were assured he wasn't missing, but had gone off with a several old friends for a short visit. This individual bearing the information, who will remain nameless, had been asked by Max to tell us of his plans and forgot to.

Now it was definitely *Miller time*, and the next day off for a *vacation* on the Forks and Marble Cone Fires in California.

F. Dale Robertson *Robertson joined the Forest Service in 1961. He worked on the Deschutes NF in R-6, in Texas and Oklahoma, in the Washington Office and was Forest Supervisor on the Siuslaw and Mt. Hood NFs in R-6. He was the twelfth Chief of the Forest Service serving from 1987 to 1993.*

This story happened while I was the Forest Supervisor of Mt. Hood NF in the late 1970s. When I arrived at work one Monday morning, all our employees were standing out in the parking lot. No one was going inside. I was told that there had been a bomb scare and that the Federal Protective Police were inside looking for a bomb!

After some time waiting outside, the police came out and asked all of the employees to go into the building and quickly look around their office surroundings to see if they could see anything suspicious. They were then to return to the parking lot.

Like all the other employees, I followed their instructions. When I checked my office I was surprised to see a large grocery bag with the top folded over sitting right in the middle of my desk. I immediately reported this to the police. A couple of employees overheard my report and the news quickly spread among the employees that the

Forest Supervisor had a bomb on his desk! You can imagine the kind of excitement this created!

The police went back inside and very carefully lifted the grocery bag off of my desk and inched it out of the building with minimum disturbance. Once they had it in a safe place in the parking lot, with all the employees looking on from a distance, the police ripped open the bag and ----- out popped a woman's bathing suit! This created quite a stir among the employees!

Here's how that mysterious bag and its contents appeared on my desk. Over the weekend our Fire Staff Officer John Wilson and his wife Bonna hosted a pot luck and swim party at his house for the Mt. Hood staff, celebrating the end of the fire season. My wife happened to leave her bathing suit at the Wilson's house after the party. John had a trip to the Barlow Ranger District scheduled for Monday and being an *old-timer*, John believed in being at a Ranger Station when District employees came to work. So, he left the Supervisor's Office very early that Monday morning in order to be in Dufur by 8:00 am and that is when he left the bathing suit on my desk.

As it turned out, the bomb scare was generated by one of our summer employees who got a kick out of seeing all the commotion. The chances of having the one and only bomb scare on the Mt. Hood NF on the very morning that John left my wife's bathing suit in a grocery bag on my desk were indeed very slim - but it happened and the employees got a big laugh out of it!

Donna Short *Short received a permanent appointment in 1979 on the Umpqua NF. She was responsible for Botany, Fisheries, Heritage, Public Affairs, Timber Sale Planning, and Wildlife on the Sweet Home Ranger District on the Willamette NF in 2005.*

On December 2, 1979, I started work for the Forest Service at the Steamboat Ranger District on the Umpqua NF as a planning forester. I had spent the last year and a half working for Georgia-Pacific in Cottage Grove for a blatantly discriminatory manager. The Forest Service job seemed like one that would better utilize my forestry training and had more career potential.

I was also the first female field forester on the Ranger District. Looking back from the 21st century it is strange to think about how I was charting new territory at the time. George Moyers, the District silviculturist, was my supervisor and seemed quite interested in mentoring new employees regardless of gender. He asked me to shadow Alan Ward, the other Planner, to help me figure out what timber sale planning was all about. I also started working with Lou Wolf and Larry Barlow on the tree improvement program.

It wasn't long before I felt like I wasn't really being all that helpful following Alan around. George agreed and assigned me a sale area all my own. On my part there was also a feeling that I needed to prove I could do the job. I learned a lot that first year and most of my colleagues were very supportive. I did have a small issue with the Ranger calling me *honey* but I wasn't quite sure what to do about it at the time.

It was a good time. We were living 40 miles from town on the North Umpqua River, one of the most beautiful rivers in Oregon. We had bought our first home, a mobile one planted on the Forest Service compound, but it was still ours. I was making new friends. The women of the compound formed a softball team and we played the women from Toketee several times over the summer. It was a good way to get to know the wives. Even though I was married at the time, it was still a new circumstance having a young woman out in the woods with their husbands. At District social functions I made sure I found topics that I could discuss with the wives to help ease the situation.

In early October, the District hired a second female forester named Beth Willhite to work in small sales. We would soon find that we had a lot in common. Later that month I found out that I was pregnant. I needed to tell George but for at least a week I tried to find the words or right way to start the conversation and couldn't. And I didn't usually have trouble talking to anyone about anything! Finally I decided that I should put my writing and new NEPA skills to work. So I wrote a very short Environmental Assessment Report. It read:

Project: Steamboat Population Expansion
Affected Environment: Foucht House

456

Expected Impact: Addition of one small human
Date of Expected Impact: June 5 (give or take a week)
Management Requirements and Constraints: No effect on ability to recon until size becomes a factor in balance and agility. Should be able to continue other responsibilities until due date unless doctor orders otherwise.
Consultation with Others: Eric M. Foucht was consulted

I put the paper on George's desk then went back to mine and tried to concentrate. A few minutes later he came by and said, "It will probably be late." That was it. Then he headed to that day's staff meeting. When he returned he gave me back the EA with the Ranger's signature under FOSI (Finding of Significant Impact) and related the following:

"I started by saying that I had some news - Donna is pregnant and is due the first week of June. The Ranger said, 'Oh, great'. Then Woody Coates (the TMA) spoke up and said 'Well I have some news too. Beth is pregnant and is due the last week of May!'"

I can't remember what George said after that probably because Beth's news was so unexpected I didn't really hear what he said.

Now we were really charting new territory but what a blessing it was to be doing it together. Beth and I were able to share the changes and challenges of our pregnancies in a way that our male colleagues could not do. We were both committed to working in the field as long as possible, which we did into our ninth month. We had our baby shower together. We were due exactly a week apart and our children were each born two days early exactly a week apart with the whole District cheering for us.

Three years later history repeated itself. By this time I was working in small sales and didn't even bother trying to start the conversation. I just wrote a Sale Area Improvement and KV Collection Plan!

<u>Bob Tokarczyk</u> *Tokarczyk started as a temporary on the Umpqua NF in 1948 and received a permanent appointment on the Gifford Pinchot NF in 1952. He worked on the Siskiyou, Willamette and Deschutes NFs, and was Forest Supervisor of*

the Gifford Pinchot NF when Mount St. Helens erupted. He retired in 1983.

Several days after the eruption of Mount St. Helens I received a call early in the morning from someone aboard President Jimmy Carter's Air Force One airplane. They said the President and his entourage were enroute to Washington State to view the damage caused by the eruption, the plane was in the air somewhere over the Mississippi River and could we host the President in about three hours? I said we could and had space for his group.

Twenty to thirty minutes later several Secret Service personnel arrived in the Gifford Pinchot NF Supervisor's Office and proceeded to start covering the office windows with paper and talking to my employees. I immediately phoned the Regional Forester Dick Worthington and asked that he come over to assist in our welcoming President Jimmy Carter and his staff at our Vancouver office. Three hours later Dick Worthington and I welcomed President Carter and his many staff, along with Dixie Lee Ray, Governor of Washington and the Governors of Idaho and Oregon.

My staff and I proceeded to brief the President on the many activities which were occurring because of the active volcano. I took him up to the War Room where we were monitoring radio activity with our plane over the volcano and the rescue activity which was in process. I started to lead the group into a different room when I was tapped on the shoulder by a Secret Service agent who whispered to me that the President always walks through the door first. I didn't realize there was a photographer inside the doorway. I stepped aside.

After four or five hours of briefing, the President and his team headed for the Marriott Hotel in Portland and as they left they asked if I could be available to act as a guide for a helicopter flight to the volcano the next morning. Of course I agreed. President Carter left his tan raincoat, that he carried over his shoulder, in my office. My secretary, Penny Hiatt, suggested we should cut it up in small squares and sell them as souvenirs for $5.00 apiece, but I returned his raincoat the next day.

The next morning I arrived at PDX and was asked to sit opposite President Carter in the big Huey chopper with the red phone and all.

On board we had the Governor of Washington, the Governor of Idaho and the Air Force officer who accompanies the President. We all had headphones, but after Governor Ray demanded federal funds over and over again, the President tapped my knee and said his headphone didn't work, so that meant I was the only source of communication to him. They took us to Kelso with a stop at a middle school then on to the volcano. His staff followed in a Chinook helicopter. We flew over Spirit Lake where I had to instruct the President's pilot to turn around because of low clouds and poor visibility as he wanted to fly farther than was deemed safe.

We later landed in Portland and President Carter was on the news that night explaining our Red Zone and how the Forest Service was managing the volcano and public safety. He stated the *superintendent* would make adjustments for public safety as needed.

Jim Bull *Bull started as a temporary in 1958, and received a permanent appointment in 1962. He worked on the Siuslaw and Deschutes NFs, and was District Ranger on the Mt. Adams Ranger District of the Gifford Pinchot NF when he retired in 1995.*

It was a lovely spring morning in 1980. My wife and I were still in bed enjoying our second cup of coffee while watching *Sunday Morning*. Along with the songs of birds, the sound of our son Gary shooting hoops wafted through the open windows.

The sound of the bouncing basketball stopped and a moment later the back door burst open and our son came running down the hallway saying, "Dad, Mom, come look. There's some monstrous storm clouds and lightning heading toward the mountain." We got up and went to the front porch and got our first glimpse of the huge ash cloud that resulted from the explosive eruption of Mount St. Helens. A quick dash to the remote base radio in the kitchen to turn up the volume and the constant radio traffic confirmed that an eruption had occurred.

At the Mt. Adams District, we, along with all other Gifford Pinchot NF employees, had been aware of the increased levels of seismic activity centered on Mount St. Helens for the previous six or seven weeks. Dave Gibney, Jr., Resource Assistant at Mt. Adams, had spent many hours in aerial reconnaissance of the mountain flying with

459

George Woodruff, the contractor for aerial detection flights out of Trout Lake. Local snowmobilers, including my family and me, and fellow employee Jim Massey, had observed one or more small ash plumes from the Sawtooth Berryfields while enjoying the snow-covered hills that winter. And Trout Lake, as did most communities within a 50-mile radius of Mount St. Helens, had experienced at least one dusting of fine ash particles in that time.

By the time I got dressed, grabbed a bite to eat and got to the office, a verbal order had gone out to keep everyone from entering the Forest. The dispatcher had sent fire patrols to the three major access points from the Trout Lake side and was lining up people for two others. The engineering zone in Willard had been contacted and the two southern access points were about to be covered. By 10:00 am or so, a copy of the formal closure order was faxed to the District and copies made for posting.

I took several copies, along with orange traffic cones, road closed signs, and some wooden barricades from the barn and headed over Guler Mountain to deliver them to the zone employees at the two entry points in the Little White Salmon River drainage. As I came to the viewpoint on the northwest side of Guler Mountain, I was able to see for the first time the immensity of the ash cloud. By now it covered the entire northern horizon from its source to well east of Mt. Adams. It looked like a huge head of cauliflower, a mixture of blacks, grays, and dark blues and purples accentuated by flashes of lightning. And I had taken off without my camera!

As the day wore on, many people stopped at the roadblocks on their way *out* of the forest. Fishing season had opened and both Goose and Mosquito Lakes were popular early season destinations. Greg Meyer, proprietor of Trout Lake Grocery, had been at Mosquito Lake and told of finding himself in a boat in the middle of the lake with mud balls up to the size of a softball landing all around him. He and a couple of others beat a hasty retreat to shore, loaded up their gear and headed to town as fast as they could. His eyes, when he was relating this to me a couple of days later, were still as big as saucers.

In my then 18 years of experience with the Forest Service, I had experienced closures of various kinds, including those associated with the cancellation of hunting season. But never had I envisioned the immensity of closing down the Forest to **ALL users, 24 hours a day, for an indeterminate period of time.**

As I recall we had 10 to 12 principle access points to the Forest. Getting each of those points established as a roadblock, properly signed and staffed with two employees on a 24-hour basis was the first chore. In addition there were patrols out at night. As a result of that effort it was quickly learned that there were at least 12 to 15 *wheel track* access points, several from adjoining ownerships. More than two weeks passed contacting those owners, letting them know we were going to *tank trap* those roads and lining up contractors with equipment to accomplish the task.

Establishing a standard gate design, then ordering and installing gates at all the points followed this effort. Once installed, this eliminated the need for a graveyard shift at the main access points. But most of the Mt. Adams District was in the *Blue Zone* and gates still needed to be open from 5:30 am to 8:00 pm to check in and out contractor employees who opted to continue working on various contracts on the Forest along with our own force account crews. Once this operation was standardized the Forest was spending about $25,000.00 per day just to restrict access.

Additional temporary employees were hired as gate guards and patrols. FEMA supplied three singlewide trailers and the necessary wiring, plumbing and septic tanks, and drain fields were installed to provide additional housing. With the Young Adult Conservation Corps (YACC) members and staff, total employment at Mt. Adams approached 250 at the peak of the season, a level not seen before or since.

To be sure, it wasn't business as usual. Operating guidelines for work in the *Blue Zone* (operations were limited to equipment removal only in the *Red Zone*) required a contractual relationship, increased communications capabilities, entry permits limited to daylight hours, pre-defined travel routes, and in the case of FS employees, a three day supply of rations, water and face masks for all crew members.

461

Establishing all this protocol was one thing; communicating it to the whole range of contractors, permittees and all other forest users became the next hurdle. Meetings were scheduled with timber sale purchasers to outline the options for extensions or operation, and if the latter was chosen, the conditions under which operations could be conducted. Similar meetings were arranged for planting, thinning and timber stand exam contractors. Having the only grazing allotments on the Forest, I also had to meet with the three C&H permittees to outline how things would have to work that summer. However, it was a tough call to the sheep permittee. Because of the *no overnight stay* requirement, there would be no sheep permit that year.

Another tough meeting was with the twin Lloyd brothers, Darryl and Darvel. They had been operating The Mount Adams Institute out of the Flying L Ranch in Glenwood for over ten years. The institute provided outdoor and environmental education through excursions into the Mount Adams Wilderness. And the Mount Adams Wilderness, along with Goat Rocks Wilderness, was in the *Red Zone*, where no operations could be conducted. These areas were included in the *Red Zone* not because of imminent danger like the approximately 12 - initially 20 - mile radius around Mount St. Helens, but because of the difficulty in communicating an emergency situation to users and the travel times needed to leave the area if such an emergency arose. Canceling the Lloyd's Special Use Permit doomed the Institute and it never recovered.

One of the first briefings on the overall situation included a statement by Fire Staff Officer Paul Stenkamp that "there was fire everywhere" north and east of the mountain and because of the ash cloud no estimate of acreage burning was possible. A decision was made to establish a fire camp at Trout Lake because of the private air strip used for aerial detection and the availability of an old re-load site on DNR lands with both electricity and phone lines present. Soon the first overhead team of many started their tour of *Volcano Fire* duty. The YACC provided a camp crew par excellence for all these teams as activities continued to develop through the summer.

As spring turned to summer I was approached by several local business interests in Trout Lake. Needless to say the financial impact on their businesses had been significant, and with the rapidly ripening

462

huckleberry crop, they were pleading to have the *Blue Zone* boundary changed to open at least the eastern part of the Forest to recreationists. Their visit with Supervisor Bob Tokarczyk, known by many in the Trout Lake community from his days as District Ranger there, and much in-depth discussion at the next Forest management team meeting in mid- July resulted in a decision to shrink the *Blue Zone* boundary to *enforceable points* east of the crest of the Cascades. That meant more gates had to be ordered and installed.

The Yakama Nation had lobbied to have the Sawtooth Huckleberry Fields included in the new *White Zone*, but the new *enforceable points* were established at Smokey Creek Organizational site and the Big Tire Junction. I recall a visit by several members of the tribal council who still were expressing desires to camp and pick at their usual and accustomed places. In the course of the day, after stopping at several locations where the berry crop was good and now accessible to the public, Tony Washines started to chuckle with gusto. "This is ironic," he said. "Here we have a couple of white men showing their usual and accustomed locations to the natives and encouraging the tribal members to pick there." It was a fun day and the start of an ongoing relationship over the next 15 years that led to several jointly executed projects in the Sawtooth Berryfields.

The hunters, first deer and then elk, followed the berry pickers. My experience of hunting season the previous three years at Mt. Adams was that there was a fair amount of pressure during deer season, but that elk hunting was a pretty low key event. Not that year! With both the Green and Toutle River drainages closed on the north end of the Forest, and a major article in the *Seattle Post-Intelligencer* exposing the east side of the Gifford Pinchot as an alternative, there were elk hunters everywhere. Much to the delight of the local businesses, I might add.

If you were to ask the line and staff officers, I'm sure all would say that, if not a unique experience in the history of the Forest Service, the total closure of the Gifford Pinchot NF was for sure an event that was for all of us a career defining experience.

Al Thompson *Thompson received a permanent appointment in 1960. He worked on the Targhee, Sawtooth, Wasatch, and Fishlake NFs and in the Regional Office in R-4. He was the Forest Engineer on the Wenatchee NF in R-6 when he retired in 1988.*

I had 15 great years as a forest engineer on the Wenatchee N F. It's always fun to get together with the old crew and talk about some of the crazy things that happened.

I recall one incident (in the early 1980s) that occurred on location of a portion of the Pacific Crest Trail. We constructed many miles of the PCT on my watch but the section where this incident occurred was on the Cle Elum Ranger District just north of Snoqualmie Pass. We had a five-man crew camped out on the ridge with a small lake nearby. Bob Bailey was the crew chief and locator.

I was asked by Bob to go up and review his located line. It was about a five-mile hike to get to their camp (straight up) and I arrived about mid-morning. The crew was out working and I could hear them over the ridge a ways so I headed in that direction. I hadn't gone more than a 100 yards or more when the side slopes became extremely steep. The surveyors had laid out several hundred yards of rope in that area so they would have something to hold on to while they traversed back and forth. I finally found Bailey down the line and we proceeded to review his tagged location.

About 30 minutes later we heard a scream from over the ridge. When we topped the ridge, one of the crew yelled and said some hikers down below had fallen and a couple of our guys were on their way to give them a hand. The report from our guys said their injuries were serious. A decision was made to call in a helicopter which could set down near a small lake below the injured folks. The chopper did come in several hours later and loaded them out.

By then it was getting late in the day, and we all headed for camp. When we arrived back in camp someone said, "Where's John Smith (not his actual name)?"

No one knew so Bailey said, "I'll go back and find him." For part of that afternoon I had sat next to John on the steep side slope as we

464

watched the drama below us unfold. During that time he was sitting next to a big stump. Bailey finally returned to camp at dusk but no John. Bob said that John was so frightened by the afternoon events and the steep slopes that he froze up and couldn't move. He was still sitting by the stump so Bob took a rope and tied him to that stump where he stayed the night. John was flown out by helicopter the next morning and shortly thereafter was assigned to the road crew.

<u>Jeff Sirmon</u> *Sirmon received a permanent appointment in 1958. He worked on NFs in Alabama and South Carolina, and in the Regional Office in R-8, on the Lassen NF and in the Regional Office in R-5, and in the Washington Office. He was Regional Engineer in R-1, Deputy Regional Forester and Regional Forester in R-4, Regional Forester in R-6, Deputy Chief for Programs and Legislation in the Washington Office and was Deputy Chief for International Forestry in the Washington Office when he retired in 1994.*

In an early 1980s election campaign for Mayor of Portland, Oregon, a popular pub owner of the Goose Hollow Tavern, Bud Clark, was one of the candidates. He had no experience in elected offices, was an ex-beatnik and became the populist candidate. His popularity was further advanced by a photograph of him dressed only in a raincoat with his back to the camera, coat flung open toward a statue with the caption, *Expose Yourself to Art.* This picture was flashed around the world in many newspapers.

During the campaign one hot-point issue was the protection of Portland's water supply from the Bull Run watershed in the Mt. Hood NF. Some long-term opponents of any kind of activity in the watershed by the Forest Service made statements about how the FS was putting quality water in danger and the next mayor must take action to protect Portland's water. Bud Clark took the bait and made promises about how he would examine and stop activities by the Forest Service which threatened water quality.

After Bud Clark was elected, Dick Pfilf, Mount Hood Forest Supervisor, arranged a tour for the mayor, some of his staff, the press and the Regional Forester and some of his staff. The day of the field trip came and Dick and his folks put on a first class *show and tell* with quality documentation showing Bull Run as perhaps the most protected and monitored watershed in the nation. The mayor was impressed.

At one point during the field trip at one of the scheduled stops the mayor needed to relieve himself. As I recall, there were no females on the trip. (Not sure that would have made any difference with Bud.) The mayor walked over to the side of the road and started to unzip his pants. I move around in position with my camera and had it aimed at him. "What are you trying to do?" he said.

To which I replied, "Take a picture to go along with tomorrow's *Oregonian* headlines, "MAYOR PROTECTS YOUR WATERSHED!""

Needless to say, this stopped the mayor. He took it all in good humor. It was even more ironic since one of the protective measures the Forest had taken in one of their horse-logging projects was to require the horses to wear diapers. A picture of this also made the rounds at an earlier time.

<u>Mark Hinschberger</u> *Hinschberger started as a temporary in 1978, and received a permanent appointment in 1979. He worked on the Bridger-Teton NF in R- 4 and the Wenatchee NF in R-6. He was a Wildlife Biologist on the Wind River Ranger District of the Shoshone NF in R-2 in 2005.*

The peregrine falcon was listed as an endangered species by the US Fish and Wildlife Service in 1970. Since that time, hundreds of captive-bred juvenile peregrines have been released to restore wild populations to their former ranges. This process called *hacking* was so successful in re-establishing breeding populations in the northeastern and eastern United States that in 1984, the Peregrine Fund built a permanent facility and headquarters, the World Center for Birds of Prey, in Boise, Idaho, to continue their recovery efforts in the west.

The first peregrine falcon hacking program on the Wenatchee NF began on the Naches Ranger District in 1989 on Divide Ridge as a cooperative effort between the Wenatchee NF, the Washington Department of Wildlife, the Peregrine Fund, Boise Cascade Corporation, and the Washington chapter of the Audubon Society. Twenty-seven young peregrines were released at two hack sites on the

466

Naches District between 1989 and 1992. These birds returned to natal areas or nearby, established natural nest sites and helped re-establish wild peregrine falcon populations in the west.

This hacking method, used by falconers for centuries to train hunting birds, had been adapted for use by the Peregrine Falcon Recovery Program. A large wooden box, with a metal grate front, solid top and sides, a feeding hole at the top, was placed in a high, relatively inaccessible location. On the Wenatchee NF the locations were Divide Ridge and Fifes Ridge. The young birds were placed in the closed box and provided with a steady supply of food, dead quail. When the young were fully feathered and able to fly, the front of the box was opened and the birds got up enough nerve to try their first flights.

The hack site attendants, who remain at the site for eight to ten weeks, provide food for the juveniles, who continue to return to the box until their hunting skills have improved to the point that they can fend for themselves completely. The young birds usually abandon the hack box completely by late summer.

Besides their foster-care duties, the [Wenatchee NF] attendants provided security and monitored their young charges' every activity. This included many very long days. Although the falcons had numbered leg bands, the attendants came up with some interesting names for their individual falcons, such as the names from Camelot for the Fifes Ridge falcons in 1991. In 1992 at Fifes Ridge, different attendants named their six birds after characters from Gilligan's Island (Thurston, Lovie, Skipper, Mary Ann, Professor and Ginger).

The peregrine falcon was delisted in August of 1999.

<u>Bonnie Wood</u> *Wood started as a temporary with the Forest Service in 1974 and received a permanent appointment with the Bureau of Land Management in 1975. She worked on the Siuslaw, Willamette, Siskiyou, Western Washington (Gifford Pinchot, Mt. Baker-Snoqualmie, and Olympic), and Malheur NFs and in the R-6 Regional Office. She was the National Fire Plan Executive Director in 2005.*

One of my more memorable experiences since I started working for the Forest Service in 1974 would have to be an encounter I had while I was the Gold Beach District Ranger.

About 1992 I was driving over the Bear Camp road from Galice to Gold Beach. I decided to take a look at a timber sale operation and the layout of a temporary road of another sale along the Burnt Ridge Road. It was a sunny summer afternoon, me proudly driving, in my Forest Service uniform, the recognizable Forest Service green vehicle, a four-wheel drive Jeep.

A vehicle came slowly around a corner toward me. As was standard for me when I was alone, I called the District office with a license and a vehicle description; they acknowledged my call. As the vehicle pulled alongside me, I rolled my window down just in time to receive a barrage of questions coming from the pleasant voice of the woman driving; she later told me she was "-in her mid-60s." She was so delighted to see a *Forest Ranger* so she could ask questions, she was nearly squealing.

Suddenly she stopped mid-sentence, her mouth dropped open and her eyes got wide. She quickly composed herself and said with delight, "Well look at you! They let you out to drive in these woods all by yourself?"

I couldn't help but acknowledge that she was driving around by herself, too, and actually I got out in the woods quite often, although rarely without others who work on the District. She then asked me if I knew anything about this area because she had LOTS of questions, and again declared herself lucky to run into a *Forest Ranger*.

Of course, she had no way of knowing that I really was the *Forest Ranger* and that I had grown up just a short ways from where we stood. I told her I was quite familiar with the area and she started asking her questions. Such occasions always result in pulling a map out and laying it over the hood of the truck. She was quite an explorer, curious about everything with little fear of anything. At one point during our conversation over the map, the District called me on the radio; they were getting concerned as I hadn't checked back in.

My new friend seemed to be so tickled that I had a radio and it worked just like on the TV shows, I must be for real!

Just when I thought the questions were coming to an end she had to ask me if we ride horses anymore and how many *Forest Rangers* are there really? I couldn't disappoint her so I told her on the east side of Oregon, *Forest Rangers* still ride horses. (Six years later I would learn that Forest Supervisors do, too.) Then I told her I actually was the District Ranger, which would be the 1992 version of a *Forest Ranger*. Without hesitation, she grabbed me with a big hug and shouted, "GOOD FOR YOU!"

The next series of questions were, of course, inquires about how I came about being a District Ranger, and why there? Since the sun had moved west quite a distance, I chose the shorter version and simply told her I was born into the Forest Service and had it in my blood. Most of my life I couldn't imagine doing anything but working for the Forest Service and that my father had been the District Ranger on the Galice District, just across the draw when I was growing up. I had to agree with him and many others, being a District Ranger is the best job in the outfit; I think it still is.

WIVES' TALES: "The Superintendent followed me out to the car that morning and asked me if I would be willing to teach music, including band."

<u>Kelly Allen Qualls</u> *Qualls was introduced to the Forest Service when her husband, Ed Allen, started work in 1961. Ed worked on the Mt. Hood, Okanogan, Siuslaw, Wallowa-Whitman and Colville NFs. Ed was working in the R-6 Regional Office in Rural Community Development when he retired in 1994. Qualls taught school when they were on the Mt. Hood and Colville NFs, and again when they moved to Portland. She gave private piano lessons everywhere they lived, sometimes having up to 35 students each week. She felt fortunate that her career as a teacher could follow Ed's even though it meant "starting over" each time they moved. She continued to teach private piano lessons until 2002.*

During our career in the Forest Service, my husband and I spent years working at two Job Corps Centers. We were at Timberlake Job Corps

Center in the 1960s for two years, and Ed was the Center Director at Curlew Job Corps Center four years in the late 1970s and early 1980s.

Curlew Job Corps Center is located ten miles from Curlew, Washington. The town of Curlew boasts a grocery store/post office, a restaurant and little else. While we were there, the center had about 225 boys and they ranged in age from 16 to 22. We had the usual offerings for the boys - things like working toward their GED and learning a trade such as brick-laying, mechanics, carpentry, forestry and cooking to name a few.

We were required to move into a house that the corpsmen had built located within walking distance of the middle of the center. Those of you that have done it know that moving into a small town is not an easy thing to do. When I took our teenaged daughter, Valerie, to enroll in the school, I asked to have her placed in the band since she played the tenor saxophone. I was told that they didn't have a band. I suggested then that they at least put her in chorus. Again I was told that they didn't have chorus. I guess I mentioned that I thought that it was a state requirement to offer music, but continued to get her classes in order so that she could start school. The Superintendent followed me out to the car that morning and asked me if they were to find a spot to do it, would I be willing to teach music including band. After some thought, I said that I would.

The music program included music for everyone from kindergarten through high school in that little school of 200 students. We started the band with six high school students and when we moved, there were 32 high school students and 28 junior high students in the band program. Two things stand out during that time. One was right after we were told that public schools could not have Christmas religious music in their *Winter* program. The entire basketball team approached me with an idea. They wanted to sing *Silent Night* in the all-school program given for their parents and friends, and they wanted my help to *do it right*. I asked the superintendent about it, and he said to go ahead. It was one of the highlights of the program. The second was that when we were to be transferred to Portland, the superintendent called me in and said, "Do you realize what you have done to me?" I couldn't imagine. He said, "I have to replace you!" That was the best

470

news I could have heard! In four years, music had become an important part of the school program in Curlew.

I grew up riding horses. When we lived in Winthrop, Washington, I went on my first cattle drive and loved it! When we lived in Unity, Oregon, I would go home after school, change clothes and head to a local ranch, saddle up and do something with cattle. Again, I loved it.

When we moved to Curlew, the corpsmen owned twelve horses. We bought a horse, but it soon became Valerie's. One of the locals had a horse that needed to be ridden - a beautiful Morgan. In good weather, after dinner each evening at 6:30, I would saddle the horse and ride to the other end of the center to the corral where they kept the horses. Corpsmen were sitting on the top rail of the fence waiting. The first twelve would come in, halter the horses, groom them and saddle them. Off we would go for about a half-hour ride. Then I would lead the next twelve out on a ride. This continued until dusk when the last twelve took the saddles off, brushed the horses and put the tack away in a uniform manner. Watching the way the boys learned how to care for a horse and how enthusiastic they were about the program had to help them in their everyday life. It felt good to have them all so glad to see me ride up to the corral and equally good to see them lose their fear and become able to ride and care for an animal.

I am proud that we worked a part of the time that we spent in our career with the Forest Service working for the Job Corps Program. I was proud when the center received the Center of the Year awards. I was proud when one of the boys had a success in their life such as achieving their GED. Sometimes, a boy that you had taken into your heart would disappoint you by messing up, but you picked up the pieces and moved forward. The real satisfaction was when, after a year outside working, a corpsman would let you know that they were doing well and were happy.

HORSES and MULES: "I heard from a Snake River outfitter there was a dead horse lying in a creek just upstream from the river and it was getting rather ripe."

<u>Glen Hetzel</u> *Hetzel received a permanent appointment in 1960 as the first Wildlife Biologist to work on the Siuslaw NF. He*

worked on the Malheur, Umatilla, Wallowa-Whitman, and Ochoco NFs in R-6, in the R-5 Regional Office, and as Assistant Director of Range Management in the Washington Office. He was Director of Range, Wildlife, Fisheries and Ecology; then Director of Renewable Resources in R-2 when he retired in 1994.

I served as District Ranger in Halfway, Oregon, on the Pine RD, Wallowa-Whitman NF from 1966 to 1971. In June 1970, Forest Supervisor John Rogers called and informed me he had received a message from Senator Bob Packwood's father-in-law saying they regrettably had to abandon one of their saddle horses along the Snake River Trail a few miles below the Hells Canyon Dam, and asked if we would keep an eye out for it. The Senator and his family had spent the previous week in the canyon getting a first-hand look at the area that was later to become the Hells Canyon National Recreation Area. About the same time, I heard from a Snake River outfitter there was a dead horse lying in a creek just up stream from the river and it was getting rather *ripe*.

I realized this was going to be a dirty job, since the area is very remote and there was no possibility of using equipment. As everyone knows, there is no budget for this type of duty, and it was a weekend task. I didn't have the heart to ask any of my staff to volunteer. I worked a deal with the outfitter, Jim Zanelli, to have the Senator pay him for his time and jet boat services if he would join me in cleaning up the mess. We used a come-along winch and made progress one inch at a time. The weather was *hot* and the stench was sickening. After several hours, we drug the horse, a white mare, out of the creek and into a nearby trench we had dug and covered her up.

I then penned a letter to John Rogers and explained in some detail the whole ordeal and told him the job was done. He responded with a signed *Red Card* qualifying me as a *Class One Horse Grave Digger*.

<u>Gordon Jesse Walker</u> *Walker, a long-time packer on the Rogue River NF, laments the passing of a good friend in 1982 and the coming end of the era of large pack strings.*

Big Red, a government mule, was born in 1949. No one seems to know exactly where, but it could have been in Missoula, Montana.

There used to be a remount station there where they broke mules to pack and then sold them to various agencies who used the pack mules. He had a one-inch slit at the top of his right ear indicating he was broke to packing and ready to sell.

Big Red came to me in the late 1960s. We traveled hundreds of miles together clear up to the fall of 1981, when he made his last trip packing a cast iron stove on his back. Big Red and I put on several shows at the Union Creek Campground amphitheater over the years and we enjoyed every one of them. He liked having his picture taken best of all because he'd pose just like a professional.

Big Red showed signs of ailing about the first of March after wintering quite well. He was taken to Crater Animal Clinic for treatment. The vets floated his teeth and he was dewormed. I gave him some liquid vitamins mixed with oats. His appetite picked up, but he still didn't gain any weight.

On March 31, he started to slow down on eating. By Friday, April 2, he wouldn't touch a thing. On April 3, I took him back to the clinic. When he climbed into the trailer he fell, never to stand again. At the clinic two doctors worked on him and tried to save his life. He couldn't get up and it was quite evident that he was suffering a lot of pain. The doctors agreed he would never stand again, and there was only one choice; that was to put Big Red to sleep. It was me who had to say "Go ahead." I would take care of his remains myself. I was by him when he died.

He was put to sleep in the big six-horse fifth-wheel trailer he dearly loved. He was 33 years old and probably worked for the Forest Service longer than any Rogue River mule, though I don't know for sure. I picked a site for his grace about a half mile northwest of the Prospect Ranger Station and he was buried there on Monday, April 5, 1982.

Sarah mule from Butte Falls preceded Big Red in death. Stella mule at the Prospect Ranger Station is the sole survivor, and the last of the Rogue River National Forest mules. When she dies it will mark the end of an era, never to be revived.

The good old days of the colorful, rough and tumble life of a packer has almost come to an end. I should know because I'm the last of the old Rogue River packers.

FIRE: "The wind had shifted and one or more of the fires were coming into town."

<u>Frank E. Lewis</u> *The first time that Lewis got paid on a fire job was in 1939 on the Willard Fire on the Columbia NF. His father, Melvin, was the District Ranger. Frank told two stories about his dad in Chapter One (Joining Up and Wives). Frank was Assistant Director (Suppression) of Fire Control in the R-6 Regional Office when he retired in 1980.*

Fire seasons in recent years have eclipsed many of the records set in Region 6 in 1970. However the fire busts that year still give pause to those involved even today. The following recollections are based upon several write-ups by Clarence Edgington, Regional Dispatcher, entitled, *15 Days in July* and *10 Days in August*. He wrote those summaries as the smoke was clearing.

The period July 16 through July 29 was especially noteworthy. That particular period was preceded by the 2,800 acre Quail Creek Fire on the lower Rogue River of the Siskiyou NF which started on July 13 and was controlled on July 16. On the 15th, a lightning storm along the east side of the Cascades and Central Oregon started 57 fires.

By early morning July 16, the lightning activity had moved into Washington. Activity was light on the Gifford Pinchot NF where only five fires occurred. This storm also set seven fires on the Yakima Indian Reservation. Another storm passed over the Olympic peninsula resulting in 14 fires on the Olympic NF and Olympic National Park. During the ensuing two-week period numerous man-caused fires required action throughout the state of Washington. Several storms on the 16th originated on the west side of the Snoqualmie NF, resulting in 227 fires on the Snoqualmie, Mt. Baker, Okanogan and Wenatchee NFs. These same storms ignited 29 fires in the Mount Rainier and North Cascades National Parks along with 65 additional fires on State of Washington Department of Natural Resources lands and seven more on the Colville Indian Reservation.

Forest Service rappelling crew on the Lake Chelan Ranger District,
Wenatchee NF – 1975

Smokejumpers heading out from the Intercity Smokejumpers Base,
Okanogan NF – 1976

Forces to combat these various fires including overhead, organized crews and equipment were mobilized from every region along with many other agencies in the country. Aircraft use developed into the largest operation ever experienced in Region 6 up until that time. Traffic became so great that FAA control towers were established at Intercity and Omak airports. Helicopters numbered 35 including large Vertol machines to supply many remote fires. Some 15 air tankers dropped 636,000 gallons of retardant and bucket-equipped helicopters made countless water drops. Smokejumpers (176) from Regions 1, 4, 5 and 6 made almost 500 jumps on fires. The military provided trucks, messing and shower units along with some of the large helicopters. Thirty-one tractors and 78 tanker/pumper units were utilized, too. The maximum number of people assigned reached 6427 in the suppression efforts.

Most of the fires that became large were inaccessible, most notably the Bunker Hill Fire in the Pasayten Wilderness Area which burned into Canada even though 64 smokejumpers were committed to it. The Lucky Fire on the Mt. Baker NF required eight hours for ground crews to hike into it to relieve the initial attack smokejumpers although roads on either side of the fire were less than a mile apart! Rehab work was initiated on the 28,468 burned acres before mop-up was completed.

The above series of fires merely set the stage for what was to happen in late August and September. Region 6 was still engaged in cleaning up after the July episode when on August 21st lightning again moved in over the Region. First reports came from the Willamette and Deschutes NFs where 70 new fires were set by the 24th. The storms continued on up the Cascades and ignited 91 new fires, primarily on the Wenatchee NF. By then the region had sustained 176 new lightning fires and human carelessness had added another 26. Records confirm that burning conditions in the Wenatchee area were the most extreme in 30 years; hence, the many lightning strikes coupled with the build-up in flammable material resulted in numerous fires reaching blow-up intensities very rapidly.

By dawn on the 25th, it was evident that a number of fires would become campaign size; hence, mobilization began immediately. By the 28th, 8103 people were engaged, directly or indirectly, supporting suppression efforts on 226 fires; 26 of which had become large.

Several in the Entiat drainage of the Wenatchee NF had burned together by the 29th. A storm originating in northern California moved into the Region on the 30th, and by the end of the next day had ignited 453 new lightning fires. Another 55 human-caused fires were also added. During the next two days 139 lightning fires and 15 more man-caused were added; mainly from *sleepers* after the storms on the 29th - 31st of August.

Mobilization involved overhead and crews from throughout the nation. On the 31st, 11,248 people (8,581 on the Wenatchee NF alone) were involved. Aircraft included 70 helicopters and 18 air tankers along with 109 tractors and 199 ground tankers. Over 350 smokejumpers from Redmond, North Cascades, Siskiyou, LaGrande, Missoula, Grangeville, McCall, Redding and Fairbanks were deployed. The military contributed 253 people and 120 vehicles along with kitchen, shower and laundry units. The National Guard set up a control tower at Pangborn Field in Wenatchee which the FAA used to control air traffic. Local civil defense and rural fire districts assisted in the protection of homes and property in the Entiat River valley. Sheriff deputies and state patrolmen controlled traffic on county roads and state highways in and adjacent to the fire areas. Other agencies assisted, including recruiting units in Alaska for Native crews. An order for *seal oil* to supplement their duties confounded even Regional Forester Charlie Connaughton at the time!

Again rehab began and went on until the next spring before embers had cooled on the 111,600 burned acres - all but 600 on the Wenatchee and Okanogan NFs. Total cost, exclusive of resource loss, were beyond the initially estimated three to five million dollars by several more million.

<u>Jack Rae</u> *Rae was a Fire Control Officer on the Mt. Hood NF at the time of this story.*

This story happened on the Zizag RD, Mt. Hood NF, during the 1970s. It was a beautiful summer day. The sky was cloudless. Just a perfect day to be alive in the Pacific Northwest working on a Ranger District in the mountains.

The Ranger was Dick Buscher, and I was the Fire Control Officer. Dick had scheduled us for a walk-through inspection of the compound grounds and buildings. Kind of a housekeeping inspection.

The same morning 60-some miles to the west in the Portland area, a family was busy loading a 16 foot tandem flat bed trailer with side racks. It was loaded with a couch, lazy boy chair, mattress, beds and other furniture. The family was headed for the Bend area. A big Cadillac was pulling the trailer. It was a perfect day for trailering with an open bed trailer. No rain in the forecast. The family was starting on a new adventure. Little did we realize that our paths were soon to cross.

Dick and I were winding down our inspection. We were walking down toward the highway. The fire warehouse was on one side of us and the gas house on the other when this Caddy and trailer pulled over to the side of the highway just in front of us. Smoke and flames were coming from the trailer. The man jumped from behind the wheel and started to holler for help. Dick and I could not believe what we were seeing. (Dick had hired me that spring to fill a FMO vacancy slot at Zigzag. I remember one of my first tasks was to check all the fire extinguishers on the District. The larger 20 and 30 pounders had cartridges that had to be weighed among other things. These were ABC extinguishers.)

Back to the story. I told Dick to grab the 30-pounder on the gas house and I went to the fire warehouse and got the 20-pounder. As we were charging to the fire, Dick looked at me with a questioning look, and said, "Are you sure these things are going to work?"

I replied, "Trust me."

He replied, "If they don't, you are going to have a very short career." By this time the wife and kids were also out of the car jumping up and down screaming and looking toward their heroes bearing down on them.

The extinguishers worked and in a few minutes, the fire was knocked down. I got a hose and was mopping up. Forest Service employees make up the main nucleus of many rural fire departments, so this was a piece of cake.

Meanwhile Dick and driver-father were in a deep discussion trying to figure out just what caused the fire. I piped up, "It's no mystery to me what happened!"

Dick turned to me and asked, "How do you know what happened?"

I replied, "Look at his ashtray. Its full of cigarette butts, so he tossed the last one out the window."

At that moment his wife jumped in. She pointed her finger at him and said, "I told you to stop throwing your butts out the window!"

The guy just stood there, his mouth wide open but nothing was coming out. Then to my amazement, Dick opened up on him. Smokey Bear would have been proud of Dick. There was nothing more for me to say. So we loaded everything back into the trailer. I told the driver where the town dump was. He just gave me a sick look and continued on to Bend.

I thought to myself as I was carrying the extinguisher back to the fire warehouse to reload, John Boy, you just passed muster.

Jerilyn Levi *Levi was a seasonal firefighter from 1974 to 1980 on the Los Padres NF in R-5, the Chugach NF in R-10, the Bureau of Land Management in Alaska, and the Willamette NF in R-6. She received a permanent appointment on the Willamette NF in 1980, then worked on the Siuslaw NF and in the Washington Office, where she was the Assistant Director for Policy, International Programs in 2005.*

When I worked at Lowell Ranger District in 1980, I was asked why a nice (educated) girl like me was working on a fire crew. Of course, I said that it was because I liked it - and had liked firefighting since I took my first step test on the Los Padres in 1974. In the late 1970s, I had worked in Alaska for both the US Forest Service and BLM and was awestruck with interior Alaska's 300,000-acre fires, disturbance ecology and the native Alaskan villagers. After several years of *far north* adventures, I had ventured south to Oregon.

In 1981, I spent the fire season on the Redmond Hotshot Crew led by Tim Sexton and Dave Craycroft. They were smart, funny and new tons about fire suppression and fire ecology. It was quite fun. That summer Logan Lee and I were the first women on the crew at Redmond, and the crew bosses from Prineville came over to watch. Of course Logan could outwork, outwit and ask more questions than anyone. We laugh about it to this day.

<u>Bob Devlin</u> *Devlin started as a temporary in 1957 and received a permanent appointment in 1958. He worked on the Allegheny NF in R-7, the Klamath, Sequoia and Stanislaus NFs in R-5, and the Rogue River and Umpqua NFs in R-6. He was Director of Natural Resources in the R-6 Regional Office when he retired in 2000.*

The 1987 fire season was late in southwest Oregon and northern California. The major storm system that traveled through that area came on Labor Day weekend. Not only did the area get hot with hundreds of lightning strikes, it came at a time when many crews were breaking up due to students going back to school. The big news was the Silver Fire on the Siskiyou Forest, but there were other problem areas also.

One that I am most familiar with is the multiple fire complexes in Douglas County on both FS/BLM and private lands. I still remember the storm and the phone call from our dispatch shop on the Umpqua that informed me of the multiple strikes and many fires showing up. As I look back on it, I have a lot of pride in the effort the Forest put into battling those fires. The Forest had numerous folks on Regional and area teams so we were short-handed right from the start. One thing that saved our butts was the fact that Assistant Fire Staff Dick Wessel placed an order for 20 crews the first night of the storm. By the next day, it was obvious that the Region and our partners were facing a major problem with the multiple fires around northern California and southwestern Oregon. A multiple area command system was established immediately and all prior orders for crews were honored. Although the Umpqua was low on the priority list for resources due to the proximity of many of the fires on other Forests, we did get our 20 crews first. Dick Wessel was very astute with that initial order.

The effort to control our fires (Angel, Clover, Apple and one in the wilderness on the Tiller District) was a major combined Forest effort. The communities of Roseburg and surrounding communities helped us immensely. The rest and recuperation camp at Umpqua Community College was first class and we had many comments from out-of-Region crews that they had never been treated better. I believe we went over 20 days without air support due to smoke and inversions.

The fires were controlled and timber was salvaged within one year after control. The emergency rehabilitation was completed before the snow flew. The area outside the wilderness was reforested in two years. The folks who worked on the Umpqua at that time should be proud of the effort of all.

Dick Grace *Grace started as a temporary with the National Park Service at Olympic National Park in 1956. He was a temporary with the Forest Service in 1958, and received a permanent appointment in 1961. He worked on the Kaniksu NF in Region 1, and the Malheur, Winema, Wenatchee, Mt. Hood, Ochoco, Umpqua, and Willamette NFs in Region 6. He was Deputy Director for Recreation, Lands and Minerals Resources in the R-6 Regional Office when he retired in 1996.*

The year was 1990 and the west had no relief from four years of drought that produced fires such as Yellowstone and Silver. In mid-August, the Ochoco and Malheur NFs received a dry lightning storm that triggered several hundred fires. The fires were organized into fire complexes and five incident management teams were assigned to the complexes. An area command team was assigned to the Ochoco and Malheur NFs to coordinate and prioritize resources for the five complexes. The incident complexes were named: Whiting with Dave Brown Incident Commander (IC); Pine Springs with Roy Montgomery IC; Buck Springs with Gary Starkovich IC; Snowshoe with Ken Lindsey IC and Sheep Mountain with Wayne Long IC. Area Commanders were Mike Edrington USFS and Rusty Lafferty Oregon Department of Forestry.

It was day three into the campaign and all fires were at maximum energy levels by mid-afternoon with 40,000 foot smoke columns dominating the skyline. At 10:00 pm, area command team leader

Edrington, and team members Schmidt, O'Neal and Grace discovered what appeared to be snow filling the night air in downtown Hines. It was ash fall! This could mean only one thing. The wind had shifted and one or more of the fires were coming into town (Hines and Burns)! A quick look and we could see a long line of fire in the sagebrush west of town. What makes this a story worth telling is what happened in the next few hours to prepare for the worst.

Montgomery's team was at the Harney County fairgrounds near town and was the first to be notified. We quickly started calling the incident command posts on fires within our command directing them to send their lowboys with dozers to the west end of town to tie in with Montgomery's team. Edrington immediately left for town to meet with the highly alarmed citizens gathered at the County Courthouse. A near panic was developing as public emergency services were trying to shout each other down on who was going to do what. It was apparent that someone needed to take charge and start making preparations for the rapidly-approaching fire.

Edrington walked into the room and looked for the most influential person there. County Commissioner Dale White was taken aside and Mike asked Dale to get the attention of the crowd and then give him the floor. After Dale had their attention, Mike explained what the firefighting agencies were doing to protect the town. He assured them that the incident command teams assembled in their town were the most competent wildland fire teams in the world and the commanders were well experienced in protecting towns from wildfire. The crowd quieted immediately. County sheriff officers laid out what they would do. The City Fire Departments displayed their plans. Citizens were organized and the scene went from a mob mentality to an organized, confident team of professionals ready to do their job.

The westside of town quickly got dozer fire lines pushed in ahead of the fire. Structural fire engines were strategically placed in the community and we waited for the fire to come to us. About 1:00 am the wind died down and like all sagebrush fires, once the wind died down, the fire stopped running. Several cows and an out-building or so were lost that night but the town was safe and the wildland fire fighters led by Mike Edrington showed that they had the right stuff.

GRAZING: "After a lot of effort, they managed to get only one of the small herd into a makeshift corral."

<u>Glen Hetzel</u> *Hetzel describes a cattle trespass impoundment that went awry.*

I served as a principle staff officer on the Umatilla NF in the early 1970s. The Pendleton Ranger District had a cattle trespass problem from unauthorized livestock crossing the forest boundary above Milton-Freewater. The District posted notices of intent to impound livestock and after appropriate warning decided to impound. After a lot of effort, they managed to get only one of the small herd into a makeshift corral. They notified the owner and presented him with a bill for collection. The owner, after looking at the bill, said the cow was not worth the cost, and the Forest Service could just keep her!

The heifer was transported to the Pendleton District work center and locked in the coral with feed and water. They scheduled an auction to sell her to the highest bidder to help recover some expense. In the meantime the heifer escaped from the pen and was on the loose at the time the sale was to take place. After several unsuccessful attempts to round her up, they called the local Oregon State wildlife biologist to assist tranquilizing her. The tranquilizer worked - too well. The heifer died even after a frantic attempt to revive her.

Now for the rest of the story. The owner, who came to observe the auction, was quite upset to have his prize purebred heifer treated so poorly and made a rather large claim against the FS.

RECREATION: "Be careful what you ask for."

<u>Bob Devlin</u> *Devlin was the Forest Supervisor of the Rogue River NF at the time of this story.*

In the early 1980s the Rogue River NF was working closely with the Army Corps of Engineers on the design and construction of the recreational facilities at the newly-filled Applegate Reservoir which was part of the flood control projects on the Rogue River. Under Don Smith's leadership and the great staff work of Dick Marlega, Bob Lichlyter and Jurgen Hess, the Forest Service was very involved with the Corps on the details of the development of this great recreation

Ranger and stockman checking an allotment, Wenatchee NF – 1970

Ranger and stockman moving cows on an allotment, Umatilla NF – 1976

attraction. As we often do with that type of involvement, especially with another federal agency who is actually paying for all of our ideas, Dick, Bob and Jurgen were relentless in assuring that the recreational facilities were top-notch and the latest in design features. It didn't come easy to get the Corps to agree but the Rogue was very successful in accomplishing this chore.

When the project was complete and the administration of the recreation sites was passed to the Forest Service, we were elated. Not only had we inherited these great increases in recreation capacity for the public, we also were proud to showcase the design aspects of the sites. Then the problem appeared.

It didn't take long to discover that our internal budget process was not very timely in accepting a large increase in recreation capacity let alone the unit costs that these modern facilities would require. There were many meetings, memos and pleas with the recreation staff in the RO to somehow get the Forest the allocations they would need to maintain these sites. The public was spoiled quickly and demanded that the sites not deteriorate. This was especially difficult for the Applegate District and the Rogue River NF, after all the beating they had done on the Corps to get the sites constructed as they were.

It worked out over the long run but I remember a long discussion that I had with Regional Forester Dick Worthington about our dilemma and Dick's response was, "Be careful what you ask for."

<u>Dave Scott</u> *Scott started as a temporary on the Superior NF in R-9 in 1948 while still in high school. His first permanent job was on the Shasta NF in R-5. He worked on the Shasta, Shasta Trinity and San Bernardino NFs in R-5, in the R-8 Regional Office, and was the Assistant Director of Recreation in the Washington Office. He was the Director of Recreation in the R-6 Regional Office when he retired in 1987.*

Change is constant. You live long enough you should know that, but often the older you get the tougher it is to change.

In 1986, the year before I retired, the Umpqua National Forest had a bunch of construction money for one of the Diamond Lake campgrounds. They were looking for ways to attract some people

485

away from lakeshore campsites to other sites a bit further away to minimize wear and tear on the most popular sites. Recreation Staff Dick Arney figured that if they installed shower facilities far enough away from the lakeshore, people would be attracted to those locations thus reducing environmental damage to the lakeshore.

At the time there were no showers in any R-6 campgrounds nor in any campgrounds service wide, except in R-8 and a few in R-9. There was a regional policy against them. Dick presented his ideas to the regional office and eventually his proposal landed on my desk for a decision. I had spent years in recreation jobs and was imbued with the idea that National Forests campgrounds were not *state parks*. If people wanted showers, they could camp at state parks. The National Forest camper was a tougher *breed of cat* who went without showers as part of the camping experience.

In any case I dragged my feet over making the decision for a month or so. Several people on the staff kept on my case to make a decision. To tell the truth I was in a real personal struggle and didn't know why, although I thought it was important that people find a different outdoor experience on the National Forests than in state parks. Finally Forest Supervisor Devlin called me and requested I say something even if it was wrong. I figured the time had come to make a decision and wrote a one-page note saying "no showers in R-6" and explaining my position. I thought I had done a good job albeit a bit late.

I slept well that night and for several months afterward until early in 1987 when after 34 years of service I retired. One of the retirement gifts was a plastic bag *sun shower* which I used several times in primitive camping conditions and it worked great. Anyhow those that were privy to the earlier shower decision got a great kick out of it as did I.

I don't know exactly when, but sometime in the next six months I learned that showers were under construction at Diamond Lake, almost immediately upon my retirement. At first I was a bit upset. Finally, upon reflection, I realized that while I wished the National Forest camper of today was still the tough kind that didn't need showers, our constituency had indeed changed their expectations and I had not changed my way of thinking. In all these years that followed I

486

have often wondered how much my ability to accommodate change had to do with my retirement date. Having been retired for 18 years I am truly happy with my life and my retirement and I take a shower every day wherever I am.

<u>Phil Hirl</u> *Hirl was the R-6 Assistant Director of Engineering at the time of this story.*

Region 6 promoted several roads in the early 1980s as *Scenic Roads*, so when the Forest Service established the National Scenic Byway program in 1988 we had a number of candidates ready to nominate.

Dick Arney, John Sloan and Ned Davis on the Umpqua NF and Dave Ewing on the Rogue River NF thought the drive along the North Umpqua River to Diamond Lake and then along the Rogue River towards Medford would be a good candidate. Pat Gallagher and Bill Shenk on the Colville NF promoted the Sherman Pass Byway. Bill Martin on the Deschutes NF and Doug Macdonald on the Willamette NF proposed the McKenzie Pass/Santiam Pass loop. Art Carroll and Jurgen Hess on the Columbia Gorge National Scenic Area suggested the historic Columbia River Highway. The Mather Memorial Parkway from Naches to Enumclaw through Mt. Rainier National Park was an easy choice to nominate. Big supporters of this were Don Rotell and Al Thompson on the Wenatchee NF, and Ted Lewis and Walt Weaver on the Mt. Baker/Snoqualmie NF.

Then in 1991, Congress passed the Intermodal Surface Transportation Efficiency Act (ISTEA called Ice Tea). It contained two provisions that helped our scenic byway program. First it established a national scenic byways program, encouraging each state to do the same, and secondly, it required the states to spend 10% of their Federal allocation for roadside enhancements.

That was not required with the forest highway program which improves county and state roads that benefit National Forests, but it sounded like a great idea to me, so I went to Jim Hall, Director of the Federal Highways Administration project office in Vancouver and suggested we do the same 10% with forest highway funds. I had spent many hours on the road with Jim looking at various projects so knew him fairly well. I thought he might be receptive and he was. Then we had to convince the state and county people. This was $1.5 million that could enhance roadways. They never would have agreed before but ISTEA set the tone and they did agree.

So the next time we asked for forest highway proposed projects we included criteria for roadside enhancement projects. One principal was the project should be a *Scenic Byway*. We had no trouble getting proposals. I retired not long after the first projects were selected, but it is still an active program in 2004.

TIMBER: "He wanted to negotiate with the purchaser to leave some standing snags in each of the units and leave a buffer strip along the creeks in each of the units."

Ralph Jaszkowski *Jaszkowski started as a temporary in 1951 and received a permanent appointment in 1955. He worked on the Kaniksu and Lolo NFs in R-1, and the Fremont, Wenatchee, Siskiyou and Willamette NFs in R-6 and in the R-6 Regional Office. He was the R-6 Regional Silviculturist when he retired in 1988.*

Originally the tree seeds used for reforestation were collected from caches of cones gathered by squirrels. Eventually it was decided to collect cones from specific trees selected for their superior characteristics. Boom trucks proved to be expensive and were limited to high standard roads. Climbing trees to collect cones was hazardous and also expensive. About 1970 the Missoula Equipment Development Center (MEDC) took the problem in hand.

For many years nuts had been harvested by machines that literally shook the trees causing the nuts to fall to the ground for easy collection. MEDC modified one of these machines to successfully harvest cones from conifer trees in the Northern Rocky Mountain Region but wanted to test the device on coastal Douglas-fir. That's where this story begins.

In the summer of 1971 we received word at the Siskiyou NF Supervisor's Office in Grants Pass that we would be given the honor of conducting the test. I assigned the project to John McCullough, the other half of our Silviculture staff. At first John thought it was a joke but soon enough realized that this was for real.

Sorting Douglas-fir seedlings at the Wind River Nursery,
Gifford Pinchot NF – 1978

The shade house with Douglas-fir seedling plugs,
Beaver Creek Nursery, Siuslaw NF – 1978

On a beautiful, late summer day in August, MEDC delivered the tree shaker to Grants Pass on a large, green flatbed truck. The Forest Service shields on the doors were as large as dinner plates. We had hired an operator for the shaker who was apprehensive but who needed the job. The equipment development guys were to train him. The machine was unloaded just outside town in a grove of unsuspecting trees belonging to an even more unsuspecting cooperative landowner. A small entourage had gathered which included Ralph *Sparky* Reeves, our shop foreman; John McCullough; the MEDC trainers; the operator; and a few *rubberneckers* such as myself and Bill Warner from the Galice Ranger District.

The tree shaker, an odd-looking device, included a hydraulic boom which could be extended to grab a chokehold on a tree trunk about fifteen feet above the ground. The boom was mounted on a large, stripped-down truck chassis and was vibrated by an eccentric reciprocating weight. This machine shook the cones out of a tree in three to five seconds. Shaking beyond that time span would begin to destroy the tree as six to ten foot chunks broke out of the top.

Training was completed in short order, the MEDC boys took off for Missoula and that's when trouble started. Sparky Reeves directed the operator to drive the shaker to the Siskiyou NF shop for some agreed-upon modifications by following a frontage road paralleling I-5. An Oregon State Policeman traveling I-5 spotted the shaker, took the next exit, came flying down the frontage road and pulled our tree shaker over. He walked around the machine about three times rubbing his chin. As I recall, his first words were, "It isn't every day you catch the feds."

Someone innocently asked, "What's wrong officer?"

The reply crackled in the air, "I'll give you a list of what's right, it'll be shorter. No windshield, no wipers, no lights, no license plates, etc., etc."

So our newly hired shaker operator received a citation which immediately set him off, "I work for you guys two days and end up with a violation on my professional driving record." The situation was deteriorating but the patrolman finally left which allowed the operator to calm down enough to get the machine to the shop. I can say that the tree shaker made it through the shop just fine but I am not at liberty to say how the operator's citation was resolved.

A trailer was required to haul the tree shaker over the long distances it would have to travel so John began searching for a rental. For some reason all the suitable trailers in the area were in use, except one that John found out in the country somewhere. It appeared suitable but later proved to have a unique problem which may have contributed to its being idle.

As the warm summer days changed to shorter, cool fall days, the cones ripened for harvest. The tree shaker traveled in and out of the Siskiyou NF, along Highway 101, around the horn up the winding Smith River Canyon to the Cave Junction and Galice Ranger Districts and back again. Cone ripening moved up in elevation as the season progressed, requiring repeat trips into higher and higher elevations. The cones were coming in by the ton with burlap sacks full of cones being shipped regularly to Wind River Nursery for seed extraction. The Siskiyou had been desperately short of tree seed and now we were getting well.

One day, a long way up in the woods from Gold Beach, the trailer developed a flat tire. Of course, the spare wheel didn't fit this maverick piece of equipment and a closer inspection showed that the tire was ruined. The tree shaker wheels didn't fit the trailer. The spare wheel on the Forest Service truck didn't fit either. Nothing to do but take the busted tire and wheel the many miles into town and have a new tire mounted. John McCullough and the shaker operator headed into Gold Beach to a likely-looking business establishment and asked to have a replacement mounted. The tire man studied the busted tire at length, craned his neck to read the dusty sidewall markings and grunted, "Hell, this is an airplane tire. You won't find one in this town."

I won't take up all the space required to relate how the dilemma was resolved. Know only that somewhere in a dark corner on the Siskiyou NF is a dusty file containing John McCullough's official report to the Missoula Equipment Development Center. The tree shaker? It was last seen on a large green truck with huge white door shields heading east on I-5 out of Grants Pass.

<u>Bruce Kaufman</u> *Kaufman started as a temporary in 1957 and received a permanent appointment in 1970. He worked on the Kootenai NF in R-1, the Challis and Sawtooth NFs in R-4, and the Mt. Hood and Umatilla NFs in R-6. He was the Public Affairs Officer for the Wallowa-Whitman NF when he retired in 1994.*

In the spring of 1977, I was Timber Management Assistant on the Bear Springs District of the Mount Hood NF. The Forest had a policy of holding a timber sale review on each Ranger District. That spring it was our turn for a presale review by the Forest Supervisor and his staff.

Lou Best, our Pre-Sale Forester, was fairly new at his job, having been reassigned from his Small Sales Forester position the fall before when Jerry Hofer transferred to the Rogue River. We chose Lou's first timber sale effort, the Pistol Sale, for the annual sale review both because it was a challenging sale and to give Lou a chance to present his work before the Forest Supervisor and his staff .

The Pistol Sale was located on the slope above the White River along our boundary with the Barlow District. On the appointed day, District Ranger Eric Morse and his District staff met Forest Supervisor F. Dale Robertson, Deputy Bill Morden, Timber Staff Officer Wendall Jones and the rest of Dale's staff at the junction of Highway 35 and the White River Road. A short distance down the White River Road, we left the vehicles and began following Lou on a game trail for what was to be a short hike to the sale boundary and one of the cutting units.

After what seemed like an awfully long time of trying to keep up with Lou's long stride, I still had not seen any sale boundary markers or unit boundary signs. Lou kept up the pace and everyone seemed to be enjoying the outing. I was beginning to get nervous and looked back at our sale planner, Lloyd Musser. Lloyd had that impish little grin on his face that he always had when things were about to go south in a hand basket. Now I was really starting to panic. All of a sudden Lou stopped and motioned for us to sit. He then began to expertly explain the silvicultural prescription, the unit design, and the logging system and how each would achieve the objectives outlined in the environmental analysis report. He fielded questions from the Supervisor and staff and his answers were well thought out and clearly spoken. When all were satisfied with what they had heard, Lou led us back down to the rigs where we were to drive up to Timberline Lodge for the review of the paper-work for the sale.

As soon as the Supervisor and his staff were loaded up and out of earshot, I said "Lou, you had no idea where you were. Did you?"

He said, "No, I was on the wrong trail. I just kept going until I came to a stand of timber that looked a lot like the unit I was trying to find, and I decided to wing it. That also is not all, I left the maps and briefing papers for the rest of the review on my desk in the office."

Lloyd Musser called the District Office on the radio and had Ted Ladoux gather up the sale papers from Lou's desk and head up to Timberline Lodge with them. The rest of us plotted how we could hold off the S.O. folks until Ted got to the lodge. All went as planned and the rest of the sale review went off without a hitch.

That evening, back at Bear Springs, we were congratulating Lou on falling in the proverbial privy and coming out covered in ice cream, when he said, "You know, I should have known what the day was going to be like. This morning I climbed in the shower and saw white stuff running down my chest. I had lathered up and forgot to use the razor."

Ron Walters *Walters received a permanent appointment in 1963. He worked on the Wenatchee and Mt. Hood NFs, and in the R-6 Regional Office. He was the Regional Landscape Architect when he retired in 1990.*

My days as the Region 6 Landscape Architect were filled with the design of new campgrounds, administrative site planning and finding ways to soften the visual impact of clearcut logging. Our budgets were well attended and we were able to offer some really fine recreation programs and facilities. Then, as it so happened, the environmental movement of the 1970s began to loom large on the Forest Service agenda and my job took a sharp turn.

Flying crane harvesting pine,
Okanogan NF – 1971

Scanning a mosaic of timber stand ages, Willamette NF – early 1980s

Once in the late seventies I was tapped to represent R6 Recreation on the annual Oregon State Parks Advisory Committee field trip. A distinguished honor I thought at the time. The bus was loaded with many influential Oregon citizens. I was ask to give a talk at Gilchrist, Oregon, the heart of the timber industry, about the efforts the Forest Service was making to reduce the destructive appearance of logging on the landscape. Our old friend, Stub Stewart, was the timber industry's representative on that trip and immediately took offense at my suggestion that the timber industry should begin to take heed of the growing environmental movement's objection to the wasteful appearance of clearcut logging. If you knew Stub, you will understand the root of my consternation. Stub made it clear, in his usual verbose manner, that the timber industry had nothing to worry about and should continue on with business as usual. Talk about sticking your head in the lion's mouth! I was the most unpopular person in that room full of loggers. Stub and I battled for two days on that trip.

Well, as it turned out, *business as usual* was one of the reasons the timber boat sank. I still wish I could tell old Stub, "I told you so."

<u>Hillard M. "Lil" Lilligren</u> *Lilligren compares the way proposed timber sales were described in the late 1970s with an earlier times description.*

This environmental adjustment will consist of controlled site enhancement to provide three 30-acre wildlife openings. Disturbed soil areas will be stabilized by planting with vegetation to provide game food and improve soil fertility.

Sufficient standing dead trees and residual unused limbs and decayed wood will be left on the ground to provide nesting and resting areas for songbirds, squirrels, and chipmunks. Some residual woody material will be removed by controlled burning to provide the nutrients necessary to speed the regrowth of trees and wildlife foods. Some species of rodents will be temporarily displaced during the first year to preserve seed necessary to revegetate the area.

The wildlife biologist will prepare the selective woody material and revegetation plans, and supervise the execution to assure that the environmental manipulation maximizes wildlife enhancement.

-OR-

There will be three clearcut areas on the sale. Logging debris will be burned. The area will be poisoned to kill the rodents so seed will survive to produce a new crop of lumber.

<u>Glen A. Horner</u>   *Horner started as a temporary in 1963 and received a permanent appointment in 1967. He worked on the Siuslaw, Deschutes, Ochoco, Gifford Pinchot, and Mt. Hood NFs. He was Forest Service Representative (FSR) for timber sales contracts on the Umatilla NF when he retired in 1994.*

Somewhere around 1978 or 1979, when I was a sale administrator on the Mt. Adams District of the Gifford Pinchot NF, we had a sale that was located just below the boundary of the Mt. Adams Wilderness. If memory serves me correctly it was called the Twin Sale. It was a series of clearcuts, some were designated as tractor logging units and some were designated as cable logging units. There were a series of tractor units that were each about 40 acres in size and consisted of a mix of species. It seems like each unit had a nice creek running down one side of it and there were a number of snags in each unit as there would be in any unit. All of these units were designated as clearcuts and the creeks were the unit boundaries.

Art Currier was the Timber Management Assistant on the District and he called me aside one day and said "Let's do something a little different with those tractor units on that sale." What he wanted to do was negotiate with the purchaser to leave some standing snags in each of the units and leave a buffer strip along the creeks in each of the units. This was in the days before more formal contract modifications, so we did a little horse trading with the purchaser and the logger. They agreed to leave a number of snags and I ran a new boundary line leaving a small buffer strip along each of the creeks in each of the tractor units. After they were logged, these clear cuts looked very strange at the time. For years we had been arguing with loggers and purchasers to cut all the snags even for a 200-foot distance outside of the cutting boundary. Now we had these units that had a number of snags within the units and a strip of timber along the creeks.

As things happen, this sale was selected as a sale to review by the Supervisor's Office staff as they did every year on every District.

They would form a team in the SO and randomly pick a sale to review each year on each District. The practice was to review the layout plans, how the layout went, the contract, the administration of the contract and some active logging to see how all was being carried out.

I'll never forget the look on Barret Couglan's, the Timber Staff, face that day when we rolled up to one of these units that we had taken upon ourselves to change. We got out of the rigs and had the usual amount of standing in a circle and kicking rocks in the road while we explained what we had done and why we had done it. The general consensus was that clearcuts should be clearcuts. Why were these snags left in there, and how were we ever going to get back and harvest those strips of timber left along the creeks? The snags and buffer strips were not looked upon very favorably that day.

I thought about that day many times in the future when I was arguing with purchasers and loggers to leave more snags in units for wildlife purposes and making sure nothing interfered with the buffer strips that were designated along dry gullies. How things change!

Frank Johnson   *Johnson describes timber sale work after the Mount St. Helens eruption.*

On January 1, 1981, I arrived on the Gifford Pinchot NF as Timber Staff, just in time to start a big salvage program on the Mount St. Helens volcano-killed timber. It was a fight all the way. One group didn't want us to sell anything, there was no timber market. Washington State Department of Labor and Industries said we could not log or haul near a snag and we had to leave snags. All we could see was snags for miles. Chief Peterson said you could not understand the size of the blast zone until you flew over it.

We got 400 million board feet the first year which was our target. In three years with the aid of some very good hands and the cooperation of adjacent Forests, we salvaged all that the law would allow. The area we could harvest kept changing. We had high lead machines, tractors and helicopters everywhere. There was a place or two where you could see 15 to 20 sides at one time. In addition, we were chipping culls and had those trucks moving about. I am sure we broke the record for the number of trucks you can put on a one-lane road.

Ron Humphrey (With help from Patti Rodgers, Mike Strange and Ron Kintzley) *Humphrey started as a temporary in 1962 and received a permanent appointment in 1965. He worked on the Payette and Toiyabe NFs in R-4, the Hiawatha and Huron-Manistee NFs in R-9, the Gifford Pinchot, Wallowa-Whitman, Malheur, Mt. Hood, and Willamette NFs in R-6, the Kootenai NF in R-1, and the Tongass NF (Stikine Area) in R-10. He was Forest Supervisor of the Olympic NF in R- 6 when he retired in 1998.*

The following incident was one of the finest examples of teamwork on a Ranger District that I saw in my 33 years with the USFS.

The situation began on a stormy night in 1984 on the Lowell Ranger District of the Willamette NF, which is now part of the Middle Fork District which combined Lowell, Rigdon and Oakridge Districts after the major workload changes brought on by the NW Forest Plan. Lowell was a relatively small (154,000 acres or so), lower elevation District close to Eugene along the Willamette River. The District had significant timber/fuels/reforestation, watershed, fish and wildlife, special forest products and recreation programs. Of special note to the recreation program were a number of low elevation trails that provided nearly year-round opportunities for hikers coming principally from the Eugene/Springfield communities. Some of those trails were on Hardesty Mountain which abutted the Cottage Grove District on the Umpqua NF to the south.

Hardesty Mountain contained an inventoried roadless area which had been analyzed during RARE I and RARE II. In 1984, the Oregon Wilderness Bill had been passed and Hardesty had not been included, essentially releasing the area back to its previous management which permitted a wide-range of multiple use activities, including timber harvest.

Back to the stormy night. A major windstorm event occurred that night, blowing down a fair amount of timber on Hardesty in the Goodman Creek area. Blowdown ranged from two areas, less than 20 acres each of concentrated blowdown, to other areas of variable blowdown. The District had an aggressive salvage program and quickly assessed the situation. Hardesty Mountain vegetation had been influenced over the years by large wildfires. Although there was some classic old growth, mixed species forest on Hardesty, the majority of the area was dominated by Douglas-fir aged 90 to 120 years. Quality of the timber was excellent and per acre volumes quite good. There was a strong desire among the District staff to quickly salvage as much of the blowdown as possible.

One issue adding impetus to move quickly was the fear of Douglas-fir bark beetle buildups in the blowdown. The District's experience was that this type of blowdown would be quickly infested by the bark beetle, populations of beetles would expand rapidly and they would in turn infest standing green timber. A rule-of-thumb the salvage crew and silviculturists used was that for every blowndown tree, two more green trees would be killed by the beetles before the populations crashed and subsided. This concern was proven real. As spring rolled around and we were conducting our numerous field trips designed with help from Public Affairs staff Jerry Mason to collect input, we observed lots of beetle entry holes and frass on the downed trees.

Closely following the National Environmental Policy Act (NEPA) process, an interdisciplinary team was formed to do an environmental analysis and to prepare an environmental assessment (EA). As we anticipated, during the public involvement process concerns were raised by hiking groups and some of the environmental groups from Eugene. A variety of issues were identified including: the roadless nature of the affected area, blowdown along and across the main Hardesty trail, sensitive plants, inventoried Northern Spotted Owl habitat, and the need to harvest the blowdown to stem the beetle attack. The sale planners developed a range of alternatives, including no harvest.

The ball was now in my court as District Ranger to make a decision. I discussed the options with our diverse constituents and considered the various impacts of action vs. no action. My decision was to proceed with a salvage sale that included two small clearcuts and individual tree salvage where the blowdown was more scattered. The timber sale was to be entirely helicopter-logged with no new roads to be built thus maintaining the roadless character. In areas of the least intensive blowdown, we would try using a newly-developed pheromone treatment to prevent beetle reproduction and further beetle-induced mortality. The spotted owl area would not be salvaged. And finally, I committed to put together a broad-based consensus group to help the Forest develop an alternative for Hardesty that would be included among the alternatives considered in the land management plan being prepared for the Willamette, under the tutelage of Rolf Anderson. A *Finding of No Significant Impact* and *Decision Notice* were prepared. An appeal was filed by the Oregon Environmental Council, but our decision was upheld by the Forest Supervisor, Mike Kerrick.

Timber sale prep proceeded and the Rotor sale was advertised and sold. Mission accomplished by a finely-tuned District team! Not quite! On a Monday morning shortly after the sale was sold, we received one of those notes you often hear about in hostage cases - a piece of paper with different letters and words cut out of various sources. The note essentially said that the blowdown trees had been spiked! It was signed *the Hardesty Avengers*.

Of course we had heard of tree-spiking in California by this time, but I think this was the first time I'd heard of it in Oregon. We immediately dispatched a team to the field to investigate. Sure enough, they found other signs posted in the woods within the timber sale and after a cursory examination they found a lot of large nails had been driven into the trees.

Perplexed, I sat in our office on South Pioneer Street in Lowell and discussed the situation with some of our District staff and members of the Lowell Action Group (LAG). The LAG was made up of the technicians, young foresters, biologists and other specialists who really got the job done on the ground. Some of staff like Tom Hussey, Mike Strange, Monty Megargel, John Robison, Fran Hemm and Don Gray, plus myself, were contemplating a recommendation to the Forest Supervisor that we unilaterally terminate the sale.

"No way!" said members of LAG: Ron Kintzley, Bill Pratt, Bob Slimp, Norm Michaels, Steve Rhineberger, Lenny Diaz, Lynn Sullivan, Jerry Smith, Ranotta McNair and Dave Bishop.

"OK, what's your plan?" I asked. These folks had surprised me numerous times before with their resourcefulness and determination. Their response was that Kintzley and Pratt had already checked out the availability of metal detectors to rent and they would proceed to pull all the nails as soon as I signed the purchase order to rent the detectors.

We figured what the heck, it was worth a try and I signed the purchase order. But we called the timber sale purchaser, Seneca Lumber, and told them what we were up to. If they wanted out, they could request the sale be cancelled. They cautiously agreed to see how we would do.

Working most of the week and over the weekend, the fire and fuels crew climbed over, under and around a lot of blowdown and pulled around 30 pounds of nails from the down trees, mostly in areas designated for clear cuts. The crew consisted of Randy Green, Frank Harrington, John Iturra, Bob Walker, and Ross Williams. When they finished, the crew leaders, Kintzley and Pratt, came to me and said they had the done the job and the sale could proceed. The purchaser looked it over and decided it was worth the risk to get the wood, plus to send a message to the eco-terrorists. As Columbia Helicopter logged the sale and hauled the volume to the Seneca Mill in Eugene, the Timber Sale Administrator, Mike Mullen, reported that they employed a log inspector who scanned each log with a metal detector before they went to the head saw. They found *one more* nail!

I was so tremendously proud of that team of ground-pounders! They got the job done once again. The sale was completed, pheromone was sprayed, clearcuts successfully planted and the trails were opened to use with little disruption. The consensus group met for over a year and developed a plan for Hardesty that became part of the preferred alternative in the Willamette Land Management Plan Environmental Impact Statement, and the media got a lot of mileage out of whole process. The eco-terrorists were never apprehended.

<u>Bill Ciesla</u> *Ciesla started as a temporary in 1957 and received a permanent appointment in 1960. He worked in Forest Pest Management Field Offices in Asheville, North Carolina and Pineville, Louisiana in R-8, in R-1, and in the Washington Office. His last job with the Forest Service was Director of Forest Pest Management in R-6. He was the Forest Protection Officer for the Food and Agriculture Organization in Rome, Italy, when he retired in 1994.*

In the spring of 1988, the Region was struggling with the most massive outbreak of western spruce budworm in its history. Several million acres were involved, including portions of the Mt. Hood NF, the Warm Springs Indian Reservation, and the Blue Mountains. Ironically, during the previous summer, my wife, Pat, and I made a summer camping trip into Oregon. One evening, while camped on the eastern slopes of Mt. Hood, we marveled at the extent of the damage the forests were suffering. "Why doesn't the Forest Service do something about this mess?" I asked out loud. About two months later my question was answered. I was transferred from Fort Collins, Colorado, to Portland to assume the duties of R-6 Director of Forest Pest Management. And my first priority task was to *do something* about the spruce budworm outbreak.

When I arrived on the job, planning for a large spray project was already well underway. An EIS was in preparation, contracts for pesticide, aircraft and related equipment were being written and an overall organizational approach was under development. Within a few weeks of my arrival, Regional Forester Jim Torrence announced that we should plan for spraying up to one million acres of forest, provided that this many acres met the budworm population criteria. It was going to be a busy summer.

Several things about this project would be unique. For the first time ever, we were committing ourselves totally to the use of a biological insecticide, *Bacillus thuringiensis*, for a large insect suppression effort. Also, with the encouragement of Mary Jo Lavin, who had also just come on board as Deputy Regional Forester for State and Private Forestry, we adopted the incident command system as the overall organizational structure to manage the project.

Because of the magnitude of the project, we organized five Incident Command teams: two for the Mt. Hood NF, one for the Warm Springs Indian Reservation, one for the Umatilla NF and another in LaGrande, Oregon, for the Blue Mountains. In addition we established an area command in the RO to coordinate the five teams. Woody Williams,

Determining spray areas for spruce budworm control, Wenatchee NF – 1976

Helicopter spraying on the spruce budworm control project,
Wenatchee NF – 1976

who was fire management officer on the Willamette NF at the time, headed up the area command with Jim Hadfield, of the R-6 FPM staff as his deputy.

When the aircraft bids arrived we found ourselves classic victims of the laws of supply-and-demand. The project required a fleet of about 80 helicopters and fixed-wing aircraft. This meant that every spray contractor in the West was ensured a piece of this pie. The bids were high, much higher than expected, and required a last minute request for additional funds to cover the project costs.

After successfully resolving some last-minute problems pumping the heavy, viscous liquid spray formulations through helicopter spray systems, we began spray operations in mid-June. The project required mobilization of several hundred people from around the Region for about two months, many with extensive project fire experience. We also had a number of detailers assigned to the project, mostly entomologists from other Forest Service Regions. The spirit at each of the incident command centers was outstanding. The people worked well together. At each center, a team member with some artistic talents designed a project tee-shirt, which was proudly worn by the team members. Evening picnics and barbeques were almost daily events.

Operations went smoothly until one morning when a spray helicopter crashed on the Warm Springs IR resulting in the death of the pilot. I happened to be on site the day of the crash. When I looked over the fleet of helicopters working that unit, I saw a rag-tag outfit of ships, many lacking the required emergency dump systems. Somehow the name *Polish Air Force* came to mind. Since Ciesla is a classic Polish name, I got away with so designating this fleet. That name stuck for the remainder of the project, especially among the members of the area command team. I grounded the helicopters lacking the emergency dump systems. Within days, the contractor had installed the required systems and we were back in business.

The only other mishap that occurred was a close call on one of the Mt. Hood units, when a spray helicopter got down too low in a canyon and began chopping branches out of the tops of some huge trees with the rotor. Happily, the pilot was able make it back safely to the heliport but with a cabin filled with Douglas-fir branches.

Fortunately the weather was favorable throughout the spray window and we got all of the qualifying area, about 600,000 acres, successfully treated. Thanks to Woody Williams, the alligator (as in *up to your ass in alligators*) became the project's symbol. As each incident command completed spraying their designated unit and began to demobilize, the incident commander made a trip to the RO and proudly presented Regional Forester Jim Torrence with a large plastic alligator, hog-tied into a bizarre position.

For me, this project was one of the biggest challenges of my Forest Service career. Moreover, seeing the deep commitment of all those involved in the project was a wonderful introduction to R-6. And the project was a great success. All of the spray units achieved the stated objective of reducing the budworm population down to less than one larva per 15-inch branch. One year later, Tommy Greg and Cathy Sheehan of the R-6 forest pest management staff conducted an analysis using aerial survey data and a geographic information system to demonstrate a significant reduction in budworm defoliation over previous years. And we did it all with a biological insecticide. Quite an accomplishment!

RESEARCH: "I remember hosting a delegation of Russian scientists - -."

Jerry Patchen *Patchen started as a temporary in 1951 and received a permanent appointment in 1954. He worked on the Wallowa-Whitman, Wenatchee, Malheur, Winema, and Willamette NFs in R-6. He was on the R-6 Regional Office Lands & Minerals staff when he retired in 1988.*

In 1975, I was transferred to the Willamette NF. It was a good time (for me anyway) to be a Forest Service employee and a good time to be on the Willamette. The workload was humongous and Forest employees were, in my opinion, well-trained and competent. The technology needed to manage Forest lands for multiple use to me was sophisticated and expanding. Because of the workload and the pace, it seemed like the Forest managers were constantly in the spotlight

Art Tiedeman, PNW researcher, sampling water quality in a burned area
in the Entiat Watershed, Wenatchee NF – 1974

Research scientist Fred Swanson
conducting studies in the newly
designated Mount St. Helens
National Volcanic Monument,
Gifford Pinchot NF – c1980s

locally (being in Eugene did not make matters easier, either) and nationally. A significant portion of manager and staff time was spent responding to inquiries or hosting visitors.

One such visit I remember was with Jerry Franklin of the Pacific Northwest Research Station hosting a delegation of Russian scientists who were on the H.J. Andrews Experimental Forest to look at a part of the International Biome network. There were four people: a stern-looking, older woman; a burly, granite-visaged Ukrainian man; a young, articulate man name *Yuri*; and a *smashing blonde* woman who was a US citizen and spoke fluent Russian. (This woman was also going to be an interpreter at the Olympic games in Moscow, but the US ended up boycotting those games). At first, the two older people communicated solely through the interpreter, but Yuri spoke fluent English. It seemed like Yuri and I hit it off famously. He was open and frank about Russia and its government and was a very knowledgeable biologist. Of course, the Russians had a ton of questions. However, after a few hours of going through the interpreter, the two older people began speaking English. After that, the interpreter was seldom used. At the end of the second day as we said farewells, Yuri and I traded various items with each other - e.g. my Forest Service field cap and some kind of honorary medallions. A few days after their departure, I was talking with Jerry Franklin about the trip. He asked me who I thought the KGB agent in the group was. I said it was probably the Ukrainian but Jerry said, "No, it was Yuri!"

Glenn A. Cooper *Cooper started as a temporary in 1952 and received a permanent appointment in 1956. He worked on the Rogue River and Gifford Pinchot NFs and in the R-6 Regional Office, at the Central States Research Station, and in research in the Washington Office. He was Deputy Director of the Pacific Northwest Research Station when he retired in 1986.*

Cooper was the newly appointed Deputy Director for the Pacific Northwest Research Station when he led a trip to the Forestry and Range Sciences Laboratory at La Grande, Oregon, to review the wildlife and range management research work of Project Leader Jack Ward Thomas. The people mentioned in this ditty are: Dawg - PNW Deputy Director Glenn Cooper; Captain Jack - Project Leader Jack Ward Thomas; Wiseman Bob - Associate Deputy Chief of Research Bob Harris; Cookie - Wildlife Biologist

507

*Larry Bryant; Ranger - Range Scientist Jon M. Skovlin; Evie
Owler - Wildlife Biologist Evelyn Bull.*

THE DAWG AND PONY SHOW

Out near Starkey in spring '81
This saga of research was planned for fun.
The crew from LaGrande was loaded for bear,
Knowing the Dawg soon would be there.

Loaded with food and a bootlegged barn
Captain Jack was a man of charm.
The quarters were polished and horses in place.
Everyone coached in extending his grace,

From Portland came the Deputy Dawg
With wise man Bob along for the jog.
They wanted to see the many improvements
Fostered by Jack's unusual movements.

A bright afternoon greeted their arrival
Dawg and Bob never questioned survival.
Cookie Bryant had gassed up the ponies
That Jack had rented to carry his cronies.

Two clans of horses were for these riders
With Kitty and Casey strictly one-siders.
Luke and Kate were such bosom brothers
They laid back ears when near those others.

Well, Dawg got on Kitty to take the jaunt
While Jack straddled Casey, to good luck flaunt.
Bob mounted Luke' cause Kate had the Cook
And they rode to the ranges for a Research look.

The grass was great, and the forest fine
They rode in peace through flower and pine.
They talked of succession and good reproduction
While D. Dawg's butt underwent reduction.

Casey spied Luke trot up beside her
Then curled her lip for a stiff reminder.
And arching her back, she threw back her head.
Mightily trying her rider to shed.

Jack instinctively made a grab for the horn
But the McClellan saddle on which he was borne
Was light and easy for the horse to stand
'Cept it provided nothing for a clutching hand.

"Leave the saddle and save your hair,"
Thought Jack as he bounced high in the air.
He leaned ahead to maintain his pose,
But Casey swiveled and her head hit his nose.

The horse reeled with a cut on her snoot
And the rider flew with head under boot.
Jack hit the road with a sickening smack,
And rolled from the hooves to avoid their crack.

Cookie jumped off to check on the Duke
While Kitty blocked Casey, and Bob held Luke.
"Are you hurt? Asked Cookie before Jack spoke,
And Jack sputtered out, "Mah nose's broke."

"Ah knows yer nose's broke, but are you hurt?"
Were the famous words that Cookie spurt.
And Jack just groaned, "Mah nose's broke."
But anyone less would've had a stroke.

With a bloodied beak and two bleary eyes,
Jack rode again over Casey's cries.
The man and the beast had had their fight
And the first day ended with the sun still bright.

The morning came with Jon the Ranger
Hauling sewed up Jack to face more danger.
The feisty horses were wild as goats
Even old Kitty was feeling her oats.

That was a day of falling and prancing
All the critters were jumping and heartily dancing.
First it was Dawg swinging on Kitty
Trying to mount during a stumble and ditty.

Then Luke dumped Bob with his hocks in the mire
And the wise Old Timer then walked to the wire.
But the show of the day went to Casey the mare
Who waited for Jack with an innocent stare.

With Jack on her back, again starting the show
She pitched and reared like in the rodeo.
Jack jumped clear and landed on the turf
While Casey stomped demons into the earth.

Four jumps, two rears, and a step from the wood,
Then three more big ones to show that she could.
Soon Jack got on her and they pushed up a hill
To take out her wind and dampen her will.

Evie the Owler was never in a wrangle,
She rode the saddle with her feet at a dangle.
Always banging on trees plumb full of holes
She obviously favored the busted up boles.

And long Ranger Jon burned stumps everywhere,
While Deputy Dawg fretted for poor Smokey Bear.
No fires got away but the smoke was so thick
That LaGrande thought it was a St. Helens' trick.

Thus the day ended in a much better way
As all the critters were led to the hay.
But Dawg told Jack as they ended the run,
"Fill in completely the damn CA-1."

Thomas M. Quigley *Quigley received a permanent employee on the Rio Grande NF in R-2 in 1976. He transferred to the Pacific Northwest Research Station in 1977, starting and finishing in La Grande, Oregon, and doing tours in Fort Collins, Colorado, and Walla Walla, Washington. He transferred to the Rocky Mountain Research Station in Ogden, Utah, and then came back to PNW as the Station Director in 2003. Quigley is a third generation Forest Service employee. His grandfather was a District Ranger and Assistant Forest Supervisor on the old LaSal NF in Utah and his father was a District Ranger on the Fishlake NF in Utah.*

Jack Ward Thomas was a long-time fixture in northeast Oregon, long before he became a symbol of the spotted owl wars and our Chief. Jack was not only a colorful actor in natural resource debates, he was also a target. When Jack and a few of his colleagues cooked up the idea that the Starkey Experimental Forest and Range would be used to test the concepts of elk, deer, and cattle interactions they knew they had a big selling job on their hands, but did not realize how much of a target that might make Jack personally. As the concept grew into a proposal to put elk-proof fencing around nearly 25,000 acres of Starkey, word began to spread among long-time users of the area.

One small, mostly unknown, group was using Starkey as a training ground for their paramilitary maneuvers. This group would dress in camouflage, carry rifles of various types and scatter among the trees. We had paid them no real attention, as they were essentially undetected. We really don't know what their intentions were beyond spending their spare time tracking each other in the woods around Starkey.

What was once an apparent retreat for playing soldier in the woods turned a different color when pictures were posted around Starkey with what looked to be Jack's face centered within the crosshairs of a rifle scope. It took some degree of investigation and some pointed private conversations before the pictures disappeared and the camouflage clad crowd moved their operations elsewhere or disbanded. Jack took all this in stride and after many long meetings, much persuasion, considerable analysis, and a long-narrow timber sale (about the width of a fence right-of-way), the Starkey elk-proof fence was in place. This seemed to condition Jack for the threats he would receive while fighting the owl wars of the Northwest.

LAND AND RESOURCE MANAGEMENT PLANNING: "The National Forest Management Act of 1976 has had considerable influence on the Forest Service and the way it conducts business."

Gerald W. "Jerry" Williams   *Williams received a permanent appointment as a sociologist in 1979. His training and role as a sociologist gave him a unique perspective for participating in Forest Service planning activities. Williams worked on the Umpqua and Willamette NFs and in the R-6 Regional Office. He was the National Historian in the Washington Office in 2005.*

In the spring of 1979, the Umpqua was just starting into the National Forest Management Act (NFMA) planning process. I was placed on the *core* planning team along with Jamie Stone, Leonard Morin, and soon, Bill Connelly, forest economist. Others were added later. It was a fast track learning course for me. I had never taken any forestry, wildlife, or geology courses in my many years of college. In order to understand what the other specialist team members were saying, as well as meaning, I had to read and listen. What an education! I once asked Jack Wright to send me to some type of formal training in a number of specialties, but he refused. He said, essentially, that he did not want me to be indoctrinated, rather to step back to hear what was being said and written by the specialists, being a neutral observer. It fit my personality perfectly (I had been a bartender during college days at Ashland).

When the draft forest plan EIS was finally produced in 1988, there was an uproar from the local timber companies. The Douglas Timber Operators (DTO), a group of small mill owners, had hired a small staff to promote increased or at least not reduced timber from federal and state lands. The Association of Oregon and California Counties, Douglas County and others did not like the plan. During the draft EIS, the DTO organized a letter-writing campaign against the preferred alternative. Over 95% of all 15,500 letters came from the timber industry. I was put in charge of a team of about 25 Umpqua employees to sort through the letters. As most of them were form letters from the timber side, it became fairly easy to analyze the results. However, the industry form letter was actually a *check-the-box letter*. Thus, every letter had to be looked at and analyzed. In the Umpqua area, at that time, there was only a small environmental

512

community. They were overwhelmed by the timber industry and the pro-industry viewpoint of the county. The process of recording the 216,000 comments onto a data base took about three weeks. It took some doing to not just *count votes* when the interdisciplinary team was revising the draft plan. The final EIS was printed in 1989.

Robert T. Meurisse *Meurisse started as a temporary in 1958, and received a permanent appointment in 1962. He worked on the Gunnison, Shoshone, Medicine Bow, and Black Hills NFs in R-2, the Prescott, Coconino, Sitgreaves, Kaibab, Apache, and Tonto NFs in R-3, in the Washington Office, and at the Intermountain Forest and Range Experiment Station. He was the R-6 Regional Soil Scientist when he retired in 1998.*

The National Forest Management Act of 1976 has had considerable influence on the Forest Service and the way it conducts business. One of the features of the act was that it required more emphasis on some of the basic resources such as water, soils, and native plants. A key provision required *identification of the suitability of lands for resource management and ensure that timber will be harvested only where soil, slope, or other watershed conditions will not be irreversibly damaged.* The NFMA also required *there is assurance that such lands can be adequately restocked within five years after harvest.* In the common parlance, lands that didn't meet these criteria were considered *unsuited for timber management.* It was up to the Regions to determine how to identify the above conditions.

Soil scientists in the Regional Office developed preliminary criteria for determining where irreversible damage might occur and where soil and other site conditions were such that satisfactory regeneration could not be achieved in the required time period. The preliminary guides were then reviewed by Forest silviculturalists, soil scientists and others, as well as the Regional Office timber management staff.

The irreversible damage criteria focused on situations where accelerated landslides would be probable. The ability to regenerate harvested sites criteria focused on soil moisture availability and ability to physically secure seedlings in the soil. The primary source of data for both of these criteria was from the soil resource inventories that had been conducted on each National Forest.

513

As forests began to identify their *unsuited* lands for incorporation into the Forest land and resource management plans, some concerns began to arise that there were too many acres identified as unsuited. Region 6 had identified a large number of acres, more than any other region. It prompted a review by the Chief's Office, but after further evaluation, the criteria remained largely intact.

A particularly striking example of some lands found to be unsuited was on the Willamette NF. What was even more amazing was that a large number of acres are where stands of about 250 to 500 year old Douglas-fir, with some noble fir and Pacific silver fir, had as much as 100,000 board feet per acre. During one Regional Forester staff meeting, Regional Forester Dick Worthington commented that there were *no unsuited lands on the Willamette National Forest.* This was before he had seen the data from the Forest. Later I brought it to his attention that there was substantial acreage there that was unsuited, and much of it was due to the inability to meet reforestation criteria.

At the time, the Willamette NF had a soil scientist by the name of Harold (Hal) Legard. Hal was a highly professional, experienced, *can do* person who had worked on the original soil resource inventory and remained on the Forest as the Forest soil scientist. The Forest also had a highly skilled, and respected, silviculturalist by the name of Ralph Jaszkowski. Hal and Ralph worked very closely together, and they knew the Forest. For a few years they had been observing an area with beautiful stands of old growth, but where some limited harvests in these stands were not getting regenerated. Hal and Ralph began some *experiments* to see if they could get seedlings to grow. They tried some rather unconventional things such as packing in more soil, rigging an irrigation system and fertilizing, but even with these methods success of seedlings was poor. They had done their homework.

In my discussions with Dick Worthington I had described this situation to him. He remained skeptical. But, I said, "Why don't you go and have a look for yourself." So, he did. Dick had a healthy respect for the land and really did want to do what was best for the land. He also was committed to a strong, high quality soils program for guiding resource management.

In my view, the process of identifying lands unsuited for timber management in the late 1970s, based primarily on data from the soil resource inventories more than paid for the cost of the surveys. It also was a time when the relatively young soils program gained considerable respect in the Pacific Northwest Region and the nation. It also afforded a great amount of credibility to the development of the forest plans based on the application of a fundamental ecosystem science.

<u>Jack Ward Thomas</u> *Thomas began his career as a wildlife researcher with the Texas Game and Fish Commission in the late 1950s. He joined the Forest Service in Morgantown, West Virginia, in 1966 and worked in research in Massachusetts and at the Blue Mountains Research Lab in La Grande, Oregon. He headed the Forest Ecosystem Management Assessment Team (FEMAT) to present a resolution based on the best scientific evidence to resolve the spotted owl crisis in the Pacific Northwest and northern California. He was the thirteenth Chief of the Forest Service serving from 1993 to 1996.*

During the last six years of my 30-year Forest Service career, circumstances dictated that I was *in the public eye* a bit more than was common for a wildlife biologist. At the start of that period, I was *drafted* by the heads of the Forest Service, Bureau of Land Management, National Park Service and the Fish and Wildlife Service to head up a team to develop a strategy for managing the northern spotted owl.

It was becoming clear that the owl was associated with old growth and a century of harvesting had reduced such forests to a tiny fraction of what once existed. And what old growth remained was being harvested rapidly and fragmented into smaller and smaller blocks. The handwriting was on the wall that the owl would be listed as *threatened* or *endangered* under the Endangered Species Act.

Clearly, that would severely reduce the amount and rate of cutting of old-growth resulting in significant consequences to the timber industry that had so long been such a large part of the economy of Oregon, Washington, and northern California. Politicians had done all they could to delay the day of reckoning - but the string had run out. The

Presidential election of 1992 pitting President George H. W. Bush against Bill Clinton and H. Ross Perot, was a year in the future. And the owl would be a wild card affecting the outcome in the Pacific Northwest - and, perhaps, the nation.

I was essentially given carte blanche to gather a team and the resources to do the job. I gathered the *best and the brightest* of the biologists working with spotted owls or having special talents useful to the effort. We had six months to do the job. The core team was made up of Jared Verner, Barry Noon and Eric Forsman of the Forest Service; E. Charles Meslow of the Fish and Wildlife Service; Joseph Lint of the Bureau of Land Management and me. There was a supporting cast of dozens of highly skilled professionals. We toiled for six months to produce the plan that had been requested.

Toward the end of the exercise, the agency heads gathered in Portland to hear what we had to say. The meeting was held in a hotel near the Portland airport. When we arrived several hundred demonstrators from the timber industry carrying signs and chanting slogans greeted us. They were hard-working folks scared for their livelihood and their way of life.

We gave our briefing. The Chief was obviously shaken, but he expressed appreciation for a job well done. The Director of the Fish and Wildlife Service praised the quality of the work. The Parks Service Director remained silent as his agency was not really affected. The Director of the Bureau of Land Management was red in the face and blurted out, "This will cost me my political career!"

A week later, we finished putting the final touches on our report for Congress. That last morning in Portland, I came back from breakfast to pick up the briefing documents and prepare to board a plane for Washington. The office that had been so busy for six months was now empty. My footsteps echoed as I moved about. When I reached my office, sitting in my chair was a picture from a children's book. It depicted a boy in overalls with a straw hat and a bundle of clothing swinging from a stick over his shoulder. He was walking up a path toward a fork in the trail. There was a sign at the fork that read *the rest of your life* pointing one way and *no longer an option* pointed the other. An owl was perched on the top of the signpost. There was prophecy in that cartoon - and I knew it. I didn't know what was to come but surely, things would be very different.

The hearings before the House and Senate Committees were more polemic castigation and posturing than an effort to gain information. Members of Congress performed for the newspapers and television cameras. I struggled to remain calm and reminded myself that this was my *ten minutes of fame* that Woody Allen had said we, each and everyone, was due. This too would pass - and none too quickly.

Two days later, I was on my way home to La Grande, Oregon. La Grande was so far off the beaten track that you *couldn't get there from here*. My plane from Washington took me to Denver. Then, there was a plane to Portland. By the time I made my way to the *bull pen* that served as the exit point for the commuter airline in Portland, I was exhausted. I sprawled on a bench of chairs. The three men sitting across from me were looking me over carefully and whispering back and forth.

Finally, one spoke. "Say, Mister, did anyone ever tell you that you look just like that biologist fellow? What's his name? Jack Ward Thomas?"

"Well, yes, several people have told me that over the years."

"Geez, fellow, that must REALLY piss you off?"

"Sometimes."

I picked up a newspaper from the seat next to me and pretended to read. The image of that little pilgrim in the cartoon approaching that fork in the trail jumped into my mind. Things were never going to be the same again - not ever.

ADMINISTRATION: "The best part of the system, where messages could be sent instantaneously anywhere in the country to other employees, was wonderful."

Harold Welborn *Welborn received a permanent appointment in 1962. He worked on the Mt. Hood, Okanogan, and Siuslaw NFs*

517

in R-6. He was an Assistant Forest Supervisor and the Administrative Officer on the Willamette NF when he retired in 1986. The construction of the first Ranger Station by the Job Corps on the Siuslaw NF is described by Wendall Jones in a story earlier in this Chapter (All in a Day's Work).

In the late 1960s and early 1970s there was a rapid buildup of professional specialists of all kinds in the Forest Service in response to increased sensitivity to environmental concerns. The increase in personnel was especially strong on Forests with a sizable annual allowable timber harvest and even larger when sensitive soils were present such as on the Siuslaw NF. The Siuslaw built up a large corps of scientists and engineers very quickly to be able to get out the cut in an environmentally safe manner. This created an acute shortage of office space on the Forest. It left us with offices often less than half of what was needed.

At the same time the Siuslaw's Angell Job Corps Conservation Center was looking for substantial, challenging building projects. Angell had a new carpentry apprentice program which was operated by the carpenter's union. Angell had quickly run through a number of small buildings such as campground restrooms and picnic shelters and wanted bigger and more challenging projects for the corpsmen trainees.

I was the Forest administrative officer (AO) and the Forest Job Corps staff officer. Job Corps Center Director Millard Mitchell and I decided we had a good fit by putting the two needs together. The Forest had a need for five Ranger Station expansion projects. After discussions on funding and design with Regional and Forest personnel with responsibility and concerns it was decided to move ahead with office construction projects. The Forest Ranger/staff group together with the Forest Supervisor prioritized the District needs. The jobs began when Spencer T. (Tenny) Moore was Supervisor and went through the tenure of F. Dale Robertson.

The first station selected was the Hebo Ranger Station, located at Hebo, Oregon. Wendall Jones was Ranger at that time from beginning through dedication. That project took the longest to get off the ground. There were many concerns to work through for the initial project that went easier on the following projects. Funding was always a concern. A very strong concern was engineering design and project supervision. The design was a custom design due to site constraints and the fact that the existing office building was to be incorporated into the new one. Of course, the District personnel had to continue operating through the construction and the Corpsmen were housed in Hebo.

That project was concluded successfully and was dedicated in a fine ceremony on Labor Day with participation of the Forest Service and the Labor Department. The principal speaker was then Senator Mark Hatfield.

Following the Hebo project were the Alsea and Waldport offices. The projects were a great thing for the corpsmen trainees, the Job Corps and the Forest Service. Many corpsmen were trained as apprentice carpenters on challenging jobs while the Forest Service gained three offices worth several hundred thousand dollars when need was high and funds were fought over for competing needs.

I was AO there from 1969 to 1975. In that short six years, we built or had underway three new offices and got leases completed or underway for the other three. We doubled the Supervisor's Office space and stayed in the building while doing it, only moved most people once, some twice.

Jerry Gause *Gause started as a temporary in 1958 and received a permanent appointment in 1963. He worked on the Sierra, Angeles, and Inyo NFs in Region 5, in the Washington Office, and in the R-6 Regional Office. He was the Regional Program Manager for the Clean Air Act in R-5 when he retired in 2003.*

I remember very well in 1980 when RF Dick Worthington and I took the editors of the *Oregonian* and the *Portland Journal* on a flight to tour FS facilities in Oregon. Rogue River NF Supervisor Don Smith met us at the airport and we had a fine tour of the new J. Herbert Stone Nursery by its newly appointed manager. We then returned to the airport for a big lunch and then a flight to the Umpqua to meet Forest Supervisor Dick Swartzlander at the Toketee airstrip.

I noticed somewhere high above Crater Lake that the Regional Forester's head was sort of bobbing around. I presumed he was having a nap. About five minutes later, the pilot says, "Where is the Toketee airstrip?" No one knew and someone said we may want to wake up Dick. We did, and all of us started looking around. Dick aimed the pilot to the east, and that didn't work, so we flew several dog legs, and finally Dick yelled and pointed, "There it is!" Dick laughed in his usual way. We spent a great evening at Lemolo Lake and returned with our happy editors the next day, after overflights on the Deschutes and Mt. Hood NFs.

Gause tells another story about a well-known R-6 personality.

The brightness and humor of Jack Usher was outstanding. Jack worked on the Fremont NF and other places as well, serving as Timber Manangement Director in R-1 and R-6. Jack was a man of immense proportions, mentally and physically. You always knew when he was in the room.

I recall one day (about 1983) in the Conference Room of the Multnomah Building where we had a serious meeting going on. Jack walked in about 15 minutes after the hour, grabbed a chair and flopped down. He pulled out a cigarette, kept it unlit and fumbled with it near the ash tray. He listened hard and soon engaged in the conversation. After a while, he just took over the meeting with numerous ideas on how things should be settled. The vocal activity in the room raised. Everybody was talking out of turn, agreeing and disagreeing! Then all of a sudden Jack says, "What meeting is this?" We told him. He said, "My gosh, I guess I am in the wrong meeting." He then scurried out the door leaving behind chaos and a lot of laughter.

Julia S. Duncan *Before joining the Forest Service, Duncan was an Electronic Technician at White Sands Proving Grounds. She was the first female Electronic Technician hired by the FS nationwide, beginning her career as a temporary in 1977 and receiving a permanent appointment in 1978. She worked on the Mt. Hood NF and in the R-6 Regional Office. In 2005 she was the Lead Telecommunication Technician for Customer Service Area 1, including the R-6 Regional Office, PNW Research Lab, the Mt. Hood, Gifford Pinchot, Olympic and Mt. Baker-Snoqualmie NFs, and the Columbia River Gorge National Scenic Area.*

Prior to 1982, the communication system was mainly by radio, for those in the woods or on fires, and leased telephones within the offices. These Forest Service radio systems in use in every region, were designed by Forest Service employees, and consisted of the mountaintop radios, the District control radios, as well as portable and mobile radios, that accessed the mountaintops. This provided a means of communication between resource personnel who traveled into the woods, and between these same field-going personnel and their District offices.

In 1982, the electronic communication within the Forest Service started to change. The telephone industry was hit with the breakup of AT&T. A directive followed stating that the federal agencies were no longer allowed to lease equipment, but must provide their own telephone equipment. This resulted in the communication shop designing telephone systems, installing, and maintaining equipment for telephone service in each Forest Service office. Voice mail came several years later, approximately 1992, as part of the phone systems.

In 1983 to 1984, the Forest Service was introduced to the Data General (DG) computer system, one of the first federal agencies to have an interconnected computer system. The expertise gained in the installation of telephone wiring was put to use for this computer system as well as all computer equipment, such as printers and plotters. The introduction of this computer system and the interconnection of offices put the Forest Service electronic communication system ahead of most federal agencies and other business enterprises, because we had electronic messaging - the forerunner of e-mail as we know it today. The DG computers were replaced begining in 1991 with the more widely used personal computer (PC) type system, the IBM, which we still have in 2003.

Today the electronic communication within the Forest Service includes radio systems for the field-going personnel, telephone systems with digital phones and voice mail for those who remain in the office, and computers for everyone, with e-mail, filing systems, and the capability to access the World Wide Web. The newest technology, already in place in some locations, will be VoIP (Voice over Internet Protocol) and Radio over IP. All of these electronic communication upgrades provide communication tools for the use of the resource people as they go about their duties in the Forests, or on fires, and while in the offices.

<u>Gerald W. "Jerry" Williams</u> *Williams shares some insight on the early use of computers.*

The advent of computers really changed the agency, but not without some grumbling.   In 1985, when the new Data General (DG) computers were about to be installed on the Umpqua, Dick Swartzlander said at the end of a meeting I attended that he did not like the idea of computers on each desk, especially for his staff. As I recall his words they were something like "typing is for typists, I want my managers to manage, not type!" But guess where the first DG terminal was placed? On Swartzlender's desk! Then they were placed on the desks of each staff, then down the ladder to the typing pool. This procedure was followed in almost every FS location across the country. I found out later that this was a deliberate strategy, otherwise the computers would have started in the typing pool and stayed for many years. Where once the Umpqua had three to four typists, within a year there was one.

The DG system was the first government agency contract to provide computers to every employee. The best part of the system, where messages could be sent instantaneously anywhere in the country to other employees, was wonderful. I heard that when the DG system was put in Chief Max Peterson's office, he sent a daily message to the Regional Foresters with some kind of request that required a response. It was Max's way of making sure that the RFs used the new computer system!

"Ecosystems are not only more complex than we think, they are more complex than we can think."

-Frank E. Egler

CHAPTER SIX

<u>1993 to 2005</u> END of the CENTURY; NEW DIRECTION

It was difficult to obtain stories for this chapter. They haven't yet been written. Certainly, they are happening, just as they have for the previous 100 years, but many haven't had enough time to develop from an informal oral recount into a fond remembrance, demanding to be documented and shared with a wide audience. The further we look back, what seemed to be everyday occurrences have evolved into cherished memories that we want to continue to recall. So it has been with collecting stories for this book - the closer we approached current times, the more difficult it was to find or coax out stories. It is not easy to look back when the events are still so close.

That said, this time period marks another major transition for the Forest Service in Region Six. Gone are the big budgets and major new programs of prior years, replaced by the dual challenge of drastically reducing the workforce while still accomplishing the program of work, including implementation of the Forest Plans. Ranger Districts and Forests have been combined to reduce overhead and many jobs have been combined or have disappeared. But there is still much work to be done, and nature still calls the shots. The stories we found for this chapter tell of fires and a flood, and the return of some old timers.

This chapter includes stories about Land and Resource Management Planning, All in a Day's Work, Fire and Research.

LAND AND RESOURCE MANAGEMENT PLANNING: "Whether intended or not, the overriding objective of the management of the federal lands in the Pacific Northwest has evolved to be the preservation of biodiversity."

<u>Mike Kerrick:</u> *Kerrick was Forest Supervisor on the Willamette National Forest when the Northern Spotted Owl was listed as an Endangered Species in 1990. He retired in 1991.*

As I viewed the 90s unfold from my perch as a recent retiree who was actively involved in a number of natural resource management issues, I watched what was happening with the implementation of the Northwest Forest Plan. I often thought of the quote from Frank Egler that Jack Ward Thomas used in his opening remarks to President William Clinton's 1993 " Forest Summit." Thomas told the gathering, "Ecosystems are not only more complex than we think, they are more complex than we can think." [Frank E. Egler was a noted plant ecologist of the 1940s and 50s].

Later, in that same testimony, Thomas went on to say, "Whether intended or not, the overriding objective of the management of the federal lands in the Pacific Northwest has evolved to be the preservation of biodiversity."

Those two statements seemed to frame the struggle the Forest Service had with implementing the "Plan." Timber sale quantities dropped like a rock along with budgets and personnel. A number of biological surveys were required, prior to timber sales, to ensure we would maintain species diversity in these complex ecosystems; meanwhile Congress sat on their hands except to provide relief to counties that were suffering from the lack of receipts from federal lands. It had to be a frustrating period for Forest Service managers.

ALL IN A DAY'S WORK: "The sign did not say the road was closed, only high water."

Gerald W. "Jerry" Williams *Another story by Williams, this one on a light note.*

During the fall of 1998, there was a research meeting dealing with Adaptive Management Areas (AMA) from the Northwest Forest Plan. The meeting was held in Cispus, Washington, on the Gifford Pinchot NF. It had been raining and storming a great deal, but it never seemed to matter in the PNW as this was typical of all the winters. Anyway, after the end of the first day, we were to sleep over in the Cispus Learning Center housing. I guess I didn't read far enough down the message about the conference where it said to bring a sleeping bag. I had none. Neither did Tim Tolle, the Regional AMA Coordinator. We decided to drive into Packwood, the nearest town where there was a hotel.

Only one problem - the roads were in bad shape. I took the back way out, hoping to avoid the area that had been severely damaged by another storm. The back route worked just perfect until we came to a sign on Road 25 that said *High Water*. It seemed that the Cowlitz River had risen above flood level at this low spot. We had no place to go. I was driving my wife's red Chevy Cavalier station wagon. The sign did not say the road was closed, only high water. After one attempt, we backed out. Tim suggested that we go forward until we couldn't see the white line on the road. We lost the line after about 20 yards. Since we could see car lights about a quarter of a mile away, I decided to press on. After all, how deep could it get? I was about to find out.

Soon, water was washing against the floor-boards, then above the door sills. The engine was still going strong, so I applied a little more gas. When the headlights were shining *through* the water, I became worried. We were causing quite a wake! Tim didn't say anything, but he was probably wondering how much swimming he would have to do. Water was soon pushing above and ahead of the front end of the wagon, but we were getting closer to dry land which was another 100 yards or so. The engine didn't sputter and finally the water started getting shallower. After what seemed like 30 minutes - although probably only five - we were back on dry land. No leaks, but the undercarriage of the wagon was thoroughly washed! The water did burn out the low beams on the headlights, but high beams still worked. After that incident, I referred to the station wagon as the *red submarine*.

<u>Alice C. Smith</u> *Smith started as a YACC on the Rogue River NF in 1979. She worked on the Wallowa-Whitman NF in fire and has been a botanist on the Willamette NF since 1987.*

Along with the Northwest Forest Plan in 1994 came a long list of survey-and-manage species. Over 200 fungi, lichens, mosses and liverworts, not to mention animals, were to be protected and we were to start looking for them by 1999. What a learning experience! I had never heard of most of the species and now I had to go find them. The field season extended from April (spring fruiting fungi) to December (fall fruiting fungi). The requirement to survey for fungi only lasted

Alice Smith using a handlens and a flashlight to locate and identify a tiny
lichen (Leptogium), Willamette NF – 2005

two years before being amended by another EIS, but for me those two years spent traipsing through the forest looking for brilliant red corals and orange cups and blue chantrelles were an exciting time. I learned about fungi with names you can't forget: Greening Goat's-Foot, Brown Elfin Saddle, Starving Man's Licorice, Stalked Orange Peel Fungus and Violet Hedgehog to name a few.

The best part of the survey-and-manage program was a component called Strategic Surveys. Vegetation plots were randomly selected throughout Wilderness and Late Successional Reserves for intensive searches of survey and manage species. Many of the plots could only be accessed by backpacking into them. Now, being paid to go backpacking is quite satisfying. We visited Ollalie Mountain and Fuji Mountain, Mink Lake and the headwaters of French Pete. But lest you think it was too much fun let me remind you of two variables to be considered - time and place. Each plot had to surveyed four times and one of those was as soon as the snow melted, in order to see that group of fungi that fruits as the snow retreats.

Anyone who has spent much time in the high country knows to avoid the snowmelt season for one reason, well actually a million reasons – *mosquitos!* Thousands of them whining at us, trying to get in our noses and in our eyes and bite us through our clothes. I remember following my fellow botanist down the trail and noting that hundreds of mosquitoes were covering his shirt and a thousand more swarmed behind him and I was continually walking into that swarm. And one day I was out there getting really cold and wet and feeling sorry for myself when I heard someone sneezing - it was the wildlife biologist, poor soul, whose job it was to look for tiny slugs and snails, less than one-quarter inch long, also survey-and-manage species.

Then there's the place to consider. Sure we saw some great country but we also saw some places no one in their right mind would go. Two of our plots turned out to be in the huge expanse of lava that dominates McKenzie Pass. We pleaded with no avail to the Regional Office to drop those plots - how could there be any hope of finding survey-and-manage species out in the treeless lava? One of those plots took six hours of walking and clambering across the lava to reach, and of course, no survey-and-manage species were found.

Archeologist inspecting artifacts at a homestead site in Hells Canyon,
Wallowa-Whitman NF – 1992

Fisheries biologist checking fish improvement structures,
Mt. Hood NF – 1994

From the manager's perspective survey-and-manage species were an expensive headache. First, the project level surveys were labor intensive: every unit had to be surveyed seven times, including three spring fungi visits, one summer visit for plants and lichens and another three visits for fall fruiting fungi. And that doesn't include the wildlife surveys. But even worse, we found so many sites, each one having a buffer, that soon proposed roads and units were dropped left and right and logging systems had to change when a site popped up at a proposed landing. Negotiations were held with purchasers, contracts rewritten, boundaries remarked and appraisals done over and over again.

One species that caused a lot of problems is a small orange fungi called Donkey Ears. The trick to finding it on a rainy fall day when the forest is dark and dripping is to crawl around under the western hemlock trees with a flashlight. We found so many sites of Donkey Ears that it was eventually dropped from the survey-and-manage list, which meant more boundary changes, reappraisals and more negotiations. That was a recurrent problem - species that were thought to be rare turned out to be common once we started looking for them.

However, most survey-and-manage species have maintained their rare status. Take *Bridgeoporus nobelissimus*, also called the Fuzzy Sandozi, named for the Sandoze brothers who first collected it. It's a huge conk that only grows on large diameter noble fir stumps and snags. Even after five years of surveying, it's known from only 60 sites in Oregon and Washington combined. Many other species are known from only a handful of locations, for instance, the Blue Vinyl lichen is known from only about a dozen.

The survey-and-manage program officially died with another EIS in 2004. Most of the species are now cloaked as sensitive under the sensitive species program. It works out that the truly rare still get protected and I still get to search for Blue Vinyl, the Fuzzy Sandozi and a host of others.

Rick McClure   *McClure started as a temporary on the Gifford Pinchot NF in 1981 and received a permanent appointment in 1983. He was made the Forest Archaeologist in 1991. He was the Archaeologist and Heritage Program Manager for the Gifford Pinchot and Mt. Hood NFs in 2005.*

It goes without saying that career Forest Service retirees - *Old Smokeys* - have a strong affinity for the National Forests and their histories. Over the years, retirees in Region Six have participated in a number of projects aimed at rehabilitation and preservation of historic buildings - old cabins, stations, and fire lookouts - that remind us of the early days of the Forest Service. Recently, one such building, the Government Mineral Springs Guard Station, within the Gifford Pinchot NF, was resurrected from abandonment and put back in service to the public. The rescue of this historic building was made possible through the efforts of Forest Service retirees, Passport-in-Time program volunteers, AmeriCorps volunteers and local Ranger District personnel. It was a highly skilled cadre of *Old Smokeys*, however, that led this project over its greatest hurdles.

Government Mineral Springs Guard Station is located within the Government Mineral Springs Recreation Site, fourteen miles north of Carson, Washington, in an area that is now part of the Mt. Adams Ranger District (formerly Wind River Ranger District). The site is a little over an hour's drive from the Portland-Vancouver area. The cabin was built in 1937 by Civilian Conservation Corps enrollees from Company 944, Camp Hemlock, under the general supervision of a Forest Service foreman. Cabin design was similar to other Region Six rustic style buildings, reminiscent of the Cascadian style architecture seen in the famous Timberline Lodge on Mt. Hood, Oregon. The station was built within a campground also developed by the CCC, and was intended for use by the campground manager, a Forest guard also responsible for fire protection activities in the area.

The forest at the Government Mineral Springs Recreation site is impressive. Giant Douglas-fir and cedar trees rise skyward like massive pillars. Some of the old trees had become unstable and fallen, leading to the closure of the popular campground in 1975. With the closure, there was no longer a need to station Forest Service personnel at the site and the guard station was abandoned. Time, weather and vandalism took their toll. By 2001, a roof leak and other moisture damage had resulted in floor structure rot, delamination of interior plywood walls and ceilings, and other structural damage. Vandals had removed shutters, broken windows and done other damage. Some Forest Service personnel felt that it was time to bulldoze the building.

Pacific Northwest Forest Service Association members Vern Clapp,
Dave Jay, Dave Scott and Lloyd Musser contemplate the next step during the
Government Minerals Springs Guard Station Restoration project,
Gifford Pinchot NF – 2001

Forest Service retiree Lloyd Musser, a long-time employee of the Mt. Hood NF and Regional Office recreation program, visited Government Mineral Springs Guard Station in June of 2000 and believed the building was worth saving. Lloyd had previous experience with rehabilitation of similar buildings at Clackamas Lake Ranger Station on the Mt. Hood. With the support of the Heritage Program, Gifford Pinchot NF, a plan was developed to start work on the cabin at Government Mineral Springs the following spring. The overall goal was to restore and rehabilitate the cabin and reopen the facility for public use as a historic cabin rental. Historic cabin and lookout rentals have become increasingly popular among recreation users throughout the Region in recent years. Facilities personnel from the Mt. Adams District would provide project oversight. Musser went to the *Old Smokeys* and pitched the idea of organizing a work party to assist in the restoration and rehabilitation of the guard station. Seven members signed on for the project.

Work began in May 2001, with an AmeriCorps crew handling the demolition of rotten flooring and the removal of damaged wall and ceiling material. More complex structural repairs were left to the team of retirees who arrived the following week and were housed at the nearby historic Wind River Training Center. In addition to organizer Lloyd Musser, the group included Dave Scott, past director of recreation for Region Six and his wife Audrey; Clay Beal and Dave Jay, past District Rangers at Wind River; Vern Clapp, a former Station resident and his wife Jessie; and Ron Walters, past Regional landscape architect.

Several of the team had gone into carpentry businesses after retiring from the Forest Service and had run up against a wide range of problem-solving in home building and remodeling projects as contractors. On the first day, as they gathered around each other's pickup trucks showing off the latest in top-of-the-line power tools, the group took stock of the situation. As Dave Scott recalls, "The bottom 18 inches of the structure from the foundation plate through the rim joints and into the stud wall was essentially rotted out and had to be replaced. This was done by jacking up the structure section by section, tearing out the rot and adding new treated members. A sledgehammer was a great help and an occasional curse word was heard."

Government Mineral Springs Guard Station after restoration by a group of Forest Service retireees, Gifford Pinchot NF – 2004

The newly reconstructed entrance and visitor area of the McKenzie River Ranger Station, Willamette NF – 2004

Indeed, there were some moments when it seemed as though the problems encountered were just too much. Someone would pull off some siding and discover even more hidden rot, and the group would stand around scratching their heads and poking about in crumbling wood until a solution was seen and the saws were again running and the hammers flying. Several crew members repaired and painted broken windows and siding. Probably the greatest collective moaning occurred when the group discovered rot up half the kitchen wall around the sink and drainboard. The practice of splicing 2 x 4s was taken to a high art form to get that wall back in line!

We fondly recall the late Clay Beal hunched over a sawhorse for many hours replacing window panes. Alfred Albert, the former forest guard who had been the first occupant of the guard station back in 1938, joined the crew for a couple of days. Albert had worked for the Forest Service from 1929 to 1940 as a seasonal fire patrolman and guard. His time living at Government Mineral Springs left him with many memories and he was very pleased to see the interest in preserving the historic cabin. Though 92 years of age, Albert jumped right into the work, single-handedly removing porch supports and assisting with other aspects of structural repairs. Forest Supervisor Claire Lavendel and other Forest staff members also joined the retirees for a very productive workday.

The following weeks brought crews of volunteers participating in the National Passport-in-Time program of the Forest Service, the return of the AmeriCorps, and the assistance of a Corrections Department crew from the Skamania County jail. Throughout the fall of 2001, a series of contractors came and went, attending to specialized jobs. Contracted work included chimney cleaning and repair, installation and finishing of new tongue-and-groove flooring, door jamb repair, and installation of the new gas heater, lights and stove. In the spring of 2002, attention shifted to interior details such as trim and painting. Surplus, donated and purchased furniture was collected for the cabin. By June, the historic guard station was available for rent to the public. Through the summer, work continued on a water system and new toilet.

In October 2002, a formal rededication ceremony was held at Government Mineral Springs Guard Station. The ceremony honored the legacy of the CCC and several surviving members of Company 944 turned out for the occasion. Volunteers who participated in the restoration and rehabilitation project, including *Old Smokeys*, were honored as a part of the ceremony. Speeches and remarks were offered to mark the occasion. E. Gail Throop, Regional Historian for the Forest Service, spoke about the historic significance of the guard station as an excellent example of a distinctive rustic architectural expression, the manifestation of an earlier Forest Service and a reminder of the magnitude of the CCC program.

Since re-opening to the public, the guard station has proven quite popular. Maintenance costs are fully recovered by the use fees and reservations for peak periods of use are booked a year in advance. An average of 30 people a month enjoy the use of the cabin, and even without running water, they love it! Journal entries from the logbook kept on a living room table suggest that the historic character and ambience provided by the ancient forest setting are major drawing points for visitors.

FIRE: "Even so, there are times when it is really scary."

<u>Douglas D. Porter</u>   *Porter's first fire as a National Incident Commander was one to remember.*

It was Friday, July 25th, 1994, just after lunch. I was at the Pro-Am Fred Meyer Challenge at the Oregon Golf and Country Club, sitting next to the seventh green watching Clint Eastwood and John Daly walking up the fairway towards me. My pager started to vibrate just as they were preparing to putt! I just had to watch them finish the hole before heading for a phone. I called dispatch and they told me my fire team had been activated. We were assigned to the 60 acre Hatchery Creek Fire near Leavenworth, Washington, one of several fires in the area started by lightning over the last couple of days. This was my first assignment as a National Incident Commander.

I thought that was a pretty small fire for a national team, but dispatch was concerned that there was a number of fires showing up and wanted a Type 1 Team in the area. Our 39 member team arrived in Leavenworth that evening, attended a briefing from the Forest personnel and received our marching orders and delegation of authority. We spent the night at the Leavenworth Ranger Station gathering as much information on the fire as possible and took over the fire, which had grown to 250 acres, the next morning, July 26th.

Due to the number of fires in the vicinity an area command group was put into place. Their job was to set priorities for equipment and personnel among the many fires. My main contacts were Gordie Schmidt and Stan Kunzman. Our fire was considered low priority and we only had a few crews to put on the line for the day shift. We were also assigned a second fire, Round Mountain (200 acres). These two fires formed the Hatchery Complex. On the 27th, a third fire, Eight Mile, was added, as well as initial attack responsibility for the Leavenworth and Wenatchee Districts.

The Hatchery Creek fire grew to 400 acres and crossed Highway 2 and the Wenatchee River. This initiated evacuation of the Tumwater Canyon area. Now there was fire on two sides of Leavenworth. Fires continued to pop up and we were assigned three small fires in the wilderness - Escondido, Blackjack 1 and Blackjack 2. We were moving up in priority with more equipment and personnel now coming our way. Even though we were making reasonable progress on the fires they continued to grow due to the hot weather and winds.

We started July 28th with high spirits and were optimistic about our progress. We now had three or four aircraft and about 20 crews. The Hatchery Fire was on the west side of Leavenworth, Eight Mile was on the southwest, and Round Mountain was to the north. We had evacuation plans for Leavenworth in place but hoped we would not have to implement them. The 28th ended with Hatchery Fire at about 2500 acres.

On the 29th, the Forest was closed to all visitors and several other communities were alerted to the possibility of evacuation. At about 4:30 pm on the 29th, a new start was reported in Icicle Creek, southwest of Leavenworth. We had two crews, a strike team of five engines, a helicopter and two fixed-wing retardant planes on the fire within five minutes, but with the temperature in the 90s and winds at 40+ miles per hour we could not catch it. At 6:30 pm it had grown to 20 acres and began one of the most dramatic runs I have ever seen. It was named the Rat Fire and was headed down Icicle Creek, straight at the south end of Leavenworth with Cashmere and Wenatchee out in front!

There was nothing but a red glow at the mouth of Icicle Creek as the Rat Fire prepared to come out. We evacuated homes along the creek and other communities in the projected path and alerted the communities of Leavenworth, Cashmere and Wenatchee of the situation. This fire ran four miles in 90 minutes, consuming about 4500 acres. We lost 14 homes in Icicle Canyon in the initial run. At about 2:30 am on the 30th, it made another run of about two miles over Wedge Mountain to the southeast and crossed Highway 97 where we lost one more home. Flame heights topped 300 feet and a huge vertical plume developed, reaching heights of over 25,000 feet. Fortunately, there was no loss of life and no injuries during these two runs.

Now we were number one priority! We had all we could handle, so we asked for another Type 1 team to take the Round Mountain Fire which had grown to 3100 acres. J. T. Richer from Montana was assigned. By the end of the day on the 30th, the Rat Fire was at 5000 acres and the Hatchery Fire at 3500 acres. The next couple of days brought intense fire behavior - running, crowning and spotting. It also brought VIPs, including Secretary of Agriculture Mike Espy, Governor Mike Lowry, Regional Forester John Lowe, Wenatchee Forest Supervisor Sonny O'Neal, Congressman Jay Inslee and Commissioner of Public Lands Jennifer Belcher.

We had all the fire we wanted as running and spotting continued. We were using explosives to build fire line on the backside of Tumwater Mountain, trying to prevent fire from coming over the face and into Leavenworth. The face of that mountain is in every picture of Leavenworth and some folks placed its value over human life. On August 2nd, we watched the neighboring fire, Tyee, blow up on Sugarloaf Mountain creating a 40,000 foot plume and growing to 100,000 acres. We continued building fireline, chasing spots and protecting communities.

August 4th brought our largest and most aggressive assault on the Rat and Hatchery fires as the weather gave us a break. We were at about 1900 firefighters, 17 aircraft, with 700 National Guardsmen scheduled to arrive. It was also our busiest day for heliport operations, dropping 150,000 gallons of retardant. About 100 rural engines arrived on the fire from all over Western Oregon. I understand they were all staged and then convoyed to the fire. Reports say it was quite a site on the freeway.

August 6th was our peak day with about 2500 firefighters. The Hatchery Fire was 8300 acres and the Rat Fire was 21,000 acres. We were unable to stop the Hatchery fire on the backside of Tumwater Mountain. Hot Shot Superintendent Steve Morefield led the line construction on Tumwater and made an all-out effort to cut it off but needed a few more hours. When it crossed over the top the terrain was too rugged to put firefighters on it. With a *pingpong machine* [polystryene spheres that resemble ping pong balls are released from a helicopter, triggering a chemical reaction with ignition occuring in about 20 seconds, putting a lot of fire on the ground in a short period of time] to keep the line even and helicopters to knock down the flare-ups, we were able to back the fire down the face of Tumwater Mountain to the edge of Leavenworth. We had a very nervous community for the next three days but we could not have had a more successful backfire burn.

When August 7th dawned, we had the upper hand. We began to demobilize people and equipment on the 8th. I was given the key to the city by Leavenworth Mayor Mel Wyles, who owned the Old Post Office Tavern (yes, I stopped by). The Leavenworth District Ranger, Becky Heath, did an outstanding job with the community as well as my team. I will always remember our conversations and her trust in me as Incident Commander.

> Final Tally :
> Fatalities - None.
> Injuries - None serious.
> Homes Protected - 2700.
> Homes Saved - 540 where the fire burned immediately adjacent to the structure.
> Homes Destroyed - 19 homes verified lost from the Rat Fire (human caused).
> Evacuations Alert - Leavenworth, Peshastin, Dryden, and Cashmere among other areas.

Evacuations - Tumwater, Freund, Spromberg, Sunitsch, Brender, Brisky, Mission Creek, Yaksum, Icicle Canyon, and areas by Hatchery, Highway 97, and Camas.
Hatchery Fire 11,200 acres; Rat Fire 28,915; Total Acres 41,273

On August 15th, my team transitioned with Wenatchee's Type 2 Incident Management Team (Jim Furlong Incident Commander) and we went home for a couple days of rest and recuperation. We had been on the fire for 22 days and during that time I celebrated my 55th birthday and received word from Mary Paulson that my friend Sam Fischer had passed away. Three days later, my team was activated to the Libby Complex in Montana and, of course, that is another story.

James Roden *Roden started as a temporary on the Bridger-Teton NF in R-4 in 1978 and received a permanent appointment the next year on the Eldorado NF in R-5. He worked on the Nez Perce NF in R-1 and was a Forester on the Mt. Hood NF in 2005. He was a firefighter on the Hashrock Fire on the Ochoco NF near Prineville in 2000.*

When I got home from the Hashrock Fire my niece asked me if I was ever scared fighting fires. I told her we go to special training to help us be safe and recognize situations that could be hazardous. Even so, there are times when it is really scary.

When fire is moving fast, roaring and showering burning embers all around, the smoke stings your eyes and burns your lungs, and you look around trying to remember which way you're supposed to run if the time comes to get to the safety zone, that's scary! When it's night and trees that have burned at the base are falling and crashing to the ground without any warning, that's scary! When you're in a helicopter being taken to some ridge top and you wonder when the last time this pilot got a good night's sleep, that's scary! When a bunch of angry yellow jackets chases you, that's scary!

But the scary times are actually few and far between. Firefighting actually consists more of tedious hard work, boredom while waiting for instructions, driving and hiking to and from, fighting off fatigue, getting dirty, and during all of this, the camaraderie of sharing stories of the glory of past fires and how scary they were.

Firefighter cutting out the line, Okanogan NF – 1993

Cable thinning in a Douglas-fir stand, Willamette NF – 1992

<u>Linda Goodman</u> *Goodman began her career on the Olympic NF in 1974 and has worked in a wide variety of administrative and managerial roles at every level of the organization. She worked on five different National Forests in R-6, ran the agency's Job Corps Field Office in Denver, and was the first Director of the 18 FS Job Corps Centers. She was Acting Chief of Staff for the Forest Service in Washington, DC, and was named Regional Forester for R-6 in 2002.*

One of the toughest moments I've experienced was an evening phone call [on July 10, 2001] and hearing, "We've lost four firefighters at a remote canyon in northern Washington." My heart dropped, and I was stunned. The hardest part of it was meeting their families and fellow co-workers and seeing the suffering and pain these people were experiencing. The death of anyone is hard, but the death of these four young and talented people seemed to resonate profoundly in everyone's heart. It was a tough time and like many, I agonized over how we could help others with their healing process.

And at that dark time, I am proud to say the Forest Service came through. At the time I was the Deputy Regional Forester, and like others, felt a ceremony honoring their lives was in order. What I experienced wasn't just a ceremony, but an outpouring of heartfelt love by the local Yakima community, other natural resource agencies (federal, state, and local), and our nationwide Forest Service community. The Chief and members of the Forest Service National Leadership team came, Forest Supervisors and District Rangers from our Region and others came, the Regional Directors came, busloads of employees came, and the retired community came in droves.

I was proud to board an aircraft and find nearly all of the living retired Forest Service R-6 Regional Foresters present *for duty*. They all came, because they were part of the Forest Service and felt that's where they should be.

The parade honoring our fallen firefighters took nearly an hour, and that was just at the starting line, as hundreds of Forest Service, other federal and state agencies, community fire trucks, water tenders, and other vehicles drove the route. At the Yakima Sun Dome, thousands of people gathered crying, praying and at times, smiling together as the lives and loves of the firefighters were recalled. It was an event of intense emotions and love.

Pride is what I felt leaving the ceremony. Pride in the lives of these four and how they lived. Pride in their families, who had raised them with such joy and love. And pride in the Forest Service, in seeing people wear their uniforms in honor of their fellow workers, and pride in our retirees, who truly are still part of the *long, green line.*

<u>Jack Berry</u> *Berry had a number of temporary appointments and also did contract work for the Forest Service. After a fifteen-year career in the news business he was visiting a friend in Baker in 1978-79 and ended up editing the first management plan for the Hells Canyon National Recreation Area. He went on to edit a number of federal agency documents, mostly for the Forest Service, including those associated with Alpine Lakes, Mount St. Helens, and the Silver and Biscuit Fires.*

Berry interviewed Richard Boothe, Two Rivers Fire Zone Fire Management Officer, Illinois and Gallice RDs on the Rogue River - Siskiyou NF about the initial stages of the Florence Fire. This fire combined with the Biscuit Fire to become the largest fire in North America in 2002 (499,965 acres on the Siskiyou NF in R-6 and the Six Rivers NF in R-5), and one of the largest fires in the recorded history of Oregon. Chapters Two and Three also have stories about the fire-prone southwest corner of Oregon.

When you don't have the troops, you attend to what is most critical. In this case, Merlin, Oregon, or, according to a worst possible case scenario, Grants Pass were at risk.

After the Florence Fire jumped the Illinois River on July 24, 2002, the possibility of flames entering the Briggs Creek drainage and thence into the Rogue River corridor was *very real.* With pernicious winds that could have been grave indeed. Also at risk were a number of structures on Oak Flat. Some of them didn't make it.

Difficult decisions confronted Glen Joki when his Type 2 IMT (Incident Management Team) arrived from Arizona. Four separate fires were burning and there were very few fire suppression resources available. Much of the Northwest seemed to be on fire in the summer of 2002. Because the origin of what became the Biscuit Fire was in the Kalmiopsis Wilderness, it had lower priority for those resources.

"The worry was that if we didn't get it tied off from Flat Top to Brushy Bar it would get into the Briggs Creek drainage and we'd have to back way out to the north, to the Onion Mountain Road."

Talking is Dick Boothe, who was the Zone FMO when a blizzard of lightning strikes ignited the biggest fire in Oregon's recorded history.

"They basically had to burn out and construct fire line, improve that fire line, and walk (continue constructing) that line down six miles into Briggs Creek from Flat Top. And the change in elevation from Flat Top to Briggs Creek is about 2,600 feet on the back side of Oak Flat." For an enterprise this daunting, Type 1 hotshot crews are normally required.

"They were probably half way down the ridge, half way down the line, when the fire jumped the Illinois River and made its first run at Oak Flat."

When this happened, people were pulled off the line "and we were concerned at the end of the shift and throughout the evening that we'd lost all that line. But it held. And the next day we started burning it back out again."

Then the fire spotted again when they were down at Brushy Bar, "and it was the time of day when all the aircraft were timed out, when helicopters had run up all their hours. They tried to chase it with a dozer, two dozers they had down there at Brushy Bar, but they didn't pick it up. The piece that spotted over took another run at Oak Flat the next day and some more of the structures were lost. They again regrouped and continued constructing and burning out the line to the east on better roads."

"There were so few options or opportunities, places where they could construct and burnout a line with the resources they had. The place where they brought it down, on that old jeep trail to Briggs Creek, if it

543

wasn't there, it was miles and miles and miles back." When Lohrey's Type 1 IMT assumed command of the Florence Fire on July 31, the north end was anchored and they could concentrate on finishing the construction and burnout of the east line towards the California border. This line would prevent fire from reaching the valley floor and thousands of residents in the Illinois Valley.

Eventually, the weather cooperated. "Once they had hooked that piece off the north and headed back toward Squaw Peak, the east/northeast wind flow was a good thing for the burnout operation. The wind just pushed the fire into itself. Initially, the wind was pushing out of the west, associated with the canyons. And that was the fear, that it was going to run with the west/southwest flow up Briggs Creek."

Boothe could not recall any memorable quotes uttered by people involved in this critical turning. His speech tends toward the laconic. "Like I say, they did a good job of getting that early work accomplished and securing that piece of line."

RESEARCH: "- - the most enjoyable part of the whole experience was right during the event when there were so many interesting things to see and hear."

Fred Swanson *Swanson received a permanent appointment in 1978. He has spent his whole career at the Pacific Northwest Research Station Forestry Sciences Laboratory in Corvallis, Oregon, where he was a Research Geologist in 2005.*

As I drove up the McKenzie River in heavy rain on the evening of February 6, 1996, reflections on earlier floods in the region came to mind. I first came to the west coast in the summer of 1965. To the eyes of this easterner, an undergraduate geology major, the landscape of north coastal California on the heels of the December 1964 flood was incredible. Massive landslides in the rugged mountains had torn off whole hillsides, including the roads we were trying to travel, and blocked rivers; signs posted well above the highway marked high river levels.

In 1972, I began working in the H.J. Andrews Experimental Forest in the Oregon Cascades. My studies concerned landslides, river channel change, and the history and function of big wood in streams and rivers.

544

From those perspectives, signs of the 1964 flood were everywhere on the land and in the minds of others studying landscape change. The experienced hands had great stories of being out in the storm, hearing debris flows rumbling down stream channels, snapping old-growth trees and blocking roads. Dick Fredriksen and Al Levno (both of PNW Research Station) had a harrowing, night-time tale of hiking out of the Andrews to the McKenzie River during that storm and almost being swept away by the flood. Al had thick glasses that fogged up, so in some stages of the trip Dick had to lead him by the hand, through the darkness in pouring rain.

That storm affected the Andrews Forest and the workers there in more ways than just triggering landslides, reshaping streams, and limiting access. It also stimulated a great deal of study by Fredriksen, Ted Dyrness (PNW Research Station), and their colleagues on effects of roads and logging on soil erosion, including studies in experimental watersheds and inventories of landslides over larger areas. The storm taught lessons that led to changes in forestry and road construction practices, resulting in improved watershed management.

Coming into the Andrews Forest landscape eight years after the 1964 flood, I tried to learn more about how the watershed functioned, including effects of that flood and other forces of change. I extended Ted Dyrness's 1964 flood landslide inventory to span the first 25 years of forest management in the Andrews Forest and started tree-ring studies of wildfire history for the past 500 years. Jim Sedell, George Lienkaemper (both of PNW Station), other colleagues and I began work on big wood in streams, recognizing its many natural ecological and geomorphic functions. This was part of bigger, integrated ecosystem studies based at the Andrews Forest led by Jerry Franklin (PNW Station) and Dick Waring (Oregon State University) and carried out through good cooperation with the Willamette NF.

So, driving up the McKenzie more than three decades after the 1964 flood, I wondered if we were heading into a replay of that event - the snowpack, river discharge, present and forecasted rainfall, and our guts all said, "Yes!" I was traveling with 1964 flood veteran Al Levno, fellow disasterologist Gordon Grant (PNW Station), Beverley Wemple, an Oregon State University PhD student studying road hydrology and several others. We arrived at the Andrews Forest offices in late afternoon. In the dim winter light we checked out a few gauging stations on small watersheds. Flows were up and muddy, the rain steady and the snow soggy when we departed for dinner at the Rustic Skillet diner (locally termed the *Rusty Skillet*). Returning after dinner in the dark we found that debris flows had ripped through two experimental watersheds including wiping out one of the gauging stations where its predecessor had been destroyed in the 1964 flood. We went to bed knowing the storm was still building.

The next morning the rain was steady and water flowed everywhere, including many places where we had never before seen streams. Gordon, with video camera in hand, and I went to Lookout Creek and excitedly viewed the flood waters. Massive, old-growth logs that had been lying in the channel for 15 years or more were gone! Tips of a toppled 30-year-old alder stand that had grown on a gravel bar in mid-channel poked up through the surface of the muddy flood water. We shared a childish enthusiasm shouting, "Rip city!" as we watched old-growth logs (*aircraft carriers*) charging length-wise down the channel. We had a combined four decades of study of wood in rivers and had never before seen really big pieces on the move. Gordon caught it on videotape, which we have revisited on many occasions to study the scenes which were so full of information of great interest to us that we could not digest it all at the time - there was just too much to absorb for these kids in the candy store.

Gordon and I spent several days during the 1996 flood tromping around the Andrews landscape and along the upper McKenzie River. Small watersheds at low elevation were pumping out lots of water, with rainfall supplemented by snow-melt, but higher elevation watersheds were not flowing so high, perhaps because a thicker snowpack was temporarily storing the rainfall. The flood waters were turbid rather early in the event, but movement of the big boulders over the streambed did not begin until flow was appreciably higher. Early in the morning of February 7, we could hear the deep, *thunk-thunk* of passing boulders rolling down the bed of Lookout Creek and we could still hear it well into the next day, more than 24 hours after the flood peak on Lookout Creek.

The small landslides and debris flows occurred during several different brief periods of intense rainfall when flow in the small watersheds peaked in the evening of the 6th and early morning of the 7th, but the mainstem of Lookout Creek did not peak until about 1 pm

Flood damage to a road in the H.J. Andrews Experimental Forest,
Willamette NF – 1996

on the 7th. Log movement in the larger channels occurred on the rising flood waters and then ceased; most logs in small channels did not move unless they were swept up by debris flows. Muddy water persisted for days on the waning limb of the flood peak. Thus, some processes occurred early in the event and shut down while others continued throughout the flood. Some processes operated only in small streams while others were relegated to the larger channels.

Thinking more broadly, we considered how the stage was set by events leading up to the floods of 1964 and 1996. The 1996 flood itself was set up by snow in the previous week and then a prolonged period of warm rain, which saturated the soil and melted much of the snow. The Andrews Forest watershed had experienced little logging or road construction in nearly 25 years prior to the 1996 flood, so it was not as sensitive to flooding as it had been in the 1964 flood, which came after 15 years of clearcutting, broadcast burning, and road construction under early management standards and it occurred in the unstable, lower-elevation parts of the Lookout Creek watershed. Comparing the number of landslides in the two floods, we found similar amounts of landsliding in forest areas, but less in cuts and roads in 1996 than in the 1964 event, apparently due to regrowth in plantations and earlier sliding of the most unstable parts of the landscape. So flood effects reflected the interaction of lots of water with the condition of the watershed at the time of the flood.

During our walks in the flood, Gordon and I commented that there would be much follow-up work to do and the most enjoyable part of the whole experience was right during the event when there were so many interesting things to see and hear. That proved true. In the following years we took part in flood studies, report writing, public discussion and debate among scientists about the effects of forestry on floods and landslides, interactions with reporters, and other communications work. But when we got frustrated with the business end of the deal, we could always reflect on the excitement of witnessing the flood and trying to understand how it worked.

These experiences highlight the value of places like the Andrews Forest which are dedicated to long-term ecological and watershed research where information grows over time and is passed from generation to generation.

REUNION: "We had an objective in mind."

<u>Dave Scott</u> *Scott is one of the organizers for the National Forest Service Reunion in 2005.*

The 100 year anniversary celebration of the Forest Service and the National Forest Service Reunion held in Portland, Oregon, in 2005 were inspirations for this book. Thus, a story about the reunion is a fitting last story. Because we wanted our book to be available at the reunion, this story had to be written before the actual event.

Glenwood Springs, Park City, Missoula and now Portland. Starting in 1991 and every five years since 1995, one of these towns has hosted a Forest Service Reunion. The Portland event planned for September 2005, will be a 100 year celebration of the Forest Service and the National Forests as well as a reunion. We will celebrate 100 years of putting Grover Blake's description, "We Had an Objective in Mind" into practice. All active employees as well as retirees are welcome to attend and participate.

It was the fall of 2000 after returning from the Missoula reunion, that President John Marker and the Board of Directors of the then "30 Year Club" agreed to host the gathering in 2005. Little did we know at the time how much we bit off. It was good planning or good luck that prompted John to ask Bob Tokarczyk to chair the search committee and who in turn convinced Bob Williams to chair the whole shooting match. In any case Bob Williams took the bit in his mouth, shook his head a couple times and took off at a full gallop. Drawing on his extensive background as a line officer he immediately gathered a highly competent and confident staff around him. Each of his staff in turn recruited their own group of helpers up to the point where there are at least 75 people working to be sure the party is a success. That number may double during the active days of the reunion. Because of the large number of people volunteering, I have chosen to not name names for fear of forgetting someone. Suffice it to say they are all hard workers.

Bob and his committee met quarterly for about three years, met bimonthly for a year and met monthly for this last year. Remember this is a group of people who thought they were done with meetings once they retired. The Gifford Pinchot NF furnished meeting space. The Regional Office, an active participant in almost every meeting, offered aid when needed. The Washington Office helped with publicity by making sure every active employee is notified. Using the word of the day, this has been a truly collaborative effort. Adding a special attraction to the gathering, the Chief and staff as well as the Regional Foresters and Directors scheduled their annual working meeting in Portland at the same time as the reunion. They, of course, have their own agenda during the day but will join the crowd for the social evenings.

A big feature of the event will be the tours, starting off with a Lewis and Clark 200 year anniversary tour from Portland to Astoria and return. In addition attendees can choose day trips to Mt. St. Helens, northern Oregon wineries, the Columbia River Gorge, Timberline Lodge, and the "Spruce Goose" at the Evergreen Air Museum.

The two days of programs are packed with featured speakers and presentations and space will be available for exhibitors to display their products. A small store selling memorabilia and an extensive silent auction will raise funds to defray expenses of the reunion as well as provide seed money for the next get together.

We have also gathered a collection of retirees and spouses who have found a new life in the fields of cultural arts. We will have eight to ten authors with their books on display. There will be six or seven artists represented with works available at the silent auction, and several craftsmen will demonstrate their skills and wares. And three musical groups, comprised primarily of retirees from Denver, Prineville and Vancouver, will entertain us. We hope to show there really is a connection, as these artisans demonstrate, between forestry, nature and the cultural arts.

While this is a comprehensive program with many things to do none of us should forget the primary objective is to gather for a great visit with old friends. It is this visiting time I have always found most rewarding

550

- a chance to reaffirm that yes, the Forest Service is indeed a family and an important part of our lives then and now.

Bob Tokarczyk, current president of PNWFSA, will welcome us to the reunion. It is here that many of the stories you have read in this book will take on a new life. They will be told several times over and embroidered somewhat with each retelling. Thus the reunion enhances the book and the book enhances the reunion. The "book committee" hopes this storytelling will inspire the work lives of today's Forest Service employees by giving them an insight into the hardships and difficulties, humor and spirit of Forest Service life in Oregon and Washington from 1905 to 2005. And, while this book is about the Forest Service in Oregon and Washington, we know similar stories can and have been told about early and modern day experiences all over the United States wherever there are National Forests and Research Stations.

With this attention to story-telling, we hope recent retirees and current employees will begin to think about recording their own stories, documenting experiences for future readers. Perhaps a new book will be available to help celebrate the 2010 reunion!

EPILOGUE

Looking Back

"I have heard some of the old-timers, in speaking of the halcyon days of the past, imply that the interesting days of the Service were gone and now it was merely humdrum. I hope none of the younger men subscribe to that idea. Of course youth has advantages over middle age, but I would not grant that the Forest Service is much past adolescence. It is fun to do firsts; I enjoyed pioneering in putting in permanent sample plots, buying the first official automobile and adding machine for District Six, proposing the first natural area, making the first yield tables, drawing up the first real research program, getting the first of the Regional forest surveys started. But there are lots of firsts yet to be done. There may not be new tree species to discover, but there is plenty of opportunity for pioneering, for originality, for enterprise. There is yet a long way to go before forest management, forest protection, forest utilization, forest land economics are utopian."   -Thornton T. Munger - 1943

"The Forest Service has been my life for 34 years. I couldn't have found any occupation so satisfactory, so respectable, so totally remunerative, giving such security and such a wide range of interests and activities and such a wide acquaintance with people. Had I the opportunity to choose again I could not find a better."
                                                -John G. Clousten – 1957

"There are days though, that I pine for being back in the woods. The clamor of yarders and skidders. The arguments with the purchasers and the loggers. The smell of diesel smoke filtering through the fir and pine. Those things have become a relic of the past. I know in the older days, 1930s, 1940s, and 1950s, what I was doing would have been considered wimpy. I always had a pick-up truck to drive to get me places. Most nights I was able to go home and sleep in my own bed. In the old days you would have gone in somewhere by foot or horse-back and camped out until the job was done. It just goes to show that times and the environment change and nothing stays the same. Life is dynamic and you have to learn to adapt. If not, you become like the Spotted Owl and die out. Time to move on."
                                                -Glen Horner – 2004

Looking Forward

"This book is about the past century of the Forest Service in the Pacific Northwest Region. It is told through stories by its employees; stories of heroic actions, every day life, and wives tales. Told by people who were proud to work for a great outfit, people who made it the envy of other Agencies in Government.

In the beginning and throughout the first century, the Forest Service was guided by the principle that decisions would be made to benefit the greatest number for the greatest good in the long run. A period that began with communicating by mail, and a small manual called the "Use Book" that could be carried in your pocket, and ended with instantaneous messaging via networking computers, wireless phones and an on-line manual system that would fill over 30 feet of shelf space if printed.

Given this platform where is the Forest Service in the Pacific Northwest headed in the next 100 years? What stories will employees tell and what will the work be like? Will the mission still be "caring for the land and serving people?" How will the big issues at the end of the first century play out in the second? What stories will be told about the effect of and dealing with climate change, sustainable management, adaptive management, the application of best available science and listening to our public. Where will technology take us and what stories will be told of how we got there? What natural disasters lay ahead and how will they affect employees and communities?

An organization is only as good as its people. If the answers to the above questions are positive it will be because the Forest Service was able to attract good people, was successful in involving the public in the critical decisions about their forests and was able to obtain the resources to implement those decisions.

What fun to be around in 2105 and read an anthology about the second 100 years!"

- Mike Kerrick - 2005

PACIFIC NORTHWEST REGION

Regional Forester	Years Served
EDWARD T. ALLEN	1908-1909
CHARLES S. CHAPMAN	1909-1911
GEORGE H. CECIL	1911-1925
CHRISTOPHER M. GRANGER	1925-1930
CLARENCE J. BUCK	1930-1939
LYLE F. WATTS	1939-1943
HORACE J. ANDREWS	1943-1951
J. HERBERT STONE	1951-1967
CHARLES A. CONNAUGHTON	1967-1971
REXFORD A. RESLER	1971-1972
THEODORE A. SCHLAPFER	1972-1977
RICHARD E. WORTHINGTON	1977-1981
JEFF M. SIRMON	1982-1985
CHARLES T. COSTON	1985-1986
JAMES F. TORRENCE	1986-1989
JOHN F. BUTRUILLE	1989-1992
JOHN E. LOWE	1992-1996
ROBERT W. WILLIAMS	1996-1999
HARV FORSGREN	1999-2002
LINDA GOODMAN	2003-

PACIFIC NORTHWEST RESEARCH STATION

Station Director	Years Served
THORNTON T. MUNGER	1924-1939
STEPHEN N. WYCKOFF	1939-1945
J. ALFRED HALL	1945-1951
ROBERT W. COWLIN	1951-1963
PHILLIP A. BRIEGLEB	1963-1971
ROBERT E. BUCKMAN	1971-1975
ROBERT F. TARRANT	1975-1979
ROBERT L. ETHINGTON	1979-1987
CHARLES W. PHILPOT	1987-1995
THOMAS J. MILLS	1995-2002
THOMAS M. QUIGLEY	2002-

PACIFIC NORTHWEST REGION and PACIFIC NORTHWEST RESEARCH STATION – Dates of Interest

February 1905:	Jurisdiction and management of the Forest Reserves was transferred from the General Land Office in the Department of the Interior to the Bureau of Forestry in the Department of Agriculture
July 1905:	Bureau of Forestry renamed Forest Service
1907:	Forest Reserves renamed National Forests
1908:	North Pacific District (District Six) established
1913:	Wind River Experiment Forest established
1921:	Alaska made a separate District
1924:	Pacific Northwest Forest Experiment Station established
1930:	North Pacific District renamed North Pacific Region (Region Six)
1937:	Pacific Northwest Forest Experiment Station renamed Pacific Northwest Forest and Range Experiment Station
1948:	North Pacific Region renamed Pacific Northwest Region
1986:	Pacific Northwest Forest and Range Experiment Station renamed Pacific Northwest Research Station

ESTABLISHMENT and DISCONTINUATION of FOREST RESERVES/NATIONAL FORESTS in the PACIFIC NORTHWEST REGION

This document was prepared from Forest Service document FS-612, 1997; Establishment and Modification of National Forest Boundaries and National Grasslands – A Chronological Record 1891 – 1996. A more complete listing of Reserve and Forest boundary modifications can be found in Publication FS-612. Forests grouped together for administration, but not officially consolidated, are not listed.

Forest Reserve/ National Forest	State	Year of Action	Effect of Action
Ashland	Oregon	1893	Established Reserve
		1908	Added with other land to establish Crater NF
Baker City	Oregon	1904	Established Reserve
		1906	Combined with Blue Mountains Reserve
Blue Mountains	Oregon	1906	Established Reserve
		1908	Distributed among Whitman, Malheur, Umatilla, and Deschutes NFs
Bull Run	Oregon	1892	Established Reserve
		1908	Combined with lands from Cascade Reserve to establish Oregon NF
Cascade	Oregon	1907	Name changed from Cascade Range Reserve
		1933	Combined with Santiam to establish Willamette NF
Cascade Range	Oregon	1893	Established Reserve
		1907	Name changed to Cascade Reserve

Chelan	Washington	1908	Established Forest from lands from Washington NF
		1955	Name changed to Okanogan NF
Chesnimus	Oregon	1905	Established Reserve
		1907	Combined with Wallowa Reserve to create the Imnaha Reserve
Columbia	Washington	1908	Established Forest from lands from Rainier NF
		1949	Name changed to Gifford Pinchot NF
Colville	Washington	1907	Established Reserve
Coquille	Oregon	1907	Established Reserve
		1908	Land combined with Siskiyou NF
Crater	Oregon	1908	Established Forest
		1932	Name changed to Rogue River NF
Deschutes	Oregon	1908	Established Forest from lands from Blue Mountains NF
Fremont	Oregon	1906	Established Reserve
Gifford Pinchot	Washington	1949	Established Forest Name changed from Columbia NF
Goose Lake	Oregon	1906	Established Reserve
		1908	Combined with Fremont NF
Heppner	Oregon	1906	Established Reserve
		1908	Combined with Blue Mountains NF lands to establish Umatilla NF

Imnaha	Oregon	1907 1908	Established Reserve Name changed to Wallowa NF
Malheur	Oregon	1908	Established Forest from lands from Blue Mountains NF
Maury Mountain	Oregon	1905 1907	Established Reserve Combined with Blue Mountains Reserve
Minam	Oregon	1911 1920	Established Forest Combined with Whitman NF
Mt. Baker	Washington	1924	Name changed from Washington NF
Mt. Hood	Oregon	1924	Name changed from Oregon NF
Mt. Rainier	Washington	1897 1907	Name changed from Pacific Reserve Name changed to Rainier Reserve
Ochoco	Oregon	1911	Established Forest
Okanogan	Washington	1911 1920 1955	Established Forest Combined with Chelan Name discontinued Re-established from Chelan NF
Olympic	Washington	1897	Established Reserve
Oregon	Oregon	1908 1924	Established Forest from Cascade and Bull Run NFs Name changed to Mt. Hood NF
Pacific	Washington	1893 1897	Established Reserve Name changed to Mt. Rainier Reserve

Paulina	Oregon	1911 1915	Established Forest Distributed among Crater, Deschutes and Fremont NFs
Rainier	Washington	1907 1933	Name changed from Mt. Rainier Reserve Distributed among Columbia, Snoqualmie and Wenatchee NFs
Rogue River	Oregon	1932	Established Forest from Crater NF
Santiam	Oregon	1911 1933	Established Forest Combined with Cascade NF to form Willamette NF
Siskiyou	Oregon	1906	Established Reserve
Siuslaw	Oregon	1908	Established Forest from Tillamook and Umpqua NFs
Snoqualmie	Washington	1908	Established Forest from lands from Washington NF
Tillamook	Oregon	1907 1908	Established Reserve Distributed among Siuslaw and Umpqua NFs
Umatilla	Oregon	1908	Established Forest from lands from Blue MountainsNF
	OR/WA	1927	Land added
Umpqua	Oregon	1907	Established Reserve

Wallowa	Oregon	1905	Established Reserve
		1907	Combined with Chesmimus Reserve to create the Imnaha Reserve Name discontinued
		1908	Re-established Forest from Imnaha NF
Washington	Washington	1897	Established Reserve
		1924	Name changed to Mt Baker NF
Wenaha	OR/WA	1905	Established Reserve
		1920	Combined with Umatilla NF
Wenatchee	Washington	1908	Established Forest from lands from Washington NF
Whitman	Oregon	1908	Established Forest from lands from Blue Mountains NF
Willamette	Oregon	1933	Established Forest from Santiam and Cascade NFs
Winema	Oregon	1961	Established Forest from Rogue River NF and other lands

AUTHOR INDEX

ACRONYMS and ABBREVIATIONS

AWS   Aircraft Warning Service
CCC   Civilian Conservation Corps
CWA   Civil Works Administration
DF   Douglas-fir
DR   District Ranger
EA   Environmental Assessment
FS   Forest Service or Forest Supervisor
GS   Guard Station
NF   National Forest
NEPA   National Environmental Policy Act
PNW   Pacific Northwest
PNWFRES   Pacific Northwest Forest and Range Experiment Station
PNWRS   Pacific Northwest Research Station
RD   Ranger District
RF   Regional Forester
RO   Regional Office
RS   Ranger Station
R-1   Region One or Northern Region (Montana, northern Idaho, North Dakota, South Dakota)
R-2   Region Two or Rocky Mountain Region (South Dakota, Nebraska, Kansas, Wyoming, Colorado)
R-3   Region Three or Southwestern Region (Arizona, New Mexico)
R-4   Region Four or Intermountain Region (southern Idaho, western Wyoming, Utah, Nevada)
R-5   Region Five or Pacific Southwest Region (California, Hawaii)
R-6   Region Six or Pacific Northwest Region (Oregon, Washington)
R-7   No longer in existence. Previously in the northeast
R-8   Region Eight or Southern Region (Texas, Oklahoma, Arkansas, Louisiana, Mississippi, Alabama, Georgia, Florida, North Carolina, South Carolina, Virginia, Kentucky, Tennessee)
R-9   Region Nine or Eastern Region (Minnesota, Iowa, Missouri, Illinois, Michigan, Wisconsin, Indiana, Ohio, West Virginia, Maryland, Delaware, New Jersey, Pennsylvania, New York, Connecticut, Rhode Island, Massachusetts, Maine, New Hampshire, Vermont)
R-10   Region Ten or Alaska Region (Alaska)
SO   Supervisor's Office
USDA   United States Department of Agriculture
USFS   United States Forest Service
WO   Washington Office
WPA   Works Progress Administration
WW I   World War One
WW II   World War Two
YACC   Young Adult Conservation Corps
YCC   Youth Conservation Corps

IN RECOGNITION

Editor Rolf Anderson truly "had an objective in mind." He obviously has a love affair with the Forest Service and its history. Rolf enjoyed a long career with the Forest Service, serving on several National Forests in the Northwest. His final assignment before retiring was District Ranger of the Sweet Home Ranger District on the Willamette National Forest.

When the PNWFSA was looking for a volunteer to edit this anthology Rolf did not hesitate to step forward. As a result he has spent countless hours, days, and weeks over two and one-half years nurturing this book to completion. It took focus, energy, and unrelenting hard work to make this happen.

The members of PNWFSA, the Forest Service employees and retirees and the people of Oregon and Washington owe Rolf a resounding thank you.

Thanks Rolf, you have met your objective.

Order copies of <u>We Had an Objective in Mind</u>

Over 300 stories chronicling the hardships and difficulties, humor and spirit of Forest Service life in Oregon and Washington from 1905 to 2005

The book is $16 per copy plus $3 for shipping and handling for a total of $19 per copy

Mail this coupon and check to:

PNWFS Assn., PO Box 5583, Portland, OR 97228-5583

Name: _____

Address:_____

_____

I wish to order _____ copies of the book,

<u>We Had an Objective in Mind</u>
<u>The U. S. Forest Service in the Pacific Northwest</u>
<u>1905 to 2005</u>
<u>A Centennial Anthology</u>.

Enclosed is a check for $_____made out to PNWFS Assn.